T0301247

Behavioral Game Theory

The Roundtable Series in Behavioral Economics

The Roundtable Series in Behavioral Economics aims to advance research in the new interdisciplinary field of behavioral economics. Behavioral economics uses facts, models, and methods from neighboring sciences to establish descriptively accurate findings about human cognitive ability and social interaction and to explore the implications of these findings for economic behavior. The most fertile neighboring science in recent decades has been psychology, but sociology, anthropology, biology, and other fields can usefully influence economics as well. The Roundtable Series publishes books in economics that are deeply rooted in empirical findings or methods from one or more neighboring sciences and advance economics on its own terms—generating theoretical insights, making more accurate predictions of field phenomena, and suggesting better policy.

Colin Camerer and Ernst Fehr, Series Editors

The Behavioral Economics Roundtable

Henry Aaron	George Loewenstein
George Akerlof	Sendhil Mullainathan
Linda Babcock	Matthew Rabin
Colin Camerer	Thomas Schelling
Peter Diamond	Eldar Shafir
Jon Elster	Robert Shiller
Ernst Fehr	Cass Sunstein
Daniel Kahneman	Richard Thaler
David Laibson	Richard Zeckhauser

Behavioral Game Theory

Experiments in Strategic Interaction

Colin F. Camerer

Russell Sage Foundation, New York, New York
Princeton University Press, Princeton, New Jersey

Copyright © 2003 by Russell Sage Foundation
Requests for permission to reproduce materials from this work should be sent to
Permissions, Princeton University Press

Published by Princeton University Press,
41 William Street,
Princeton, New Jersey 08540
In the United Kingdom: Princeton University Press,
3 Market Place, Woodstock, Oxfordshire OX20 1SY

and Russell Sage Foundation,
112 East 64th Street, New York, New York 10021

All Rights Reserved

Library of Congress Cataloging-in-Publication Data

Camerer, Colin, 1959–
    Behavioral game theory : experiments in strategic interaction / Colin F. Camerer.
      p. cm.
    Includes bibliographic references and index.
    ISBN 0-691-09039-4
    1. Game theory. 2. Statistical decisions. 3. Negotiation—Mathematical
  models. 4. Decision making. I. Title. II. Series.
  HB144 .C364   2003
  330′.01′5193—dc21   2002034642

British Library Cataloging-in-Publication Data is available

This book was composed in ITC New Baskerville with ZzTEX by Princeton Editorial
Associates, Inc., Scottsdale, Arizona

www.pup.princeton.edu
www.russellsage.org

10 9 8 7 6 5 4 3 2 1

To my parents

Contents

Preface

IN ECONOMICS AT THE UNIVERSITY OF CHICAGO in the late 1970s, game theory was considered a messy analytical swamp between monopoly and perfect competition. My intermediate price theory teacher explained cynically how von Neumann and Morgenstern had both solved one problem that was no longer a problem (by giving a method to measure utilities, which was not needed after the ordinal revolution) and failed to solve the hard problem (uniqueness of equilibrium in all games). In class we therefore stuck to the important polar cases and hoped that two firms would be perfectly competitive, so we didn't need game theory. Fortunately, my first job in 1981 (a de facto postdoc) was up the road at Northwestern which had an unbelievable all-star team of game theorists in its MEDS Department—Bengt Holmstrom, Ehud Kalai, Paul Milgrom, Roger Myerson, John Roberts, Mark Satterthwaite. You couldn't help but learn some game theory, and get excited about it, just breathing the air in seminars. But my background in cognitive psychology and behavioral decision research also made it natural to look at games and ask how people with cognitive limits and emotions—i.e., *normal* people—would behave.

So the roots of this book go back at least that far. A conference organized to honor Hilly Einhorn, who died tragically young, gave me a chance to put ideas on paper (published in 1990) and coin the term "behavioral game theory" for the empirical, descriptive approach rooted in data and psychological fact.

People who have influenced me intellectually (in loosely chronological order) include my thesis advisors, Hilly and Robin Hogarth, Charlie Plott (who taught a Ph.D. course at Chicago in 1980 which changed the course of my research), Ken MacCrimmon, Howard Kunreuther, Daniel Kahneman, Paul Slovic, Amos Tversky, John Kagel, George Loewenstein, Jon Baron, Eric Johnson, Dick Thaler, Matthew Rabin, Marc Knez, Teck Ho, Kuan Chong, and my students and many other collaborators.

This book has been a long time in the making, and it has benefited from ideas of many people. It was supported by a wonderful year at the Center for Advanced Study in the Behavioral Sciences in 1997–98. (Is it possible to have a *bad* year there? It poured rain the whole time and it was still fun.) Hundreds of seminar participants, and my colleagues in the MacArthur Norms and Preferences Network, have shaped my thinking over the years. Students in my Psychology 101 class at Caltech, colleagues Bruno Broseta, Miguel Costa-Gomes, John Kennan, Roberto Weber, and in particular Vince Crawford, and three anonymous referees all commented helpfully on the manuscript. Research assistants Chris Anderson, Dan Clendenning, Ming Hsu, and Angela Hung helped with graphics and editorial support. Gail Nash, Rachel Kibble, and especially the tireless Karen Kerbs did amazing work on the manuscript with great aplomb. Thanks also to Peter Dougherty of Princeton University Press for unflagging cheerleading, sage advice at all the right moments, and some cool free books. Timely moral support was provided throughout by Peter, and by a fortune cookie from the local Chinese delivery place. Their message arrived just before I finished the tedious process of reviewing the copyediting. It said—no lie—"You are soon to achieve perfection."

The book is written so that the reader can either "dive" or "snorkel." Snorkeling means swimming along the surface, looking at the pretty fish but not going so deep that you need special equipment (e.g., intimate knowledge of game theory) to breathe. Snorkelers should appreciate highlights of crucial facts about what has been learned from experiments relative to theory, and how those findings suggest new theory (summarized in section summaries). Divers will want to explore the details of studies and make their own judgments about what was learned and important.

I have also skimped on, or omitted, extremely important areas because they are either well covered elsewhere or simply overwhelming—especially experiments on cooperative games, unstructured bargaining (see Roth, 1995b, for more on this subject), public goods and prisoners' dilemma games, and auctions (see Kagel, 1995, or Kagel and Levin, in press).

I have followed certain writing conventions. My goal is to convey the regularities that have been discovered in experimental studies of game theory, and a feeling for the care, craftsmanship, and conventions of the experimental method. Some studies have been overemphasized and some deemphasized. My preference is to describe the first or last studies and the most solid or interesting results. In summarizing results, the goal is full disclosure without clutter and irrelevance. If you are curious about a detail of the experiments or data that have not been reported, they probably were omitted because they do not matter (or were omitted in the original published reporting); however, I would be horrified if you took this as an excuse to forgo looking at the original article if you are *really* curious.

For example, when the data from various periods of an experiment are lumped together and reported as an average, that usually means there is no interesting learning across periods.

Details of how experiments are conducted (e.g., matching protocol, incentive levels) have been collected in the appendix at the end of the book to keep you from being distracted as you read.

Interested in teaching from this book? Start with Chapter 1 (duh) and have the students actually play the three games in that chapter to get a feel for what piques their curiosity. Pick and choose other material to suit the interests and technical mastery of the students. Chapters 2 and 7 will be of broadest interest to noneconomists, Chapter 6 is heavy on econometrics, and Chapter 8 (and parts of Chapter 4) is the most technically demanding.

Behavioral Game Theory

1
Introduction

GAME THEORY IS ABOUT WHAT HAPPENS when people—or genes, or nations—
interact. Here are some examples: Tennis players deciding whether to serve
to the left or right side of the court; the only bakery in town offering a discounted price on pastries just before it closes; employees deciding how hard
to work when the boss is away; an Arab rug seller deciding how quickly to
lower his price when haggling with a tourist; rival drug firms investing in a
race to reach patent; an e-commerce auction company learning which features to add to its website by trial and error; real estate developers guessing
when a downtrodden urban neighborhood will spring back to life; San Francisco commuters deciding which route to work will be quickest when the Bay
Bridge is closed; Lamelara men in Indonesia deciding whether to join the
day's whale hunt, and how to divide the whale if they catch one; airline
workers hustling to get a plane away from the gate on time; MBAs deciding what their degree will signal to prospective employers (and whether
quitting after the first year of their two-year program to join a dot-com
startup signals guts or stupidity); a man framing a memento from when
he first met his wife, as a gift on their first official date a year later (they're
happily married now!); and people bidding for art or oil leases, or for knick-
knacks on eBay. These examples illustrate, respectively, ultimatum games
(bakery, Chapter 2), gift exchange (employees, Chapter 2), mixed equilibrium (tennis, Chapter 3), Tunisian bazaar bargaining (rug seller, Chapter
4), patent race games (patents, Chapter 5), learning (e-commerce, Chapter 6), stag hunt games (whalers, Chapter 7), weak-link games (airlines,
Chapter 7), order-statistic games (developers, Chapter 7), signaling (MBAs
and romance, Chapter 8), auctions (bidding, Chapter 9).

In all of these situations, a person (or firm) must anticipate what others will do and what others will infer from the person's own actions. A game is a mathematical x-ray of the crucial features of these situations. A game consists of the "strategies" each of several "players" have, with precise rules for the order in which players choose strategies, the information they have when they choose, and how they rate the desirability (or "utility") of resulting outcomes. An appendix to this chapter describes the basic mathematics of game theory and gives some references for further reading.

Game theory has a very clear paternity. Many of its main features were introduced by von Neumann and Morgenstern in 1944 (following earlier work in the 1920s by von Neumann, Borel, and Zermelo). A few years later, John Nash proposed a "solution" to the problem of how rational players would play, now called Nash equilibrium. Nash's idea, based on the idea of equilibrium in a physical system, was that players would adjust their strategies until no player could benefit from changing. All players are then choosing strategies that are best (utility-maximizing) responses to all the other players' strategies. Important steps in the 1960s were the realization that behavior in repeated sequences of one-shot games could differ substantially from behavior in one-shot games, and theories in which a player can have private information about her values (or "type"), provided all players know the probabilities of what those types might be. In 1994, Nash, John Harsanyi, and Reinhard Selten (an active experimenter) shared the Nobel Prize in Economic Science for their pathbreaking contributions.

In the past fifty years, game theory has gradually become a standard language in economics and is increasingly used in other social sciences (and in biology). In economics, game theory is used to analyze behavior of firms that worry about what their competitors will do.[1] Game theory is also good for understanding how workers behave in firms (such as the reaction of CEOs or salespeople to incentive contracts), the spread of social conventions such as language and fashion, and which genes or cultural practices will spread.

The power of game theory is its generality and mathematical precision. The same basic ideas are used to analyze *all* the games—tennis, bargaining for rugs, romance, whale-hunting—described in the first paragraph of this chapter. Game theory is also boldly precise. Suppose an Arab rug seller can always buy more rugs cheaply, an interested tourist values the rugs at somewhere between $10 and $1000, and the seller has a good idea of how

---

[1] Game theory fills the conceptual gap between a single monopoly, which need not worry about what other firms and consumers will do because it has monopoly power, and "perfect competition," in which no firm is big enough for competitors to worry about. Game theory is used to study the intermediate case, "oligopoly," in which there are few enough firms that each company should anticipate what the others will do.

impatient the tourist is but isn't sure how much the tourist likes a particular rug. Then game theory tells you *exactly* what price the seller should start out at, and *exactly* how quickly he should cut the price as the tourist hems and haws. In experimental re-creations of this kind of rug-selling, the theory is half-right and half-wrong: it's wrong about the opening prices sellers state, but the rate at which experimental sellers drop their prices over time is amazingly close to the rate that game theory predicts (see Chapter 4).

It is important to distinguish *games* from game *theory*. Games are a taxonomy of strategic situations, a rough equivalent for social science of the periodic table of elements in chemistry. Analytical game *theory* is a mathematical derivation of what players with different cognitive capabilities are likely to do in games.[2] Game theory is often highly mathematical (which has limited its spread outside economics) and is usually based on introspection and guesses rather than careful observation of how people actually play in games. This book aims to correct the imbalance of theory and facts by describing hundreds of experiments in which people interact strategically. The results are used to create behavioral game theory. Behavioral game theory is about what players *actually* do. It expands analytical theory by adding emotion, mistakes, limited foresight, doubts about how smart others are, and learning to analytical game theory (Colman, in press, gives a more philosophical perspective). Behavioral game theory is one branch of behavioral economics, an approach to economics which uses psychological regularity to suggest ways to weaken rationality assumptions and extend theory (see Camerer and Loewenstein, 2003).

Because the language of game theory is both rich and crisp, it could unify many parts of social science. For example, trust is studied by social psychologists, sociologists, philosophers, economists interested in economic development, and others. But what *is* trust? This slippery concept can be precisely defined in a game: Would you lend money to somebody who doesn't have to pay you back, but might feel morally obliged to do so? If you would, you trust her. If she pays you back, she is trustworthy. This definition gives a way to measure trust, and has been used in experiments in many places (including Bulgaria, South Africa, and Kenya; see Chapter 3).

The spread of game theory outside of economics has suffered, I believe, from the misconception that you need to know a lot of fancy math to apply it, and from the fact that most predictions of analytical game theory are not well grounded in observation. The need for empirical regularity to inform

---

[2] To be precise, this book is only about "noncooperative" game theory—that is, when players cannot make binding agreements about what to do, so they must guess what others will do. Cooperative game theory is a complementary branch of game theory which deals with how players divide the spoils after they have made binding agreements.

game theory has been recognized many times. In the opening pages of their seminal book, von Neumann and Morgenstern (1944, p. 4) wrote:

> the empirical background of economic science is definitely inadequate. Our knowledge of the relevant facts of economics is incomparably smaller than that commanded in physics at the time when mathematization of that subject was achieved. . . . It would have been absurd in physics to expect Kepler and Newton without Tycho Brahe—and there is no reason to hope for an easier development in economics.

This book is focused on experiments as empirical background. Game theory has also been tested using data that naturally occur in field settings (particularly in clearly structured situations such as auctions). But experimental control is particularly useful because game theory predictions often depend sensitively on the choices players have, how they value outcomes, what they know, the order in which they move, and so forth. As Crawford (1997, p. 207) explains:

> Behavior in games is notoriously sensitive to details of the environment, so that strategic models carry a heavy informational burden, which is often compounded in the field by an inability to observe all relevant variables. Important advances in experimental technique over the past three decades allow a control that often gives experiments a decisive advantage in identifying the relationship between behavior and environment. . . . For many questions, [experimental data are] the most important source of empirical information we have, and [they are] unlikely to be less reliable than casual empiricism or introspection.

Of course, it is important to ask how well the results of experiments with (mostly) college students playing for a couple of hours for modest financial stakes generalize to workers in firms, companies creating corporate strategy, diplomats negotiating, and so forth. But these doubts about generalizability are a demand for more elaborate experiments, not a dismissal of the experimental method per se. Experimenters *have* studied a few dimensions of generalizability—particularly the effects of playing for more money, which are usually small. But more ambitious experiments with teams of players, complex environments, communication, and overlapping generations[3] would enhance generalizability further, and people should do more of them.

---

[3] See Schotter and Sopher (2000).

1.1 What Is Game Theory Good For?

Is game theory meant to predict what people do, to give them advice, or what? The theorist's answer is that game theory is none of the above—it is simply "analytical," a body of answers to mathematical questions about what players with various degrees of rationality will do. If people don't play the way theory says, their behavior has not proved the mathematics wrong, any more than finding that cashiers sometimes give the wrong change disproves arithmetic.

In practice, however, the tools of analytical game theory *are* used to predict, and also to explain (or "postdict"[4]) and prescribe. Auctions are a good example of all three uses of game theory. Based on precise assumptions about the rules of the auction and the way in which bidders value an object, such as an oil lease or a painting, auction theory then derives how much rational bidders will pay.

Theory can help explain why some types of auction are more common than others. For example, in "second-price" or Vickrey auctions the high bidder buys the object being auctioned at a price equal to the *second*-highest bid. Under some conditions these auctions should, in theory, raise more revenue for sellers than traditional first-price auctions in which the high bidder pays what she bid. But second-price auctions are rare (see Lucking-Reilly, 2000). Why? Game theory offers an explanation: Since the high bidder pays a price other than what she bid in a second-price auction, such auctions are vulnerable to manipulation by the seller (who can sneak in an artificial bid to force the high bidder to pay more).

How well does auction theory predict? Tests with field data are problematic: Because bidders' valuations are usually hidden, it is difficult to tell whether they are bidding optimally, although some predictions can be tested. Fortunately, there are many careful experiments (see Kagel, 1995; Kagel and Levin, in press). The results of these experiments are mixed. In private-value auctions in which each player has her own personal value for the object (and doesn't care how much others value it), people bid remarkably close to the amounts they are predicted to, even when the function mapping values into bids is nonlinear and counterintuitive.[5]

In common-value auctions the value of the object is essentially the same for everyone, but is uncertain. Bidding for leases on oil tracts is an example—different oil companies would all value the oil in the same way but aren't sure how much oil is there. In these auctions players who are most optimistic about the value of the object tend to bid the highest and win.

---

[4] In some domains of social science, these kinds of game-theoretic "stories" about how an institution or event unfolded are called "analytical narratives" and are proving increasingly popular (Bates et al., 1998).

[5] See Chen and Plott (1998) and the sealed-bid mechanism results in Chapter 4.

The problem is that, if you win, it means you were much more optimistic than any other bidder and probably paid more than the object is worth, a possibility called the "winner's curse." Analytical game theory assumes rational bidders will anticipate the winner's curse and bid very conservatively to avoid it. Experiments show that players do not anticipate the winner's curse, so winning bidders generally pay more than they should.

Perhaps the most important modern use of auction theory is to prescribe how to bid in an auction, or how to design an auction. The shining triumphs of modern auction theory are recent auctions of airwaves to telecommunications companies. In several auctions in different countries, regulatory agencies decided to put airwave spectrum up for auction. An auction raises government revenue and, ideally, ensures that a public resource ends up in the hands of the firms that are best able to create value from it. In most countries, the auctions were designed in collaborations among theorists and experimental "testbedding" that helped detect unanticipated weaknesses in proposed designs (like using a wind tunnel to test the design of an airplane wing, or a "tow-tank" pool to see which ship designs sink and which float). The designs that emerged were not exactly copied from books on auction theory. Instead, theorists spent a lot of time pointing out how motivated bidders could exploit loopholes in designs proposed by lawyers and regulators, and using the results of testbedding to improve designs. Auction designers opted for a design that gave bidders a chance to learn from potential mistakes and from watching others, rather than a simpler "sealed-bid" design in which bidders simply mail in bids and the Federal Communications Commission opens the envelopes and announces the highest ones. One of the most powerful and surprising ideas in auction theory— "revenue equivalence"—is that some types of auctions will, in theory, raise the same amount of revenue as other auctions that are quite different in structure. (For example, an "English" auction, in which prices are raised slowly until only one bidder remains, is revenue-equivalent to a sealed-bid "Vickrey" auction, in which the highest bidder pays what the second-highest bidder bid.) But when it came to designing an auction that actual companies would participate in with billions of dollars on the line, the auction designers were not willing to bet that *behavior* would actually be equivalent in different types of auctions, despite what theory predicted. Their design choices reflect an *implicit* theory of actual behavior in games that is probably closer to the ideas in this book than to standard theory based on unlimited mutual rationality. Notice that, in this process of design and prescription, guessing accurately how players will actually behave—good prediction—is crucial.[6]

---

[6] Howard Raiffa pointed this out many times, calling game theory "asymmetrically normative."

Even if game theory is not always accurate, descriptive failure is prescriptive opportunity. Just as evangelists preach *because* people routinely violate moral codes, the fact that players violate game theory provides a chance to give helpful advice. Simply mapping social situations into types of games is extremely useful because it tells people what to look out for. In their popular book for business managers, *Co-opetition*, Brandenburger and Nalebuff (1996) draw attention to the barest bones of a game—players, information, actions, and outcomes. Both are brilliant theorists who *could* have written a more theoretical book. They chose not to because teaching MBAs and working with managers convinced them that teaching the basic elements of game theory is more helpful.

Game theory is often used to prescribe in a subtler way. Sometimes game theory is used to figure out what it is likely to happen in a strategic interaction, so a person or company can then try to change the game to their advantage. (This is a kind of engineering approach too, since it asks how to improve an existing situation.)

1.2   Three Examples

This chapter illustrates the basics of behavioral game theory and the experimental approach with three examples (which are discussed in more detail in later chapters): ultimatum bargaining, "continental divide" coordination games, and "beauty contest" guessing games. Experiments using these games show how behavioral game theory can explain what people do more accurately by extending analytical game theory to include how players feel about the payoffs other players receive, limited strategic thinking, and learning.

The three games use a recipe underlying most of the experiments reported in this book: pick a game for which standard game theory makes a bold prediction or a vague prediction that can be sharpened. Simple games are particularly useful because only one or two basic principles are needed to make a prediction. If the prediction is wrong, we know which principles are at fault, and the results usually suggest an alternative principle that predicts better.

In the experiments, games are usually posed in abstract terms because game theory rarely specifies how adding realistic details will affect behavior. Subjects make a simple choice, and know how their choices and the choices of other subjects combine to determine monetary payoffs.[7] Subjects are

---

[7] These design choices bet heavily on the cognitive presumption that people are using generic principles of strategic thinking which transcend idiosyncratic differences in verbal descriptions of games. If choices are domain specific then the basic enterprise this book describes is incomplete; varying game labels to evoke

actually rewarded based on their performance because we are interested in extrapolating the results to naturally occurring games in which players have substantial financial incentives. The games are usually repeated because we are interested in equilibration and learning over time. An appendix to this chapter describes some key design choices experimenters make, and why they matter.

1.2.1 Example 1: Ultimatum Bargaining

I once took a cruise with some friends and a photographer took our picture, unsolicited, as we boarded the boat. When we disembarked hours later, the photographer tried to sell us the picture for $5 and refused to negotiate. (His refusal was credible because several other groups stood around deciding whether to buy their pictures, also for $5. If he caved in and cut the price, it would be evident to all others and he would lose a lot more than the discount to us since he would have to offer the discount to everyone.) Being good game theorists, we balked at the price and pointed out that the picture was worthless to him (one cheapskate offered $1). He rejected our insulting offer and refused to back down.

The game we played with the photographer was an "ultimatum game," which is the simplest kind of bargaining. In an ultimatum game there is some gain from exchange and one player makes a take-it-or-leave-it offer of how to divide that gain. Our picture presumably had no value to him and was valuable to us (worth more than $5 in sentimental value). A price is simply proposing a way to divide the gains from exchange between our true reservation price and his cost. His offer to sell for $5 was an ultimatum offer because he refused to negotiate.

In laboratory ultimatum games like this, two players, a Proposer and a Responder, bargain over some amount, say $10 (the sum used in many experiments). The $10 represents the value of the gain to exchange (or "surplus") that would be lost if the trade wasn't made. The Proposer offers x to the Responder, leaving herself $10 − x$. The Responder can either take the offer—then the Responder gets x and the Proposer gets $10 − x$—or reject it and both get nothing.

Because the ultimatum game is so simple, it is *not* a good model of the protracted process of most naturally occurring bargaining (and isn't intended to be). It *is* the right model of what happened to us after the cruise,

---

domain-specific reasoning is the next step. The study by Cooper et al. (1999) of ratchet effects in productivity games using Chinese factory managers—who face such effects in planned economies—is a good example (see Chapter 8).

and what happens in the waning minutes before a labor strike is called, or on the courthouse steps before a lawsuit goes to trial. It is a model of the last step in much bargaining, and hence is a building block for modeling more complicated situations (see Chapter 4).

Simple games test game-theoretic principles in the clearest possible way. Ultimatum games, and related games, also are useful for measuring how people feel about the allocations of money between themselves and others.

The analytical game theory approach to ultimatum bargaining is this: First assume players are "self-interested"; that is, they care about earning the most money for themselves. If players are self-interested, the Responder will accept the smallest money amount offered, say $0.25. If the Proposer anticipates this, and wants to get the most she can for herself, she will offer $0.25 and keep $9.75. In formal terms, offering $0.25 (and accepting any positive amount) is the "subgame perfect equilibrium".[8] By going first, the Proposer has all the bargaining power and, in theory, can exploit it because a self-interested Responder will take whatever she can get.

To many people, the lopsided distribution of the $10 predicted by analytical game theory (with self-interest) seems unfair. Because the allocation is considered unfair, the way people actually bargain shows whether people are willing to take costly actions that express their concerns for fairness. In the cruise-picture example, offering $1 instead of the $5 price the photographer offered added $4 to our surplus and subtracted $4 from his. If he thought this was unfair to him, he could reject it and earn nothing (even though everyone suffers—he earns no money and we don't get a picture we would like to own). The lab experiments simulate this simple game. Will Responders put their money where their mouths are and reject offers that seem unfair? If so, will Proposers anticipate this and make fair offers, or stubbornly make unfair offers?

In dozens of experiments conducted in several different countries, Proposers offer $4 or $5 out of $10 on average, and offers do not vary much. Offers of $2 or less are rejected about half the time. The Responders think much less than half is unfair and are willing to reject such small offers, to punish the Proposer who behaved so unfairly. Figure 1.1 shows data from a study by Hoffman, McCabe, and Smith (1996a). The *x*-axis shows the amount being offered to the Responder, and the *y*-axis shows the relative frequency of offers of different amounts. The dark part of each frequency bar is the number of offers that were rejected. Most offers are close to half

---

[8] Note also that every offer is a "Nash equilibrium" or mutual best-response pattern because *x* is the optimal offer if the Proposer thinks the Responder will reject any other offer. (This belief may be wrong but, if the Proposer believes it, she will never take an action that disconfirms her belief, so the wrong belief can be part of a Nash equilibrium.)

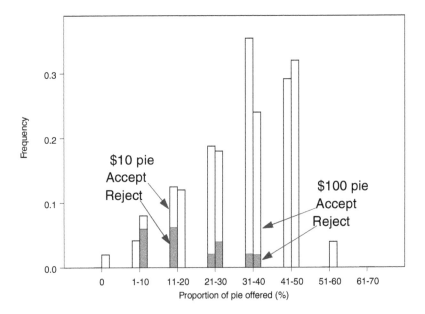

Figure 1.1. *Offers and rejections in high- and low-stakes ultimatum games. Source: Based on data from Hoffman, McCabe, and Smith (1996a).*

and low offers are often rejected. Figure 1.1 also shows that the same pattern of results occurs when stakes were multiplied by ten and Arizona students bargained over $100. (A couple of subjects rejected $30 offers!) The same basic result has been replicated with a $400 stake (List and Cherry, 2000) in Florida and in countries with low disposable income, including Indonesia and Slovenia, where modest stakes by American standards represent several weeks' wages.

There are many interpretations of what causes Responders to reject substantial sums (see Chapter 3). There is little doubt that some players define a fair split of $10 as close to half and have a preference for being treated fairly. Such rejections are evidence of "negative reciprocity": Responders reciprocate unfair behavior by harming the person who treated them unfairly, at a substantial cost to themselves (provided the unfair Proposer is harmed more than they are). Negative reciprocity is evident in other social domains, even when monetary stakes are high—jilted boyfriends who accost their exes, ugly divorces that cost people large sums, impulsive street crimes caused by a stranger allegedly "disrespecting" an assailant, the failure of parties in legal "nuisance cases" to renegotiate after a court judgment even when both could benefit (Farnsworth, 1999), and so on.[9]

This explanation for ultimatum rejections begs the question of where fairness preferences came from. A popular line of argument is that human experience in our ancestral past created evolutionary adaptations in brain mechanisms, or in the interaction of cognitive and emotional systems, which cause people to get angry when they are pushed around because getting angry had survival value when people interacted with the same people in a small group (see Frank, 1988). A different line of argument is that cultures create different standards of fairness, perhaps owing to the closeness of kin relations or the degree of anonymous market exchange with strangers (compared with sharing among relatives), and these cultural standards are transmitted socially through oral traditions and socialization of children.

Remarkable evidence for the cultural standards view comes from a study by eleven anthropologists who conducted ultimatum games in primitive cultures in Africa, the Amazon, Papua New Guinea, Indonesia, and Mongolia (see Chapter 2). In some of these cultures, people did not think that sharing fairly was necessary. Proposers in these cultures offered very little (the equivalent of $1.50 out of $10) and Responders accepted virtually every offer. Ironically, these simple societies are the *only* known populations who behave exactly as game theory predicts!

Note that rejections in ultimatum games do not necessarily reject the strategic principles underlying game theory (for example, Weibull, 2000). The Responder simply decides whether she wants both players to get nothing, or wants to get a small share when the Proposer gets much more. The fact that a Responder rejects means she is not maximizing her own earnings, but it does not mean she is not capable of strategic thinking. Recent theories attempt to explain rejections using social preference functions which balance a person's desire to have more money with their desire to reciprocate those who have treated them fairly or unfairly, or to achieve equality. Such functions have a long pedigree (traceable at least to Edgeworth in the 1890s). Economists have resisted them because it seems to be too easy to introduce a new factor in the utility function for each game. But the new theories strive to explain results in different games with a *single* function. Having a lot of data from different games to work with makes this enterprise possible and imposes discipline.

---

[9] My sister Jeannine told me that in Atlantic City the casinos sometimes have problems with lucrative "high-roller" customers stealing luxurious towels, robes, and other items from their (complimentary) hotel rooms after losing at the casinos. In their minds these losers are simply taking things they have paid for.

The new theories make surprising new predictions. For example, when there are two or more Proposers, there is no way for any one of them single-handedly to earn more money *and* limit inequality. As a result some theories predict that both Proposers offer almost everything to the Responder even though they *do* care about equality. (If there had been *two* photographers on that damn boat, we would have gotten our picture for $1.)

New social preference theories should prove useful in analyzing bargaining, tax policy, the strong tendency of tenant farmers to share crop earnings equally with landowners (Young and Burke, 2001), and wage-setting (particularly the reluctance of firms to cut wages in hard times, which is puzzling to economists who assume changes in the price of labor will equalize supply and demand, and other phenomena).

1.2.2 Example 2: Path-Dependent Coordination in "Continental Divide" Games

In coordination games, players want to conform to what others do (although they may have different ideas about which conformist convention is best). For example, in California there is an ongoing struggle over the physical location of the "new media" firms, such as internet provision of film and entertainment. New media people could gravitate toward Silicon Valley, where web geeks congregate, or toward Hollywood and Southern California, where many movies and TV shows are produced. Which geographical region is the better location depends on whether you think the location of internet firms is central, and "content" producers should follow them, or whether the internet is merely a distribution channel and content providers are king.[10]

This economic tug-of-war can be modeled by a game in which players choose a location, and their earnings depend on the location they choose and the location most other people choose. A game with this flavor has been studied by Van Huyck, Battalio, and Cook (1997). Table 1.1 shows the payoffs (in cents). In this game, players pick numbers from 1 to 14 (think of the numbers as corresponding to physical locations—low numbers are Hollywood and high numbers are Silicon Valley). The matrix in Table 1.1 shows the row player's payoff from choosing a number when the *median* number everyone in a group picks—the middle number—is the number in the different columns. If you choose 4, for example, and the median is 5, you earn a healthy payoff of 71; but if the median is 12 you earn −14 (bankruptcy!). The basic payoff structure implies you should pick a

---

[10] Of course, this example is undermined by the fact that cyberspace is everywhere and nowhere, so content providers might be able to stay put in the swank Hollywood Hills and still do business "in" Silicon Valley without moving.

low number if you think most others will pick low numbers, and pick a high number if you think most others will pick high numbers. If you aren't sure what others will do, pick a number such as 6, which gives payoffs ranging from 23 to 82 (hedging your bet).

In the experiments, players are organized into seven-person groups. The groups play together fifteen times. After each trial you learn what the median was, compute your earnings from that trial (depending on your own choice and the median), and play again. Since the game is complicated, think for a minute about what you would actually do and what might happen over the course of playing fifteen times.

The payoffs have the property that, if a player guesses that the median number is slightly below 7, her best response to that guess is to choose a number smaller than the guess itself. For example, if you think the median will be 7, your best response is 5, which earns 83 cents. Thus, if medians are initially low, responding to low medians will drive numbers lower until they reach 3. Three is an equilibrium or mutual best-response point because, if everyone chooses 3, the median will be 3 and your best response to a median of 3 is to choose 3. If players were to reach this point, nobody could profit by moving away. (The payoff from this equilibrium is shown in italics in Table 1.1.)

Table 1.1. *Payoffs in "continental divide" experiment (cents)*

	Median choice													
Choice	1	2	3	4	5	6	7	8	9	10	11	12	13	14
1	45	49	52	55	56	55	46	−59	−88	−105	−117	−127	−135	−142
2	48	53	58	62	65	66	61	−27	−52	−67	−77	−86	−92	−98
3	48	54	*60*	66	70	74	72	1	−20	−32	−41	−48	−53	−58
4	43	51	58	65	71	77	80	26	8	−2	−9	−14	−19	−22
5	35	44	52	60	69	77	83	46	32	25	19	15	12	10
6	23	33	42	52	62	72	82	62	53	47	43	41	39	38
7	7	18	28	40	51	64	78	75	69	66	64	63	62	62
8	−13	−1	11	23	37	51	69	83	81	80	80	80	81	82
9	−37	−24	−11	3	18	35	57	88	89	91	92	94	96	98
10	−65	−51	−37	−21	−4	15	40	89	94	98	101	104	107	110
11	−97	−82	−66	−49	−31	−9	20	85	94	100	105	110	114	119
12	−133	−117	−100	−82	−61	−37	−5	78	91	99	106	*112*	118	123
13	−173	−156	−137	−118	−96	−69	−33	67	83	94	103	110	117	123
14	−217	−198	−179	−158	−134	−105	−65	52	72	85	95	104	112	120

Source: Van Huyck, Battalio, and Cook (1997).

But there is another Nash equilibrium. If players guess that the median will be 8 or above, they should choose numbers that are *higher* than their guesses, until they reach 12; 12 is also a Nash equilibrium because choosing 12 gives the highest payoff if the median is 12.

This is a coordination game because there are *two* Nash equilibria in which everybody chooses the same strategy. Game theorists have struggled for many decades to figure out which of many equilibria will result if there are more than one.

This particular game illustrates processes in nature and social systems in which small historical accidents have a big long-run impact. A famous example is what chaos theorists call the "Lorenz effect": Because weather is a complex dynamic system, the movement of a butterfly in China can set in motion a complicated meteorological process that creates a storm in Bolivia. If that butterfly had just sat still, the Bolivians would be dry! Another example is what social theorists call the "broken window effect." Anecdotal evidence suggests that, when there is a single broken window in a community, neighbors feel less obligation to keep their yards clean, replace their own broken windows, and put fresh paint on their houses. Since criminals want to commit crimes in communities where neighbors aren't watchful and other criminals are lurking (so the cops are busy), a single broken window can lead to a spiralling process of social breakdown. Policymakers love the broken window theory because it suggests an easy fix to problems of urban decay—repair every window before the effect of a few broken ones spreads throughout the community like a virus.

I call the game in Table 1.1 the "continental divide" game. The continental divide is a geographic line which divides those parts of North America in which water will flow in one direction from the parts in which water flows in the opposite direction. If you stand on the continental divide in Alaska, and pour water from a canteen as I once did, some drops will flow north to the Arctic Ocean and others will flow to the Pacific Ocean. Two drops of water that start out infinitesimally close together in the canteen end up a thousand miles apart.

The game is called the continental divide game because medians below 7 are a "basin of attraction" (in evolutionary game theory terms) for convergence toward the equilibrium at 3. Medians above 8 are a basin of attraction for convergence toward 12. The "separatrix" between 7 and 8 divides the game into regions where players will "flow" toward 3 and players will flow toward 12.

Which equilibrium is reached has important economic consequences. The 12 equilibrium pays $1.12 for each player but the 3 equilibrium pays only $0.60. On this basis alone, you might guess that players would choose higher numbers in the hopes of reaching the more profitable equilibrium. Before glancing ahead, ask yourself again what you think will happen. If you

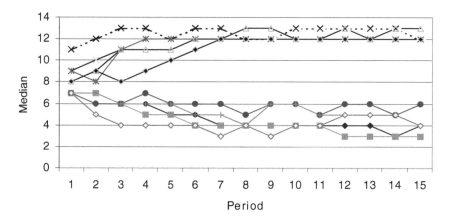

Figure 1.2.   *Median choices in the "continental divide" game. Source: Based on data from Van Huyck, Battalio, and Cook (1997).*

have studied a lot of game theory and still aren't sure what to expect, your curiosity about what people actually do should be piqued.

Figure 1.2 shows what happened in ten experimental groups. Five groups started at a median at 7 or below; all of them flowed toward the low-payoff equilibrium at 3. The other five groups started at 8 or above and flowed to the high-payoff equilibrium.

The experiment has two important findings. First, people do *not* always gravitate toward the high-payoff equilibrium even though players who end up at low numbers earn half as much. (Whether they would if they could play again, or discussed the game in advance, is an interesting open question.) Second, the currents of history are strong, creating "extreme sensitivity to initial conditions." Players who find themselves in a group with two or three others who think 7 is their lucky number, and choose it in the first period, end up sucked into a whirlpool leading to measly $0.60 earnings. Players in a group whose median is 8 or higher end up earning almost twice as much. One or two Chinese subjects choosing 8—a lucky number for Chinese— could bring good fortune to everyone, just as the butterfly brought rain on the Bolivians.

No concept in analytical game theory gracefully accounts for the fact that some groups flow to 3 and earn less, while others flow to 12 and earn more. Indeed, the problem of predicting which of many equilibria will result in games such as these may be inherently unsolvable by pure reasoning. Social conventions, communication, subtle features of the display of the game, analogies players draw with experiences they have had, and homespun ideas about lucky numbers could all influence which equilibrium is reached. As

Schelling (1960) wrote, predicting what players will do in these games by pure theory is like trying to prove that a joke is funny without telling it.

1.2.3 Example 3: "Beauty Contests" and Iterated Dominance

In Keynes's famous book *General Theory of Employment, Interest, and Money*, he draws an analogy between the stock market and a newspaper contest in which people guess what faces others will guess are most beautiful: "It is not a case of choosing those which, to the best of one's judgment, are really the prettiest, nor even those which average opinion genuinely thinks the prettiest. We have reached the third degree, where we devote our intelligences to anticipating what average opinion expects the average opinion to be. And there are some, I believe, who practise the fourth, fifth, and higher degrees" (1936, p. 156). This quote is perhaps no more apt than in the year 2001 (when I first wrote this), just after prices of American internet stocks soared to unbelievable heights in the largest speculative bubble in history. (At one point, the market valuation of the e-tailer bookseller Amazon, which had never reported a profit, was worth more than all other American booksellers combined.)

A simple game that captures the reasoning Keynes had in mind is called the "beauty contest" game (see Nagel, 1995, and Ho, Camerer, and Weigelt, 1998). In a typical beauty contest game, each of N players simultaneously chooses a number x_i in the interval $[0,100]$. Take an average of the numbers and multiply by a multiple $p < 1$ (say $p = 0.7$). The player whose number is closest to this target (70 percent of the average) wins a fixed prize. Before proceeding, think about what number you would pick.

The beauty contest game can be used to distinguish whether people "practise the fourth, fifth, and higher degrees" of reasoning as Keynes wondered. Here's how. Most players start by thinking, "Suppose the average is 50". Then you should choose 35, to be closest to the target of 70 percent of the average and win. But if you think all players will think this way the average will be 35, so a shrewd player such as yourself (thinking one step ahead) should choose 70 percent of 35, around 25. But if you think all players think that way you should choose 70 percent of 25, or 18.

In analytical game theory, players do not stop this iterated reasoning until they reach a best-response point. But, since all players want to choose 70 percent of the average, if they all choose the same number it must be zero. (That is, if you solve the equation $x^* = 0.7x^*$, you've found the unique Nash equilibrium.)

The beauty contest game provides a rough measure of the number of steps of strategic thinking that subjects are doing. It is called a "dominance-solvable game" because it can be "solved"—i.e., an equilibrium can be computed—by iterated application of dominance. A dominated strategy is one that yields a lower payoff than another (dominant) strategy, regardless of what other players do. Choosing a number above 70 is a dominated strategy because the highest possible value of the target number is 70, so you can always do better by choosing a number lower than 70. But if nobody violates dominance by choosing above 70, then the highest the target can be is 70 percent of 70, or 49, so choosing 49–70 is dominated if you think others obey one step of dominance. Deleting dominated strategies iteratively leads you to zero.

Many interesting games are dominance solvable. A familiar example in economics is Cournot duopoly. Two firms each choose quantities of similar products to make. Since their products are the same, the market price is determined by the total quantity they make (and by consumer demand). It is easy to show that there are quantities so high that firms will lose money because flooding the market with so much supply will drive prices too low to cover fixed costs. If you assume your rivals won't produce that much, then somewhat lower quantities are bad (dominated) choices for you. Applying this logic iteratively leads to a precise solution.

In practice, it is unlikely that people perform more than a couple of steps of iterated thinking because it strains the limits of working memory (i.e., the amount of information people can keep active in their mind at one time). Consider embedded sentences such as "Kevin's dog bit David's mailman whose sister's boyfriend gave the dog to him." Who's the "him" referred to at the end of the sentence? By the time you get to the end, many people have forgotten who owned the dog because working memory has only so much space.[11] Embedded sentences are difficult to understand. Dominance-solvable games are similar in mental complexity.

Iterated reasoning also requires you to believe that others are thinking hard, and are thinking that *you* are thinking hard. When I played this game at a Caltech board of trustees meeting, a very clever board member (a well-known Ph.D. in finance) chose 18.1. Later he explained his choice: He knew the Nash equilibrium was 0, but figured the average Caltech board member was clever enough to do two steps of reasoning and pick 25. Then why not pick 17.5 (which is 70 percent of 25)? He added 0.6 so he wouldn't tie with people who picked 17.5 or 18, and because he guessed that a few people would pick high numbers, which would push the average up. Now that's good behavioral game theory! (He didn't win, but was close.)

What happens in beauty contest games? Figure 1.3 shows choices in beauty contests with $p = 0.7$ with feedback about the average given to

---

[11] Seeing the sentence on the written page makes it easier; try reading it aloud to somebody who must remember the words and cannot refer back to them.

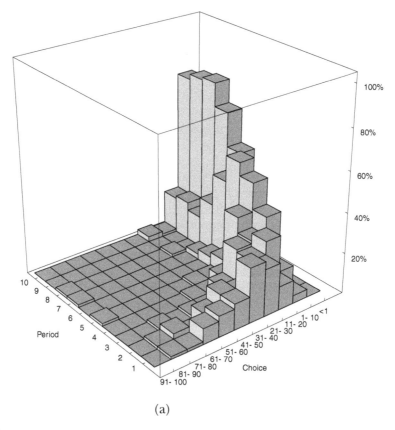

(a)

Figure 1.3.   *Convergence in low-stakes and high-stakes "beauty contest" games. Source: Unpublished data from Ho, Camerer, and Weigelt.*

subjects after each of ten rounds (unpublished data from Ho, Camerer, and Weigelt). Bars show the relative frequency of choices in different number intervals (on the side) across ten rounds (in front). The first histogram shows results from games with low-stakes payoffs (a $7 prize per period for seven-person groups) and the second histogram shows results from high-stakes ($28) payoffs.

First-round choices are around 21–40. A careful statistical analysis indicated that the median subject uses one or two steps of iterated dominance. That is, most subjects roughly guess that the average will be 50 and choose 35, or guess that others will choose 35 and choose 25. Very few subjects chose the equilibrium of zero in the first round. In fact, they should *not* choose zero. The goal is to be *one* step ahead of the average but no further and choosing zero is being too smart for your own good!

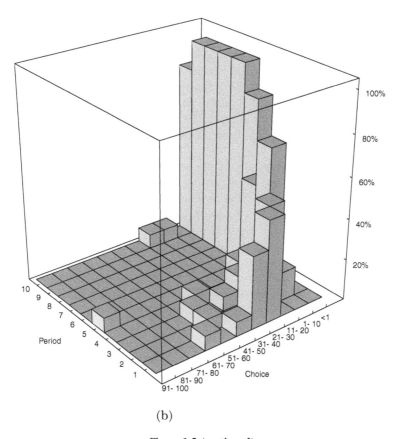

(b)

Figure 1.3 (continued)

Although the game-theoretic equilibrium of zero is a poor guess about initial choices, players *are* inexorably drawn toward zero as they learn. Behavioral game theory uses a concept of limited iterated reasoning to understand initial choices and a theory of learning to explain movement across rounds.

The beauty contest has been replicated in dozens of subject pools (see Chapter 5 for details), including Caltech undergraduates,[12] trustees on

---

[12] Caltech students are a useful subject pool because they are extraordinarily analytically skilled. In many years, the incoming first-year class has a median math SAT score of 800. Recently, the average test scores of the *applicants* have been higher than the average of those students who are *accepted* at Harvard. Studying how these students play simple games establishes whether very analytical students can figure the games out. Generally they do not play much differently than students at other colleges.

the Caltech board (including a subsample of corporate CEOs), economics Ph.D.s and game theorists, and readers of business newspapers (the *Financial Times* in the United Kingdom, *Spektrum* in Germany, and *Expansion* in Spain). The results in all these groups are very similar: Players use 0–3 levels of reasoning, and few subjects choose the Nash equilibrium of zero. Comparing Figures 1.3(a) and 1.3(b) shows that increasing the prize by a factor of four, leading to average earnings of $40 for a 45-minute experiment, has only a small effect. (In the high-stakes condition there are more low-number choices in periods 5–10).

The limited iterated reasoning measured in these games provides one explanation for persistence of phenomena such as the stock price bubbles Keynes had in mind. Even if all investors foresee a crash, they do not "backward induct" all the way to the present. They guess that others will sell a couple of steps before the crash, and plan to sell just before that exodus. This reasoning process does not unravel all the way (because doubt "reverberates"), which explains why bubbles can persist even if everyone knows they will eventually burst. Allen, Morris, and Shin (2002) make their argument precise and Camerer and Weigelt (1993) and Porter and Smith, (1994) show that bubbles can happen in the lab.

1.3 Experimental Regularity and Behavioral Game Theory

This book is a long answer to a question game theory students often ask: "This theory is interesting . . . but do people actually play this way?" The answer, not surprisingly, is mixed. There are no interesting games in which subjects reach a predicted equilibrium immediately. And there are no games so complicated that subjects do not converge in the direction of equilibrium (perhaps quite close to it) with enough experience in the lab.

Consider the three examples above. In ultimatum bargaining, players are far from the perfect equilibrium-assuming self-interest, but they are roughly in equilibrium when the Responder's preference for being treated fairly is taken into account (because offers maximize expected profit given observed rejection rates). Behavioral game theory explains these results by combining new theories of social utility with analytical game theory (see Chapter 2). In the continental divide and beauty contest games, players start far from equilibrium and converge close to it in ten periods or so. Behavioral game theory explains these results using concepts of limited reasoning as players first think about a game (see Chapter 5) and precise theories of learning (see Chapter 6).

Sherlock Holmes said, "Data, data! I cannot make bricks without clay." Experimental results are clay for behavioral game theory. The goal is not to "*dis*prove" game theory (a common reaction of psychologists and sociologists) but to *im*prove it by establishing regularity, which inspires new theory. Without some sort of observation, theoretical assumptions are grounded in casual pseudo-empirical work—informal opinion polls in seminar and office discussions and using one's own intuitions (a one-respondent poll). Biologists don't just ask "If I was a robin foraging for food, how might I do it?" They watch robins forage, or ask somebody who has. Theorist (and part-time experimenter) Eric Van Damme, among others, worries about the effects of having too few data of this sort in game theory (1999, p. 204):

> Without having a broad set of facts on which to theorize, there is a certain danger of spending too much time on models that are mathematically elegant, yet have little connection to actual behaviour. At present our empirical knowledge is inadequate [precisely the same word von Neumann and Morgenstern used fifty years before!] and it is an interesting question why game theorists have not turned more frequently to psychologists for information about the learning and information processing processes used by humans.

Data are particularly important for game theory because there is often more than one equilibrium (see Chapter 7) and how equilibration occurs is not perfectly understood (see Chapter 6). Pure mathematics alone will not solve these problems.

Why has empirical observation played a small role in game theory until recently? One possibility is that early experimentation was thought to have "failed". In a 1952 RAND conference, several theorists (including eventual Nobel laureate Nash) gathered to think about game theory. They also did some experiments, the results of which did not confirm theory and reportedly discouraged Nash and perhaps others (Nasar, 1998).[13] Interest in data also suffered from the fact that so many interesting mathematical puzzles were open for solution in game theory for such a long time.[14] From about 1970 onward, developments in the theory of repeated games, games of incomplete information, and applications to important fields such as principal–agent relations, contracting, and political science led to an

---

[13] I think these early experimenters made a mistake by concentrating too much on games with mixed-strategy equilibria. In those games, players have low monetary incentives and predictions depend on assumptions about risk tastes, which are difficult to measure or even control.

[14] Many "modern" ideas in behavioral game theory were first proposed early in the history of game theory, and left aside or forgotten. In his thesis Nash (1950) described a "mass action" interpretation of equilibrium similar to modern evolutionary game theory (Weibull, 1995). Weighted fictitious play (see Chapter 6), which seems to have been revived by empiricists around 1995, is described in the amazingly insightful book by Luce and Raiffa (1957). Selten (1978) emphasized how players perceive the game they play, a topic being revived by Rubinstein (1991), Camerer (1999), and Samuelson (2001), among others. Rosenthal (1989) first proposed a "quantal response equilibrium" version, later refined and applied by McKelvey and Palfrey (1995, 1998) and Goeree and Holt (1999).

explosion of theory. There is no doubt that this pursuit has been extremely insightful and necessary, but it was conducted with little empirical guidance of any sort. There is also little doubt that it is high time to raise the ratio of observation to theory. It is also encouraging that some theorists have turned serious attention to modeling bounded or procedural rationality formally (e.g., Rubinstein, 1998).[15]

Of course, experimental data are only one component of behavioral game theory. Detailed facts about cognitive mechanisms and field tests are important too.[16] The result of controlled experiments, field observation, and theorizing working together is summarized by Vince Crawford (1997, p. 208):

> The experimental evidence suggests that none of the leading theoretical frameworks for analyzing games—traditional non-cooperative game theory, cooperative game theory, evolutionary game theory, and adaptive learning models—gives a fully reliable account of behavior by itself, but that most behavior can be understood in terms of a synthesis of ideas from those frameworks, combined with empirical knowledge in proportions that depend in predictable ways on the environment.

Rapid development of behavioral game theory will depend on how scientists react to data. Reactions vary.

If you are smitten by the elegance of analytical game theory you might take the data as simply showing whether subjects understood the game and were motivated. If the data confirm game theory, you might say, the subjects must have understood; if the data disconfirm, the subjects must have not understood. Resist this conclusion. The games are usually simple, and most experimenters carefully control for understanding by using a quiz to be sure subjects know how choices lead to payoffs. Furthermore, by inferring subject understanding from data, there is no way to falsify the theory. Physicists and biologists would not have the same reaction if a theory about particles were falsified by careful experimentation ("The particles were confused!") or if birds didn't forage for food as predicted ("If they had more at stake [than survival?] they would get it right!"). Game theorists should be similarly open-minded to what behaving humans can teach them about human behavior.

In fact, evidence cited as confirmation of game theory often supports a key element of *behavioral* game theory—namely, that equilibration may take a long time, perhaps years or decades (and equilibration is therefore a crucial component of any theory). In the foreword to Roth and Sotomayor's

---

[15] This includes finite automata, ϵ-equilibrium, evolutionary and dynamic theories, non-partitional information structures, and so on. Most of this work is not directly inspired or disciplined by data, however.

[16] Roth's work on matching for college bowl games, sorority rush, and medical residency are rare, impressive examples (e.g., Roth and Xing, 1994).

(1990) book about the theory of matching markets, the brilliant mathematician Robert Aumann notes that

> the Gale–Shapley [matching] algorithm had in fact been in practical use already since 1951 for the assignment of interns to hospitals in the United States; it had evolved by a trial-and-error process that spanned more than half a century. . . . in the *real* real world—when the chips are down, the payoff is not five dollars but a successful career, and people have time to understand the situation—the predictions of game theory fare quite well.

Note that the "time to understand the situation" Aumann refers to was fifty years![17] Over such a span, a learning or equilibration theory is essential.

Another reaction you may have is to criticize details of experimental design. Aumann, again, writes (1990, p. xi):

> It is sometimes asserted that game theory is not "descriptive" of the "real world," that people don't really behave according to game-theoretic prescriptions. To back up such assertions, some workers have conducted experiments using poorly motivated subjects, subjects who do not understand what they are about and are paid off by pittances; as if such experiments represented the real world.

Aumann is alluding to an earlier generation of experiments in the 1960s and 1970s which were not sensitive to subject comprehension and incentives. This book largely ignores those experiments (though some are described in Chapter 3). The modern experiments described in this book—mostly from the past ten years—fully respect concerns such as Aumann's and are designed with them in mind. Subjects are typically analytically skilled college students who are quizzed and highly motivated.

Another reaction you are likely to have when behavior does not conform to analytical game theory is that subjects were playing a different game than the experimenter created. Such explanations are useful if they can be tested and falsified. However, these explanations make experimenters bristle when they are made in ignorance of the extraordinary care taken to ensure subject comprehension, control for anonymity when trying to create one-shot games, and variation in stakes and subject pool to check for robustness.

---

[17] A similar point is made by Dixit and Skeath (1999). Stephen Jay Gould (1985) argued that baseball batting averages converged in the 20th century because of dynamic adjustments in field, pitching, and hitting. Dixit and Skeath describe this as an "encouraging tale, drawn from real life, of how players learn to play equilibrium strategies." But the learning was on the order of decades, which means a behavioral learning theory is just as important (or more so) than an equilibrium concept.

For example, a common interpretation of the fact that Responders reject offers in ultimatum games is that the Responders think they might be playing a repeated game because they will meet the Proposers again. But experimenters go to great lengths to ensure that subjects won't meet again and know that. For example, some experimenters pay subjects one at a time, with a short lag between each payment, and stand in the hall to be sure subjects don't wait for others to leave. Under these conditions, the faux-repeated-game explanation of ultimatum results is simply wrong. Others (such as the famously careful Ray Battalio) are known to end an experiment immediately if a subject says something aloud that others hear, breaking the experimenter's control. The reaction that subjects are playing a different game than the experimenter intended should disappear as more theorists learn about what actually happens in laboratories and come to believe in the quality of the data that are produced.

Still another reaction you may have is that behavior which is not rational can't be modeled. For example, several years ago Abreu and Matsushima (1992b) said experimental results are frequently inexplicable by "even approximately rational explanation." I disagree: Virtually all the results reported in this book can be accommodated by including behavioral components—social utility, limited iterated reasoning, and learning—into analytical theory. They go on to ask, "Should we then give up the rationality paradigm?" Of course not. It is too useful as a source of sharp predictions, and it is often a good prediction of limiting behavior. Behavioral game theory *extends* rationality rather than abandoning it. The last chapter of this book shows how.

1.4 Conclusion

This chapter described three examples which illustrate experimental regularity, and hinted how that regularity is formalized in behavioral game theory.

In the ultimatum game, Proposers typically offer close to half of a sum to be divided, and Responders reject offers that are too low because they dislike unfairness. The game is so simple that it is impossible to believe Responders rejecting money are confused, and the result has been replicated for very high stakes (up to $400 in America, and comparable sums in foreign countries). According to behavioral game theory, Responders reject low offers because they like to earn money but dislike unfair treatment (or like being treated equally). In the continental divide game, players gravitate toward equilibria over time and often end up in Pareto-inefficient equilibria they could have avoided. Behavioral game theory explains this by assuming that players aren't sure what to do (at the beginning of the game), so they pick numbers in the middle; then they respond to history according to simple statistical learning rules. In the beauty contest game, players seem to do one or two steps of reasoning about others, then stop. (Analytical game theory assumes they keep going until they reach a mutual best-response equilibrium.) And they learn over time. Later chapters expand on these results and describe other classes of games (mixed equilibria, bargaining, signaling, and auctions).

APPENDIX

A1.1 Basic Game Theory

This appendix introduces basic ideas in game theory.[18] The goal is to equip the novice reader to understand the gist of the rest of the book. If you do not have some other background in game theory, and are serious about understanding the experimental results described later, you should read other books. A good introductory book (low on math) is Dixit and Skeath (1999). More mathematical books include Rasmusen (1994) and Osborne and Rubinstein (1995). Gintis (1999) includes fresh material on evolutionary theory and experimental data, and tons of problems. The heavy tomes that are used in graduate classes at places such as Caltech include Fudenberg and Tirole (1991).

Notation: Player i's strategy is denoted s_i. A vector of strategies, one for each player, is denoted $s = s_1, s_2, \ldots, s_n$. The part of this vector which removes player i's strategy (i.e., every other player's strategy) is denoted s_{-i}. The utility of player i's payoff from playing s_i is $u_i(s_i, s_{-i})$.

A1.1.1 Dominance

Definition A1.1.1 *The strategy s_i^* is a dominant strategy if it is a strict best response to any feasible strategy that the others might play*

$$u_i(s_i^*, s_{-i}) > u_i(s_i', s_{-i}) \ \forall s_{-i}, s_i' \neq s_i^*.$$

The strategy s_i' is dominated if there exists $s_i'' \in S_i$ such that

$$u_i(s_i'', s_{-i}) > u_i(s_i', s_{-i}) \ \forall s_{-i}.$$

---

[18] Thanks to Angela Hung for writing much of this appendix.

The strategy s_i' is weakly dominated if there exists $s_i'' \in S_i$ such that

$$u_i(s_i'', s_{-i}) \geq u_i(s_i', s_{-i}) \; \forall s_{-i},$$

$$u_i(s_i'', s_{-i}) > u_i(s_i', s_{-i}) \quad \text{for at least one } s_{-i}.$$

Example A1.1.1 *Consider the simple normal-form game below. In a normal-form (aka strategic-form or matrix) game players are presumed to move simultaneously so there is no need to express the order of their moves in a graphical tree (or extensive-form). Each cell shows a pair of payoffs. The left payoff is for the row player (1) and the right is for the column player (2). The payoffs are utilities for consequences. That is, in the original game the consequences may be money, pride, reproduction by genes, territory in wars, company profits, pleasure, or pain. A key assumption is that players can express their satisfaction with these outcomes on a numerical utility scale. The scale must at least be ordinal—i.e., they would rather have an outcome with utility 2 than with utility 1—and when expected utility calculations are made the scale must be cardinal (i.e., getting 2 is as good as a coin flip between 3 and 1).*

		Player 2		
		L	M	R
Player 1	U	1,0	1,2	0,1
	D	0,3	0,1	2,0

For player 2, strategy R is strictly dominated by M (because M gives a higher payoff if player 1 chooses U, 2 instead of 1, and a higher payoff if player 2 chooses D, 1 instead of 0). Deleting strategy R (i.e., assuming a rational player 2 will never play it) makes D strictly dominated by U. But if player 1 plays U, then player 2 should play M. Therefore, the iterated-dominance equilibrium is (U,M).

Dominance is important because, if utility payoffs are correctly specified (one need get only their *order* right) and players care only about their own utility, there is no good reason to violate strict dominance. One step of iterated dominance is a judgment by one player that the other player will not make a dumb mistake. This often tells a player what she herself should do. In the example, player 1 might consider choosing D because of the chance of earning the 2 payoff in the lower right (D,R) cell. But will she ever earn that payoff? Only if player 2 does something that is dominated. If player 1 assumes player 2 won't do that, she can rule out R, and her hope of earning 2 disappears. Then she should obviously choose U.

Example A1.1.2 *(Battle of the Sexes)*

Player 2

		L	M
Player 1	U	2,1	0,0
	D	0,0	1,2

The game is not dominance solvable. Neither strategy is dominant (or dominated) for either player because there is no one strategy that is always best. Put differently, each strategy might be best depending on what you think the other person will do.

A1.1.2 Nash Equilibrium

Definition A1.1.2 *The strategy profile $s^* = (s_i^*, s_{-i}^*)$ is a Nash equilibrium (NE) if each player's strategy is a best response to the other players' strategies. That is, no player has incentive to deviate, if no other player will deviate. (If players find themselves in equilibrium, there is no reason to move away.)*

$$u_i(s_i^*, s_{-i}^*) \geq u_i(s_i', s_{-i}^*) \ \forall s_i' i.$$

Note that, if a strategy profile is an iterated-(strict) dominance equilibrium, then it is a Nash equilibrium. This is not true of equilibria created by iterated application of *weak* dominance.

Example A1.1.3 *(Battle of the Sexes) Solving for pure-strategy Nash equilibrium:*

Player 2

		L	R
Player 1	U	2,1	0,0
	D	0,0	1,2

If player 1 plays U, 2's best response is L. If player 1 plays D, 2's best response is R. If player 2 plays L, 1's best response is U, and if 2 plays R, 1's best response is D. Therefore, U is a best response to L, and L is a best response to U. Likewise, D is a best response to R and R is a best response to D: Pure strategy NE are (U,L) and (D,R).

A1.1.3 Mixed Strategies

A mixed strategy for player i is a probability distribution over all the strategies in S_i.

Example A1.1.4 *(Battle of the Sexes) Solving for mixed-strategy Nash equilbrium:*

Player 2

		L	R
Player 1	U	2,1	0,0
	D	0,0	1,2

Suppose player 1 plays U with probability p and D with probability $1-p$ and player 2 plays L with probability q and R with probability $1-q$.
    Then the expected value to 2 from playing L is

$$1p + 0(1-p)$$

and the expected value to 2 from playing R is

$$0p + 2(1-p).$$

Player 2 is indifferent iff

$$1p + 0(1-p) = 0p + 2(1-p)$$

or

$$p = \frac{2}{3}.$$

    The expected value to 1 from playing U is

$$2q + 0(1-q)$$

and the expected value from playing D is

$$0q + 1(1-q).$$

Player 1 is indifferent iff

$$2q + 0(1-q) = 0q + 1(1-q)$$

or

$$q = \frac{1}{3}.$$

As a result, a pair of (weak) best responses constitutes a mixed-strategy equilibrium:
$$\left((\tfrac{2}{3}U, \tfrac{1}{3}D), (\tfrac{1}{3}L, \tfrac{2}{3}R) \right).$$

Mixed-strategy equilibrium is a curious concept. Introducing mixed strategies makes the space of payoffs convex (i.e., for any two points in the space, all points in between are in the space too), which is necessary to guarantee existence of a Nash equilibrium (in finite games). Guaranteed existence is a beautiful thing and is part of what makes game theory productive: For *any* (finite) game you write down, you can be sure to find an equilibrium. This means that a policy analyst or scientist trying to predict what will happen will *always* have something concrete to say.

However, the behavioral interpretation of mixing strategies is dubious. By definition, a player desires to mix only when she is indifferent among pure strategies, which means she does not (strictly) desire to mix with particular probabilities; she just doesn't care what she does. Furthermore, one player's equilibrium mixture probabilities depend *only* on the *other* player's payoffs, which is odd. A modern interpretation of mixed-strategy equilibrium (called "purification") is that one player might appear to be mixing but is actually choosing a pure strategy conditional on some hunch variable they privately observe. Mathematically, this works the same way— as long as each player's *belief* about the other players' choice matches the predicted probabilities, the mixed equilibrium is a mutual best-response point. Chapter 3 gives more detail.

Example A1.1.5 *A three-strategy example*

| | | Player 2 | | |
		$L(r)$	$M(s)$	$R(1-r-s)$
Player 1	$T(p)$	30,30	50,40	100,35
	$M(q)$	40,50	45,45	10,60
	$B(1-p-q)$	35,100	60,10	0,0

Player 1:

$$30r + 50s + 100(1 - r - s) = 40r + 45s + 10(1 - r - s)$$
$$= 35r + 60s + 0(1 - r - s),$$

or

$$r = \frac{22}{83},$$

$$s = \frac{56}{83},$$

$$1 - r - s = \frac{5}{83}.$$

Because the game is symmetric,

$$p = r = \frac{22}{83},$$

$$q = s = \frac{56}{83},$$

$$1 - p - q = 1 - r - s = \frac{5}{83}.$$

A1.1.4 Constant-Sum Games

In a constant-sum game, the sum of the payoffs of the players is constant across outcomes. Constant-sum games are actually extremely rare because even when the sum of physical payoffs is constant (like bargaining over money or food-sharing) the players' utilities probably do not add to a constant. For two-person, constant-sum games, minimax, maximin, and Nash equilibrium all select the same strategy.

Definition A1.1.3 *The strategy s_i^* is a maximin strategy if it maximizes i's minimum possible payoff; that is,*

$$s_i^* = \arg \max_{s_i} \left[\min_{s_{-i}} u_i \right].$$

Definition A1.1.4 *The strategy s_i^* is a minimax strategy if it minimizes the other players' maximum possible payoff; that is,*

$$s_i^* = \arg \min_{s_i} \left[\max_{s_{-i}} u_{-i} \right].$$

Example A1.1.6 *(Matching Pennies)*

		Player 2	
		L	R
Player 1	U	1,0	0,1
	D	0,1	1,0

If the game is expanded to include mixed strategies, then the maximin strategy for the row player 1 is to randomize equally over U and D, which gives an expected utility of 0.5 for both L and R. Hence, 0.5 is the maximin value. It is also the minimax strategy because it guarantees that the column player 2 makes no more than 0.5 (in expected utility). It is also the unique Nash equilibrium.

In constant-sum games, minimax is a heuristic way of respecting the fact that the other player's best responsiveness (as in Nash equilibrium) will necessarily give you the lowest payoff, because the players' interests are strictly opposed. If you best-respond, I'll get the least; my best response to that likelihood is to maximize the least I can get.

A1.1.5 Extensive-Form Games and Information Sets

An extensive-form game is used to model games where there is a specific order of moves. An extensive-form game is (1) a configuration of nodes and branches running without any closed loops from a single (root) starting node to its end (terminal) nodes; (2) an indication of which node belongs to each player; (3) probabilities that "nature" (an outside force) uses to choose branches at random nodes; (4) collections of nodes, which are called information sets; and (5) utility payoffs at each end node.

Definition A1.1.5 *An information set for a player is a collection of decision nodes satisfying:*

1. *The player has the move at every node in the information set, and*
2. *When the play of the game reaches a node in the information set, the player with the move does not know which node in the information set has been reached.*

A1.1.6 Subgame Perfection

An equilibrium for an extensive-form game specifies what each player will do at each information set, even those not reached. Subgame perfection imposes the further restriction that players will actually play their equilibrium strategy if the subgame is reached (Selten, 1965). (A subgame is the continuation game from a singleton node—i.e., a node which has no other nodes in its information set—to the end nodes which follow from that node.) In my view, this "refinement" of Nash equilibrium simply patches up an omission in Nash's concept, which was not evident until theorists began thinking about extensive-form trees rather than matrices.

Example A1.1.7 *Mini-ultimatum game*

Player 2

Player 1	E	5,5	
		A	R
	U	8,2	0,0

In this mini-ultimatum game, player 1 moves first and offers an even (E) split of 10, paying (5,5), or offers an uneven (U) split. If E is chosen, the game ends and both players earn 5. If U is chosen, player 2 is "on the move" and can choose to accept (A), in which case player 1 gets 8 and player 2 gets 2, or can reject (R), in which case both get nothing.

The strategy profile (E, R|U) is a Nash equilibrium because it specifies moves at each node, and strategies are—technically—best responses. If player 1 anticipates that player 2 will choose R after a move of U, then player 1 should choose E to earn 5. And if player 1 is going to choose E, it makes no difference what player 2 does—"planning" to respond with R to U is not penalized because, in equilibrium, player 2 is never called upon actually to play. Playing U after R is a weak best response because in this equilibrium R never results. Subgame perfection requires that, if the U node *is* reached, then player 2's subsequent strategy must be a best response. But since R earns 0 for player 2 and A earns 2, the best response in the subgame that results when player 1 chooses U is to play A. Anticipating this, player 1 should choose U. Therefore, (U, A|U) is a Nash equilibrium and is also subgame perfect.

A1.1.7 Bayesian-Nash Equilibrium

In games of incomplete information, at least one player is uncertain about the other players' payoff function(s). This is traditionally represented (after Harsanyi, 1967–68) by having "nature" move at the beginning of the game and determine a player's "type." Players observe their own types but not the types of others. (In formal terms, the player who knows her type knows which branch emanating from the start node nature chose. The player who does not know the other player's type has an information set containing nodes that emanate from both branches following from the start node.) However, the probability distribution of types is common knowledge (the "common prior" assumption). Bayesian-Nash equilibrium adds two features to Nash equilibrium: (i) Along the equilibrium path (i.e., for all moves that occur in equilibrium with positive probability), players must update their beliefs about player types using Bayes' rule. Bayes' rule states that $P(H_i|D) = P(D|H_i)P(H_i)/ \sum_k^n = 1P(D|H_k)P(H_k)$, where H_i are n different hypotheses (e.g., possible player types) and D is the observed data (e.g., a player's move). (ii) Off the equilibrium path (i.e., after moves that never occur in equilibrium), players should have *some* belief about player types. Note well that Bayes' rule does not restrict what these beliefs should be, because an off-path move has probability zero (i.e., $P(D|H_i) = 0 \ \forall H_i$). Then the denominator of the updating equation is zero and Bayes' rule breaks down. Hence, Bayesian-Nash equilibrium imposes the minimal a-Bayesian restriction on what off-path beliefs should be—namely, they should be *something*! This simply rules out the possibility that players will violate dominance after observing an off-path move.

A1.1.8 Trembling Hand Perfection

Selten (1975) suggested a clever way to subject off-equilibrium-path beliefs to the discipline of Bayes' rule, called "trembling hand perfection." The idea is to suppose that, even in an equilibrium, there is a small chance that a player's hand trembles when she chooses, so that *all* paths through the tree are taken with positive probability. Then Bayes' rule can be used to update beliefs. A trembling hand perfect equilibrium is the limit of the Bayesian-Nash equilibria with trembling, as the tremble probability goes to zero. Many others have suggested further refinements which try to codify, logically, what sort of beliefs after off-path moves seem intuitive or sensible. Sequential equilibrium (Kreps and Wilson, 1982a) is a kissing cousin of trembling hand perfection and is generically the same (i.e., the only games in which the two differ are knife-edge cases, in a way that can be made mathematically precise). Myerson (1978) suggested that the tremble probabilities should be smaller when payoff differences between equilibrium and nonequilibrium strategies are larger, leading to a concept of "proper" equilibrium. Some other refinements are discussed in Chapter 8, on signaling games.

A1.1.9 Quantal Response Equilibrium

In a quantal response equilibrium (QRE), players do not choose the best response with probability one (as in Nash equilibrium). Instead, they "better-respond," and choose responses with higher expected payoffs with higher probability. In practice, the QRE often uses a logit or exponentiated payoff response function:

$$P(s_i) = \exp\left(\lambda \sum_{s_{-i}} P(s_{-i})u_i(s_i, s_{-i})\right) \Big/ \sum_{s_k} \exp\left(\lambda \sum_{s_{-i}} P(s_{-i})u_i(s_k, s_{-i})\right),$$

where $\exp(x)$ denotes e^x and the sums are taken over all strategies for $-i$ (all other players) and i. Intuitively, QRE says that players fix a strategy and form beliefs about what others will do ($P(s_{-i})$), and compute expected payoffs given those beliefs. Making this calculation for each strategy gives a profile of expected payoffs for each possible strategy. Then player i better-responds by choosing noisily according to the strategies' expected payoffs. The parameter λ is a measure of their sensitivity to differences in expected payoffs.[19] Note that since player I is calculating $P(s_i)$, and others are too, the system of equations is recursive: A player's behavior determines expected payoffs, which determine other players' behavior. When $\lambda = 0$, players just choose each strategy with the same equal probability. As λ rises, they become more and more responsive, converging to Nash equilibrium in which they always choose the best response.[20] Thus, Nash equilibrium is a kind of "hyperresponsive" QRE.

I used to say in classes and seminars that, if John Nash had been a statistician rather than a mathematician, he might have discovered QRE rather than Nash equilibrium. (Such an early discovery would have automatically presolved the problem of refining away incredible Nash equilibria, which required the development, much later in the 1960s and 1970s, of subgame and trembling-hand perfection.) When I mentioned this at a talk in Princeton in the fall of 2001, some audience members grinned and nudged each other (Nash was, after all, a hometown hero in Princeton). People later said they were grinning and nudging because, unbeknownst to me, Nash had been in the audience! Since Nash didn't *protest* when he heard my counterfactual speculation about his would-be early discovery of QRE, I later stretched the truth and said "Nash didn't *deny* that he would have discovered QRE." Still later, in December 2001, I had a chance to meet Nash and asked him point blank about QRE. He said he had been working on a similar stochastic best-response model of bargaining just recently; so we can count him as recently converted to, or at least sympathetic toward, a quantal response approach.

A1.2 Experimental Design

The way in which an experiment is conducted is unbelievably important. Just as all thoroughbred racehorses are descended from four horses, most American experimental economics began in the 1960s and 1970s at a small number of institutions (particularly Caltech, Arizona, Purdue, and Texas A&M) and grew slowly. (A similar effort occurred in parallel in Germany.) As a result, the experimental community is tight-knit and has established clear conventions for experimental practice which permit a high degree of comparability across data sets. Smith (1976) is an early rulebook which also summarizes many regularities. For example, most articles include raw data and instructions to enable readers to judge for themselves what was learned. (If you asked a psychologist for data or instructions he or she might

---

[19] Goeree and Holt (1999) use $1/\mu$ instead to emphasize their interpretation of the noise as computational mistakes; when μ is large, the mistake rate is high and players are very insensitive, and vice versa.

[20] This is not quite true, technically. The limit of a sequence of QREs as λ increases can converge to something that is not a Nash equilibrium (see McKelvey and Palfrey, 1995).

be insulted, because the convention in that field is to give the writer the benefit of the doubt.)

This appendix sketches some important design choices. To learn more, see Friedman and Sunder (1993), Davis and Holt (1993), and Kagel and Roth (1995).

A1.2.1   Control, Measure, or Assume

Any variable can be evaluated in one of three ways: control, measurement, or assumption.

Control means taking an action to affect the value of a variable, often with a "manipulation check" to be sure the control worked. Induced value is an important kind of control which creates preferences for actions by associating those actions with payoffs in a currency that subjects value (typically money, but sometimes grade points, ranking of points earned, and so forth).

Measurement refers simply to measuring the value of a relevant variable through psychometric measures ("Describe how angry you are when someone offers you $2 out of $10?"), methods for measuring risk-aversion (e.g., certainty equivalents) or probability judgments (scoring rules). Types of measurement that are less familiar in economics, but worth exploring, include content analysis of videotapes, physiological measures such as heartrate or galvanic skin response, information acquisition (see Johnson et al., 2002, in Chapter 4, and Costa-Gomes, Crawford, and Broseta, 2001, in Chapter 5), and even fMRI brain imaging (Smith et al., 2002).

Assumption is pseudo-control in which the experimenter is willing to accept a maintained hypothesis about the value of a variable.

As an illustration of all three methods, consider the classic economic experiments in which agents are endowed with costs and valuations for an object, and one would like to test theories of competitive equilibrium (CE), which predict that prices will converge to the point where supply meets demand. One strategy is to hand out everyday objects, such as CD recordings or coffee mugs, and make an assumption about how much subjects value them. This is generally a bad design because CE predictions are very sensitive to the valuations of marginal traders, and the valuations are not likely to be well understood by experimenters.[21] Another strategy is to

---

[21] A beautiful exception, which proves the rule, is the Kahneman, Knetsch, and Thaler (1990) experiments with coffee mugs. They were interested not in prices at all, but only in the quantity of trade, and in showing that aversion to losses creates an "endowment effect" that is present with everyday objects and *not* with induced-value tokens. They were able to use everyday objects because they did not care about the level of homemade valuations, but needed only to assume that mean valuations were similar in samples that (randomly) did and did not receive mugs.

measure valuations for each individual (using, say, the incentive-compatible Becker–DeGroot–Marschak procedure) and then assume those measured valuations represent the subjects' costs and reservation prices and construct demand and supply curves from the measurements. This is a defensible procedure but has rarely been used (see Knez and Smith, 1987). A third strategy is to "induce" or control valuations by making the objects of trade valueless tokens, and telling subjects that they can trade tokens for specific money values. This form of induced valuation, first used by Chamberlin (1948) and tirelessly refined by Vernon Smith beginning in 1956, is surely the crux move in the development of experimental economics. Smith's later insistence on actually tying money payments to the induced valuations led to credibility among nonexperimenters and reliability in actual behavior, which enabled exploration of extremely subtle hypotheses and rapid progress.

A1.2.2 *Instructions*

Instructions tell subjects what they need to know. It is scientifically very useful to have a clear instructional "script" that enables precise replication, particularly across subject pools who may vary in language comprehension, obedience, intrinsic motivation, and so on. (Precise replication is surprisingly rare in other social sciences, in psychology for example.) Reading instructions out loud is a common practice to establish "public knowledge" (e.g., what subjects know everyone else has been told, and what everyone else knows everyone else has been told), which is as close as we can practically come to the common knowledge usually assumed in game theory.

The overwhelming convention in modern (post-1975) game theory experiments is to explain how each sequence of moves by each player leads to payoffs (including payoffs to other subjects, and also including asymmetric information à la Harsanyi). This practice arose because experimenters wanted to be sure that subjects had enough information to compute an equilibrium. (Earlier experiments on markets deliberately withheld information about values of others, to test the Adam Smith/Hayek hypothesis that, even if players knew only their own values, they could still converge to a Pareto-efficient equilibrium.) More recently, learning models have been proposed that do not always assume players have complete knowledge of all possible payoffs. As an empirical matter, it is quite interesting to know how people learn in these environments (since players may have poor information about payoffs in many naturally occurring situations). So some recent experiments have deliberately withheld information about payoffs from the instructions (e.g., Van Huyck, Battalio, and Rankin, 2001). This design choice also raises a problem—when subjects are *not* told something about the environment they are placed in, their default assumption may be wrong.

Here is an example. A large literature on "probability matching" studies subjects (including nonhuman animals) making one of two choices (left L and right R). On each trial one of the levers is "armed" to deliver a reward and the other delivers nothing. Subjects choose one lever and receive a reward if it is armed. Typically, there is a chance p that L is armed and $1 - p$ that R is armed, and *which lever is armed is determined independently of previous trials.* From the experimenter's view, the rewards from choosing L are independent Bernoulli trials. But what do subjects think? If they are not told that the lever-arming process is independent and identically distributed (with fixed p), they might entertain an array of possibilities of how rewards are delivered. It might be much more plausible, to a subject, that the experimenter is interested in whether they can figure out an elaborate pattern of variation in which levers are armed rather than figure out that L has an independent p chance each time. Empirically, subjects typically "probability match" by choosing L on about p of the trials. If subjects knew the process was independent and identically distributed, this would be a mistake (they should always choose the arm with the higher p). Does probability matching tell you that subjects are making a mistake, or that they fail to guess the strange (uninteresting) environment the experimenter has placed them in? What the experimenter observes in a low-information probability-matching experiment is a combination of the subjects' revealed perceptions about the statistical process of reward and their decision rule for choosing. Withholding statistical information is not necessarily a bad design choice. But, by not revealing information about the environment, there is no guarantee that subjects will guess accurately what they are not told. Since the guesses are hard to observe directly (without additional measurement), it will be difficult to conclude whether subjects are playing rationally or not.

A1.2.3 Anonymity

If the subjects know the identity of the person they are bargaining with, their knowledge might influence what they do for many reasons. They might like the way the person looks and want to make them happy, or fear retribution or embarrassment if they make a stingy offer and see the person after the experiment. Unless these possibilities are precisely the focus of the experiment, most of the experiments described in this book try to create anonymity—sometimes to a dramatic degree—by making it as difficult as possible for subjects to know precisely who they are playing with. Anonymity is obviously *not* used because it is lifelike. It is used to establish a benchmark against which the effects of knowing who you are playing can be measured, if those effects are of interest.

A1.2.4 *Matching Protocols and Reputation Building*

Experiments are usually designed with several periods of play so subjects can learn from experience. But if a pair of subjects play together several times, the possibility of "reputation building" can affect the prediction that game theory makes. For example, in the ultimatum game it may pay for a Responder to build up a reputation for being "tough" by rejecting large offers in the first few periods, to "teach the proposer a lesson" and get larger offers in later periods. Put more formally, when the same pair (or group) of players play together several times, there may be game-theoretic equilibria for the repeated game that differ from the one-shot, stage-game equilibrium. Unless we are explicitly interested in the nature of reputation formation and repeated-game strategies (as some experiments are), this possibility is avoided by having subjects play with each other only once in an experimental session.

There are various ways in which players can be matched with different players in a stage game that is repeated. The most common protocol is no-repeat rematching (or a "stranger" design)—players are never rematched with a former match, to reduce the possibility of reputation building. (It is not known, by the way, whether no-repeat rematching actually does disable reputation building. I suspect it does not, but more work on this is needed.) In a "no-contagion" design, players are never rematched, and are never rematched with somebody who will be matched with somebody they will later be matched with, and so forth. In random rematching, players are rematched randomly (so they may be rematched with their partner from the previous period, but typically the probability of consecutive matches is low and they do not know whether they are rematched anyway). In a mean-matching or population protocol, each player plays every other player and earns the average payoff from all those matches.

A1.2.5 *Incentives*

Vernon Smith (1962) reported the earliest experiments comparing the behavior of subjects who were rewarded in points with that of subjects whose points were converted into dollars that they were actually paid. Vernon observed that subjects paid only in points tended to approach competitive equilibrium more erratically, and seemed to grow bored with the experiment faster than those who were paid money. He suggested that, although people may have enough intrinsic motivation to earn lots of points, hypothetical rewards were typically more "erratic, unreliable, and easily satiated"

(1976) than money. Put differently, by inducing value using money payments, the experimenter need rely only on the assumptions that everybody likes having more money and nobody gets tired of having more of it. These are safe assumptions, and substantially safer than figuring out whether somebody is motivated by having their name posted if they did best (some people might be embarassed by it), is likely to give up if they are far behind when payoffs have a tournament structure, and so forth. (If you know anybody who is tired of getting more money let me know; I'll take their leftovers!)

Paying subjects their earnings quickly became the norm in experimental economics (in sharp contrast to most of modern experimental psychology, with important exceptions such as Ward Edwards and Amnon Rapoport). Does it matter whether performance is rewarded, and how much? The evidence is mixed. Experimenters should not abandon the practice of paying performance-based incentives, but few results that disconfirm theory have been overturned by paying more money. Smith and Walker (1993) review a couple of dozen studies and argue that paying money reduces variance of responses around a rational prediction (first noted by Dave Grether in a 1981 working paper). Hogarth and I (Camerer and Hogarth, 1999) conducted a more thorough review and draw several conclusions. Paying money *does* reduce variation and outliers, which may be particularly important in settings that are sensitive to variation, such as "weak-link" coordination games (see Chapter 7) or asset markets with potential for speculative bubbles. (In those tasks investigators should certainly pay money.) Paying money improved performance most reliably in judgment and decision-making tasks, when there are returns to thinking harder (see also Hertwig and Ortmann, 2001). But in tasks that are quite easy ("floor effects") or very hard ("ceiling effects") paying money usually does not matter. We also point out that there is no empirical reason to obsess only about money, because the effect of experience is just as large. Labeling strategies, individual differences, and other variables can have comparably large effects and should be investigated further.

In the 1980s a controversy erupted over whether money payments established what Vernon Smith called "dominance," which means that the money at stake is enough to induce subjects to think hard. The controversy was ignited by Harrison (1989), who pointed out that the size of a deviation from theory in payoff terms may be much lower than the deviation in the strategy space. (The same point—the "flat maximum critique"—was made almost two decades earlier, in 1973, by Von Winterfeldt and Edwards.) For example, in a mixed-strategy equilibrium, if other players are using their mixture strategies, then a subject has absolutely no financial incentive to play her equilibrium mixture instead, regardless of the level of money payoffs in the game. Similarly, in first-price private-value auctions, a bidder who overbids by, say, $1 does not actually lose a dollar. Overbidding reduces her prospective earnings but raises the chance of winning the auction, and the net effect may reduce her expected payoff by only pennies.

Experimenters never developed an ideal solution to the flat maximum problem. The critique did sensitize us to the need to worry about marginal costs of deviation (and see Fudenberg and Levine, 1997) and to seek designs with steep marginal incentives where possible. (For ultimatum game Responders, for example, the cost of the error from rejecting is exactly equal to the deviation in strategy space, and is often very large.) Furthermore, the fact that very large variations in stakes typically have only modest effects muted criticisms that payoffs were not large enough. At least two dozen studies have been done in foreign countries where purchasing power is so low that modest sums by the standards of developed countries amount to several weeks' or months' earnings. The results are generally very close to those with smaller stakes.

Finally, Rob Kurzban mentioned a great example of poor reasoning in a very high-stakes situation. In the final round of the first edition of the popular *Survivor* television show, survivor Greg Buis was deciding which of two others to vote for based on their answers in a simple number game. (The winner got $1 million and the runner-up $100,000, so the stakes are huge.) The two finalists, Richard Hatch and Kelly Wigglesworth, were asked to pick integers between 1 and 9 and the person whose number was closest to Buis's would win. (Whether Buis actually committed to his number, or simply used the contest to create an illusion of fairness, is hard to tell.) Hatch chose 7. Astonishingly, Wigglesworth then chose *3*, a choice that is dominated by choosing 6, because 6 would win for any choice by Buis of 6 or below whereas 3 would lose if Buis picked 6 and tie if he picked 5. If Buis had picked randomly, by choosing 3 after Hatch's 7 Wigglesworth lost an expected $160,000. And, unless one had a reason to think Buis would go high or low, picking 5 would have been a better choice by Hatch than 7. (Buis claimed he chose 9 and so Hatch won the $1 million.)

A1.2.6 Order Effects

Experiments often involve two treatments, A and B. If they are always done in the same order, denoted AB, then any difference in the two treatments might be due to the fact that A came first and B came second (an "order effect"). Order is "confounded with" (perfectly correlated with) the treatment. This is easily controlled by running some sessions in the reverse order, BA, and including an order dummy variable in statistical analyses.

A1.2.7 Controlling Risk Tastes

Even though subjects should be risk-neutral toward small lab gambles (Rabin, 2000), it would be useful to have a procedure for creating payoffs that subjects are risk-neutral towards (i.e., so they are indifferent to the dispersion of possible payoffs around a fixed mean). There *is* such a procedure—the binary lottery procedure.

In the binary lottery procedure, subjects are paid in lottery tickets, which are later used to determine their chance of winning a lottery for a fixed prize (see Roth and Malouf, 1979). If players reduce compound lotteries to single-stage lotteries, they should be neutral toward mean-preserving spreads in their ticket distribution—that is, they should have linear utility over tickets. For example, if they regard a 0.32 chance of winning fifty tickets (and otherwise getting none) as the same as having sixteen tickets, they are risk-neutral toward tickets. (In theory, the procedure can be extended to induce any shape of utility function by transforming payoff units to tickets nonlinearly; see Schotter and Braunstein, 1981, and Berg et al., 1986.)

Unfortunately, there is little evidence that the binary lottery procedure works as it should in theory (and a couple of studies showing it does not work). For example, in direct tests, players who make choices with monetary payoffs and players who make choices with lottery ticket payoffs exhibit the same patterns, so the binary lottery procedure does not change apparent risk-aversion over money into risk-neutrality over tickets (Camerer and Ho, 1994; Selten, Sadrieh, and Abbink, 1999). On the other hand, Van Huyck and Battalio (1999) found that players behaved consistently with risk-neutrality over tickets (though see their footnote 9 for an opposite result). In the most careful study, Prasnikar (1999) found that risk-aversion coefficients estimated from choices among gambles over tickets were close to their predicted coefficient values. The method worked best for the minority of subjects who obeyed reduction of compound lotteries.

It is surprising that many experimenters use the binary lottery procedure despite so little careful evaluation of when it does induce risk-neutrality (and given the evidence that it often doesn't). To paraphrase G. B. Shaw's wisecrack about marriage, faith in the procedure seems to be a triumph of hope over data. There are two alternatives to trying to induce risk tastes: assume risk-neutrality, or measure risk tastes over money independently and use those measures to calibrate an individual subject's risk preferences in a game (which several experimenters have done). In any case, it would be good to see more careful research (à la Prasnikar, 1999) establishing when the procedure works and when it does not.

A1.2.8 Within-Subjects and Between-Subjects Design

In a "within-subjects" design, a single subject is observed in different treatments. (The subject serves as "her own control group".) In a "between-subjects" design—the norm in experimental economics—different subjects are tested in treatments A and B. Statistical variation across the subjects then muddies the waters of what is observed by comparing A and B. Within-subject designs are more statistically powerful than between-subject designs because they automatically control for individual differences, which are often a large source of variation, and hence allow the effect of a treatment to shine through when the nuisance of individual difference is controlled for.

There is a curious bias against within-subjects designs in experimental economics (not so in experimental psychology). I don't know why there is a bias, and I can't think of a compelling reason always to eschew such designs. One possible reason is that exposing subjects to multiple conditions heightens their sensitivity to the differences in conditions. This hypothesis can be tested, however, by comparing results from within- and between-subjects designs, which is rarely done.

A1.2.9 Experimetrics

"Experimetrics" are econometric techniques customized to experimental applications. Although I'm an amateur econometrician, I am a huge fan of experimetrics. The next generation of experimenters should feel obliged to use the very latest inferential tools—the best microscopes—to see patterns in data as clearly as possible. The work by Crawford, El-Gamal, McKelvey and Palfrey, Stahl, and Van Huyck and Battalio described in this book sets a high standard other experimenters should emulate.

A new tool in experimetrics which has not become widely adopted is optimal endogeneous experimental design (e.g., El-Gamal, McKelvey, and Palfrey, 1993). In many experiments, the experimenter has one or more hypotheses that she can put prior probabilities on. A crisp prior, and specification of the hypotheses, can be used to compute the information value (in the sense of dispersion of posterior probabilities relative to dispersion of priors) of different experimental design parameters. This motivates the choice of "optimally informative" design parameters. Furthermore, because of increases in computing power, for the first time in human history we can alter the experimental design in real time—while subjects are waiting, for seconds rather than days—to optimize the amount of information collected in an experiment. (Seen this way, all previous experimental designs are heuristic approximations to endogeneously optimized designs.) Information-optimized designs have rarely been used. The younger generation should embarass us older folks by taking them up with a vengeance.

2
Dictator, Ultimatum, and Trust Games

IN 1982, GÜTH, SCHMITTBERGER, AND SCHWARZE reported the kind of empirical finding that surprises only economists. They studied an "ultimatum" game in which one player, the "Proposer," makes a take-it-or-leave-it offer, dividing some amount of money between herself and another person. If the second person, the "Responder," accepts the division, then both people earn the specified amounts. If the Responder rejects it, they both get nothing. The ultimatum game could hardly be simpler. If Responders maximize their own money payoffs, they should accept any offer. If Proposers also maximize and expect Responders to maximize, they should offer the smallest amount.

In experiments, Proposers offer an average of 40 percent of the money (many offer half) and Responders reject small offers of 20 percent or so half the time. The data falsify the assumption that players maximize their own payoffs as clearly as experimental data can. Every methodological explanation you can think of (such as low stakes) has been carefully tested and cannot fully explain the results.

Since the equilibria are so simple to compute (the Responder's move is just a choice of a payoff allocation), the ultimatum game is a crisp way to measure social preferences rather than a deep test of strategic thinking (see Marwell and Schmitt, 1968). Measuring social preferences in money terms is important because concepts such as fairness and trust figure prominently in private negotiation and public policy. But many cynics (especially economists) think fairness is simply a rhetorical term used by people who deserve the short end of the stick for trying to get more, and that people will not sacrifice much to punish unfairness or reward fairness. As George

Stigler (1981, p. 176) wrote: "[When] self-interest and ethical values with wide verbal allegiance are in conflict, much of the time, most the time in fact, self-interest-theory . . . will win."

Ultimatum games are a way to test whether Stigler was right. A Responder who rejects an offer of $2 from a $10 sum puts a $2 price tag on how much she dislikes being treated unfairly ("negative reciprocity").

The emotional reaction to unfairness which is highlighted by the ultimatum game can work at many levels. A reviewer suggested a dramatic illustration from political history. At the Federal Convention in 1787 in Philadelphia, delegates from the original thirteen American states debated how to treat new states that would join later, as western lands were annexed. Gouverneur Morris argued they should be admitted as second-rate states, so they could not outvote the original thirteen. George Mason argued that offering second-rate status would be like offering somebody an unfair portion, and the western states might reject it. He said, "They [new western states] will have the same pride and other passions which we have, and will either not unite with or will speedily revolt from the Union, if they are not in all respects placed on an equal footing with their brethren" (Farrand, 1966, pp. 578–79). Mason's argument that western states might reject an unequal offer (and the moral appeal of equal treatment, independent of the threat of rejection) eventually won over the delegates. (If he hadn't, I might be writing this in the great *country* of California, under the political aegis of California President Arnold Schwarzenegger and Vice-President Shaquille O'Neal, rather than under the rule of George Bush, the minority choice of voters in the impoverished neighbor country America, to our east.)

This chapter discusses several other games that measure aspects of social preference (see also Bolton, 1998; Sobel, 2001). Dictator games are ultimatum games with the Responder's ability to reject the offer removed. Dictator games establish whether Proposers in ultimatum games make generous offers because they fear rejection or because they are purely altruistic. (The answer is mostly fear and a little altruism.) Trust games are dictator games with an initial investment by an Investor that determines how much the dictator, or Trustee, has to allocate. The Investor "trusts" that the Trustee will give back enough to make her initial trust worthwhile. Trust games are simple models of contracting with moral hazard and no contractual enforcement. The amount of investment measures trust; repayment measures trustworthiness. The "centipede" game (see Chapter 5) is a trust game with several stages. A multiplayer trust game is "gift exchange" in labor markets: Firms offer wages to workers who accept offers and choose effort levels. Effort is costly to workers and valuable to firms but cannot be enforced by firms, so firms must trust workers to work hard. Experimentation with ultimatum, dictator, and trust games has exploded recently. These games are popular

Table 2.1. *Prisoners' dilemma*

	Cooperate	Defect
Cooperate	H,H	S,T
Defect	T,S	L,L

Note: Assumes $T > H > L > S$.

because they model key features of economic situations and experiments are easy to run.

Two other important games are prisoners' dilemma (PD) and public goods games. Although these games have been studied in literally thousands of experiments, I will say only a little about them because the results are well known and nicely summarized in many other sources (Davis and Holt, 1993; Colman, 1995, Chapter 7; Ledyard, 1995; Sally, 1995).

Table 2.1 shows payoffs in a typical PD. Mutual cooperation provides payoffs of H for each player, which is better than the L payoff from mutual defection. However, if the other player cooperates, a defector earns the T(emptation) payoff, which is better than reciprocating and earning only H (since $T > H$ in a PD). A player who cooperates against a defector earns the S(ucker) payoff, which is less than earning L from defecting. Since $T > H$ and $L > S$, both players prefer to defect whether the other player cooperates or not. Mutual defection is the only Nash equilibrium but it is Pareto dominated (worse for both players) than mutual cooperation.

In public goods games, each of N players can invest resources c_i from their endowment e_i in a public good that is shared by everyone and has a total per-unit value of m.[1] Player i earns $e_i - c_i + m(\sum_k c_k)/N$. Assuming $m < 1/N$, the payoff-maximizing outcome is to contribute nothing ($c_i = 0$). If everyone contributed, however, the players would collectively earn the most.

PD and public goods games are models of situations such as pollution of the environment, in which one player's action imposes a harmful "externality" on innocent parties (cooperation corresponds to voluntarily limiting pollution), villagers sharing a depletable resource such as river water, and production of a public utility such as a school or irrigation system that non-contributing "free riders" cannot easily be excluded from sharing (see Ostrom, 2000). Low rates of voluntary cooperation and contribution in these games can be remedied by institutional arrangements such as government

---

[1] Assume $m < 1$ so that a player does not benefit enough personally to contribute for private gain, and $mN > 1$ so all players contributing is Pareto improving.

taxation (which forces free riders to pay up), or informal mechanisms such as yelling at people who throw trash out of their cars (ostracism). And when players in PD and public goods games are matched together repeatedly, it can be an equilibrium for all players to cooperate until one player defects.

In experiments, subjects cooperate in one-shot PD games about half the time and contribute about half their endowments in public goods game (although there is wide dispersion; most subjects contribute either all or nothing—see Sally, 1995; Ledyard, 1995). Changes in monetary payoffs have predictable effects: Lowering T and raising S increase cooperation in the PD; and raising the marginal return m raises public good contribution. Preplay communication, which should have no effect in theory, is the non-payoff variable that raises the rate of cooperation by the most.

When the games are repeated with random "stranger" rematching, cooperation and contribution dwindle to a small core of persistent contributors. Figure 2.1 shows a typical pattern of average contributions over time from Fehr and Gächter (2000c) in stranger treatments. The figure also shows the strong effect of punishment. If free-riding is prevalent because of self-interest, then players should not incur a private cost to punish free riders (they should free ride on punishment by others, a "second-order" free-riding problem). This prediction is wrong: Yamagishi (1986) and Fehr and Gächter (2000c) showed that costly punishment works very well, raising steady-state contributions to more than half of endowments, as shown in Figure 2.1. (In partner protocols with rematching, contributions are nearly 100 percent. Then the punishment mechanism is "free" because, when contributions are that high, nobody punishes.)

Players who contribute are more likely to say they expect others to contribute than free riders are. This correlation between beliefs and choices implies that cooperation is conditional or reciprocal. Contributions are also higher when the same players are paired together in partner protocols (e.g., Andreoni, 1993), which is consistent with "folk theorems" about the efficiency gains from repeated play.

PD and public goods games are important in economic life, but they are blunt tools for guiding theories of social preference. These games cannot distinguish between players who are altruistic and players who match expected cooperation. Nor can they distinguish between players who are self-interested and those who have reciprocal preferences but pessimistically think others will free ride. The other games described in this chapter are sharper tools for making these sorts of distinctions than PD and public goods games.

Before proceeding, it is crucial to emphasize again (as Weibull, 2000, has) that evidence of public good contribution, dictator allocation, ultimatum rejection, and trust repayment does *not* falsify game theory, per se. Games lead to utilities over allocations, and one player's concern for how

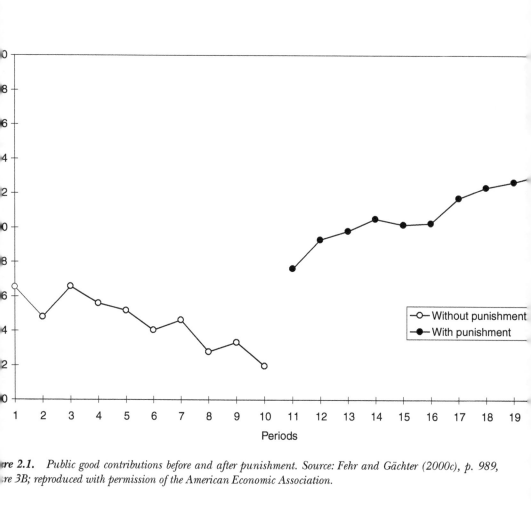

Figure 2.1. *Public good contributions before and after punishment. Source: Fehr and Gächter (2000c), p. 989, Figure 3B; reproduced with permission of the American Economic Association.*

much another player earns (whether positive or negative) can certainly affect her utility. In experiments, however, games are played in money. Since we cannot easily measure or control players' preferences over how much others earn, we always end up testing a joint hypothesis of game-theoretic behavior coupled with some assumption about utilities over money outcomes.

Offering $4 out of $10 could be an equilibrium offer in an ultimatum game, if the Proposer correctly believes that the Responder has a strong dispreference for unequal allocations and will reject a lower offer. But offering $4 could also be a disequilibrium offer, if the Proposer's belief about the Responder's likely behavior is wrong.

Thus, the trick in explaining these data from simple bargaining and public goods games is to seek a parsimonious specification of how observable payments (such as dollars paid to each individual subject) map into an individual's "social preferences," then test the *joint* hypothesis that players have a particular kind of social preferences and play game-theoretically. Throughout the chapter, you will see that the joint hypothesis of game-theoretic behavior *and* social preferences that value only one's own payment (what is often, casually but imprecisely, called "the" game-theoretic prediction) is easily rejected. Then the interesting question is, "Are the rejections due to the pure self-interest part of the joint hypothesis, or to the game-theoretic reasoning part (or both)?"

The answer seems to be "both"; so both parts of the joint hypothesis are in need of repair. Deciding whether to accept an ultimatum offer requires no strategic thinking (it is simply a choice), so rejections clearly indict the self-interest assumption as the culprit. At the same time, direct evidence of how people think during the game (in Chapter 4) and of limited strategic thinking in constant-sum dominance-solvable games (in Chapter 5) shows that game-theoretic reasoning is limited even when self-interest is a reasonable assumption. So is game theory dead? Of course not; it is simply being renovated, or generalized in a precise way. Simple parsimonious models of both social preferences (see Section 2.8 in this chapter) and limited strategic thinking (e.g., Chapter 5 and Camerer, Ho, and Chong, 2001) have already emerged and should continue to be a hot topic of research.

2.1 Ultimatum and Dictator Games: Basic Results

In a typical ultimatum experiment, subjects are paired with anonymous others, and a Proposer makes an offer that the Responder then accepts or rejects. Two common variants on this baseline design either repeat the game (rematching with a new player each time) or ask the Responder to state a minimum acceptable offer (MAO) rather than simply decide whether to accept a specific offer. The MAO method has the huge advantage of measuring likely reactions to all possible offers, which is important if the most interesting offers (such as very low ones) are rare. For some reason, economists are generally reluctant to use the MAO method (even if very little is learned about rejection behavior by using the specific-offer method).[2]

Tables 2.2 and 2.3 compile statistics from many studies of ultimatum games. These studies used specific offers in one-shot games, unless noted otherwise. Each line of the tables lists a study, the amount being divided, and the number of pairs of subjects. The data are relative frequencies of offers in each percentage interval (Table 2.2) and the relative frequency of rejections conditional on each percentage offer (Table 2.3). The median offer percentage is printed in italics. Mean offers and overall rejection rates are shown in the rightmost columns of each table. (Percentages are fractions of the total amount being divided unless stated otherwise.) Significant differences across conditions within a study are noted by lettered "significance codes." Conditions with the same letter are not significantly different; conditions with different letters are significantly different at $p \leq 0.05$.

The results reported in the tables are very regular. Modal and median ultimatum offers are usually 40–50 percent and means are 30–40 percent. There are hardly any offers in the outlying categories of 0, 1–10, and the hyper-fair category 51–100. Offers of 40–50 percent are rarely rejected. Offers below 20 percent or so are rejected about half the time.

It is useful to distinguish the emotions or reasons that cause Responders to reject behavior (call it "anger") from the emotion A might feel when B does something unfair to a third party, C (call it "indignation"). Anger is more personal, and often motivates an aggrieved party to administer justice herself. An indignant A is cooler and is more likely to be happy if B is punished in some other way. (These delicate emotions are important in shaping proceedings such as war tribunals, as in the Nuremberg trials or the South African Truth and Reconciliation Commission. Indignation by parties who were not directly harmed, but are appalled that others were, is important but probably less powerful a force than personal anger.) Indignation is cooler. In recent work, Ernst Fehr and colleagues have been exploring "third-party punishment" games in which A can spend money to punish B for treating C unfairly.

Generous offers could come about because Proposers are fair-minded or because Proposers are afraid of having low offers rejected (or both). The two explanations can be easily separated in a dictator game, which removes the Responder's ability to reject offers. If Proposers offer positive amounts

---

[2] There is a vague sense that Responders demand more when stating MAOs (see Weber and Camerer, 2001), but this difference is neither well established nor (if true) well understood.

Frequencies of ultimatum offers

ental condition	Amount($)	No. of pairs	Offer frequencies (percent offered)								Mean offer	Signif. code	Comments
			0	1–10	11–20	21–30	31–40	41–50	51–60	61–100			
zwick (1995)													
ultimatum	4	20	< 0.45 >			*0.25*	0.05	0.00	0.25		0.24	a	Offers imp
lind (ZK)	4	20	<0.50>			*0.25*	0.00	0.00	0.25		0.22	a	series of
999)													
an rupiah	5K	101	0.08	0.02	0.12	0.06	0.20	*0.38*	0.03	0.11	0.42	a	"Problems"
an rupiah	40K	35				0.17	0.17	*0.63*		0.03	0.45	b	
an rupiah	200K	37	0.03	0.03	0.03	0.08	0.24	*0.57*	0.03		0.42	a	
6)													
l	10	26	0.00	0.04	0.04	0.04	0.25	*0.57*	0.07		0.45	a	Data from
ned	10	28	0.00	0.12	0.15	0.15	*0.23*	0.31		0.04	0.36	b	paper
ossman (2001)													
	5	96	0.01	0.01	0.11	0.14	*0.52*	0.21	0.01	0.01	0.41	a	Numbers e
	5	95	0.01	0.04	0.12	0.22	*0.45*	0.18	0.01		0.39	a	from fig
cCabe, Shachat, and Smith (1994); Hoffman, McCabe, and Smith (1996a)													
lication	10	24				0.13	*0.38*	0.50			0.44	a	
	10	24		0.08	0.25	*0.25*	0.33	0.08			0.31	b	
lication	100	27	0.04			0.11	0.26	*0.52*	0.07		0.44	a	
	100	23			0.17	0.26	*0.26*	0.22	0.11		0.29	b	
tberger, and Schwarze (1982)													
	4–10	21	0.10		0.14	0.10	0.24	0.43			0.37		Payment in
ced	4–10	21		0.05	0.11	*0.29*	0.24	0.24			0.33		9 and 12 ga

Okuno-Fujiwara, and Zamir (1991)

ound 1	10	27			0.04	0.11	0.22	*0.56*	0.04	0.04	0.47	
ound 1	30	10						*0.80*	0.20		0.52	
ound 1	400K	30			0.03	0.07	0.13	*0.73*	0.03		0.46		Payment in dinar
1	2000	29		0.07	0.07	0.14	0.14	*0.41*	0.07	0.07	0.42		Payment in yen
1	20	30		0.17	0.07	0.10	*0.20*	0.43	0.03		0.37		Payment in sheke
ound 10	10	27			0.04		0.33	*0.63*			0.46	a	
ound 10	30	10				0.10		0.80	0.10		0.49	a	
ound 10	400K	30			0.03		0.27	*0.70*			0.47	a	Payment in dinar
10	2000	29				0.17	*0.34*	0.48			0.43	b	Payment yen
10	20	30		0.03	0.13	0.20	*0.57*	0.07			0.35	c	Payment in sheke

z, Savin, and Sefton (1994)

	10	24			0.04	0.04	0.17	*0.71*	0.04		0.47	a	
	5	43			0.09	0.02	0.23	*0.53*	0.11		0.45	a	
	5	48	0.04		0.06		0.31	*0.48*	0.08	0.02	0.44	a	Two sessions diffe

Cabe (1996b)

splay), period 20		16			0.06		0.19	*0.75*			0.44	a	MAOs; U3 report
splay), period 20		16		0.31	*0.50*	0.19					0.13	b	human data on
r), period 1	20	16			0.12	0.19	*0.56*	0.06	0.06		0.46	a	
r), period 15	20	16			0.19	*0.81*					0.14	c	

nt (1997)

ontrol)	7	51	0.02	0.12	0.10	0.13	0.04	*0.57*	0.02		0.38	a	1/3 paid; nos. fro
guage	7	54	0.06	0.08	0.02	0.13	0.02	*0.67*	0.02		0.41	a	figures (study 1

li, and Potter (1996)

			$0–0.99	1–1.99	2–2.99	3–3.99	4–4.99	5–6.99	7–8.99	9–max			Proposers inform
orm [0,30]	[0,30]	10	0.13	0.08	0.16	0.10	*0.08*	0.25	0.10	0.11	0.31	a	make $ offers
orm [5,25]	[5,25]	10	0.04	0.01	0.08	0.16	0.17	*0.23*	0.18	0.12	0.38	b	2 ten-period phas
orm [10,20]	[10,20]	10		0.01		0.06	0.16	*0.52*	0.18	0.07	0.41	c	roles switched

(con

(continued)

ntal conditio Amount($)		No. of pairs	Offer frequencies (percent offered)								Mean offer	Signif. code	Comments
			0	1–10	11–20	21–30	31–40	41–50	51–60	61–100			
ndali, and Seale (1996)		Class:	1	2	3	4	5	6	7	8			Proposers informe
ıniform [0,30]	[0,30]	20	0.13	0.07	0.17	0.12	*0.18*	0.13	0.12	0.08	0.28	a	
ıniform [5,25]	[5,25]	20	0.04	0.09	0.15	0.19	*0.12*	0.17	0.19	0.04	0.34	b	
ıniform [10,20]	[10,20]	20	0.14	0.08	0.06	0.16	*0.14*	0.19	0.12	0.08	0.35	b	
ss, and Zapater (1996)													
?	10	17			0.06	0.18	0.12	*0.53*	0.12		0.45	a	
∫o stages	10	18		0.17	0.17	0.17	*0.06*	0.17	0.25	0.06	0.41	a	
Roth (1998)													
·s	60	240			0.01	0.03	0.16	*0.75*	0.06		0.45	a	Payment in
stakes	300	330		0.04		0.07	0.20	*0.66*	0.07		0.42	a	Slovak crowns
es	1500	250		0.01	0.06	0.04	0.12	*0.69*	0.07		0.43	a	
rry (2000)													
·s	20	290			0.28	0.10	*0.17*	0.36	0.09		0.34	a	Offers < 25 perce
es	400	270			0.27	0.17	*0.17*	0.34	0.04		0.32	a	in (11,20) inter

s in italic represent median offers.

quencies of rejections in ultimatum games

condition	Amount($)	No. of pairs	Conditional rejection frequencies (percent offered)								Rejection rate	Comments
			0	1–10	11–20	21–30	31–40	41–50	51–60	61–100		
(1995)												
natum	4	20	< 1.00 >		0.78	0.57	0.12	0.08			0.38	Offers imputed fro
(ZK)	4	20	< 1.00 >		0.70	0.07	0.07	0.13			0.30	series of games
piah	5K	101	1.00	1.00	0.75	1.00	0.08	0.03	0.00	0.00	0.17	"Problems" exclude
piah	40K	35				0.40	0.17	0.00		0.00	0.09	
piah	200K	37	1.00	1.00	1.00	0.00	0.00	0.05			0.12	
	10	26		0.00	1.00	1.00	0.00	0.00	0.00		0.07	Data from working
	10	28		0.00	0.00	0.25	0.00	0.00		0.00	0.04	paper
an (2001)												
	5	96	1.00	0.50	0.35	0.23	0.03	0.00	0.00	0.00	0.10	Numbers estimate
	5	95	0.00	1.00	0.50	0.40	0.05	0.00	0.00		0.14	from figures
e, Shachat, and Smith (1994); Hoffman, McCabe, and Smith (1996a)												
ion	10	24				0.33	0.11	0.00			0.08	
	10	24		0.00	0.50	0.00	0.00	0.00			0.13	
ion	100	27				0.00	0.14	0.00	0.00		0.04	
	100	23		0.75	0.00	0.33	0.00	0.00	0.00		0.21	
er, and Schwarze (1982)												
	4–10	21	0.50		0.33	0.00	0.00	0.00			0.10	Payment in DM
	4–10	21		1	0.50	0.33	0.00	0.20			0.25	9 and 12 games ex

(continued)

ntal condition	Amount($)	No. of pairs	\multicolumn{8}{c}{Conditional rejection frequencies (percent offered)}								Rejection rate	Comments
			0	1–10	11–20	21–30	31–40	41–50	51–60	61–100		
kar, Okuno-Fujiwara, and Zamir (1991)												
h, Round 1	10	27			0.00	0.67	0.17	0.07	0.00	1.00	0.19	
h, Round 1	30	10						0.25	0.00		0.20	
a, Round 1	400K	30			1.00	0.50	0.25	0.23	0.00		0.27	Payment in dinars
und 1	2000	29		0.50	0.50	0.50	0.25	0.08	0.50	0.00	0.24	Payment in yen
und 1	20	30		0.80	0.50	0.33	0.00	0.15	0.00		0.27	Payment in shekels
h, Round 10	10	27			1.00		0.22	0.12			0.19	
h, Round 10	30	10				0.00		0.13	0.00		0.10	
a, Round 10	400K	30			1.00	0.63	0.05				0.24	Payment in dinars
und 10	2000	29				0.20	0.10	0.14			0.14	Payment yen
und 10	20	30		0.00	0.25	0.17	0.12	0.00			0.13	Payment in shekels
owitz, Savin, and Sefton (1994)												
	10	24			0.00	0.00	0.25	0.00	0.00		0.04	
	5	43			0.50	0.00	0.10	0.00	0.00		0.07	
ay	5	48	1.00		0.67		0.27	0.00	0.00	0.00	0.17	Two sessions differe
cCabe, Shachat, and Smith (1994)												
lication	10	24				0.33	0.11	0.00			0.08	
l Contest	10	24			0.00	0.00	0.00	0.00			0.00	
e	10	24			0.00	0.25	0.00	0.00	0.00		0.08	
e and Contest	10	24		0.00	0.50	0.00	0.00	0.00			0.13	
d McCabe (1996b)												
ic display), period 1	20	16	1.00	0.87	0.74	0.61	0.36	0.00	0.00	0.00	0.11	MAOs; U3 reports
ic display), period 15	20	16	1.00	1.00	0.00	0.00	0.00	0.00	0.00	0.00	0.31	human data only
puter), period 1	20	16	1.00	1.00	1.00	0.94	0.63	0.51	0.00	0.00	0.68	
puter), period 15	20	16	1.00	0.00	0.00	0.00	0.00	0.00	0.00	0.00	0.00	

at (1997)

ontrol)	7	51	0.98	0.67	0.58	0.46	0.37	0.03	0.00	0.00	0.30	1/3 paid; nos. from
uage	7	54	0.70	0.48	0.37	0.26	0.26	0.04	0.00	0.00	0.15	figures (study 1); MAC

, and Potter (1996)

			\$:0-.99	1-1.99	2-2.99	3-3.99	4-4.99	5- 6.99	7-8.99	9-max		
												Proposers informed,
rm [0,30] [0,30]	10	0.68	0.40	0.19	0.20	0.06	0.00	0.00	0.05	0.18	make \$ offers
rm [5,25] [5,25]	10	0.86	0.40	0.31	0.18	0.09	0.02	0.00	0.00	0.12	2 ten-period phases,
rm [10,20] [10,20]	10		1.00		0.67	0.67	0.18	0.00	0.00	0.25	roles switched

, and Seale (1996)

	class:	1	2	3	4	5	6	7	8		
										Proposers informed	
rm [0,30] [0,30]	20	0.29	0.22	0.09	0.18	0.01	0.16	0.15	0.30		
rm [5,25] [5,25]	20	0.65	0.22	0.12	0.06	0.10	0.04	0.11	0.13		
rm [10,20] [10,20]	20	0.55	0.39	0.22	0.15	0.09	0.07	0.02	0.06		

d Zapater (1996)

	10	17		1.00	0.33	0.50	0.00	0.00		0.18	
ges	10	18	1.00	0.33	0.33	0.00	0.00	0.00	0.00	0.28	

1998)

	60	240		1.00	0.67	0.42	0.11	0.07	0.18	Payment in Slovak crown
s	300	330	0.85		0.31	0.17	0.07	0.05	0.16	
	1500	250	0.50	0.50	0.58	0.07	0.03	0.00	0.14	

2000)

	\$20	290		0.72	0.43	0.30	0.13	0.12	0.35
	\$400	270		0.55	0.28	0.17	0.08	0.00	0.26

in a dictator game, they are not payoff maximizing, which suggests some of their generosity in ultimatum games is altruistic rather than strategic.

In the first dictator game experiment, Kahneman, Knetsch, and Thaler (1986) gave subjects a choice between dictating an even split of $20 with another student, or an uneven ($18,$2) split favoring themselves. Their results are shown in Table 2.4, which compiles statistics from many dictator game experiments. Three-quarters chose the equal split ($10,$10).

Reaction to the striking dictator results got the literature off on the wrong interpretive foot. Many people thought the main question about the ultimatum findings was whether offers were fair or were strategic (merely avoiding rejection). But the tail that wags the proverbial dog is the *rejections by Responders*, which force Proposers to make generous offers. Forsythe et al. (1994) did the first thorough comparison of dictator and ultimatum results where dictators could offer any amount they wanted (rather than simply choosing one of two allocations). Their dictators show less generosity than Kahneman et al. reported, but the mean allocation is about 20 percent, showing that there is some pure altruism. The fact that dictator offers are much lower than Proposer offers in ultimatum games, but positive, shows that Proposers are being both strategic (avoiding more to avoid rejection) *and* altruistic.[3] Early results showed that average offers are close to the offer that maximizes expected payoffs given the actual pattern of rejections (e.g., Roth et al., 1991), which implies Proposers are simply being strategic. More sophisticated analyses then showed that actual offers are more generous than payoff-maximizing offers, even controlling for risk-aversion (Henrich et al., 2001; cf. Lin and Sunder, 2002). In a model allowing nonequilibrium beliefs (and learning), Costa-Gomes and Zauner (2001) found that Proposer beliefs were generally a little too pessimistic.

The many studies on ultimatum and dictator games have varied the conditions in the game or identity of subjects to explore a wide variety of issues. Variables fall into five categories. *Methodological* variables change how the experiment is conducted—stakes, anonymity, and repetition. *Demographic* variables measure how different groups of people behave. (Few

---

[3] I suspect that Proposers behave strategically in ultimatum games because they expect Responders to stick up for themselves, whereas they behave more fair-mindedly in dictator games because Recipients cannot stick up for themselves. This behavior could be codified in a theory of reciprocal fairness that includes responsibility. Define the last-moving player who affects player i's payoff as the only one 'responsible' for i. If that responsible player is not i then she must take some care to treat i fairly; otherwise, she can treat i neutrally and expect i to be responsible for herself. This idea is exemplified by former Philadelphia mayor Frank Rizzo, who was asked whether he ever gave money to the city's many homeless beggars. Rizzo was a notorious law-and-order autocrat (for example, the number of civilians shot by policemen fell dramatically after he retired as police chief), so I expected a gruff answer about how the homeless don't deserve handouts. Instead, Rizzo said he made a judgment about whether the person asking for money was capable of working (based on apparent physical or mental disability), and gave money to those beggars who appeared unable to work. Rizzo is providing social insurance.

locations in dictator games

condition	$	No. of pairs	Percent allocated to other person										Mean	Signif. code
			0	1–10	11–20	21–30	31–40	41–50	51–60	61–70	71–90	91–100		
(1997)														
	13	18	0.11		0.06	0.17	*0.22*	0.44					0.35	a
- info.	13	25		0.04	0.04	0.04	0.20	*0.28*	0.12	0.12	0.04	0.12	0.52	b
ad Zwick (1998)														
·d	10	28	0.93	na	na	na	na	0.07	na	na	na	na		
	10	28	na	na	na	na	0.89	0.11	na	na	na	na	na	
ard	1	25	0.40	0.04	*0.36*	0.16		0.04	na	na	na	na	0.16	a
ard	1	25	0.40	0.08	*0.24*	0.20		0.08	na	na	na	na	0.20	a
	10	33	0.37	*0.18*	0.15	0.03	0.12	0.09		0.03			0.17	a
·d	10	27	*0.52*	0.15	0.07	0.07		0.15	na	na	na	na	0.13	a
(1998)														
	40	40	0.38	0.05	0.05	*0.15*	0.16	0.19			0.03		0.23	
	40	40	0.28	0.16	0.05	*0.05*	0.05	0.12	0.12	0.05	0.13		0.31	
z, Savin, and Sefton (1994)														
	10	24	0.21	0.17	*0.13*	0.29		0.21					0.24	b
	5	45	0.14		0.11		*0.26*	0.47			0.02		0.38	a
	5	45	0.35		*0.28*	0.05	0.09	0.18	0.05				0.23	b
(1995)														
d	13	39	0.28	0.08	0.03	0.10	*0.18*	0.30	0.03				0.26	a
	13	28			0.07			*0.082*		0.04		0.07	0.50	b
communication	13	17	0.06	0.06		0.12	0.05	*0.41*	0.12			0.18	0.48	b

(continued)

ntal condition	$	No. of pairs	Percent allocated to other person											Signi code
			0	1–10	11–20	21–30	31–40	41–50	51–60	61–70	71–90	91–100	Mean	
Oppenheimer (1997)														
	10	22	0.34	0.18		0.05	0.09	0.23				0.11	0.27	a
ates	10	19	0.47	0.20	0.05			0.26					0.16	a
d Eckel (1993)														
ind 1	10	12	0.58		0.08	0.08	0.17	0.08					0.15	
recipient	10	48	0.27	0.10	0.23		0.08	0.17			0.04	0.10	0.31	
Cabe, Shachat, and Smith (1994)														
labels	10	24	0.21	0.04	0.04	0.42	0.17	0.12					0.27	a
nd exchange	10	24	0.42	0.17	0.21	0.17	0.04						0.13	b
ind 1	10	36	0.64	0.19	0.06	0.03		0.06			0.03		0.10	c
ind 2	10	41	0.59	0.20	0.02	0.07	0.02	0.10					0.10	c
Cabe, and Smith (1996b)														
ication	10	28	0.18	0.18	0.07	0.18	0.07	0.25		< 0.07 >			0.24	
ation	10	28	0.43		0.11	0.14	0.11	0.18		< 0.04 >			0.20	
nd 1	10	37	0.41	0.27	0.11	0.05	0.03	0.14					0.15	
nd 2 (dec. form)	10	43	0.42	0.21	0.12	0.05	0.05	0.09		< 0.07 >			0.13	
Knetsch, and Thaler (1990)														
hoice	20	161	na	0.24	na	na	na	0.76	na	na	na	na	na	
s, and Zapater (1996)														
(control)	10	16	0.13	0.06		0.25	0.06	0.44				0.06	0.39	a
stages	10	16	0.31		0.19	0.31	0.13			0.06			0.23	b

demographic effects have proved to be large or replicable, although there are intriguing effects of race, age, and beauty.) *Culture* seems to be important when sampled broadly: In simple societies with more "market integration," ultimatum offers are closer to even splits. *Descriptive* variables change the description of the game but not its structure. *Structural* variables change the game by adding moves. Methodological, demographic, and descriptive variables have proved to have modest effects that are often not robust across studies. Cultural and structural variables have bigger effects and are more helpful for building social preference theories.

2.2 Methodological Variables

Methodological variables were vigorously studied as interest in the ultimatum games first reported in 1982 caught fire several years later.

2.2.1 Repetition

Several experiments have used stationary replication to see whether repeating simple bargaining games matters. Roth et al. (1991), Bolton and Zwick (1995), Knez and Camerer (1995), Slonim and Roth (1998), and List and Cherry (2000) repeated ultimatum games using stranger-matching. Bolton and Zwick did not observe an experience effect; the other studies show a slight (usually insignificant) tendency for offers and rejections to fall over time.

Subjects may adjust offers over time more strongly when they know what all other subjects have done, or when playing with programmed subjects with unusual tastes (e.g., pure self-interest). Harrison and McCabe (1996b) measured these effects. Providing information about the offers and MAOs of all other subjects lowered offers and MAOs drop to around 15 percent by period 15.[4] Either Responders quit punishing unfair Proposers if they see that many others are not doing so, or their perceptions of what is fair are shaped by what others are doing. In another condition, when data from sixteen human subjects were reported to subjects along with sixteen additional random offers and MAOs of 1–14 percent, human offers and MAOs fell substantially over time.

Taken together, these studies show only a small effect of experience (lowering offers and rejections) unless the population is 'seeded' with self-interested computerized players. Note that a drop in rejections could be

---

[4] See Harrison and McCabe's (1992) working paper.

learning, or it could be temporary satiation of a taste for revenge. If rejections are emotional expressions of distaste for being treated unfairly, those expressed tastes might temporarily satiate like other tastes with a visceral component (such as food, exercise, or sex). For example, Aristotle opined that "men become calm when they have spent their anger on someone else." And, in trials of collaborators in German-occupied countries after 1945, those who were tried later generally received milder sentences (holding severity of the crime constant). Workers in less-developed countries speak of "donor fatigue," when charitable impulses are worn out by overwhelming solicitation by the poor.

A very easy way to distinguish satiation from learning is to "restart" the experiment after a break of a day or a week. If subjects stopped rejecting in one session because they got tired of expressing their anger, the frequency of rejections should rise again after the break. If they stopped rejecting because they learned not to, the break should have little effect.

2.2.2 Methodology: Stakes

If I had a dollar for every time an economist claimed that raising the stakes would drive ultimatum behavior toward self-interest, I'd have a private jet on standby all day. Many experimental studies *have* raised stakes (see Camerer and Hogarth, 1999).[5] In simple tasks such as ultimatum games, paying extra usually does not make much difference in how hard players think because the task is easy. But higher stakes might change the relative weight players put on their own payoffs and the payoffs of others. In fact, most sensible theories predict that, as stakes rise, the *amount* that Responders will reject goes up but the *percentage* they will reject goes down. (That is, they are more likely to reject $5 out of $50 than out of $10, and are more likely to accept 10 percent of a $50 pie than of a $10 pie.)

Studies show some stakes effect of this sort, but the effects are surprisingly weak. The earliest studies in the United States show no significant effect on rejection rates (Roth et al., 1991; Forsythe et al., 1994; Hoffman, McCabe, and Smith, 1996a; Straub and Murnighan, 1995). (These studies are handicapped, however, because the specific-offer method is used and low offers are rare, so the statistical power to detect changes in rejection rates is low.)

---

[5] Across many different experiments, the largest effect of raising incentives comes when subjects are paid some performance-related incentive, compared with being paid nothing, and when the task is neither so difficult that thinking harder doesn't help nor so easy that very little thinking is required (for both extremes the performance improvement from extra payment is low). Once subjects are paid some incentive, multiplying the stake by two or ten makes little difference for average responses. However, paying more generally reduces outliers and shrinks variance.

Inventive studies have been done in foreign countries where modest stakes (by American standards) have large purchasing power. Cameron (1999) did the first study in Indonesia. Her stakes were 5K, 40K, and 200K rupiah (about one day's to one month's wages); stakes made little difference. In the Slovak Republic, Slonim and Roth (1998) found significantly fewer rejections in medium- and high-stakes conditions pooling ten rounds of play (matching with no repetition in matching). List and Cherry (2000) did a clever high-stakes experiment in Florida (which is considered a foreign country by Californians) with an important twist: Subjects who answered more general knowledge questions correctly "earned" the right to make offers from a $400 pie rather than a measly $20 pie. List and Cherry conjectured, correctly, that entitlement would generate more low offers and therefore more statistical power to detect any difference in rejections for the two pie sizes (and change over time). Indeed, rejection rates are a little lower for the $400 pie and decline modestly over time.

Taken together, these studies show that very large changes in stakes (up to several months' wages) have only a modest effect on rejections. Raising stakes also has little effect on Proposers' *offers*, presumably because aversion to costly rejection leads subjects to offer *closer* to 50 percent when stakes go up.[6] The frequent number of rejections of large dollar amounts is striking. In Hoffman, McCabe, and Smith (1996a) two subjects (out of six) rejected $30 offers out of $100. In List and Cherry (2000) a quarter of the subjects who were offered $100 out of $400 rejected it. It is tempting to conclude that these subjects were "confused," but this explanation is acceptable only if confusion is measured independently of whether a subject's behavior deviated from somebody's pet theory.

A different kind of incentive effect changes the "price" at which people indulge tastes for vengeance or altruism. Andreoni and Miller (2002) ran dictator games in which they multiplied the amount allocated to the Recipient. A multiplier greater than one models situations in which charitable contributions are "matched" by employers (or by the government through tax deduction). If Dictators have preferences over dollar allocations between themselves and Recipients, they should allocate (weakly) more when the multiplier is high. Their subjects were endowed with forty to one hundred tokens (worth $0.10). Tokens could be "held" for a value from 1 to 3 to the Dictator, or "passed," giving a value of 1 to 3 for the Recipient. By varying the "price" of altruism—the ratio of token values—they are able to classify subjects into three categories (and forecast contributions in other public

---

[6] At a conference at Penn years ago, several of us discussed how much we'd offer from a $1 million stake. As I recall, Al Roth said he'd offer something like $400,000, below the equal split but well above the self-interest equilibrium. Bob Aumann said, "Al, you must be rich! I'd offer $500,000." Aumann was unwilling to bet so much money on the rationality and self-interest of a random person he was paired with.

goods games accurately): Half are selfish (maximize own earnings π_s), one-third are Leontief or Rawlsian (maximize $\min(\pi_s, \pi_o)$, where π_o is earnings of others), and the rest are utilitarian (maximize $\pi_s + \pi_o$). The representative subject gives as much money to the Recipient as she keeps if the relative payoff for others is about three to four times as large as for herself.

2.2.3 Anonymity and Experimenter "Blindness"

Psychologists have long known that details of experimental protocol or instructions could be taken by subjects as implicit "demands" about what the experimenter intends or hopes to happen. A problem arises if subjects derive utility from "helping" the experimenter by satisfying the demands they perceive. Concerned about these effects, Hoffman et al. (1994) took extreme care to reassure each subject that the experimenter would not know how they behaved in two "double-blind" dictator game experiments.

Dictators got an opaque envelope containing ten dollar-sized blank slips of paper and ten $1 bills. Dictators went, one at a time, inside a large cardboard "phone booth" and took out a combination of ten dollars and blank slips, leaving ten pieces of paper (dollars or slips) in the envelope. (As the dictator left the phone booth the experimenter could not tell from the thickness of the envelope how many dollars were left inside because, even if the subject took all the dollars out, the blank slips were left and simulated the heft of dollar bills.) Then they put the envelope in a large box. After all the envelopes were placed in the box, the experimenter checked all the envelopes to learn the *distribution* of allocations; but since the envelopes were unmarked she did not know what any individual subject had left. Then each Recipient subject took an envelope out of the box and kept whatever money was left.

As Table 2.4 reports, more than half the subjects left nothing and the mean allocation was only 10 percent, significantly less than in control conditions without double-blindness. Hoffman, McCabe, and Smith (1998) also reduced dictator allocations using subtle treatments that they interpret as increasing the 'social distance' between subjects (through instruction changes) or between subjects and the experimenter (through double-blindness) (Frey and Bohnet, 1997). Bolton, Katok, and Zwick (1998) also studied anonymity in dictator games. In their treatment "1 Game 6 Card" in Table 2.4, half the Dictators left nothing and a sixth split the money equally, but they did *not* offer less in the "anonymity" condition.

Bolton and Zwick (1995) imposed experimenter-blindness in ultimatum games. Guaranteeing Proposers that the experimenter will not know their decision is much more difficult in these games, because Proposers need to convey their decision to a specific Responder, *and* find out what that Responder did; and the experimenter needs to record all these decisions. Their "zero-knowledge" design uses an ingenious scheme, passing boxes back and forth. Tables 2.2 and 2.3 show the results.[7] Anonymity lowers rejections very slightly.

Concerns about experimental "blindness" create both challenge and opportunity. Distancing the experimenter from the subject might undermine experimental credibility, which creates a challenge. Frohlich and Oppenheimer (1997) found that dictator subjects who allocated less were more likely to doubt that there were actually human Recipients on the receiving end (see Table 2.4). Opportunity comes from the fact that anonymity can be easily created in field experiments which complement lab experiments. An example is the "lost letter paradigm" used in the 1950s. Researchers dropped sealed letters containing slugs the size and weight of coins around a town. (Others used "lost wallets" which contain identification so the "recipient" identity can be experimentally manipulated.) The number of letters returned to the experimenter unopened is a measure of altruism. These paradigms sacrifice knowledge of who the subjects are but create experimenter–subject anonymity and have a lifelike feel.

Summary: Studies of methodological variables have tested the robustness of ultimatum rejections to the "usual suspect" explanations that are always raised whenever data conflict with economic theory: repetition, stakes, and—a newer concern—anonymity of subjects from experimenter scrutiny. Repetition makes little difference; there is a weak effect of stakes on the rejection of fixed-percentage offers (although subjects reject larger *dollar* offers when stakes go up); and anonymity sometimes lowers Dictator allocations but has little effect in ultimatums.

2.3 Demographic Variables

Many researchers are fascinated by the possibility of demographic differences in strategic behavior and social preferences. Gender, academic major, and culture are the demographic variables studied most often, but there is also limited evidence on other variables.

---

[7] Their results are reported in an unorthodox way to fit in the table. Because subjects do not have a free choice of offer percentages, I used the fraction of times when Proposers offered x instead of the even split $2 to construct a cumulative distribution function (cdf), then used differences in the cdf as estimates of the percentage of subjects making offers in each interval. For example, in the zero-knowledge condition, fifteen of twenty subjects offered the ($3,$1) split instead of an even split, and ten of twenty offered the ($3.40,$0.60) split instead of an even split. This implies that five of twenty subjects (25 percent) would choose an ideal offer, if allowed, between $0.61 and $0.99. Since this range of offers has an average equal to 20 percent of the stake, 25 percent of the offers are reported in the interval [11,20].

2.3.1 Gender

It is widely thought that women are more likely to sacrifice their own interests for the sake of preserving harmony in relationships, whereas men are more competitive and apply moral principles that override personal relations (e.g., Gilligan, 1982). The contrast can be seen when children play. If a scraped knee interrupts a game, girls gather around the injured player, sympathizing. Boys are more likely to help the player off the field and keep playing. An economic reason to study gender is the gender gap in wages: Women seem to be paid less for equivalent work (even adjusting for such variables as age, job seniority, and education and skill requirements). Perhaps this gap is partly caused by the different bargaining strategies of women and men, which can be measured in simple experiments (even in the field; see Ayres and Siegelman, 1995).

Eckel and Grossman (2001) measured gender differences in ultimatum bargaining (see also Eckel and Grossman, in press). Some results are summarized in Tables 2.2 and 2.3. Although male and female offers are similar, Eckel and Grossman (and Rapoport and Sundali, 1996) found that women reject less often. Bolton, Katok, and Zwick (1998) and Frey and Bohnet (1995) found no gender difference in dictator games. Solnick (2001) found that both genders demanded more from women, and offered more to men.

Eckel and Grossman (1996b) studied gender in a dictator game with an opportunity for "third-party" punishment. Subjects could divide $12 evenly between themselves and a type A player who had behaved unfairly toward somebody else in an earlier dictator game, or they could divide a smaller sum x (either $10 or $8) evenly between themselves and a fair type B. Females punished more overall and are "better shoppers" (more price sensitive): They punished more often than males when it cost less ($x = \$10$) and punished less often when it cost more ($x = \$8$).

Andreoni and Vesterlund (2001) studied gender in the Andreoni–Miller dictator game with varying values of tokens to a Dictator and Recipient. Overall, women and men allocate the same *dollar* amount to others but this aggregate result hides a big difference: Half the men were purely self-interested, whereas more than half the women were Rawlsian. The mixed effects suggest gender does not have a simple "main effect" on social preferences (such as "women are nicer"—note that they punish more often in the Eckel–Grossman third-party game[8]). Instead, gender seems to interact with many other variables (prices, perhaps beliefs about others), which makes it both a slippery and a rich topic.

---

[8] Hell hath no fury like a woman scorned?

2.3.2 Race

Modern social scientists are often afraid to study race but it is an interesting variable. Simple games could be used to measure discrimination and whether racial differences account for wage and employment gaps in the economy. Evolutionary psychologists believe that ethnolinguistic differences (which are usually easy to see and hear) are "essentialist" distinctions people are adapted to notice and respond to.

Three studies show interesting distinctions; daring, thoughtful researchers should look for more. In Eckel and Grossman's (2001) ultimatum games designed to study gender effects, they actually found a stronger effect of race: Black students offer more and reject more often. Glaeser et al. (2000) found a small racial effect in their trust games: White students did not repay the trust of Asians. Fershtmann and Gneezy (2001) found a strong difference between behavior toward eastern (Ashkenazic) and western (Sephardic) Jews in Israel; the Ashkenazics were treated more poorly by everybody.

2.3.3 Academic Major

A few studies measure whether students' academic backgrounds affect their allocations. Carter and Irons (1991) ran ultimatum experiments with students majoring in economics and in other fields. Economics majors offered 7 percent less and demanded 7 percent more than others. Because the offer gap did not change when contrasting first-year students and seniors they conclude that the economics-major effect is "born, not made": Students who self-select to study economics tend to behave more self-interestedly (and expect others to), but do not change after four years of economics courses. Other studies have shown mixed effects. Economics and business students offer *more* in Kahneman, Knetsch, and Thaler (1986) and Frey and Bohnet (1995) and behave the same as other majors in Eckel and Grossman (1996) and Kagel, Kim, and Moser (1996).

2.3.4 Age

Developmental studies of how children and adults behave at various ages are important for figuring out whether fairness tastes are innate (as evolutionary theories suggest) or learned through socialization. There are only two studies of age effects. Damon (1980) suggests that children pass through three phases. Before age 5, they are primarily self-interested. From ages 5–7 they focus on strict equality as a way of preventing conflict (even asking to divide a single M&M candy in half to achieve perfect equality when the

number of candies is odd!). After age 7 they begin to think in terms of equity
(e.g., rewards proportional to inputs, perhaps coinciding with an increase
in cognitive ability to grasp fractions).

To look for these phase changes, Murnighan and Saxon (1998) used
children in kindergarten, 3rd grade, and 6th grade. Because of the subjects' young age, fears about comprehension loom large (like cross-cultural
research, crossing adult and child cultures). The children divided M&M
candies and money. In imperfect information conditions, children did not
know how much the other child was dividing; in perfect information conditions they did. The children were not paid, on the advice of teachers. When
dividing money, the 3rd graders offered less than the 6th graders (30 percent versus 50 percent). Responders stated an average MAO of 10 percent
in the complete information condition, about half as large as in other studies with adults. There were no effects of age on candy offers or responses.
However, kindergartners accepted 70 percent of the offers of one penny or
one candy, compared with 30–60 percent for the older children.

Harbaugh, Krause, and Liday (2000) did a similar study with 2nd, 4th–
5th, and 9th graders in Oregon. Children bargained over ten tokens, which
were worth $0.25 each to the 9th graders and could be used by the younger
children to buy supplies or toys. Each child played both roles in ultimatum
and dictator games. Dictator allocations look like those of adults: About two-
thirds of the children gave nothing and the rest gave half or less. Ultimatum
offers were the lowest among the youngest children (2nd graders) and
got slightly more generous for older children (means were 35 percent, 41
percent, 44 percent). The 2nd graders also were more inclined to accept
low offers. There is also a striking effect of *height*: Taller children (adjusting
for gender) offered less in the dictator game and the ultimatum games.
(There is also a "height premium" in wages and other domains. For example,
American Presidents tend to be taller than average; see Persico, Postlewaite,
and Silverman, 2001.)

Harbaugh et al. draw a nicely worded conclusion:

> This result gives a new twist to work by others on cross-cultural differ-
> ences in economic behavior. Explanations of these cultural differences
> are either really about genetic differences, or they require that there be
> some way that different cultures persuade people with the same genes to
> behave differently. We suggest that this process happens in childhood,
> and we provide evidence of substantial behavioral changes in a sample
> of children from the same culture, over ages 7 to 14. (2000, p. 20)

Note that in these studies, the youngest children in both studies are
closer to the self-interest prediction of game theory than virtually any adult
population! This is a huge hint that experience does *not* teach people

to behave like payoff-maximizing game-theorists, as is often presumed. If anything, the opposite seems to be true: Grown-up fair-mindedness is the result of the swing of a pendulum from pure self-interest (at young ages), to obsession with strict equality (in 3rd grade), to an adult compromise. These facts cast doubt on a strong version of the hypothesis that an instinct for acting tough in repeated interactions evolved because it was adaptive in our ancestral past. At best, people may have adapted the ability to *learn* to react to perceived unfairness over time (much as a piece of exposed film gradually becomes a picture in a chemical bath; but what chemicals are used affects the exposure). But the innate learning hypothesis is difficult to distinguish from learning that is not innate at all.

2.3.5 Brains, Biology, and Beauty

If ultimatum rejections are mistakes, then subjects who make mistakes in judgment problems should be more likely to reject offers. Clark (1997) tested this hypothesis by having subjects engage in two judgment tasks (probability matching tasks and the Wason four-card logic problem) and a dictator-like allocation task. Subjects who are generous in the allocation task are slightly *better* in the judgment tasks, contrary to the mistake hypothesis. However, reasoning does seem to matter somewhat because Carter and Irons (1991) found that subjects who figured out the perfect equilibrium correctly in the ultimatum game offered and demanded about 5 percent less than others.

Ideally, social preference theories should say something about where preferences come from. An unusual step in this direction is Burnham (1999), who measured testosterone levels (T) using saliva samples. T is positively correlated with willingness to behave aggressively, social status, and profession (actors, National Football League players, and firemen are high in T; doctors, salesmen, and ministers are low; professors are in the middle, along with the unemployed). Burnham hypothesized that higher-T males have a stronger incentive to preserve their reputation by behaving aggressively in ultimatum games and rejecting offers. In his constrained ultimatum game, Proposers offer either $5 or $25 out of $40. High-$T$s were more likely to reject the $5 offer, as hypothesized, but were also more likely to choose the generous offer of $25, contrary to intuition.

Physical attractiveness is economically interesting because there is a well-established "beauty premium" in wages (Hamermesh and Biddle, 1994). To investigate the effect of beauty and gender, Schweitzer and Solnick (1999) had seventy University of Miami students make ultimatum offers and state MAOs. Each subject's picture was taken and rated on attractiveness. Then the most and least attractive 10 percent of the pictures were shown to a second group, who played ultimatum games against the person whose picture they saw (using the pictured subjects' earlier offers and MAOs).

In the first stage, there was no substantial difference in the offers and MAOs of the most and least attractive subjects. The second group of subjects had a small tendency to offer more to the more attractive subjects, and also to demand more from them. The largest effect is surprising. Men were not especially generous toward attractive women, but women offered about 5 percent more to attractive men than to unattractive men. In fact, the average female offer to good-looking guys was $5.07; this is the only Western group ever found in which the average offer is *more* than half! This extra-fair average results because few women offer less than half to cute guys, and 5 percent offer almost the whole pie ($8–10). The results imply a 10 percent beauty premium (the increase in expected earnings for the attractive compared with the unattractive) and a 15 percent gender premium (men earn more). The fact that the beauty and gender premiums in earnings evident in field data can be reproduced in laboratory bargaining is really interesting and deserves more exploration.

Summary: Demographic variables generally have weak effects on ultimatum and dictator behavior, although they are often significant and always intriguing. There are mixed effects of race; very mixed effects of gender and subject academic background (men and economics majors are often more self-interested); and mild effects of testosterone (high-T males reject more often, but are also more generous) and beauty (many women give more than half to attractive guys). The effect of age is strong—young children are more self-interested, then become fair-minded as they grow older. This developmental effect is crucial because it suggests fairness norms are not innate; they change as children develop.

2.4 Culture

Culture is a very interesting variable, but cross-cultural comparison raises at least four difficult methodological problems: Stakes, language, experimenter interactions, and confounds.

- *Stakes.* Controlling for stakes requires the experimenter to match the purchasing power of the stake in two different cultures.[9] Converting

---

[9] In less-developed cultures researchers may have to construct a cost-of-living index by measuring local prices of commonly used items such as pots, knives, radios, sugar, salt, and cooking fat.

a baseline sum into local exchange rates is a good approximation. An alternative solution is to control for stakes in terms of labor supply by equalizing the number of hours of work required to earn the stake amount (Beard, Beil, and Mataga, 2001).

• *Language.* Keeping the meaning of instructions as constant as possible is important. The standard method is "back translation": Have instructions in language A translated to language B, then have the language B version translated back to language A *by a different translator*. If the versions differ, fiddle with the language until it translates back and forth unambiguously.

• *Experimenter effects.* The identity and behavior of the experimenter can sometimes affect what subjects do. Reading from a common script, with as few deviations as possible, controls much of behavior. The biggest mistake in controlling for identity is to use a different experimenter in each culture; then you cannot statistically distinguish the effect of the experimenter from the effect of the culture. The "main effect" of experimenter identity can be controlled by having *each* experimenter conduct an experiment in one culture (e.g., each member of the team of Roth et al., 1991, conducted one session in Pittsburgh), but more care is needed if there are potential experimenter-place interactions.[10] The ideal experimenters speak both languages and are perceived similarly in both cultures (e.g., the first author and experimenter in the Buchan, Johnson, and Croson, 1997, team, who compared Japan and the United States, is Japanese-American).

• *Confounds with culture.* It is extremely difficult to avoid the effects of potentially important variables that are confounded with culture (causing "identification problems" in econometrics terms). For example, suppose you go to two universities in different countries, recruit students from economics classes, and find a difference in their behavior. The difference may be due to culture, or it may be that overall behavior is the same (if people are sampled randomly) but students in one culture are less representative of the population than students in the other culture (e.g., they are older because of pre-college army service, or only the wealthiest go to college). That is, student status may be proxying for unobserved variables that cause the observed behavior, leading to the spurious conclusion that culture matters. The best solution is to match the two cultural samples on as many demographic variables as possible, and measure any variables you can't control (see Botelho et al., 2002).

---

[10] For example, a female experimenter may be less credible in one culture than another; or there may be a stronger identification between subjects and a same-culture experimenter in one culture than another. The only conclusive control is to have each experimenter do an experiment in each location.

Roth et al. (1991) ran the first thoughtful comparison of bargaining games in America, Israel, Japan, and Yugoslovia. From an anthropologists' point of view, the cultures in these countries are actually very similar, but the paper of Roth et al. still marked an important start. Tables 2.2 and 2.3 summarize results from rounds 1 and 10 in each of the four countries. Offers in the United States and Slovenia were initially more generous and closer together than in Japan and Israel, which were 10 percent lower. By round 10, all offer distributions were more tightly clustered around the initial mean and the 10 percent gap persisted. Players also rejected offers less often in Japan and Israel, especially compared with Slovenia. A key point is that, whereas the Japanese offers are lower and the Israeli offers even lower, rejection rates are no higher in these countries. Roth et al. conclude that "what varies between subject pools is not a property like aggressiveness or toughness, but rather the perception of what constitutes a reasonable offer under the circumstances" (1991, p. 1092).

Buchan, Johnson, and Croson (1997) also compared ultimatum bargaining in Japan and America. They conjectured that the relatively collectivist culture in Japan would exhibit a stronger sharing norm; they were right. Their finding that offers were higher in Japan is the opposite of what Roth et al. observed. The difference illustrates how subtle and interactive cultural effects may be. Buchan et al. used the MAO method and Roth et al. used the specific-offer method, which may have caused differences. A different mixture of students in Japan in the two experiments is another possible explanation.

The most dramatic cross-culture bargaining experiments so far are a remarkable interdisciplinary collaboration between eleven anthropologists and several economists (Henrich et al., 2001, 2002). It began when an enterprising graduate student, Joe Henrich (2000), ran ultimatum experiments during fieldwork with Machiguenga farmers in Peru. He found that Machiguenga offered much less than had been observed in any other subject pool—an average of 26 percent with a mode at 15 percent—and accepted all but one offer! When Henrich came back to UCLA and showed the data to Rob Boyd and me, he wasn't sure whether he had screwed up the experiment or had discovered the first group of people who behave close to the game-theoretic (self-interest) prediction. A close replication in the United States (controlling for stakes) showed the usual result—a huge spike of 50 percent offers—and confirmed that Henrich had found a huge effect of culture.

An anthropology colleague of Henrich's noted that the Machiguenga are quite socially disconnected. The economic unit is the family; families hunt, gather, and practice swidden ("slash and burn") manioc farming. Anonymous transactions within a village are rare. Their society is the opposite of the bar on the television series *Cheers* ("where everybody knows

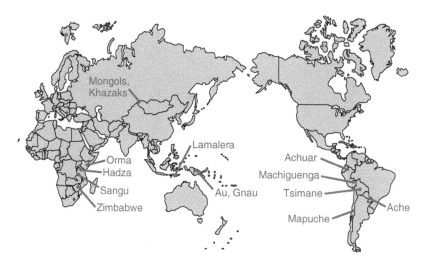

Figure 2.2. *Map of filed sites for "experimental economics in the bush" project. Source: Henrich et al. (2002).*

your name")—they don't have proper names for other Machiguenga except for relatives. Perhaps the extreme social and economic isolation of the Machiguenga explains why they have no sharing norm. The best way to test such hypotheses, of course, is to compare many cultures. So Henrich and his advisor Rob Boyd assembled a team of anthropologists and one economist to run ultimatum and public goods games in many different cultures which vary in important ways. Figure 2.2 shows a map of the amazing places they did experiments. Figure 2.3 pictures anthropologist David Tracer explaining the ultimatum game to an experimental subject in Papua New Guinea (and her infant who, contrary to appearances, is not for sale).

Their results are described in Henrich et al. (2002). Table 2.5 summarizes some features of the ultimatum game results. In about ten of the cultures (the top rows of the table), average and modal offers are lower than we have seen in many developed countries. Rejection rates are generally low, but vary across cultures. A careful statistical analysis shows that offers are persistently above the utility-maximizing offer (controlling for risk-aversion). Proposers appear to be "rejection-averse" beyond the loss of utility from being rejected. Many subjects said they offered a lot because rejections would cause turmoil in the village. The attentive reader will notice two unusual cultures at the bottom of the table—the Ache headhunters of Paraguay and the Lamelara whalers of Indonesia—who offer *more* than half on average! The anthropologists think these hyperfair offers represent either a norm of

Figure 2.3.   *Anthropologist David Tracer explaining the ultimatum game to an experimental subject in Papua New Guinea and her child. Photograph courtesy of David Tracer.*

oversharing because game caught in a hunt cannot be consumed privately, or a potlatch or competitive gift-giving. Accepting an unusually generous gift (such as excess meat caught in a successful hunt) incurs an obligation to repay even more, and is considered something of an insult (since it implies that the giver is a better hunter than the receiver). Hyperfair offers are often rejected, consistent with the competitive gift-giving interpretation. These offers are a reminder not only that self-interest is typically violated in these games, but also that offers and rejections are a language with nuance and cultural variation.

The big payoff from a cross-culture comparison is finding variables that can explain cultural variation. Differences in subject comprehension (rated by experimenters), arithmetic skills, education, anonymity of exchanges, and privacy (i.e., how much the neighbors know about your business) don't seem to matter. Two variables *do* predict differences in offers with a multiple $R^2 = 0.68$: the amount of cooperative activity or economies of scale in production (e.g., collective hunting for whales and big game); and the degree of "market integration." Market integration is an index combining the existence of a national language (rather than a local dialect), the existence of a labor market for cash wages, and the farming of crops for cash. Cultures

nmary of ultimatum bargaining games

Country	N	Stake size	Mean	Mode (percent of sample)	Standard deviation	Rejection rate (percent)	Rej of <
Peru	21	2.3	0.26	0.15/0.25 (72 percent)	0.14	4.8	1
Tanzania	29	1.0	0.27	0.20 (38 percent)	0.15	28	3
Bolivia	70	1.2	0.37	0.50/0.30/0.25 (65 percent)	0.19	0	
Ecuador	13	1.0	0.27	0.25 (47 percent)	0.16	015	5
Mongolia	10	8.0	0.35	0.25 (30 percent)	0.09	5	
Mongolia	10	8.0	0.36	0.25	0.09		
Chile	30	1.0	0.34	0.50/0.33 (46 percent)	0.18	67	2
Papua New Guinea	30	1.4	0.43	0.30 (33 percent)	0.14	27	
Papua New Guinea	25	1.4	0.38	0.40 (32 percent)	0.19	40	5
Tanzania	26	1.0	0.40	0.50 (28 percent)	0.17	19	8
Tanzania	20	1.0	0.41	0.50 (35 percent)	0.12	25	1
Zimbabwe	31	1.0	0.41	0.50 (56 percent)	0.14	10	3
Ecuador	16	1.0	0.42	0.50 (36 percent)	0.20	0	
Tanzania	20	1.0	0.42	0.50 (40 percent)	0.09	5	
Kenya	56	1.0	0.44	0.50 (54 percent)	0.092	4	
USA	27	0.28	0.45	0.50 (52 percent)	0.096	22	
Zimbabwe	86	1.0	0.45	0.50 (70 percent)	0.10	7	5
USA	15	2.3	0.48	0.50 (93 percent)	0.065	0	
Paraguay	51	1.0	0.51	0.50/0.40 (75 percent)	0.15	0	
Indonesia	19	10.0	0.58	0.50 (63 percent)	0.14	20	

modes are listed, the first is more common and the second less common. Fractions of the total sample at all modes are in
a, cigarettes were used (they are like currency) and lower "sham" offers were used to test whether subjects would reje
on rates are for the sham offers.

with more cooperative activity and market integration have sharing norms closer to equal splits.

There are important lessons for social science in this project. One is that interdisciplinary research is hard work but worthwhile. The project came together only after Boyd, Henrich, and other anthropologists learned enough about game theory and experimental methods to produce clean data. The anthropologists repay the debt by producing surprises and broadening economists' vision.

The effect of market integration is extremely important. A presumption in economic theory is that, since market exchange can lead to efficient outcomes even if agents are purely self-interested, active markets and self-interest may somehow go hand-in-hand. This project suggests this view might be fundamentally wrong. In cultures with the most market integration, people bargain the least self-interestedly. The anthropologists' very broad view is also a reminder that comparing, say, America and Japan is hardly a study of culture at all because those countries are quite close together in important cultural features.

Summary: In their pioneering study, Roth et al. found persistent cross-national differences in ultimatum offers (Japan and Israel are lowest). The key point is that countries have different sharing norms, and comparable rejection rates imply that those different norms are well acccepted (or rapidly learned in the lab) in each country. A remarkable project doing ultimatum (and other) games in a dozen simple societies in remote places such as Papua New Guinea, the Amazon basin, and Africa reveals more dramatic differences across cultures. This project shows some societies in which the self-interested game-theoretic prediction is accurate, and others where there are many "hyperfair" offers that can be interpreted as competitive gift-giving insults. Average offers are strongly correlated with the degree of "market integration," which implies that either market experience creates norms of equal division or the propensity to share evenly permits impersonal markets to flourish.

2.5 Descriptive Variables: Labeling and Context

Since Schelling's (1960) work on "psychological prominent" focal points in coordination games (see Chapter 7), it has been well understood that the way in which strategies are described could focus expectations on them and affect the way people play. A related literature in the psychology of decision making shows that the way options are described or "framed" can influence choices. Thus, it is sensible to ask whether alternative descriptions of ultimatum games affect the way they are played.

Hoffman et al. (1994) found that describing an ultimatum game as an exchange—a seller setting a price for a good that a buyer can take or leave—lowers offers by almost 10 percent and leaves rejection rates unchanged. Larrick and Blount (1997) pointed out that ultimatum games are strategically similar to "resource dilemmas" in which players make sequential claims from a fixed common pool of resources and get nothing if their claims add up to more than the pool. When one player makes a claim from the pool, her claim essentially "offers" the second player a chance to claim the remaining amount (or veto it by claiming more), just as in an ultimatum game. They test strategic equivalence by comparing an ultimatum game with a sequential resource dilemma. Offers in the dilemma frame are slightly more generous, and rejections less frequent. They conclude that the language of "claiming" creates a sense of common ownership that makes both sides more generous.

Hoffman, McCabe, and Smith (2000) asked Proposers to "consider what choice you expect the buyer [Responder] to make. Also consider what you think the buyer expects you to choose." These "prompting instructions" raised offers 5–10 percent. They hypothesize that prompting increases Proposer fears of rejection.

Summary: Changing the way games are described can have modest effects. Calling it a seller-buyer exchange encourages self-interest. Describing it as a claim from a shared resource pool encourages generosity. There is little doubt that describing games differently can affect behavior; the key step is figuring out what *general* principles (or theory of framing) can be abstracted from labeling effects. Work on framing in matching games, risky choice, and PD games shows how this abstraction might proceed. [11]

2.6 Structural Variables

A structural variable changes the way the tree describing the ultimatum game is drawn, typically by adding a move. (Descriptive variables simply change the way the moves or information nodes are labeled.) In my view, structural variables are the most useful to study because they connect simple games to richer economic structures (e.g., adding competition) and also

---

[11] Work on unpacking focality in matching games (see Chapter 7) points to the roles of distinctiveness and perception. Framing effects in risky choice are understood to occur because of the interaction between shifts in reference points for encoding gains or losses, and systematic gain–loss differences. Pilutla and Chen (1999) found that calling a prisoners' dilemma an "investment game" decreased cooperation compared with a "social event game" description. If players are reciprocal, the labeling could change their beliefs about what others will do and trigger an effect that is self-fulfilling.

provide the most direct clues to the psychology underlying social preference (for example, Konow, 2000, 2001).

2.6.1 Identity, Communication, and Entitlement

Some studies varied how much players know about the identity of the person they are playing with, and whether they communicate. Identification may activate empathy or contempt (for example, Jenni and Loewenstein, 1997).

Bohnet and Frey (1999) did experiments using one-way identification in which Recipients held a number in their hands, which paired Dictators in a classroom could use to identify "their" Recipient (but not vice versa).[12] Allowing Dictators to see their Recipient decreased the number leaving zero but did not change the mean significantly. However, when the Recipients stood up and talked briefly about themselves (their name, birthplace, hobbies, and major), the average allocation rose to half and 40 percent of the Dictators give *more* than half. Knowing something about their "charity" seems to activate target-specific[13] sympathy in the Dictators. In a similar study, Eckel and Grossman (1996a) found that allocations doubled when the Recipient was a well-known charity, the Red Cross. In a Swedish experiment,[14] Johannesson and Persson (2000) found no differences between allocations to other students and to members of the general population (other students aren't considered either a good or bad "charity").

Many studies have shown that bargaining face-to-face improves efficiency (see also Roth, 1995b, pp. 295–96). It is not known what components of face-to-face bargaining account for these large effects.

Inspired by earlier research by Hoffman and Spitzer (1982, 1985), Hoffman et al. (1994) allocated the right to propose an offer to the person who answered more general knowledge questions. This shift in "entitlement" lowered offers by about 10 percent (see also List and Cherry, 2000) and reduced Dictator allocations by half. However, it does not appear that this sense of entitlement is entirely shared by ultimatum Responders: rejection rates go up

---

[12] In earlier experiments (Frey and Bohnet, 1995), both two-way identification between a Dictator and Recipient in a class, and private discussion between the two for ten minutes, doubled mean allocations from 25 percent to about half. However, their design did not control for the possibility of post-experiment interaction.

[13] Frey and Bohnet (1997) studied three-person dictator games in which the Dictator could identify (ID) or talk to one of the Recipients but not the other. When ID and communication were allowed, allocations were about twice as large to the identified Recipient. This means the identification effect is target specific and is not the result of general sympathy toward others activated by looking or talking at one recipient.

[14] The results are interesting from a cross-cultural perspective because Swedes pay high taxes and spend a lot on social services, but their overall rate of Dictator allocation is comparable to that of other countries.

(even in $100 ultimatum games), perhaps owing to self-serving judgments about the legitimacy of entitlement.

2.6.2 *Competitive Pressure and Outside Options*

In psychological terms, whether people have behaved unfairly toward us depends on what forces we think caused their unfair behavior (i.e., what "attribution" we make for cause). Careening through a red light is socially acceptable when rushing to the maternity ward, but not when rushing to the video store before it closes, though both acts endanger other drivers equally. The law distinguishes carefully between degrees of accident and deliberation in punishing people for harm to others.

In surveys, consumers say price increases are justified if competition threatens a firm's survival, but not when they exploit a surge in demand (Kahneman, Knetsch, and Thaler, 1986). Using the same intuition, Schotter, Weiss, and Zapater (1996) ask whether competitive pressure could provide an excuse for self-interested behavior. They used two-stage games in which players were allowed to play in a second stage (with a different partner) only if the amount they earned placed them in the top half of earnings among all subjects playing in their role. Dictators certainly used competitive pressure as an excuse—30 percent kept all the money in the two-stage condition, compared with 13 percent in a standard one-stage control. Proposers in two-stage ultimatum games also offered about 10 percent less, and Responders appeared to accept less using the specific-offer method, but not using the MAO method.

Knez and Camerer (1995) added an outside option to ultimatum games (i.e., players earn a nonzero payoff if offers are rejected). If a Proposer's division of a $10 pie was rejected, the Proposer earned $2 and the Responder earned $3. Introducing options creates multiple focal points for how to divide the pie fairly. One focal point is to offer $5, half of the $10 pie. Another is to offer the Responder just enough to get her to accept, such as $3.25 (the self-interested subgame perfect equilibrium). Still another solution is to award each player half the surplus (the gains beyond their outside options), which gives *more* to the Responder ($5.50) if the Responder's option is better.

The rate of disagreement in these games with options is very high—nearly 50 percent, compared with 10–15 percent in most experiments. The high disagreement rate implies that something about the game's structure is undermining the Proposer's willingness to share what the Responder expects, or his ability to guess what Responders will accept. The cause is self-serving bias in judgments of fairness (see Chapter 4): Proposers are more likely to offer $5 or $3.25, but Responders often state MAO demands for the equal-surplus offer $5.50. However, over five trials the disagreement rate falls somewhat, as Responders' demands fall.

2.6.3 *Information about the Amount Being Divided*

Several experiments have explored how information affects ultimatum offers and rejections. In a typical experiment, Proposers know the exact amount of money to be divided and Responders either know nothing at all or know the probability distribution of possible amounts (see Huck, 1999, for a short review).

Limited information complicates the game in two ways. First, when the pie is unknown the Proposer's offer conveys information to the Responder about the pie size, which complicates the game substantially. Second, if the Responder does not know the Proposer's end of the bargain, the Responder has no way to evaluate whether his share is too low. If Responders accept less when they do not know the Proposer's share, that is very strong evidence that rejections are an expression of preference when they *do* know the Proposer's payoff.

Most studies show that Responders do accept less in the low information condition. Proposers generally do not hesitate to exploit this behavior and offer little when the amount being divided is large. Camerer and Loewenstein (1993) published the first study of this sort. In standard conditions, undergraduate subjects at different schools (Carnegie-Mellon and Penn) made offers and stated MAOs for each of the pies $1, $3, $5, $7, and $9. In the incomplete information condition, Proposers knew the pie size but Responders knew only that the pie was equally likely to be any of the sizes. In both conditions, the median and mean offers were 40–50 percent of each pie. When the pie size was known to Responders, they demanded mean MAOs around 30 percent and the overall disagreement rate was a typical 15 percent. In the incomplete information case, Responders demanded a mean of $1.88 (with substantial variation; many demanded zero). As a result, when pies were small, Proposers could not meet this demand and disagreements were common (39 percent across all pie sizes). Knowing possible pie sizes were $1–9 seemed to focus the Responder's attention on an intermediate pie size, which meant offers were sure to be rejected if the pie was low.

Different results were observed by Mitzkewitz and Nagel (1993), Straub and Murnighan (1995), Croson (1996), and Rapoport, Sundali, and Potter (1996). They all compared bargaining over known pie sizes with incomplete information where players either knew the distribution of possible pies (in Mitzkewitz and Nagel and in Rapoport et al.) or were told nothing at all (in the other studies). In each case Responders seem to give Proposers the benefit of the doubt: Since a low offer *could* be fair if the pie is small, rejecting it might punish the Proposer unfairly, so lower offers tended to get accepted more often in the face of uncertainty. Proposers generally take advantage of this by offering less. Güth and Hück (1997) ran an interesting study where Proposers knew whether a pie was DM 38 or 16 and a single Responder did not. Responders usually accepted an offer of 8 (half the small pie), but they rejected offers of 7 or 9 half the time, apparently suspecting that an offer that was not *exactly* half of the small pie was probably a small part of the larger pie.

Kagel, Kim, and Moser (1996) ran ultimatum games in which players bargain over a hundred chips with different values to the two players (cf. Roth and Murnighan, 1982; see Chapter 4). Chips were worth $0.10 to one player and $0.30 to another. When only Proposers knew the chip values, they offered around 45 percent when their own chip value was higher, and about 30 percent when the Responder's value was higher, so they are exploiting their information to get more chips for themselves when their value is lower. When the Responders knew the Proposers' chips were more valuable, they tried to squeeze the Proposers to offer more than half in order to equalize dollar earnings; as a result the rejection rate was high (40 percent).

Abbink et al. (2001) ran an ultimatum game in which only the Responders knew how much the Proposer was getting, ex ante, in the event of a rejection. Rejections were more frequent when the Proposer's rejection payoff was lower, which implies that Responders are either envious or deliberately punishing Proposers when it hurts most.[15]

Fairness explanations of ultimatum bargaining leave open the possibility that fairness norms evolve with experience. One way for norms to change and adapt is that players take actions of others as evidence of what is fair or, oppositely, what they can get away with. A way to explore the sensitivity of fair-mindedness to the behavior of others is to provide players with information on what other players have done, and see whether it changes what they do. Two studies show modest effects of social influence. Knez and Camerer (1995) found that ultimatum offers were affected by how much others offered (cf. Harrison and McCabe, 1996b). Cason and Mui (1998) explored social influence in dictator games. Players made two Dictator offers in consecutive rounds. In the second round, players were paired with another subject and told what the other subject offered in the first round (call it P_1). There was some social influence, because subjects generally offered more when the other subject's offer was higher.

---

[15] In Abbink, Sadrieh, and Zamir (1999), rejections are slightly more common when Responders know that the Proposers will know what happened (compared with a condition in which Proposers won't know). But rejections are common even when Proposers won't know they were punished, which means Responders are taking private pleasure in punishment.

2.6.4 Multiperson Games

Games with several players raise two important questions: What norms of fair division apply to more than two players? And are players willing to punish unfairness in the same way when their punishment might affect an 'innocent' party? (see Kagel and Wolfe, 2001).

Güth, Hück and Ockenfels (1996) ran a two-stage, three-person game in which the first player learns whether a pie is large (DM 24.60) or small (DM 12.60), then proposes an offer x of that amount to two other players who don't know the pie size. One of the two players can reject x and end the game, or accept it and make an ultimatum offer dividing x with the third player. Notice that sharing the small pie equally among all three means players 1 should offer 8.40 to the other two players. However, when the amount was small only a sixth of the player 1s offer as much as 8.00. When the amount was *large*, 70 percent of the player 1s offer an amount x around 8.40 (pretending the total amount was small). Player 1's exploitation of the other players' uncertainty works because offers are usually accepted. And player 2s generally offered about half of what they were offered to player 3.

Güth and Van Damme (1998) ran a three-person game combining ultimatum and dictator games with and without information about pie sizes. A single Proposer divides 120 points (about $6.80) by making a three-way offer (x, y, z) which gives y to an active Responder and z to an inactive Recipient (leaving x for the Proposer). The Responder can reject the offer, leaving everyone nothing, or accept it on behalf of the inactive Recipient (who does nothing). There are three information conditions: the active Responder knows the entire allocation (y, z) (and can infer x), knows only the "essential" information y, or knows only the "irrelevant" information z. This design tests whether an active Responder cares how much the Proposer allocates to an inactive third party, and what Proposers do in different information conditions.

When the Responder knows her own share, the Proposer offers 30–40 percent of the amount being divided, as in two-person games, and leaves only a little (5–10 percent) for the inactive Recipient. When the Responder does not know her own share, but knows what the inactive Recipient was offered, the Proposer leaves more to the inactive Recipient than in the other cases (12 and 15 percent), trying to signal that she is not too selfish. Overall rejection rates are low (around 5 percent) and Responders don't seem to care much about how inactive third parties are treated.

A dramatic effect of multiple players occurs when there is competition among many Proposers or Responders. Roth et al. (1991) first showed this in their "market games," in which nine Proposers made simultaneous offers to a single Responder (who accepted the highest offer). In the first round offers were dispersed but much higher than in two-person ultimatum games (most offers are above half). The highest offer was usually large—around 95 percent of the pie—and by the second round virtually all Proposers offered almost all the pie. This result is important because it presents a challenge to theories of the ultimatum game results. As I will note in Section 2.7 below, most theories *do* predict more self-interested behavior in the face of competition. In the market games, a Proposer who is outbid earns no money and ends up being treated unequally. The only way to reduce disadvantageous inequality and earn more is to bid higher. A similar effect of competition is observed when Responders compete (Güth, Marchand, and Rulliere, 1998) and in experimental markets with excess demand or supply (Smith and Williams, 1990; Cason and Williams, 1990).

2.6.5   Intentions: Influence of Unchosen Alternatives

An important effect of attribution of cause (or "intentions") was first shown by Sally Blount-Lyon (1995; then Sally Blount). First note that a Responder faced with an (8,2) split, for example, might reject it for two different reasons: She might dislike being treated unfairly by somebody who benefits from unfair treatment; or she might just dislike unequal payoffs. If she dislikes unfairness but does not mind inequality, then she will reject the (8,2) division if it was made by a Proposer, but accept the same (8,2) division made by a random device or third party (e.g., a court or regulation). Indeed, Blount-Lyon found that players stated lower MAOs when offers were made randomly than when they were made by Proposers.

Falk, Fehr, and Fischbacher (in press) investigated whether "intentions" matter using three discrete ultimatum games (see also Brandts and Sola, 2001; and Andreoni, Brown, and Vesterlund, 2002). A Proposer can offer either (8,2) or one of the divisions (5,5), (2,8), or (10,0). The question is how Responders react to the (8,2) offer depending on which of the unchosen alternatives was possible (see Table 2.6). Each alternative generates a different psychological evaluation of the intentions lying behind the offer (8,2). Offering (8,2) instead of (5,5) is relatively unfair; the Proposer's intentions are selfish. Offering (8,2) instead of (10,0) means the Proposer intends to be nice, helping the Responder get something instead of zero. Offering (8,2) instead of (2,8) means that the Proposer had to choose between two lopsided divisions, and chose the one which was better for her (she did not intend to take the short end of the stick if somebody had to do so).

The relative frequencies of (8,2) offers and rejections of that offer are shown in Table 2.6. Intentions matter because frequencies of rejection of (8,2) do vary substantially with the unchosen offer. When the unchosen offer is the equal split (5,5), nearly half the Responders rejected (8,2). When the unchosen offer was the selfish (10,0), only 10 percent rejected (8,2).

Table 2.6.   *Ultimatum games with varying unchosen paths*

Unchosen offer	Interpretation of (8,2) offer	How often the (8,2) offer is	
		Rejected	Proposed
(5,5)	Relatively unfair	0.44	0.31
(2,8)	Not sacrificial	0.27	0.73
(8,2)	Neutral	0.18	—
(10,0)	Relatively fair	0.09	1.00

Source: Falk, Fehr, and Fischbacher (in press).

The Proposers seem to anticipate these differences in likely rejection rates, because they offer (8,2) only a third of the time when the alternative is the equal-split (5,5), and offer (8,2) most of the time in the other conditions. Since forgone alternatives matter, theories that evaluate social preferences by applying a utility function to terminal node outcomes are incomplete (see Section 2.7).

Summary: Changing structural variables in simple games is very helpful for understanding what is going on and extrapolating to complex settings. Creating entitlement by letting a contest winner be the Proposer lowers offers. Knowing who you are allocating money to and hearing them talk raises average Dictator allocations, and many give much more than half. (Fund raising agencies know this and create "identifiable victim" sympathy with tragic pictures of victims of disaster and hunger.) When Responders don't know how large the pie being divided is they usually accept less because they are reluctant to reject low offers that might be fair offers from small pies (even if they are probably unfair offers from large pies). Proposers take advantage of this "benefit of the doubt" by offering less.

Multiperson games show that the social preferences are not based on judgments about another player's overall generosity, but are based on judgments about another player's fairness toward oneself. For example, in three-person ultimatum games, active Responders accept offers that give very little to an inactive third party.

When Proposers and Responders compete, there is no way for fair-minded players to earn money *and* enforce fairness, so outcomes consistent with self-interest result (in practice and in theory). This does not imply that players are self-interested in markets per se. It just means that in some exchange institutions it is impossible to express social preferences for fairness or low inequality, so only preferences for earning more money (self-interest) are expressed.

Some studies show that intentions—the influence of unchosen alternatives on the psychological evaluation of a chosen alternative—matter. In ultimatum games with competitive pressure (high-earning Proposers get to play again), the need to compete is an excuse for Proposer greed, so Responders accept lower offers. Responders are also more likely to accept unequal offers generated by a random device than by a Proposer who benefits from the inequality; they are punishing the person who benefits from the unfair action rather than simply rebelling against inequality.

Many of these findings are tentative. They deserve replication and further exploration because they will put a lot of empirical constraint on theories of social preference. Good theories must not just explain why some players reject ultimatum offers. They must also explain why randomly generated offers are accepted more often, why the nature of unchosen offers affects rejections, why competing Proposers give everything to a single Responder, why Responders don't care how much is offered to a silent Responder, and so forth. A theory that can explain a broad range of these phenomena will be extraordinarily useful in designing organizational contracts, explaining intrahousehold bargaining, understanding everyday concepts of fairness and justice, and so forth. These phenomena also suggest a way to put variables from psychological and sociological theories into a game-theoretic language that could unify some aspects of social sciences.

2.7 Trust Games

Trust is an elusive concept which cuts across many disciplines. Marriage therapists talk about rebuilding trust after an affair. Sociologists are interested in how social networks produce or inhibit trust. Economists emphasize trust as a way of reducing the costs of transacting, "lubricating" the economy (e.g., Arrow, 1974). Whenever there are gains from trade, there is a productivity advantage to any institution or norm that assures traders that the other side will hold up their end of the deal. Legal contracts, third-party assurance (e.g., a mutual friend vouches for the trustee's honor), family solidarity, and threats of violence can provide assurance but they cost something. Trust is cheap.

Development economists and pundits think differences in trust (or "social capital") can explain why some countries or cultures are rich and others struggle. For example, Knack and Keefer (1997) found a strong cross-country correlation between economic growth and the fraction of citizens who said they generally trust people. Such explanations will live or die on accurate measurement of trust and social capital. But, as Putnam (1995) laments, "Since trust is so central to a theory of social capital, it would be desirable to have strong behavioral indicators of trends in social trust or misanthropy. I have discovered no such behavioral measures."

Here are some examples of trust:

1. When I was visiting the University of Iowa from Chicago, people there constantly told me how friendly small-town living was compared with life in the big city. Driving to the airport, my host's car had trouble. He pulled over at a nearby farm and peered under the hood helplessly. A farmer came out in his truck to see what the problem was. My host, who didn't know the farmer, explained that he had to get me to the airport quickly. The farmer then *lent us his truck* to drive to the airport. Before we hopped in the truck, my host went to hand over the keys to his sleek, ailing BMW to the farmer as collateral. The farmer said "Hell, just keep 'em, I wouldn't know what to do with those anyway. Just come on back and we'll take care of your car."

2. Tokyo's lost and found center is famous for its ability to return lost items to their owners (*Los Angeles Times*, 1999b). About 72 percent of items (measured by value) are returned to their owners, including a bag with $90,000 in cash. The system mixes a tradition of teaching children to turn in lost property at police kiosks (*koban*), a golden rule that creates empathy for how the owner of the lost item must feel, and straightforward incentives (by law and social convention, the owner must give 5–20 percent of the item's value to the finder as a thank-you).

3. Why do firms prefer to lay off workers during a downturn rather than cut wages? Since risk-averse workers should prefer wage cuts, the preference for layoffs is a major puzzle. Managers inexorably refer to the fact that workers get upset when wages are cut. Since workers have a lot of leeway to do good or bad work, keeping wages up is a kind of insurance to guarantee reasonable work performance (see Bewley, 1998). Similarly, despite the rise of the "war on drugs," during record lows in unemployment in the late 1990s firms were reluctant to test employees for drug use because "drug testing, particularly without probable cause, seems to imply a lack of trust and presumably could backfire if it leads to negative perceptions about the company" (*Los Angeles Times*, 1999a). Furthermore, drug testing is most common in lower-level white- and blue-collar jobs, even though drug use surely harms overall productivity much more in professions such as movie direction, surgery, floor trading on Wall Street, and politics. But firms say mandatory drug testing would upset these high-level professionals and undermine trust.

4. Noncontractual reciprocity occurs even in a domain that is notorious for greed and ruthlessness—Hollywood. When the film *Titanic* was running spectacularly over budget, many critics forecast the biggest flop

in film history. Director James Cameron surrendered part of his fees and "points" (profit percentage) to comfort panicky studio executives (a classic example of signaling; see Chapter 8). The film went on to become the third-highest-grossing film of all time, and the fees and points Cameron waived had lost him $50 million. Giddy studio executives gave Cameron the biggest tip in history by returning those fees. Increases in director fees of this magnitude never occur just because films do well and studios want the director to make more hits for them (as repeated-game models could explain). What was special was the fact that Cameron had waived the fees to begin with. The studio's payment was clearly a repayment of his sacrifice.

A beautiful simple game to measure trust was proposed by Berg, Dickhaut, and McCabe (1995; and earlier by Camerer and Weigelt, 1988). In their game, the Investor has X, which she can keep or invest. Suppose she invests T and keeps $X - T$. The investment of T earns a return, at a rate $(1 + r)$, and becomes $(1 + r)T$. Then another player, the Trustee, must decide how to share the new amount $(1 + r)T$ with the Investor. (The Trustee is playing a dictator game in which the amount to be allocated was determined by the Investor.) Suppose she keeps Y and returns $(1 + r)T - Y$. Then the total payoffs are Y for the Trustee and $(X - T) + (1 + r)T - Y$ for the Investor, which is $X - Y + rT$.

In this game, trust is the willingness to bet that another person will reciprocate a risky move (at a cost to themselves). Trust is risky because the Investor will regret having entrusted if she doesn't get much back.[16] T measures the amount of trust. The amount returned, $(1 + r)T - Y$, measures trustworthiness. If players maximize their earnings, the Trustee will keep it all ($Y = (1 + r)T$); the game has moral hazard or hidden action which cannot be guaranteed contractually. Anticipating this, a self-interested Investor should keep the money rather than invest it.

Trust must be risky. Trustworthiness must also go against the Trustee's self-interest, to test whether people are willing to sacrifice to satisfy moral obligation.[17] Sociologists and psychologists usually object that this game doesn't capture all there is to trust because the two-person one-shot game does not include relationships, social sanctions, communication, and so many other rich features that may support or affect trust. That's precisely the point—the game requires *pure* trust. It also provides a plain benchmark

---

[16] A prisoners' dilemma played sequentially is also like a trust game; the first player cooperates, exposing herself to possibly earning the lowest payoff, trusting the second player to reciprocate by cooperating back.

[17] Otherwise the game does not measure trust, it is simply a bet on the rationality and self-interest of others, like the Beard–Beil games in Chapter 5.

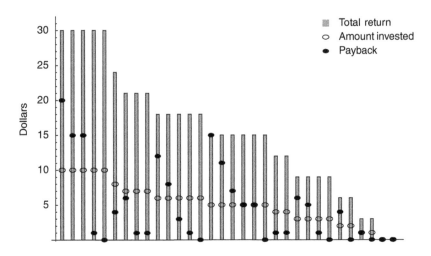

Figure 2.4. *Investment and repayment in a trust game. Source: Based on Berg, Dickhaut, and McCabe (1995).*

against which trust under more complicated conditions can be compared, like a wire mannequin that can be dressed up with clothing.

The trust game caught on quickly. Berg, Dickhaut, and McCabe (1995) played it with an initial amount $X = \$10$, a rate of return $r = 2$, and an elegant mailbox design to ensure "double-blindness." Their results are shown in Figure 2.4. Points are arrayed from left to right according to the amount of the investment. The open circle in each bar shows what was invested (T). The height of the bar is the amount available to split, $3T$. The dark circle shows how much was returned. If the dark circles are above the open circles, then trust is repaid. On average, Investors put in about 50 percent; five of thirty-two invested it all and only two invested none. The average amount repaid was about 95 percent of what was invested (or, equivalently, about a third of the tripled amount), with a wide dispersion—half repaid either nothing or an insulting $1. The fact that the return to trust is around zero seems fairly robust (e.g., Bolle, 1995).

The substantial amount of blind trust and trustworthiness Berg et al. observed among students in Minnesota has been generally replicated in various places, with some interesting variation. In Massachusetts, Ortmann, Fitzgerald, and Boeing (2000) experimented with variants of the Berg et al. design, prompting subjects by asking how much they expected and giving "social history" about what others had done. Investments ranged from 40–60 percent across treatments and repayments averaged 110 percent. Koford

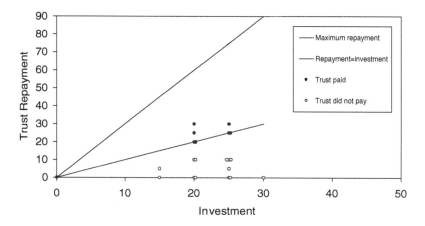

Figure 2.5. *Investment and repayment in a trust game in Kenya. Source: Based on data from Ensminger (2000).*

(1998) found Bulgarian students were surprisingly[18] trusting, investing 70 percent and getting 150 percent back. He speculates that Bulgarians are used to trusting among themselves precisely because their trust in authority is so low. Willinger, Lohmann, and Ususnier (1999) found the French trusted much less that the Germans, but both nationalities returned about 40 percent. Ensminger (2000) found very little trust and trustworthiness among Orma herders in Kenya (see Figure 2.5). In Figure 2.5, closed circles represent repayments greater than investment (trust paid); open circles represent repayments less than investments. The Orma invested 40 percent of 50 currency units—only one invested more than half; and they repaid only 55 percent (so most of the points in Figure 2.5 are open circles close to the zero-repayment *x*-axis). Note that Kenya is considered one of the more corrupt countries in the world, measured by indices of "transparency," which guess the extent of bribery, bureaucratic corruption, and black market trade, so it is encouragingly consistent that this simple game shows low levels of trust also.

Jacobsen and Sadrieh (1996) conducted a trust experiment in Germany in which subjects made decisions as groups of three and their discussions

---

[18] Subjects were thirty-two undergraduate students in economics and business at Sofia University playing for 1,000 leva (roughly two hours' wages). Koford reports Bulgaria is a typical East European country with little trust in authority and high levels of fraud, corruption, and bribery, including widespread cheating on exams, and professors accept bribes to give good grades.

Table 2.7. *Payoffs in a trust game*

	Trustee move	
Investor move	Repay trust	Don't repay trust
Don't trust	P, P	P, P
Trust	R, R	T, S

Source: Snijders and Kerens (1998).
Note: $S < P < R < T$.

were videotaped. They invested 60 percent and were repaid 110 percent. In their discussions, all Investor groups mentioned the chance of earning more by investing, most discussed whether to invest all or none, and about half talked about charity and altruism toward the other side. *All* Trustee groups talked about reciprocity (often using the German verb *honorieren*). The students were well aware that there was risk of moral hazard in a one-shot anonymous game (though some fantasized about possibilities for post-experiment punishment), which casts doubt on the popular hypothesis that they do not distinguish between one-shot and repeated games.

Snijders and Keren (1998) varied payoffs across binary-choice trust games with the structure (in the normal form) in Table 2.7. If trust is not repaid, the Investor earns a payoff S below the no-trust guarantee of P (like the "sucker" payoff in PD) and the Trustee earns the highest payoff, T. If trust is repaid, both earn R ($> P$, so reciprocated trust helps both sides). They derive some propositions from a simple "social orientation" model proposed by Edgeworth (1881) and studied extensively by social psychologists in the 1970s, $u_i(x_i, x_j) = x_i + \alpha_i x_j$.[19]

The model predicts trust will be lower when "risk" $(P - S)/(R - S)$ is high and "temptation" $(T - R)/(T - S)$ is high (risk is probably influenced by anticipated temptation, of course), and players will be less likely to repay trust when temptation is high. (The Fehr–Schmidt model of inequality-aversion, see section 2.8.2 below, also points to the temptation factor $(T - R)/(T - S)$ as the key predictor of Trustee behavior.[20])

Across thirty-six payoff structures, a probit regression of the dummy variable "trust" showed a strong effect of risk and a smaller effect of temptation. (Subjects who carried an organ donor card also trusted more.) Regressions

---

[19] See McClintock (1972). Like simple altruism models, it is incomplete because the social orientation weight α_i can empirically change sign depending on the game and beliefs about a player's opponent. The great triumph of new models such as Rabin's (1993), discussed below, is that they endogenize α_i in a parsimonious, falsifiable way.

[20] In their model, the Trustee repays iff $T - \beta(T - S) < R$, or $\beta < (T - R)/(T - S)$, where β is a coefficient measuring the disutility of advantageous inequality (or guilt).

of the dummy "repay trust" showed a strong effect of the temptation ratio $(T - R)/(T - S)$, as predicted by their model and by Fehr–Schmidt, and a weak gender effect (men are less trustworthy). An important fact is that including a dummy variable for each game improves fit very little, which means virtually *all* the impact of the payoff variables is captured by the risk and temptation measures.

Van Huyck, Battalio and Walters (1995, 2001) studied a trust game modeled after a "peasant" who must decide how much to plant (at various possible rates of return r) when a Dictator landowner decides how much to confiscate by "taxation." In their discretion condition, Dictators announce a tax rate *after* the peasants' decisions (as in the trust games above). Peasants believe they cannot trust the Dictators, so they invest very little (the median is zero) and the Dictators usually grab everything.[21] In another condition, when Dictators can precommit to tax rates they usually choose rates that induce efficient investment and create gains for everyone. Median investment is 100 percent and median tax rates are close to the efficient level, although Dictators share surplus more evenly than predicted when returns r are high. In a third reputation condition, Dictators have discretion but are matched repeatedly with the same peasant (with a continuation probability of 5/6). Allowing reputation building creates outcomes midway between the discretion and commitment conditions, with some convergence to optimality over time. These results are important because they find the *least* trust seen so far in the discretion treatment, and also show that reputation in repeated matching is a partial substitute for precommitment.

2.7.1   Is Trustworthiness Just Altruism?

Trustee repayments are usually thought to reflect moral obligation or positive reciprocity toward Investors who took a risk that benefits the Trustee. But this conclusion is right only if repayments from X by Trustees are larger than allocations in a game where a dictator allocates a sum X that did not result from an Investor move. Two studies suggest, surprisingly, that only a small amount of the repayment by Trustees is owing to positive reciprocity.

Dufwenberg and Gneezy (2000) studied a trust game in which the Investor could let the Trustee divide 20 Dutch guilders between them, or could take an outside option and earn x for herself, ranging from 4 to 16 Dutch guilders (giving nothing to the Trustee). The average amount Trustees returned is one-third, insignificantly larger than the average allocation of 30 percent in a 20-guilder Dictator game. Furthermore, the amount Trustees

---

[21] The Dictator's dilemma is sometimes called the "paradox of omnipotence": A Dictator above the law is unable to commit herself to be unable to do something in the future.

repaid did not depend significantly on the sure option value x that the Investor passed up to the Trustee (and herself).

Cox (1999) also compared trust repayments $r(3t)$ (given investments of t determined by Trustees) with the amounts allocated out of $3t$ in dictator games. (That is, the size of the Dictator pie was matched to the amount Trustees repaid in the trust game.) The difference between repayments and allocations, $r(3t) - 3t$, is significantly positive (\$1.20) but small (around 10 percent), which indicates only a small extra effect of positive reciprocity. Cox also compared decisions of individuals with their later decisions as part of a three-person group. Groups give and repay less and appear to be disproportionately influenced by the least trusting and trustworthy members.

2.7.2 Indirect Reciprocity, Karma, Culture

In the trust games discussed so far, Investors know that the Trustee they are paired with will repay money to them (or not). Many social transactions are less direct. For example, dealing with bureaucrats, firm employees, or spouses in a household, there is usually a presumption that a repayment that is agreed to by one person will be honored by his or her spouse or fellow bureaucrat or employee if the original Trustee is not around.

To measure the strength of this sort of "indirect reciprocity," two studies see what happens when Investors know they will be repaid money by a different Trustee than the one they entrusted their money to. Buchan, Croson, and Dawes (2000) used three experimental conditions.

1. The *pairs* condition is a standard control replicating the many studies described above.
2. In a *foursome* condition, there were two Investors and two Trustees but each Trustee repaid the opposite Investor (i.e., A invested with B and C invested with D but D repaid A and C repaid B). That is, a person was repaid by the Trustee whom "their" Trustee's Investor invested with (try saying that three times quickly).
3. In a *society* condition, Investors and Trustees were in separate rooms and which trustee paid money to a particular Investor was random.

The group and society conditions model situations in which moral obligations to repay are passed around, as if Investors believe in "karma" (good deeds will eventually be repaid by somebody else doing a good deed). Like blind trust itself, karma sounds silly to economists but many religions include some concept like it; and note that a society in which karma is widely believed in will be more productive than one without it.

Buchan et al. also measure how sharply trust drops off from pairs to foursomes to societies in different countries (United States, Japan, Korea, and China). Their interest in these countries is motivated by claims such as the popular 1980s' (pre-bubble collapse) idea that trust was responsible

Table 2.8. *Trust game results across three conditions and four countries*

Countries	Pair	Foursome	Society	Overall
Fraction invested				
American–Chinese	0.76	0.49	0.49	0.54
Japanese–Korean	0.51	0.48	0.28	0.41
Mean	0.64	0.48	0.39	0.47
Fraction of tripled investment returned				
American–Japanese	0.28	0.13	0.11	0.15
Chinese–Korean	0.41	0.25	0.18	0.25
Mean	0.35	0.19	0.15	0.20

Source: Buchan, Croson, and Dawes (2000).

for fast economic growth in Japan, the idea that the non-market-oriented Chinese might be less trusting, and the importance of family and business groups as economic units in the Asian countries.

Table 2.8 (pooling separately for each measure across countries with similar results) shows that the Chinese were most trusting and trustworthy, and the Japanese least. Overall investment was about 60 percent and the amount repaid was 105 percent of the investment, quite close to other results reported above. Trust and repayment did drop off in the group and society conditions in most countries, although there is substantial belief in karma even when the Trustees didn't know who would repay them.

Dufwenberg et al. (2000) also compared pairs and foursomes (which they call direct and indirect reciprocity) with $r = 2$. In the pair condition, they added incomplete information about whether the return was $r = 1$ or 3 (known to the Trustee but not the Investor), to see whether the Trustees would give less when they could hide behind the possibility of a small return as an excuse (as we observed in ultimatum games). Results are shown in Table 2.9. Trust and repayment are essentially the same in all conditions and comparable to amounts seen in earlier studies.

Table 2.9. *Trust game with pairs and foursomes*

	Complete information		Incomplete information
	Pair	Foursome	Pair
Fraction invested	0.60	0.53	0.55
Fraction returned	0.28	0.37	0.26

Source: Dufwenberg et al. (2000).

Table 2.10. *Contribution rates for high-cost conditions*

Previous contributions	History condition		Recipient history
	Donor		
	History	No history	
0 of last 6	0.02	0.00	0.24
1 of last 6	0.42	0.21	0.45
2 of last 6	0.48	0.31	0.51
3 of last 6	0.65	0.44	0.60
4 of last 6	0.71	0.58	0.73
5 of last 6	0.78	0.70	0.77
6 of last 6	0.85	0.98	0.94
Overall	0.70	0.25	

Source: Seinen and Schram (1999)

Seinen and Schram (1999) study indirect reciprocity, inspired by biological thinking about how an organism's "image"—its observed record of cooperativeness—induces others to cooperate with it (e.g., Nowak and Sigmund, 2000). The idea is similar to repeated-game equilibria in which a player i anticipates reciprocity by an unknown future player who conditions her contribution on whether i contributed. In each period, a player could donate 250 to another randomly chosen player at a cost of 150 to themselves.[22] In a history condition, players were told the last six decisions made by their target recipient (and knew their own history would be reported). In the no-history condition, no such history was reported.

Table 2.10 shows that reporting history has a huge effect, raising the contribution rate from 25 percent to 70 percent (Wedekind and Milinski, 2000, replicated this result). The middle two columns show that contribution rates by a donor are strongly increasing in that donor's own history (this reflects persistent individual differences; some just donate a lot and others do not). The right column shows that donors give more often to those recipients who contributed recently. There is also a small decay in contributions over time (as in most public goods games with stranger matching). Reliable individual differences can be used to forecast later contributions with 75 percent accuracy.

[22] Their game is a dictator game with a multiplier greater than 1 on allocations made to others. They also studied a low-cost condition in which the donor's cost was 50. Overall contribution was higher (86 percent) than in the high-cost condition but the image results are basically the same so the text reports only the high-cost results.

2.7.3 A Complex Omnibus Game

McCabe, Rassenti, and Smith (1998) used a complex Big Tree game which illustrates concepts of reciprocity. Many of the experiments in this book (and particularly this chapter) use a decomposition principle in design: Pick a game that isolates which features of game theory are violated if predictions prove wrong.[23] The Big Tree game illustrates an opposite design strategy: Use a complex game where several forces operate at once. The top panel of Table 2.11 sketches the payoffs.[24] Player 1 either chooses an outside option which ends the game (it is a nuisance and rarely picked) or gives the move to player 2, who chooses a left or right branch (the left and right halves of Table 2.11). Choosing right gives player 1 a chance to take a (30,60) node or pass to player 2, who can choose (40,40) or pass back to player 1, who has two bad choices ((15,30) and (0,0), which is omitted from the table). Choosing left gives player 1 a chance to enforce (50,50) or pass to 2, who can choose (60,30) or pass back to player 1 for a poor choice of (20,20) and (0,0) (omitted). Assuming self-interest, the subgame perfect prediction (in italics) is that player 1 rejects the option, player 2 moves right, and player 1 passes to 2, who chooses (40,40). Note, however, that players can earn (50,50) if player 2 moves left and player 1 chooses the (50,50) endnode (although 1 will pass if she believes 2 will take the self-interested outcome of (60,30)). This reciprocity-based outcome is marked in bold. A version of this game called game 2 flips around the location of the (50,50) and (60,30) outcomes on the left branch of the tree so that (60,30) comes first and can be chosen by player 1 right away.

Their game pits the self-interested subgame perfect outcome (right, (40,40)) against a loose concept of reciprocity which leads to the (left, (50,50)) outcome. The paper is informal about game-theoretic details. The authors compare "one-shot" games, with a partner-matching treatment (called "same"). In a treatment where players know only their own payoffs ("private payoff information"), social preferences and reciprocity are disabled.

The overall frequencies of player 2 choosing left or right, and conditional frequencies of each of the other possible outcomes, are shown in Table 2.11. The reciprocal and subgame perfect outcomes are reached about equally often in one-shot games and reciprocity is much more

---

[23] For example, the PD game is a *bad* decomposition because defectors could be self-interested, envious, or conditionally cooperative and pessimistic; so defection, by itself, does not pin down a defector's motives. The ultimatum is a *good* decomposition because rejections by Responders isolate negative reciprocity (if they reject more often when offers come from Proposers rather than random devices). Rejections are a clear indication of negative reciprocity and nothing else (e.g., they have nothing to do with failures of strategic thinking, as in Chapter 5, or reputational considerations, as in Chapter 8).

[24] Terminal nodes that result in (0,0) are omitted because they are rarely chosen.

Table 2.11.   *Conditional frequencies of choices in multimove game*

	Payoffs (player 1 on top, player 2 on bottom)						
	Left branch			Right branch			
Player move		1	2	1		1	2	1
		50	60	20		30	40	15
Treatment	% left	50	30	20	% right	60	40	30
One-shot 1	43	**0.85**	0.08	0.08	57	—	*0.94*	0.06
One-shot 2	46	**0.50**	0.50	—	54	0.00	*1.00*	—
Same 1	82	**0.88**	0.04	0.06	18	0.04	*0.85*	0.05
Same 2	62	**0.84**	0.16	—	38	0.17	*0.70*	0.13
Private payoff information 1	16	**0.43**	0.56	0.02	84	0.14	*0.84*	0.02

Source: McCabe, Rassenti, and Smith (1998).
Note: Subgame perfect outcomes are in *italics*; reciprocal outcomes are in **boldface**.

common in partner-matching. When payoff information is private, how-ever, reciprocity falls apart and the subgame perfect (40,40) outcome is usually reached.

2.7.4 Multistage Trust Games

In multistage games, trust can usually be supported by repeated-game rep-utation building, so multistage games are not evidence of blind trust and therefore make a different point than the studies in this chapter do. How-ever, some experiments on multistage trust games are described in Chapters 5 and 8, and two new studies of "centipede" games are worth noting here.

A centipede game is a multistage trust game in which players alternate moves. Each player can "take," ending the game, and take some percentage of the available surplus. Or the player can "pass," increasing the surplus, and allow the other player a chance to take or pass. The game ends with a terminal node where one player must take. Because there is a terminal node, self-interested players will always take at the end. If players backward induct, this leads to unraveling—taking at *all* nodes. The typical finding (McKelvey and Palfrey, 1992; see Chapter 5) is that players pass until a couple of steps from the end. (Play in finitely repeated prisoners' dilemmas, a cousin of centipede games, is similar.)

Ho and Weigelt (2000) did four-move centipede games in which the surplus doubled with each move, players could take as much as they wanted at each node, and the terminal node is (0,0). Subjects gave normal-form strategies (i.e., they stated in advance whether they would take at each possible node). They did experiments in China, America, and Singapore (which is quite Westernized, a convex combination of China and America). They observed much more self-interest than in other studies—about 30 percent (50 percent) of player 1s (2s) took at their first node, and players took almost all the surplus (95 percent).

Rapoport et al. (in press) ran a three-person centipede game with nine nodes for very large stakes (subjects could have earned $1,500 if everybody always cooperated). Like Ho and Weigelt, they observed early taking consistent with self-interest—one-third of the games ended at the first or second node. These two studies are inconsistent with what McKelvey and Palfrey found (and see also Chapter 8 results); the difference is probably due to the presence of a (0,0) terminal node.[25] In the study by Rapoport et al., playing with *two* other players, rather than one, is a big psychological step, because it requires a player to trust each of two others, *and* to trust that the others both trust each other, and so on.

2.7.5 Gift Exchange in Experimental Labor Markets

Fehr and many collaborators did a series of experiments on labor markets (summarized in Fehr and Gächter, 2000b). Their studies illustrate the virtues of a steady, ambitious, cumulative research program. In their paradigm (e.g., Fehr, Kirchsteiger, and Reidl, 1993) firms offer a wage w and workers who accept it then chose an effort level e. Firms earn $(q - w)e$ and workers earn $w - c(e)$, where $c(e)$ is a convex cost function over effort levels from 0.1 to 1.0. There is an excess supply of labor (eight workers and six firms). In most of their experiments, firms post offers which workers accept or reject (usually in random order). Firms cannot contract with specific workers and do not know their identities, so workers cannot build up reputations. The experiments have ten to twenty periods, to observe equilibration over time.

Once workers are hired, firms cannot control workers' effort and self-interested workers will choose the minimal effort (0.1). Anticipating this, profit-maximizing firms should pay the market-clearing wage of 1. An alternative theory is "gift exchange" (Akerlof, 1982): Workers reciprocate a firm's "gift" of an above-market wage by exerting more effort than they have to. This reciprocation is *not* a repeated-game equilibrium because workers

---

[25] Many explanations of passing in centipede games rely on the idea that some fraction of "nice" players will pass even at the last node, owing to social preferences, and self-interested players have a reputational incentive to mimic the nice ones until near the end (Camerer and Weigelt, 1988; McKelvey and Palfrey, 1992). But there is no sensible social preference that would explain passing from an advantageous division for oneself to a (0,0) payoff. Without the possibility of such niceness, self-interested players have no incentive to build trust in early stages.

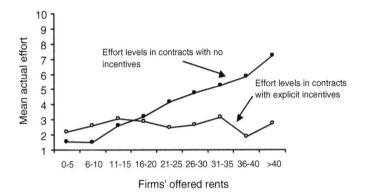

Figure 2.6. *Job rents (wage-effort cost) and effort levels, with and without shirking fines. Source: Fehr and Gächter (2000b), p. 171, Figure 3; reproduced with permission of the American Economic Association.*

and firms are matched anonymously for one period at a time. If reciprocation occurs, it is purely because of a social norm or moral obligation workers
feel (which firms anticipate). Furthermore, the firms' marginal profit from
increases in effort e is much larger than the workers' marginal cost, so a gift
exchange norm creates higher wages, higher effort, and higher profit.[26]

The gift exchange account is similar to "efficiency wage theory"—wages
are paid above the market-clearing level so that workers have something
valuable to lose (the job rent) if they shirk and are caught by (costly)
monitoring. In equilibrium, workers should therefore not shirk. The gift
exchange and efficiency wages are hard to distinguish empirically with field
data[27] so an experiment is ideal.

A good statistic to summarize results is the "job rent," $w - c(e)$, offered
by the firm. In Fehr and Gächter (2000a) effort levels vary from 1 to 10 and
firms offer a wage plus a suggested effort level e'. Figure 2.6 plots the job
rents offered by firms ($w - c(e')$) against actual effort levels. In the treatment
with no disincentive for shirking (black dots), workers respond reciprocally
by choosing higher effort levels when the offered job rent is higher, just as

[26] Naturally, whether gift exchange emerges spontaneously may be sensitive to the firm's productivity
gains from effort, relative to its disutility to workers. In most of the experiments by Fehr et al., the total
surplus from increasing effort is large. It would not be difficult to create an experimental environment in
which the joint gains from effort are lower and convergence to the low-wage/low-effort equilibrium results.
Regardless, the experimental data are an existence proof that reciprocity can be very important even in
competitive environments in which moral hazard is predicted.

[27] In the efficiency wage story, firms should auction off scarce jobs by charging an upfront fee, equal to
the discounted value of the rent stream lucky workers will receive, but in practice this is rarely observed.

gift exchange theory predicts (even when stakes are a couple of months' wages; see Fehr and Tougareva, 1995).

Keep in mind that workers are *not* rematched with the same firms over time, so the degree of gift exchange is striking and not explained by standard concepts in game theory such as reputation building. However, the boundaries of this result remain to be thoroughly established. Hannan, Kagel, and Moser (in press) report much less gift exchange among American undergraduates, and Charness, Frechette, and Kagel (2001) find much less gift exchange when subjects are shown an explicit payoff table giving net profits for all wages and effort levels.

Another treatment in Fehr and Gächter's (2000a) study adds explicit disincentives for shirking (as in standard agency theory models). Firms can impose a preannounced fine (up to some maximum) if workers exert less effort than the required effort e' and their shirking is detected (with probability $1/3$). In their experiment, workers should choose $e = 4$ when faced with the maximum fine. Figure 2.6 shows that, in fact, workers exert *less* effort when threatened with fines! Their effort also does not respond reciprocally to offered job rents. Because there is sometimes shirking in the markets with fines, firms earn more in the treatment with fines, but total surplus is lower because effort levels are never very high. These classic monitor-and-fine incentive schemes reduce total output because leaving effort up to the worker risks moral hazard but actually triggers reciprocation; and, given the firm's profit function, the higher reciprocated effort creates a large surplus. Put differently, explicit incentives "crowd out" homegrown intrinsic incentives.[28]

Fehr, Gächter, and Kirchsteiger (1997) extended their design by adding a third stage in which firms can punish or reward workers after observing their efforts (in addition to probabilistic fines). In the third stage firms choose a number p between 0 and 2. Their worker's job rent $(w - c(e))$ is multiplied by p, so that workers are rewarded with a bonus $(p > 1)$ or punished by sanctions $(p < 1)$. Choosing a value of p further from 1 is costlier to the firm, so profit-maximizing firms will never reward or punish. In the two-stage design (with no multiplier p), it is impossible to incentivize workers to exert more than 10 percent of the maximal effort (since the maximum expected fine is equal to the worker disutility from exerting 10 percent

---

[28] Psychologists and others have argued that extrinsic incentives crowd out or extinguish intrinsic incentives in other ways. For example, children who like to color pictures do more coloring when they are suddenly paid a small piece-rate fee per picture, but they "go on strike" and reduce their coloring (to a level of output below their pre-fee rate) when the piece-rate is taken away. In my view, this is an extremely important phenomenon but has not been carefully separated from other forces. For example, in a multitasking environment, if people are suddenly rewarded for one type of output but not the other, they will naturally shift effort to what they're paid for. If this is bad for a company then it's poor incentive design.

effort). Firms ask for 30 percent effort but most workers exert less than 10 percent effort. Adding the third bonus/sanction stage improves effort and profitability dramatically. Firms ask for 90 percent effort and workers respond with about 80 percent. Firms *are* willing to punish and reward by choosing $p \neq 1$. When workers shirk ($e < e'$), they exert hardly any effort, and more than half the firms choose a low multiple (an average of 0.20). When workers work as hard as firms ask ($e = e'$), the firms pay substantial bonuses half the time (mean $p = 1.6$). As in Fehr and Gächter's (2000c) public goods games with punishment, the mere threat of punishment or bonus awards—although not credible in a world of profit-maximizing firms—is carried out often enough that it supports high effort levels and large gains from exchange.

Fehr and Falk (1999) went a step further. Their earlier experiments use a posted-offer institution reflecting how most labor markets seem to operate: Firms post wages and workers either take the jobs or don't. Fehr and Falk used a double auction institution in which both sides post offers. In a complete contract condition, the experimenter (playing the role of a regulatory institution or union contract) specified an effort level. In an incomplete contract condition, effort was unspecified. In the complete contract condition, workers ask for a wide range of wages and firms just hire those who will work for the least (since there is no need to overpay to induce worker goodwill, because workers are required to exert the demanded effort).

Figure 2.7 shows the time series of worker wage offers (dashes) and mean offers accepted by firms (connected dots) over ten periods, when offered contracts were *incomplete*. In the incomplete contract condition, workers compete fiercely for jobs by offering to work for less and less. But firms persistently hire the workers who ask for the *highest* pay. Hiring the most expensive workers actually pays because those workers usually choose higher effort levels, "repaying" the firm's "gift" of supramarginal wages. These results can be interpreted as firms knowing that it pays to share the productivity benefits of having highly motivated workers, a result often seen in field data (e.g., Krueger and Summers, 1987).

In all the experiments above, firms cannot identify a worker and recontract with the same worker repeatedly. Brown, Falk, and Fehr (2002) add the possibility of firms making private wage offers that are earmarked to specific workers. Within five periods, half the firms make private offers. If the worker they hired exerts enough effort, the firms often offer a "raise," but if effort is disappointing (relative to the firms' expectations, which are measured) the workers are "fired" (not rehired). A two-tier labor market emerges in which some workers and firms pair repeatedly, workers work hard and firms pay them well, and other firms offer a low wage to whomever is unpaired. This extension to private earmarked offers should prove a very useful paradigm

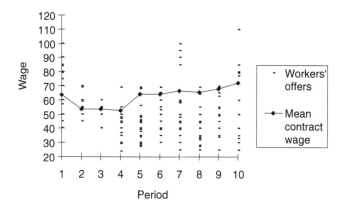

Figure 2.7. *Worker wage offers (dashes) and accepted offers (connected dots) in double auction labor markets with incomplete contracts. Source: Fehr and Gächter (2000b), p. 174, Figures 4a and 4b; reproduced with permission of the American Economic Association.*

to study insider/outsider models, the stigma of unemployment, and other labor market phenomena which are often difficult to understand fully in field data.

One way to digest what gift exchange experiments tell us is to start with two caricatures of organizational design. Firms adopt rigid incentive schemes, requiring certain effort levels, punishing shirkers with fines or firing, and hiring the cheapest workers. (This scenario may describe manual labor jobs where monitoring is easy, such as service industry "McJobs.") Or, oppositely, firms eschew explicit threats and rely on worker goodwill, perhaps hiring those who ask for the *highest* pay. These scenarios loosely correspond to discussions in organizational literature contrasting the "theory X" assumption that workers are basically lazy and must be incentivized and monitored, with the "theory Y" assumption that good job design provides motivation to workers who are eager to take satisfaction from a job well done, and workers will not reliably take advantage of loopholes if they feel some moral obligation to "their" company. Economic models mostly dwell on the gloomy theory X scenario and how contracts can minimize moral hazard. The experimental results suggest that it is easy to create an experimental theory world in which moral hazard is solved by norms of reciprocation. Furthermore, in the presence of reciprocity, incentive-based solutions may do more harm than good by extinguishing the beneficial effects of reciprocation.

A careful study of successful high-tech startups suggests the "soft" gift exchange model can work well in practice. Baron, Hannan, and Burton (2001) classified 175 Silicon Valley firms into several organizational design categories and followed their progress for several years in the 1990s. About one-fifth of the firms used a "commitment blueprint" in which the basis for recruitment and retention was a person's fit in the company's "community" and workers were controlled and coordinated by peers and company culture (rather than monitoring or formal processes). Most CEOs thought the community-type firms would be the first to go. In fact, they were the *most* successful (i.e., went public most rapidly).

Summary: In a pure (or blind) trust game, an Investor invests money with a Trustee she does not know, talk to, or meet again. The investment earns a return. Then a Trustee decides how much to repay. This is a classic game with moral hazard because the Trustee's repayment is not contractually enforced at all. In most experiments subjects invest about half their endowment (exceptions are the peasant–dictator games of Van Huyck et al., in which there is little trust, and in Kenya, where they invest a quarter). Repayments are generally equal to the original investment or slightly less than the original investment (trust does not quite pay). Trustees appear to repay because of a moral obligation they feel, or (put differently) a positive reciprocation of the Investor's risky action which benefits them. However, in two studies Trustees repay only slightly more than Dictators allocate (matching the amount at stake), which suggests repayments are mostly the result of altruism and are increased only a little by reciprocation.

In two-person games, trust and trustworthiness can be justified by emotional links (even if anonymous). Such links might be severely weakened when the person who repays you is not the one you trusted initially. Three studies show the opposite: There is substantial indirect reciprocity of this type (karma, in the extreme), though it is probably weaker than direct reciprocity. Any such effects suggest that "me and my group," although hardly a natural unit of analysis in game theory (contagion effects aside), could be a helpful concept for explaining evidence of substantial indirect reciprocity. An economics without concepts of group identity (cf. Akerlof and Kranton, 2000) may be missing something very important.

Gift-exchange labor markets are multiperson trust games in which firms post wage offers and workers (who outnumber firms) accept them or not. Then workers exert costly effort which firms cannot control or penalize. Self-interest predicts workers will shirk, and firms, anticipating this, offer minimum wages. In the experiments, however, firms offer large wages and workers reciprocate by working hard. Explicit incentives such as fines after probabilistic detection of shirking—the textbook solution—backfire because they undermine reciprocity. Reciprocity solves the moral hazard problem very well, and explicit incentives substitute a poor solution for a very good one.

2.8 Theory

The regularities above can be explained by maintaining the assumptions that players maximize utility (and that Proposers believe Responders do so), but allowing the utility to reflect a social preference for what others get. Theorists worry—justifiably—that altering the utility function allows one to explain anything. One unpublished working paper concluded, "This [finding] puts the basis of our modeling on unobservable preferences, and raises the specter of extensive ad hoc modeling with a basis primarily in psycho babble."[29]

Comments such as this do not appreciate how constructive and parsimonious behavioral economics strives to be (and how different it is from psychology in that respect). The goal is *not* to explain every different finding by adjusting the utility function just so; the goal is to find parsimonious utility functions, supported by psychological intuition, that are general enough to explain many phenomena in one fell swoop, and also make new predictions.

Several theories are good candidates. In the earliest theories, players care about the commodity bundles (Becker, 1974) or utilities (Edgeworth, 1881) of others, or get a "warm glow" from acting charitably that is independent of its impact on a recipient (e.g., Andreoni, 1990). Modern theories can be loosely classified into two kinds. Many theories substitute a social utility for a vector of payoffs. "Inequality-aversion" theories assume people care about their own payoff and their relative payoff (see Bolton, 1991, and Chapter 4; Fehr and Schmidt, 1999; and Bolton and Ockenfels, 2000). Charness and Rabin (2002) present a "Rawlsitarian" me-min-us theory in which players care about their own payoffs and the minimum payoff and total payoffs.

Others assume that the ways other players behave affect whether a player cares positively or negatively about that player. Rabin (1993) is the pioneering paper in this approach (cf. Hirshleifer, 1987). Sally (2002b) uses a similar framework, in which players can choose a level of "sympathy" that affects utilities, to study collusion and sympathetic solutions to the lemons problem. Levine (1998) proposed a signaling-type explanation which is closely related to Rabin's. Dufwenberg and Kirchsteiger (1998) and Falk and Fischbacher (1998) extended Rabin's approach to extensive-form games.

Now I sketch several of the theories and compare the intuitions they embody.

---

[29] Although I've included this sentence because it represents the views some economists articulate about the ability of psychology to inform economics, I've withheld the citation because the sentence was edited out from a later version of the paper.

2.8.1 Pure and Impure Altruism

An obvious starting point for a theory of social utility is that one player's utility increases in the other player's consumption or utility ("pure altruism").
Alternatively, a player may get utility from the act of contributing to others
("impure altruism"; Andreoni, 1990).

Sugden (1982) notes that if players in linear public goods games (discussed at the beginning of this chapter) have altruistic preferences, and
concave utility, then when others contribute a lot, the marginal return from
the altruism component of utility is low, so altruistic players will *reduce* their
contributions. (That is, altruistic giving is "crowded out" if others give.) Theories in which players have reciprocal or inequality-averse preferences (see
below) predict the opposite pattern: Contributions and beliefs will be positively correlated. Direct measurement of contributions shows that about
half of subjects are "conditional cooperators" (they give more if others give
more) and a third or so free ride (Fischbacher, Gächter, and Fehr, 2001; see
also Croson, 1999). This strong correlation between beliefs and behavior
goes against the altruistic model and in favor of reciprocity theories. Theories of purely altruistic preferences fall short because they do not gracefully
explain why players sometimes act negatively toward others (rejecting ultimatum offers, for example) and sometimes act positively (giving generously
in dictator games and reciprocating trust). (Or imagine a romantic marriage and bitter divorce, in which the *same two people* treat each other first
very positively, then very negatively!) Of course, it is easy to "explain" this
switch by flipping the sign of the coefficient on other players' utilities. But a
good theory should be able to do this *endogeneously*, based on the structure
of the game and on beliefs. (Many of the theories described in the rest of
this section do that.)

2.8.2 Inequality-Aversion Theories

Fehr and Schmidt (1999) propose a model of "inequality-aversion" (or
envy and "guilt"[30]) in which players care about their own payoffs and the
differences between their payoffs and those of others. Player i's utility for the
social allocation $X \equiv \{x_1, x_2, \ldots, x_n\}$ is

$$U_i(X) = x_i - \frac{\alpha}{n-1} \sum_{k \neq i} \max(x_k - x_i, 0) - \frac{\beta}{n-1} \sum_{k \neq i} \max(x_i - x_k, 0). \quad (2.8.1)$$

---

[30] Guilt is not quite the right word since it is usually induced by actions, which are not part of these brand
of inequality-aversion models. And note that when guilt is created by outcomes alone, like the "survivor's
guilt" felt by those who survive accidents their loved ones don't survive, it is considered irrational.

They assume $0 \leq \beta_i < 1$ and $\beta_i \leq \alpha_i$. Intuitively, players feel envy and guilt: They dislike having lower allocations than others (with envy weight α_i) and also dislike (somewhat less) having higher allocations (with guilt weight β_i). Given these utilities, Fehr and Schmidt apply standard equilibrium concepts and derive values of the envy and guilt weights needed to explain experimental results.

In ultimatum games, the Responder should reject an offer less than $\alpha_R/1 + 2\alpha_R$ (where α_R denotes the Responder's envy weight). Proposer offers depend on the guilt weight β_P and the Proposer's guess about the distribution of rejection thresholds. In games with proposer competition, several Proposers make offers to a single Responder. As noted above, Proposers quickly and reliably begin offering almost everything to the Responder. Inequality-aversion can explain this result. Players who are outbid get no money and feel envious; if they outbid the highest-bidding player they can earn money and feel guilt rather than more envy. If $\beta_i \leq \alpha_i$ they prefer to bid higher and, in equilibrium, they give the Responder almost everything. Note that this result does *not* depend on the number of Proposers (as long as there are at least two).

Güth, Marchand, and Rulliere (1998) studied Responder competition. A single Proposer (such as a monopolist seller) makes an offer and two or more Responders indicate whether they will take it or not. If more than one says yes, the Proposer randomly allocates the offer. If there are two or more Responders, Fehr–Schmidt prove there is an equilibrium in which Responders will accept any offer, the Proposer will offer zero iff $\beta_P < n - 1/n$, and the highest (perfect) equilibrium offer is

$$\min_{k \in \{2, \ldots, n\}} \alpha_i/(\beta_i + 2\alpha_i + (n - 1)(1 - \beta_i)).$$

In contrast to Proposer competition, there is a role for the amount of competition in this game because increasing n increases the denominator of the minimum, lowering the highest possible offer. Somebody should do an experiment comparing the effects of the number of competing Proposers (which shouldn't matter according to Fehr–Schmidt) and the number of competing Responders (which should).

In public goods contribution games, both contribution and costly punishment can emerge if players are guilty and envious enough. Suppose player i contributes $g_i \in [0, y]$, $G \equiv \{g_1, g_2, \ldots, g_n\}$ and earns $x_i(G) = y - g_i + m \sum_{k=1}^{n} g_k$, where m is the marginal private return from the public good. In a two-stage version of the game with punishment, after contributions are made all players are informed about G. Player i can punish k one unit with a punishment p_{ik}, which costs the punisher $c < 1$.[31] The standard model with

---

[31]The payoff function in the public goods game with punishment is $x_i(G) = y - g_i + a \sum_{k=1}^{n} g_k - \sum_{k=1}^{n} p_{ki} - c \sum_{k=1}^{n} p_{ik}$.

no social preference predicts complete free riding in the public good game ($g_i = 0$) and no costly punishment in the two-stage game ($p_{ik} = 0$). As noted at the beginning of the chapter, although repeated public goods games do converge close to complete free-riding, in games with punishment there is a small amount of punishment that generates convergence to substantial rates of contribution. (Note that the effectiveness of punishment might also be linked to the cost to the punisher—punishees might feel worse if the punisher went out of her way to teach them a lesson.)

Fehr and Schmidt prove several properties of behavior in public goods games when there is envy and guilt. Players with $\beta_i < 1 - a$ will always free ride; if k players free ride and $k > a(n - 1)/2$, then everyone free rides; if there are a small enough number of free riders and enough inequality-averters of the right sort ($(a + \beta_k - 1)/(\alpha_k + \beta_k) > k/(n - 1)$ for players with $\beta_k < 1 - a$) then the free riders contribute nothing and others contribute some amount $g_k \in [0, y]$. In the game with punishment, suppose there are n^* players who are sufficiently guilty ($\beta_i \leq 1 - a$) and also sufficiently envious ($\alpha_i > c(n - 1)(1 + \alpha_i) - c(n^* - 1)(\alpha_i + \beta_i)$). These "conditionally cooperative enforcers" guarantee the possibility of a perfect equilibrium with some positive contribution. The n^* enforcers will be willing to punish defectors (which reduces the inequality in their payoffs since it hurts the punishee more than it costs the defector), which supports cooperation.

Bolton and Ockenfels (2000) proposed a very similar model of inequality-aversion that they call "ERC" (for equity, reciprocity, and competition). In ERC, players care about their own payoffs and their *relative* share, so

$$U_i(X) = U\left(x_i, \frac{x_i}{\sum_{k=1}^{n} x_k}\right). \qquad (2.8.2)$$

In ERC, players strictly prefer a relative payoff that is equal to the average payoff $1/n$ (i.e., $v_2^i(x_i, 1/n) = 0$, $v_{22}^i < 0$), which means players will sacrifice to move their share closer to the average if they are either below or above it.

Like Fehr and Schmidt, Bolton and Ockenfels combine standard game-theoretic concepts with their specification of social preference and prove several propositions about what will happen in different games which match the empirical facts nicely. In dictator games, people will give between half and all of the pie. (This result does not come from Fehr–Schmidt preferences unless concave utilities are included.) In ultimatum games, Responders will reject zero offers all the time, the rejection rate will fall with increasing percentage offers and decrease in the pie size (fixing percentage offer), and Responders will never reject 50 percent offers. Ultimatum offers will be less than half, and will be greater than Dictator allocations. In the three-player combination ultimatum–dictator games of Güth and Van Damme (1998), ERC predicts that the allocation to the inactive Recipient will be ignored, which is roughly what is observed.

2.8.3 Fairness Equilibrium (Rabin)

Rabin's (1993) "fairness equilibrium" approach is motivated by the fact that people both behave nicely toward those who treat them nicely, and behave meanly toward those who harm them. A model that can explain these stylized facts must include players' judgments of whether others are nice or mean, so Rabin adopts the psychological games framework of Geanakoplos, Pearce, and Stacchetti (1989) in which utilities can depend directly on players' *beliefs*.[32] Suppose there are two players, denoted 1 and 2. Denote strategies by a_i, i's beliefs about the strategy of the other player by b_{3-i} (i.e., b_2 is 1's belief about what 2 will do, and b_1 is 2's belief about what 1 will do), and beliefs about beliefs by c_i. The central construct in Rabin's approach is a player's "kindness" (and perceived kindness).

To assess kindness, take a player's point of view, and fix their belief about what the other player will do. For example, suppose player 1 has the belief b_2 about what player 2 will do. Then from player 1's point of view, her own choice is an allocation to player 2 of a possible payoff out of the set of possible payoffs we denote $\Pi(b_2)$. Call the highest and lowest of these payoffs, for player 2, $\pi_2^{\max}(b_2)$ and $\pi_2^{\min}(b_2)$. Define an equitable (or fair) payoff by $\pi_2^{\text{fair}}(b_2)$. (Rabin assumes $\pi_2^{\text{fair}}(b_2)$ is the average of the highest and lowest payoffs, excluding Pareto-dominated payoff pairs, but this particular definition is not essential to most of what follows.) Then player 1's kindness toward 2, which depends on her actual choice a_1, is

$$f_1(a_1, b_2) = (\pi_2(b_2, a_1) - \pi_2^{\text{fair}}(b_2))/(\pi_2^{\max}(b_2) - \pi_2^{\min}(b_2)). \quad (2.8.3)$$

Thus, kindness is a fraction of the way above or below the fair point (scaled by the range of payoffs player 1 could have dictated) that player 2's actual payoff lies. A positive $f_1(a_1, b_2)$ is kind because it means player 2 got a payoff higher than the fair one; a negative value is mean because player 2 got a lower than fair payoff.

For player 1 to decide how kind player 2 is being toward her, she forms a perceived kindness number,

$$\tilde{f}_2(b_2, c_1) = (\pi_1(c_1, b_2) - \pi_1^{\text{fair}}(c_1))/(\pi_1^{\max}(c_1) - \pi_1^{\min}(c_1)). \quad (2.8.4)$$

This perceived kindness is a conjecture about what player 2's own kindness toward 1 is. To form this conjecture player 1 must guess what player 2 thinks player 1 will do, so player 1's iterated belief plays a role.

---

[32] This generalization allows phenomena such as surprise, in which players may actually get pleasure from having their belief that they won't get a gift (for example) proved wrong. See Ruffle (1999) for an application.

Table 2.12.   *Prisoners' dilemma with social preferences*

		Cooperate	Defect
Cooperate	C	$4 + 0.75\alpha, 4 + 0.75\alpha$	$0 - 0.5\alpha, 6$
Defect	D	$6, 0 - 0.5\alpha$	$0, 0$

Source: Rabin (1993).

Rabin assumes that player 1's social preferences are

$$U_i(a_i, b_j, c_i) = \pi_i(a_i, b_j) + \alpha \tilde{f}_2(b_2, c_1) + \alpha \tilde{f}_2(b_2, c_1) \cdot f_1(a_1, b_2). \quad (2.8.5)$$

That is, players care about their monetary payoffs (the first term), whether they are being treated kindly or not (the second term), and the product of the kindness they expect and their own kindness. The weight α simply weighs fairness utilities against money.[33]

By multiplying a player's kindness, and the kindness she expects, this social preference function captures reciprocity motives—players prefer to be nice (positive kindness) to people who act nice to them, and to be mean (negative kindness) toward people who act mean.

Rabin then applies an equilibrium concept in which players maximize social utilities, and their beliefs are rational expectations of what actually happens—i.e., $a_i = b_j = c_i$ (beliefs about what others will choose are correct, and beliefs about what others will believe are correct also). He calls this a "fairness equilibrium." Empirical bite comes from the assumption that the fairness term becomes relatively less important as the payoffs π_i get larger.

An easy example is the prisoners' dilemma. Table 2.12 shows payoffs adjusted for fairness. The (C,C) money payoffs are (4,4), the (D,D) payoffs are (0,0), and the (C,D) payoffs are (0,6).

Consider the row player's payoffs. When α is large enough, she feels worse choosing C when she expects her opponent to choose D, because D is a mean choice by the column player. Oppositely, if she expects the column player to choose C then she earns $4 + 0.75\alpha$ from reciprocating cooperation, because doing so is nice (it gives column a better payoff than if row defected), and column is also being nice by not taking advantage and defecting.

Thus, mutual cooperation is a fairness equilibrium when α is large enough and the monetary payoffs relatively small. In this view, PD is a coordination game in which players try to coordinate their emotions or levels of niceness. This jibes nicely with the experimental observation that

---

[33] The weight α isn't in Rabin's original approach, but I've added it to highlight how self-interest can be a special case.

Table 2.13. *Chicken with social preferences*

	Dare	Chicken
Dare	$-2,-2$	$2, 0 - 0.5\alpha$
Chicken	$0 - 0.5\alpha, 2$	$1 + 0.75\alpha, 1 + 0.75\alpha$

Source: Rabin (1993).

players who expect others to cooperate are more likely to cooperate also (i.e., the belief in C and the tendency to choose C are correlated), which is hard to explain in many models.

Another interesting example is "chicken," with fairness-adjusted payoffs shown in Table 2.13. The Nash equilibria ($\alpha = 0$) are (C,D) and (D,C)—one player backs down and chooses C when the other is expected to choose D. However, when α is large enough (above 4), a player who expects the other to D(are) would rather choose D, earning -2, than choose C(hicken) and let the mean player take advantage, suffering a loss of 0.5α. Similarly, when $\alpha > 4/3$ then reciprocating the choice of Chicken with Chicken pays because it repays the other player's kindness. Thus, if fairness effects are large then (C,C) and (D,D) are fairness equilibria. In this lovely example, the set of outcomes allowed by fairness is completely opposite those required by standard equilibrium. The game also captures both the mutually happy and the mutually angry aspects of social preference, like a couple who sacrifice to please each other, only to end up in an ugly *War of the Roses* divorce in which their sole goal is to harm the other person who harms them. Some experimental evidence is also supportive of the (C,C) and (D,D) outcomes (Rutström, McDaniel, and Williams, 1994).

Rabin proves several propositions about the existence and characterization of a fairness equilibrium. He also describes an application to monopoly pricing: Firms cannot extract all the surplus because a buyer will reciprocate a price that seems too high by withholding demand.[34] An application to gift exchange in employment also shows how a worker will reciprocate a high wage with high effort.

2.8.4 Extensive-Form Fairness Equilibrium

Dufwenberg and Kirchsteiger (1998) extended the Rabin framework to extensive-form games. They define strategies to be behavior strategies which assign to each of a player's information sets a probability distribution of possible choices at that information set. One difference from Rabin is that

---

[34] There is some evidence of demand withholding in monopoly pricing experiments (e.g., Ruffle, 2000).

Pareto-inefficient strategies are defined as those that yield weakly less for all players than some other strategy *for all subgames*. This is a subtle departure from Rabin, who defines inefficient strategies as those that yield less for everyone on the equilibrium path (i.e., for the player's beliefs about the others' strategies).

Their social preferences differ from Rabin's slightly. First they define kindness functions as differences between payoffs and fair payoffs, so i's kindness to j is

$$f_i(a_i, b_j) = \pi_j(a_i, b_j) - \pi_j^{\text{fair}}(b_j), \quad \text{where } \pi_j^{\text{fair}} = (\pi_j^{\max}(a_i, b_j) + \pi_i^{\min}(a_i, b_j))/2$$

(where the max and min payoffs are defined for efficient strategies only). Their utility function is

$$U_i(a_i, b_j, c_i) = \pi(a_i, b_j) + Y_i \sum_{j \neq i} f_i(a_i, b_j)\tilde{f}_j(b_j, c_i).$$

Their specification of social preferences differs from Rabin in three ways: They do not scale the kindness terms by the range of $\pi^{\max}$ and $\pi^{\min}$ as Rabin does; the kindness of player(s) j does not enter directly; and the product of i's kindness and i's perceived kindness is summed across players j. They prove the existence of a sequential reciprocity equilibrium (SRE) in which players maximize social utility, and strategies match beliefs. They also show that using normalized kindness functions and a belief-dependent definition of efficiency destroys the guarantee of existence.

Dufwenberg and Kirchsteiger apply the model to sequential prisoners' dilemma (PD) and ultimatum games. In sequential PD, the second player always reciprocates defection and she reciprocates cooperation if her value of Y_i is high enough. The first player's behavior is not sharply restricted, unfortunately. For example, if $Y_2 > 1$, then player 1 either cooperates for any value of Y_1, defects if $Y_1 > 1$, or cooperates with probability $(Y_1 - 1)/2Y_1$.

Behavior in ultimatum games is also somewhat indeterminate. The Responder has thresholds of offers she always accepts and always rejects (which depend on the Responder's parameter Y_R). There is always an SRE in which the Proposer offers the minimum acceptable amount, but if the values of Y_i are large enough there is also an SRE in which the Proposer's offer is rejected.

Falk and Fischbacher (1998) also use psychological game theory to incorporate reciprocity in extensive-form games. Their innovative approach departs from Rabin's in two interesting ways—measuring intentions more directly and (like Dufwenberg and Kirchsteiger) measuring kindness by differences across players' payoffs. Since they are interested in applications to extensive-form games, they define emotional terms at each node. Denote i's strategy by s_i, i's belief about j's choice by s_j', and i's belief about

j's belief about i's choice by s_i''. As in Rabin, fixing beliefs and second-order beliefs, i regards j's choice as allocating a payoff to i, from the set of possible payoffs. Then their outcome term $\Delta(n)$ at node n is defined by $\pi_i(n, s_i'', s_j'') - \pi_j(n, s_i'', s_j')$. That is, players measure fair treatment by the difference between their own expected payoffs and the other player's payoff. This is a fundamentally different approach than Rabin's, which judges kindness by how much a player gets relative to some "fair" payoff for themselves (for example, the average of their own possible payoffs). In Falk and Fischbacher's approach, kindness as measured by $\Delta(n)$ is multiplied by a factor measuring how *intentional* j's kindness was. The intention function $\Omega(\pi_i, \pi_j, \pi_i^0, \pi_j^0)$ compares a set of possible payoffs π_i^0, π_j^0 with alternative payoffs π_i, π_j. Roughly speaking, intention is equal to 1 when player j gives more to i than to herself and she could have given i less, or when she gives less to i and could have given more. Intentions are equal to a value ϵ_i if j gives i more than to herself but could have given even more, or if j gives i less but could have given even less. Fixing a node and set of beliefs s_i', s_i'', the intention factor $v(n)$ is the maximum of the intention factors defined above across all alternative payoffs π_i, π_j available at node n.

Denote the node following n, on a path to endnode f, by $v(n, f)$. Then player i's reciprocation of j is measured by $\sigma(n, f) = \pi_j(v(n, f), s_i', s_i'') - \pi_j(n, s_i', s_i'')$. This reciprocation is the difference between what player j expected at node n, and what i actually "awards" at the subsequent node $v(n, f)$. Then player i's utility at an endnode f is given by

$$U_i(f) = \pi_i(f) + \rho_i \sum_{n \to f} v(n)\Delta(n)\sigma(n, f), \qquad (2.8.6)$$

where $n \to f$ is the set of nodes n that precede f (either directly or indirectly).

This utility includes both "material payoffs" $\pi_i(f)$ and "emotional" payoffs, which sum up the products of intention, kindness, and reciprocation across nodes on the path to f. The factor ρ_i is the weight i places on emotional payoffs (if this is zero, the self-interested model results as a special case). The intention term is an important innovation. When $\epsilon_i = 1$, then $v(n)$ is always 1 and the model reduces to one in which players care only about differences in payoff allocations, and not about possible differences on unchosen paths (i.e., they don't care whether players could have treated them worse or badly).

Falk and Fischbacher apply standard equilibrium concepts with the additional restriction (as in Geanakoplos et al. and Rabin) that beliefs are correct in equilibrium ($s_i'' = s_j' = s_i$). They apply their model to several games mentioned in this chapter, to see how well its predictions correspond to the data. They get a very impressive array of precise predictions that loosely correspond to stylized facts.

For example, in the prisoners' dilemma they predict less cooperation in the simultaneous-move game than in sequential games, and predict cooperation following cooperation in the sequential game (if ρ_i is large enough). In dictator games, the Dictator offers $d^* = \max(0, 0.5 - (1/2\epsilon_1\rho_1))$; if the outcome concern parameter ϵ_i and reciprocation taste ρ_i are high enough, Dictators will give something (but never more than half).

In ultimatum games, offers are the maximum of the Dictator offer (with $\epsilon_i = 1$) or $c^* = (1 + 3\rho_2 - \sqrt{1 + 6\rho_2 + \rho_2^2})/(4\rho_2)$. Acceptance thresholds are $c/[\rho_2(1 - 2c)(1 - c)]$, which start at zero and rise in a convex function toward 1. In the ultimatum game where offers are made by a third party (as in Blount, 1995), the acceptance threshold is $c/[\epsilon_2\rho_2(1 - 2c)(1 - c)]$, which is larger if $\epsilon_2 < 1$. (Intuitively, the intention measurement term ϵ_1 is in the ultimatum game but can be lower in the random-offer version, reflecting the Responder's awareness that the beneficiary of a low offer had no mean intentions if the offer was generated by somebody else.)

The model makes a sharp prediction about ultimatum and "best-shot" public goods games. Compare the mini-ultimatum game, in which player 1 can choose a left branch with payoffs (5,5) and (0,0) or a right branch with uneven payoffs (8,2) and (0,0). Now replace the equal payoff node (5,5) with an unequal payoff node (2,8), creating a sequential battle of the sexes (BOS). Theories that evaluate only the social utility of endnode payoffs regard player 2's choice between the (8,2) and (0,0) nodes in both games as identical (what's on the unchosen branch doesn't matter). As Falk, Fehr, and Fischbacher (in press) showed, forgone payoffs *do* matter. In the Falk–Fischbacher model, the probability of player 2 choosing the (8,2) outcome from the right branch is $\max(1, 5/12\rho_2)$ in the mini-ultimatum game and $\max(1, 5/12\epsilon_2\rho_2)$ in the best-shot game. Thus, for concern parameters $\epsilon_2 < 1$ players are more likely to accept unequal payoffs in the best-shot game (BOS) because player 1's intentions are not so mean in that game (as Andreoni, Brown, and Vesterlund, 2002, confirmed).

2.8.5 Comparing Approaches

Since many of the theories just described make similar predictions, a busy and important area of current research is finding games in which the theories differ and testing them.

ERC (Bolton–Ockenfels) and guilt–envy (Fehr–Schmidt) theories of inequality-aversion differ in two ways: ERC assumes players care about relative shares whereas guilt–envy assumes players care about absolute differences; and ERC does not compare one player's payoffs with each other player's (it sums other players' payoffs) whereas guilt–envy does.

Both features of ERC appear to be the wrong modeling choices. Consider a payoff allocation to three players $(x, x - \epsilon, x + \epsilon)$. ERC predicts that

Table 2.14.   *Two games that distinguish social preference theories*

Offer	Responder action		Rejection frequency	Predicted rejection frequency			
	Accept	Reject		Bolton—Ockenfels	Fehr—Schmidt	Dufwenberg—Kirchsteiger	Falk—Fischbacher
Equal	5,5	0.5,0.5	—	—	—	—	—
Unequal	8,2	0.8,0.2	0.38	None	Some	Some	Some
Equal	5,5	3,3	—	—	—	—	—
Unequal	8,2	6,0	0.19	None	None	Some	Some

Source: Falk, Fehr, and Fischbacher (in press).

the preference of the first player (who receives x) is independent of ϵ; since she gets an equal share of the total, she is neutral toward total-preserving spreads in payoffs of others. Guilt–envy predicts utility will fall as ϵ increases (if guilt is weaker than envy). Charness and Rabin (2000) report that preferences do fall with ϵ as guilt–envy theory predicts, contrary to ERC.[35] And in public goods games with punishment, guilt–envy theory predicts, correctly, that players punish the biggest free riders to reduce the largest envy gaps, whereas ERC makes no prediction about *who* is punished.

The difference between relative share and absolute difference specifications can also be explored with variants of ultimatum games, shown in Table 2.14. In the game in the top panel, a Proposer offers (5,5) or (8,2). If the Responder rejects, the payoffs are 10 percent of the original offer. Since the relative shares are the same whether Responders accept or reject, and they earn less money by rejecting, ERC predicts they should never reject. The linear guilt–envy specification predicts indifference (but it is easy to explain rejections by allowing concave utilities for money, guilt, and envy). As Table 2.14 shows, almost 40 percent of unequal offers are rejected, contrary to ERC.

Another important distinction among theories is whether utilities of terminal-node payoffs are separable from the path through the tree and from payoffs on unchosen branches. Inequality-aversion theories assume separability. Separability is analytically useful because it allows a modeler simply to substitute social utilities at terminal nodes and then use standard concepts (e.g., subgame perfection) to derive equilibria.

Some evidence suggests separability is systematically violated. As noted above, players are less likely to reject ultimatum offers generated at random compared with those of Proposers who benefit from lopsided offers

---

[35] In contexts such as social processes of taxation, voters' reaction to this sort of "neutral" income inequality is important because it will determine how middle-class voters in the middle of a national income distribution will react to attempts to reduce income inequality.

(Blount, 1995). Similarly, there is (weak) evidence that Trustees in trust games repay more when their stake was generated by an initial investment (compared with a control dictator game). Experimental results of Falk, Fehr, and Fischbacher (in press) (see Table 2.6), discussed in detail above (see also Brandts and Sola, 2001), also show modest violations of separability which have plausible psychological interpretations. The bottom panel of Table 2.14 shows a modified ultimatum game which tests separability further. If the Responder rejects, two units are subtracted from both players' payoffs. Since this subtraction lowers the relative share of unequal offers, and keeps the difference in payoffs constant, both ERC and guilt–envy theories predict Responders should never reject unequal (8,2) offers. But they do so about 20 percent of the time. Dufwenberg–Kirschteiger and Falk–Fischbacher's theories allow such rejections.

Other evidence suggests separability is a good approximation. For example, Bolton, Brandts, and Ockenfels (1998) found that whether one player takes a cooperative move (sacrificing to help the other) is roughly independent of whether the first player sacrifices or not. And, as noted above, the difference between Trustee repayments and Dictator allocations from equal sums is not very large (and is zero in one study). Although these findings are in urgent need of further study, they suggest that players sometimes exhibit stronger social preferences when they are punishing or rewarding actions of others. Charness and Haruvy (2002) estimate a general model that tests many of the theories above, and they find support for several forces, especially reciprocity, in gift exchange settings.

Inequality-aversion theories also require a careful specification of *which* other players' payoffs a person is comparing herself to. This is an important question that is rarely discussed. A natural assumption is that a subject in an experiment compares herself with others she is playing with, but there are other possibilities—Why not compare with all others in the same experimental session? Or in all sessions of the same experiment?—which have different implications.[36] Exploring the boundaries of social comparison will prove important in generalizing these results to applications such as job titles and firm structure.[37]

---

[36] For example, why not worry about other players in the same experimental session? Consider two players in an ultimatum game in an experimental session with N other pairs. If N is very large, and a player cares about the payoffs of all $N - 1$ other players (who are likely to earn some money), then her relative share will fall with N, and envy will increase, which should guide her toward self-interest.

[37] There are well-known industry-wide and firm-specific wage differentials (e.g., janitors at a fancy law firm where top attorneys are well paid are paid more than janitors at a fast-food restaurant). Wages are presumably driven by social comparison with those in the same firm. One response is to outsource low-cost work (e.g., the janitors at Stanford University work for a private company, not for Stanford), which has implications for firm structures.

Summary: Several parsimonious theories have been proposed to explain a broad sweep of data with a single model of social preference (and some parametric flexibility). In theories of pure and impure altruism, players care about the utilities of others or get satisfaction from treating others kindly. In inequality-aversion approaches, players care about earning more money and earning the same as others. In Rabin's reciprocal approach, players make a judgment about whether another player's action is kind or mean (i.e., gives the target player a good or bad relative payoff) and have a taste for reciprocating both kindness and meanness with the same. Rabin's theory, developed for normal-form games, was extended by Dufwenberg and Kirschsteiger and by Falk and Fischbacher.

Most data support either inequality-aversion or the reciprocal approaches. Altruism theories do not explain both negative and positive behavior toward others without crudely changing the signs of coefficients exogenously. Inequality-aversion theories are very promising but predict a kind of separability—utilities of terminal-node allocations are independent of how those allocations arose, and of allocations from unchosen alternatives—that is psychologically suspect and violated in several experiments.

I like the reciprocal approaches because they get the psychology right. Furthermore, the main argument in favor of inequality-aversion is analytical simplicity. But the history of economic thought shows how quickly the profession can learn to use a tool that seems too unwieldy at first. After all, applying the reciprocity approaches to interesting games cannot possibly be more difficult than the incredibly complicated mathematics now being done in areas such as asset pricing, macroeconomics, epistemological game theory, and econometrics. At the same time, when the empirical dust settles, both approaches may prove useful in different technical applications, much as theories of consumer choice and production sometimes use Cobb–Douglas functions and sometimes use CES (constant elasticity of substitution) or linear expenditure.

2.9 Conclusion

This chapter describes experimental regularities in simple bargaining games, an area of research that is growing rapidly because the games are so useful for shaping theories of social preference. In dictator games, players offer modest sums to others (about 20 percent of the amount being divided). When others have entrusted the Dictators with large sums, the Dictators tend to return more (and trust is repaid, on average, although results vary widely). Proposers offer nearly-equal splits in ultimatum games (about 40 percent) for fear of having low offers rejected. Offers around 20 percent *are* rejected half the time. We know a rejection is a punishment by the Responder to a Proposer who has behaved unfairly because Responders are more likely to accept offers when they don't know how much the Proposer is earning, when uneven offers are generated by chance, and when rejecting does not hurt the Proposer as much as it hurts the Responder.

It is sometimes said that fairness is simply a label for the behavior rather than an explanation. This is no longer true because the many experimental results *do* suggest an explanation: Fairness is a judgment people make about an action players take or its consequences, and that judgment affects their preferences for actions and allocations. Whether an action is judged fair, and what players do as a result, respond to observable variables in intuitive ways. It is fair to keep more if you became the Proposer by winning a contest, or if keeping more is the only way a Proposer can play a second time and earn more money.

The fabric of fairness perceptions and their effects on behavior have been explored in studies that control or measure five kinds of variables: methodological, demographic, cultural, descriptive, and structural.

Methodological studies have concentrated on the amount being divided, whether the game is repeated or not, and whether experimenters know exactly what each subject did. There is little evidence that stakes matter much once subjects are paid something (although Responders reject larger amounts, and reject percentage offers less often, when stakes rise). Repeating the game does not matter much. Anonymity of subjects' actions from the experimenter lowers Dictator allocations in some experiments but does not affect ultimatum behavior.

Despite much interest in whether or not people in different demographic groups play differently, only the effect of academic major has replicated reliably (economics majors offer and accept less), and often it has no effect. Gender effects on offers and rejections have not proved reliable, except that women are more price sensitive in punishing unfairness and allocating money. Age effects are important because young children are actually very self-interested, which implies that deviations from self-interested strategic predictions are learned as children grow up, and are not mistakes that more learning will undo.

Perhaps the most intriguing experiments are those that cross cultures. For example, the Machiguenga farmers in Peru are one of the least-educated groups ever studied . . . and also conform *most* closely to the game-theoretic model (based on self-interest). Comparing cultures is also informative because the degree of market integration is positively correlated with equality of offers across a dozen or so small-scale societies, as if market exchange either requires or cultivates norms of equal sharing.

Descriptive variables can matter. For example, calling an ultimatum game a buyer–seller exchange lowers offers. These effects are like other kinds of context-dependent etiquette. In Beijing it is considered acceptable to spit on the sidewalk and disgusting to blow your nose into a handkerchief that you then carry around. In Los Angeles the opposite is true. Similarly, in bargaining, monopoly sellers are allowed to gouge buyers by charging a high price which leaves little consumer surplus, but two people jointly claiming money are expected to share.

Structural variables that add moves to the game have proved most interesting. Inducing a sense of entitlement, by allowing the winner of a contest to be the Proposer, lowers offers. If Responders aren't sure how much Proposers get, they accept less. Games with multiple players suggest that Responders care about whether Proposers are unfair to *them*, but don't care much how Proposers treat others. Competition among Proposers or Responders drives offers to extremes.

The effects of multiple players and limited information suggest a general conjecture about bargaining and markets. In two-person games with perfect information about how much each side is earning, fairness concerns loom largest. As players are added, competition can create very lopsided allocations. And, as the Responder's knowledge about the Proposer's gain becomes hazier, Responders become more tolerant of low offers (since they aren't sure how unfair the Proposer is being). The concern for fairness evident in two-player perfect information games therefore disappears in large markets. That does *not* mean traders in such markets do not care about fairness per se. They may care, but they behave self-interestedly because they aren't sure whether others are being fair and can't easily punish unfairness. A competitive market is simply a place in which it is hard to express your concern for fairness because buying or selling (or refusing to do so) will not generally change your inequality much. This does not mean that "fairness doesn't matter in important situations"; it just means that people will then express social preferences about unfair market outcomes through "voice" (protest, newspaper editorials), regulation, and law. For example, many states that are disaster prone have laws prohibiting "gouging," which is defined as raising prices of basic commodities such as water and gasoline after a shortage due to a disaster. These laws codify a social norm of fairness.

At this point, we should declare a moratorium on creating ultimatum game data and shift attention toward new games and new theories. Good new theories codify precisely what fairness *is*, organize observed regularities, and make new predictions.

Rabin's reciprocity-based theory suggests that the way players feel about others depends on how they expect to be treated. Theories based on inequality-aversion (Fehr–Schmidt and Bolton–Ockenfels) suggest that players dislike getting less than a fair share *and* (less intuitively) dislike getting more than a fair share. The latter assumption serves as a kind of proxy for reciprocity, since it often motivates players to refuse to take advantage of others who have made themselves vulnerable.

The reciprocity-based view is surely more psychologically correct because players do care about the intentions of other players and unchosen paths. At the same time, inequality-aversion is easy to use analytically because social utilities can just be substituted into cells of a payoff matrix, or nodes of a tree, before doing standard equilibrium analyses.

Another idea often espoused to explain these results, but rarely formalized, is an evolutionary explanation. The argument is that, when the human brain and body physically evolved in our ancestral past, people lived in small hunter–gatherer bands. In these groups, the argument assumes, one-shot interactions were rare, protecting property (such as the spoils of a hunt) was important, but sharing norms were useful as social insurance against the risks of bad harvests or hunts. The evolutionary argument is that repeated-game behavior (like rejection in ultimatum games to teach Proposers to offer more) was ingrained in the ancestral environment. When our caveman brains play one-shot games in modern laboratories, we cannot suppress repeated-game instincts or acquired habits, much as our evolved caveman tastes for fatty foods lead to widespread obesity when unleashed in a world of 15,000 McDonald's restaurants and guaranteed half-hour delivery of pizzas with cheese *inside* the crust.

There is surely some truth to the evolutionary argument. But it is difficult to falsify and there is collateral evidence against it. Subjects are usually well aware that one-shot games are strategically different than repeated ones—they say so on Jacobsen and Sadrieh's (1996) videotapes—and they *do* reject more in repeated ultimatum games with partner-matching where they can build reputation (see Slembeck, 1998). More importantly, the evolutionary account has not produced clear fresh predictions. It is time either to make the evolutionary theory precise (Samuelson, 2001, is an important start), derive surprising implications, and test them; or to quit talking about evolution as if it were an obviously better explanation than other theories that *have* passed such tests.

There are many potential applications of all these theories. Obvious examples include bargaining which seems to exhibit costly delay that can partly be ascribed to social preferences—labor–management strikes, ugly divorces, and custody battles. Social comparison of workers with others, and the implications of those comparisons for wage-setting, may also be neatly modeled by these theories. Dictator game experiments may help us understand the determinants of charitable giving. Trust games seem extremely helpful for investigating how 'social capital' affects the development of different economies, favors exchange inside organizations (Prendergast, 1999b), and so forth.

All these applications will also require further development of our understanding of other psychological aspects of social preferences. For example, do angry workers consider "management" to be a single monolithic player, and get angry at "management" the same way they get angry at a spouse who threatens to leave them or a driver who cuts them off on the LA freeway? Perhaps they do, perhaps not. Whom do workers in a firm compare themselves to when their utilities are altered by perceptions of inequality? The cognitive boundaries of comparison groups will matter for most applications, and need to be investigated.

More experimental studies, a new wave of 'second-generation' experiments testing the theories described above, and a lot of applications to field phenomena promise to provide a coherent theory of social preference which should replace the simple caricature of self-interest in economic theory.

Finally, it is important to keep in mind that all the social preference theories permit the possibility that many people are self-interested much of the time. Institutional arrangements can be understood as responding to a world in which there are some sociopaths and some saints, but mostly regular folks who are capable of both kinds of behavior. Dawes and Thaler (1988, p. 195) tell a story which makes this point nicely:

> In the rural areas around Ithaca it is common for farmers to put some fresh produce on a table by the road. There is a cash box on the table, and customers are expected to put money in the box in return for the vegetables they take. The box has just a small slit, so money can only be put in, not taken out. Also, the box is attached to the table, so no one can (easily) make off with the money. We think that the farmers who use this system have just about the right model of human nature. They feel that enough people will volunteer to pay for the fresh corn to make it worthwhile to put it out there. The farmers also know that if it were easy enough to take the money, someone would do so.

3
Mixed-Strategy Equilibrium

IN GAMES WITH MIXED-STRATEGY EQUILIBRIA (MSE) players are predicted to choose probabilistic "mixtures" in which no single strategy is played all the time. Common examples are zero-sum games in which your win is my loss—as in sports, perhaps war and diplomacy, and some other domains. In these games, if I always choose a particular strategy, and you anticipate that strategy, then you will win; so I shouldn't behave so predictably. The only equilibrium will involve unpredictable mixing. Randomizing is also sensible when a little genuine unpredictability will deter another player from doing something you dislike. (Think of random searches of passengers boarding U.S. airlines after the September 11, 2001, attacks, or the liquor store in the South with a large sign outside—"This establishment is guarded by a vicious dog three nights a week. . . . See if you can guess which nights.")

Games with mixed equilibria do not have some of the complications of other games described in this book. The games reported in this chapter do not have multiple equilibria, so there is no question about which equilibria are selected (as in Chapter 7). And in constant-sum games it is not possible for one player to help another without hurting herself, so social preferences and reciprocation (recall Chapter 2) play no role.

Furthermore, in constant-sum MSE games the maximin solution—in which players just choose strategies that maximize the minimum they can get—is also a Nash equilibrium.[1] Maximin leads straight to Nash equilibrium

---

[1] I shall use the terms maximin and minimax interchangeably.

in zero-sum games because players' interests are strictly opposed: If others will do whatever they can to get the most, their actions will give me the least, so I should try to maximize the least I can get. Since maximin is a particularly simple decision rule and coincides with Nash, in these games there is a good chance that the Nash equilibrium will describe what players do in these games.

That's the good news. The bad news is that, from a behavioral point of view, MSE games raise difficult challenges for Nash equilibrium and for learning.

One way to think about the complexity of reaching an equilibrium in a game is to ask what assumptions about players' mutual rationality and understanding of each other's likely behavior are mathematically required to derive an equilibrium. (These assumptions are called "epistemic foundations"; e.g., Brandenburger, 1992.) In dominance-solvable games, for example (Chapter 5), players need only to have several steps of mutual rationality–that is, faith that others are thinking rationally. But in games with mixed equilibria, in equilibrium players must somehow accurately guess each other's strategies (or infer these from knowing the other players' beliefs, and believing they are rational). This is a tall order.

Perhaps mixed equilibria can be easily learned. But learning dynamics that assume players move toward strategies with higher expected payoffs ("gradient processes") are known to spiral *away* from mixed equilibria (Crawford, 1985); so it is not clear how equilibrium can actually be reached by learning. And in an MSE the expected utility payoff to each strategy used in the mixture is exactly the same (by definition), so there is no positive incentive to mix "properly" or to stick to an equilibrium mixture if it is ever reached.

Furthermore, MSE presumes that players use a probability mixture, or—importantly—appear to (and use the same mixture over time). If randomization is unnatural for players, or undesirable,[2] they will not randomize independently when they play repeatedly. In fact, when experimental subjects are asked to produce random sequences, they produce sequences that reliably deviate from random ones: There are too few long runs, too many alternations, and, consequently, sample relative frequen-

---

[2] For example, if preferences are quasi-convex then players dislike mixtures of equally preferred items and will dislike randomizing (although equilibrium existence can still be rescued as an equilibrium in beliefs; see Crawford, 1990). This may seem unlikely, but it does point out that, although MSE games are simple in some respects, probability predictions require assumptions about preferences over mixtures (typically the expected utility hypothesis), which is a stronger assumption than is needed to compute equilibria in other games (which typically just use monotonic utilities).

cies are too close to event probabilities. These misconceptions also affect field phenomena such as patterns of betting on lottery numbers (people quit betting on a number for a few days after it has won, until it gradually becomes "due" again; see, e.g., Clotfelter and Cook, 1993; cf. Rabin, 2002).

Another question that is special to games with MSE is raised by experiments in which players are randomly matched with others in a population. In a population-matching protocol, it is possible for an MSE to occur in the *population*, even though *individual* players are not adhering to the MSE. Consider matching pennies, in which two players choose H(eads) or T(ails). The row player wins one if she matches the column player, and the column player wins one if they mismatch. In the unique MSE, both players randomize equally and both guarantee an expected 0.5 chance of winning.

Now imagine a population in which row and column players are randomly rematched and do not know their partner's identity (or, equivalently, forget their history). Then the MSE can be reached at a population level if half the players *always* choose H and half *always* choose T. This population-mixture interpretation is common and persuasive in theoretical biology. It is plausible that different animals adopt pure strategies but selection pressures guide a population toward an equilibrium mixture in which each pure strategy has the same expected payoff. In experiments we can observe both individuals and populations so we can see whether populations appear mixed, in the aggregate, even if individuals are not mixing.

An interesting puzzle is why this sort of stable polymorphic population distribution argument should apply to individual subjects in a group in the lab. One mechanism is learning but, as noted above, this is problematic because players who have learned by switching their strategies have no incentive *not* to switch once they reach equilibrium. How exactly this process works is an interesting open question.

A preview of what lies ahead can be seen in Fig. 3.1. Each point in this figure corresponds to a single strategy in a particular experiment. The graph shows the predicted MSE probability with which that strategy will be played (on the *x*-axis) against the actual relative frequency of play throughout the experiment (*y*-axis). Although there is dispersion, the MSE predictions are not bad. There is a slight tendency for low-probability strategies to be played too often (e.g., strategies that should never be played are actually played about 5 percent of the time) and high-probability strategies are not played often enough. Nevertheless, the strong relation across all the points shows that MSE has a lot of predictive power.

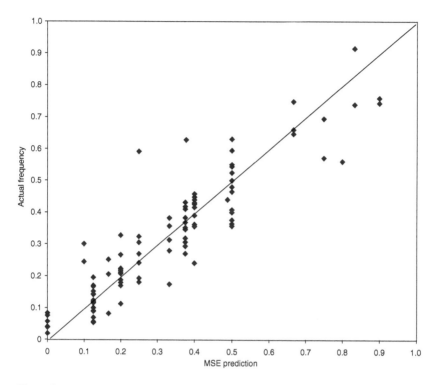

Figure 3.1. *Frequencies of different strategy choices predicted by mixed-strategy equilibrium and actual frequencies.*

3.1 Early Studies

The first wave of studies on games with MSE occurred in the late 1950s. An important early study was Kalisch et al. (1954), who were discouraged by a perceived failure of game theory predictions. Atkinson and Suppes (1958) and Suppes and Atkinson (1960) were interested in simple one-person models of learning in low-information environments. Their designs treated humans like "lower" animals. In many of their experiments subjects are not told they're playing a game (or, worse, are told they are *not* playing a game when they are) and do not know the matrix of payoffs. Despite being unable to compute equilibria, subjects tend to learn in the correct direction, and long-run frequencies are often close to MSE predictions.

A common early design used one person playing against a computerized strategy. This design is certainly useful for answering some questions. But nothing in game theory says players should use MSE mixtures against a computerized opponent. And the results are often hard to interpret because subjects usually were not told details of what the computerized opponents were doing. These experiments end up being about subjects' intuitions about the contents of computer programs created by experimenters, rather than about game theory per se.[3]

Nevertheless, the basic result in these experiments—relative frequencies of choices are somewhere between equiprobable and the MSE prediction—has held up in more recent studies. To illustrate the early style and results, I will describe a few studies in some detail (see also Estes, 1957).

Lieberman (1962) studied the 2×2 zero-sum game in Table 3.1. The payoffs are the row player's payoff in pennies; in a zero-sum game the column player's payoff is always the row player's times -1. So only row payoffs are shown. In condition O, row subjects play against the experimenter (who use MSE probabilities "in an optimal manner"). We are not told whether the experimenter choices are actually "iid" (independent and identically distributed) draws, although the choices are fixed in advance and are the same for all subjects. Lieberman reports that "subjects tended to look for patterns in the experimenter's play and anticipate his response on each trial in an attempt to win the small amounts of money involved" (1962, p. 213).

In condition O, the experimenter used the MSE probability ($P(E1) = 0.75$)) for 300 trials. Condition N had 100 trials using the MSE probabilities and then switched to 200 trials in which E1 and E2 were played equally often. In a second experiment (Malcolm and Lieberman, 1965), pairs of subjects played each other.

There is little learning across trials so only aggregate results are reported in Table 3.1. (I shall use this convention throughout: aggregate results are reported if there is little learning.) The row player frequencies for each row strategy are reported in the row corresponding to that strategy; similarly for column strategy frequencies.

Contrary to the MSE prediction, row subjects in condition O play S1 less than half the time (40.9 percent) against the properly mixing column experimenter. However, subjects *are* sensitive to the experimenter's behavior, because they switch to S2 substantially more often (65 percent) when the experimenter switches to playing E1 and E2 with equal frequency in condition N, when S2 is a strict best response. When pairs of subjects played each other in experiment 2, their frequencies were roughly halfway between equiprobable and MSE.

Lieberman also experimented with a zero-sum game with a saddle point (pure strategy equilibrium). Both he and Brayer (1964) found strong sup-

---

[3] These are the games that Aumann (1990), cited in Chapter 1, justifiably complains about.

yoffs (in pennies) and results in a 2 × 2 game

| | Column player (computer) | | | Experiment 1 | |
	E1	E2	MSE probability	Condition O frequency	Condition N frequency
	3	−1	0.75	0.409	0.651
	−9	3	0.25	0.591	0.349
	0.25	0.75			
ondition O frequency	0.250	0.750			
ondition N frequency	0.500	0.500			
requency	0.306	0.694			

1an (1962); Malcom and Lieberman (1965).

port for equilibrum play in these zero-sum games with a pure equilibrium (see also Binmore, Swierzbinski, and Proulx, 2001). These results establish that the very simplest game-theoretic concepts (which do not involve mixing) are well supported even under old-fashioned experimental conditions.

Subjects in Kaufman and Becker (1961) played five 2×2 zero-sum games. Each game has a maximin payoff of 0.95 points, and MSE probabilities ranging from 0.5 to 1.0. The subjects actually give mixtures (allocations of 100 choices in any mixture they wanted). The twist is that subjects play an impossible-to-beat rule implemented by the experimenter: The experimenter observes the subjects' mixture, and then randomizes among all experimenter mixtures that give the subject *less* than his or her maximin outcome. Because they are forced to tip their hand to the experimenter, the best subjects can do is to play maximin.

Subjects played each of the five games fifty times. The results are underreported so it is impossible to compile them in a table, but the accuracy of the MSE prediction is not bad. Absolute probability deviations averaged from 0.10 to 0.20, and decline across the five-game sequence. A surprising number of subjects converge to the exact MSE mixture on every trial until the end, and the fraction of these true MSE players rose from 10 percent to 65 percent across the five-game sequence. This unique study shows that players do choose maximin when deviations are punished by playing sequentially.

Messick (1967) studied the 3×3 game shown in Table 3.2. His subjects played against computerized opponents programmed with one of three strategies: Maximin (MSE mixtures); and two variants of fictitious play learning rules.[4] Subjects were told:

> The computer has been programmed to play so as to make as much money as possible. Its goal in the game is to minimize the amount of money you win and to maximize its own winnings. In one way the computer will have an advantage since it can remember every choice you have made and use this information to decrease your winnings. You, on the other hand, have the advantage of being human, of possessing intelligence and complete freedom and flexibility of choice which should allow you to capitalize on any weakness you perceive in the play of the machine. (Messick, 1967, p. 35)

This instruction illustrates the difficulty of interpreting results from this sort of experiment. Referring to the computer's memory seems to suggest that the computer is tracking previous choices, although it is *not* when it plays MSE.

Results from the condition in which the computerized player plays MSE are summarized in Table 3.2. Choice frequencies in the first seventy-five

---

[4] In fictitious play, a player's belief is simply an arithmetic average of what her opponent has done in the past. See Chapter 6 for details.

Table 3.2. *Payoffs and results in a 3 × 3 game*

| Row choice | Column player (computer) | | | MSE probability | Actual frequency | |
	A	B	C		Periods 1–75	Periods 76–150
a	0	2	−1	0.400	0.270	0.250
b	−3	3	5	0.111	0.390	0.290
c	1	−2	0	0.489	0.340	0.460
MSE probability	0.556	0.200	0.244			

Source: Messick (1967).

periods are close to equal, but there is movement toward MSE (increased play of strategy c) in the last seventy-five periods.

Perhaps surprisingly, subjects who played against computerized strategies using variants of fictitious play were able to beat the stuffing out of the computerized strategies. Subjects also tend to use the same strategy after a win (59 percent "stay") but switch after a loss (38 percent). This "win–stay, lose–shift" heuristic is a coarse version of reinforcement learning and shows up in many other games (e.g., the "email game" described in Chapter 5).

Summary: In early 1960s' studies, incentives were low and subjects often played against computerized rules. These results are frequently hard to interpret because there is no control over what subjects thought their computerized opponents were doing. In two cases, however, there is strong support for MSE. In Kaufman and Becker's experiment, subjects moved first and the experimenter's rule exploited deviations from MSE. Most subjects learned to play exactly the MSE within fifty periods. In Malcolm and Lieberman's experiment, pairs of subjects playing each other generated choice frequencies that lie between equal randomization and the MSE prediction.

3.2 Modern Studies

Because the interpretation of these early results was discouraging, research on zero-sum games waned. Modern work was revived by O'Neill (1987). He noted that predicted mixture probabilities depend on players' utilities for outcomes (i.e., risk-aversion), unless there are only two possible outcomes in a game. To avoid concerns about unmeasured utilities, and to improve power, O'Neill constructed a 4 × 4 zero-sum game with row payoffs (shown in Table 3.3). The game has four strategies, represented by playing cards 1–3 and joker (J). The payoffs are a 5 cent win or loss for each player, so that any monotonic utility function in which players prefer to win gives the

Table 3.3.   *Row player payoffs (in cents) and results in a 4 × 4 game*

Row choice	Column player 1	2	3	J	MSE probability	Actual frequency	QRE estimate
1	−5	5	5	−5	0.20	0.221	0.213
2	5	−5	5	−5	0.20	0.215	0.213
3	5	5	−5	−5	0.20	0.203	0.213
J	−5	−5	−5	5	0.40	0.362	0.360
MSE probability	0.20	0.20	0.20	0.40			
Actual frequency	0.226	0.179	0.169	0.426			
QRE estimate	0.191	0.191	0.191	0.426			

Source: O'Neill (1987).
Note: QRE estimate is $\hat{\lambda} = 1.313$.

same mixture probabilities. The unique MSE probabilities are 0.20 each for cards 1–3 and 0.40 for J. His subjects were matched in fixed pairs. Results are summarized in Table 3.3. The overall relative frequencies are remarkably close to the MSE predictions. Row players are predicted to win 40.0 percent of the time in MSE and actually win 41.0 percent of the time.

Also reported in Table 3.3 are estimates from the quantal response equilibrium (QRE) of McKelvey and Palfrey (1995) and Chen, Friedman, and Thisse (1996) (cf. Rosenthal, 1989). In a quantal response equilibrium (QRE), players do not choose the best response with probability 1 (as in a Nash equilibrium). Instead, they "better-respond" and choose responses with higher expected payoffs with higher probability. In practice, the QRE often uses a logit payoff response function:

$$P(s_i) = e^{\lambda \sum_{s_{-i}} P(s_{-i}) u_i(s_i, s_{-i})} \bigg/ \left(\sum_{s_k} e^{\lambda \sum_{s_{-i}} P(s_{-i}) u_i(s_k, s_{-i})} \right). \quad (3.2.1)$$

QRE uses one parameter (λ) to measure how noisily players respond to expected payoffs, and typically generate predictions somewhere between equal randomization and MSE. In the O'Neill game the QRE estimates fit the joker frequency very accurately, but mistakenly estimate, as MSE does, that other card probabilities will be equal.

Brown and Rosenthal (1990) criticized O'Neill's interpretation of his results as overly supportive of MSE. They noted that aggregate tests lack the power to distinguish MSE from alternative theories, and finer-grained analyses reject the assumption that players mix independently using the MSE probabilities. Their analysis set the stage for several other experiments described below.

Table 3.4. *Tests for temporal dependence in zero-sum games*

Effect	Coefficient	Percentage of players with significant ($p < .05$) effects			
		BR	RB exp. 1	RB exp. 2	BR94
Guessing	b_0	8	8	5	10
Previous opponent choices	b_1, b_2	30	42	35	12
Previous outcomes	c_1, c_2	38	28	20	6
Previous choices and outcomes	b_1, b_2, c_1, c_2	44	55	38	12
Previous own choices	a_1, a_2	48	48	42	42
All effects	a_i, b_i, c_i	62	72	50	52

Sources: Brown and Rosenthal (1990); Rapoport and Boebel (1992); Budescu and Rapoport (1994).
Notes: BR denotes Brown and Rosenthal (1990); RB denotes Rapoport and Boebel (1992); BR94 denotes Budescu and Rapoport (1994). $J_{t+1} = a_0 + a_1 J_t + a_2 J_{t-1} + b_0 J_{t+1}^* + b_1 J_t^* + b_2 J_{t-1}^* + c_1 J_t J_t^* + c_2 J_{t-1} J_{t-1}^*$.

They first noted that win rates across specific pairs range from 30 percent to 54 percent. Much of the variation in these win rates comes from correlation between the players' choices.[5] Where is the correlation coming from? To investigate, Brown and Rosenthal ran a logit regression of players' choices of J in period $t + 1$, denoted J_{t+1}, against two lags of opponents' choices (denoted J_{t+1}^*), and own choices and the interaction between own and opponent choices. If players are randomizing and are not able to detect nonrandomization in others' choices,[6] all the coefficients (other than the constant a_0) should be zero.

Column BR in Table 3.4 reports results from a suite of regressions that Brown and Rosenthal ran exploring different types of temporal dependence. For more than half the players (62 percent), the null hypothesis that all lag coefficients are zero can be rejected (at 0.05). For about half the subjects, the coefficients on their own lagged choices (a_1, a_2) are significant, which means players are *not* randomizing independently (typically, they play J twice in a row too rarely). A third of the subjects had significant coefficients (b_1, b_2) on lags of their opponent's J choice, which means they are trying to guess their opponent's temporal dependence. Only 8 percent

---

[5] That is, the win rate is substantially different from what it would have been if players used their observed frequencies but made draws across the 105 periods.

[6] As we shall see, the typical deviation from independent randomization is to alternate too frequently. But a player who thinks that an H is due after a string of Ts should therefore be able to guess the over-alternation and beat her opponent. So there must be some cognitive limit, or interference from a player trying to control her own randomization, that prevents widespread exploitation of nonrandomness.

of the players had a significant coefficient of contemporaneous choice J^*_{t+1}; thus, although players did respond to what they had seen (and done) in the past, they were *not* able to use this information to guess what their opponent would do in the current period. Brown and Rosenthal conclude that there is little support for the maximin hypothesis.

A sensible interpretation of what's going on follows from the "purification" interpretation of mixed equilibrium (due to Harsanyi and Aumann). Suppose a player does not think she is consciously randomizing—for example, she observes a hunch variable and conditions play on that variable. If the other player does not see the variable that generates nonrandomization, then the other player believes she faces a mixture. MSE can then be an equilibrium in *beliefs* rather than in mixtures.

A key fact in Brown and Rosenthal's reanalysis is this: Even though there is substantial temporal dependence in choices, very few players are able to detect dependence in their opponent's choice and outguess what their opponent will do (as evidenced by very few significant b_0 coefficients). Thus, there *are* substantial deviations from maximin, but players cannot detect them so the equilibrium-in-beliefs interpretation is supported. That is, although players are not mixing randomly, opponents' departures are not being detected.

Rapoport and Boebel (1992) replicated O'Neill's study with four small differences.[7] Their overall results, reported in Table 3.5, replicate O'Neill's. Actual frequencies of play are generally between MSE predictions and equal probability, but the MSE predictions can be rejected by a χ^2 test for 85 percent of the subjects. Frequencies are similar across win/loss conditions in experiments 1–2, so strategic equivalence holds.[8] Note that QRE estimates do an adequate job of capturing deviations from MSE, especially for row players.

An interesting fact is that there are no persistent skill differences in these games, because the correlation between a single subject's win rates in his or her two different sessions is only 0.17. Rapoport and Boebel also replicated the Brown–Rosenthal findings on temporal dependence (see Table 3.4) and found a little support for a behavioral model in which mixture proportions depend on the proportion of "wins" in the matrix.

Mookerjhee and Sopher (1997; see also 1994) studied four constant-sum games, with an emphasis on learning (described later in Chapter 6).

---

[7] They used a 5×5 game; stakes were higher; subjects play as both row and column players; and they test for strategic equivalence by varying win and loss payoffs in a way that should not affect MSE probabilities.

[8] It would be useful to have an alternative theory of why strategic equivalence might *not* hold for these particular parameters. For example, in standard utility theory the win and loss utilities can simply be set to 0 and 1, so they should be invariant to the absolute magnitude of the win and loss payoffs. But if win and loss utilities are cardinally scaled, and losses loom larger than gains ("loss-aversion"), then MSE predictions will differ in the two cases. It would be useful to work through specific predictions along these lines, and to choose design parameters in which strategic equivalence is most likely to be rejected in the direction of a plausible alternative.

Payoffs and results in 5 × 5 games

| | Column choice | | | | | MSE | Actual frequency | | QRE estimates | |
e	C	L	F	I	O	probability	Experiment 1	Experiment 2	Experiment 1	Experi
	W	L	L	L	L	0.375	0.293	0.306	0.286	0.2
	L	L	W	W	W	0.250	0.305	0.324	0.302	0.2
	L	W	L	L	W	0.125	0.123	0.100	0.138	0.1
	L	W	L	W	L	0.125	0.119	0.115	0.138	0.1
	L	W	W	L	L	0.125	0.160	0.155	0.138	0.1

m probability	0.375	0.250	0.125	0.125	0.125
quency (experiment 1)	0.352	0.180	0.218	0.099	0.151
quency (experiment 2)	0.346	0.193	0.202	0.116	0.143
ate (experiment 1)	0.412	0.169	0.140	0.140	0.140
ate (experiment 2)	0.410	0.184	0.135	0.135	0.135

oport and Boebel (1992).

) payoffs are ($10,−$6) in experiment 1, ($15,−$1) in experiment 2. QRE estimate parameters are $\hat{\lambda}_1 = 0.248$, $\hat{\lambda}_2 = 0$

Table 3.6.   *Row payoffs and results in games 1 and 3*

Row choice	Column choice				MSE probability	Actual frequency
	1	2	3	4		
1	W	L	L	W	0.375	0.318
2	L	L	W	W	0.250	0.169
3	L	W	$\frac{2}{3}$W	$\frac{2}{3}$W	0.375	0.431
4	L	L	$\frac{1}{3}$W	W	0.000	0.083
MSE probability	0.375	0.250	0.375	0.000		
Actual frequency	0.383	0.308	0.270	0.040		

Source: Mookerjhee and Sopher (1997).
Note: L, W, pW denote loss, win, and a p chance of win.

Table 3.7.   *Row payoffs and results in games 2 and 4*

Row choice	Column choice						MSE probability	Actual frequency
	1	2	3	4	5	6		
1	W	L	L	L	L	W	0.375	0.410
2	L	L	W	W	W	W	0.250	0.241
3	L	W	L	L	W	L	0.125	0.048
4	L	W	W	L	L	L	0.125	0.069
5	L	W	L	W	L	W	0.125	0.195
6	L	L	W	L	W	W	0.000	0.038
MSE probability	0.375	0.250	0.125	0.125	0.125	0.000		
actual frequency	0.368	0.269	0.099	0.166	0.080	0.019		

Source: Mookerjhee and Sopher (1997).

Their games are shown in Tables 3.6 and 3.7. To test for the effects of doubling stakes, a win (denoted W) is worth 5 rupees in games 1 and 3 and 10 rupees in games 2 and 4.[9] Game 1 is like game 2 except that strategies 3–5 from game 2 are collapsed into a single strategy 3 in game 1. Under the maximin hypothesis these games should be equivalent.

Pooled results across all forty periods are shown in Tables 3.6 and 3.7. Although the multinomial MSE prediction can be rejected, the results are close to MSE. Weakly dominated strategies are rarely played (2–8 percent of the time). Strategic equivalence from combining strategies 3–5 in game 2

---

[9] Monthly room and board in a student dorm is 600 rupees, so these stakes are large.

Table 3.8.   *Games and results*

Row choice	Column choice			MSE probability	Actual frequency
	7	8	9		
Game 1					
1	20,0	8,16	8,16	0.167	0.311
2	5,12	20,4	5,10	0.333	0.313
3	0,12	0,12	20,8	0.500	0.376
MSE probability	0.167	0.333	0.500		
Actual frequency	0.163	0.313	0.524		
Game 2					
1	0,0	12,16	12,16	0.167	0.074
2	15,12	0,4	15,10	0.333	0.382
3	20,12	20,12	0,8	0.500	0.544
MSE probability	0.167	0.333	0.500		
Actual frequency	0.462	0.174	0.364		
Game 3					
1	4,0	10,12	12,16	0.167	0.235
2	15,15	0,6	15,10	0.333	0.357
3	18,10	0,12	14,8	0.500	0.408
MSE probability	0.167	0.333	0.500		
Actual frequency	0.321	0.279	0.400		

Source: Tang (2001).

into a single strategy in game 1 holds on average, although columns play the combined strategy more often and rows play it less often.

Tang (1996a–c, 2001) reports experiments on three games with mixed-strategy equilibria and estimates a dizzying variety of learning models on those data. The games are shown in Table 3.8. All three games have a mixed-strategy equilibrium in which the row players play strategies 1–3 and column players play strategies 7–9, with probabilities (1/6, 1/3, 1/2). In addition, game 2 has two other classes of equilibria in which only the column player mixes.[10] The pattern of results should be familiar by now to readers who are paying attention: Deviations from the MSE proportions are small

---

[10] In one class of equilibria, the row player chooses 3, and the column player chooses any mixture of strategies 7 and 8. In the other class, the row player chooses 1 and the column player mixes between 8 and 9, with a probability of choosing 8 between 0.2 and 0.6.

Table 3.9.   *Game 1–5 row payoffs and results*

Row choice	Column choice		MSE probability	Actual frequency
	1	1		
Game 1				
1	−2	3	0.167	0.251
2	−1	−2	0.833	0.749
MSE probability	0.833	0.167		
Actual frequency	0.915	0.085		

Row choice	Column choice			MSE probability	Actual frequency
	1	2	3		
Game 2					
1	−3	−2	−3	0.000	0.044
2	−1	−1	0	1.000	0.888
3	3	−3	−3	0.000	0.068
MSE probability	0.000	1.000	0.000		
Actual frequency	0.011	0.918	0.071		

Row choice	Column choice			MSE probability	Actual frequency
	1	2	3		
Game 3					
1	−2	3	−3	0.167	0.205
2	−1	−3	0	0.000	0.056
3	0	−1	1	0.833	0.739
MSE probability	0.667	0.333	0.000		
Actual frequency	0.647	0.279	0.075		

but significant, and the predicted ranking of strategies by MSE probability corresponds to rankings of actual frequencies in most cases.

Binmore, Swierzbinski, and Proulx (2001) conducted an ambitious study with eight different games. Their view is that equilibrium play can *only* come about from learning, which implies that equilibration *necessarily* generates temporal dependence of the sort Brown and Rosenthal pointed out. Dependence is therefore *evidence* of equilibration.

The five main zero-sum games they study are shown in Table 3.9 (game 5 is O'Neill's game). Since they observe some convergence toward MSE over time, only frequencies from the last third of the experiment are reported

Table 3.9.   *(continued)*

Row choice	Column choice			MSE probability	Actual frequency
	1	2	3		
Game 4					
1	0	2	−1	0.167	0.207
2	2	0	−1	0.167	0.133
3	−1	−1	0	0.667	0.660
MSE probability	0.167	0.167	0.667		
Actual frequency	0.081	0.171	0.748		

Row choice	Column choice				MSE probability	Actual frequency
	1	2	3	4		
Game 5						
1	1	−1	−1	−1	0.400	0.439
2	−1	−1	1	1	0.200	0.187
3	−1	1	−1	1	0.200	0.224
4	−1	1	1	−1	0.200	0.150
MSE probability	0.400	0.200	0.200	0.200		
actual frequency	0.448	0.266	0.112	0.174		

Source: Binmore, Swierzbinski, and Proulx (2001).

in these tables. Relative frequencies are again close to the MSE predictions, with a slight bias toward 0.5. Fine-grained analyses show that the most frequent observations are close to the MSE on average, although the deviations are statistically significant.[11] The learning dynamics are generally consistent with best response: About 60 percent of the changes in the overall frequencies of the choice are a best response to history. Players are also very sensitive to the moving averages of their own payoffs (they switch more when their moving average is lower).

Summary: Modern studies have all used pairs of subjects playing against each other, for modest to very large stakes (in Mookerjhee and Sopher,

---

[11] Since MSE predictions are multiples of 1/6, and there are six pairs in each period, the datum from a single period can be placed into forty-nine bins representing each of the combinations of frequencies (0, 1/6, 2/6, . . . , 1) for each of the row and column players. Call the bin that has the most points in it, after all the period data are placed in bins, the "best unit predictor" (BUP).

Binmore et al. have nice plots of boxes around this BUP (1/3 wide in probability terms) and show their location relative to the MSE. In three cases the BUP boxes just graze the MSE prediction, in one game (3) the BUP box is centered right on MSE, and in game 5 it includes the MSE.

1997), in games with several strategies and (typically) only win–loss payoffs so risk tastes can't possibly matter. Actual frequencies are not far from the MSE predictions. The deviations are smallest in the experiments by Binmore et al., in which players play for 150 periods and can track moving averages of the payoffs of themselves and others. However, deviations are usually highly significant, either at the individual level or in the aggregate. Most subjects also exhibit temporal dependence—their choices depend on previous choices by themselves and others.

3.3 Subjective Randomization and Mixed Strategies

Rapoport and Budescu wrote several papers linking MSE games with psychological studies of subjective perceptions of randomness. The idea is to see whether the implicit randomization that players should do (if they want to reduce predictability in their choices when playing opponents who know their history) is similar to the kind of randomization evident when subjects are asked to produce or recognize sequences.

Many psychology studies use "production tasks" in which subjects generate random sequences or arrange a sample of outcomes in a random order. Other studies use "recognition tasks" in which subjects are asked to rate how random different series appear to be. Many conditions and response modes have been explored (see Bar-Hillel and Wagenaar, 1991).

The studies show that people reliably produce sequences whose features resemble the underlying statistical process more closely than short random sequences actually do. For example, in a class exercise I ask some students actually to flip a coin twenty times, and I ask other students to generate a sequence of flips that looks as much like a coin flip sequence as possible.[12] Student-generated sequences can usually be recognized by three tell-tale clues: (1) The number of heads is more likely to be exactly 10, and less likely to be below 8 or above 12, than the actual coin sequences; (2) there are too few runs of identical flips in the student-generated sequences (there is an average of $(n + 1)/2$ in a random sequence); and (3) the longest run in the student sequences is usually only three or four flips, whereas maximum length runs of five or six are common in actual sequences.

Alternating outcomes ("negative recency") are common, with two interesting exceptions: Children don't seem to learn this misconception until after fifth grade (Ross and Levy, 1958); and subjects trained to produce many sixty-trial sequences with extensive feedback are able to produce remarkably random sequences (Neuringer, 1986). The evidence from children is im-

---

[12] This can be done in an incentive-compatible way by telling the students who produce artificial sequences that they win money if they can fool a statistical algorithm or person who is trying to tell their sequence apart from a random one.

portant because it implies that misrandomizing is *not* a mistake that is easily erased by learning. Quite the opposite: It is a mistake that is *caused* as developing minds acquire the erroneous intuition that small samples should have all the properties of large ones (the facetiously named "law of small numbers").

Rapoport and Budescu (1992) were the first to compare sequences from a production task with strategies in a constant-sum game. Their study was motivated by four criticisms of the production and recognition paradigms: Instructional biases or vagueness may cause subjects to generate nonrandom sequences;[13] tests for randomness are problematic; few studies paid performance-based rewards; and production tasks are artificial (they don't correspond to anything people explicitly do in everyday life). All these criticisms are overcome by using games in which randomized mixing is desirable.

Rapoport and Budescu's study had three conditions. In condition D, subjects played a game of matching pennies 150 times in the usual trial-by-trial way; in condition S, subjects gave an entire sequence of 150 plays at once (which were then paired with elements of an opponent's sequence to determine 150 outcomes and payoffs); and in condition R subjects were asked to "simulate the random outcome of tossing an unbiased coin 150 times in succession."

As usual, subjects produced sequences with too many runs: Z-tests on individuals reject the iid hypothesis for 40 percent, 65 percent, and 80 percent of the subjects in conditions D, S, and R. (Note that twice as many subjects show temporal dependence in the production condition R as in the game condition D.) The game-playing environment seems to reduce deviations from randomness.

Budescu and Rapoport (1994) extended their earlier paper to a 3×3 version of a zero-sum matching pennies game. The players choose one of three colored cards; if the colors match, row wins 2 and, if they mismatch, row loses 1. The MSE is for both players to choose all three cards equally often. They again compared a game-theoretic condition D with a random-generation condition R. Regressions show significant temporal dependence, as in earlier studies (see Table 3.4, column BR94). More of the R subjects exhibit temporal dependence (typically over-alternation).

Table 3.10 reports frequencies of selected patterns. The pattern (x,x) denotes *any* of the three possible runs of two identical cards in a row, and (x,y) denotes any pair of non-identical cards. Patterns are predicted to be uncommon (compared with iid) if they are "unbalanced" and have streaks, and are predicted to be more common if they are balanced. For example, the pattern (x,x,x) has only one run and one color of card, and is thus highly

---

[13] For example, Ayton, Hunt, and Wright (1989) note that, in many experiments, subjects are told not to generate sequences with "identifiable patterns." This may discourage them from generating long runs, leading to over-alternation.

Table 3.10.   *Frequency of selected patterns in a three-strategy experiment*

Pattern length	Pattern type	Predicted frequency relative to iid	Frequency in condition		Expected frequency if iid
			D (game)	R (production)	
2	(x,x)	Lower	0.269	0.272	0.333
	(x,y)	Higher	0.731	0.728	0.667
3	(x,x,x)	Lowest	0.073	0.063	0.111
	(x,x,y)	Lower	0.196	0.209	0.222
	(x,y,y)	Lower	0.196	0.210	0.222
	(x,y,x)	Higher	0.237	0.160	0.222
	(x,y,z)	Highest	0.297	0.359	0.222
4	(x,x,x,x)	Lowest	0.020	0.018	0.037
	(x,x,x,y)	Lower	0.053	0.045	0.074
	(y,x,x,x)	Lower	0.054	0.045	0.074
	(x,y,x,x)	Lower	0.056	0.035	0.074
	(x,x,y,x)	Lower	0.058	0.037	0.074
	(y,x,z,x)	Higher	0.096	0.078	0.074
	(x,y,x,z)	Higher	0.099	0.079	0.074
	(x,y,z,x)	Highest	0.121	0.173	0.074

Source: Budescu and Rapoport (1994).
Note: iid = independent and identically distributed.

unrepresentative (and predicted to occur too rarely in subjects' choices). The pattern (x,y,z) contains one of each of the three choices and is most representative. There is strong statistical bias in which actual patterns are most and least frequent, in the direction of balance. The bias is larger in the random-generation condition R than in the game-playing condition D.

In the second part of their paper (based on Budescu, Freiman, and Rapoport, 1993) they contrast two different explanations for why game-playing subjects exhibit less temporal dependence. One hypothesis is that the game-playing subjects have a clearer goal and more motivation than sequence-generators: maintain unpredictable play so your opponent cannot outguess you. An alternative explanation is "interference": Working memory is so overwhelmed keeping track of one's own choices *and* the opponent's choices that game players literally remember less of what they did in the past, which leads them closer to "memoryless" randomization. In this view, game players are not "more rational" per se; instead, the constraint of bounded memory inhibits their ability to *mis*randomize because playing a game increases the memory constraint. This hypothesis predicts that departures from short-run randomness will be similar for D and R subjects, but departures based on more "distant memory" (such as three- and four-outcome patterns) will be stronger for R subjects. The data in Table 3.10 are consistent with this prediction.[14]

Rapoport and Budescu (1997) propose an elegant model to explain departures from randomization in a production task (cf. Rabin, 2002). It is a useful example of how good psychological modeling works. Their model combines limited working memory with the intuition behind the "representativeness heuristic." Representativeness is a heuristic used to judge conditional probabilities $P(hypothesis|evidence)$ by how representative the evidence is of the hypothesis (see Tversky and Kahneman, 1982). The idea is that a hypothesis and a piece (or sample) of evidence both have statistical properties (mean, variance, and so forth), but also have features or proximity to a category exemplar. People judge the likelihood of a hypothesis, given evidence, by how well the features of the evidence match features of the hypothesis. The same psycho-logic can extend to judgments such as $P(category|example)$. For example, if you meet a very attractive person in a Los Angeles nightclub, is he or she more likely to be a schoolteacher or a model? Since all exemplars in the category "model" are attractive, it is common to overestimate the chance the person you met is a model, neglecting the fact that the overall frequency, or base rate, of schoolteachers is much larger. The psychology of representativeness judgments is fundamentally different than Bayesian statistical reasoning because there is no natural place in it for concepts such as sampling variation, regression toward the mean in a time series, and use of base rates (priors) (see Kahneman and Frederick, 2002).

The same heuristic can be applied to producing a random sequence of coin flips. When generating samples to match the coin-flip process, subjects who are feature matching will generate samples that are "too balanced" in percentages of H and T elements. Similarly, when people are not sure about the statistical properties of a time series, if they see surprisingly long runs they may mistakenly infer serial correlation where there is none. A surprising and well-established example is the mythical belief in the "hot hand" in basketball shooting (see Gilovich, Vallone, and Tversky, 1985).[15]

In the Rapoport and Budescu model, subjects remember only the previous m elements in their sequence and use the feature-matching heuristic. They choose the $m + 1$st element to balance the number of H and T choices in the last $m + 1$ flips. If the memory length m is not very large, subjects will

---

[14] To investigate interference, Budescu et al. gave an unexpected memory quiz, asking subjects to write down as many of their own and their opponent's choices as they could remember after a matching pennies game. Subjects in the game condition D remembered fewer previous choices and were less accurate at recalling basic features of their sequences, consistent with interference.

[15] Hot hand beliefs also affect betting odds for National Basketball Association games (Camerer, 1989). Odds set, in effect, by the (dollar-weighted) median bettor were biased in favor of teams with winning streaks and against teams with losing streaks.

alternate choices too frequently. The model makes very specific predictions. For example, in two experiments with binary outcomes, H and T subjects had an estimated $P(H|H) = 0.42, P(H|HH) = 0.32, P(H|HHH) = 0.21$. The model yields predictions very close to these actual numbers if memory length m is around 7. This implied constraint on short-term memory is amazingly close to the "7 plus or minus 2" discussed almost fifty years ago in a classic psychology article by Miller (1956).

Summary: In experiments comparing randomization by subjects playing games with MSE and subjects producing sequences, the sequence-generating groups show more temporal dependence. One study suggests that the difference in behavior is due to the cognitive demands of playing the game and attending to the opponents' choices. Playing a game ties up limited working memory and interferes with the players' instinct to randomize incorrectly. Over-alternation is consistent with remembering about seven previous choices and making new choices to balance the remembered portion of the sequence.

3.4 Explicit Randomization

Three modern researchers allow players to randomize deliberately over strategies. (None knew that Kaufman and Becker, 1961, had done this thirty years earlier!) "Controlled randomization" is important because it allows players who would *like* to use iid draws, but find it hard to do so, an explicit device that helps them randomize. In addition, it gives experimenters a chance to observe explicit randomization that is rarely observable in the field.

Bloomfield (1994) studied a 2×2 game, shown in Table 3.11. His subjects controlled randomization by allocating a total of fifty choices to either of their two strategies. For example, the row player could execute the MSE ($p(A) = 0.4$) by allocating twenty choices to row A and thirty choices to row B. Players were paired randomly and each player's payoff was the *expected* payoff given both players' distributions.[16]

Bloomfield told subjects their opponent's actual (mixed) strategy and the expected payoffs they would have earned from every possible mixture. In an extra "disclosure" condition, subjects were also told their opponents' ex post expected payoffs for all strategies, to see if this information would create anticipatory or sophisticated reasoning and speed up equilibration. These information treatments are influenced by Bloomfield's interest in an adaptive dynamic in which a player's strategy probability p is adjusted by a

---

[16] For example, if the row player submitted 20 As and 30 Bs, and the column player allocated 10 Xs and 40 Ys, the row player's payoff would be $(0.4)[(0.2)80 + (0.8)40] + (0.6)[(0.2)40 + (0.8)100] = 72$.

Table 3.11. *A 2 × 2 game and results*

	Column player		MSE	Actual frequencies	
	X	Y	probability	Control	Disclosure
Row player					
A	80,40	40,100	0.400	0.416	0.397
B	40,80	100,40	0.600	0.584	0.603
MSE probability	0.600	0.400			
Actual frequency					
Control	0.545	0.455			
Disclosure	0.556	0.444			

Source: Bloomfield (1994).

fraction of the payoff gradient (the derivative of the expected utility with respect to p) based on the previous period's outcome. Adjustment based on payoff gradients leads players to spiral *away* from the MSE.[17]

Results are reported in Table 3.11. Once again, the aggregate proportions are close to the predicted MTE frequencies. Regressions of the actual mixed-strategy proportions against a player's previous probability and the payoff gradient give significant coefficients of 0.45 and 0.14, respectively, for the control conditions. The corresponding coefficients are 0.24 and 0.04 in the disclosure condition. The effect-of-payoff gradient is therefore reduced by a factor of about three by disclosure, which is consistent with players anticipating adjustment by others predictably and responding less to experience.

Ochs (1995b) also allowed explicit randomization in three versions of a matching pennies game (shown in Table 3.12), in which the payoff to the row player from the (1,1) upper-left match varied. Players choose an allocation of ten plays to each of the strategies 1 or 2. This is used to produce a randomized sequence (without replacement) of ten actual plays, which are then matched with ten plays from their opponent.

Table 3.12 shows the games, results, and estimates of steady-state frequencies derived from a useful difference equation.[18] When the row player's (1,1) match payoff changes, the row player's MSE probabilities *should not*

---

[17] To see this, suppose players are at the point $p = P(A) = 0.5$ and $q = P(X) = 0.5$. Then the expected utilities for the row and column players are $70 - 10p$ and $70 - 10q$, so the payoff gradients are both -10. The new probabilities will be $p' = p - 10h$ and $q' = q - 10h$ (where h tunes the sensitivity to the gradient). Calculation shows that (p', q') is further from the MSE of $(0.4, 0.6)$ in squared (Euclidean) distance than the starting point $(0.5, 0.5)$ is. See Crawford (1985) for details on how general this result is.

[18] The difference equation is $X_t = a + bX_{t-1} + e_t$, where X_t is "the relative frequency of 1s played as of round t." The estimator $\hat{b}/(1 - \hat{a})$ gives an estimate of the steady-state frequency, an idea first used to my knowledge in experimental economics by Camerer (1987).

Table 3.12.   Games and results

Row choice	Column choice 1	Column choice 2	MSE probability	Actual frequency	Steady-state estimate	QRE estimate
Game 1						
1	1,0	0,1	0.500	0.500	0.502	—
2	0,1	1,0	0.500	0.500	0.498	—
MSE probability	0.500	0.500				
Actual frequency	0.480	0.520				
Steady-state estimate	0.482	0.518				
Game 2						
1	9,0	0,1	0.500	0.600	0.631	0.649
2	0,1	1,0	0.500	0.400	0.369	0.351
MSE probability	0.100	0.900				
Actual frequency	0.300	0.700				
Steady-state estimate	0.350	0.650				
QRE estimate	0.254	0.746				
Game 3						
1	4,0	0,1	0.500	0.540	0.534	0.619
2	0,1	1,0	0.500	0.460	0.466	0.381
MSE probability	0.200	0.800				
Actual frequency	0.340	0.560				
Steady-state estimate	0.562	0.438				
QRE estimate	0.331	0.669				

Source: Ochs (1995b).
Note: Actual frequencies are estimated from Ochs's Figure 2. QRE parameter estimates are $\hat{\lambda}_2 = 3.24$, $\hat{\lambda}_3 = 2.66$. See McKelvey and Palfrey (1995) for details.

change, but the column player's probability of playing strategy 1 should fall. This wacky prediction is surprisingly close to correct. The relative frequencies of the row player choosing 1 vary only from 0.50 to 0.60 across games, while the frequencies of the column player choosing strategy 1 fall from 0.48 to 0.30 across games. QRE estimates account for the deviations from MSE in games 2 and 3 fairly well. Furthermore, a large number of players are strictly best responding rather than mixing—there are spikes at all-1 and all-2 allocations of the ten plays for most players.

Table 3.13.   *Choice frequencies in 4 × 4 O'Neill game*

Row choice	Column choice				MSE probability	Actual frequency	z-statistic
	1	2	3	J			
1	0.051	0.049	0.039	0.073	0.200	0.212	(1.60)
2	0.045	0.045	0.044	0.088	0.200	0.222	(2.93)
3	0.045	0.044	0.039	0.082	0.200	0.210	(2.47)
J	0.075	0.069	0.065	0.147	0.400	0.356	(−4.76)
MSE probability		0.200	0.200	0.200	0.400		
Actual frequency		0.216	0.207	0.187	0.390		
z-statistic		(3.46)	(1.52)	(−2.81)	(−1.08)		

Source: Shachat (2002).

Shachat (2002) also allowed explicit randomization. His treatment 1 uses the four-strategy O'Neill game with minor changes. His randomization procedure corrects a very subtle flaw in earlier procedures.[19] In treatment 2, players specify a probability distribution by filling a computer-displayed "shoe" of 100 cards with a composition of actions. The shoe is shuffled and the computer selects the "top" card as the realized strategy. Subjects learn their opponent's realized strategy after each period. In treatment 3 they *also* learn the opponent's mixture.

Shachat's results closely replicate O'Neill's. All three information treatments give similar results, so only pooled results are shown in Table 3.13. The table shows the relative frequencies of choices, with z-statistics testing MSE predictions in parentheses. Attentive readers can sing along with the familiar refrain: Deviations from MSE are small in size but significant.

Shachat did a more sophisticated test for temporal dependence than Brown and Rosenthal did. The independent variable is the *joint* realization

---

[19] Consider Ochs's design, in which subjects give K pure strategies and they are played (without replacement) in each of K pairings. Consider $K = 4$ in a matching pennies game with an MSE of 0.5 on each of two strategies. The unique solution in this design is for each player to designate two H and two T strategies. When they are played without replacement, however, the distribution of the number of wins for a particular player, from 0 to 4, is 1/6, 0, 2/3, 0, 1/6. This is different from the binomial distribution (1/16, 1/4, 3/8, 1/4, 1/16) that would result in a series of one-shot games in which players randomize. The difference is owing to the fact that the H and T strategies are drawn without replacement, so that wins across the K periods are negatively correlated, which spreads probability toward the chances of never winning, winning exactly twice, and always winning. In principle, feedback from these slightly "distorted" win totals could hinder the subjects' ability to learn the mixed equilibrium. Bloomfield's design errs in the opposite direction—since the expected payoff is used rather than a sample of realizations, the distribution of payoffs is a spike which gives players an average payoff more often than they would get from mixing in a series of stage games.

of a pair of J plays, using only one time lag. Tests for independence from *own* and *opponent* previous choices reject for 15 percent and 22 percent of the players, respectively, compared with 24 percent of O'Neill's players. About 10 percent of Shachat's subjects are "purists" who used pure strategies (all 100 cards of one type) in most periods. Half the subjects sometimes mix and sometimes use pure strategies. The overall card proportions used by the purists and the mixers, as groups, closely approximate the MSE mixtures. The rest of the subjects rarely used pure strategies (nine times or less). Their strategies are biased away from MSE toward equiprobable play. (Several subjects mix equally among the four strategies most of the time.)

Summary: Three studies allowed subjects explicitly to mix by choosing allocations of tickets to different strategies. The results in these controlled randomization experiments replicate earlier ones. Most subjects do not choose mixtures that correspond to the MSE proportions, and a large fraction often use pure strategies (either best-responding to what their opponent has done, or speculating on the success of a particular strategy). However, population mixtures across subjects are close to MSE predictions.

3.5 Patent Race and Location Games with Mixed Equilibria

This section describes two games that model specific examples of economic interest. Other interesting examples are omitted (e.g., mixing in posted-offer markets with market power; see Holt and Solis-Soberon, 1992; Davis and Wilson, in press).

Rapoport and Almadoss (2000) studied an investment game.[20] In the symmetric game, two firms each have an equal endowment e (such as an R&D budget) they can invest in a patent race in integer amounts. Firms keep the amount of their budget they do not spend. The firm that invests the most wins a fixed prize r; if the firms spend the same amount, neither earns the prize (reflecting, say, dissipation of gains through patent disputes). There is a unique symmetric MSE in which firms invest their entire endowment with probability $(r - e)/r$ and invest all smaller integer amounts with equal probabilities $1/r$.

Results are reported in Table 3.14. Guess what? The results are close to MSE. What a shock! Subjects do choose 0 too often, but actual choices of 1–4 are about equally frequent and close to the MSE prediction of $1/r$. The

---

[20] Amaldoss and Jain (2002) analyze a related game in which players have asymmetric mixed strategies. They find good support for the mixed-strategy equilibrium.

Table 3.14.   *Results in a symmetric patent race*

Investment	Game L ($e = 5$, $r = 8$)		Game H ($e = 5$, $r = 20$)	
	MSE probability	Actual frequency	MSE probability	Actual frequency
0	0.125	0.169	0.050	0.141
1	0.125	0.116	0.050	0.055
2	0.125	0.088	0.050	0.053
3	0.125	0.118	0.050	0.053
4	0.125	0.090	0.050	0.069
5	0.375	0.418	0.750	0.628

Source: Rapoport and Almadoss (2000).

modal choice is to bet the whole endowment of 5, as predicted.[21] Individual choices show some purification because there is a wide dispersion in the number of times a subject invests the entire endowment. In game L, for example, one-fifth of the subjects hardly ever invest the whole endowment e and a similar number invest it almost every period.

Collins and Sherstyuk (2000) looked at a simultaneous spatial location game (à la Hotelling). Three subjects simultaneously chose integers in [0,100] which correspond to "locations" of firms. Simulated customers are located at each of the 100 points and buy units from the firm nearest to them. Firm profits are proportional to units sold. Thus, subjects want to choose a location that is as far away from the other firms as possible so they can sell the most units to nearby customers (knowing other firms are trying to do the same).

Brown-Kruse, Cronshaw, and Schenk (1993) studied the classic two-firm location game, in which firms should snuggle together back-to-back at 50 (and do, experimentally). Hück, Müller, and Vriend (2002) studied a four-firm game in which firms should locate in two clusters, at 25 and 75. They found clustering at those locations, but also disequilibrium clustering in the middle.

The three-firm game is interesting because firms should avoid clustering in the middle so that they do not get squeezed by firms on both sides. Shaked (1982) showed that the unique symmetric MSE is for each firm completely to avoid locations below 25 and above 75, and to randomize uniformly over the

---

[21] Rapoport and Amaldoss estimate three learning models discussed in Chapter 6: experience-weighted attraction (EWA), reinforcement, and belief learning. EWA fits slightly better than reinforcement, but there is not much learning and none does a good job at fitting the data over time.

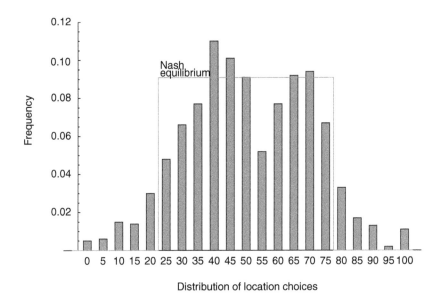

Figure 3.2.   *Frequency of location choices in three-person simultaneous Hotelling game. Source: Based on Collins and Sherstyuk (2000).*

interval [25,75]. This is a bold prediction: It implies that half of the locations will never be chosen, and all others will be chosen with equal frequency.

Distributions of locations were similar across sessions and over time, so the aggregate distribution is shown in Figure 3.2 (along with the Nash equilibrium, a thick line). Choices look like a smoothed version of the equilibrium: Low (< 25) and high (> 75) choices are rare, and most choices are in the middle. There is a dip at 55 and two prominent modes at 40 and 70—subjects are avoiding the center for fear of being squeezed. The center-avoidance can be explained by adding risk-aversion to MSE or assuming behavior is consistent with approximate (ϵ) equilibrium.[22]

Summary: Experiments modeled after patent races and three-firm spatial location show strong, and surprising, consistency with counterintuitive MSE predictions.

---

[22] The expected payoff for each of the locations [25,75] is the same, but the standard deviation is highest at 50 (because of the "squeeze risk") and falls as you move to either side. Risk-aversion may therefore explain why subjects avoid the center and cluster around 40 and 70. Collins and Sherstyuk also compute ϵ-equilibria (in which subjects choose strategies that are within $1 - \epsilon$ of best-response utility) and show that behavior is consistent with these equilibria with $\epsilon = 1$ percent or 5 percent.

3.6 Two Field Studies

In sports, players must randomize a physical move—where a pitch is thrown, a soccer ball is kicked, a tennis ball served—or be vulnerable to exploitation by another player who can guess where the ball is heading. Tennis is a good game to study because serves are hit to the left (L) or right (R) side of the opponent's court, and it is easy to see where the serve went. In a mixed equilibrium with competitive players, the expected payoffs from serving L or R should be equal.[23] If the payoffs from L and R are different, the players are not mixing properly.

Walker and Wooders (2001) collected data from ten matches between famous tennis pros, for the period 1974–97. They chose important matches (Grand Slam and Master's tournaments) that were long enough that many points were generated, to permit powerful statistical tests.[24] Testing the equilibrium prediction is simple: Are the relative frequencies of winning on L and R points close together?

The answer is yes. Each match has two players serving from two different halves of the court (called the "ad" and "deuce" court), so the data have a total of forty comparisons from the ten matches. The L and R winning frequencies are statistically different (at $p < .10$) in only two of the forty comparisons, compared with fifteen out of fifty win-rate differences in O'Neill's (1987) experiment.

The over-alternation of strategies observed in the lab is present in the tennis data too, although weaker: In eight of forty comparisons, there are either too many (six of the eight) or too few (two of the eight) runs at the $p < .10$ level.

Those who don't think experimental results generalize to natural settings are tempted to crow, "See! When the stakes are high among experienced players game theory *does* work!" Walker and Wooders (2001, p. 1535) draw a more thoughtful and even-handed conclusion:

> We do not view these results as an indictment of the many experiments that have been conducted to test for equilibrium play. The experiments have established convincingly that in strategic situations requiring unpredictable play, inexperienced players will not generally mix in the

---

[23] This isn't generally true, of course. If Pete Sampras serves to me, he can always serve to the same side of the court and still win every point. The MSE holds when players are competitive enough that consistently serving to one side of the court reduces a player's expected payoff, compared with an interior mixture.

[24] Miguel Costa-Gomes (personal communication) pointed out that choosing long matches could create a selection bias. In matches where one player is deviating from the proper MSE, that player is likely to lose more quickly; so excluding such matches may create a selection bias in favor of matches that are unusually close to MSE. Since the Walker–Wooders results *are* quite supportive of MSE, this unmet criticism is a real concern. Measuring the magnitude of any such selection bias requires comparison of long and short matches, which hasn't been done yet.

equilibrium proportions. . . . There is a spectrum of experience and expertise, with novices (such as typical experimental subjects) at one extreme and our world-class tennis players at the other. The theory applies well (but not perfectly) at the "expert" end of the spectrum, in spite of its failure at the "novice" end. There is a very large gulf between the two extremes, and little, if anything, is presently known about how to place a given strategic situation along this spectrum.

Note that there are two interesting ways in which previous experiments *do* jibe with what is found in tennis. First, Neuringer (1986) found that in experiments with very large amounts of training—perhaps comparable to the thousands of hours of practice serious tennis players engage in—subjects in the lab *could* learn to randomize. The tennis study is a kind of field replication of this experimental finding. Second, the tennis players over-alternate just as lab subjects do. Indeed, the presence of equal L–R win rates *and* statistically significant temporal dependence suggests that players receiving serves were not able to detect patterns in the serves. This is a reminder that behavior consistent with MSE could come about in two very different ways: Players could be truly randomizing; or they could exhibit temporal dependence which their opponent doesn't detect. The latter possibility means MSE is still an equilibrium in beliefs, but players' beliefs do not use information that they could (namely, temporal dependence).

Palacios-Heurta (2001) essentially replicated the Walker and Wooders paper, using data on penalty kicks in European soccer. Penalty kicks occur after certain penalties, and allow the kicker to place the ball on a penalty mark 12 yards from the goal. Other players can line up between the kicker and the goal but must be 10 yards from the ball. (Players usually bunch together in the middle, in effect forcing the player to kick either left or right.) Since it takes only 0.3 seconds for the ball to zoom into the net, the game is essentially a simultaneous-move game: The kicker usually aims for a left (L) or right (R) corner, and the goalie must commit, leaping to the kicker's L or R, before seeing where the ball is headed.

An advantage of Palacios-Huerta's study is that he is easily able to code the moves of *both* goalie and kicker, so he can tell whether they are in a mutual best-response equilibrium. (Recall that Walker and Wooders code only the direction of the serve, so it is possible given their results that servers are not minimaxing and *receiver* win rates from standing left or right are not equal.) Another advantage is that he has a sample of *all* penalty kicks, so there is no possible bias toward selection of matches that are more likely to be in equilibrium, as in Walker and Wooders.

He finds the same basic result as Walker and Wooders: Win rates for L and R kicks, and L and R goalie moves, are quite close. Aggregate results are summarized for left- and right-footed kickers in Table 3.15. The table

Table 3.15. *Scoring rates for left and right moves in soccer*

| Kick direction | Goalie move direction | | Overall |
	L	R	
Left-footed kickers			
L	0.62	0.95	0.76
R	0.94	0.61	0.81
Overall	0.76	0.80	0.78
Right-footed kickers			
L	0.50	0.94	0.76
R	0.98	0.73	0.83
Overall	0.77	0.82	0.80

Source: Palacios-Huerta (2001).

shows scoring rates for each combination of L and R kicks and goalie moves, and overall rates. The overall rates are very close for L and R for both kicks (rightmost column) and goalie moves (bottom row), for both types of kickers. The differences between L and R scoring rates on a player-by-player basis are very close to what you would expect under randomness. There is also no serial correlation in players' moves. But this is not surprising because there are long time lags between kicks (there are only a couple per game, and usually not by the same kicker) so the bias toward small-sample representativeness of temporally local sequences probably does not occur. Chiappori, Levitt, and Groseclose (2001) find basically the same result from European penalty kicks.

Summary: In MSE, serving to the left and right sides of the court or kicking toward the left or right of a soccer goal should yield the same frequencies of winning points. This prediction is confirmed in data from ten major tennis tournaments and from soccer matches.

3.7 Conclusion

This chapter has reviewed studies in which subjects play games (mostly zero-sum) with unique mixed-strategy equilibria (MSE). These games are important because MSE can be derived without the sophisticated logic required in later chapters, and social preferences to help or hurt others are limited, so game theory may predict better than in other games. At the same time, players may not actually choose equilibrium mixtures because the incentives to learn MSE are weak and proper randomizing conflicts with intuitive misperceptions of what random sequences look like.

Early studies of games with MSE are difficult to interpret because performance-based incentives were low or nonexistent, and subjects usually played against a computerized strategy whose details were not known (so there was no reason for them to choose an MSE mixture). Modern studies use higher incentives, control for possible risk-aversion, and pit two people against each other. The typical result in these modern experiments, replicated very reliably, is that aggregate frequencies of play are surprisingly close to the MSE predictions in magnitude, but the deviations are large enough to be statistically significant. The results can be summarized visually in Figure 3.1 (previewed earlier), which uses most of the data reported in this chapter. Each point in Figure 3.1 graphs the MSE prediction for a specific strategy against that strategy's observed relative frequencies.[25] The actual frequencies are sprinkled around the MSE predictions. Frequencies are a little too high for low MSE predictions, and too low for high MSE predictions. The mean absolute deviation is only 0.057 and the R^2 is .84.

MSE does well in two important senses. First, the MSE predictions are precise and counterintuitive. If you were to give these payoff matrices to somebody who knew little about game theory, and asked them to predict the probabilities with which people choose different strategies, it is unlikely that they would derive anything remotely as accurate as the MSE predictions. Many people would be surprised at where the MSE predictions come from, and might be even *more* skeptical after you go through the calculations! Good theories are not just right, they are boldly and surprisingly right. Using these criteria, MSE is a good theory, although the deviations are significant.

Second, deviations are damning only if they suggest a better alternative theory. However, it is hard to think of a radical alternative to MSE to explain observed deviations. Learning theories are a natural candidate, but there is often little apparent learning in these MSE games and the data are too statistically noisy to permit accurate identification of how players are learning (see Chapter 6).

A candidate alternative theory is quantal response equilibrium (QRE). Figure 3.3 plots observed frequencies against QRE estimates, for the subsample of games where QRE estimates have been computed (reported throughout this chapter). The points are a little closer to the identity line in Figure

---

[25] The graph uses $n - 1$ data points from games with n strategies, since using all the data creates an obvious "double-counting" because the relative frequencies in a game add to one. In games with three or more strategies, the strategy with an MSE proportion closest to 0.50 is excluded, unless there are two or more strategies with equal predicted frequencies; then one of the strategies predicted to be equiprobable is excluded. Furthermore, strategies that are predicted to be played with zero probability are always included, to see at a glance how often weak dominance is violated.

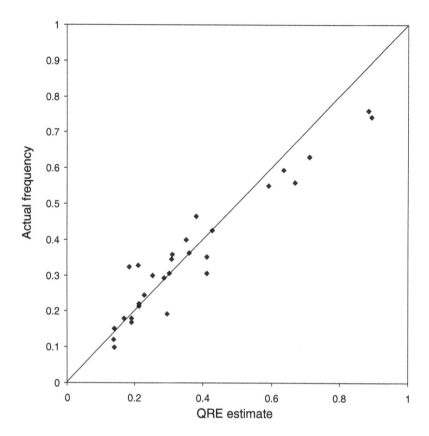

Figure 3.3.   *Frequencies of different strategy choices predicted by quantal response equilibrium and actual frequencies.*

3.3 than in Figure 3.1, which is visual evidence that QRE is reducing deviations.[26] However, QRE predicts certain kinds of payoff sensitivity which are not observed in the data (see McKelvey, Palfrey, and Weber, 2000), so there is room for improvement (see also Goeree, Holt, and Palfrey, 2000).

In repeated games with the same partner, a player should choose randomly from an iid distribution so an opponent cannot see any temporal dependence in a player's sequence of choices and outguess her. In fact, there is pronounced temporal dependence in virtually every game where

[26] The R^2 for the QRE–actual Figure 3.3 plot is .92, compared with .84 for the corresponding subsample of points out of all those in Figure 3.1. (Not all Figure 3.1 points are in Figure 3.3 because there are not QRE estimates for all the games.) The mean absolute deviation is 0.047, compared to 0.067 for the same points in the MSE-actual comparison.

scientists have looked for it: Players alternate choices too frequently. It appears that players have limited working memory (recalling seven to eight previous plays, consistent with the typical measured size of short-term memory) and try to balance the number of previous choices to represent the MSE proportions. These two ingredients lead to over-alternation, and are parametrically quite accurate in explaining the sequences subjects produce. The fact that younger children do *not* over-alternate is an important part of the psychological story too—as their minds develop, they learn away from randomization toward the mistaken idea that short sequences should represent the properties of the underlying statistical process.

A modern interpretation of MSE is that players need not actually randomize, as long as other players cannot guess what they will do. An MSE can be an "equilibrium in beliefs": Players' beliefs about the likely frequency with which their current opponent will choose different strategies are correct on average, and make them indifferent about which strategy they play. Three recent studies allowed players explicitly to randomize, so that the experimenter could observe whether they are truly mixing or not. Many players *do not* explicitly mix in any given period, but aggregate frequencies are close to the MSE proportions, which is consistent with an equilibrium in beliefs.

A clever field study by Walker and Wooders using data from tennis tournaments exploits the fact that, in an MSE, a player's expected payoffs to different strategies should be equal if other players are randomizing. The percentage of points won when serving to the left- and right-hand sides of the court, in a sample of ten major tennis tournaments, is statistically very close, as MSE predicts. These top professional players also over-alternate as we see in the lab (although less strongly). Seasoned pros with much at stake and decades of experience seem to have learned how to mix; laboratory subjects have not. Since most naturally occurring game playing probably lies between these extremes, having both sorts of data available is useful. What we should be doing now is searching for general theory to explain the full range of behavior.

4
Bargaining

BARGAINING IS THE PROCESS by which economic agents agree on the terms of a deal. Defined this broadly, bargaining is possibly the most basic activity in economic life. Even in thick, competitive markets where traders closely resemble the "price-takers" of economic theory, haggling occurs over time of delivery, repairs, side payments, and quality, as well as price. Prices on commodities exchanges, for example, are actually bargains between traders who shout at each other in the pit.

Since bargaining is central to economic life, it has been the subject of constant attention. Edgeworth (1881) created the famous "Edgeworth box" to show the range of possible outcomes of a bargain, but was frustrated by his inability to reach a unique solution. Zeuthen (1930) and Hicks (1932) later defined theories of bargaining which proceeded in several steps, to describe bargaining as it often takes place and to come to a sharp prediction about what outcomes would result. Nash (1950, 1951) approached bargaining in two different ways. First, he proposed a series of axioms that any reasonable bargaining solution should obey, and showed that maximizing the product of the agents' utilities (beyond their utilities from an exogeneous "threat point") was the solution that uniquely satisfied his axioms (subsequently called the "Nash bargaining solution"). Second, in a quite different paper, he proposed a "noncooperative" solution in which predicted outcomes depend on the structure by which the bargaining took place. Nash envisioned a unification of the two approaches—the "Nash program." The unification finally came in the 1980s, when Binmore, Rubinstein, and Wolinsky (1986) showed that subgame perfect equilibria of noncooperative games with a certain alternating-offer structure were the same as the utility product maxima prescribed by the Nash bargaining solution.

Because bargaining seems so indeterminate, experiments on what happens proved useful (beginning with Fouraker and Siegel, 1963). This chapter reviews experimental studies of bargaining. As throughout the book, I primarily describe cumulation of regularities from experiments by comparing behavior with sharp theoretical predictions. Empirical regularity then suggests psychological principles that can be formalized in behavioral game theory. The interested reader should also read Roth's (1995b) chapter in the *Handbook of Experimental Economics*, which covers much the same ground with important differences.

Paralleling Nash's two-pronged approach, experimental studies of bargaining can be divided into two classes: In *unstructured* bargaining, the details of how the bargaining proceeds (the type of messages players can send, the order in which they make offers, and so forth) are left up to the players; in *structured* bargaining, the details of the bargaining procedure are specified by the experimenter. Structured experiments have the advantage of enabling an observer to predict what bargaining outcomes might occur from theories of noncooperative equilibrium behavior. Unstructured bargaining tells us what results when players are free to invent their own rules, and is arguably a better model of naturally occurring bargaining.

A quite different approach to the study of unstructured bargaining has flourished in applied psychology, under the rubric of "negotiation research" (see Bazerman et al., 2000, for a review). Negotiation research blends three elements: an early interest among social psychologists (beginning in the 1960s) in negotiation as an area of application; Raiffa's (1982) use of elements of game theory and decision theory to improve negotiating skills; and the idea from 1980s behavioral decision research that we can identify systematic ways in which negotiators depart from the prescription of decision analysis.

In one of several widely used negotiation paradigms (Bazerman, Magliozzi, and Neale, 1985), participants negotiate over numerical or categorical levels of each of several issues (e.g., prices or quality) using free-form communication with a time deadline. They each have a private point schedule that shows how many points they earn depending on how each issue is resolved (but little information about what other players' point schedules might look like). Since subjects have clear preferences, it is easy to evaluate whether an agreement is Pareto-efficient, which side benefits most, and so forth. One general finding is that deals are not Pareto-efficient, and are affected by systematic heuristics (e.g., players instinctively assume points sum to a constant, so the negotiation is purely competitive), normatively irrelevant factors (e.g., whether points are positively or negatively "framed"), and other cognitive variables that are not part of game-theoretic bargaining theories.

To date, there has been little mutual influence between negotiation research and the game theory experiments reported in this chapter (though some researchers do both, and the overlap is growing). Most negotiation researchers think game theory assumes too much rationality to be descriptively accurate, while experimental economists view game theory as an approximation that can be improved by careful observation. Many negotiation researchers are psychologists who care more about cognitive processes, rather than simply focusing on outcomes as economists typically do. The style of experimentation in negotiation research also makes it hard to know which kind of game theory to apply (since the negotiations are dynamic games of incomplete information designed to reflect the complex world of actual negotiation rather than the simplified world of theory). Many negotiation researchers also teach in business or policy schools and don't find game theory the most useful prescription for improving negotiation. It is tempting to conclude that the research interests of experimental economists and negotiation researchers are simply more different than they appear at first blush; so both sides can safely ignore each other. But many of the research questions *are* the same, and are arguably converging (especially as experimental economists become more interested in issues such as mental representation, learning, and bounded rationality, which have long been on the minds of negotiation researchers). And there are surely some unexploited gains to intellectual exchange between the two fields.

4.1   Unstructured Bargaining

4.1.1   Unstructured Bargaining over Ticket Allocations

Early studies centered around the cooperative Nash bargaining solution. Because the bargaining solution did not specify a protocol or set of rules, these experiments usually gave subjects a period of time in which to bargain and did not restrict communication at all.

Nash's solution assumes that the key structural features in any bargaining situation are the set of feasible agreement points (S) and the disagreement point (d_1, d_2). Nash showed that there is a unique Pareto-optimal solution point S^* which obeys several appealing axioms.[1] The Nash solution is the point that maximizes the *product* of the utility gains above the disagreement point, i.e., $S^* = \text{argmax}_{(x_1,x_2)}(x_1 - d_1)(x_2 - d_2)$.

A crucial assumption is that points in S are assumed to be measures of the preferences a player has for various bargaining outcomes. In practice, of course, this requires some specification of a utility function for outcomes. In early tests, when the Nash solution predicted unequal monetary payoffs,

---

[1]The axioms are symmetry (if $d_1 = d_2$, if the point (x_1, x_2) is in S^* then (x_2, x_1) is also); independence of irrelevant alternatives (if the solution to a game (S, d) is contained in a subset T of S, then that point is the solution to (T, d) also); and independence of the solution from affine transformations of payoff utilities.

players often deviated in the direction of equal payoffs (e.g., Nydegger and Owen, 1975; Rapoport, Frenkel, and Perner, 1977). However, these early experiments did not control for the way in which payoffs yield utility. As a result, a rejection of the theory is a rejection only of the *joint* hypothesis that the solution is being applied *and* that payoffs are mapped into utilities in a particular way (typically risk-neutrality).

This realization led Roth and Malouf (1979) to look for a procedure that might permit them to know how bargaining payoffs lead to utilities. There are three general strategies for controlling preferences in experiments: assume, measure, or induce (see Chapter 1 for more discussion of methodology). Early studies assumed preferences were risk neutral. An alternative strategy is to elicit measures of utility for various bargaining outcomes, and plug these measurements into the theory to generate predictions (e.g., Murnighan, Roth, and Schoumaker, 1988). Yet another alternative is to try to induce (or control) preferences.

Roth and Malouf (1979) used a "binary lottery" technique to induce risk-neutrality, first proposed by Cedric Smith (1961) and later generalized to induce any risk preference by Schotter and Braunstein (1981) and Berg et al. (1986). The idea is that players bargain over a distribution of one hundred lottery tickets. Each player has a fixed cash prize, and the number of lottery tickets they get by bargaining determines their chance (out of one hundred) of earning the fixed prize. A player who bargains for seventy-two tickets, for example, has a 0.72 chance of winning her fixed prize and a 0.28 chance of winning nothing.

The binary lottery technique induces risk-neutral preferences if subjects are indifferent between compound lotteries and their single-stage equivalents (e.g., if they are indifferent between having a 0.5 chance of thirty-two tickets, or having sixteen tickets for sure). I am cautiously pessimistic about success of the binary lottery technique, because reduction of compound lotteries has failed repeatedly in many direct and indirect tests. Furthermore, there are *no* published studies showing that paying in lottery tickets actually works and gives different results than paying money (though Prasnikar, 1999, is supportive). However, the technique may prove useful once the conditions under which it works are better established (see Chapter 1 for a longer discussion.)

Nash's theory takes as an axiom that bargaining solutions should not be sensitive to affine transformations of payoffs (i.e., adding a constant or multiplying by a positive constant). This is actually quite a strong property. It implies, for example, that bargaining over lottery tickets should not be sensitive to the size of the monetary prizes players can earn if they win their lotteries (or to their information about those prizes). Roth and several colleagues conducted a thorough series of tests, which generally reject this property and suggest an alternative.

Table 4.1. *Results in binary lottery bargaining games*

Information condition	Money prizes	Number of tickets for player 2							Fraction of disagreement
		20	25	30	35	40	45	50	
Full	($1,$1)	0	0	1	0	1	0	20	0.00
	($1.25,$3.75)	1	6	3	2	2	1	4	0.14
Partial	($1,$1)	0	0	0	0	0	1	14	0.06
	($1.25,$3.75)	0	0	0	0	0	3	13	0.00

Source: Roth and Malouf (1979).

In Roth and Malouf (1979), players bargained over allocations of one hundred lottery tickets. Tickets determined the chance of winning either equal prizes ($1) or unequal prizes ($1.25 for player 1 and $3.75 for player 2). They also varied whether both subjects knew both prizes ("full information"), or each subject knew only her own prize ("partial information").[2] Under all conditions, the Nash bargaining solution predicts the 100 chips would be divided evenly.

The number of agreements giving different fractions of lottery tickets is shown in Table 4.1. Although the sample is very small (only nineteen bargaining pairs), the results are very clear, and replicate earlier findings in which tickets were converted into money at different rates (e.g., Nydegger and Owen, 1975). Agreements cluster heavily on 50–50 splits and disagreement is rare except when *both* subjects know that prizes are unequal.[3] When player 2 has the larger $3.75 prize, the allocation of twenty-five tickets to her and seventy-five to player 1 equalizes the expected *dollar* payoffs of the players. When prizes are known to be unequal, players seem to be torn between dividing tickets evenly (giving fifty to player 2) and dividing tickets unevenly to equate dollar payoffs (giving twenty-five to player 2), and there are also many agreements between these two modes. Players are clearly sensitive to

[2] They also varied the maximum number of tickets that player 2 could earn. In their games 1 and 3 the maximum was one hundred; in games 2 and 4 the maximum was sixty. This variation is important because a solution proposed by Raiffa (1953) is sensitive to the maximum payoff a bargainer can get. Raiffa's idea is that the hypothetical ideal point, $(\bar{x}_1, \bar{x}_2)$, consisting of the maximal feasible payoffs each player might get, could influence the bargaining (even though this point is usually not itself a feasible outcome). Raiffa suggested that the *ratio* of the players' gains, relative to the disagreement point, should equal the ratio of the gains from the disagreement point to $(\bar{x}_1, \bar{x}_2)$. Kalai and Smorodinsky (1975) later showed that Raiffa's solution is the unique solution following from the four Nash axioms, with a property called individual monotonicity substituted for independence of irrelevant alternatives. In fact, behavior in games 1 and 2 is quite similar, and behavior in games 3 and 4 is quite similar, so that Raiffa's idea is rejected in this experiment.

[3] This strong tendency to conform to a simple focal division is also observed in the field; see Young and Burke (2001) on sharecropping contracts in Illinois.

money payoffs which result from various ticket allocations, violating the axiom of independence from affine transformations.[4] There are also more disagreements (14 percent) when prizes are known to be unequal. Roth and Murnighan (1982) replicated this result in a more complex design (see Roth, 1995b, for details).

Murnighan, Roth, and Schoumaker (1988) pointed out an interesting regularity in several of their earlier experiments: Virtually all pairs settled in the final minutes of the nine to twelve minutes allotted. The obvious explanation is that players are trying to convey private information about stubbornness or costs of delay (see Roth, 1995b, 323–27).

Roth and Schoumaker (1983) explored focal points in bargaining with a neat twist: Players bargained with a computer that was programmed (unbeknownst to them) to give the subject a disproportionate share. As a result, the players developed expectations about receiving disproportionate shares. Then players began to bargain with other human players, and all players' histories were commonly known. Players who had "strong reputations," having received generous agreements in the past, were able to get generous agreements when playing against the new subjects. Reputations that were developed exogenously determined later equilibrium allocations.

A similar focal point effect in bargaining was documented by Mehta, Starmer, and Sugden (1992). In their games two players divide £10 in a "Nash demand game." Both players state a demand. If the demands add to £10 or less, they get their demands; otherwise they get nothing. Before bargaining, subjects are dealt four cards randomly from a deck with eight cards: four aces and four deuces. Since subjects know the composition of the deck, they can tell from their own hand how many aces the other subject has (namely, four minus their own number). Subjects were told that all four aces were worth £10 together, so that to earn money they had to pool their aces and agree on how to divide the £10 in unstructured bargaining. The game is like two players bringing resources to a partnership, which are worthless outside of the partnership but which might be perceived as affecting how much of the gains they are entitled to. The aces were worthless—having more of them did not improve a person's outside option payoff—but they might still create focal points. For example, if a person who was dealt one ace thought that the person with the three aces would demand £7.50, then the first person should demand only £2.50.

---

[4] Roth and Malouf propose an alternative axiom, in which allocations are independent of transformations of payoffs that preserve ordinal preferences, and that preserve information about which player makes larger gains at any given payoff. They show, rather remarkably, that substituting this alternative axiom in lieu of Nash's, along with Pareto-optimality, symmetry, and independence of irrelevant alternatives, implies a unique solution that yields the largest *minimum* gain from disagreement for the two players. This point always equalizes gains, and has a maximin or Rawlsian flavor. If players are bargaining over expected dollar payoffs rather than tickets, this solution is the (25,75) point frequently observed in the data.

Table 4.2. *Bargaining demands by number of aces held*

	Number of aces		
Demand	1	2	3
£2.50	11	0	0
£3.00–£4.50	5	1	1
£5.00	16	40	17
£5.50–£7.00	0	1	11
£7.50	0	0	4
Sample size	32	42	33

Source: Mehta, Starmer and Sugden (1992).

Table 4.2 shows the distribution of demands.[5] When both bargainers had two aces, there is a very sharp agreement on an equal split (demanding £5). However, when one had one ace and the other had three, about half the subjects demanded half the pie, and the other half demanded a fraction equal (or near) to the fraction of aces they held. As a result, there is 22 percent disagreement in cases with one and three aces. These results show how descriptions of the game that are completely payoff irrelevant can affect bargaining substantially (and, by introducing competing focal points, also create disagreement).

Roth (1985) proposes a simple way to explain outcomes, and disagreement rates, as the result of coordination among multiple focal points. Suppose players make simultaneous proposals to divide one hundred tickets either $(50,50)$ or $(h, 100 - h)$, which gives a fraction h to player 1 and $1 - h$ to player 2. This coordination game has a mixed-strategy equilibrium in which player 1 demands the larger amount h with probability $(h - 50)/(150 - h)$ and player 2 demands $(50,50)$ with probability $(h - 50)/(h + 50)$. The mixed-strategy equilibrium predicts a very specific disagreement rate, $(h - 50)^2/[(150 - h)(50 + h)]$. Roth's earlier (pre-1985) experiments with different values of h that equalize dollar payoffs allow a test of the theory. Predicted disagreement rates in the mixed-strategy equilibrium in three different h conditions are 0, 7 percent, and 10 percent. The corresponding observed disagreement rates are 7 percent, 18 percent (22 percent in Mehta et al.), and 25 percent. The observed disagreement

---

[5] No subjects were dealt zero or four aces, although their behavior would be interesting.

rates are too high, but they do rise with h as predicted and are close enough to encourage a further test.

Murnighan, Roth, and Schoumaker (1988) designed a test with a wider range of prize pairs, creating equal-dollar focal points at h values of 60, 70, 80, and 90. The disagreement frequency was constant across h, although it should vary from 1 percent to 19 percent if the coordination failure model is right, so the coordination model did not hold up as well as hoped.

4.1.2 Self-Serving Interpretations of Evidence in Unstructured Bargaining

Serious bargaining disputes, such as divorces, wars, and strikes, are often inflamed by a difference in the bargainers' perceptions about what is fair. This difference is often "self-serving": Players believe that what is better for them is also fair.

For example, in the studies by Roth et al. described in the previous subsection, the self-serving bias predicts that players will be drawn to the focal point that gives them more. Indeed, Roth and Malouf (1979) report that, in the messages players sent to one another, arguments in favor of the (50,50) split of lottery tickets almost always came from high-prize players (who get more than from equal-ticket splits than they would from equal-payoff divisions). The model of disagreement as coordination failure could be easily extended to incorporate self-serving bias if players choose the equilibrium demand that benefits themselves with a probability that is *greater* than the mixed-strategy equilibrium probability. This extension would raise the predicted disagreement rate, bringing it closer in line to the data.

Kagel, Kim, and Moser (1996) report evidence consistent with self-serving biases from ultimatum game bargaining (see Chapter 2). Closely related examples are games in which the presence of an outside option can create multiple focal points and disagreement results if players favor the focal points that are better for themselves (see Knez and Camerer, 1995, in Chapter 2). Similar results are reported in outside option games by Binmore, Shaked, and Sutton (1989) and Binmore et al. (1998) (see below). When outside options are large enough to create a substantial gap between the equal-split and equal-surplus points, disagreement is common.

There is a large body of literature in psychology, some of which has seeped into economics, on the degree to which preferences influence beliefs self-servingly (see Babcock and Loewenstein, 1997). Self-serving biases come in many varieties.

Many studies show that people are overconfident about how they compare with others. For example, *everyone* thinks their sense of humor is above average. In a College Board study of a million high school students, virtually all students rated themselves as being at least average at "getting along well with others" and a quarter of the students said they ranked in the top

1 percent. A related phenomenon is "wishful thinking"—the belief that good outcomes are particularly likely.[6] However, these expressed beliefs have been linked to monetary rewards in only a few studies.[7]

Loewenstein et al. (1993) and Babcock et al. (1995, 1997) conducted a thorough series of experiments on self-serving biases (see also Thompson and Loewenstein, 1992, and Gächter and Reidl, 2000, for a clever recent paper). In their studies, pairs of subjects bargained over how to settle a legal case, adapted from an actual suit and consisting of twenty-seven pages of background, depositions, and exhibits. In the case, a motorcyclist plaintiff sues an automobile driver defendant for $100,000 in damages for injury. Subjects had thirty minutes in which to settle the case by agreeing on a payment from the defendant to the plaintiff. Every five minutes, both sides incurred $5,000 in legal fees. If the case did not settle after six periods, an award was imposed by a judge (an actual retired judge who presided over such cases). Before negotiating, subjects guessed the amount the judge would award and what they thought was fair. Subjects were paid either in dollars, scaling $10,000 case dollars to one actual dollar, or in grade points derived by comparing the performance of each player in a given role to others in the same role.[8] Subjects were students at Carnegie-Mellon (in public policy), Penn (undergraduate business), Texas (law), and Chicago (MBA).[9]

Some summary statistics are shown in Table 4.3. In the two control conditions, settlement takes three to four five-minute periods on average and about 70 percent of the cases settle. The gap between the plaintiff's guess about the expected judgment and the defendant's (shown in the second-from-right column) is about $20,000, which is a substantial disagreement for a case worth up to $100,000. The difference in expected judgments is also highly predictive of whether bargaining pairs settle or not.

---

[6] Forsythe, Rietz, and Ross (1999) show wishful thinking effects in experimental "political stock markets." Bar-Hillel and Budescu (1995) note that wishful thinking is often hard to establish empirically. A likely explanation is that wishful thinking is partly offset by "defensive pessimism," which leads people who strongly prefer an event to occur to hedge their emotional bet by downplaying its likelihood to reduce ex post disappointment.

[7] Camerer and Lovallo (1999) found that overconfidence about their relative skill in trivia led subjects to enter a competitive market, in which more skilled players earned more, too frequently. The result was that, collectively, entrants were guaranteed to lose money. Another example is the reaction of traders in the Iowa "experimental political stock market" to common news. In those markets, traders purchase shares that pay a dividend if a particular candidate wins an election (see Forsythe, Rietz, and Ross, 1999). After a televised presidential election debate between Bush and Dukakis, traders who were pro-Bush supporters before the debate bought more Bush shares (i.e., shares that paid a dividend if Bush won the election) and pro-Dukakis supporters bought more Dukakis shares. Both sides thought their candidate won the debate, and were willing to bet money that they were right.

[8] There was no significant difference in paying dollars or grade points. Indeed, a casual calculation in Camerer and Loewenstein (1993) suggests the grade-point scheme might create very large financial incentives, to the extent that superior grades help students get better-paying jobs.

[9] There were no differences among these subject pools.

Table 4.3. *Settlement and judgment bias in "sudden impact" experiments*

Experimental condition	No. of pairs	Settlement statistics			Difference in E (judgment)	
		Frequency	No. of periods	Standard error	Mean	Standard error
Control (knew roles)	47	72%	3.75	.28	$18,555	3,787
Did not know roles	47	94%	2.51	.21	−$6,275	4,179
Significance		(< .01)	(< .01)		(< .01)	
Control	26	65%	4.08	.46	$21,783	3,956
List weaknesses	23	96%	2.39	.34	$4,676	6,091
Significance		(.01)	(.01)		(.02)	

The cause of the self-serving bias, and a way to get rid of it, are established by different treatment conditions. The top panel shows the difference between a control condition, in which bargainers are informed of their role *before* they read the case, and a treatment condition, in which they read the case first, *then* find out their role, state what they think is fair and what they expect the judge to award, and bargain (see Babcock et al., 1995). If the self-serving bias occurs during the process of encoding case information, there should be no bias in the "did not know roles" condition.[10] Indeed, these subjects have no significant bias, and settle more rapidly (2.51 periods) and more frequently (94 percent) than the control group. Of course, assigning roles *after* learning about the case is not a practical way to reduce self-serving biases in practice because prospective defendants and plaintiffs know their roles in advance.[11] Therefore, Babcock et al. (1997) investigated other "debiasing" techniques that could reduce the self-serving bias and increase settlement. The bottom panel of Table 4.3 shows one technique that works—weakness listing. In this condition, after learning their roles and reading the case (but *before* saying what was fair and guessing what the judge awarded), these subjects were told about possible bias and asked to list weaknesses in their case. Listing weaknesses works: 96 percent of pairs settle, in an average of 2.39 periods, and there is no self-serving bias in expectations about the judge's award. Psychologists feel that they understand a phenomenon when they can "turn it on and off." (Affecting policy also

---

[10] Similar "top–down" encoding biases occur routinely in perception, categorization, and other cognitive processes. For example, after buying a new car, people suddenly notice more of the same type of car on the road.

[11] However, many lawyers say that part of their job is precisely this sort of "debiasing," by drawing a veil of ignorance in front of their clients' eyes or helping them see their cases as others would.

relies on this kind of understanding.) Weakness listing passes this test.[12] Formal models of self-serving bias could be built by allowing preferences to influence beliefs, then applying Bayes' rule (see Rabin and Schrag, 1999).

Summary: Bargaining outcomes are affected by focal points—psychologically prominent divisions which are noticed by both players. The dependence of outcomes on chip value observed by Roth et al. violates a basic assumption in the bargaining solution (that affine transformations of utility should not matter). Experimental outcomes can be interpreted as the result of bargainers trying to coordinate when there are multiple focal points (although a precise model of this sort did not predict well in the one study designed to test it). Self-serving biases occur when players think that an outcome that favors themselves is particularly likely. Experiments by Babcock, Loewenstein, Issacharoff, and myself show such biases in bargaining over a legal case, and the size of the bias in a pair predicts the length of costly delay and chance of settlement. The bias occurs largely during the encoding phase—when reading case facts, one's role biases what information is attended to.

4.2 Structured Bargaining

There are many experiments on structured bargaining. In this section I describe results from alternating-offer games with finite and "infinite" horizons, and games with random termination and outside options.

4.2.1 Finite Alternating-Offer Games

In naturally occurring bargaining, players often alternate offers (perhaps because making two offers in a row is a sign of weakness). Delay is costly because the amount being bargained over loses value (owing to conventional time discounting, impatience, or perishability), or because there is a fixed cost to delay (owing to opportunity costs from lost wages and profits in a strike, for example).

---

[12] Weakness listing helps because it improves the settlement rate, reducing the joint costs to delay. An interesting, unanswered, question is whether having one side list weaknesses benefits that side, if the other side does not. The net effect could go either way: The side that lists weaknesses is more inclined to settle, but might also settle on unfavorable terms. These "sudden impact" studies also illustrate how the contextual domain of the experiment can affect behavior. If self-serving biases occur because preferences affect how ambiguous information is encoded, or retrieved from memory, then it is important to conduct experiments in which encoding and retrieval biases may occur. Explicit random devices such as draws from bingo cages may produce different results since it is hard to misperceive the color of a bingo ball (though see Forsythe, Rietz, and Ross, 1999).

There is much theory about alternating-offer bargaining with costly delay, and several experiments as well (see Stähl, 1972; Rubinstein, 1982).[13] In theory, the player with the higher discount factor[14] has a large advantage (if others players know this). More patient players can afford to wait out a protracted process of bargaining and extract concessions from impatient players. An example is wealthy tourists travelling in relatively poor countries, trying to buy goods from local merchants. The merchants know that the tourists are in a hurry, and can often exploit their impatience by drawing out haggling over many minutes or hours. Children also have a knack for sensing disparities in waiting costs, realizing that a well-timed temper tantrum or "work slowdown" ("I *am* hurrying. . . . You know I just learned how to tie my shoes!") when a parent is in a hurry may give them power to bargain for candy or a cool car.

The first alternating-offer experiments were conducted by Binmore, Shaked, and Sutton (1985). They used a two-period game. In the first period player 1 offers a division of 100 British pence to player 2. If player 2 rejects it, then the "pie" being divided shrinks to 25p (i.e., $\delta = 0.25$) and player 2 makes a counteroffer to player 1. If player 1 rejects that counteroffer, the game is over and neither player gets anything (i.e., the second round of the game is an ultimatum game). The subgame perfect equilibria are centered around an initial demand of 75p, leaving 25p for player 2.

In the first period, there is a sharp mode around the equal split point (50p), some offers near the subgame perfect equilibrium of 25p, and quite a few offers between those two points. After the first play, subjects in the role of player 2 made hypothetical opening demands as player 1 in a second game B.[15] Their opening offers shift dramatically toward the perfect prediction of 25p.

Binmore et al. concluded that the experience subjects had in the player 2 role in the first game led them to realize that a sensible player 2 would accept any offer that leaves them 25p. Then they "exploit" this imagined behavior in their new roles as player 1 in the second game, offering only 25p. Further studies with this kind of "role reversal" protocol sometimes

---

[13] Rubinstein is careful to note that he does not think having a truly infinite horizon is crucial. Instead, the key point is simply that there is no end that is commonly known by the players, so the periodicity exploited to derive the solution is conceivable.

[14] The discount factor δ refers to the multiplier on future gains that measure their present value. The discount rate r is related to δ by $\delta = 1/(1 + r)$.

[15] The comparison of player-2 offers in the hypothetical second game with player-1 offers in the first game creates a triple "confound" in experiment conditions: The second-game offers could be different because of experience (second game versus first game), role reversal (player 2s making opening offers versus player 1s), or incentives (they were hypothetical in the second game versus real in the first game). The confounds are unfortunate because these data are the strongest evidence of rapid learning of perfect equilibrium.

Table 4.4. *Frequencies of offers and rejections in alternating-offer bargaining*

Offer category ($)	Two rounds		Three rounds		Five rounds	
	Offer	Rejection	Offer	Rejection	Offer	Rejection
> 2.50	—	—	0.10	—	—	—
2.50	0.05	—	*0.70*	—	0.05	—
2.01–2.49	—	—	0.05	—	—	—
1.71–2.00	0.03	—	0.08	—	0.38	0.067
1.70	—	—	—	—	*0.35*	0.071
1.51–1.70	—	—	—	—	0.10	—
1.26–1.50	*0.45*	0.11	0.08	0.67	0.05	—
1.25	0.38	0.20	—	—	—	—
< 1.25	0.10	1.00	—	—	0.08	1.000

Source: Neelin, Sonnenschein, and Spiegel (1988).
Note: Medians are in italic type.

show learning (see Harrison and McCabe, 1992, described below), but the learning is not as fast as Binmore et al. observed.

These data inspired a skeptical partial replication by Neelin, Sonnenschein, and Spiegel (1988). In their design, players participated in a two-round game like that of Binmore et al., with payoffs $5.00 and $1.25, a three-round game with pie sizes of $5.00, $2.50, and $1.25, and a five-round game with pies of $5.00, $1.70, $0.58, $0.20, $0.07.[16] By design, the subgame perfect equilibria are the same in all three games (player 1 should offer $1.25). Subjects were eighty undergraduate students at Princeton in an intermediate microeconomic theory course.

The results are shown in Table 4.4. The two-round game fails to replicate the Binmore et al. result, because there is a large frequency of opening-round offers of $1.25, close to the perfect equilibrium prediction. Opening-round offers are around $2.50 in the three-round game and $1.70 in the five-round game. The modal offer is just the second-round pie size, as if players truncate each game to just two stages and play the perfect equilibrium.

The difference between these results and those of Binmore et al. is curious. A likely explanation is that the subjects were economics undergraduate students, who learned one step of backward induction in an example involving a two-stage game, or perhaps simply induced it, then "overapplied" the two-round heuristic in the three- and five-round games.

---

[16] The games were played one after the other, in that order, so there was no attempt to control for an effect of the order in which a game was played, which is a small design flaw.

There are noticeable differences in the instructions between the Binmore et al. and Neelin et al. experiments as well. The key differences are subtle—only one sentence—but are worth dwelling on as a case study in methodology.

Binmore et al. were worried that subjects might think the experimenters expected them to be fair-minded, and would respond to this "demand effect." So they included a sentence (in capitals) stating, "YOU WOULD BE DOING US A FAVOR IF YOU SIMPLY SET OUT TO MAXIMIZE YOUR WINNINGS." Of course, this instruction risks bending over too far and inducing fair-minded subjects to behave "too" self-interestedly.

The instructions of Neelin et al. mention that "You will be discussing the theory this experiment is designed to test in class." This kind of instruction breaks a conventional rule in experimental economics: Try to isolate subjects' behavior in the lab from other uncontrolled influences that might affect their motivation.[17] A reminder that results will be discussed in class might have led subjects to conform more closely to some theory they were being taught. Since the Neelin et al. results *do* show more conformity with subgame perfection than in Binmore et al. in the two-round game, the possibility that subjects were trying extra hard to please the experimenter is consistent with the data and can be ruled out only by further experimentation.

Responding to the earlier conflict in results, Ochs and Roth (1989) ran a more complex experiment. Their design combined old and new structural features: The number of rounds was two or three, the discount factors were 0.4 and 0.6, and discount rates could be different for different players.[18]

Table 4.5 shows the parameter configurations, and perfect equilibria (dollars offered to player 2 out of $30 total). The first four cells of the design, when $T = 2$, are simplest: In theory, player 1 should just offer player 2 the number of chips equal to her discount factor (δ_2) times $30 (since the second period is an ultimatum game in which player 2 will claim all the chips). Comparing cells 1–4 ($T = 2$) and cells 5–8 ($T = 3$) shows that adding a third period lowers the amount player 2 should be offered, because being able to counteroffer in the third period gives player 1 extra bargaining power.

---

[17] For example, many experimenters pay subjects privately one at a time, in a separate room, while other subjects sit inside the lab for their names to be called, to make it more difficult for subjects to compare monetary earnings or implement post-experiment sharing between well-paid and poorly paid subjects. In addition, experimenters avoid using students in the same class, particularly in situations where their behavior might be scrutinized later in a public forum such as a class discussion.

[18] To implement different discount rates, players bargained over one hundred chips (worth $0.30 each), but the amount of money the chips were worth was reduced each period according to each player's discount rate.

Table 4.5.   *Predictions and offers in alternating-offer bargaining*

Cell	Number of rounds (T)	Discount factors		Perfect equilibrium	Average opening offer		Rate of rejection
		δ_1	δ_2		Round 1	Round 10	
1	2	0.4	0.4	12.00	13.19	12.03	0.10
2	2	0.6	0.4	12.00	14.73	14.34	0.15
3	2	0.6	0.6	18.00	13.88	14.70	0.13
4	2	0.4	0.6	18.00	14.67	13.57	0.20
5	3	0.4	0.4	7.20	13.02	12.81	0.12
6	3	0.6	0.4	4.80	14.04	13.17	0.14
7	3	0.6	0.6	7.20	13.93	13.70	0.15
8	3	0.4	0.6	10.50	13.90	14.23	0.29

Source: Ochs and Roth (1989).

Table 4.5 reports average opening offers in rounds 1 and 10, and the rate of first-round rejections across all ten rounds. Offers average around $14, and do not vary nearly as much across cells as they are predicted to. There is significant learning between rounds 1 and 10 in cells 1, 3, and 4, but the change is in the wrong direction in cell 4.

Many of the predictions across cells go in the wrong direction, or are statistically weak. When $T = 2$, offers should not depend on player 1's discount factor δ_1 but later offers actually fall with δ_1. Player 2 should be offered less when $T = 3$ compared with $T = 2$, but this difference is significant in only two of four comparisons (cells 2–6 and 3–7). However, Ochs and Roth's statistical tests are conservative.[19] In fact, evidence for subgame perfection is mildly favorable when all comparisons are taken together: Across pairs of cells, there are twenty-five predicted differences in opening offers; seventeen differences go in the correct direction ($p = .05$ by a binomial test).

The analysis above concerns only opening offers to player 2. How often are offers rejected? And what happens when they are? The rightmost column of Table 4.5 shows rejection rates in each cell. The overall rejection rate of 16 percent figure is quite similar to the rates in earlier studies (15 percent in Binmore et al., 14 percent in Neelin et al.) and in ultimatum games (see Chapter 2). Counteroffers that follow rejections have two interesting properties. First, second-period counteroffers are rejected more often

---

[19] Their cross-cell tests use only round 10 data, comparing just ten offers with ten other offers, which lacks the power to detect modest effects. A better test would use all the data while somehow controlling for dependence over trials, or use a within-subjects design in which a single subject is exposed to different cells (i.e., a subject "acts as her own control group").

(40 percent) than opening offers are, and third-period rejections are even more common (54 percent).[20] Second, most (81 percent) counteroffers are "disadvantageous"—a player who rejects an offer then makes a counteroffer that leaves herself *less* than she was offered. Disadvantageous counteroffers are also common in the studies by Binmore et al. (75 percent) and Neelin et al. (65 percent), and *all* rejections in ultimatum games are disadvantageous (since they leave the Responder with nothing).

There are two plausible reasons for disadvantageous counteroffers: Either players do not try to maximize their own monetary payoffs (the "social utility hypothesis"); or players do not think ahead sufficiently to realize that, by rejecting X, they may be forced to earn less than X (a form of "limited computation").[21] Social utility and limited computation probably both contribute to the frequency of disadvantageous counteroffers, because there is evidence for both forces in other studies. Support for the limited computation hypothesis is found in "Mouselab" studies, described below, and Chapter 2 describes evidence of social utility.

One social utility model is worth noting here. Bolton (1991) conjectured that players care about money earnings *and* their relative share of earnings, and demand more money when their relative share is low. Now suppose players earn money only from their rank in a constant-sum "tournament," in which their rank and tournament earnings depend only on their bargaining performance relative to other players in the same role as they are. Bolton notes that players should never reject equilibrium offers in the bargainining games if they care only about their tournament earnings and their share of tournament money (and don't care about the nominal amounts "earned" in the bargaining that determines their tournament rank).

Why? Because rejecting an equilibrium offer only reduces the amount they can earn from the tournament and it *also* reduces their share of the

---

[20] The rise in rejection rate across rounds could be due to heterogeneity and sample selection bias—some combative or demanding player 2s both reject opening offers and propose stingy counteroffers, so that the samples of subjects in round 1 and in later rounds are systematically different. Or the difference could be due to negative reciprocity (player 1s whose offers were rejected fight back by rejecting player 2's counteroffer).

[21] Limited computation could include players guessing incorrectly, at the time that they reject an offer, about how large a counteroffer they could make in the next period without risking rejection. For example, take $T = 2$ games. A player with $\delta_2 = 0.6$ might reject a low offer of forty chips, worth $12, because she thinks she may get up to $18 in the subgame (which is an ultimatum game). Upon reaching the subgame, she begins to worry whether player 1, angered by the first-period rejection, would accept a very lopsided division of the $18 so she may end up offering an equal split, disadvantageously counteroffering $9 for herself after rejecting $12. In this story, the limit in computation is her inability to imagine player 1's likely reaction to counteroffers at the time at which she rejects the initial offer. Such an inability to project out of one emotional state to another has been well documented in a variety of contexts by Loewenstein and Schkade (1999), who call it a "hot–cold empathy gap."

tournament money (which is fixed). Bolton then compared regular and tournament incentives in experiments. The results are mixed. Tournament offers among inexperienced subjects are about the same as in the regular bargaining control groups, except that the variance is higher and there are some differences in rejection rates. When bargainers return for a second session, tournament incentives nudge offers about a quarter of the way closer to the perfect equilibrium, but subjects in a third tournament session move back toward the equal split, *away* from perfect equilibrium. Carter and McAloon (1996) also report that tournament incentives in ultimatum games do not move offers and acceptances toward self-interest, as Bolton's idea predicts.

4.2.2 Limited Computation

What about learning? Perhaps players do not respect the equilibrium impact of structural features on bargaining power right away, but they learn to over time. Binmore et al. found that a single period of role reversal produced rapid convergence to equilibrium. Ochs and Roth, and Bolton, however, observed little convergence in ten periods. Since most of the subjects in the latter studies suffered only one or two rejections, they might not have experienced subgame play often enough to learn from it.

Precisely this concern motivated a clever paper by Harrison and Mc-Cabe (1992). They begin by pointing out that in pricing finitely lived assets (Forsythe, Palfrey, and Plott, 1982) and learning to vote strategically rather than sincerely (Eckel and Holt, 1989) players learn a backward induction solution only by playing through subgames. Applying the same idea, their subjects played seven three-round games with pie sizes of 100, 50, and 25 points, alternated between seven two-round games with pies of 50 and 25 points. The pie sizes in the two-round game are precisely those in the subgame that begins in the second round of the three-round game. In theory, subjects could learn from the two-round games what to expect if their first-round offer was rejected in the three-round game and play then proceeded to the second-round subgame. Across the seven three-round games, opening offers averaged 47, 40, 41, 35, 34, 30, and 29, converging close to the equilibrium prediction of 25. (Offers in the two-round games averaged 24–25 in every sequence.)

In the Harrison-McCabe design, the perfect equilibrium in the two-round subgame, 25, is the same as an equal split. This coincidence helps ensure that the perfect equilibrium is reached in the two-round game, leading to equilibrium in the three-round game. To test the robustness of this finding, Carpenter (2000) alternated two-round games with discount factors of either 0.75 or 0.25 with a one-period ultimatum game that was exactly the same as the second round of the associated two-round game. (That is, a two-round game with pies of 100 and 25 was compared with an ultimatum dividing 25, in the $\delta = 0.25$ condition.) The results did not replicate Harrison and McCabe's strong conclusion. Offers averaged 40 percent of the pie in all games. There was a very slight, insignificant, drift toward equilibrium in the two-round game.

Since learning effects are mixed to weak, the main question about alternating-offer bargaining is what combination of stable social preference and failures of backward induction explains what happens. To study limitations on strategic calculation, Camerer et al. (1994) and Johnson et al. (2002) ran experiments using two novel design features. One design feature was having subjects play against computerized opponents that were programmed to maximize their own earnings (and think their opponents are trying to maximize earnings too). If human subjects are able to calculate perfect equilibria, they should make equilibrium offers to the robots. If they do not make equilibrium offers, it must be that they don't know how to calculate them.

The second design feature is that the "pie sizes" in each of three rounds of bargaining were hidden in boxes on a computer screen. The boxes could be "opened," revealing the pie size, only by moving a cursor into the box. When the cursor moved out, the box closed. Figure 4.1 shows the computer display subjects saw, with the first-round box open, showing a pie size of $5.00. This "mouselab" system has been extensively used to study individual decision making. It provides a "subject-eye view" of what information players are using to test hypotheses about reasoning. The mind is treated like a "thinking factory." Measuring the flow of inputs (information) into the factory and the length of time between input arrivals enables one to draw inferences about the unobserved production process going on inside the factory.[22]

Subjects bargained over three periods in which the pie sizes were around $5.00, $2.50, and $1.25. To prevent memorization, the pie sizes were perturbed in each period such that the subgame perfect prediction ("equilibrium" hereafter) was fixed at $1.25. The bargaining results replicate earlier

---

[22] Taking subgame perfection to follow from a specific computational process is obviously a departure from the "as if" conception in positive economics. But, since the equilibrium prediction is rejected, we know that either the computational process subjects use is not backward induction, or subjects are in an equilibrium modified by social preferences. Studying information processing is the most efficient way to determine which hypothesis is true. The direct approach has at least two admirers. Rubinstein (1999, p. 163) called it "one of the most beautiful experiments I have ever come across." And Costa-Gomes, Crawford, and Broseta (2001) later used Mouselab to study iterated reasoning (see Chapter 5).

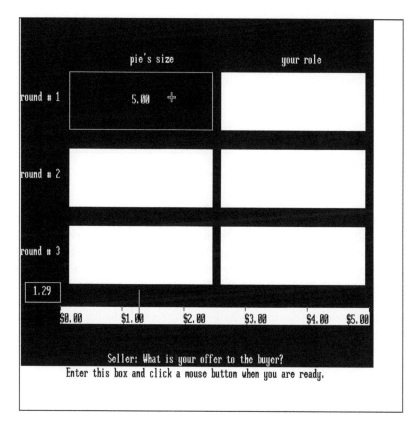

Figure 4.1. *The information display in alternating-offer mouselab experiments. Source: Johnson et al. (2002), p. 22, Figure 1; reproduced from* Journal of Economic Theory *with permission of Academic Press.*

findings. Most offers were between $2.50 and $2.00, averaging $2.11. Offers less than $1.80 were rejected about half the time. The overall rejection rate was 12 percent.

What did subjects pay attention to? Let's start with player 1s who are deciding how much to offer in the first round. Table 4.6 shows the average number of lookups (the number of times each box was opened in a period), total gaze time (the number of seconds that each round's box was open), and the number of transitions from the box representing one round to another round. (The number 2.55, for example, means that on average subjects moved the cursor from the round 1 box to the round 2 box between two and three times per trial.)

Table 4.6.   *Average lookups, gaze times, and transitions by player 1s*

| | Pie size | Number of | Fraction of periods | Gaze | Number of transitions from row round to column round | | |
Round	($)	lookups	with zero lookups	time	1	2	3
1	5.00	4.38	0.00	12.91	—	2.55	0.65
2	2.50	3.80	0.19	6.67	2.10	—	1.24
3	1.25	2.12	0.10	1.24	0.50	0.88	—

Source: Johnson et al. (2002).

Table 4.6 shows that players looked longest at the first-round box and about half as long at the second-round box, and barely glanced at the third-round box.[23] They also made slightly more forward box-to-box transitions (upper-right entries) than backward (lower-left). A key fact is that players did not open the second- and third-round boxes at all on 19 percent and 10 percent of the trials, respectively.[24] The fact that they don't always open the future boxes is a death blow to the strong form of the backward induction hypothesis.

Grouping trials by the offers player 1s made and comparing their information-processing patterns provide a test of whether offers and information processing are correlated. Figure 4.2 shows an "icon graph" cooked up by my collaborator Eric Johnson to represent attentional statistics. The figure represents the statistics graphically, as features of icons. The three rectangular boxes represent data from each of the three-round boxes subjects saw on their screens (the top one represents round 1, and so forth). The fraction of each box that is shaded is proportional to the relative gaze time for that box. The width of each box is proportional to the number of lookups. And the thickness of the arrows pointing down and up is proportional to the average number of transitions from box to box (if there was less than one transition on average, no arrow is shown).

The icon graph shows at a glance that the round 1 box is opened more often (it's wider) and gazed at longer (it's more shaded). Most of the transitions from box to box are back and forth between the first- and second-round pie sizes. Comparing across offer categories, player 1s who made the

---

[23] Rubinstein (1999) found a similar result with a simpler method: Subjects were asked the order in which they wanted to see the first- and second-round pies in a two-round game. Nearly two-thirds chose to see the first-round pie size first.

[24] The results were not due to a top–down display bias, because a control experiment in which the boxes were displayed "upside down" (with the third-round on top) showed the same pattern of search across rounds.

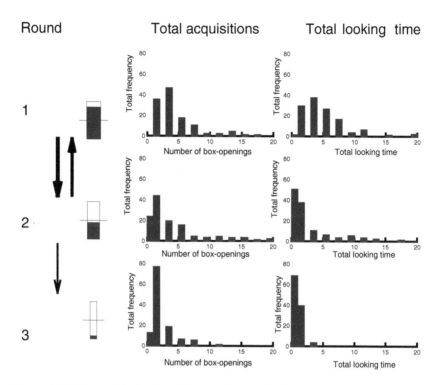

Figure 4.2. *Icon graphs for player 1's attention statistics in alternating-offer experiments. Source: Johnson et al. (2002), p. 29, Figure 3; reproduced from* Journal of Economic Theory *with permission of Academic Press.*

lowest offers (below $2.00) looked at the second-round pie size more often and longer than those who made higher offers. The relation between offers and looking patterns means you could use the subject's looking patterns to predict what offer they would make, before they even made it. After player 1 made an offer, player 2s could then look at the boxes and decide whether to accept the offer or not. Players who accepted the low offers spent more time looking at the round 2 pie size compared with players who rejected similar offers.

Violations of the subgame perfect prediction could come from subjects doubting the rationality or self-interest of others. We tested this explanation by having human subjects play computerized opponents who are known to maximize their own earnings (and were known to expect their opponent—the human subject—to do the same). Subjects who are self-interested and able to make equilibrium calculations should offer $1.25 to the computerized opponents. The average offer to the computerized opponents in these

Round

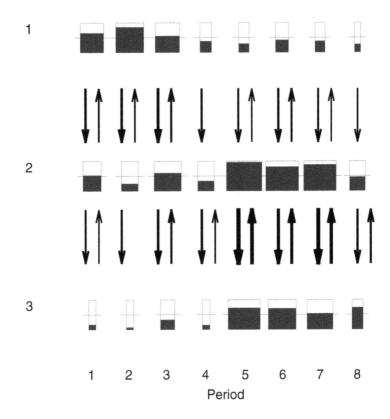

Period

Figure 4.3. *Icon graphs for player 1's attention statistics before (periods 1–4) and after (periods 5–8) instruction. Source: Johnson et al. (2002), p. 34, Figure 6; reproduced with permission of Academic Press.*

periods was $1.84, compared with $2.11 to human subjects but well above $1.25, so erasing doubts that opponents are rational does *not* induce equilibrium play.

Figure 4.3 shows icon graphs across eight periods with robots—four before instruction, and four after brief instruction about backward induction. After brief instruction in backward induction, subjects' lookup patterns and gaze times were quite different: They looked mostly at the second- and third-round boxes, and made more transitions between those boxes. The average offer in those periods was $1.22, just pennies away from the equilibrium prediction.

A final experimental session combined untrained subjects with trained subjects who had learned to make equilibrium offers to the computerized opponents. Who "trains" whom? The result was a "tug-of-war" between the two types of subjects. Untrained subjects often rejected the trained subjects' lower offers, but they also learned to offer less. The trained subjects gradually raised offers after rejections. The result was an average offer of $1.60. Injecting some trained subjects into an untrained population therefore does have an effect, but it does not guarantee population convergence to perfect equilibrium.

Where does this leave us? One modeling approach is to assume that players' mental representations of games are truncated games in some way (compared with the true game), then they operate on the truncated game using simple decision rules or equilibrium concepts (see Camerer, 1998, and Johnson et al., 2002). (Including some decision cost or exogeneous cognitive constraint could lead to "optimally suboptimal" versions of this approach; see Samuelson, 2001.) Another approach is to posit decision rules that predict both observed decisions (e.g., offers and acceptances) and particular patterns of cognitive processing; then use both decisions and attentional statistics to infer decision rules (see Costa-Gomes, Crawford, and Broseta, 2001; Chapter 5 of this volume).

Of course, evidence that heuristic procedures are used in place of equilibrium reasoning does not imply that social preferences don't exist as well. It simply means modeling social preference is *insufficient* to explain everything we see. Note well that the attentional statistics and results from computerized opponents also reject the new generation of theories which assume social preferences along with equilibrium reasoning (e.g., Rabin, 1993; Fehr and Schmidt, 1999; Bolton and Ockenfels, 2000). Note also that subjects are able to learn backward induction quickly, and they transfer their skills to games with different pie sizes. This means backward induction is not computationally difficult; it is simply unnatural to learn without guidance (like learning to ride a bike, compute a present value, or windsurf).

Summary: Opening offers in alternating-offer bargaining lie somewhere between equal splits and equilibrium predictions and are fairly insensitive to structural parameters. Some rejections occur, which are usually followed by disadvantageous counteroffers. Learning was not evident except in one study (Binmore et al.) and in a study designed to expose subjects to subgame play even if opening offers were accepted (Harrison and McCabe), although the latter study's finding did not replicate with a different game (Carpenter). Three experimental findings show that limited computation (or limited understanding of how bargaining power emerges from structure) is part of the explanation for deviations from perfect equilibrium. First, in many trials players do not even look ahead to how much will be divided one or two periods ahead if an offer is rejected; second, when human players bargain with computerized opponents (so that social preferences for fairness are turned off) they still do not make equilibrium offers; and third, after training in backward induction, they *do* make equilibrium offers to computerized opponents (so they *are* cognitively capable of backward induction, they just don't do it instinctively).

4.2.3 Random Termination

One interpretation of discounting in bargaining is that players realize an exogenous force may suddenly terminate bargaining, with a known probability. Examples include regulatory intervention in a merger, the sudden appearance of a better bargaining partner, management turnover, physical disruption such as travel restrictions or communication snafus, or random emotional disruptions, which players can anticipate statistically but are helpless to resist once they occur.

To test the equivalence between time discounting of future payoffs and termination, Zwick, Rapoport, and Howard (1992) had players alternate offers of how to divide $30 with a random termination probability of $1 - p$ if an offer is rejected. If players are risk neutral, then bargaining in this way is equivalent to bargaining over a pie that is discounted by a discount factor p; instead of a portion of the pie shrinking, the probability of termination induces a probability of the entire pie shrinking. In practice, bargaining could be different if players have certain kinds of social preferences.[25] And since each subgame is identical (the pie does not shrink), random termination also allows a kind of repeated experience with subgames, which may speed up learning.

Zwick et al. used three continuation probabilities: 0.90, 0.67, and 0.17. The subgame perfect predictions are 14.21, 12.00, and 4.29 in the three conditions. As in earlier studies, offers were below the equal split point ($15) in the direction of perfect equilibrium and there was little learning. The rate of rejections was high (36 percent in the last six trials). The averages of accepted *final* offer across the three conditions were 14.97, 14.76, and 13.92. The corresponding averages in studies with pie shrinkage are 14.90, 14.64, and 13.57,[26] so termination and discounting results are very close.

---

[25] The Ochs–Roth "minimum acceptable offer" idea, for example, will predict a lot more later-period rejections in the shrinkage design, and hence more overall rejection, than in the random termination design. The Bolton (1991) theory makes the same prediction. The Fehr–Schmidt (1999) theory predicts equivalence.

[26] The first number comes from Binmore, Shaked, and Sutton's (1989)'s control group, and the latter two from Weg, Rapoport, and Felsenthal (1990). The amounts reported are rescaled for pie size to match the $30 scale.

4.2.4 Games with Fixed Delay Costs and Outside Options

In many bargaining situations, the costs of delay are fixed. In litigation, each party runs up legal bills that are essentially independent of any final settlement. In strikes, the costs of delay are lost wages and profits. Games with fixed delay costs have very lopsided equilibria: The side with the lower delay cost should get almost everything. Suppose player i has delay cost c_i and player 1 moves first. Then player 1 should get the *whole* pie if her delay cost is lower ($c_1 < c_2$) and should get only c_2 if her delay cost is higher ($c_1 > c_2$). This is an equilibrium because prolonged bargaining just gives a larger and larger incentive for the higher-cost bargainer to settle, so the high-cost bargainer can never do better than accepting a pittance right away. When the bargainers have equal costs, there is a range of equilibria in which the first-mover gets something between the (common) delay cost and the entire pie.

Rapoport, Weg, and Felsenthal (1990) examined bargaining with fixed costs. Their players divided 30 Israeli shekels, and the fixed costs for players 1 and 2 were 0.10 and 2.50 or 0.20 and 3.0. They created a pseudo-infinite horizon by telling subjects the experiment would be terminated if it lasted too long.

Table 4.7 shows the average final offer (gross of delay costs), and the proportion of trials ending in the first trial. The results go strongly in the predicted direction, and get closer over trials. In the strong condition, for example, strong players are offering only 4.4–7.9 out of 30 shekels in the final block, and the weak player 2s accept these low opening offers 60–80 percent of the time. Weak first-movers are reluctant to accept the cold fact that higher delay costs undermine their bargaining power, so only 30 percent of their first offers are accepted. The horrible truth sinks in quickly, however. In the second round of weak-condition games, 35 percent settle, and another 22 percent settle in the third or fourth rounds.

In Binmore, Shaked, and Sutton (1989), players bargain over a £7 pie and player 2 has an outside option that is commonly known (£0, £2, or £4). Cooperative theories, such as the Nash bargaining solution, prescribe and predict that bargaining outcomes will divide the surplus that can be gained *beyond the players' threat points*. These concepts do not ask whether the threat to quit bargaining is credible or not. Suppose player 2's threat point is £2 (and the other's threat point is £0). Since cooperative theories do not question the credibility of the implicit threat to quit, player 2 should get £2 plus some fraction of the £5 surplus to be gained. But if player 2's likely total is greater than £2, why would she ever exercise the implicit threat? And if she won't exercise it, why should the threat point matter?

Noncooperative theories incorporate this skepticism by evaluating whether threats would be carried out in equilibrium, and ignoring those that will not. For example, Rubinstein–Stahl alternating-offer bargaining

Table 4.7. *Fixed-cost bargaining results*

	Trials			Equilibrium prediction
	1–6	7–12	13–18	
Experiment 1				
Strong ($c_1 = 0.10 < c_2 = 2.5$)				
Mean final offer	9.2	7.4	4.4	0.00
Percent accepted on first trial	50	67	83	1.00
Weak ($c_1 = 2.5 > c_2 = 0.10$)				
Mean final offer	20.0	23.2	25.4	29.9
Percent accepted on first trial	39	28	33	1.00
Equal ($c_1 = c_2 = 2.5$)				
Mean final offer	14.8	16.1	15.6	[0,27.5]
Percent accepted on first trial	78	83	83	1.00
Experiment 2				
Strong ($c_1 = 0.20 < c_2 = 3.0$)				
Mean final offer	12.8	8.6	7.9	0.00
Percent accepted on first trial	44	39	61	1.00
Weak ($c_1 = 3.0 > c_2 = 0.20$)				
Mean final offer	17.9	18.5	21.6	29.8
Percent accepted on first trial	28	22	28	1.00
Equal ($c_1 = c_2 = 3.0$)				
Mean final offer	14.8	14.6	14.7	[0,27.0]
Percent accepted on first trial	94	94	94	1.00

Source: Rapoport, Weg, and Felsenthal (1990).

predicts a solution in which player 2 gets a fraction $\delta/(1 + \delta)$ of the surplus (where δ is the common discount factor). If δ is close to 1, this solution predicts divisions that are close to equal splits. Since player 2 is predicted to get around half of the £7 pie, or £3.50, player 2's outside option should not matter if it is £2. However, if player 2's option is more than what she can expect to get in equilibrium, then player 2 should just get her outside option.

The noncooperative equilibrium that ignores outside options less than $\delta/(1 - \delta)$ is called "deal-me-out." Solutions that divide the surplus net of the outside options are called "split-the-difference" solutions. In the experiments by Binmore et al., the discount factor is $\delta = 0.9$. Deal-me-out predicts that player 2 will get 47 percent of the pie when the outside option is £0 or £2, and 57 percent (=£4/£7) when the outside option is £4. Split-the-difference predicts 47 percent, 64 percent, and 76 percent for the three option values. Subjects bargain by exchanging alternating offers.

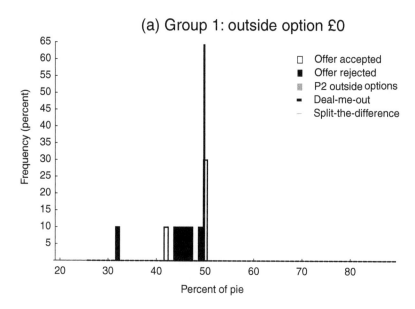

Figure 4.4.   *Distribution of outcomes in outside option games. Source: Based on Binmore, Shaked, and Sutton (1989).*

Figure 4.4 shows the final outcomes, in terms of the percentage amount offered by player 2 as a fraction of the original £7 cake, in three option value conditions (groups 1–3 correspond to option values of £0, £2, and £4). The deal-me-out and split-the-difference predictions are indicated by thick and dotted lines, respectively. Dark bars indicate offers rejected in the first round and light bars indicate offers accepted in the first round. Gray bars indicate cases in which player 2 took the outside option. Deal-me-out predicts much better than split-the-difference: There is a large spike of agreements around 50 percent when the outside option is £0 or £2, and agreements cluster around 57 percent when the option is £4. Player 2 does not get much more when the outside option is £2 than when it is £0.

Figure 4.4 illustrates important subtlety in how these bargaining outcomes are reached. Notice that when player 2's outside option is £2 (group 2), there are several cases where initial offers are rejected (black bars) and the final agreements give player 2 about a third of the original pie. In those cases, player 2s are not taking their outside options, and usually get about half of the remaining pie, because bargaining lasted about three rounds. It takes player 2s a couple of rounds of costly pie shrinkage to learn that they are unlikely to get more than half. Thus, the value of the outside option does

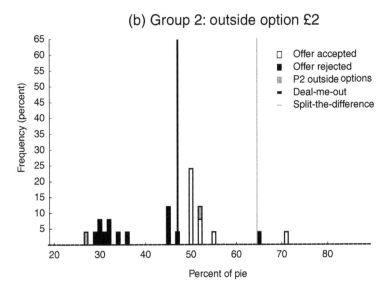

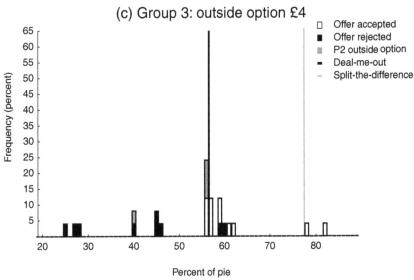

Figure 4.4 (continued)

affect *equilibration*—it produces some costly delay—but it does not affect the distribution of the discounted pie.

Binmore et al. (1998) were interested in cases where one player's option is very attractive, so the joint gains from partnership are small. Their players divide $10. Player 2 has an option worth α ($0.90, $2.50, $4.90, $6.40, or $8.10). Player 2 can take the option or give it up and play a Nash demand game. In the demand game, both players write down demands, and if they sum to less than $10 each player gets her own demand (otherwise they get nothing). Since players in $10 Nash demand games almost always demand close to $5, the interesting cases are when the option is worth $6.40 or $8.10: Is the option player willing to bet that the other player will essentially concede, allowing the option-rejecting player to earn at least $6.40 or $8.10?[27]

The same subjects played repeatedly with different values of α. The results, reported in Table 4.8, support the deal-me-out theory. The third column shows that the option player 2s claim close to $5 when $\alpha < \$5$ and claim exactly α when α is $6.40 or $8.10.[28] There is variation in what the player 1s demand. For example, when $\alpha = \$8.10$, the median player 1 demand is an accommodating $1.65, but the (0.05,0.95) interval ranges from $0.95 to $4.50. Player 2s wisely opt out more than half the time when $\alpha = \$6.40$ and about 80 percent of the time when $\alpha = \$8.10$. Using the actual player 1 behavior, one can calculate the expected profits for player 2s who did not opt out. These expected payoffs are below the option value when α is $6.40 or $8.10.

Forsythe, Kennan, and Sopher (1991a) ran outside option experiments motivated by a "joint-cost" theory of strikes.[29] The idea is simple: Strikes in which joint costs are higher should be less likely. The top of Table 4.9 shows their design parameters. The total gain from exchange is the revenue minus the threat points; this per period difference, multiplied by the number of periods, is the "pie size." In every case, the stronger player's threat point is $7/12$ or 58 percent of the available revenue R, so the strong player should always demand at least this much. The Nash split-the-difference solution and the deal-me-out solution, which gives the strong player the maximum of half and their 58 percent threat point, are also shown in Table 4.9. Bargaining took place by exchange of free-form messages over a computer network.

----

[27] Notice that this experiment tests forward induction (see also Chapter 7), since player 1s should know that rational player 2s who choose to play will expect to earn at least their outside option, and should accordingly demand less.

[28] Between 5 percent and 10 percent of player 2s actually opt in and demand *less* than α when it is $6.40 or $8.10. This is either a dumb mistake or an expression of the guilty belief that they do not deserve to earn that much from the bargaining, even when they can earn it for sure by opting out.

[29] See Kennan (1980) and experiments by Sopher (1990).

Results in outside option experiments

ue of option α ($)	Percent of player 2s opting out	Median claim of player 2s when opting in ($)	Median claim of player 1s ($)	Percent of pl demands leavin; less thar
0.90	0.0	4.97	4.90	0.0
2.50	1.0	4.95	4.90	0.0
4.90	33.4	5.00	4.65	0.9
6.40	59.8	6.40	3.20	11.1
8.10	80.9	8.10	1.65	17.0

rce: Binmore et al. (1998).

Table 4.9. *Design and results in strike-cost experiments*

	Pie size $4		Pie size $8	
	Game I	Game II	Game III	Game IV
Per-period revenue	$2.40	$1.20	$2.40	$1.20
Number of periods (T)	4	8	8	16
Threat points (strong, weak)	($1.40,0)	($0.70,0)	($1.40,0)	($0.70,0)
Average strike length	0.74	1.17	1.47	1.44
Average total payoffs to (strong, weak)	(5.77,3.09)	(6.49,2.53)	(11.62,6.14)	(12.50,5.97)
Predictions				
Nash	(7.60,2.00)	(7.60,2.00)	(15.20,4.00)	(15.20,4.00)
Deal-me-out	(5.60,4.00)	(5.60,4.00)	(11.20,8.00)	(11.20,8.00)

Source: Forsythe, Kennan, and Sopher (1991a).

Results from the condition in which players negotiate period-by-period are shown in Table 4.9. A "strike period" is a period in which players failed to agree and earned only their threat points. The joint-cost avoidance theory predicts shorter strikes in games I and III because more net revenue is at stake; this prediction is wrong because average strike lengths were similar. Average payoffs support the deal-me-out prediction: Weak players were able to get about 70 percent of the surplus (beyond threat points); strong players got only 5–10 percent of the surplus; and the rest was lost owing to inefficient strikes.

The paper by Forsythe et al. reports the messages players sent, which document a verbal tug-of-war strongly rooted in everyday concepts of fairness and game-theoretic concepts of bargaining power. Strong bargainers persistently reminded their weak partners that, even if they failed to agree, the strong would earn plenty of money. The weak bargainers begged the strong to charitably offer equal divisions (implicitly favoring the weak; this plea usually fell on deaf ears), or at least split the surplus equally. Subjects promised to logroll across periods, grabbing a large share in one period but making it up generously in the next. One subject described how "cute" he is, and his partner groped vaguely for decisive social connections ("Are you in a frat? If so maybe I'll deal and maybe I won't. Depends on whatever."). Another negotiation erupted into a hateful war of words lasting for several periods, ending with all gains dissipated ("Go back to Burge [dormitory] and roll in the barf," followed by "I'm a junior and live in Mayflower and I'd love for you to stop by sometime and visit"). These transcripts are a reminder of the ambitious possibility of mapping a large space of socially nuanced announcements into sharp predictions of who gets what.

Finally, Binmore et al. (1991) compared exercising outside options with exogenous (forced) termination. If termination is exogenous, then even low option values (below the noncooperative equilibrium share) matter because the options may be credibly exercised "by accident." They found that options do influence bargaining differently when exercising them is voluntary or exogenous, as predicted by equilibrium theory. Furthermore, subjects were asked afterwards what divisions seemed most fair, and their answers were influenced by their experience, which is the first direct evidence that fairness conceptions may be malleable.

Summary: Random termination and discounting of future payoffs yield very similar bargaining outcomes, except that there are more rejections when termination is random. There is a big difference between the lopsided divisions in the fixed-cost games and the persistent tendency toward equal splits in fixed-discounting games seen previously in this chapter. The difference is an important puzzle. Theories of social preference that can explain the equality-biased results in fixed-discounting games should also be able to explain these highly *unequal* results in fixed-cost games. Experiments in which players have outside options vindicate the noncooperative view, in which options matter only if they yield more than the perfect equilibrium offer, compared with the Nash bargaining solution or "threat point" approach in which players with better options should always get more. However, it takes time for the high-option players to learn that they will get little of the surplus.

4.3 Bargaining under Incomplete Information

In theory, asymmetries in information fundamentally change the nature of how people bargain. Introducing asymmetries undermines efficiency because bargaining strategies then serve two different purposes: Players bargain both to get the most they can and to convey information. The two purposes usually conflict (and, in some models, inevitably do; e.g., Rubinstein, 1985). A typical outcome is that players who would like to accept a pending offer must turn it down to convey something about how patient they are to the other players, or to signal how good their outside options are.

So far, few experiments have been done to control information asymmetry and test theory. There are two sorts: a little work on "strikes" by Forsythe et al.; and a larger body of work on the sealed-bid mechanism under incomplete information, primarily by Radner and Schotter and by Rapoport et al.

4.3.1 One-Sided Buyer Information with Seller-Only Offers

In Rapoport, Erev, and Zwick (1995), the seller has a good that is worthless to her, and the buyer has private information about his reservation price (which is uniform from $(0,1)$). Only the seller can make offers. This kind of situation is common in retail selling.[30] Assuming a common discount factor of δ, there is a unique sequential equilibrium in which the seller offers $p_0 = \gamma(1-\delta)/(1-\gamma \cdot \delta)$ in the first period (where $\gamma = [1 - (1-\delta)^{0.5}]/\delta$) and $p_t = \gamma^t \cdot p_0$ in subsequent periods t. A buyer with value v accepts if and only if the price is below $v(1-\delta)/(1-\gamma \cdot \delta)$.

Although the math is messy, the economic intuition is not. Low-valuation buyers simply cannot afford to accept high prices. This enables the seller to price discriminate—offering high prices at first, then gradually lowering them. But why don't high-value buyers wait for the price to drop? The reason is that equilibrium prices decline exponentially, so the amount of price reduction slows down rapidly. The surplus that high-value buyers earn does not grow much if they wait, so the *discounted* surplus falls if they wait too long. High-value buyers are forced to buy early, and low-value buyers must wait till the price drops to where they can afford it. The results are obviously sensitive to the discount factor δ. If δ is close to 1, the high-value buyers can wait and wait, and so the seller is forced to offer a low price right away. If $\delta = 0$ (all the buyers have to catch a plane immediately), the seller maximizes expected profit by setting a price equal to half of the highest value.

To test the effect of δ, Rapoport et al. used three values: H (0.90), M (0.67), and L (0.33). The time series of average prices in each bargaining period is shown in Figure 4.5 for the three discount factor conditions. Look first at first-period prices. The predicted opening prices are 24, 36, and 45 for H, M, and L. Initial offers are higher than predicted, and vary with the discount factor in the opposite of the predicted direction. However, offers *do* decline across periods at rates amazingly close to the rates predicted by the sequential equilibrium. The predicted exponential factors (γ) are 0.76, 0.68, and 0.55 across H, M, and L conditions. The estimated exponential declines are 0.81, 0.68, and 0.55.

Buyers' acceptance decisions are close to those predicted by theory in one sense. Buyers should accept offers that maximize their discounted surplus, $\delta^t(v - p_t)$. This means that whenever an offer is accepted, the discounted surplus that was passed up in previous rounds should not be larger than the discounted surplus they end up with. This "no regret" condition is

---

[30] Ausubel and Deneckere (1992) proved that, if the time between periods is short (or, equivalently, the discount factor is close to 1), then it is never optimal for buyers to make offers, which justifies restricting attention to the case where only the seller makes offers.

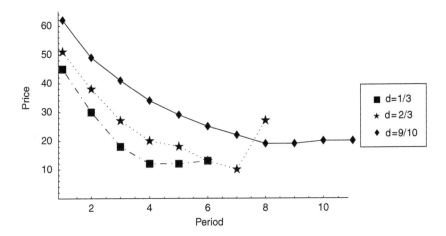

Figure 4.5. *Average prices in seller-offer bargaining with unknown buyer valuations. Source: Based on Rapoport, Erev, and Zwick (1995).*

rarely violated in those cases where a deal was eventually made.[31] Although buyers rarely regret waiting, they often accept offers too soon. Buyers typically accepted the first offer that was below their value v, or the second such offer, but could have done better by waiting. Because the buyers jump too quickly, sellers ask prices that are too high and end up with a larger share of profit than is predicted by the equilibrium. The fact that buyers accept offers too quickly is probably sensitive to information conditions.[32] If buyers were allowed to observe the price sequences offered by all sellers, they could see the "sale prices" in later periods and might learn to be more patient.

4.3.2   One-Sided Private Information and Strikes

Forsythe, Kennan, and Sopher (1991b) analyzed games in which the amount to be divided is either large or small (π_g or π_b, for "good" or "bad" states, whose probabilities are commonly known), and only one of two bargainers (the informed one, I) knows that amount.

    Can predictions be made if the details of how bargaining occurs are not known? Amazingly enough, the answer is Yes. In one of the most beautiful

---

[31] Ten of the thirteen violations occurred when buyers had valuations above 50. Rapoport et al. speculate that these high-value buyers are waiting too long to punish sellers (at a cost to themselves) for asking too much and cutting their prices too slowly, which may reflect some expression of preference for fairness. As a result, these buyers end up taking prices too late, which give them less discounted surplus.

[32] This regularity is related to patterns of price convergence in posted-offer auctions for perishable goods (see Holt, 1995), in which sellers' prices tend to start above the competitive equilibrium, and gradually come down as sellers undercut each other.

pieces of modern economic theory, Myerson (1979) showed that *any* Nash equilibrium of the bargaining game, regardless of its rules, is equivalent to a "direct revelation game" in which the informed bargainer announces the state truthfully, the pie is reduced to amounts $\gamma_g \pi_g$ and $\gamma_b \pi_b$, and the uninformed bargainer, U, gets the amounts x_g and x_b. (These reductions and payments are together called a "mechanism.")

The truth-telling constraint has enormous analytical power because it severely restricts the possible values of the reduction factors γ_g and γ_b, and the shares x_g and x_b. The uninformed player U's shares must make I better off, announcing that the state is good when it really is, given the amount that she will then get, and announcing that the state is bad when it really is. A little algebra shows that these two constraints imply[33]

$$(\gamma_g - \gamma_b)\pi_b \le x_g - x_b \le (\gamma_g - \gamma_b)\pi_g. \qquad (4.3.1)$$

Since $\pi_g > \pi_b$, the only way both inequalities can hold is if $\gamma_g - \gamma_b$ is positive—i.e., there is more shrinkage when the state is claimed to be bad. (This shrinkage keeps I from claiming the pie is large when it really is small.)

We can say more. Suppose the mechanism is "interim incentive efficient" (hereafter, just "efficient") in the sense that the payoff profile to the three pseudo-players—U, I in the good state, and I in the bad state—is Pareto optimal. Then it pays to make $\gamma_g = 1$ and make x_g and x_b as large as possible, which implies $x_g - x_b = (1 - \gamma_b)\pi_g$. A little more logic implies that strikes can be efficient only when a "strike condition" $p\pi_g > \pi_b$ holds (where p is the probability of the bad state), but there are efficient mechanisms that yield strikes when $p\pi_g < \pi_b$. Thus, the revelation principle and the presumption of efficiency yield a very strong prediction: There should be no strikes when $p\pi_g < \pi_b$, and strikes are expected when $p\pi_g > \pi_b$. (A stike occurs when time ends and players did not agree how to divide the pie.)

This theory predicts when strikes will occur but says nothing about players' shares. Further assumptions make a precise prediction about the shrinkage factors and the shares they imply.[34] Social scientists who are interested in bargaining should be flabbergasted that such sharp prediction can be derived from thin air (and that theorists would take it seriously!). If the

---

[33] If the state is good, the payoff from a truthful announcement to I is $\gamma_g \pi_g - x_g$ and the payoff to lying is $\gamma_b \pi_g - x_b$. If the state is good, the payoffs to truth-telling and lying are $\gamma_b \pi_b - x_b$, and the payoff to lying is $\gamma_g \pi_b - x_g$. Requiring truth to be more profitable than lying and combining the two inequalities gives the inequality in the text.

[34] Suppose players would agree to a fair (random) mixture of the mechanisms (i.e., the shrinkage factors and shares for U) each would impose if they had dictatorial power. This "random dictator" (RD) axiom yields very precise predictions: $\gamma_g = 1$, $x_g = \pi_g/2$, $\gamma_b = 1/2$, $x_b = 0$ when $p\pi_g > \pi_b$ and $\gamma_g = 1$, $x_g = \pi_b/2$, $\gamma_b = 1$, $x_b = \pi_b/2$ when $p\pi_g < \pi_b$. Thus, there should be exactly 50 percent strikes when the strike condition is on and the state is bad. The RD axiom also yields precise predictions about how much U gets, depending on whether the strike condition holds or not.

Table 4.10.   *Results in incomplete information bargaining*

Game	Probability of bad state	State	Pie size (π)	Payoffs U	Payoffs I	Value of information	Total payoff	Percentage inefficiency
I	0.5	Bad	1.00	0.31	0.30	−0.01	0.61	39.0
		Good	6.00	1.78	3.70	1.92	5.48	8.7
		Mean	3.50	1.05	2.00	0.95	3.05	13.0
		Prediction		1.50	1.75	0.25	3.25	7.1
II	0.75	Bad	2.30	1.06	0.84	−0.21	1.90	17.2
		Good	3.90	1.53	2.07	0.54	3.59	7.9
		Mean	3.50	1.41	1.76	0.35	3.18	9.3
		Prediction		1.46	1.75	0.29	3.21	8.3
III	0.5	Bad	2.80	1.47	1.18	−0.29	2.66	5.2
		Good	4.20	1.52	2.41	0.89	3.93	6.5
		Mean	3.50	1.50	1.80	0.30	3.29	6.0
		Prediction		1.40	2.10	0.70	3.50	0.0
IV	0.25	Bad	2.40	1.08	1.04	−0.04	2.12	11.8
		Good	6.80	1.58	5.03	3.45	6.61	2.9
		Mean	3.50	1.21	2.04	0.83	3.24	7.4
		Prediction		1.20	2.30	1.10	3.50	0.0

Source: Forsythe, Kennan, and Sopher (1991b).

theory is even close to right, that would be a triumph. If it is not, the nature of deviations may tell us something about which assumptions underlying the theory need replacement (and by what). The stage is set for an experiment that cannot fail. In their experiments, Forsythe et al. conducted ten-minute bargaining sessions in which players bargained through handwritten messages prescribing how much U would get. Messages were passed between rooms, to limit the strong effect of face-to-face communication.

Averages from pooling all sessions are shown in the action-packed Table 4.10. In games I and II, the strike condition is on; in games III and IV, the strike condition is off. The RD-based theory predicts 50 percent strikes in the bad state in games I and II, and no strikes in all other conditions (good states in I and II and all states in III and IV). Although the sharp predictions of the theory are not that close to the data in absolute terms, the predicted differences across conditions are confirmed. There are frequent strikes in the bad states in games I and II (17 percent–39 percent, when theory predicts 50 percent), and fewer strikes in bad states of games III and IV (around 10 percent, when theory predicts none).[35]

Thus, although game-theoretic predictions are sometimes inaccurate in their details, the presumption that very complicated bargaining can be approximated by direct mechanisms (which is the central principle in this body of theory) passes a difficult test. Furthermore, most of the deviations can be accounted for by small deviations from self-interest (bargainers are not as ruthless as the theory assumes).

4.3.3 Sealed-Bid Mechanisms for Bilateral Bargaining

A simple way to determine a price in bilateral buyer–seller bargaining is for both sides to write down a price and to trade at the average of their prices if they overlap (i.e., if the seller names a selling price larger than the buyer's bid). When there are many buyers and sellers bargaining simultaneously, this "sealed-bid mechanism" is known as a "call market" and has been studied a fair amount experimentally (e.g., Cason and Friedman, 1999; Hsia, 1999). Call markets are used to create an opening price at the Paris Bourse and in some other naturally occurring markets.

The two-person sealed-bid mechanism is ripe for empirical testing because there is much theory about it. Suppose the valuations of the buyer and seller, V and C, are drawn from a uniform distribution $[0,100]$, which is commonly known. Chatterjee and Samuelson (1983) showed that there existed a piecewise-linear equilibrium in which buyers bid their values up to 25, then "shaved" their bids, bidding $(25/3) + (2/3)V$ for values $V \geq 25$. Similarly, sellers bid their cost if $C \geq 75$ and otherwise overbid $25 + (2/3)C$. While there are other equilibria,[36] Myerson and Satterthwaite (1983) proved that the piecewise-linear equilibrium maximizes the ex ante gains from trade that can be achieved by *any* Bayesian–Nash equilibrium (among mechanisms that are individually rational and that give all of the buyer's payment to the seller). As in the strike games described above, in theory there is an inevitable loss of surplus caused by the information asymmetry—there will be times when they should trade, but don't (or "can't").

Radner and Schotter's (1989) experimental study of the sealed-bid mechanism investigated whether players use bidding strategies such as the linear equilibrium. They ran eight sessions with various design changes. Sessions 1–2 and 8 use the uniform value distribution and had the linear

---

[35] Note that the rates of striking in the good states of the bargaining games, 2.9–8.7 percent, are within a factor of two of the rates of disagreement observed in complete information games, where strikes should also never occur.

[36] Leininger, Linhart, and Radner (1989) show that there are many other equilibrium bidding functions for the sealed-bid mechanism. There is a two-parameter family of nonlinear differentiable bidding functions, as well as discontinuous step-function equilibria.

equilibrium given above. Session 3 used a different pricing rule—subjects traded at a price of $(v + c + 50)/3$ if v exceeded c by 25 or more. Subjects should simply bid their values ($v = V$, $c = C$) under this mechanism, in equilibrium, and it should produce the same pattern of prices and efficiencies as in session 1. In session 4, the price was equal to the buyer's bid v if v and c overlapped (rather than setting the price at the midpoint); buyers should bid half their value. In sessions 5–6 they changed the value distributions to increase the number of expected trades (and, hence, learning), which reduced the bid function slope to 0.438. In session 7, subjects engaged in unstructured face-to-face bargaining.

Variation of bid function slopes across the experimental treatments can be seen from pooled regressions in Table 4.11. The results show that subjects *do* bid roughly linearly in their values (linear regressions of bids against values fit well). The table breaks observations into two samples—those below the critical values at which the slope is predicted to change, and those above the critical value—to test for piecewise linearity.[37] *T*-statistics testing whether the slope coefficient is equal to the predicted coefficient (in parentheses) are generally small, so bids are consistent with equilibrium bidding. In sessions 1–2 and 8, the slopes should be 0.67 (above the critical value for buyers, and below the critical value for sellers), and are close, from 0.58 to 1.06.[38] In sessions 4–6, the slopes should be lower (from 0.438 to 0.500) and they are. Subjects did change the degree to which they shaded their values across sessions, in the direction predicted by theory.[39] The prediction that bid functions are piecewise linear is borne out because slopes *are* generally different below and above critical values, except for buyers in session 2.

In the face-to-face session 7, efficiency is 110 percent. Some subjects truthfully revealed their values, but the variance of profits was also much higher in this condition, which means there was a large dispersion in how truthful different subjects were. The efficiency and variance of face-to-face bargaining was surprising to theorists.[40] Radner and Schotter concluded (1989, p. 210) that "The success of the face-to-face mechanism, if replicated,

---

[37] To test whether piecewise linearity holds more sharply when it is predicted to (in sessions 1–2 and 8) than when it is not predicted to (in sessions 3–4), fixing the value distribution, the table breaks observations into subsamples below and above 25 (for buyers) and 75 (for sellers) even for sessions 3–4, where no break is predicted. Then we can see whether there is more of a break in sessions 1–2 and 8 than in sessions 3–4, as there is predicted to be, holding the break point constant.

[38] Notice that the binary lottery procedure used in session 8 does not produce systematically different results than paying money in baseline session 1.

[39] An important exception is the direct mechanism session 3. In this session, subjects should simply bid their values, so the slopes should be 1. However, the estimated slope is 0.726 for buyers and 1.06 for sellers, so the mechanism works only for one side.

[40] Roth (1995b) reports a small sample of data from ultimatum games showing that players coordinate even more sharply than usual on 50–50 divisions, with essentially no rejections, when bargaining face to face.

Table 4.11.   *Estimated bid function slope coefficients*

	Below critical value			Above critical value		
Session	Predicted β	Estimated $\hat{\beta}$	t-test $(\hat{\beta} - \beta)$	Predicted β	Estimated $\hat{\beta}$	t-test $(\hat{\beta} - \beta)$
Regressions of buyer bids against values						
1	1.0	1.00	(0.01)	0.670	0.85	(4.14)
2	1.0	0.91	(−0.52)	0.670	1.06	(1.28)
8	1.0	0.91	(−0.14)	0.670	0.80	(2.32)
3	1.0	0.92	(−0.08)	1.000	0.73	(−2.64)
4	0.5	0.55	(0.66)	0.500	0.58	(2.32)
5	1.0	0.80	(−4.17)	0.438	0.50	(1.12)
6 (1–20)	1.0	.085	(−1.40)	0.438	0.40	(−0.56)
6 (21–40)	1.0	1.11	(0.70)	0.438	0.32	(−1.55)
Regressions of seller bids against costs						
1	0.670	0.58	(−1.38)	1.0	0.97	(−0.32)
2	0.670	0.74	(1.28)	1.0	1.07	(0.14)
8	0.670	0.75	(1.65)	1.0	1.07	(0.17)
3	1.000	1.06	(1.04)	1.0	0.67	(−0.58)
5	0.438	0.48	(0.87)	1.0	1.00	(0.60)
6 (1–20)	0.438	0.57	(2.16)	1.0	0.97	(−0.79)
6 (21–40)	0.438	0.52	(1.20)	1.0	0.95	(−0.69)

Source: Radner and Schotter (1989).

might lead to a halt in the search for better ways to structure bargaining in situations of incomplete information. It would create, however, a need for a theory of such structured bargaining in order to enable us to understand why the mechanism is so successful."

Schotter, Snyder, and Zheng (2000) introduced agents. Players first drew valuations (using the asymmetric distributions from Radner and Schotter's sessions 5–7). Then buyers (sellers) told an agent the maximum (minimum) they were willing to bid, and the agents bargained face to face with other agents. Agents were paid either a percentage of the surplus they earned or a fixed fee for each trade.[41]

Principals typically gave their agents a maximum reservation price below the true valuation. Regressions of the instructed reservation prices against

[41] Subjects were NYU undergraduates. Ten pairs of subjects were run in each fee condition for fifteen rounds.

values yield slopes of 0.78 in the percentage fee condition and 0.70 in the fixed-fee condition, halfway between the predicted slope of 0.438 and the truthful revelation slope of 1. The latitude subjects allowed their agents is also correlated with the apparent skill of the agents.

Rapoport and Fuller (1995) replicated the Radner–Schotter results on the sealed-bid mechanism with two important extensions. Their first experiment used uniformly-distributed values and closely replicated Radner and Schotter's results, even when subjects gave bid functions for each of twenty-five possible values (see also Selten and Buchta, 1998).

Daniel, Seale, and Rapoport (1998) first replicated Rapoport and Fuller's second experiment, which used asymmetric value distributions.[42] Buyer (seller) values were uniformly distributed over the interval [0,200] ([0,100]). The equilibrium bid function is linear for the seller ($c = 50 + (2/3)C$). The buyer's bid function is piecewise linear: Bid V for $V < 50$, bid $(50 + 2V)/3$ for values between 50 and 150, and bid a flat 116.7 for all values above 150 (since, in equilibrium, the most the seller would ask is 116.7). Median estimates of the buyer slopes for the last two intervals are 0.56 and 0.28, close to the predictions of 0.67 and 0. Daniel et al. also conducted a second experiment with more extreme asymmetry, in which seller values were distributed uniformly on the interval [0,20] and buyer values were uniform from [0,200]. With these value distributions, sellers should ask $c = 50 + (2/3)C$, marking their costs way up to exploit the fact that the buyer's value is likely to be far above their cost. Buyers should bid their value ($v = V$) for $V \leq 50$, bid $v = (50 + 2V)/3$ for $50 \leq V \leq 70$, and bid 63.3 for any value V above 70.

This equilibrium makes for an interesting empirical test. Sellers should ask a price that is much higher than any possible cost, which they may be reluctant to do. And for most of their values (above 70), buyers should bid a flat 63.3.

Figure 4.6 shows a scatter plots of bids, pooling buyers in experiment 2. It is hard to see sharp piecewise linearity in the buyers' bid functions, but buyers are clearly bidding a smaller fraction of their values when the values are high than when values are low. Sellers do mark up their costs dramatically; their bids are widely dispersed and a little below the equilibrium prediction.

Table 4.12 shows means or medians of estimated intercepts and slopes of the bid functions across subjects, for experiments 1 and 2 separately. The same predictions are made across experiments, although the type of bidder and value interval to which the prediction applies vary. To look for piecewise linearity, bid function slopes are estimated using spline regression.[43]

---

[42] Their replication had fifty periods (rather than thirty), used a computerized network (rather than message passing), and showed each subject her complete history (which Rapoport and Fuller did not).

[43] The spline regression allows the slopes to vary but constrains the intercepts so the segments meet.

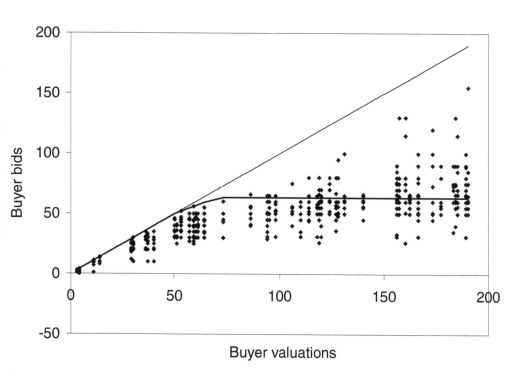

Figure 4.6. *Buyer valuations and bids in sealed-bid mechanism bargaining. Source: Based on data from Daniel, Seale, and Rapoport (1998).*

Table 4.12. *Estimated bid function parameters*

	Seller estimates			Buyer slope estimates			
				Buyer value ranges			
	Intercept	Slope	R^2	0–50	51–150	151–200	R^2
Prediction	50.0	0.67	—	1.00	0.67	0.00	—
Means (DSR exp. 1)	39.0	0.73	0.67	0.88	0.61	0.16	0.87
Medians (RDS exp. 1)	26.3	0.84	0.83	0.89	0.64	−0.08	0.88
				Buyer value ranges			
				0–50	51–70	71–200	
Medians (DSR exp. 2)	34.0	0.66	0.05	0.78	0.46	0.21	0.76
	Buyer estimates			Seller estimates			
				151–200	51–150	0–50	
Medians (RDS exp. 2)	15.0	0.71	0.80	0.95	0.62	0.05	0.91

Source: Daniel, Seale, and Rapaport (1998) and Rapaport, Daniel, and Seale (1998).

In Daniel et al. (DSR) experiment 2, the estimated slopes are fairly close to the equilibrium predictions, and R^2 values are high. There is also substantial learning: Bidders with high values often bid way too much in the first ten periods but learn to bid much lower after a while (which poses a challenge for learning models; e.g., Camerer, Hsia, and Ho, 2002).

Rapoport, Daniel, and Seale (1998) replicated DSR's experiment 1, and conducted a second experiment (with fixed pairings of subjects rather than random rematching). Seller costs C were uniformly drawn from [0,200] and the buyer values were uniformly drawn from [100,200]. The linear equilibrium then flips around the bid functions of the buyer and seller. As in Daniel et al., the median slopes are quite close to those predicted.

Following Radner and Schotter (1989), Valley et al. (2002) studied the effect of communication in the sealed-bid mechanism in more detail. In their studies, buyers and sellers drew values uniformly in the interval [0,$50] and bargained by stating bids. There were seven trading periods with no repeat rematching. Half the subjects participated in a no-feedback condition in which they received no feedback about the other subjects' bids. In a no-communication condition, players had two minutes to think about what to bid. In a written-communication condition, players exchanged written messages (through couriers) for thirteen minutes, then submitted final bids. In a face-to-face condition, players discussed anything they wanted, in person, then returned to separate rooms and submitted final bids.

Valley et al. (2002) report two studies. In their second, larger study Valley et al. find that communication enhances efficiency of trade. This can be seen in Figure 4.7, which plot pairs of buyer values v (on the y-axis) and seller costs c (on the x-axis), for the cases where mutually profitable trade is possible (i.e., $v > c$), across the three communication conditions. Pairs who made a trade are plotted as diamonds; failures to trade are plotted as open squares. The linear equilibrium predicts trade should not occur when v exceeds c by less than 12.5 (intuitively, when there is too little gain from trade, the possible gains do not overcome the incentive subjects have to shade their valuations). This "no-trade zone" is the area between the two thick lines. In theory, the no-trade zone should be filled with squares, and the larger zone to the upper left should be filled with diamonds. This prediction is accurate in the no-communication condition. But when there is written and face-to-face communication, however, there are a lot of trades (diamonds) in the no-trade zone.

The special contribution of Valley et al. is to figure out where the added efficiency comes from. They first note that regressions of bids against

(a) No communication

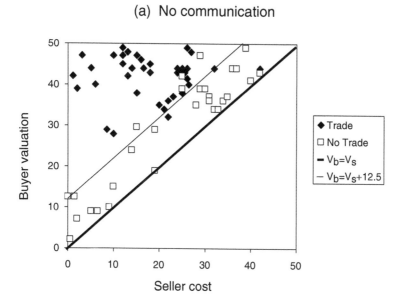

Figure 4.7. *Buyer-seller value pairs and trade incidence. Source: Valley et al. (1998), p. 138, Figure 3; redrawn from original with permission of Academic Press.*

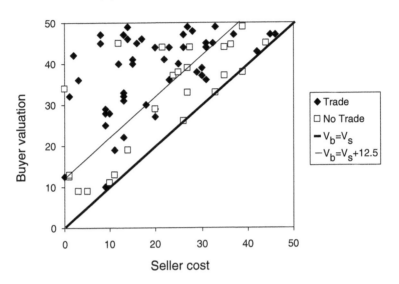

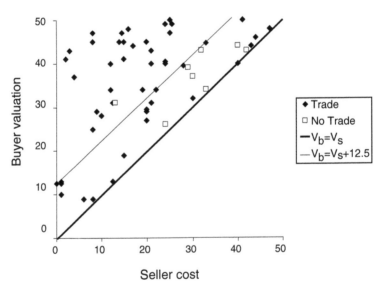

Figure 4.7 (continued)

valuations show empirical bid functions (slopes around 0.7) that are quite close to the linear equilibrium slope of 0.67. If the subjects were using these bid functions, there should be few trades in the no-trade zone in the communication conditions. But there *are* many trades in the no-trade zone. What gives?

The key clue comes from running a regression of the buyer's bid on the buyer's value *and* the seller's bid. The regression slope of buyer bids against seller bids is 0.60, which means the buyer *somehow* knows to bid higher when the seller is bidding higher. Further analysis shows three ways a pair of bargainers (a dyad) coordinate their behavior: mutual bidding of values; mutual revelation of values (they tell each other their true values); and coordinating on a price (i.e., agreeing on a single bid they both will make, so the buyer's bid will exactly match the seller's and they will trade at that bid price). Mutual value bidding and mutual revelation of values are rare,[44] but coordinating on a single price is common: It happens about 40 percent of the time with written communication and 70 percent of the time with face-to-face communication.

Thus, communication does enhance efficiency dramatically, but mostly *not* by encouraging mutual truth telling.[45] Subjects apparently feel each other out for approximate revelations of values—with a healthy dose of actual lying—then coordinate on a price that gives each side enough surplus to make her happy. The modal result is an equal split of surplus (i.e., the agreed-upon price is halfway between their values). Communication also doubles the variance of surplus shares because bidders who reveal values are often matched with others who don't.

Summary: Several experiments have been run in which some bargainers know something about their values that others don't know, but the uninformed side knows that the others are better informed. This is surely how most bargaining works. Experimental results are surprisingly supportive of theories that are bold and often counterintuitive, although sometimes wrong on key details. In one-sided bargaining in which sellers make a sequence of offers (and buyers know their own values), initial offers are higher than predicted, but they decline at close to the predicted rate. In bargaining games with large and small surplus, predictions about when "strikes"

---

[44] Mutual revelation and value bidding are more common in their first study, where subjects are students who know each other from a class, and norms of honesty among acquaintances apparently encourage truth telling. This is a reminder that the social context of bargaining matters.

[45] In the written and face-to-face conditions, only one-third of subjects truthfully revealed their actual values and another third actively misrepresented their values (more so in writing). Truth telling is not coordinated within dyads, because in only 4 percent and 8 percent of dyads did *both* players reveal in the written and face-to-face conditions.

(failures to agree) will occur, and how much players will earn, are roughly confirmed.

In the sealed-bid mechanism (or bilateral call market), buyers and sellers learn their own valuations and bid, and they trade at the halfway price if the seller offers less than the buyer bids. Strategies resemble the piecewise-linear equilibria predicted by theory to a remarkable degree. Changes in parameters lead to changes in bids in the predicted direction.

Preplay communication has two effects: Talking reduces strategic misrepresentation, resulting in efficiency that is *higher* than predicted (owing to a combination of norms, empathy, nonverbal cues, etc.); and players use communication to agree on a "one-price" equilibrium (an agreed-upon price at which both will bid) that is self-enforcing.

4.4 Conclusion

This chapter has surveyed dozens of experiments on bargaining. I will recap the key regularities and note directions for productive future research. In unstructured bargaining, players gravitate toward focal divisions, such as equal splits. When players bargain over chips that are converted to money at different rates, there are competing focal points: equal-chip divisions, and unequal divisions of chips that equalize money payoffs. Roth et al. showed that having two focal points leads to bimodality in agreements and increases the disagreement rate. Research on environments with richer information, which permits larger self-serving biases in perception, helps explain the rate of disagreement. Loewenstein, Babcock, Issacharoff, and myself showed that interested bargainers encode information self-servingly—they say that arguments that favor them are more important. Self-serving bias is not merely cheap talk, because it is correlated with the length of costly delay. The bias can be erased by having subjects absorb case facts before they know which side of the bargaining they are on (which clearly implicates cognitive encoding as a primary cause of self-serving bias) or by having subjects describe the weaknesses in their own case.

Theoretical work by Rubinstein (1982) and others led to many experiments on alternating-offer bargaining in which players strictly alternate offers and delay is costly because future gains from agreeing are discounted or there is a fixed cost to delay. Several experiments study alternating-offer bargaining with discounting. Generally, players deviate from (perfect) equilibrium predictions in the direction of equal splits, and offers are only weakly sensitive to the structural factors that are predicted to matter by game theory (e.g., bargaining horizon and discount factors). There is a little evidence that "suitable experience" creates convergence to perfect equilibrium, but these conditions seem to be special and fragile (playing separate games corresponding to subgames of a larger game in one study, or special instruction in backward induction).

Formal theories have been developed to explain deviations from self-interest in simple bargaining games, by incorporating a distaste for unequal divisions of money or an (indirect) taste for reciprocating behavior (see Chapter 2). Only one study applies these theories to complex bargaining games, with promising results (see Goeree and Holt, 2001).

These theories replace the self-interest assumption but retain the assumption of equilibrium. However, my work with Johnson et al. using computer displays to record attentional statistics showed deviations from equilibrium that cannot be attributed to social preferences. Players in a three-round game did not look ahead to the second and third rounds as much as backward induction requires—in 15 percent of trials, they did not even bother to open a box showing the "pie size" a round or two ahead. Their lookahead is limited even when they play computerized opponents that are self-interested and rational. Although it is not clear how to integrate limited computation formally with social utility theories, doing so would be an important breakthrough.

Binmore et al. and others have explored how outside options or threat points affect bargaining. The evidence squarely supports the noncooperative game theory view that outside threats affect bargaining divisions *only* if the divisions themselves make it credible for players to exercise the threats. (Cooperative solution concepts, such as the Nash bargaining solution, do not endogenously determine whether threats are credible, and hence are sensitive to threat points even when the subjects are not.)

One unusual result deserves mention. In bargaining with fixed costs of delay, equilibrium divisions give nearly everything to the player with a lower fixed cost (since a weaker player who holds out suffers relatively more and more as bargaining drags on). In the only experiment on these games, results are quite close to the equilibrium predictions, which are very unequal, in sharp contrast to results from shrinking-pie discounting games. It would be nice to know why perfect (self-interested) equilibria are reached when delay costs are fixed, but not in other structures.

Given the prominence of information asymmetries in naturally occurring bargaining, and the number of theoretical models of such situations, there are relatively few experiments with controlled differences in information. In an early study, Forsythe et al. found that the revelation principle, coupled with a "random dictator" assumption, does a remarkably good job of explaining when disagreements occur. Rapoport et al. investigate a "bazaar mechanism" in which a seller does not know a buyer's value, and makes a series of offers which decline over time. Offers decline as the theory predicts, but respond to changes in discount rates in the wrong direction. Buyers also accept offers too early, so there is scope for learning which should be explored in further experiments.

A few experiments study bilateral bargaining with two-sided incomplete information. These experiments use the "sealed-bid mechanism" in which both sides state a bid, and trade at the point halfway between the bids if the buyer bids more than the seller asks. Bids tend to lie somewhere between truthful revelation (bidding one's value) and piecewise-linear equilibria, which require buyers to bid less, and sellers to ask more, than their values. When the piecewise-linear bid function bends sharply, the empirical bid function usually bends as well.

Radner and Schotter (1989) noticed that in face-to-face bargaining with two-sided incomplete information players often overreveal their values (acting "too honestly," compared with what would maximize their payoffs), which leads to *more* efficiency than is predicted by individual rationality. Exploring this effect, Valley et al. (2002) found that players use the chance to communicate to agree on a single price, which they later bid—although usually not by revealing their actual values. These "one-price" agreements create more efficiency than is possible in the piecewise-linear equilibrium because players whose values are close wouldn't trade in the linear equilibrium, but are able to coordinate a mutually acceptable price when they can talk or pass messages.

It is interesting to contrast the results of the sealed-bid mechanism experiments, in which equilibrium predictions are remarkably accurate (after learning), with the results of alternating-offer bargaining, in which subgame perfection does not generally predict well. One explanation for the difference is that the sealed-bid mechanism is cognitively more transparent—players simply grope for a reasonable markdown factor and don't have to figure out how discount rates and time horizon convey bargaining power. Another explanation is that, since players in the alternating-offer games know precisely how much others are earning, fairness concerns loom larger than in the sealed-bid mechanism (in which the other player's earnings are not known ex ante because their values are not observed).

General theory that could reconcile the descriptive accuracy of game theory in the one domain with its failures in another would be a real triumph. Such a theory will probably weave together perceptions of equity (which may be shared or self-servingly disagreed about), stable social preferences for equal payoffs or fair treatment, heuristic computation, and individual differences (which necessarily create information asymmetries, since players are not sure about their opponent's patience or bargaining skill). Opening the Pandora's box of face-to-face bargaining should also be a research priority.

5
Dominance-Solvable Games

DOMINANCE IS THE MOST BASIC PRINCIPLE Strategy A strictly dominates B if the payoff from choosing A is higher than the payoff from B, for *any* strategy choice by other players' strategy. A weakly dominates B if A's payoffs are higher for some choices by others, and never lower.[1] Dominance is extremely appealing because, if A dominates B, A will turn out as least as good as B no matter *what* you think other players will do. This also means that you should choose a dominant strategy over a dominated one even if you don't know what other players' payoffs are, or how rational they are.

Assuming that other players obey dominance gives a player a way to make a simple, conservative guess about what others will do. Assuming others obey dominance can then enable a player to infer that certain payoffs from her own undominated strategies will never be realized—because they come about only if other players violate dominance. This inference can make a strategy that is initially undominated in effect dominated. Dominance can therefore be applied iteratively: First eliminate dominated strategies for all players; then check whether that first round of elimination makes some (initially undominated) strategies dominated; eliminate those (iteratedly) dominated strategies, and repeat. Games in which this process of iteratively deleting dominated strategies leads to a unique equilibrium are called "dominance solvable."

---

[1] A related concept which will occasionally come in handy is "stochastic dominance": A risky choice A stochastically dominates B if the chance of earning a fixed amount X or larger is always greater if you pick A than if you pick B.

Two examples will illustrate. Suppose driving the wrong way down a one-way street is akin to a violation of dominance. Then a pedestrian who thinks drivers obey dominance will expect cars to come from only one direction—the correct one—and need look only one way for oncoming cars. Looking both ways before crossing one-way streets therefore implies that the pedestrian thinks the driver may violate dominance.

The importance of a second level of mutual reasoning is illustrated by the words painted on the back of some large eighteen-wheeler trucks. The words are not painted very large, so drivers with normal vision (which excludes Superman and Mr. Magoo) can see them only as they get close to the truck. The words are: "If you *can* see this, I *can't* see you." That means drivers who are close enough to read the words are in the truck driver's "blind spot" (an area behind the truck not visible in the truck driver's side rear-view mirrors). The words install knowledge in the car driver's head about what the truck driver knows (or actually, what the truck driver *doesn't* know—namely, that a car is right behind). Truck drivers use this reminder because they have learned that drivers don't always realize that other drivers may not see or know the same things they themselves do, and that error causes accidents. (This "auto-autism" seems to be on the rise in modern America because drivers of jumbo sport utility vehicles often literally can't see that others can't see.)

Another example is previewed here and in Chapter 1 and is discussed much more later. In the "2/3 beauty contest" game, players choose numbers between 0 and 100. The number closest to (2/3) of the average number wins a fixed prize. Since the average will never be above 100, (2/3) of the average will never be above 67, so choosing a number above 67 violates dominance— no matter what people choose, you have a higher chance of winning by choosing 67 or below than choosing above it. Now if you think people obey dominance, then the average will be no more than 67, and (2/3) of the average will be no more than 44. Therefore, choosing above 44 violates *two* steps of iterated dominance. Choosing above (2/3)44, or 29, violates three steps of iterated dominance, and so forth.

Behavior in dominance-solvable games is an implicit measure of the extent of iterated deletion of dominated strategies. These measures could connect game theory to other social sciences, which study the beliefs people have about the beliefs and behavior of others.[2] The degree of subjects' strategic sophistication is also important in many basic social science de-

---

[2] For example, developmental psychologists have studied when and how children acquire the concept of "belief". Three year olds know that people who see inside a container know its contents, but do not know how perceptual input affects knowledge (e.g., they think that people who touch a blue ball without looking at it would know that it's blue) (see Wellman, 1990). A prominent theory of autism holds that autistics lack an understanding of beliefs of others, or "theory of mind" (Baron-Cohen, 1995).

bates. In diplomatic decisions, such as whether to impose an embargo or call a bluff, knowing how another country's leader will behave is crucial. In designing incentive contracts, it is important to guess how workers will respond to incentives. In a review of empirical work, Prendergast (1999) noted that workers usually respond rationally (e.g., by working harder when a piece rate payment for output is imposed), but firms do not usually use contracts that are predicted by theory to work best. This broad pattern is consistent with companies maximizing profits but being unwilling to bet heavily that workers will optimize. In political science it is often assumed that people vote "strategically"—i.e., they will vote against their most preferred candidate if doing so can increase the utility they get from the likely outcome. Evidence suggests however that people often vote surprisingly "sincerely" (Alvarez and Nagler, 2002). In the 2000 U.S. presidential election, for example, 4% of people voted for Ralph Nader, who had no real hope of winning. Most of these voters strongly preferred Al Gore over George Bush. Gore would have won if the Nader fans had voted for him; because they didn't, Bush won, giving the Nader voters their worst outcome.

Knowing how many steps of iterated reasoning players use is also essential for giving good advice. In the beauty contest game, for example, the unique Nash equilibrium is zero. But actually choosing zero in an experiment is a mistake, because the goal is to be one step in reasoning ahead of others, *but no further*. Good advice depends on having a good idea of what others will do.

As we shall see below, the number of steps of iterated thinking people use is limited for several reasons. The assumption that *others* obey dominance has a very different cognitive status than strict dominance: It is a guess about the rationality of other players (and about what the other players' payoffs are). Although it seems quite reasonable for players to obey dominance, it is less obvious that you should always expect others to obey dominance. Iterating further, to think that others will think *you* obey dominance is a guess about what somebody else thinks about you. As players proceed up this hierarchy of iterated reasoning, the scaffolding they climb gets more and more wobbly. The psycholinguist Herbert Clark jokes that the grasp of three or more levels of iterated reasoning "can be obliterated by one glass of decent sherry" (Clark and Marshall, 1981).

The experiments establish empirical bounds on the number of steps of reasoning players use. This approach has been rapidly successful. The first papers along these lines are less than ten years old, but in that time-span regular behavior has been observed in a very wide range of games. What have we learned? It is important to note one definition and a qualification. I define obeying dominance to be *one* step of iterated deletion of dominated strategies. Thus, when I say "players seem to use one level of iterated dominance," that means they obey dominance but do not believe that others will obey dominance. The qualification is that game payoffs are defined as utilities, and therefore measuring whether people violated dominance requires measuring utilities. But we can control money payoffs in experiments and make guesses about how utilities depend on payoffs. Therefore, for the purposes of measuring dominance violations, I will assume that players' utilities depend only on their own payoffs. Otherwise, it is difficult to tell whether a player is violating dominance, per se, or exhibiting a utility for something other than her own payoffs (see Chapter 2).

Nearly all people use one step of iterated dominance (i.e., they obey dominance).[3] However, at least 10% of players seem to use each of two to four levels of iterated dominance, and the median number of steps of iterated dominance is two. A conclusion this sharp is of course a simplification; readers who want a more precise answer should keep reading.

The chapter is divided into five sections. Section 5.1 is a warmup which reports results from the simplest games, in which iterations of dominance eliminate one or two strategies, and a "patent race" game in which iteration eliminates some strategies but not others. Section 5.2 discusses the "p-beauty contest" games mentioned above, in which players choose numbers and the player whose number is closest to p times the average of the numbers wins a fixed prize. Section 5.3 discusses games economists have studied for various purposes, in which iterated applications of dominance *reduce* the collective payoffs to players: Centipede, I and S games (akin to centipede and prisoners' dilemma), price competition, travelers' dilemma, and email games. Section 5.4 is about the "dirty faces" game used in logic, which has the opposite property of the games in the third section—namely, an increase in the number of steps of iterated dominance *increases* payoffs. Section 5.5 is a betting game. Section 5.6 describes two ambitious studies which posit a set of "types" (who use different amounts of iterated reasoning, or various decision rules) and estimate the frequency of types statistically. Section 5.7 draws conclusions and suggests ways that game theory might be modified to account for limited iterated reasoning.

Here is some tour-guide advice: The basic regularities that appear again and again throughout the chapter—one to three steps of iterated reasoning—can be grasped from the simpler games in Sections 5.1 and 5.2. Understanding the games in Sections 5.3 and 5.4, and the econometrically intensive studies in Section 5.6, requires more knowledge of game theory

---

[3] There is an important exception to the rare-violation rule: Dominance violations are common when doing so is an expression of social preference. For example, cooperating in the prisoners' dilemma manifests cooperativeness; contributing in dictator games manifests generosity; paying back money in a trust game manifests trustworthiness; and rejecting ultimatum offers manifests vengeance, even though all these actions violate dominance (assuming own-payoff maximization).

and more patience. Pick and choose games in Section 5.3 to read about based on your tastes: The centipede game is easy to grasp and closely related to trust games, discussed in Chapter 2. The I and S games of Van Huyck et al. illustrate subtleties of trigger strategy logic in repeated games. The price competition game and traveler's dilemma are relatively simple. The email game is tricky but illustrates how learning can create a surprising degree of equilibration. Sefton and Yavaş's fine mechanism experiment illustrates a rare showdown between "high theory" and experimental observation.

5.1 Simple Dominance-Solvable Games

Several experiments measure behavior in games that can be solved with only two or three levels of iterated dominance.

5.1.1 Games Solvable by Two Steps of Iterated Dominance

The simplest study, and one of the earliest, was done by Beard and Beil (1994). Their study was motivated by an example of Rosenthal (1981) designed to question the descriptive accuracy of backward induction (or, in a normal form game, iterated dominance). Payoffs in the game (in dollars) are shown in Table 5.1.

Player 1 moves first and can earn $9.75 for herself by choosing L (giving $3 to player 2). Or she can choose R, putting player 2 on the move. If player 2 behaves self-interestedly she responds with r, giving the two players $10 and $5, respectively. If player 2 violates dominance by choosing l, they earn $3 and $4.75. Subgame perfection selects the solution (R,r), if player 1 is self-interested and thinks player 2 is self-interested also.

This game tests whether player 1 is willing to bet heavily that others will obey dominance. By varying the game payoffs, Beard and Beil tested for various influences on frequency of subgame perfection and on player 1's

Table 5.1. *Beard and Beil's iterated dominance game*

Player 1 move	Player 2 move	
	l	r
L	9.75, 3	
R	3,4.75	10,5

Source: Beard and Beil (1994).

Table 5.2.   *Payoff treatments and results in Beard and Beil*

Treatment	Payoffs from			Frequency of		Number of pairs	Threshold $p(r|R)$
	(L, l)	(R, l)	(R, r)	L	r|R		
1 (baseline)	(9.75,3)	(3,4.75)	(10,5)	0.66	0.83	35	.97
2 (less risk)	(9,·)	(·,·)	(·,·)	0.65	1.00	31	.85
3 (even less risk)	(7,·)	(·,·)	(·,·)	0.20	1.00	25	.57
4 (more assurance)	(·,·)	(·,3)	(·,·)	0.47	1.00	32	.97
5 (more resentment)	(·,6)	(·,·)	(·,·)	0.86	1.00	21	.97
6 (less risk, more reciprocity)	(·,5)	(5,9.75)	(·,10)	0.31	1.00	26	.95
7 (1/6 payoff)	(58.5,18)	(18,28.5)	(60,30)	0.67	1.00	30	.97

Source: Beard and Beil (1994).
Note: (·,·) indicates the payoffs are the same as those in the baseline case.

beliefs about 2's likelihood of violating dominance. Table 5.2 summarizes the various payoffs and results (dots indicate the same payoffs as in the baseline treatment 1).

In the baseline treatment, 66% of player 1s choose L, while 83% of the R choices are met with the self-interested response r. The faith in 2's rationality required to justify choosing R is shown by the threshold probability $p(r| R)$; this is the belief in an r choice following R which makes R just preferable to L (if she is risk neutral). The threshold is 0.97 in the baseline treatment. Since 83% of player 2s choose r, the threshold is not quite met by actual behavior.

The "less risk" treatments 2–3 lower the risk of choosing R by lowering the L payoff to player 1. (The thresholds $p(r|R)$ fall to 0.85 and 0.57.) Player 1s then choose L less often—65% and 20%. In "more assurance" treatment 4, the gap in player 2's R payoffs is raised, providing more incentive for 2 to choose r instead of l. Player 1s respond by choosing L less often. In "more resentment" treatment 5, the payoff to player 2 from L is raised from $3 to $6. This is designed to create resentment in player 2 if 1 chooses R, which forces 2 to accept less than she would have gotten if L had been chosen. This treatment raises the fraction of nonsubgame perfect play of L to its highest level, 86%. The "more reciprocity" treatment again lowers risk for player 1, by raising player 2's R payoffs; then player 2 might feel inclined to reciprocate a "generous" choice of R by choosing r. This treatment lowers L choice to 31%. Finally, paying large stakes probabilistically, in treatment 7, does not affect the results at all relative to the baseline treatment 1 with equivalent expected payoffs.

Table 5.3.   *Goeree and Holt's credible threat games*

Condition	Number of pairs	Threshold $p(r|R)$	Payoffs (L)	(R,l)	(R,r)	Frequency of L	r|R
Baseline 1	25	.33	(70,60)	(60,10)	(90,50)	0.12	1.00
Lower assurance	25	.33	(70,60)	(60,48)	(90,50)	0.32	0.53
Baseline 2	15	.85	(80,50)	(20,10)	(90,70)	0.13	1.00
Lower assurance	25	.85	(80,50)	(20,68)	(90,70)	0.52	0.75
Very low assurance	25	.85	(400,250)	(100,348)	(450,350)	0.80	0.80

Source: Goeree and Holt (1999).

As Rosenthal conjectured, 1s do not usually have enough faith in 2's rationality and self-interest to choose the subgame perfect choice R, except when the assurance threshold is around a half (treatment 3) or player 2 seems likely to reciprocate a generous choice (treatment 6). At the same time, 2 *does* choose the self-interested response r in almost every case. Player 2s overwhelmingly obey dominance but player 1s are not willing to bet that player 2s will obey dominance.

The basic finding of Beard and Beil (1994) was replicated by Goeree and Holt (1999), in their insightful paper on "treasures and contradictions" in game theory.[4] Table 5.3 shows their results. The fraction of L moves varies from 12% to 80%. As in Beard and Beil's study, the tendency to play L responds predictably to differences in player 1's risk, and to the incentive player 2 has to play r rather than l. Starting from baseline condition 1, lowering the assurance that player 2 will move r (by making the differences between 2's payoffs in (R,r) and (R,l) closer) lowers the fraction of player 2s who *actually* move r, and raises the propensity of player 1s to move L. The same effect occurs starting from baseline 2. The *cost* of player 2's deliberate punishment or mistake affects what player 2 does, and player 1s seem to anticipate this in deciding whether to take the safe action L.

5.1.2 Iterated Dominance and Tree-Matrix Differences

Schotter, Weigelt and Wilson (1994) did a more extensive comparison of iterated dominance and subgame perfection. Their first games, 1M and 1S, are shown in Table 5.4. Games 1M and 1S are like the Beard and Beil games,

---

[4] The theme of their paper is that pairs of games which have the same kinds of equilibria can be constructed so that players choose the equilibrium in one game (treasure) but do not choose it in the equivalent paired game (contradiction). The major difference is that Goeree and Holt use the strategy method: They asked player 2s what they would do *if* player 1 chose R.

Table 5.4.   *Games 1M and 1S of Schotter et al.*

| | Player 2 | | Actual |
Player 1	l	r	frequency
Normal form (1M)			
L	4,4	4,4	(0.57)
R	0,1	6,3	(0.43)
Frequency	(0.20)	(0.80)	
Sequential form (1S)			
L	4,4		(0.08)
	l	r	
R	0,1	6,3	(0.92)
Frequency	(0.02)	(0.98)	

Source: Schotter, Weigelt, and Wilson (1994).

a test of player 1's willingness to expect 2 to obey weak dominance (game 1M) or play self-interestedly in the subgame (game 1S).

A large majority of player 2s *do* obey dominance—80% in 1M and 98% in 1S—but player 1s are willing to bet strongly on this (choosing R) only in the sequential game 1S. The difference in 1M and 1S behavior seems to be due to a matrix-tree "presentation effect."[5]

Schotter et al. also studied a hybrid game (1H) in which the game was described sequentially—players were actually shown a tree—but *played* simultaneously. In this hybrid version the fractions of R and r play were 86% and 88%, similar to results in the sequential version 1S. It appears that the physical description of the game is what matters. Perhaps the visual isolation of player 2's move in the tree makes dominance of r over l more transparent to player 1.

Their games 3M and 3S, in Table 5.5, allow investigation of three levels of iterated dominance (game 3M) and forward induction (game 3S). In 3M, B is strictly dominated for player 1. Eliminating it makes M weakly dominant for player 2. Eliminating T and B for player 2 then selects M for player 1, so (M,M) is selected by three steps of iterated dominance.

In an equivalent sequential game, 3S, player 1 can move T and end the game with payoffs (4,4), or put player 2 on the move. Player 2 can then

---

[5] Another example is the common violation of weak dominance manifested in sealed-bid second-price auctions, compared with strategically equivalent English ascending-price auctions (see Kagel, 1995; Camerer, 1998).

Table 5.5. *Games 3M and 3S of Schotter et al.*

Player 1 move	Player 2 move			Frequency
	T	M	B	
Normal form 3M				
T	4,4	4, 4	4,4	(0.82)
M	0,1	6,3	0,0	(0.16)
B	0,1	0,0	3,6	(0.02)
Frequency	(0.70)	(0.26)	(0.04)	

Sequential form 3S

				Conditional frequency
T	4,4			(0.70)
	T			
	0,1			
		M	B	
	M	6,3	0,0	(1.00)
	B	0,0	3,6	(0.00)
Frequency	(0.13)	(0.31)	(0.69)	

Source: Schotter, Weigelt, and Wilson (1994).

end the game with T, yielding (0,1), or else they play a simultaneous-move battle-of-the sexes (BOS) game with pure-strategy equilibria (M,M) and (B,B). In 3S, iterated dominance eliminates strategies in conjunction with an assumption of dynamic consistency, leading to (M, M). T is dominated for player 2 since she can guarantee more than 1 by mixing in the BOS subgame (if she is not too risk averse). And forward induction applies: If player 2 realizes that player 1 rejecting the (4,4) payoff signals 1's intention to play *M* in the subgame and get 6, then player 2 will also play M. This argument picks out the (M,M) equilibrium. The crucial difference in the game forms is that player 2 in 3S can move after *observing* what player 1 has done, rather than merely hypothesizing what 1 would do in game 3M (and 2 knowing in 3M that 1 realizes 2 is merely hypothesizing rather than "knowing").

Table 5.5 shows that in game 3M hardly any player 1s violate strict dominance by choosing B, but only a small minority of player 2s (26%) seem to anticipate that and deduce that they should play the weakly dominant

M. Thus, there is little evidence for more than one step of deletion of dominated strategies.[6]

The sequential 3S results are roughly similar. In the subgame player 1s always choose M. However, player 2s do not seem to figure this out and mistakenly choose B 69% of the time. Apparently anticipating this, player 1s mostly choose T, so the forward induction equilibrium (M,M) is rarely reached.

Overall, Schotter et al. saw very limited evidence of either much iteration of dominance (beyond one step), or subgame perfection and forward induction, except in the simplest case 1S. They speculate that more experience is needed to lead to dominance-solvable outcomes. Brandts and Holt (1995) did experiments with eight periods, however, and still observed only limited evidence of forward induction.

5.1.3 A Partially Dominance-Solvable Patent Race Game

Rapoport and Amaldoss (1997) ran a "patent race" investment game in which iterated deletion has an interesting alternating structure (see Zizzo, 2002). In their game the players are "strong" and "weak" (or deep- and shallow-pocketed firms). The strong player has an endowment of 5 and the weak player has an endowment of 4. Whichever player spends the most earns a reward of 10 (independent of what they spent), and keeps her endowment minus what she spent. If both players spend the same amount, neither one gets the reward. The payoffs are shown in Table 5.6.

Denote strong player investments of i by s_i and weak player investments by w_i. The stronger player can guarantee earning the reward by investing all 5, choosing s_5, simply outspending the weak player. Since this strategy strictly dominates investing 0 (and keeping the endowment of 5), strategy s_0 can be eliminated for the strong player. Eliminating s_0 then makes investing 1 dominated for the weak player (since investing 1 is only worthwhile if she has a chance of outspending the strong player, and she can't if the strong player never invests 0). Eliminating w_1 for the weak player then makes s_2 dominated by s_1 for the strong player, and so forth. Applying dominance iteratively leads to deletion of strategies in the following order: s_0, w_1, s_2, w_3, s_4. Further analysis derives predicted mixed-strategy probabilities for the undeleted strategies: Strong players should choose the highest investment, s_5, 60% of the time, and the weak players should throw in the towel by choosing the

---

[6] Schotter et al. also ran games 3Mb and 3Sb in which they changed the (0,0) payoffs to (2,2). This does not change the game-theoretic prediction at all but has one effect on the results. Player 2s in 3Mb chose T, M, and B 11%, 32%, and 57% of the time, respectively, rather than 70%, 27%, and 4%. Changing the 0 payoff from player 2 strategies M and B to a payoff of 2 makes the fact that T is dominated more obvious and reduces its choice frequency from 70% to 11%.

Table 5.6. *Payoffs in patent race game*

Weak player investment, w_i	Strong player investment, s_i						Prediction	Actual frequency
	0	1	2	3	4	5		
0	4,5	4,14	4,13	4,12	4,11	4,10	0.60	(0.55)
1	13,5	3,4	3,13	3, 12	3,11	3,10	0.00	(0.03)
2	12,5	12,4	2,3	2,12	2,11	2,10	0.20	(0.07)
3	11,5	11,4	11,3	1,2	1, 11	1,10	0.00	(0.14)
4	10,5	10, 4	10, 3	10,2	0,1	0,10	0.20	(0.22)
Prediction	0.00	0.20	0.00	0.20	0.00	0.60		
Frequency	(0.01)	(0.17)	(0.05)	(0.09)	(0.13)	(0.55)		

Source: Rapoport and Amaldoss (1997).

lowest investment, w_0, 60% of the time. Both should randomize equally over their other two undeleted strategies.

The predicted probabilities and actual frequencies across 160 periods are shown in Table 5.6. Conformity to this unintuitive equilibrium is quite good. Players were predicted to choose extreme investment levels 60% of the time and actually chose them 55% of the time. The fractions of play of the iteratively dominated strategies, in the order in which they are eliminated, were 0.01, 0.03, 0.05, 0.14, and 0.13. At the individual level, the fractions of players who violated one or more levels of iterated dominance at least once in 80 trials were 0.11, 0.32, 0.83, 0.70, and 0.92 (in order of increasing number of steps of iteration).[7]

Summary: In the simplest games in which iterated application of dominance deletes some strategies, few subjects violate dominance, but most subjects are also not willing to bet heavily that others will obey dominance (i.e., there is one step of iterated dominance). In the patent race games, most subjects exhibit three levels of iterated dominance, but some of their sophisticated behavior might be due to learning over 160 trials.

5.2 Beauty Contest Games

The "p-beauty contest" game first presented in Moulin (1986), and discussed earlier, is an ideal tool for measuring the number of steps of iterated deletion of dominated strategies. Each of N players i choose a number x_i in the

---

[7] That is, 11% of the strong players played s_0 at least once (89% never did), 32% of the weak players played w_1 at least once, and so on.

interval [0,100] simultaneously. A multiple p of the average of their numbers, $p \cdot \sum_{i=1}^{N} x_i/N$, defines a target number. The player whose number is closest to the target number wins a fixed prize. Before proceeding, readers should think of which number they would pick if they were playing against a group of students.

The game is called a "beauty contest" after the famous passage in Keynes's *General Theory of Employment, Interest, and Money* about a newspaper contest in which people guess which faces others will guess are most beautiful (see Chapter 1). Like people choosing the prettiest picture in Keynes's passage, players in the beauty contest game must guess what average number others will pick, then pick 2/3 of that average (knowing everyone is doing the same). The beauty contest game can distinguish whether people "practise the fourth, fifth, and higher degrees" of reasoning as Keynes wondered. Choosing a number larger than 67 violates stochastic dominance, because any such choice has less chance of winning than a choice of exactly 67 does. So numbers in the range (67,100] violate first-order iterated dominance. A player who thinks others obey dominance can infer that the target will be below (2/3)67, or 44, so an optimal choice is in the range [0,44]. Hence, a choice between (45,67] is consistent with a player obeying one step of dominance, but not two. Stepping further, choices in the range (29,44] are consistent with two steps of iterated dominance but not three. Thus, number choices in the beauty contest game place bounds on the frequency of violations of increasing degrees of iterated rationality. Infinitely many steps of iterated dominance lead to the unique Nash equilibrium of 0.

This game was first studied experimentally by Nagel (1995). She used groups of fourteen–sixteen German students as subjects. Her results from games with $p = 2/3$ are shown in Figure 5.1b. The average number is around 35, and many subjects chose either 33 (one step of reasoning from the midpoint of 50) or 22 (two steps). Very few subjects picked 0.

The first replication of Nagel's results was reported by Ho, Camerer, and Weigelt (1998). They used values of p of 0.7, 0.9, 1.1, and 1.3, to compare behavior when the Nash equilibrium is 0 (when $p < 1$) and the Nash equilibrium is the largest number (which results when $p > 1$). Subjects played one game with a particular value of p 10 times, then played another game in which p was on the opposite side of 1, so the equilibria in the two games were on opposite ends of the number interval.[8] There was an interesting effect of transfer of learning across the two games: Subjects who

---

[8] Subjects were students in Singapore in groups of three or seven playing for $3.50. Curiously, subjects in the larger groups tend to choose numbers closer to equilibrium and converge faster. We suspect that in the three-person groups, subjects think about each of the other two subjects separately, and generally want to be in the middle. In the seven-person groups, they think about the composite of the six other subjects, and want to be below the composite, which drives them closer to zero. Quantal-response equilibrium also predicts lower choices when groups are larger.

Table 5.7.   *Estimated fractions ω_k of level-k types in beauty contest games*

Estimate	Ho, Camerer, and Weigelt (1998)		Nagel (1995)	
	$p > 1$ games	$p < 1$ games	$p = 1/2$	$p = 2/3$
ω_0	0.22	0.16	0.16 (0.24)	0.28 (0.13)
ω_1	0.31	0.21	0.38 (0.30)	0.34 (0.44)
ω_2	0.13	0.13	0.47 (0.41)	0.37 (0.39)
ω_3	0.34	0.50	0.00 (0.06)	0.00 (0.03)

Note: Numbers in parentheses indicate Nagel's original estimates.

had converged toward a high equilibrium in one game (with $p > 1$) tended to start higher in the second game with $p < 1$, but also converged more rapidly, as if they "learned to learn" from one game to another (see Camerer, Ho, and Chong, 2002a,b, and Chapter 6).

In further experiments, Ho, Weigelt, and I became interested in the influence of the size of the stakes on behavior. Higher stakes might induce subjects to think harder or might lead subjects to think *others* would think harder, which would lead them to choose lower numbers. We compared low ($7) and high ($28) stakes conditions across ten periods; the results were shown in Figures 1.3a and 1.3b. There was a small effect of stakes lowering number choices (i.e., increasing the number of steps of thinking), especially in later periods when virtually all the high-stakes subjects chose numbers less than 1.

In our paper we also improved on the casual way in which Nagel measured steps of iterated reasoning. Following Stahl and Wilson (1995) (see Section 5.5 below), we assumed that a fraction ω_0 of the subjects just choose a number randomly from a normal distribution with mean μ and standard deviation σ. Call these subjects "level-0" players. A fraction ω_1 are level-1 players, who think all others are level-0 players and choose best responses with some noise. There are also assumed to be fractions ω_2 and ω_3 of level-2 and level-3 players, each of whom thinks all others are one level below them and best-respond.

Table 5.7 shows the estimated fractions of the various levels of players, using only first-round data. The estimated fractions of levels of reasoning show that players are typically using one to three steps of iterated reasoning. Nagel's informal estimates (shown in parentheses) are close to the estimates derived by our earlier procedure.

Several variants of the beauty contest game have been done. Figure 5.1 shows histograms taken from Nagel (1999). Using the median instead of the average to compute the target does not change results (Figure 5.1c).

Figures 5.1g–h show experiments by Ho, Weigelt, and myself (unpublished) in which the equilibrium is located in the *interior* of the number

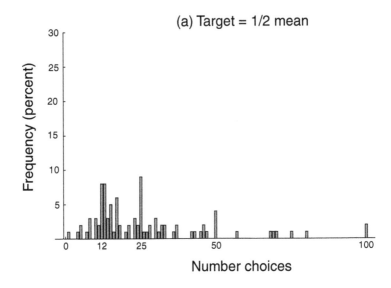

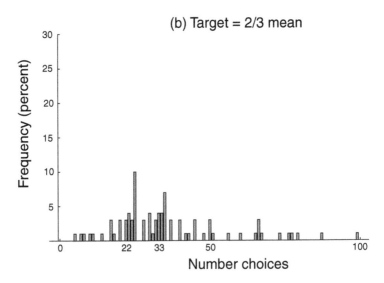

Figure 5.1.   *Beauty contest choices. Sources: Based on data from Nagel (1999) and Camerer, Ho, and Weigelt (unpublished).*

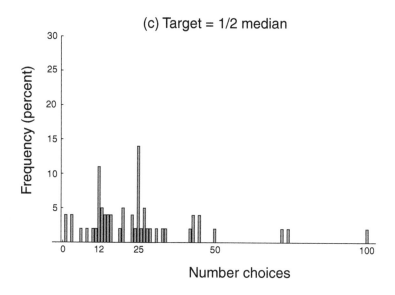

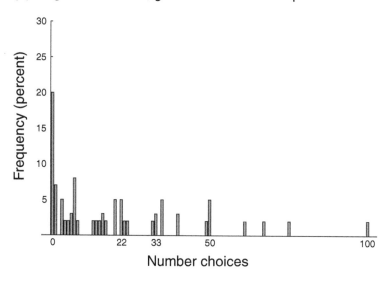

Figure 5.1 (continued)

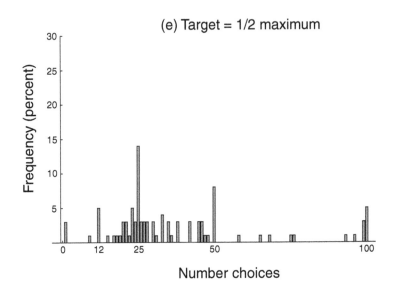

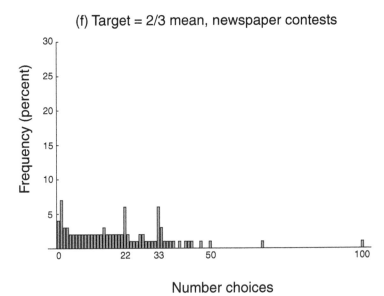

Figure 5.1 (continued)

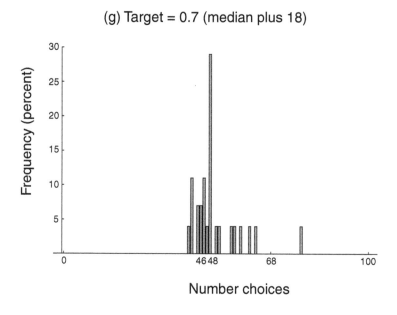

(g) Target = 0.7 (median plus 18)

Number choices

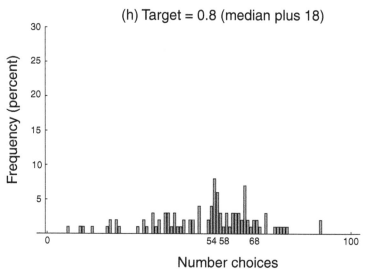

(h) Target = 0.8 (median plus 18)

Number choices

Figure 5.1 (continued)

interval. When the target is $p(M + 18)$ (where M is the median number), then the equilibrium is 42 if $p = 0.7$ and 72 if $p = 0.8$. Locating the equilibrium in the interior is useful because having an equilibrium on the boundary makes it impossible, strictly speaking, to distinguish equilibrium play plus random noise from limited iterated reasoning.

Nagel's graphs helpfully mark the x-axis with numbers that correspond to various steps of reasoning (starting from 50). For example, in the $M + 18$ game with $p = 0.8$, subjects who think others will choose an average of 50 and best-respond will choose 54; best-responding to 54 yields 58, and so forth. The distributions show spikes at numbers that correspond to one or two steps of reasoning.

The beauty contest game has been used in demonstration experiments from many exotic subject pools in public lectures. These data have less experimental control than in the laboratory, but they are informative about whether unusual groups who we cannot usually get into the lab behave like college students.

Figure 5.2 shows data from several unusual subject pools (see Camerer, 1997). Caltech students are in the front of the figure, followed by economics Ph.D.s, and so on, with portfolio managers last. One group is portfolio managers who make investment decisions on behalf of large groups of people (and who are savvy about how stock markets work). Another group is students in a graduate (Ph.D.) course in economics, who have all learned about simple game theory concepts. Still another group is Caltech undergraduates in a psychology course, using $p = 2/3$. Their average was around 24, about a half-step of reasoning lower than in other student populations. These data are useful because it is often asserted that subjects who are "smart enough" will make choices much closer to game-theoretic predictions than average college subjects will. The median SAT math score at Caltech is often 800, the maximum. The fact that the Caltech students do not choose numbers that much closer to the Nash equilibrium than average folks refutes the hypothesis that simply being good at math will automatically lead players to a Nash equilibrium.

Giving a lecture to the Caltech Board of Trustees, I had a chance to see how older adults with an amazingly wide range of personal achievements would play this game in a group of their peers. The group had a subsample of twenty CEOs, corporate presidents, and board chairmen. Members of this subsample are indeed among the titans of industry who are often thought of as the "rational decision makers" whose ideas and behavior influence the entire economy. Their results are shown in the CEO histogram in Figure 5.2.

Another interesting subject pool is readers of financial magazines. Two experiments were conducted, one by Rosemarie Nagel and Antonio Bosch in the Spanish business magazine *Expansion*, another by Richard Thaler in the British newspaper *The Financial Times*. Readers were offered a large prize

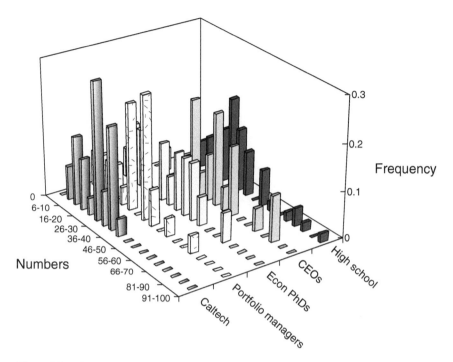

Figure 5.2.   *Beauty contest choices from various exotic subject pools. Source: Camerer (unpublished).*

if they won a $p = 2/3$ contest. The pooled results from these two newspaper contests are shown in Figure 1f. There is a sharp spike at 33 and another spike at 22. About 8% of subjects chose the equilibrium of 0. Interestingly, there is no prominent spike between 22 (two steps of reasoning) and 0. Players who did more than two steps of reasoning seemed to pick up momentum rolling down a slippery inductive slope, and continued their logical induction all the way to 0.[9]

Slonim (2001) had subjects play three beauty contests for three periods each, and mixed together players with different levels of experience. When an experienced player is suddenly mixed in with two new subjects who have not played before, what happens? One possibility is that the experienced

---

[9] It is also notable that the *Financial Times* and *Expansion* readers had a lower average number, and many fewer outlying responses above 50, than subjects in other experiments. This fact is, frankly, a little disturbing for experimenters because it points out the way in which a highly educated group of subjects, volunteering to participate in a mass public experiment, might reason more thoughtfully than students corralled together to make a choice in the usual experimental style.

player recalls what *she* did when she first played the game, and is able to use that information to outguess the newbies. Or it might be that choosing low numbers has become so natural or obvious to the experienced player, that she chooses *too low* a number (adjusting too little for the fact that new players will pick high numbers, a "curse of knowledge") and does *worse* than the new folks. It turns out that the experienced players use their experience wisely—they choose higher numbers when the new players arrive, and win almost all the time. But their edge disappears after one period.

Summary: In beauty contest games, the typical subject uses one or two steps of reasoning (starting from 50). This basic result has been obtained with the widest variety of subject pools ever sampled for a particular game. Unusual analytical skill and training in game theory move choices about one iteration closer to the equilibrium. Samples of self-selected newspaper readers also make choices closer to equilibrium.

5.3 Games in Which Iterated Reasoning Decreases Payoffs

This section discusses dominance-solvable games in which higher levels of iterated reasoning reduce the collective payoffs to players.

5.3.1 Centipede Games

By repeatedly passing, the players can enlarge the pie dramatically, but as the pie grows the temptation to choose Take does too.

A four-move "centipede" game[10] studied by McKelvey and Palfrey (1992) is shown in Figure 5.3. At each node, a player can "take" (T) 80% of a growing pie and end the game, or "pass" (P) and let the other player move, doubling the pie each period. The collective gain to passing is huge. In the four-move game, players could share $8 ($6.40 + $1.60) if they pass at every node, but if a player takes immediately they share just $0.50.

Centipede games are multistage trust games (Chapter 2 discusses one-stage trust games). They model situations such as business or personal relationships in which there are gains from exchange which grow over time (perhaps owing to learning), and a constant temptation for each player to end the relationship to grab more. Backward induction (along with self-interest) predicts that players will expect taking at the last node (since passing at that point violates dominance), which leads to taking at the next-to-last node, and so forth to the start: Players will take at *every* node. The

---

[10] The game (introduced by Rosenthal, 1981) was dubbed a "centipede" game by Ken Binmore because it has one hundred vertical terminal nodes which, graphically, resemble a centipede insect.

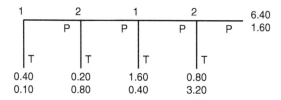

Figure 5.3.   *A centipede game with four moves. Source: Based on McKelvey and Palfrey (1992).*

game measures steps of iterated reasoning because passing at node t violates $5 - t$ steps of iterated dominance.

The centipede game illustrates an important byproduct of experimentation: Choosing a design disciplines theorizing because it forces one to be crystal clear about the conditions under which theory is really expected to apply. In centipede games, the dollar payments to subjects vary dramatically across possible outcomes. In a six-move game, the Nash equilibrium predicts the experiment will cost $.50 per trial. But if subjects completely trust each other and pass to the end it will cost $32, sixty-four times as much! Choosing the scale of payoffs requires an experimenter literally to bet money—the experimental budget—on what will happen.

The baseline game is the four-move game shown in Figure 5.3. McKelvey and Palfrey used undergraduate subjects at Caltech (CIT) and Pasadena City College (PCC), which spans a range of analytical skill. They also ran a six-move game and a version of the four-move game with payoffs multiplied by four. Table 5.8 shows results aggregated across four PCC and two CIT sessions for sequences 1–5 and 6–10.

Table 5.8.   *Results in McKelvey and Palfrey's centipede games*

Treatment	Trials	Conditional frequencies of "take" at nodes					
		1	2	3	4	5	6
Four moves	1–5	0.06	0.32	0.57	0.75		
	6–10	0.08	0.49	0.75	0.82		
Four moves,	1–5	0.08	0.46	0.60	0.80		
high stakes	6–10	0.22	0.41	0.74	0.50		
Six moves	1–5	0.00	0.06	0.18	0.43	0.75	0.81
	6–10	0.01	0.07	0.25	0.65	0.70	0.90

Source: McKelvey and Palfrey (1992).

Players rarely take in early nodes as Nash equilibrium (and four steps of iterated dominance) predict. However, conditional "take" probabilities *do* increase at each node and most subjects (around 80%) take at the last node. There is some evidence of "unraveling" toward the equilibrium, because take probabilities are higher at every node in trials 6–10 than in the earlier trials 1–5. There is little effect from quadrupling the stakes.

By design, the subgame consisting of the last four moves in the low-stakes condition (beginning with the third node) is *exactly* the same as the four-move game with high stakes. If players build up trust over time, then they should be more likely to pass at the third node of the longer six-move game than at the start of the four-move game. Actually, the opposite is true. Having had two periods of prior trust in the six-move game does not enhance tendency to pass.

Following the insight of the famous "gang of four" paper on the repeated prisoners' dilemma (Kreps et al., 1982), McKelvey and Palfrey explain the high rates of passing with an equilibrium model in which a small percentage (7%) of altruistic players truly prefer to pass, and a large percentage of normal players mimic the altruists by passing up to a point in order to earn more.[11] Gradual unraveling is explained by including an error rate that shrinks over time (see also Zauner, 1999).

Fey, McKelvey, and Palfrey (1996) control for the influence of social preferences using a constant-sum centipede game. The players divide $3.20. At the first take node, the sum is divided evenly; as players pass, the division of the $3.20 gets more and more lopsided. If players pass in the regular centipede game just to create more surplus to share (as if conspiring against the experimenter), they will take right away in the constant-sum version of the game. In fact, players do take much more often. In the last half of the experiment, the conditional rates of playing take are more than half at the first node and around 80% at the second node. A quantal response equilbrium (QRE) model with an increasing response sensitivity (a reduced-form model of learning) fits the data reasonably well.

Nagel and Tang (1998) ran normal-form centipede game experiments with extensive-form feedback: Players state the first node at which they would "take"; the player who took at the later node is told the node at which the other player took but not vice versa (i.e., if you took first you don't know when the other player would have taken). Players take about halfway through the game, and there is no evidence of learning to take earlier. In fact, there is a slight movement toward taking *later*, away from the Nash equilibrium (see Ho, Wang, and Camerer, 2002).

---

[11] This idea was first informally implemented by Camerer and Weigelt (1988; see Chapter 8) and Palfrey and Rosenthal (1988), but McKelvey and Palfrey deserve credit for the first high-tech implementation, which marked the start of more sophisticated "experimetrics."

Table 5.9.   *Centipede-type game I of Van Huyck et al.*

Row	Column strategies				
strategies	a_1	a_2	a_3	a_4	a_5
a_1	7,7	0,11	0,0	0,0	0,0
a_2	11,0	6,6	0,10	0,0	0,0
a_3	0,0	10,0	5,5	0,9	0,0
a_4	0,0	0,0	9,0	4,4	0,8
a_5	0,0	0,0	0,0	8,0	3,3

First period of repeated game I(5/6,2)

First sequence	0.20	0.20	0.40	0.18	0.03
Last sequence	0.30	0.23	0.23	0.23	0.03

Source: Van Huyck, Wildenthal, and Battalio (2001).

Rapoport et al. (in press) ran three-person centipede games with enormous stakes (subjects could have made thousands of dollars if they passed to the end . . . but they didn't). They found a very low rate of passing. In a low-stakes condition, subjects lend more often, so a sufficient condition for Nash behavior seems to be three players and high stakes. (The cognitive hierarchy model of Camerer, Ho, and Chong, 2001, can explain the difference between two- and three-player games but QRE cannot.)

5.3.2 Prisoners' Dilemma and Quasi-Centipede Games

Van Huyck, Wildenthal, and Battalio (2002) investigate two 5 × 5 dominance-solvable games, shown in Tables 5.9 and 5.10. One has a centipede structure (game I) and one is a multi-strategy prisoners' dilemma (game S). The games are denoted I and S because I is solved by *i*terated dominance and S is solved by *s*trict dominance.

In game I, strategy a_2 weakly dominates[12] a_1; eliminating a_1 makes a_2 dominated by a_3, and so forth, until only a_5 is left. However, the unique Nash equilibrium (a_5, a_5) is Pareto dominated by any other (non-equilibrium) outcome on the diagonal.

Game S is more straightforward: Strategy a_5 strictly dominates all other strategies, leading to a unique Nash equilibrium (a_5, a_5) which is Pareto dominated.

---

[12] Lower-numbered strategies can also be eliminated by strict dominance using the mixed strategy which puts 0.70 weight on a_2 and smears positive support on each of the higher-numbered strategies.

Table 5.10.   *Prisoners' dilemma–type game S of Huyck et al.*

Row strategies	Column strategies				
	a_1	a_2	a_3	a_4	a_5
a_1	7,7	0,0	0,0	0,0	0,11
a_2	0,0	6,6	0,0	0,0	0,10
a_3	0,0	0,0	5,5	0,0	0,9
a_4	0,0	0,0	0,0	4,4	0,8
a_5	11,0	10,0	9,0	8,0	3,3

First period of repeated game S(5/6,2)

First sequence	0.25	0.05	0.08	0.00	0.63
Last sequence	0.65	0.00	0.00	0.00	0.35

Source: Huyck, Wildenthal, and Battalio (2001).

Van Huyck et al. were interested in the emergence of repeated-game equilibria when the game is played with a fixed-partner protocol. They compare treatments $G(\delta, T)$, where δ is the probability of continuing the game after each period (with the same partner), and T is the length of the terminal "continuation game" after the probabilistically-repeated game ends. Specifically, they compare one-shot games I(0,1) and S(0,1) with I(5/6,2) and S(5/6,2). In the latter games, players are told that there is a 5/6 chance the game will continue after each trial. When that phase ends, they play exactly two more periods, hence the notation (5/6,2). In the repeated game, the 5/6 continuation probability is high enough that it is an equilibrium for both players to choose a_1 and to punish a defection from this equilibrium by choosing the next-best repeated-equilibrium payoff.[13]

There is a subtle strategic difference between repeated games I(5/6,2) and S(5/6,2). Axelrod (1985) pointed out that trigger strategies—such as punishing one's opponent for defecting in a repeated PD—are "clear" in the sense that there is little doubt the punishment is meant to exact revenge for an earlier defection. In game I(5/6,2), playing a_2 is itself a repeated-game equilibrium *and* is also the optimal way to defect, in the short run, from the a_1 equilibrium. To see this, suppose in game I that we are bumping along happily playing a_1, and earning 7 each time. Now one player switches to a_2. Are they "defecting," which merits punishment by reverting

---

[13] In the PD-like game S, the next-best payoff is 11 from reverting to the Nash equilibrium a_5. In the centipede-like game I, the next-best payoff is the 11 from a_2. These conditions give long-run payoffs to choosing a_1 of $7 + \delta/(1 - \delta)(7)$ and a payoff to defecting of $11 + \delta/(1 - \delta)(3)$. For $\delta = 5/6$, sticking to the a_1 equilibrium yields a higher payoff than defecting (42 rather than 26).

to the Nash equilibrium a_5, or are they switching to the a_2 equilibrium? You simply can't tell. The PD game $S(5/6,2)$ is different. In that game, if players are choosing a_1 reliably, and one player chooses a_2, that choice is not a profitable defection (since it yields a payoff of 0). Instead, a choice of a_2 is "clearly" a switch to the slightly less efficient repeated-game path of a_2. Van Huyck et al. argue that confusion about whether a defection in $I(5/6,2)$ to a_2 is a punishment, or a reversion to a new equilibrium, may undermine the effectiveness of such a punishment as a way of supporting the Pareto-efficient repeated-game equilibrium at a_1. If they are right, there will be more choices of a_1 in $S(5/6,2)$ than in $I(5/6,2)$.

In the centipede-like game $I(0,1)$, subjects paired randomly in one-shot games started out choosing a mixture of distributions with a median of a_3, and converged in about twenty rounds to a modal choice of a_5. Since the median a_3 corresponds to three steps of iterated dominance, this initial play of a_3 is roughly consistent with the other games in this chapter. In the one-shot PD-like game $S(0,1)$, subjects overwhelmingly chose the dominant strategy a_5 from the beginning, although a few persistently chose the cooperative outcome a_1.

Behavior in the repeated games $I(5/6,2)$ and $S(5/6,2)$ is interesting. Some summary statistics are reported in the bottom panel of Tables 5.9 and 5.10. The statistics show the frequency distributions across actions for the *first* period in each sequence, averaged over the first and last sequences in each of the four sessions. These statistics show how subjects start off each time they play a separate sequence, and how this initial behavior varies across sequences.

Game $I(5/6,2)$ results look like those in the one-shot game $I(0,1)$: Subjects play a_1 through a_4 with almost equal probability. These frequencies do not change much from the first of the eight sequences in each session to the last sequence. Subjects are not learning, across sequences, to coordinate on the more efficient repeated-game equilibrium a_1.

Behavior is quite different in the repeated game $S(5/6,2)$. In the first sequence more than half of subjects play the dominated strategy a_5. By the last (eighth) sequence, more than half are choosing a_1 in the first period. In the last five of the eight sequences, the median subject plays a_1 until the continuation phase is over, then reverts to a_5 in both periods of the terminal phase. Just as Van Huyck et al. conjectured, clarity of defection is able to support the efficient a_1 repeated-game equilibrium in the PD-like game $S(5/6,2)$, but not in $I(5/6,2)$.

5.3.3 Price Competition

Capra, Goeree, Gomez, and Holt (2002) studied a dominance-solvable game of imperfect price competition. Two firms choose prices, p_1 and p_2, from the interval [\$0.60, \$1.60]. Assume $p_1 < p_2$. Then the low-price firm earns p_1 and

the high-price firm earns a fraction $\alpha \cdot p_1$ (in the experiment α is 0.2 or 0.8).
If the prices are equal they each earn $(1+\alpha)p_1/2$.

The parameter α measures the degree of responsiveness of buyers to
which seller named the best price. When α is close to 1, buyers still buy from
the high-price seller, but at the lower price. This kind of structure reflects
markets with "meet-or-release" contracts, in which buyers pledge to buy from
sellers, who in turn must either meet a competitor's lower price or release
the buyer to go elsewhere. When α is low, buyers gravitate toward the low-
price seller. The effect of price competition is perhaps more relevant in the
economy than ever before, as the Internet allows consumers to search for
prices with the click of a mouse.

The imperfect price competition game is also similar to a centipede
game in which players "start" at low prices. "Passing" corresponds to raising
the price. Players have a joint incentive to raise prices by passing, but if a
player ever expects the other player to stop passing then she wants to stop
first and name the minimum price.

When $\alpha < 1$, theory predicts that Bertrand competition drives prices to
the minimum of \$0.60, the unique Nash equilibrium, regardless of how far
α is below 1. Capra et al. also derive quantal response equilibria, and prove
that raising α leads to higher QRE prices.

Figure 5.4 shows the time series of prices in each of three sessions with
$\alpha = 0.8$ (dotted lines) and three sessions with $\alpha = 0.2$ (thin lines). Averages
of same-α sessions are shown with thick lines. When $\alpha = 0.2$, prices fall from
around \$0.90 to \$0.70, converging reasonably close to the Nash prediction
of \$0.60. But when $\alpha = 0.8$, prices start around \$1.20 and do not converge
downward at all.

5.3.4 The Travelers' Dilemma

Capra et al. (1999) and Cabrera, Capra, and Gómez (2002) ran experiments
on a "travelers' dilemma" which is quite similar to their price competition
games (and also to p-beauty contests[14]). In the travelers' dilemma, two
players simultaneously state price claims, between 80 and 200, for luggage
they lost. The airline pays both players the *minimum* price. The airline also
adds a reward of R to the player who stated the lower price, and subtracts a
penalty of R from the player who stated the higher price.

Payoff-maximizing players will state prices one unit below what others
are expected to state, in order to boost the minimum price (and hence their

---

[14] Nagel (1998) has run beauty contest experiments in which the player whose number is closest to p
times the average earns the average, so that payoffs fall as equilibration occurs. This variant is closely related
to the travelers' dilemma and the imperfect price competition game.

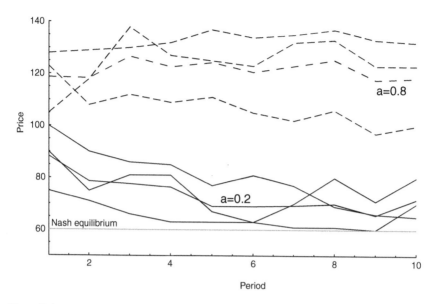

Figure 5.4.   *Time series of prices with imperfect competition. Source: Based on data from Capra et al. (2002)*

payoff) while earning the reward R. The result is a "race to the bottom" in which players should choose the minimum claim, the unique Nash equilibrium. The travelers' dilemma is like a price competition game in which consumers buy from each of two sellers at the lower price but also reward and penalize sellers who stated lower and higher prices (reflecting word-of-mouth recommendations, spitefully withholding future demand from high-priced sellers, and so forth).

Figure 5.5 shows the average price claimed across the ten rounds of part A, for six values of the reward/penalty parameter R. Prices gradually converge toward the Nash equilibrium of 80 (the lowest possible price) only when $R = 50$ or 80. When R is lower (5 or 10), players actually move slightly *away* from the Nash equilibrium, toward a collusive price of 200.

Capra et al. also discuss learning theories that attempt to explain the pattern of adjustment (see Chapter 6).[15]

---

[15] They fit a fictitious play model which gets the direction of convergence right—it fits the upward drift when $R = 5$ and 10, and the downward drift in other conditions—but it is off by a factor of four predicting the magnitude of convergence. An experience-weighted attraction EWA does better because it is responsive to forgone payoffs and also depreciates old experience, enabling larger changes across the experiment than fictitious play (see Ho, Camerer, and Chong, 2001).

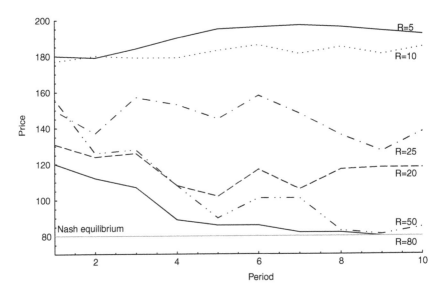

Figure 5.5.   *Time series of prices in price-matching games with varying loyalty parameters R.*
Source: Based on data from Capra et al. (1999).

5.3.5 The "Email Game"

The "email game" is an interesting dominance-solvable game, introduced
in economics by Ariel Rubinstein (1989). Rubinstein's game is based on a
well-known problem in parallel computing called the "coordinated attack
problem," described by Joseph Halpern (1986). I illustrate the argument
using the parameters from an unpublished experiment conducted by Barry
Blecherman, David Goldstein, and myself.

In our experiments there are two states, M1 and M2, which occur with
probabilities .2 and .8. Occurrence of each state triggers use of a different
payoff matrix, shown in Table 5.11. The informed player 1 *always* knows
the state (and hence the matrix). If the state is M1, then no messages are
sent to player 2. If the state is M2, a message is sent to player 2 announcing
that the state is M2. This message (and all subsequent messages) is received
by the receiver player with probability .8 and intercepted with probability
.2. When a message is received, the receiving player automatically sends
a reply acknowledging its receipt; the reply may also be transmitted or
intercepted, and so on. The message-sending process stops when a message
is intercepted. There will always be a finite time at which a message gets
intercepted and the process screeches to a halt.

In the coordinated attack interpretation of the game, players 1 and 2
are generals commanding divisions of an army. The enemy has troops at

Table 5.11.   *Payoff matrices M1 and M2 for the "email game"*

		Uninformed player 2 choice	
State M1		A	B
Informed player 1 choice	A	1,1	0,−2
	B	−2,0	0,0
State M2		A	B
Informed player 1 choice	A	0,0	0,−2
	B	−2,0	1,1

location B, but may be moving some of those troops to A. The states M1 and M2 correspond to the location of the troops—if the enemy troops are moved to A, that's state M1; if they are still massed at B, that's state M2. The payoffs reflect the fact that the two generals (players 1 and 2) together can defeat the enemy if they can coordinate their attack at the right location—if they coordinate an attack at A when the state is M1, or coordinate an attack at B when the state is M2. But the enemy always has troops left behind at B, so if a single general takes troops there by himself (choosing B when the other general chooses A), he will suffer defeat and earn a negative payoff.

First notice that if the states were common knowledge, then the players would choose A in state M1 (because choosing A weakly dominates choosing B) and B in state M2 if they use payoff dominance to select the (B,B) equilibrium. If the players do not know anything about the states (other than their probabilities), there is an equilibrium in which both players choose A, another equilibrium in which both players choose B, and a mixed-strategy equilibrium. The important point is that having common knowledge of the state is essential to achieve full coordination (that is, to agree on A when the state is M1 and on B when the state is M2). Rubinstein asks: What if the players do not have common knowledge, but have "almost common knowledge," in the sense that they know others know they know . . . up to several levels of iterated knowledge? Will they play as if they have common knowledge?

In the experiment, we tried to make this tricky game as concrete as possible. Players were shown hypothetical "information sheets" listing all the messages each player sent and received. Figure 5.6 is a tree depicting sequences of messages and the associated information sheets subjects would see. For example, suppose the state is M2 (triggering the message-sending process), player 1's first message is received, player 2's acknowledgement

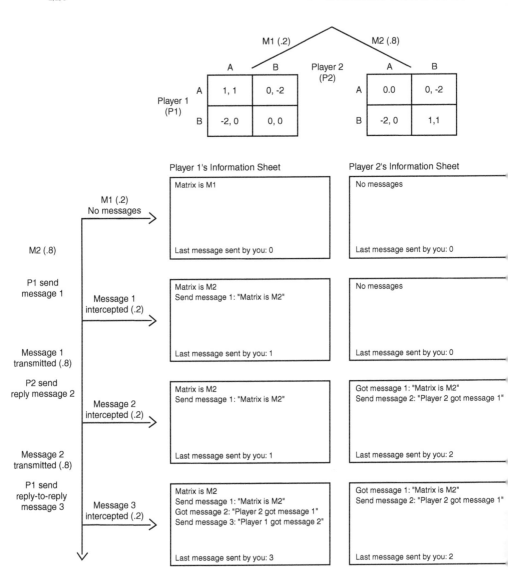

Figure 5.6. *Information tree showing information sheets of players in the "email game."*

is sent and received, but player 1's reply to player 2's acknowledgement is intercepted. Then player 2's information sheet reminds her that she received a message saying "Matrix is M2," that she sent a reply saying "Player 2 got message 1," and that she heard nothing back (the third or fourth box down on the right of Figure 5.6). The crucial point is that player 2, in this situation, cannot tell whether her message to player 1 was intercepted (third box), or whether player 1 received the message and sent a reply that was intercepted (fourth box). That is, player 1's message sheet might say "Matrix is M2, sent message" or it might say "Matrix is M2, sent message, player 2 sent reply, sent reply to reply." Since player 2 can't tell if she is in the third or fourth row of Figure 5.6, she can't be sure what player 1 knows.

However, a Bayesian probability calculation shows that the relative probabilities of being in these two situations are .56 and .44; that is, it is slightly more likely that one's message was intercepted than that the message got through and the reply was intercepted.[16]

What will actually happen if players obey iterated dominance? Start with the top row in Figure 5.6. If player 1 knows the state is M1, and obeys weak dominance, she chooses A for sure. Now consider player 2 when her information sheet says "No messages." She doesn't know whether the state is M1 (i.e., she is in the top row) or the state is M2 but player 1's message was intercepted (i.e., she is in the second row). The relative probabilities are .56 and .44. If she uses two steps of iterated dominance, she will figure out that, if she is in the top row, then player 1 will choose A. Suppose, for the sake of argument, that player 2 thinks player 1 will choose B if she is in the second row. Now if player 2 chooses A, she earns a payoff of 1 with probability .56, and a payoff of 0 with probability .44. Or she can choose B, earning a payoff of −2 with probability .56 and a payoff of 1 with probability .44. Choosing A stochastically dominates B because she has a higher chance of winning 1 (.56 instead of .44) and a lower chance of losing 2 (0 instead of .56). Therefore, player 2 should choose A if her information sheet says "No messages." It is just too risky to gamble that the state is M1 and choose B, because the state is more likely to be M1 and choosing B yields the worst payoff (−2) if player 1 obeys dominance in that state and chooses A.

Now suppose player 1 has the information sheet in rows 2–3, which says that the state is M2 and she sent a message to player 2 but no reply was received. If player 1 thinks that player 2 uses two steps of iterated dominance,

---

[16] The unconditional probability of getting to the third row of the information sheet is .8(.8)(.2)—that is, the state must be M2 (probability .8), the first message from player 1 must get through (probability .8), *and* the reply must get intercepted (probability .2). Similarly, the unconditional probability of being in the fourth row is .8(.8)(.8)(.2). These two probabilities are .128 and .1024. Thus, given that player 2 has the information sheet in the third or fourth rows, which happens with total probability .128 + .1024 = .2304, the relative probability of being in the third row is .128/.2304, or .56.

she can figure out that player 2 will choose A if her information sheet says "No messages." Suppose player 2 is likely to choose B if she has the information sheet in the third or fourth rows. Faced with her information sheet that says "Matrix is M2, send message 1" and nothing more, if player 1 chooses A then she earns 0 for sure (since she knows the matrix is M2, and choosing A always yields zero in M2). If she chooses B, she earns -2 with probability .56, and thinks she earns 1 with probability .44, an expected value of -0.68. Thus, unless player 1 is very risk seeking (or misunderstands the probability), if she thinks player 2 uses two steps of iterated dominance she will choose A.[17] The latter step in the argument is crucial. Player 1 knows for sure that the state is M2 and that choosing A guarantees a payoff of zero. But she should choose A anyway. Why? Because she knows that, if her message didn't get through, player 2 will choose A, which makes choosing B too risky.

Now consider player 2's information sheet in the third and fourth rows. (We're back where we started several paragraphs ago.) If she believes that player 1 obeys weak dominance, and that player 2 thinks she (player 1) knows this, then she will figure out that player 1 will choose A in row 3. This puts her in precisely the same decision as player 1 was, and she should choose A too—even though she knows the state is M2, and knows that player 1 knows it. The argument works by induction all the way down the tree, flipping each intuitive choice of B to a reasoned choice of A like a row of dominoes toppling one after the other. Induction leads to an unbelievable result: *No matter how many messages are passed, both players should choose A.*

Rubinstein's result is shocking because it pits a strong intuition against the steady march of inductive logic. In everyday life a couple of steps of mutual knowledge is usually enough to guarantee coordinated behavior—a message and a confirmation are all it takes. Only the most neurotic first-daters would email back and forth endlessly confirming and reconfirming in order to prevent the unraveling and mutual no-show predicted by the theory. However, the inductive logic shows that, if mismatching can be very costly to the player who chooses the nondefault option that must be talked about, then not getting a confirmation back undermines coordination, which implies that not confirming a confirmation undermines coordination, and so on. In theory, no amount of confirmation is enough![18]

---

[17] Notice that here we switch from iterations of dominance to iterations of rationality (Bayesian utility maximization).

[18] Game theorists have argued about whether other mathematical descriptions of common knowledge are more sensible than the one Rubinstein used (Monderer and Samet, 1989). In addition, Binmore and Samuelson (2001) showed that, if communication is voluntary (including the possibility of commonly understood refusal to reply to a message), then equilibria in which limited communications lead to coordination on B can occur. Their proof is important for explaining how people are able successfully to coordinate action in everyday life, but it is beside the point for our purposes—which is to use choices in the email game to measure the level of iterated reasoning.

Note that each step of the induction requires an additional iteration of dominance or rationality, so we can use the choices subjects make to measure indirectly how many iterations of dominance they apply.

To give the subjects enough experience, we created an unusual protocol combining the "strategy method" with a large number of randomized re-pairings. In each round, subjects stated whether they would choose A or B for each possible information sheet. Then, in each of 500 rounds, a subject was randomly re-paired with another subject (of the opposite type), realizations of the state and the message passing were simulated, and payoffs were determined by the realizations and the subjects' stated strategy choices. At the end of the 500 rounds, subjects were given a summary table of the number of times that each information sheet was generated, the number of times that their opponents chose A and B in those situations, their total payoffs for each information sheet, and their total payoff for the round. This prepackaged feedback was designed to make it as easy as possible for them to learn to play the equilibrium. Note that, although the monetary payoff in each of the 500 rounds is small, the total incentive is high because the player is essentially forced to stick to her strategy for 500 rounds. As a result, recording a B instead of an A for one information set could easily cost a subject a couple of dollars in one 500-period round, so the *marginal incentive* is very high.

So what happened? Each player's strategy in a round is a list of letters, either A or B, corresponding to their choice for each information sheet. Two sessions were conducted with the Table 5.11 payoffs, and the results are shown in the Appendix. Results from two other sessions (with the Table 5.11 payoff of -2 changed to -4) are shown in Figure 5.7. The figure shows the fraction of subjects choosing the equilibrium choice A for each number of messages (i.e., the information boxes in Figure 5.6), over fourteen sequences. In the first sequence, few subjects choose A after the first three information levels, corresponding to three levels of iterated dominance. As they learn, As are chosen for higher and higher levels of information, which means the frequency of B play dissipates. As the sequences progress, disequilibrium play shrivels up for higher and higher numbers of messages. Learning is strongly driven by losing money from choosing B for a particular information level, which precipitates switching to A about half the time.[19] When player 1s switch to A for one information level, choosing B at the next-highest level then becomes unprofitable for player 2s and a switch to

---

[19] With Table 5.11 payoffs, switching to A occurred eight times after a component B choice was profitable, and fifty times after B lost money. But money losing did *not* lead to switches forty-eight times. The corresponding figures for the Figure 5.7 data are nineteen switches after earnings, sixty-four switches after losing, and forty-two failures to switch. This "win–stay, lose–shift" heuristic was first reported by Messick (1967).

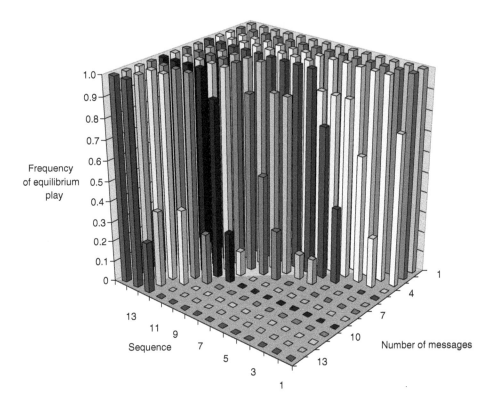

Figure 5.7. *Percentage of players choosing equilibrium given messages. Source: Camerer, Blecherman, and Goldstein (unpublished).*

A subsequently results. By sequence 13, there is *no* disequilibrium play—i.e., all subjects are playing the weird Nash equilibrium, choosing A for *all* information levels.

5.3.6 An Implementation Mechanism That Uses Iterated Dominance

Sefton and Yavaş (1996) studied iterated dominance in a neat paper on mechanism design. Consider game 1 in Table 5.12, a pure coordination game with Pareto-ranked payoffs. In pilot experiments, subjects overwhelmingly (92%) chose Red, leading to the Pareto-dominant outcome (1.20, 1.20). (Chapter 7 reports more results of this type.)

Abreu and Matsushima (1992a) consider the important problem of how a planner might implement outcomes by altering the rules of the game. For

Table 5.12. *Sefton and Yavaş's game 1*

	Column	
Row	Red	Blue
Red	1.20, 1.20	0,0
Blue	0,0	.60, .60

Source: Sefton and Yavaş (1996).

example, suppose you wanted to get the players to earn the Pareto-inferior (Blue, Blue) outcome in game 1. How would you do it?

Here's an example of this sort of mechanism design. Suppose the players are developers who are trying to decide at which of two locations, Redland or Blueland, they should build offices and homes. Suppose further that people like living near work. Then offices and homes are complements, in the sense that the office-builder wants the offices to be located near the homes— for simplicity, at the same location—and the home-builder wants people to be able to live near offices. Now suppose an outside agency, such as a city or state authority, decides they would rather have development take place in Blueland.[20] The agency would like to induce the developers to choose Blue(land).

The Abreu and Matsushima mechanism slices the game into T "pieces" or stages, dividing all payoffs by T; then the players play the T divided games in a sequence by specifying a series of Red or Blue plays for each of the T stages. The player who plays Red first in a sequence pays a fine of F. (Both are fined if they play Red at the same time.) In game 1, if the fine is greater than $1.20/T$ then neither player would ever want to play Red in the first of the T games, because they can earn at most $1.20/T$ in a particular stage but would then have to pay a fine of $F > 1.20/T$. If all T choices are specified at once then, by iterated deletion of dominated strategies, neither player will choose Red in the first stage, so neither will want to choose Red in the second stage (and be fined), and so on. The logical conclusion, after T steps of iterated dominance, is that no player should *ever* chose Red. Therefore, the fines "implement" the unnatural (Blue, Blue) outcome. Furthermore, in equilibrium, no player should deviate and pay the fine, so if the threat is credible and the mechanism is understood no fines will ever have to be collected (it should be "free"). In our developer example, the T stages are

[20] For example, there may be some other policy goal, such as providing employment in areas near Blueland, whose social payoffs are not reflected in the payoffs to the developers shown in the matrix.

like requiring developers to make partial investments or agreements along the way, and taxing or penalizing the first one to invest in Redland.

Notice that the Abreu and Matsushima mechanism could be easily implemented by setting $T = 1$, forcing the players to play Blue right away or pay a large fine of $1.20. The practical value of the mechanism is clearly in allowing the planner to make F small by making T large. Having a small fine is better, because players are more likely to think that the planner really can collect the fines.

However, as Glazer and Rosenthal (1992) pointed out, as T rises, players must do more steps of iterated deletion of dominated strategies for the mechanism to work in theory. So the main virtue of the mechanism springs from an assumption that is empirically suspect. Glazer and Rosenthal (1992, p. 1438) say they would "hesitate to give long odds" on successful implementation. Abreu and Matsushima (1992b, p. 1441) responded by saying that "[our] gut instinct is that our mechanism will not fare poorly in terms of the essential feature of its construction, that is, the significant multiplicative effect of 'fines.'"

Sefton and Yavaş's subjects play T times with $F = \$0.225$, specifying a sequence of T choices of either Red or Blue. In theory, the mechanism should induce (Blue, Blue) play when $T = 8$ or 12 but not necessarily when $T = 4$. For example, when $T = 8$ the players earn $.15 from (Red, Red) in each game piece, but are fined $.225 if they choose Red before others do, so it always pays to choose Red one stage after the other player and avoid the fine.[21] When $T = 4$, however, the potential earnings in a period from Red is $1.20/4=$.30, which is greater than the $.225 fine, so it can pay to choose Red and pay the fine anyway.

Figure 5.8 shows the proportion of all-Blue sequences for various T. In theory, there should be many all-Blue sequences for $T = 8$ or 12 and none for $T = 4$, but the opposite is true. After the first few periods, hardly any players choose all-Blue in $T = 8$ or 12, and in $T = 4$ sessions the fraction showing all-Blue rises steadily.

If subjects aren't choosing all-Blue sequences as theory predicts, what *are* they doing? After the first couple of rounds, 90% of subjects choose monotonic sequences of all-Blue followed by a series of Reds, switching to Red at some "switchpoint" round. Subjects are trying to coordinate on Red as soon as they can, to earn the higher payoff, but they try to switch from Blue to Red one period *after* the other player, to avoid the fine. In general, subjects switch in the third or fourth round (independently of T), and the switching point creeps up by about one round across the fifteen trials.

---

[21] (Blue,Blue) is uniquely rationalizable when $T = 8$ or 12, but when $T = 4$ there is also an equilibrium in which both players play Red all the time, happily paying the fine to earn more money in each period.

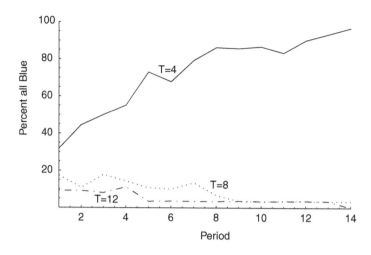

Figure 5.8.   *The percentage of all-Blue sequences (Nash is all-Blue) in implementation games.*
Source: *Sefton and Yavaş (1996).*

Glazer and Perry (1996) show how implementation can work in a sequential game via backward induction. Their idea is inspired by Glazer and
Rubinstein (1996), who suggested that deletion of dominated strategies in a
normal-form game can be made transparent as stage-by-stage comparisons
in an analogous extensive-form game (see the Schotter, Weigelt, and Wilson
experimental result described earlier). Katok, Sefton, and Yavaş (2002) did
experiments with the sequential Glazer–Perry mechanism, but it, too, does
not implement outcomes as predicted.

Katok, Sefton, and Yavaş's results are an empirical part—and the *only*
empirical part—of a dialogue among theorists and experimenters. The reply
by Abreu and Matsushima to Glazer and Rosenthal represents a rare, cogent
written statement by two clever theorists about their perceptions of the interplay between theory and observation. First they note that the mechanism
might have to be *explained* to subjects. This sort of explanation requirement
should be included as part of the theory (since it is, in an everyday sense
of the word, what is usually meant by "implementation"!), and suggests a
good experiment. They also write: "The prospect of being at the mercy of
controlled experiments is indeed intimidating" and say that "experimental
results frequently defy all attempts at even approximately rational explanation" (1992b, p. 1440). The last statement is too pessimistic. In fact, this
book strives to show that the opposite is true: There are hardly *any* experimental results that cannot be explained by some form of psychologically
plausible theory. For example, Sefton and Yavaş's results are consistent with

subjects doing three to four steps of iterated deletion of dominated strategies, guessing others will start playing Red in the third period and choosing Red one step later. Learning also causes the switchpoint to drift up over time. Both limited iterated reasoning and payoff-sensitive learning are certainly "approximately rational."

Summary: In most games reviewed in this section players exhibit two to four steps of iterated dominance in initial choices. The price competition and travelers' dilemma games are a little different because they have much larger strategy spaces (large ranges of prices). These results could be interpreted as some subjects choosing initial prices in the midpoint of a strategy space, and doing iterated reasoning in 5- or 10-point jumps. In the email game, large amounts of packaged feedback lead subjects to play an extremely counterintuitive equilibrium requiring fourteen steps of iterated deletion of dominated strategies. This result shows that the learning process can produce dominance-solvable equilibration, but perhaps only under special conditions. The Sefton–Yavaş study shows that a mechanism widely discussed in economic theory does not work as predicted because it presumes too much iterated dominance (i.e., the mechanism does not take into account "computability constraints").

5.4 When More Iteration Is Better: The "Dirty Faces" Game

A logic problem in which iterated reasoning plays a central role was first described by Littlewood (1953, pp. 3–4): "Three ladies, A, B, C, in a railway carriage all have dirty faces and are all laughing. It suddenly flashes on A: why doesn't B realize C is laughing at her? Heavens! *I* must be laughable. (Formally: If I, A, am not laughable, B will be arguing: If I, B, am not laughable, C has nothing to laugh at. Since B does not so argue, I, A, must be laughable.)" Translated from Littlewood's quaint language: If B saw A's clean face, she would infer from C's laughter that C was laughing at *her* (Ms. B), quit laughing, and start blushing (or run to the washroom to clean up). Since B doesn't blush, then A's face must be dirty too. Notice that, for A to realize this, A must think that B is rational enough to draw an inference from C, a subtle chain of reasoning. Littlewood points out that this logic can be extended link by link to an arbitrarily large number of dirty-faced ladies.

Variants of this game are widely used in conceptual discussions about iterated knowledge. The first experimental evidence is Weber (2001). In his study, players have independently drawn types, either X or O, with probabilities .8 and .2. After observing the types of *other* players—but not their own types—players take actions simultaneously in a series of rounds. At the end of each round, all the players' actions are announced. The actions

Table 5.13.   *Payoff table for the "dirty faces" game*

		Type	
		X	O
Probability		(.8)	(.2)
Action	Up	0	0
	Down	$1	−$5

Source: Weber (2001).

are choices of either Up or Down. Payoffs from combinations of actions and types are shown in Table 5.13.

If players choose Up, they earn nothing. If players choose Down, they earn $1 if they are type X and lose $5 if they are type O. A session of the game ends when one player chooses Down. Since the prior probability of being a type X is .8, the expected payoff to choosing Down, if players know nothing about their realized type, is −$0.20, so players will choose Up (unless they are somewhat risk preferring). Being in state X is like having a dirty face; and choosing Down is like knowing you have a dirty face and leaving to clean up.

When at least one player is a type X, the players are commonly told, "At least one player is type X." There are two cases to consider: XO case (one player is X and the other is O) and XX (both are X).

In the XO case, after the announcement, the player who is X should infer that, since at least one player is an X, *she* is the type X (this is analogous to a dirty-faced lady seeing that the *other* ladies' faces are clean). Then she should move Down. The fraction of X types who move Down right away in the XO case therefore measures the fraction of players who can make the simple rational inference that they are the X if they see an O.

The more interesting case is XX. Both players know there is at least one type X, and they know the *other* player is X, so they do not know anything about their own type. Rational players will therefore choose Up (unless they are substantially risk preferring). Then both players are told the other player's choice. Player 1, for example, is told that player 2 chose Up. If player 1 thinks player 2 is rational, she can infer that player 2 must have known player 1 was a type X. (Otherwise, by the logic in the previous paragraph, player 2 would have moved Down.) Then, in theory, player 1 can infer her *own* type from player 2's behavior—she must be an X, or player 2 would have moved Down in the first round. So player 1 should move Down in the second round if she does two steps of inference.

Table 5.14.   *Results for a two-player "dirty faces" game*

	Trial 1		Trial 2	
	XO	XX	XO	XX
Round 1				
UU	0	7*	1	7*
DU	3*	3	4*	1
DD	0	0	0	0
Round 2 (after UU)				
UU	–	1	–	2
DU	–	5	–	2
DD	–	1*	–	3*
Other (UD)	–	–	1	–

Source: Weber (2001).

Weber ran two-player and three-player games. The three-player results are similar so I'll report only the simpler two-player results, which are shown in Table 5.14. The predicted patterns of behavior are marked by an asterisk. Cumbersome information passing enabled Weber to do only two trials, so there is limited time for learning to occur.

In the XO condition, players pass the basic rationality test seven out of eight times by choosing Down when they are type X. In the trickier XX condition, players are predicted to choose UU in the first round, followed by DD. There *is* a lot of UU choice in the first round, but in most second rounds only one of two type Xs chooses D (i.e., DU in the table, rather than both choosing D as predicted by rationality). Counting the number of individual subjects who are behaving rationally (rather than pairs), 87% are rational in the XO condition, and 53% in the second round of the XX condition.[22] Weber also shows that three statistical variations on Nash equilibrium do a fairly good job of explaining the data.[23]

Weber's results are important because Caltech students are selected for their skill at logic puzzles such as the dirty faces game (and they know other

[22] That is, fifteen out of twenty-eight XX subjects choose D in round 2 after observing UU in round 1, pooling across trials.

[23] The three models are: a "noisy Nash" model, in which players play Nash with error, choosing correctly about 75% of the time; a probabilistic information model, which adds the assumption that players ignore information revealed by choices of others in earlier rounds with a certain probability (estimated to be around .60); and a quantal response equilibrium. All three are substantial improvements over a random choice model, and show that there is hope to modify standard concepts minimally to make sense of departures from Nash equilibrium.

students are very skilled). The extent of their iterated reasoning—half of them do not do two steps—is a plausible upper bound on iterated reasoning by most people in abstract games such as these.

Second, in the price competition, email, centipede, and mechanism games, players always do better if others have limited rationality. The dirty faces game is the opposite. If players have limited rationality they will choose Down when they should choose Up (and vice versa), harming the other players' ability to draw inferences about their own types. The fact that iterated reasoning is quite limited in the dirty faces game supports the conclusion that choices in the other games reveal limited reasoning (rather than pure cooperativeness).

5.5 The "Groucho Marx" Theorem in Zero-Sum Betting

Sovik (1999) studied a zero-sum betting game (replicating Sonsino et al., 1998). In the game there are four states, A–D, which are equally likely. Players have (commonly known) information partitions which tell them the set of possible states that may have occurred, for a particular state realization. After learning their information, players choose whether to bet or not. Betting is zero-sum, so that one player wins what another loses if both bet.

Table 5.15 shows the information partitions and payoffs for a type I and type II player. If the state is A, for example, player I knows only it could be A *or* B, but type II knows it is definitely A. The type II player should certainly bet in state D (since she knows the state is D and will win 16 if the other player bets also). Type II should certainly *not* bet in state A (since she will lose 32 for sure). If the type I player thinks type II is rational, then she knows II will never bet when the state is A, so for type I to bet when her information is the partition (A,B) means she can never win. If type II knows that type I

Table 5.15. *Information partitions in betting game*

	State			
	A	B	C	D
Type I	(A,B)		(C,D)	
I payoff	32	−28	20	−16
Type II	A	(B,C)		D
II payoff	−32	28	−20	16

Source: Sovik (1999).

is rational (and thinks, I think she, type II, is rational) then she infers I will never bet when her information is (A,B), so that betting when her own type II information is (B,C) will result in the loss of 20 (when the state is C). Iterating one more step, if type I knows that II is rational, and knows that II thinks I thinks II is rational, then she can infer that II will never bet in (B,C), so that betting in (C,D) is a lost cause for type I. Therefore, no bets will ever take place (in theory).

This result is an example of the "Groucho Marx theorem" (Milgrom and Stokey, 1982): Players who are trading only for the purpose of speculation (rather than to shift risk or to enhance the excitement of watching an event unfold), should never trade, because in zero-sum betting it never pays to bet with somebody who is willing to bet with you. (The theorem was named by Milt Harris, after the famous quip by Groucho Marx that he would never join a club that would have him as a member.) A similar intuition is present in the winner's curse in uninformed bargaining and common value auctions (namely, take somebody's willingness to trade, or to let you outbid them, as a signal—which is bad for you—about their information). But in those situations there is usually *some* trade, in equilibrium, because correcting for anticipated adverse selection still leaves some (expected) gains from trade, but in zero-sum games there are no gains and hence there should be no trade.

The Groucho Marx no-trade result is quite unintuitive, since it requires many levels of iterated reasoning. The no-trade prediction appears to be violated dramatically, in the sense that there is a huge volume of zero-sum betting in options, futures, and commodity markets—a trillion dollars worth of foreign exchange trading every day in New York—which is too high to be due to risk hedging (e.g., Sen, 2002). Experiments provide a nice clean way to see whether the basic logic underlying the no-trade result is transparent to subjects, and if not, how quickly it can be learned.

Sovik's design was motivated by an interest in the robustness of pioneering experiments by Sonsino et al. (1999). In their experiments, not betting gave a sure payoff of one Israeli shekel; betting gave the outcomes in Table 5.15 if both sides chose to bet. Sonsino et al. conducted several different designs. The minimum and maximum betting rates—the fraction of trials in which subjects chose to bet—in the first 50 periods (out of 250) and the last 50 periods are shown in Table 5.16, for each partition. Two odd regularities stick out. Type II players should never bet in state A (they know they will lose 32 for sure, rather than earning 1); yet they bet 6–24% of the time in the first 50 periods and 4–20% of the time in the last 50 periods! And they should *always* choose to bet in state D, since they cannot lose and can win if the type I player bets. But they choose to bet only 78–95% of the time in state D the first 50 trials, and 81–100% in the last 50 trials. These rates of betting at a certain loss, and failing to bet for a certain gain, are not huge, but mistake rates of this magnitude are unusual. More importantly, if

Table 5.16.   *Bet frequencies in a zero-sum betting game*

	State			
	A	B	C	D
Type I betting rates	(A,B)		(C,D)	
Sonsino et al.				
First 50 (min,max)	0.31–0.70		0.49–0.63	
Last 50 (min,max)	0.12–0.48		0.37–0.65	
Sovik				
First 12	0.44		0.50	
Sovik				
Last 12	0.11		0.60	
Type II betting rates	A	(B,C)		D
Sonsino et al.				
First 50 (min,max)	0.06–0.24	0.61–.073		0.78–0.95
Last 50 (min,max)	0.04–0.20	0.58–0.70		0.81–1.00
Sovik				
First 12	0.00	0.69		0.99
Last 12	0.00	0.55		1.00

Source: Sovik (1999).

the type IIs are betting when they should not, their aberrant behavior slows down the rate at which type Is learn not to bet when their partition is (A,B), which slows down type IIs learning not to bet when they know (B,C), and so on. As a result, Sonsino et al. see very slow convergence toward the no-trade equilibrium even over 250 trials.

Sovik altered the Sonsino et al. design in several ways: paying money rather than binary lottery points; raising the stakes (Table 5.15 points were worth 2.5 pesetas each, about $0.02, eight times higher than in Sonsino et al.); playing in random rematches as well as fixed pairings; and using only 24 periods rather than 250. In the first 12 periods players were given a specific information set and asked whether they wanted to bet. In the last 12 periods Sovik used the "strategy method," asking subjects whether they would bet for each possible partition (then one state was drawn and their full strategy was used to determine what they did do).

The results are summarized and contrasted with those of Sonsino et al. in Table 5.16. First note that type II players *never* bet when the state was A, and *almost always* bet when the state was D. Despite these lower rates of dominance violation, iterated reasoning was still quite limited because type

Is bet almost half the time when their information was (A,B) in the first 12 trials. However, this rate dropped to 11% in the last 12 trials.

The strategy method shows full information-contingent strategies. One-third of the type Is never bet, and half chose not to bet in (A,B) but bet in (C,D) (which is consistent with two levels of iterated reasoning). Type IIs chose to bet in (B,C) and in D half the time, which is inconsistent with three steps of iterated reasoning, and they bet only in D half of the time. Overall, the evidence is consistent with two steps of iterated reasoning by most players.

5.6 Structural Models of Decision Rules and Levels of Reasoning

This chapter has highlighted how games can be used to measure the frequency of violation of different numbers of steps of deletion of dominated strategies. A problem with this method is that subjects who appear to obey dominance may be doing so even though they use specific decision rules that do not *generally* respect dominance. For example, in beauty contest games, student players sometimes choose numbers such as 21, which correspond to two levels of iterated reasoning (from a starting point of 50). But they may just be choosing their age in years, rather than truly thinking iteratedly. When they turn 67 they'll start violating dominance!

The papers described in this section give a clear answer by positing decision rules directly and seeing how well they explain what players do.

Stahl and Wilson (1995) proposed a model in which players have different degrees of strategic sophistication. The model was foreshadowed by Stahl (1993) and Nagel (1995) (and also Holt, 1999, which first circulated in 1993).

They distinguished three "levels of reasoning": Level-0 players choose uniformly; and level-k players choose best responses to level-$(k-1)$ choices, for $k \in \{1, 2\}$. Obviously, one could extend the number of levels arbitrarily, but Stahl and Wilson stopped at two, and introduced some other rules as well.

Some notation is necessary to describe precisely what they did and appreciate its compact parsimony. Consider symmetric games with two players and three strategies. Let $j \in \{1, 2, 3\}$ denote strategies, and U denote a payoff matrix for game I. U_{jk} denotes the payoff to a row player who chooses j when column chooses k. Vectors p will denote beliefs about the frequency of choices by others. P_0 is the uniformly distributed belief over the three choices. The expected payoff from strategy j given belief p_i is therefore the matrix product $U_j p_i$. Denote a best response to belief p by $b(p)$. Denote the Nash equilibrium choice frequency vector by p_j^{Nash}.

First define a general family of beliefs q_j which reflect the assumption that ϵ of the population play a noisy best response to P_0, and the remaining $1 - \epsilon$ play Nash. Formally,

$$q_j(\mu, \epsilon) = \epsilon \cdot e^{\mu U_j P_0} / \sum_k e^{\mu U_k P_0} + (1 - \epsilon) p_j^{\text{Nash}}, \qquad (5.6.1)$$

where μ is a response sensitivity parameter, expected payoffs from the beliefs q_j are denoted $y_j(\mu, \epsilon) = U_j q_j(\mu, \epsilon)$. Players are assumed to choose according to expected payoffs with noise parameter γ, according to $P_j(\gamma, \mu, \epsilon) = e^{\gamma y_j(\mu, \epsilon)} / \sum_k e^{\gamma y_k(\mu, \epsilon)}$.

This simple two-step structure includes an amazing variety of decision rules corresponding to different values of the parameters μ (perceived noise in others' choices), γ (noise in a player's own choices), and ϵ (the fraction of perceived non-Nash players). Because each subject makes only twelve choices, it is hard to reliably estimate individual parameters separately, or even search for clusters. Instead, Stahl and Wilson restricted players to belong to a small set of possible types (specific parameters or ranges) and estimated a model in which the population is a mixture of those types. They posited five types,[24] with relative frequencies α_0 to α_4:

1. Level-0 types just choose each strategy equally often, so $\gamma = 0$.
2. Level-1 types assume that all others are level-0 types, so $\mu = 0, \epsilon = 1$ (i.e., all others choose randomly), and $\gamma > 0$.
3. Level-2 types assume that all others are level-1 types, so $\epsilon = 1$ and $\mu > 0$ (their beliefs about what level 1s will do are generated by noisy best responses to the belief P_0), and $\gamma > 0$.
4. Naive Nash types think others will play Nash, so $\epsilon = 0$ and $\gamma > 0$.
5. Worldly Nash types think some others will play Nash, but some players compute expected payoffs from P_0 beliefs or best responses $b(P_0)$, so $0 < \epsilon < 1$ and $\gamma > 0$.

Subjects play twelve symmetric 3×3 games, shown in Table 5.17. The games were selected to have various strategic properties.[25] The table shows payoffs to the row player and lists which decision rules select which strategies. The actual choice frequencies are also shown in the table.

---

[24] They actually include a sixth "rational expectations" (RE) type, which is assumed to know the relative frequencies of all five types and their own type. These types are estimated to be quite infrequent and are dropped from most analyses.

[25] Games 1, 5, and 12 are strict dominance solvable; games 3 and 9 are weak dominance solvable; games 4, 7, and 11 have unique mixed-strategy Nash equilibria; and games 2, 6, 8, and 10 have pure-strategy Nash equilibria (in which the Nash, $b(P_0)$, and $b(b(P_0))$ strategies are distinct). When Nash is listed more than once in the table, the probability with which each strategy is used in the mixed-strategy equilibrium is given in parentheses.

Table 5.17.   *Stahl and Wilson's payoff tables, model predictions, and actual frequencies*

				Actual frequency	Mixture model prediction	Decision rules selecting strategy
		Payoff table				
Game 1		T	M	B		
	T	25	30	100	0.15	0.19	$b(P_0)$
	M	40	45	65	0.83	0.76	Nash, $b(b(P_0))$,RE
	B	31	0	40	0.02	0.06	Dominated
Game 2		T	M	B		
	T	75	40	45	0.63	0.51	Nash
	M	70	15	100	0.25	0.28	$b(P_0)$,RE
	B	70	60	0	0.13	0.21	$b(b(P_0))$
Game 3		T	M	B		
	T	75	0	45	0.10	0.06	Dominated
	M	80	35	45	0.33	0.41	Nash,$b(b(P_0))$,RE
	B	100	35	41	0.56	0.53	$b(P_0)$
Game 4		T	M	B		
	T	30	50	100	0.54	0.56	Nash (.67),$b(P_0)$,RE
	M	40	45	10	0.31	0.25	Nash (.27),$b(b(P_0))$
	B	35	60	0	0.15	0.19	Nash (.06)
Game 5		T	M	B		
	T	10	100	40	0.29	0.22	$b(P_0)$
	M	0	70	50	0.06	0.10	Dominated
	B	20	50	60	0.65	0.68	Nash,$b(b(P_0))$,RE
Game 6		T	M	B		
	T	25	30	100	0.23	0.27	$b(P_0)$,RE
	M	60	31	51	0.42	0.43	Nash
	B	95	30	0	0.35	0.30	$b(b(P_0))$

Table 5.17.   *(continued)*

		Payoff table			Actual frequency	Mixture model prediction	Decision rules selecting strategy
Game 7		T	M	B			
	T	30	100	50	0.44	0.45	Nash $(.53), b(P_0)$,RE
	M	40	0	90	0.35	0.25	Nash $(.17)$
	B	50	75	29	0.21	0.30	Nash $(.30), b(b(P_0))$
Game 8		T	M	B			
	T	0	60	50	0.25	0.26	$b(b(P_0))$
	M	100	20	50	0.25	0.31	$b(P_0)$,RE
	B	50	40	52	0.50	0.43	Nash
Game 9		T	M	B			
	T	40	100	65	0.54	0.36	$b(P_0)$
	M	33	25	65	0.02	0.12	Dominated
	B	80	0	65	0.44	0.52	Nash,$b(b(P_0))$,RE
Game 10		T	M	B			
	T	45	50	21	0.81	0.50	Nash
	M	41	0	40	0.06	0.22	$b(b(P_0))$
	B	40	100	0	0.13	0.28	$b(P_0)$,RE
Game 11		T	M	B			
	T	30	100	22	0.27	0.42	Nash $(.37), b(P_0)$,RE
	M	35	0	45	0.08	0.19	Nash $(.13)$
	B	51	50	20	0.65	0.40	Nash $(.50), b(b(P_0))$
Game 12		T	M	B			
	T	40	15	70	0.54	0.63	Nash,$b(b(P_0))$,RE
	M	22	80	0	0.06	0.06	Dominated
	B	30	100	55	0.40	0.31	$b(P_0)$

Source: Stahl and Wilson (1995).

Table 5.18.   *Stahl and Wilson's parameter estimates for mixture models*

Parameter	Interpretation	Estimate	Standard error
γ_1	Level-1 response sensitivity	0.218	0.043
μ_2	Level-2 perceived γ_1	0.461	0.062
γ_2	Level-2 response sensitivity	3.079	0.574
γ_3	Nash-type response sensitivity	4.993	0.936
μ_4	Worldly Nash response sensitivity of non-Nash types	0.062	0.006
ϵ_4	Worldly-type perception of percentage of non-Nash types	0.441	0.077
γ_4	Wordly-type response sensitivity	0.333	0.055
α_0	Frequency of level-0 types	0.175	0.059
α_1	Frequency of level-1 types	0.207	0.058
α_2	Frequency of level-2 types	0.021	0.020
α_3	Frequency of Nash types	0.167	0.060
α_4	Frequency of worldly Nash types	0.431	0.078
Log-likelihood	-442.727		

Source: Stahl and Wilson (1995).

Maximum-likelihood parameter estimates are shown in Table 5.18. There appear to be hardly any level-2 types (2%), roughly equal numbers of level-0, level-1, and naive Nash types, and 43% worldly Nash types. Thorough further analyses show that estimates are robust to cross-game forecasting and classify most subjects reliably.[26] All these frequencies are precisely estimated.

The expected payoffs for different types given the actual data range from 43.0 for the level-0 types to 46.6 for naive and worldly Nash types. These payoffs are not significantly different, which is a reminder that payoff losses or selection pressures against boundedly rational (low-level) types may be weak (Stahl, 1993).

Costa-Gomes, Crawford, and Broseta (2001) investigated decision rules and iterated dominance using a design similar to Stahl and Wilson's, but which also measures how subjects attend to payoff information (as in Camerer et al., 1994, and Johnson et al., 2002; see Chapter 4). Subjects play eighteen two-player normal-form games with two, three, or four strate-

---

[26] Stahl and Wilson also tested for the presence of a "sophisticated" or "perfect foresight" type who chooses best responses to the actual relative frequencies observed in the experiment, but "soundly rejected" that hypothesis.

gies, with no feedback (deliberately to disable learning). The games were constructed to enable identification of several decision rules, including different levels of iterated dominance. The nonstrategic decision rules are: naive or level 1 (choose strategies with the highest average payoff, averaging payoffs equally); optimistic or maximax; pessimistic or maximin; and altruistic (maximize the sum of the two players' payoffs). There are also five strategic types (which, by definition, think about what other players might do): L2, which best-responds to naive; D1, which does one round of deleting dominated decisions, then best-responds to a uniform prior on the remaining decisions; D2, which does two rounds of deletion then best-responds to remaining strategies; sophisticated, who guess accurately the proportion of the population that chooses each nonequilbrium strategy; and (Nash) equilibrium. By design, different rules do not overlap much in the strategies they choose.[27] These games are therefore an unusually tough test for equilibrium, compared with most experiments, in which predictions of equilibrium and other decision rules overlap.

Subjects participated in one of three conditions: Baseline (B); Open Boxes (OB); and Training (TS). In Baseline (B), payoffs were hidden behind boxes that could be opened and closed only by clicking a mouse. As discussed in Chapter 4, this information display enables the experimenter to "get behind the subjects' eyes" and see what subjects see. If decision rules are treated as algorithms that demand certain kinds of information, knowing what information subjects use helps identify the rules. In the OB treatment, the boxes were always open; comparing this with the Baseline tests whether having payoffs in boxes affects what strategies subjects choose. In the training treatment, TS, subjects were rewarded only for choosing equilibrium strategies (after receiving general instruction in game-theoretic reasoning). Their behavior established an empirical baseline for how subjects who *were* reasoning game-theoretically looked up information, which could then be compared with lookups by B subjects. The results can be summarized in three parts: consistency of strategies with iterated dominance; estimates of decision rules used by subjects; and information search patterns. Table 5.19 shows the games Costa-Gomes et al. used and frequencies with which different strategies were chosen.

The fractions of B and OB subjects choosing equilibria are about 90%, 65%, and 15% when equilibria require 1, 2, and 3 levels of iterated dominance, corroborating many other results reported in this chapter. However, the trained subjects (TS conditions) are able to execute equilibrium reasoning almost perfectly, 90–100% of the time, including three levels of iterated

---

[27] In the original version of their paper, the L2, D1, and D2 types were not present and a large fraction of players were classified as sophisticated.

Table 5.19. *Games and actual frequencies of Costa-Gomes et al.*

Game	Row choice	Column choice		Actual frequency
		L	R	
2b	U	38,57	94,23	0.92
	D	14,18	45,89	0.08
Actual frequency		0.72	0.28	
3a	U	75,51	42,27	0.70
	D	48,80	89,68	0.30
Actual frequency		0.92	0.08	
3b	U	55,36	16,12	0.72
	D	21,92	87,43	0.28
Actual frequency		0.94	0.06	
4b	T	68,46	31,32	0.41
	M	47,61	72,43	0.06
	B	43,84	91,65	0.53
Actual frequency		0.89	0.11	
4c	T	51,69	82,45	0.92
	M	28,37	57,58	0.00
	B	22,36	60,84	0.08
Actual frequency		0.56	0.44	
5b	T	74,62	43,40	0.14
	M	25,12	76,93	0.11
	B	59,37	94,16	0.75
Actual frequency		0.70	0.30	
8b	T	71, 49	28, 24	0.22
	M	46, 16	57, 88	0.08
	B	42, 82	84, 60	0.70
Actual frequency		0.47	0.53	
9a	T	45,66	82,31	0.92
	TM	22,14	57,55	0.00
	BM	30,42	28,37	0.00
	B	15,60	61,88	0.08
Actual frequency		0.64	0.36	

Table 5.19.   *(continued)*

		Column choice			
		L	M	R	
4a	T	70,52	38,29	37,23	0.70
	B	46,83	59,58	85,61	0.30
Actual frequency		0.86	0.0	0.14	
4d	T	42,64	57,43	80,39	0.89
	B	28,27	39,68	61,87	0.11
Actual frequency		0.78	0.03	0.19	
6b	T	64,76	14,27	39,61	0.61
	B	42,45	95,78	18,96	0.39
Actual frequency		0.17	0.11	0.72	
7b	T	56,78	23,53	89,49	0.44
	B	31,35	95,64	67,91	0.56
Actual frequency		0.19	0.06	0.75	

		Column choice			
		L	ML	MR	R
9b	T	67,46	15,23	43,31	61,16	0.83
	B	32,86	56,58	38,29	89,62	0.17
Actual frequency		0.86	0	0	0.14	

Source: Costa-Gomes, Crawford, and Broseta (2001).

dominance. This excellent performance establishes that game-theoretic reasoning is *not* computationally difficult, per se, but is simply *unnatural* for most subjects (as seen in Johnson et al., 2002). Costa-Gomes et al. joke, only half-facetiously, that after an hour of training the subjects apply game theory better than his undergraduates do after a semester! Thus, strategic thinking seems to be more like learning to windsurf, ski, or fly an airplane, activities that require people to learn skills which are unnatural but teachable, and less like weight-lifting or dunking a basketball, where performance is constrained by physical limits.

Since different decision rules point to different strategies in each game, by looking at a player's strategy choices the player can be classified according to which decision rule she uses most often. Costa-Gomes et al. did this by assuming that each player uses one decision rule, but trembles or errs.

Table 5.20.   *Estimated frequency of decision rule types*

Decision rule	Expected payoff ($)	Information used	
		Decisions only	Decisions + search
Altruistic	17.11	0.089	0.022
Pessimistic	20.93	0.000	0.045
Naive	21.38	0.227	0.448
Optimistic	21.38	0.000	0.022
L2	24.87	0.442	0.441
D1	24.13	0.195	0.000
D2	23.95	0.000	0.000
Equilibrium	24.19	0.052	0.000
Sophisticated	24.93	0.000	0.022

Source: Costa-Gomes, Crawford, and Broseta (2001).

Subjects were then classified by finding a rule, and error rate, that maximized the likelihood of observing the pattern of choices subjects actually made. Similar procedures were used by Harless and Camerer (1994, 1995) and El-Gamal and Grether (1995).

Table 5.20 shows the fraction of subjects estimated to be of each type, using either the decisions or decisions plus information search data, and the expected dollar payoff of those rules. Using decisions alone, about 20% of the subjects are classified in each of the naive or D1 categories, and 44% are classified as L2. Adding information search data sharpens this classification substantially—then 45% are classified as naive and *none* are classified as D1. Note also that the expected payoffs to the reasoning-level, equilibrium, and sophisticated types are all around $24 for the session. Although the sophisticated types' expected earnings are highest (by definition), the L2 types earn only $0.06 less.

Information search measures can be analyzed in various ways. The basic information measures are: the number of times the boxes are opened ("lookups"), the length of time boxes are open ("gaze times"), and transitions from box to box.

The trickiest part of the project of Costa-Gomes et al. was creating plausible restrictions on how the information search measures vary with players' decision rules. This requires one to take the decision rules very seriously, and ask how information-processing measures differ across rules. Big differences come from whether players open own-payoff boxes differently than other-payoff boxes. In their display, like the usual normal-form game matrix,

Table 5.21.   *Predicted and actual payoff-box transitions (percent)*

Subject/decision rule	Up–down, own-payoff		Left–right, other-payoff	
	Predicted	Actual	Predicted	Actual
TS (equilibrium)	>31	63.3	>31	69.3
Equilibrium	>31	21.5	>31	79.0
Naive/optimistic	<31	21.1	—	48.3
Altruistic	<31	21.1	—	60.0
L2	>31	39.4	=31	30.3
D1	>31	28.3	>31	61.7

Source: Costa-Gomes, Crawford, and Broseta (2001).
Note: Pessimistic, D2, and sophisticated not classified.

players who are computing their own expected payoffs will shift *up and down* within an own-payoff column; that is, they will compare the payoffs with different row strategies (fixing a column, which corresponds to a fixed choice by the other player). Note that, in their display, the normal-form matrix is divided in half, with one's own payoffs in one half and the other's payoffs in the other half. A player who is naive, optimistic, or altruistic will make *left-to-right* transitions, comparing across columns to compute a strategy's average, minimum, or maximum payoff. Different rules also allow different transitions among other-payoff cells. For example, equilibrium players will find best responses for *other* players by making left-to-right transitions among other-payoff cells. Subtle calculations predict that equilibrium players will make up–down transitions among own-payoff cells more than 31% of the time (i.e., more than 31% of the transitions will be up–down rather than right–left). Other types will make those transitions less than 31% of the time. Therefore, the frequency of those transitions is one way of testing whether the classifications of subjects by their decisions corresponds to their information-processing behavior.

Table 5.21 shows these predictions and the actual transition frequencies for players who were classified into each type by the earlier analysis on their choices. TS subjects make equilibrium-type own-payoff transitions about two-thirds of the time; other types make those transitions less often. Equilibrium subjects also make many more left–right transitions in other-payoff cells than sophisticated subjects do, though the opposite holds for own-payoff transitions. Keep in mind that the row classification in Table 5.21 was done *purely* by using decisions. The positivist idea that decision rules are simply predictions about choices, rather than necessarily constraining details of a thinking process, allows the possibility that the decisions a player makes are uncorrelated with information-processing measures. But decisions and search patterns *are* correlated. Put the other way around, if the classification had been done by information search first, and choices were predicted from those search patterns, the cognitive data would have helped predict what subjects would actually choose.

Information measures can also be used to classify individuals. Costa-Gomes et al. explained the lookups necessary to execute each decision rule and defined several levels of compliance for these lookups. The weakest level of compliance ("occurrence") requires a subject to have *all* the necessary lookups *somewhere* in a trial's entire lookup sequence. The strong requirement ("adjacency") is that payoffs that must be compared to execute a decision rule must occur next to each other in a sequence.[28] For example, an altruistic subject is assumed to add together own- and other-payoffs in a particular cell. Occurrence states that she has both of the payoffs from a particular cell *somewhere* in her lookup sequence. Adjacency states that the payoffs must be next to each other in the looked-up sequence. Compliance with these requirements is then treated as a discrete variable that can be used to classify subjects simultaneously by strategy choice and lookup sequence compliance.

Since adjacency is a very strong requirement, subjects can be usefully classified by whether adjacency is high (occurring on 67–100% of the trials) or low (0–33%), assuming that occurrence is 100%. Cross-classifications by decisions and high and low adjacency, assuming perfect compliance with occurrence, are summarized in Table 5.22. The table shows rates of high and low compliance with predicted adjacency patterns (columns) for subjects classified into various rules (rows). For example, subjects classified as L2 by their decisions had 85% strong compliance and 3% weak compliance with adjacency lookup restrictions. A tight match between predicted lookups and resulting decisions would yield compliance rates on the diagonal (ignoring the TS row) with H (L) figures that are higher (lower) than other rates in the same column. For example, the 85% high compliance by L2 decision types with L2 lookup patterns is greater than the rate of high compliance in the same column for all other types (which range from 42 percent to 64 percent for equilibrium players) and the 3% low compliance rate is lower than all except equilibrium. In most cases the classification is not bad. For example, within-column ranks of the diagonal figures for high compliance provide answers to the following question: Judging from high compliance with type *x* lookups, how do players classified as type *x* by decisions rank (compared with the other four classified types)? Across columns, these ranks are 1, 2,

---

[28] These requirements could be considered boundary conditions on what subjects could do if they have enough working memory (weak requirement) or what they must do if they have very little working memory (strong requirement).

Decision rule classification by strategy and information lookup compliance

ssified ule (percent)	High, Low compliance with decision rule (percent)								
	Altruistic	Pessimistic	Naive	Optimistic	L2	D1	D2	Equilibrium	Sophist
	3, 50	44, 36	83, 0	86, 14	76, 0	92,1	92, 1	*96, 1*	75,
(4)	**78,11**	56,33	53,42	97,3	47,39	36,56	33,56	31,56	28,
imistic (24)	9,53	85,9	*89,3*	*96,4*	42,3	45,20	43,23	26,28	23,
	8,58	72,9	78,0	80,20	**85,3**	57,9	54,10	49,12	46,
	23,26	59,16	63,6	77,23	53,6	*48,14*	45,15	42,17	38,
m (4)	6,86	100,0	97,0	100,0	64,0	69,14	67,14	**56,19**	53,

a-Gomes, Crawford, and Broseta (2001).

nistic, D2, and sophisticated types were never classified by decision rule. *Italics* denotes cells that should have highest, L, compliance in their column; **boldface** denotes cells that should and *do* have the best compliance in their columns

3, 1, 3, 1 (random ranks would average 3). The classification is not perfect, but it is not bad. An analysis of posterior probabilities of each subject being of a particular type shows that 80% of the subjects have a posterior on one type of .90 or more.

Summary: Studies of decision rules find a wide variety of rules which explain aggregate decisions rather well. In Stahl and Wilson's classification, around 20% of subjects are level 0 (choosing randomly) or level 1 (best-responding to level 0). Another half of the subjects are "worldly Nash" who think some subjects will choose equilibrium strategies and others will make level-0 or level-1 choices, and respond accordingly. In Costa-Gomes, Crawford, and Broseta's study, large percentages appear to be naive or optimistic, and about half seem to believe that others are best-responding to random choice (level 2). They also show how measuring the information subjects gather is crucial to help figure out what their decision rules are. For example, from decisions alone about 20% of subjects appear to choose according to naive or D1 rules. But search data adjust these classifications to 45% and 0 percent. A study that used only choice data would have drawn the wrong conclusion. They also note that about 10, 35, and 85% of untrained subjects violated 1, 2, and 3 steps of iterated dominance, which is comparable with results seen throughout this chapter.

5.7 Theories

As simple bargaining and contribution games have inspired a flurry of theorizing (see Chapter 2), the regularity in limited thinking in dominance-solvable games has led immediately to different theories which are precisely specified and ready to apply to more games.

5.7.1 Multiple Types

One approach is to classify players into types, based on the number of steps of reasoning they appear to do. Stahl (1993) deserves much credit for this idea (as does Debra Holt, whose 1999 paper first appeared in 1993 and used types to analyze Cooper et al. coordination data, discussed in Chapter 7). In Stahl and Wilson's (1995) approach, the types included iterated steps of thinking and other types (such as equilibrium and "worldly" players). Costa-Gomes, Crawford, and Broseta (2001) went further down this path. Nagel (1995) used a simple iterated-types model to analyze her "beauty contest data," later done a little more formally by Ho, Camerer, and Weigelt (1998) and Nagel et al. (1999).

The roots of the thinking steps approaches can be found in Harsanyi's "tracing procedure" (e.g., Harsanyi and Selten, 1988). Searching for an algorithm that would select a unique equilibrium (and pick a "reasonable" one), Harsanyi suggested a procedure in which players start with a prior, imagine a best response, update the prior, and so forth to convergence. The thinking steps models use the same logic but assume that different players stop cold after different numbers of steps. Thus, the thinking steps and the Harsanyi model are related much as modern learning theories of fictitious play are related to the original incarnation (e.g., Chapter 6).

5.7.2 Payoff-Sensitive Noisy Iteration

The multiple-types idea does not relate the *degree* to which dominance is violated to the payoffs from strategies, which undoubtedly matters. For example, there is much more evidence against weak dominance than against strict dominance, probably because playing a weakly dominated strategy is a smaller mistake (in expected payoff terms). One way to allow limited reasoning that is payoff sensitive is to assume players form iterated beliefs and optimize (with noise), but add more and more noise at each step of iteration.

Capra (1999) was the first to suggest a way to do this and test it. Her idea was later modified and cleverly refined by Goeree and Holt (1999). They showed examples in which "increasing doubt" converges to quantal response equilibria (QRE). QRE has the right basic ingredients for explaining limited iterated dominance. Here's why: When λ, the responsive sensitivity parameter in QRE, is 0 then people choose randomly (they are "level-0 types") and will sometimes violate dominance. As λ rises, people are less and less likely to violate dominance, because dominated strategies will have low expected payoffs for any beliefs. The equilibrium assumption effectively builds in iterated deletion of dominated strategies as λ rises, because players come to believe that others are unlikely to violate dominance (if λ is large enough), that others are unlikely to play strategies that are dominated when dominated strategies are eliminated (when λ is larger still), and so forth. Then λ is a handy single-parameter index of the degree of limited iterated reasoning.

5.7.3 QRE Refinements: Differences and Asymmetry in λ

QRE is clearly a good tool for investigating limited iterated reasoning since lowering the response sensitivity λ will generally produce equilibria that look like data from limited iteration. However, two refinements of the QRE approach should also be explored.

1. In many games, there are clear spikes in the data which correspond to discrete levels of thinking. For example, in the p-beauty contests with $p = 2/3$ (see Figure 5.1b) many people pick exactly 33, optimizing against an expected average of 50; others pick exactly 22, and so on. QRE with a single λ will not produce such spikes, but allowing a *distribution* of λ values will.

2. In many games, such as the simple Beard and Beil games, almost all players behave rationally (e.g., obeying strict dominance) but players are not always willing to bet that *others* behave rationally. (This may be a special kind of overconfidence, in which everybody thinks others are dumber than they are.) This can be explained by extending QRE to make it asymmetric, so that players are all responsive to payoffs, but players also mistakenly believe others are less responsive than they really are (see Weiszäcker, 2000). That is, a player's behavioral probabilities are given by $P(s_i)$ (based on a sensitivity λ_i) but the same player believes another player's probabilities are $\tilde{P}(s_{-i})$ based on a lower sensitivity $\tilde{\lambda}_{-i}$ (where $\lambda_i > \tilde{\lambda}_{-i}$ to reflect more doubt about another person's behavior than about one's own). Note that this produces beliefs that are *not* in equilibrium, but in my view this is a "feature" rather than a "bug" because the idea of coupling equilibrium with quantal response always seemed rather unnatural to me (at least as a theory of play during equilibration). Formally, asymmetric QRE in logit form is defined by

$$P(s_i) = \exp\left[\lambda_i \sum_{s_{-i}} \tilde{P}(s_{-i}) u_i(s_i, s_{-i})\right] \Bigg/$$

$$\left(\sum_{s_k} \exp\left[\lambda_i \sum_{s_{-i}} \tilde{P}(s_{-i}) u_i(s_k, s_{-i})\right]\right), \qquad (5.7.1)$$

$$\tilde{P}(s_{-i}) = \exp\left[\tilde{\lambda}_{-i} \sum_{s_i} P(s_i) u_{-i}(s_i, s_{-i})\right] \Bigg/$$

$$\left(\sum_{s_{-k}} \exp\left[\tilde{\lambda}_{-i} \sum_{s_i} P(s_i) u_{-i}(s_i, s_{-k})\right]\right). \qquad (5.7.2)$$

Weiszäcker (2000) shows that an asymmetric QRE model organizes data from many one-shot games much better than a (symmetric) QRE can. However, the empirical asymmetry between own and perceived responsiveness (λ) largely disappears in games without dominant or dominated strategies. It appears that there is something special about players' distrust that others can do very simple kinds of logical reasoning, which suggests that a more nuanced and cognitive view will ultimately prove helpful.

5.7.4 A Poisson Cognitive Hierarchy

Teck Ho, Kuan Chong, and I (Camerer, Ho, and Chong, 2001) have been working on a cognitive hierarchy (CH) theory, which is a special kind of thinking steps model but incorporates many different elements of the approaches above. We have applied it to first-period data from dozens of games and it always predicts as least as well as Nash equilibrium, and often better (see also Gneezy, 2002). The frequency of players using K steps of thinking is given by a Poisson distribution $f(k \mid \tau)$, where τ is the mean (and the variance, in Poisson distributions) of the number of thinking steps. Players using zero steps of reasoning just choose randomly or use some other heuristic. (Random choice is useful for theoretical purposes because it means all strategies are chosen with some probability, which helps link the CH approach to equilibrium refinements.) Players using $K > 0$ steps anticipate the decisions of lower-step thinkers and best-respond to the mixture of their decisions using normalized frequencies. Formally, the expected payoff of a K-step player using strategy i is given by

$$E_i(K) = \sum_{h=1}^{m_{-i}} \pi(s_i, s_{-i}^h) \cdot \left\{ \sum_{c=0}^{K-1} \left[\frac{f(c \mid \tau)}{\sum_{c=0}^{K-1} f(c \mid \tau)} \cdot P(h \mid c) \right] \right\}, \quad (5.7.3)$$

where $P(h \mid c)$ is the chance that a c-step player chooses strategy h.

The Poisson CH has some advantages. It is very easy to compute (just iterate, starting with zero-step thinkers, on a spreadsheet), easier than QRE and even easier than Nash equilibrium in some games. It is parsimonious (only one parameter, and for empirical purposes a value of τ around 1.5 works well in many games). In most games, players who do different steps of thinking will make different decisions, but the aggregate frequency of choices will be mixed by the Poisson frequencies. Therefore, even though players are all best-responding (except zero-step thinkers), the resulting mixture will look like stochastic choice. In games with mixed equilibria, for example, the resulting predicted mixtures look a lot like data (see Camerer, Ho, and Chong, 2001, for details), but players are "purifying" since most are choosing pure strategies.

The model appears to be widely applicable to games that at first blush appear to require different sorts of models. It is obviously capable of explaining limits on iterated thinking in dominance-solvable games; but optimal choices tend to exhibit cycles in mixed games, which creates predicted mixtures close to the data. It can also explain the "magic" of coordination in entry games with market capacity (Chapter 7) because higher-step types essentially "fill in gaps" in the entry function. (To guarantee more entry as capacity grows larger requires $1 + 2\tau < e^\tau$, or $\tau < 1.25$, which is a reasonable number.) The Poisson distribution is also relatively easy to work with theoretically. For example, when τ is very large then the normalized frequencies of lower-level types, from level k's perspective, put all the weight on type $k - 1$. This means that, as τ grows large, the model will converge to Nash equilibrium in dominance-solvable games. There may also be close theoretical relations to risk dominance and perhaps to signaling game refinements (we conjecture that CH with large τ picks out sender–receiver equilibria that are "divine" or "universally divine"). Finally, the CH model predicts interesting effects of group size in beauty contest and centipede games (Chapter 5), and in stag hunt games (Chapter 7) which appear to correspond to experimental regularities.

A key difference between the CH approach (and other types-based approaches) and the QRE and noisy introspection approaches is that the latter generate a single, typically smooth, distribution of probabilities. CH will produce spikes. We are also optimistic that the steps of thinking which can be inferred from choices will be correlated with psychological measures like response time (more steps of thinking take longer, adjusting for working memory and calculating speed; cf. Johnson and Payne, 1985).

5.8 Conclusion

Eliminating dominated strategies is an irresistible decision principle because it (weakly) guarantees a better outcome regardless of what other players do. But believing that others obey dominance is a different matter because it is a guess about both the payoffs and the rationality of others. Believing that others believe *you* obey dominance is a different matter still. As a result, the number of levels of elimination of dominated strategies that people actually perform is an interesting question—and a fundamentally empirical one. This question has essentially been answered by the studies described in this chapter. At the risk of oversimplifying, the answer appears to be two to three steps of iterated dominance (where eliminating one's own dominated strategies is counted as one step of iteration). Results in this range have been derived in simple games with only a couple of strategies and in patent race games which are partially dominance solvable. Similar results appear in games where increasing elimination of dominated strategies *reduces* payoffs to players (centipede, price competition, travelers' dilemma, "email," and fine mechanism games) and in one game where increased iterated reasoning *increases* payoffs (the dirty faces game). The sharpest evidence on iterated dominance comes from p-beauty contest games, in which players try to choose numbers close to p times the average number. This simple game has been run on dozens of subject pools, including successful professionals and readers of business publications, with quite similar results corresponding to two to three steps of iterated reasoning.

It would be wonderful if the number of steps of iterated reasoning people tend to use were a universal constant, or even systematic across people and games, but that is unlikely. However, for doing applied game theory, simply knowing that iterated dominance is limited to a couple of steps is enough to improve predictions substantially. There is also no shame in making a prediction that is a range or subset of possible outcomes—set-theoretic predictions are common in cooperative game theory—since it is usually better to be approximately right than precisely wrong.

There are several ways limited iterated reasoning might be modeled formally.

Finally, it is important to note that equilibration does occur over time in the games described in this chapter, bringing players closer to playing dominance-solvable equilibrium. The "email game" is the most striking example of this: In the space of an hour or two, subjects can learn to play a Nash equilibrium that they themselves regarded as utterly bizarre in the early stages of the experiment. Thus, for predicting the time path of play in an experiment, or a naturally occurring process of trial-and-error learning, any theory of limited iterated reasoning will have to be coupled with a theory of learning (see Chapter 6).

Appendix: Raw Choices in Email Game and Additional Data

Tables 5.23–5.27 help you see the association between losses and strategy changes (learning). A capital letter denotes a strategy component (i.e., a message-specific choice of A or B) that was switched from the previous sequence. Underlining denotes a strategy component that earned a negative total payoff. If subjects switch only after losses, all capital letters will be underlined. If losses always create switches, the only letters that are underlined will be capitalized.

Table 5.23.   *Sample feedback sheet, email game (player 1 strategy abbbbbb)*

Matrix	Last message sent by You	Last message sent by Opponent	Your decision	Opponent's decision	Number of times	× Payoff	= Subtotal
M1	0	0	A	A	30	2	60
M1	0	0	A	B	0	0	0
M2	1	0	B	A	28	−4	−112
M2	1	0	B	B	0	2	0
M2	1	2	B	A	8	−4	−32
M2	1	2	B	B	3	2	6
M2	3	2	B	A	7	−4	−28
M2	3	2	B	B	5	2	10
M2	3	4	B	A	0	−4	0
M2	3	4	B	B	5	2	10
M2	5	4	B	A	1	−4	−4
M2	5	4	B	B	4	2	8
M2	5	6	B	A	0	−4	0
M2	5	6	B	B	2	2	4
M2	7	6	B	A	1	−4	−4
M2	7	6	B	B	1	2	2
M2	7	8	B	A	0	−4	0
M2	7	8	B	B	2	2	4
M2	9	8	B	A	0	−4	0
M2	9	8	B	B	1	2	2
M2	9	10	B	A	0	−4	0
M2	9	10	B	B	0	2	0
M2	11	10	B	A	1	−4	−4
M2	11	10	B	B	1	2	2
M2	11	12	B	A	0	-4	0
M2	11	12	B	B	0	2	0
						Total payoff =	−76

Source: Camerer (unpublished).

Table 5.24. *Raw choices in email game: Session 1*

	Choices for last message sent			Choices for last message sent	
	Player 1 messages 0,1,3,5,7,9,11	Player 2 messages 0,2,4,6,8,10		Player 1 messages 0,1,3,5,7,9,11	Player 2 messages 0,2,4,6,8,10
Set	Subject 1	Subject 4	Set	Subject 3	Subject 6
1	abbbbbb	abbbbb	1	bbbbbbb	abbbbb
2	abbbbbb	abbbbb	2	AAbbbbb	Bbbbbb
3	abbbbbb	abbbbb	3	aabbbbb	AAbbbb
4	aAbbbbb	abbbbb	4	aabbbbb	aBbbbb
5	aBbbbbb	aAbbbb	5	aabbbbb	abbbbb
6	abAbbbb	aabbbb	6	aabbbbb	abbbbb
7	aABbbbb	aabbbb	7	aabbbbb	abbbbb
8	aBAabbb	aabbbb	8	aabbbbb	aAbbbb
9	abBBbbb	aaAbbb	9	aabbbbb	aabbbb
10	aAAbbbb	aaBbbb	10	aaAbbbb	aabbbb
11	aBBbbbb	aaAbbb	11	aaabbbb	aabbbb
12	aAAbbbb	aaaabbb	12	aaabbbb	aabbbb
13	aBBbbbb	aaaabbb	13	aaaAbbb	aabbbb

Set	Subject 2	Subject 5
1	abbbbbb	ababab
2	aAbbbbb	abBbBb
3	aabbbbb	aabbbb
4	aabbbbb	aAbbbb
5	aabbbbb	aabbbb
6	aabbbbb	aabbbb
7	aaAbbbb	aaAbbb
8	aaabbbb	aaBbbb
9	aaabbbb	aBbAbb
10	aaabbbb	aAbBbb
11	aaabbbb	aaAbbb
12	aaabbbb	aaabbb
13	aaabbbb	aaabbb

Source: Camerer (unpublished).

Table 5.25.   *Raw choices in email game: Session 2*

	Choices for last message sent			Choices for last message sent	
	Player 1 messages	Player 2 messages		Player 1 messages	Player 2 messages
	0,1,3,5,7,9,11	0,2,4,6,8,10		0,1,3,5,7,9,11	0,2,4,6,8,10
Set	Subject 1	Subject 5	Set	Subject 3	Subject 7
1	aabbbbb	aabbbb	1	abbbbbb	abbbbb
2	aabbbbb	aabbbb	2	abbbbbb	abbbbb
3	aabbbbb	aBbbbb	3	abbbbbb	abbbbb
4	aabbbbb	aAbbbb	4	aAbbbbb	abbbbb
5	aabbbbb	aabbbb	5	aabbbbb	aAbbbb
6	aaAbbbb	aabbbb	6	aaAbbbb	aBbbbb
7	aaabbbb	aaAbbb	7	aaBbbbb	aAbbbb
8	aaabbbb	aaBbbb	8	aaAbbbb	aabbbb
9	aaabbbb	aaAbbb	9	aaabbbb	aaAbbb
10	aaaAbbb	aaabbb	10	aaabbbb	aaabbb
11	aaaabbb	aaabbb	11	aaaabbb	aaabbb
12	aaaabbb	aaabbb	12	aaaAbbb	aaabbb
13	aaaabbb	aaabbb	13	aaaabbb	aaaAbb
14	aaaaAbb	aaaAbb	14	aaaabbb	aaaabb
15	aaaaabb	aaaBbb	15	aaaabbb	aaaabb
Set	Subject 2	Subject 6	Set	Subject 4	Subject 8
1	abbbbbb	abbbbb	1	bbbbbbb	abbbbb
2	aAbbbbb	abbbbb	2	AAbbbbb	abbbbb
3	aabbbbb	abbbbb	3	aabbbbb	aAbbbb
4	aabbbbb	aAbbbb	4	aabbbbb	aBbbba
5	aabbbbb	aabbbb	5	aabbbbb	aAbbbb
6	aabbbbb	aabbbb	6	aaAbbbb	aBbbbb
7	aabbbbb	aBAbbb	7	aaBbbbb	aAbbbb
8	aabbbbb	aABbbb	8	aaAbbbb	aBbbbb
9	aabbbbb	aabbbb	9	aaabbbb	aAAbbb
10	aabbbbb	aabbbb	10	aaabbbb	aaabbb
11	aaAbbbb	aabbbb	11	aaabbbb	aaabbb
12	aaabbbb	aaAbbb	12	aaabbbb	aaBbbb
13	aaabbbb	aaabbb	13	aaabbbb	aaAbbb
14	aaaAbbb	aaabbb	14	aaaAbbb	aaabbb
15	aaaabbb	aaaAbb	15	aaaabbb	aaabbb

Source: Camerer (unpublished).

Table 5.26.   *Raw choices in email game: Session 3*

	Choices for last message sent			Choices for last message sent	
	Player 1 messages 0,1,3,5,7,9,11	Player 2 messages 0,2,4,6,8,10		Player 1 messages 0,1,3,5,7,9,11	Player 2 messages 0,2,4,6,8,10
Set	Subject 1	Subject 5	Set	Subject 3	Subject 7
1	aabbbbb	abbbbb	1	aabbbbb	abbbbb
2	aabbbbb	abbbbb	2	aabbbbb	aAbbbb
3	aabbbbb	abbbbb	3	aabbbbb	aabbbb
4	aabbbbb	aAbbbb	4	aabbbbb	aabbbb
5	aabbbbb	aabbbb	5	aaAbbbb	aabbbb
6	aaAbbbb	aabbbb	6	aaabbbb	aabbbb
7	aaabbbb	aaAbbb	7	aaabbbb	aaAbbb
8	aaaAbbb	aaabbb	8	aaabbbb	aaabbb
9	aaaabbb	aaaAbb	9	aaabbbb	aaabbb
10	aaaaAbb	aaaabb	10	aaaAbbb	aaaAbb
11	aaaaabb	aaaaAb	11	aaaaAbb	aaaaAb
12	aaaaaAb	aaaaaA	12	aaaaaAb	aaaaab
13	aaaaaaA	aaaaaa	13	aaaaaaA	aaaaaA
14	aaaaaaa	aaaaaa	14	aaaaaaa	aaaaaa
Set	Subject 2	Subject 6	Set	Subject 4	Subject 8
1	aabbbbb	abbbbb	1	abbbbbb	abbbbb
2	aabbbbb	abbbbb	2	aAbbbbb	aAbbbb
3	aabbbbb	abbbbb	3	aabbbbb	aBbbbb
4	aabbbbb	abbbbb	4	aabbbbb	aAbbbb
5	aaAbbbb	abbbbb	5	aabbbbb	aabbbb
6	aaabbbb	abbbbb	6	aaAbbbb	aabbbb
7	aaabbbb	aAbbbb	7	aaabbbb	aaAbbb
8	aaabbbb	aabbbb	8	aaabbbb	aaabbb
9	aaaAbbb	aaAbbb	9	aaaAbbb	aaabbb
10	aaaaAbb	aaaAbb	10	aaaaAbb	aaaAbb
11	aaaaabb	aaaaAb	11	aaaabb	aaaaAb
12	aaaaaAb	aaaaaA	12	aaaaaAb	aaaaab
13	aaaaaaA	aaaaaa	13	aaaaaaA	aaaaaA
14	aaaaaaa	aaaaaa	14	aaaaaaa	aaaaaa

Source: Camerer (unpublished).

Table 5.27.   *Raw choices in email game: Session 4*

	Choices for last message sent			Choices for last message sent	
	Player 1 messages	Player 2 messages		Player 1 messages	Player 2 messages
	0,1,3,5,7,9,11	0,2,4,6,8,10		0,1,3,5,7,9,11	0,2,4,6,8,10
Set	Subject 1	Subject 5	Set	Subject 3	Subject 7
1	aabbbbb	abbbbb	1	aabbbbb	abbbbb
2	aabbbbb	abbbbb	2	aabbbbb	abbbbb
3	aabbbbb	aAbbbb	3	aabbbbb	aAbbbb
4	aabbbbb	aabbbb	4	aaAbbbb	aabbbb
5	aaAbbbb	aabbbb	5	aaabbbb	aabbbb
6	aaabbbb	aabbbb	6	aaabbbb	aabbbb
7	aaabbbb	aaAbbb	7	aaaAbbb	aaAbbb
8	aaaAbbb	aaabbb	8	aaaabbb	aaabbb
9	aaaaAbb	aaaAbb	9	aaaabbb	aaaAbb
10	aaaaabb	aaaabb	10	aaaaAbb	aaaaAb
11	aaaaaAb	aaaaAb	11	aaaaabb	aaaaab
12	aaaaaaA	aaaaab	12	aaaaaAb	aaaaaA
13	aaaaaaa	aaaaaA	13	aaaaaaA	aaaaaa
14	aaaaaaa	aaaaaaa	14	aaaaaaa	aaaaaa
Set	Subject 2	Subject 6	Set	Subject 4	Subject 8
1	aabbbbb	abbbbb	1	aabbbbb	abbbbb
2	aAbbbbb	abbbbb	2	aabbbbb	abbbbb
3	aabbbbb	aAbbbb	3	aabbbbb	aAbbbb
4	aaAbbbb	aabbbb	4	aaAbbbb	aabbbb
5	aaabbbb	aabbbb	5	aaaAbbb	aabbbb
6	aaabbbb	aaAbbb	6	aaaBbbb	aabbbb
7	aaabbbb	aaabbb	7	aaaAbbb	aaAbbb
8	aaaAbbb	aaabbb	8	aaaabbb	aaabbb
9	aaaabbb	aaaAbb	9	aaaaAbb	aaaAbb
10	aaaaAbb	aaaaAb	10	aaaaabb	aaaabb
11	aaaaaAb	aaaaab	11	aaaaaAb	aaaaAb
12	aaaaaaA	aaaaab	12	aaaaaab	aaaaab
13	aaaaaaa	aaaaaA	13	aaaaaaA	aaaaaA
14	aaaaaaa	aaaaaa	14	aaaaaaa	aaaaaa

Source: Camerer (unpublished).

6

Learning

THE QUESTION OF HOW AN EQUILIBRIUM ARISES in a game has been largely avoided in the history of game theory, until recently. Equilibrium concepts implicitly assume that players either figure out what equilibrium to play by reasoning, follow the recommendation of a fictional outside arbiter (if that recommendation is self-enforcing), or learn or evolve toward the equilibrium.

Most of the research on learning and evolution is theoretical, but it is unlikely that theorizing alone will explain how people learn without the input of empirical regularity and careful testing. Theories generally use the mathematics of stochastic processes to prove theorems about the limit properties of different rules (see Weibull, 1995, and Fudenberg and Levine, 1998, for overviews). Rules with plausible limiting behavior are thought to be better descriptions. However, if limiting behavior takes months, years, or decades to unfold, then limit theorems are not as useful as being able to predict the path of equilibration.

This chapter focuses on using experimental data to test models of learning. Note that this chapter is quite different from the others in this book. The focus is not regularity in a class of games; the focus is on what types of model generally fit the path of learning, and why. Learning is defined as an observed change in behavior owing to experience. Statistical models of learning therefore predict how probabilities of future choices are affected by historical information.

Experimental data are a good way to test models of learning because control over payoffs and information means we can be sure what subjects know (and know others know, and so on), what they expect to earn from different strategies, what they have experienced in the past, and so forth.

Table 6.1. *Stag hunt game*

Row player strategies	L	R
T	3,3	0,1
B	**1,0**	1,1

Since most models make detailed predictions that require this information, laboratory control is indispensable for sorting out candidate models at this early stage in the research. Laboratory pre-screening can identify models that are likely to work well in naturally occurring situations such as auctions, firm choices of prices and quantities, bargaining outcomes in strikes and divorce, and consumer learning about preferences.[1]

6.1 Theories of Learning

There are many approaches to learning in games: evolutionary dynamics; reinforcement learning; belief learning; sophisticated (anticipatory) learning; experience-weighted attraction (EWA) learning; imitation; direction learning; and rule learning.

The stag hunt game in Table 6.1 (see also Chapter 7) helps show exactly how some of the theories work. Let's focus only on learning by the row player. Suppose in period t the row player chose B and the column player chose L, yielding payoffs of 1 and 0 respectively for row and column (printed in bold in the table). The forgone payoff from row's unchosen strategy (T) is 3.

Many theories assume strategies have numerical evaluations, which we call "attractions." Learning rules can be characterized by how attractions are updated in response to experience. Denote the attractions for strategies T and B *before* the period t play by $A^T(t-1)$ and $A^B(t-1)$. Attractions are mapped into predicted choice probabilities using some statistical rule (usually logit or power). Table 6.2 summarizes how attractions for T and B are predicted to change according to various theories.

1. *Evolutionary approaches* assume a player is born with a strategy and plays it, usually in random matching with members of a population.

---

[1] A great field application is Weisbuch, Kirman, and Herreiner (2000), who apply a reinforcement model to the development of trading relationships in the Marseilles fish market. Ho and Chong (in press) predict consumer learning about products such as ice cream and analgesics. (Their model predicts better out of sample by a substantial margin than the leading model in marketing research, and has 80 percent *fewer* parameters.)

2. *How learning theories update attractions in the stag hunt example*

	Functional form or statistic	Attraction for . . .	
		B in $t+1$ $A^B(t)$	T in $t+1$ $A^T(t)$
cement	Averaging	$\phi A^B(t-1) + (1-\phi)(1-\epsilon)(1-\rho(t-1))$	$\phi A^T(t-1) + (1-\phi)\epsilon(1-\rho$
	Cumulative	$\phi A^B(t-1) + (1-\epsilon))(1-\rho(t-1))$	$\phi A^T(t-1) + \epsilon(1-\rho(t-$
earning	Beliefs	$P_t(L) = \dfrac{3\rho+1}{5\rho+1}$	$P_t(R) = \dfrac{2\rho+0}{5\rho+1}$
	Attractions	1	$\dfrac{3(3\rho+1)+0(2\rho+0)}{5\rho+1}$
		$\dfrac{\phi N(t-1)A^B(t-1)+1}{\rho N(t-1)+1}$	$\dfrac{\phi N(t-1)A^T(t-1)+}{\rho N(t-1)+1}$
tor nics	Population proportions	$\dfrac{p^T(t+1)}{p^T(t)} = 1+\alpha(3p^L(t)-1)(1-p^T(t))$	$\dfrac{p^B(t+1)}{p^B(t)} = 1+\alpha(1-3p^L(t))$

Strategies that are relatively successful increase the player's fitness—perhaps they provide food or avoid attacks by predators—and enable players to survive longer or reproduce more frequently. Mathematical exploration of evolutionary models has been a hot topic of research recently (see, e.g., Weibull, 1995). I will discuss them in this chapter only briefly because evolutionary models apply best to animals with genetically heritable strategies, or to human cultural evolution (Boyd and Richerson, 1985), neither of which explains rapid individual learning in the lab.

2. One step up from evolutionary models in the cognitive sophistication that agents are assumed to have are *reinforcement* approaches (also called stimulus-response or rote learning). Choice reinforcement assumes strategies are "reinforced" by their previous payoffs. Reinforcement may also "spill over" to strategies that are similar to the chosen strategy (e.g., neighboring strategies, if strategies are rank ordered). Reinforcement learning is a reasonable theory for players with very imperfect reasoning ability (nonhuman animals pecking levers in the lab or foraging in the wild) or for human players who know absolutely nothing about the forgone or historical payoffs from strategies they did not choose.[2]

   Applied to our example, reinforcement theories update attractions according to $A^B(t) = \phi A^B(t-1) + (1-\epsilon)1 - \rho(t-1)$ and $A^T(t) = \phi A^T(t-1) + \epsilon$, if the attractions "cumulate." The parameter ϵ represents a spillover or generalization of reinforcement from one strategy (B) to neighboring strategies (T). (Which strategies are "neighboring" is of course an empirical question, having to do with the psychology of categorization.[3]) Note that, when $\epsilon = 0$, strategy T receives no reinforcement. In a variant of this model, attractions are weighted averages rather than cumulations, so $A^B(t) = \phi A^B(t-1) + (1-\phi)(1-\epsilon)$ and $A^T(t) = \phi A^T(t-1) + (1-\phi)\epsilon$.

3. *Belief learning models* assume players update beliefs about what others will do based on history, and use those beliefs to determine which

---

[2] There is a closer relation between evolutionary models of population learning and models of individuals learning by reinforcement than one might suspect at first glance. Börgers and Sarin (1997) show that in the Cross (1973) reinforcement learning model, if strategies are reinforced by an increasingly small fraction of their payoffs (to mimic a reduction in the time between iterations becoming smaller), as that fraction goes to zero the reinforcement dynamics converges to replicator dynamics.

[3] In his discussion of confirmation bias in gambling Wagenaar (1984, p. 109) gives an interesting example of how spillover may work in perhaps surprising ways: "[Consider] the roulette player who suddenly places a large single bet on number 24, completely out of his routine betting pattern. His reason was that 12 is always followed by a 24. After he lost his bet I enquired what had gone wrong. He said, 'It almost worked.' The number that did come out was 15, which is adjacent to 24 on the number wheel. Probably, he would have considered other outcomes like 5, 10, and 33 also confirmations, because they are nearby on the wheel. Also he could have taken the outcomes 22, 23, 25, and 26 as confirmations because their numerical value is close [to 24]."

strategies are best. A popular model is "fictitious play." In fictitious play, players keep track of the relative frequency with which another player has played each strategy in the past. These relative frequencies are beliefs about what that player will do in the upcoming period. Players then calculate expected payoffs for each strategy given these beliefs, and choose strategies with higher expected payoffs more frequently.

Fictitious play counts all previous observations equally. At the opposite extreme is Cournot best-response dynamics: Assume the strategy played most recently by others will be played again. Cournot dynamics weight the most recent past very heavily and dismiss or discard older experiences.

Weighting distant experiences less than recent ones gives a hybrid form called "weighted fictitious play" (Cheung and Friedman, 1997; Fudenberg and Levine, 1998). In our example, suppose that before period t the player had a belief $P_{t-1}(L) = 0.6$, and the strength of this belief (in units of experience) is 5 (i.e., $P_{t-1}(L) = 3/5$ and $P_{t-1}(R) = 2/5$). Then in weighted fictitious play beliefs are updated according to $P_t(L) = (3\rho + 1)/(5\rho + 1)$ and $P_t(R) = (2\rho + 0)/(5\rho + 1)$, where ρ is a decay factor. The boundary case $\rho = 0$ is Cournot best-response dynamics and $\rho = 1$ is fictitious play (keep a running count of the number of times L and R are chosen and take the ratio of L observations to total observations to be the belief $P_t(L)$). Beliefs are then used to compute expected payoffs, so $A^T(t) = [3(3\rho + 1) + 0(2\rho + 0)]/(5\rho + 1)$. Notice that the payoff the row player actually received in period t plays no special role in determining choice behavior in period $t + 1$.

4. *Experience-weighted attraction (EWA) learning* was designed by myself and Teck Ho (1999a) to combine the most appealing elements of reinforcement and weighted fictitious play in a hybrid or "gene-splice." (The Nobel laureate Francis Crick, who discovered DNA, wrote: "In nature a hybrid species is usually sterile; in science the opposite is often true" [1988, p. 150].)

   The model adds a key feature to reinforcement and belief learning: δ, the weight players give to forgone payoffs from unchosen strategies. When parameters are restricted to have certain values, EWA reduces to a simple version of choice reinforcement in which only chosen strategies are reinforced. When parameters are restricted in a different way, EWA reduces *exactly* to weighted fictitious play. So EWA is a *family* of learning rules with reinforcement and belief learning as extreme cases.

   In our example, EWA attractions are updated according to $A^B(t) = [\phi N(t - 1)A^B(t - 1) + 1]/(\phi(1 - \kappa)N(t - 1) + 1]$ and $A^T(t) = [\phi N(t - 1)A^T(t - 1) + 3\delta]/[\phi(1 - \kappa)N(t - 1) + 1]$. Notice that, if $\delta > 1/3$, a player could reinforce T more strongly than B even though T was not chosen. Players are then predicted to shift choice probability away from B and toward T. Notice that the choice of the column player plays a role in the row player's updating (because it determines the forgone payoff), and whether a payoff was received or simply imagined also matters (since the forgone payoff is weighted by δ).

5. In adaptive models such as fictitious play and EWA, players only look back at what other players have done previously. As a result, adaptive players will never shift their beliefs to expect something that they did not expect or observe before, and adaptive players will ignore information about other players' payoffs. But experiments that vary whether players know other players' history and payoffs show that players do care about what other players earn.

   Both limitations are overcome in models with *anticipatory learning* or *sophistication* (e.g., Milgrom and Roberts, 1991; Selten, 1986; Camerer, Ho, and Chong, 2002a; Stahl, 1999a). In these models, players do use information about other players' payoffs to reason more thoughtfully about what other players will do in the future.[4] These sophisticated models are a kind of belief learning because players *are* forming beliefs and best-responding according to them; it's just that their beliefs are more sophisticated than merely guessing that players will repeat their past choices.

   In the stag hunt example, adding sophistication means the row player knows that the column player earned 0, and knows the column player could have earned 1 from choosing R. If the row player thinks the column player is learning according to Cournot, therefore, she will predict that column will choose R. A sophisticated row player will therefore choose B, expecting a payoff of 1 (from column's R choice). Note that sophistication requires knowledge of the other player's payoffs (to compute her likely response). Including sophistication is also a way to model the fact that players behave differently when they are randomly rematched and when they are matched with "partners" repeatedly (see Camerer, Ho, and Chong, 2002a,b, and Chapter 8).

6. Players sometimes learn by *imitating* the strategies of others. Imitation could be independent of payoffs or could depend on payoffs—for example, players imitate the most successful player they see.

7. In *learning direction theory*, a player determines her ex post best response and adjusts her previous strategy in the direction of the best response (Selten and Stöcker, 1986). Learning direction theory combines the idea of moving toward the best response from Cournot-style

---

[4] Another example is an adaptive model in which players are assumed to detect which strategies are dominated for other players, and think others will never play those strategies (Cooper, Garvin, and Kagel, 1997b).

belief learning and the idea that one anchors on the previous strategy from reinforcement learning or habit models. It has not been generally defined for games without ordered strategies.

8. *Rule learning* assumes that people have decision rules that map histories into strategy choices. They learn about which *rules* to use, rather than about which specific *strategy* to use. Possible rules could include those listed above, and other rules such as tit-for-tat, level-*k* reasoning (see Chapter 5), and so forth.

   To illustrate using stag hunt, suppose the rules a player is considering are minimax (choose the strategy with the highest minimum payoff, which prescribes B) and a level-1 rule (best-respond to a random choice by others), which prescribes T. Given that the column player chose L, minimax would be reinforced by the payoff to the strategy it recommended (B), which is 1, and the level-1 rule would be reinforced by 0.

Most of the theories above are plausible, so it is useful to have a clear set of criteria for judging which theories are best (and for which purposes).

One way to judge plausibility is to ask what sorts of information are used by the updating rules. If there is information a theory does not require, which people use when it is available, the theory is incomplete. Theories that demand more information than people are able to integrate effectively are dubious too.

Notation is necessary to proceed further. Denote player i's jth strategy (out of m_i strategies) by s_i^j. The strategies that i and all other players (denoted $-i$) actually chose in period t are denoted $s_i(t)$ and $s_{-i}(t)$, respectively. Player i's payoff to playing s_i^j when others played s_{-i}^k is $\pi_i(s_i^j, s_{-i}^k)$. Player i's (ex post) best response is $b_i(s_{-i}(t)) \equiv \text{argmax}_k \ \pi_i(s_i^k, s_{-i}(t))$.

Table 6.3 shows the minimal information players need in different theories.[5] (Evolutionary theories are not listed because, taken seriously, they assume players use no information at all since they are born with fixed strategies.)

Actual information use depends on what information is available and on players' cognitive capacities. In high-information conditions, such as most of the experiments discussed in this chapter, all the information listed in Table 6.3 is available to players. Theories that assume players do not use

---

[5] Some kinds of information are sometimes necessary to compute other information. For example, if the payoffs are known then the choice by other players $s_{-i}(t)$ is needed to compute player i's received payoff $\pi_i(s_i(t), s_{-i}(t))$. However, it is possible to know player i's received payoff without knowing what other players did. Since Table 6.3 shows the *minimal* information needed by theories, a theory that requires knowing only the received payoffs (such as reinforcement) would *not* require knowledge of the choice $s_{-i}(t)$.

Table 6.3. *Minimal information used by various learning theories*

	Learning theories					
						Imita
Information	Reinforcement	Beliefs	Direction learning	EWA	Sophistication	Aver
i's choice $s_i(t)$	X		X	X		
$-i$'s choice $s_{-i}(t)$		X		X	X	X
i's received payoff $\pi_i(s_i(t), s_{-i}(t))$	X	X		X		
i's forgone payoffs $\pi_i(s_i^j, s_{-i}(t))$		X		X	X	
i's best response $b_i(s_{-i}(t))$			X			
$-i$'s received payoff $\pi_{-i}(s_i(t), s_{-i}(t))$					X	
$-i$'s forgone payoffs $\pi_i(s_i^j, s_{-i}^k)$					X	

all that information are implicitly assuming some constraint on cognitive capacity.

Different theories can be tested indirectly, by seeing whether behavior changes when required information is or is not available, or by measuring what information players look at. The few studies of this type show that subjects learn faster when they have full payoff information (which contradicts reinforcement), look up information about their own previous payoffs (which contradicts belief learning), and behave differently when they know the payoffs of others (implying sophistication).[6]

Another way to judge learning rules is to ask which rules would survive in an evolutionary competition (e.g., Heller, 1998). (The key to modeling this competition effectively is to specify the costs of rules of different complexity.) Josephson (2001) found that, in two-player games, EWA rules with high values of δ ("vivid imagination") tended to persist.

It is useful to list other properties we generally like theories to have. Here is one such list of desiderata: fit, coherence (or surprisingness), fruitfulness, and analytical tractability. Good theories *fit* and *predict* data well (adjusting for degrees of freedom, of course, to guard against overfitting). Good theories make *coherent* sense of unrelated phenomena; when their relation is *surprising* that's a bonus.[7] A theory that can be easily understood and applied by a broad body of scholars, and that provides a large body of solvable puzzles, is *fruitful*. And a theory should be *"analytically tractable"*— clear and parsimonious enough that theorists can prove something about what follows from assuming the theory is true. As you read, judge for yourself which theories are strongest on these criteria (or any criteria you like).

The empirical literature on fitting learning models to experimental data has grown dramatically in just a few years. I will first discuss studies that test only one approach, then discuss comparative studies.

6.2   Reinforcement Learning

Reinforcement approaches are derived from behaviorist psychology. Behaviorism was an extreme and important chapter in the history of psychology from about 1920 to 1960. The behaviorists were fed up with vague "mentalist" accounts of thinking processes that could not be directly observed. So they imposed an intellectual prohibition on speculation about cognitive

---

[6] Mookerjhee and Sopher (1994), Van Huyck, Battalio, and Rankin (2001a), and Rapoport and Erev (1998) find different learning when forgone payoff information is available. Partow and Schotter (1996) find differences when other players' payoffs are known.

[7] A theory that affirms the obvious adds nothing new to knowledge; in Bayesian terms, we seek theories that create posterior beliefs that are far from priors.

processes and insisted that all behavior could be explained as learned responses to previous reinforcement. Although the behaviorists left behind an
invaluable legacy of careful experimentation (which had not existed in psychology before), their basic framework has been largely abandoned since
then because it could not explain how people learned vicariously, and so
quickly, in domains with a vast array of possible responses and no direct reinforcement (e.g., children learning language). And cognitive constructs
were increasingly added on to explain these phenomena,[8] reinventing the
mentalist ideas that behaviorists eschewed in the first place. Note that behaviorism was never "disproved." It was largely *replaced* by fruitful analogies
between the brain and the computer, and the brain and "connectionist"
(parallel distributed processing, or PDP) neural networks.[9]

There are three waves of formal research on reinforcement learning in
decision and game theory. Fifty years ago Bush and Mosteller (1955) and
others formalized simple reinforcement rules and applied them to learning
in decisions. In a one-person second wave, Cross (1973, 1983) applied reinforcement to economic decisions. Unfortunately, his pioneering work was
largely ignored until a third wave, about ten years later, when Arthur (1991,
1994) revived the reinforcement approach and applied it to simple decisions. McAllister (1991), Mookerjhee and Sopher (1994, 1997), Roth and
Erev (1995), Sarin and Vahid (2001), and others later applied reinforcement
to games.

6.2.1 Reinforcement in Weak-Link Games

In McAllister's (1991) approach, rewards are normalized within payoff
bounds, and updated according to

$$A_i^j(t) = \phi A_i^j(t-1) + (1-\phi)\pi_i(s_i(t), s_{-i}(t))_j \qquad s_i^j = s_i(t)_j \quad (6.2.1)$$

$$A_i^j(t) = \phi A_i^j(t-1)_j \qquad\qquad\qquad\qquad\qquad\qquad \text{otherwise.} \quad (6.2.2)$$

Using an indicator function $I(x, y)$ which equals 1 when $x = y$ and 0 otherwise, the two rules can be written as

$$A_i^j(t) = \phi A_i^j(t-1) + (1-\phi)I(s_i^j, s_i(t))\pi_i(s_i(t), s_{-i}(t)). \quad (6.2.3)$$

---

[8] An example is "stimulus generalization," the indirect reinforcement of one stimulus by a different
stimulus which is similar.

[9] Reinforcement is still widely used to study animal learning and some domains of human behavior,
such as treatment of phobias, which are widely thought to tap "old brain" mechanisms for which simple
animal learning rules may also apply to humans. It is also useful for explaining learning in simple decision
environments such as slot machine gambling (e.g., Lea, Tarpy, and Webley, 1987, p. 287), where partial
reinforcement is clearly a powerful way to keep people pulling the lever.

Table 6.4.   *Simulated reinforcement learning of weak-link data*

Action	Period 1 data	Period 8 data	Period 8 simulated
1	0.019	0.654	0.25
2	0.047	0.252	0.50
3	0.047	0.028	0.13
4	0.168	0.028	0.06
5	0.318	0.009	0.06
6	0.093	0.000	0.00
7	0.308	0.028	0.00

Source: McAllister (1991).

The probability $P_i^j(t)$ of choosing strategy s_i^j in period t is updated according to

$$P_i^j(t) = (P_i^j(t) - \alpha \cdot \rho_j(t) P_i^j(t)) \Big/ \left(\sum_{k=1}^{m_i} P_i^k(t) - P_i^k(t)\alpha \cdot \rho_k(t) \right), \quad (6.2.4)$$

where α is an adjustment factor which affects the rate of learning and $\rho_j(t)$ is an adjustment ratio. Learning is faster when α is high and γ is low.

McAllister applies this model to the weak-link coordination game data of Van Huyck, Battalio, and Beil (1990) (see Chapter 7). It learns too slowly unless attractions are updated according to either actual or forgone payoffs (i.e., $A_i^j(t) = \phi A_i^j(t-1) + (1-\phi)\pi_i(s_i^j, s_{-i}(t))$). (Like others who came later, McAllister did not realize that this important change makes the reinforcement model a close relative of belief learning.) Experimenting with several parameter values, he finds that for fast updating—$\alpha = 0.75$, $\gamma = 0.5$, and $\phi = 0.5$—simulated paths converge toward the observed data in eight periods (see Table 6.4), although actual players converge more strongly to strategy 1 than the simulations do.

6.2.2   Reinforcement with Payoff Variability

Roth and Erev (1995) ask whether reinforcement learning can explain differences among three games—ultimatums, ultimatums with proposer competition ("market games"), and best-shot public goods games. In all three games the division of surplus is predicted to be extremely uneven. In experiments, however, subjects converge more strongly to uneven divisions in market games and best-shot games, and converge to nearly-equal offers in ultimatum games (see Chapter 2). Roth and Erev wanted to see whether learning models could reproduce these patterns (which are also parsimoniously explained by new models of social preference, see Chapter 2).

In the simplest form of their model, attractions cumulate according to

$$A_i^j(t) = \phi \cdot A_i^j(t-1) + I(s_i^j, s_i(t)) \cdot \pi_i(s_i^j, s_{-i}(t)), \qquad (6.2.5)$$

and are mapped into probabilities using a power function (with $\lambda = 1$). The same model was proposed earlier by Harley (1981), who suggested a neural interpretation in which reinforcements are levels of brain activation.

Cumulating attractions with a power probability function means later payoffs have less proportional impact than early ones, so learning slows down over time.[10] In earlier models (Bush and Mosteller, 1955; Cross, 1983), choice probabilities are updated directly by reinforcements, and learning slows down because an updating parameter is assumed to fall over time (Sarin, 1995).

Their model also has a scaling parameter $S(1)$ (which fixes the sum of the initial attractions to be $S(1)$ times the average game payoff) and a local experimentation parameter ϵ, which spills reinforcement of a chosen strategy over to its two neighboring strategies.[11]

Like McAllister, Roth and Erev fit the model by choosing small sets of parameter values, simulating model behavior for those values, and comparing the simulations with data informally. (Later studies choose finer-grained parameter values using a fit-maximizing technique that permits statistical tests.)

When initial conditions are matched to the data, the simulated learning paths in ultimatum games move in the right direction, but much more slowly than subjects do. In the best-shot games, players 1 and 2 choose a public good contribution 0, 2, or 4 (denoted q_1 and q_2), which is privately costly. The public good is an increasing function of the *maximum* of q_1 and q_2 and benefits both players equally. Given the payoffs, the subgame perfect prediction is $q_1 = 0$ and $q_2 = 4$.

Table 6.5 reports changes in the probabilities that q_1 is 0 or 2, and probabilities of q_2 being chosen as 0 or 2 in response to the perfect equilibrium choice $q_1 = 0$ (for the partial information condition). For player 1 choices of q_1, the simulated change from period 1 to 100 is close to the actual 10-

---

[10] The "power law of practice" refers to the fact that, in tasks such as adding numbers, recognizing previously presented sentences, or rolling cigars, the speed of performance or recall reliably obeys a power law of the amount of experience N, $P = ae^{-bN}$ (e.g., Anderson, 2000, p. 187). Of course, since the learning environment in a game is nonstationary (owing to learning by others), an exact power law usually won't hold, but the "power law" phrase is used informally to refer to a slowdown in learning.

[11] They also have a cutoff parameter μ, which sets probabilities below μ equal to 0.

Table 6.5. *Data and simulated reinforcement behavior in partial information best-shot public goods games*

Statistic	Data change Periods 1–10	Simulated change Periods 1–10	Periods 1–100
$\Delta P(q_1 = 0)$	+0.48	+0.22	+0.55
$\Delta P(q_1 = 2)$	−0.20	−0.10	−0.22
$\Delta P(q_2 = 0 | q_1 = 0)$	+0.11	−0.05	−0.09
$\Delta P(q_2 = 2 | q_1 = 0)$	−0.35	+0.04	+0.08

Source: Numbers estimated from Roth and Erev (1995), Figure 4.
Note: $\Delta P(q_1 = i)$ represents change in the proportion of player 1s choosing i over the periods indicated in the column headings. $\Delta P(q_2 = k | q_1 = i)$ represents change in the proportion of player 2s choosing k in response to a q_1 choice of i.

period change, but the simulated 10-period change is only half as large as it is in the data. However, the simulations do not capture the change in player 2 responses well.

In the market games, nine Proposers offer a division of a fixed pie to a single Responder, who takes the best offer. Offers converge very rapidly, in just one or two periods, to offering almost all the points. The reinforcement model described above cannot explain the rapid rate of convergence, because eight of nine Proposers' offers are rejected, so they get no reinforcement and do not learn to offer more. To explain the rapid rate of convergence, Roth and Erev switch to a different model, in which players' unchosen strategies are reinforced by the payoff of the *winning* bidder (which is basically belief learning). They use the same winning-payoff model to speed up learning in weak-link coordination games, where simulated learning from received payoffs is too slow to match the data (see McAllister, 1991, and Roth, 1995b, pp. 37–40).

These early studies show that reinforcement learning from own payoffs can approximate the direction of learning in ultimatum and best-shot games (thought it is too slow) but does a poor job explaining learning in market and weak-link games. Given these results, an obvious direction, taken by many later authors (including myself), was to search for more robust models which do not have the empirical weaknesses of reinforcement. Another was to acknowledge that models sometimes fail badly, but to continue to explore other domains in which reinforcement may work adequately.

Pursuing the latter path, Erev and Roth (1998) applied a variety of reinforcement models to constant-sum games with mixed equilibria. They

Table 6.6. *Average model fit (MSD) at individual level*

	Data	Experiment		
		O'Neill (1987)	Ochs (1995a)	Erev and Roth (new data)
Basic reinforcement	1st half	0.20	0.13	0.24
	2nd half	0.18	0.12	0.21
Fictitious play	1st	0.19[+]	0.14	0.24
	2nd	0.19[-]	0.15[-]	0.22
Nash equilibrium	1st	0.18[+]	0.15[-]	0.31[-]
	2nd	0.18	0.14[-]	0.30[-]

Source: Erev and Roth (1998).
Note: Superscript $-$ denotes significantly worse than basic reinforcement by paired t-test within-subject (one-tailed, $p = .05$); superscript $+$ denotes significantly better.

chose games with long spans (100 or more trials) in which equilibration is slow "to observe intermediate term as well as short term behavior." They explored various specifications and levels of analysis. One comparison fit data to individual subjects using three models: basic reinforcement ($\phi = 1$, $\epsilon = 0$), a stochastic power form of fictitious play (PFP), and Nash equilibrium. The mean squared deviations (MSDs) between observed choices and predictions are shown in Table 6.6 for the first and second halves of each of three data sets. Table 6.6 shows that equilibrium predictions are not bad in absolute terms, but are significantly worse than the learning models in two of three data sets. Stochastic fictitious play (PFP) and reinforcement are about equally accurate across the three data sets (PFP is slightly less accurate for later periods).

Erev, Bereby-Meyer, and Roth (1999) add a payoff variability term to their earlier model and apply it to risky choices. The idea is to divide attractions by the variability of received payoffs as a way of slowing down learning when the environment is variable, and sharpening convergence when the environment is stable.

Roth et al. (1999) use this model to fit and predict data from randomly sampled 2×2 games with mixed-strategy equilibria. They stress that it is good to have a precise criterion for measuring how useful a theory is (see Harless and Camerer, 1994) and propose a measure called "predictive value." A theory's predictive value is the number of observations of data (new subjects or new periods) one can save by using the theory to make predictions instead of running more subjects. (It is a measure of "labor savings.")

In more recent work on their sample of 2×2 games with mixed equilibria, reinforcement, Camerer-Ho EWA, and fictitious play models are about equally accurate, and all the learning models are substantially better than equilibrium.

6.2.3 Reinforcement with "Mood Shocks"

Sarin and Vahid (2001) propose a reinforcement model in which attractions are equal to lagged attractions plus a learning rate parameter γ times the "surprise," the difference between the received payoff and the previous attraction. That is,

$$A_i^j(t) = A_i^j(t-1) + I(s_i^j, s_i(t)) \cdot \gamma(\pi_i(s_i^j, s_{-i}(t)) - A_i^j(t-1)). \quad (6.2.6)$$

(This is just Erev and Roth's simple model with $\phi = 1$ and attractions equal to averages.) Sarin and Vahid assume that players always choose the strategy with the highest attraction, but they average across many simulations with random shocks included, so the model is observationally similar to one with stochastic choice.

Sarin and Vahid first compare frequencies of simulated choices with frequencies in block-averaged data from the games with mixed equilibria that Erev and Roth (1998) sampled. The one-parameter Sarin–Vahid model fits better than Roth–Erev's three-parameter model in seven data sets, worse in four, and slightly better overall. A subject-by-subject analysis is similar. The estimated learning parameter $\hat{\gamma}$ is 0.010, which is very small and is likely to be much larger in other classes of games. It is not clear *why* the Sarin–Vahid averaging model does modestly better than the Roth–Erev cumulation model. They attribute its relative success to the maximization assumption, but I think that's wrong because averaging simulations is noisy best response. Averaging is probably just a better description of the cognitive process in these games than cumulation is.

6.2.4 Information Conditions

Because reinforcement models assume players care only about their history of payoffs, the models can be applied in low-information and changing environments. But it also implies that players in high-information environments ignore a lot of what they know.

To test whether information matters, Mookerjhee and Sopher (1994) compared high- and low-information conditions. They found some differences, casting doubt on reinforcement models, but they used matching pennies games, which have little power to distinguish learning theories when simple statistics are used.

A more thorough test was conducted by Van Huyck, Battalio, and Rankin (2001a). They use an order-statistic coordination game with five players. A player's payoff depends on her own choice and the median choice. Strategies s_i^j are numbers in the interval [0,1]; denote the vector of all other players' strategies by s_{-i}; and $M(s(t))$ is the median of all five players' strategies. Player i's payoff is then

$$\pi_i(s_i^j, s_{-i}) = .5 - |s_i^j - \omega \cdot M(s) \cdot (1 - M(s))|. \qquad (6.2.7)$$

In their game with $\omega = 2.44$, denoted G(2.44), the maximum value of $\omega \cdot M(\cdot) \cdot (1 - M(\cdot))$ is 0.61, so any number above 0.61 is dominated. The Nash equilibria are solutions to the equation $x = 2.44 \cdot x \cdot (1 - x)$, which are 0 and 0.59.

This can be seen graphically in Figure 6.1 phase diagrams, which show how a median $M(t+1)$ (on the y-axis) depends on the previous median $M(t)$ (on the x-axis). The inverted U-shaped line plots the best-response function $M(t) = 2.44M(t)(1 - M(t))$. Equilibria are where the best-response function and equilibrium condition $M(t) = M(t+1)$ intersect (i.e., 0 and 0.59).

Van Huyck et al. (VHBR) ran four sessions with G(2.44). Subjects knew they were playing seventy-five periods with four others, and knew their own history of choices and payoffs, but did *not* know anything at all about the payoff function. The path of actual medians in the four experimental sessions are shown in the Figure 6.1 phase diagrams. Subjects zig-zag around the interior equilibrium at 0.59 for a while, then settle down after about twenty periods.

Van Huyck et al. ask whether the actual dynamic path in Figure 6.1 can be explained by the Cross (1973) reinforcement rule. The Cross rule modifies choice probabilities according to

$$P(s_i^j)(t+1) = P(s_i^j)(t) + \alpha \cdot r[\pi_i(s_i^j, s_{-i}(t))] \cdot (1 - P(s_i^j)(t) \quad s_i^j = s_i(t) \quad (6.2.8)$$

$$P(s_i^j)(t+1) = P(s_i^j)(t) - \alpha \cdot r[\pi_i(s_i^j, s_{-i}(t))] \cdot P(s_i^j)(t) \quad s_i^j \neq s_i(t), \quad (6.2.9)$$

where $r(\pi)$ is the reinforcement from payoff π.[12]

Figure 6.2 shows a simulated path of the Cross dynamic for seventy-five periods for $\alpha = 0.05$ and uniform initial conditions. The process converges much more slowly than the actual data, and often wanders into the dominated-strategy territory above 0.61 (which subjects rarely do). The Cross reinforcement rule clearly learns far too slowly to explain the behavior of subjects. The adjustment speed α can be increased but, as Van Huyck et al. note (2001a, p. 15), "when you speed up these algorithms they begin to get stuck in absorbing states that are not even close to being mutually

---

[12] They normalize reinforcements to be 0 and 1 for the lowest and highest payoffs, and try adjustment speed parameters $\alpha = 0.01$ or 0.05.

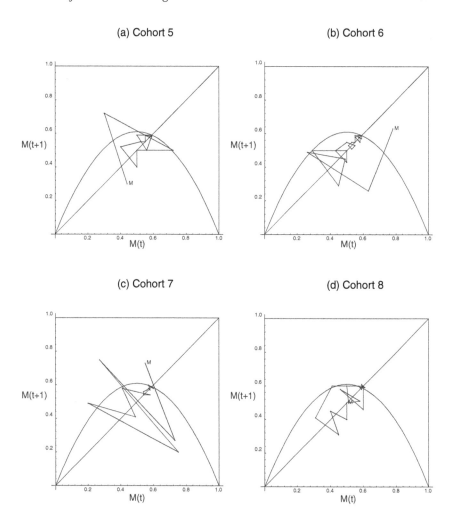

Figure 6.1. *Phase diagrams of actual period-by-period medians in Van Huyck, Battalio, and Rankin's order-statistic games. Source: Van Huyck, Battalio, and Rankin (2001a).*

consistent, something our subjects don't do, and if one continually smears probability to prevent this then the process doesn't converge, which is also something our subjects don't do." However, Sarin and Vahid (2000) show that spilling reinforcement to a chosen strategy 6–12 neighboring strategies, and decaying lagged attractions rapidly, improves the fit of the model substantially.

Van Huyck et al. compare these sessions to complete-information sessions in which subjects knew the payoff function. Reinforcement learning predicts that the additional payoff function information should not matter

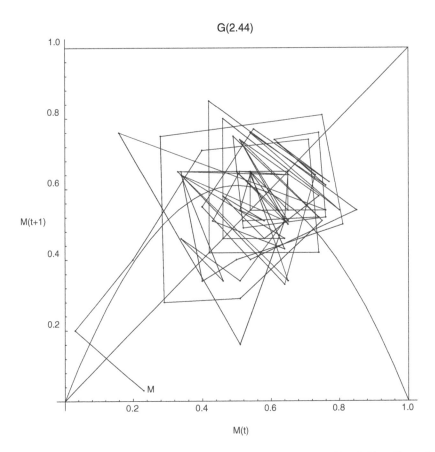

G(2.44)

M(t+1)

M(t)

Figure 6.2. *Simulated paths of Cross (reinforcement) dynamics in Van Huyck, Battalio, and Rankin's games (G(2.44)). Source: Van Huyck, Battalio, and Rankin (2001a).*

but subjects converge much faster when they know the payoff function (in five periods rather than twenty).

Summary: Reinforcement learning models in which only chosen strategies are reinforced predict the direction of learning correctly, but are often too slow to match the pace of human learning (except in games with mixed equilibria, when there is little learning and many models improve slightly over equilibrium predictions or random guessing). Underestimation of learning can be directly traced to the fact that, in environments with full payoff information, subjects use that information. One can speed up the algorithms to approximate human learning by assuming that players reinforce all strategies according to unchosen payoffs, reinforce "winning" strategies, or reinforce a wide range of strategies that are "similar" to the one they chose. Models discussed later in this chapter move in the same direction, by expanding the range of how subjects learn.

6.3 Belief Learning

An early model of belief learning dates back to Cournot ([1838] 1960), who suggested players choose a best response to behavior observed in the previous period. Theories of "fictitious play" were proposed by Brown (1951) and Robinson (1951). These theories were initially proposed to compute Nash equilibrium algorithmically, providing a story about how mental simulation could lead to immediate equilibration in a kind of cognitive tâtonnement.

   Early proofs showed that in some games, if fictitious play beliefs converged, they would converge on a Nash equilibrium. Then, in 1964, Shapley showed that, in a certain zero-sum game with three strategies, fictitious play cycles around strategies and does not converge to the unique mixed-strategy equilibrium. His counterexample took the wind out of the sails of the hope for a general guarantee that fictitious play would always converge to Nash equilibrium. Research on learning dynamics came to a screeching halt for about fifteen years.

   In the 1980s, theorists dusted off fictitious play and reinterpreted it as a theory of how players might learn from periods of actual behavior rather than from mentally simulated trials (Fudenberg and Kreps, 1995).

6.3.1 Weighted Fictitious Play

Cheung and Friedman (1997) were the first to study belief learning thoroughly using data. They use a weighted form of fictitious play and a stochastic response function. Weighted fictitious play beliefs are defined by

$$E_i(s^j_{-i})(t) = \frac{I(s^j_{-i}, s_{-i}(t)) + \sum_{k=1}^{t-1} \phi_i^k \cdot I(s^j_{-i}, s_{-i}(t-k))}{1 + \sum_{k=1}^{t-1} \phi_i^k} \qquad t = 1, 2, \dots \quad (6.3.1)$$

(i.e., observations t periods back are weighted by ϕ^{t-1}). Adding the weight ϕ is sensible because standard fictitious play ignores *when* another player made various choices in the past. Cournot best-response dynamics errs in the opposite direction by taking into account only what happened last time. Weighted fictitious play is a sensible compromise. When $\phi = 1$, weighted fictitious play is original fictitious play; when $\phi = 0$, it is Cournot.[13]

---

[13] A further generalization allows ϕ to vary with time (e.g., Crawford, 1995). For example, ϕ might grow over time if players recognize that other players are changing their strategies more frequently at the beginning of a game than at the end (e.g., Ho, Camerer, and Chong, 2002).

Table 6.7. *Games used by Cheung and*
Friedman

Game	Matrix	
Hawk–dove	−2, −2	8, 0
	0, 8	4, 4
Coordination	5, 5	−1, 4
(stag hunt)	4, −1	1, 1
Buyer–seller	2, 2	0, 3
	3, −1	−1, 4
Battle of the sexes	1, 3	−1, −1
	−1, −1	2, 1

Source: Cheung and Friedman (1997).

Their games are shown in Table 6.7. They varied the matching and history protocols in interesting ways. In a (standard) random pairwise (RP) condition, players were randomly rematched in each period. In a "mean matching" (MM) condition, each player chose one strategy and earned the mean of their payoffs averaged over matches with every other player. In the (standard) no history (NH) condition, each player knew only their own personal history; in a history (H) condition players knew the distribution of *all* strategies chosen previously.

Parameters are estimated separately for each individual. There are many estimates in outlying categories, greater than 1 or below 0 (which implies parameters are not estimated too precisely). The median fictitious play weights ϕ are between 0.25 and 0.50, closer to the Cournot prediction of 0 than the fictitious play prediction of 1.

Table 6.8 classifies individuals into types according to the value of ϕ.[14] For example, Cournot types are those for whom the hypothesis that $\phi_i = 0$ can be accepted but $\phi_i = 1$ can be rejected. Adaptive types are those for whom both $\phi_i = 1$ and $\phi_i = 0$ can be rejected. Most estimates of ϕ tend either to include one extreme but not the other (Cournot and fictitious play), or to include both (uninformative). The type distribution is not significantly different across the four games. Cheung and Friedman note that, since players have more information when they know all players' histories, or are matched to everyone and paid the average, they should weight new

[14] The two "imprinting" types with $\hat{\phi} > 1$ (also known as "primacy effects" in cognitive psychology) are excluded.

Table 6.8. *Number of subjects classified by estimated fictitious play weight*

Game type	Fickle	Cournot	Adaptive	Fictitious play	Uninformative
Accept	$\phi_i < 0$	$\phi_i = 0$	$0 < \phi_i < 1$	$\phi_i = 1$	$\phi_i = 0,1$
Reject	$\phi_i = 0$	$\phi_i = 1$	$\phi_i = 0,1$	$\phi_i = 0$	
Hawk–dove	15	31	8	31	41
Coordination	5	25	6	18	22
Buyer–seller	4	37	9	17	25
Battle of the sexes	4	51	6	18	18

Source: Cheung and Friedman (1997).

information more heavily (higher ϕ_i) and respond more sensitively (higher λ_i) in those conditions. These predictions are correct.

6.3.2 General Belief Learning

Crawford (1995; and see Crawford and Broseta, 1998) proposes a belief-type approach to model how the interaction of dispersed initial beliefs and adaptive dynamics explain convergence patterns in order-statistic coordination games studied by Van Huyck, Battalio, and Beil (1990, 1991) (see Chapter 7). The model allows common changes in beliefs and player-specific shocks.

In these games, players choose a number from 1 to 7 and a player i's payoff depends on the number she chose, $s_i(t)$, and on an order statistic of all the numbers, $y(t)$. Payoffs are generally increasing in $y(t)$ and decreasing in deviation between $s_i(t)$ and $y(t)$. In Van Huyck et al. (1990) the order statistic was the median. In these games, players are penalized quadratically for choosing a number higher or lower than the median number, which induces a desire for conformity. In Van Huyck et al. (1991) the order statistic was the minimum. In these "weak-link" games, players were penalized if their choice was above the minimum, but everyone wanted the minimum to be high.

In the median game, there is some dispersion in initial choices, with frequent choices of 4–5, and a fast convergence to the initial median in a couple of periods. In minimum games with large groups, the dispersion in initial choices means that the minimum of those choices is usually low, and the large groups *always* converge to the minimum of 1, usually within a few periods.

Crawford's analysis exploits the fact that, since players are penalized for deviating from the order statistic, there is no need to distinguish between players' *beliefs* about the order statistic and their *choices*. Following the literature on adaptive control, he assumes that player i's initial choices $s_i(1)$ and adapted choices $s_i(t)$ are given by

$$s_i(1) = \alpha_0 + \zeta_{i0} \qquad\qquad\qquad\qquad\qquad\qquad\qquad (6.3.2)$$

$$s_i(t) = \alpha_t + (1 - \phi_t)y_{t-1} + \phi_t s_i(t-1) + \zeta_{it} \quad (t = 1, 2, \ldots). \quad (6.3.3)$$

In each equation, an individual player's response depends on common parameters and a player-specific term ζ_{it}.

The intercepts α_t capture period-specific drift in choices, which is common across players. A lower value of the weight ϕ_t represents quicker responsiveness to experience. The terms ζ_{it} represent idiosyncratic player-specific initial beliefs and shocks to beliefs.[15]

Under special parametric restrictions, the model reduces to fictitious play or Cournot. But the full model is a generalization of these approaches, which allows time-varying history weights and idiosyncratic changes in beliefs (owing to bursts of insight or correlated shocks due to public events). Solving recursively, Crawford shows that for a given set of parameter values there is a unique path of choices and order statistics. If the weights $(1 - \phi_t)$ lie in an interval $(0, 1 - b)$ for some $b < 1$, and the summed common drift terms α_t and shock variances $\sigma^2(\zeta_{it})$ are finite, all players eventually choose the same number. Intuitively, this means a group will equilibrate (reaching a mutual best-response point) as long as they continually respond to experience and the drift and shock terms dampen over time.

These conditions imply convergence will occur, but *which* equilibrium the players converge to will depend stochastically on initial conditions and parameter values (i.e., even an observer knowing only the initial conditions and parameters cannot predict exactly what will happen). As Crawford emphasizes, this is a kind of proof that experimental observation is necessary: Theorizing alone cannot predict which paths will occur, so putting people in these games and observing what happens is necessary to understand the system fully.

Some econometrics is used to estimate the model's parameters. To conserve degrees of freedom, some innocuous restrictions are imposed. The estimate of α_0 is 4.75, which matches the central tendency in the data to choose 4 or 5 in the first period. The variance of the first-period player-specific shock is $\sigma^2(\epsilon_t) = 1.62$, implying a standard deviation of 1.27 of initial choices across players. The learning coefficient $\hat{\phi}$ is 0.42, which means that

---

[15] If the conditional variance $\sigma^2(\zeta_{it}|x_{it-1})$ is 0, then all players who chose the same number in the last period have the same idiosyncratic change in beliefs. This can be shown to imply, surprisingly (see Crawford's footnote 18), that the order statistic y_t must converge to its initial value y_0. Since this path-dependence is evident in median games, Crawford infers that the conditional variance of the player-specific shocks must be small.

players weight their previous observed median y_t slightly more (0.58) than their own previous choices (0.42).

In minimum-action games with large groups, the drift term α_t is constrained to be constant across periods t, but is allowed to be nonzero. It is estimated to be -0.27, reflecting the downward drift across periods evident in the data. The estimated inertia coefficient $\hat{\phi}$ is larger, 0.75, indicating that players are more inertial than in the median-action games.

Broseta (2000) adds an ARCH (autoregressive conditional heteroskedasticity) modification to the Crawford model. In ARCH, the unconditional shock variances in each period t, $\sigma^2(\zeta_{it})$, are positively autocorrelated over time. That is, $\sigma_t^2 = \kappa_{0t} + \kappa_1 \sigma_{t-1}^2$, where κ_{0t} is a period-specific component of unconditional variance and κ_1 captures the correlation between player-specific variances in adjacent periods. If $\kappa_1 > 0$, when player i has an idiosyncratic shock in a period that is large in absolute value (meaning that ζ_{it}^2 was large for i in period t), she is likely to have large shocks in subsequent periods (ζ_{it+1}^2 will be large too). Under mild conditions on the conditional variances (κ_{0t}s converge to 0 quickly enough, and κ_1 is not too close to 1), the ARCH process leads to convergence of players' choices in the limit, as in Crawford's setup.

The ARCH specification is like an omnibus correction for omitted variables which persistently influence players' forecasts. Allowing correlation of error variances across time will improve the overall fit, without requiring one to specify precisely what the omitted variable is. As Broseta (2000, p. 34) explains:

> To gain some intuition, suppose that for unknown cognitive reasons, subject k expects a high value of the order statistic and, accordingly, tends to play a high effort level at time t. We should then expect to observe, ex post, a large (and in this case, positive) prediction error ϵ_{kt}. After the value of y_t is publicly announced, all players update their beliefs. But if they do so sensibly . . . idiosyncratic differencs are likely to persist in the near future. In particular we would expect that, as he or she clings to "optimistic" beliefs, agents k will still expect a high value of y_{t+1}, which is then likely to result, ex post, in a large (and positive) value of ϵ_{kt+1}.

The ARCH model fits substantially better even though it is simpler. Broseta imposes some economizing restrictions. Most coefficients are similar to Crawford's. The ARCH persistence coefficient κ_1 is estimated to be 0.40 and 0.63 in median and minimum games, which is large.

Many other papers study belief models but are not discussed in detail here. Cooper, Garvin, and Kagel (1997a,b) apply belief learning models to signaling models of entry deterrence. Chapter 8 discusses their work and related work on belief learning in signaling games by Brandts and Holt (1993,

1994) and Anderson and Camerer (2000). In a study of the dominance-solvable "travelers' dilemma" (see Chapter 5), Capra et al. (1999) fit a fictitious play model, which goes in the right direction but underpredicts the magnitude of change by a factor of four. Sefton (1999) models learning in coordination games with fictitious play.

6.3.3   Learning Direction Theory

Learning direction theory settles for predicting only the *direction* in which choices will change, in low-information environments where players may know only the ideal direction of change. Selten often uses the example of an archer shooting an arrow toward a target. If the arrow misses to the left of the target, the archer knows to aim further to the right, but may know little more.

Although learning direction theory has never been fully specified, it can be interpreted as a relative of belief learning which combines elements of Cournot dynamics—moving toward the ex post best response—with habit or inertia. Learning direction theory was first used to analyze experimental data on finitely repeated prisoners' dilemmas (PDs) by Selten and Stöcker (1986). Their subjects played twenty-five sequences consisting of a ten-period repeated PD. They define a "cooperative play" of a sequence as one in which both players choose C for at least four periods, one player chooses D in at least one subsequent period, and both players choose D in all subsequent periods. Since most sequences are played this way, it is reasonable to characterize sequences by the first period in which defection occurs. Table 6.9 shows the average period in which deviations were intended to occur, averaged across blocks of three sequences for six experimental sessions.[16] Sessions vary—for example, defection occurs around periods 6–7 in groups I and IV, and in period 8 or later in others. Players also defect earlier and earlier across sequences.

In their learning direction model, each subject has an intended deviation period k. Players who intended to defect later than their opponent actually did (i.e., the opponent defected before them) lower their k by one unit with probability α. Players who defect at the same time as their opponent lower their k by one unit with probability β.[17]

---

[16] "Intended" defection is either a player's first D period, or their intended period from an analysis of written responses. Means greater than 10 occur because period 11 denotes cooperation through all ten periods.

[17] Presumably $\alpha > \beta$, because players learn more and react more strongly to a defection that precedes their defection than to a defection that occurs at the same time. Notice that this intuition uses a concept of forgone payoff in the background, but the amount of the loss from defecting later does not enter directly into a calculation about the switch rates α and β.

Table 6.9. *Mean intended defection periods in ten-period prisoners'
dilemma*

Sequences	Session						
	I	II	III	IV	V	VI	Total
13–15	7.7	8.8	10.1	7.6	10.0	10.2	9.1
16–18	7.0	8.5	9.9	7.3	9.3	9.9	8.7
19–21	6.4	8.0	9.8	6.8	9.2	9.2	8.2
22–25	5.7	7.8	9.5	6.1	8.7	8.5	7.6

Source: Selten and Stöcker (1986).

If a player defects *before* her opponent she increases k by one unit with probability γ. In most cases (65 percent) players change their defection period as predicted by direction learning; in 35 percent of the cases players changed in the wrong direction. Counting the relative frequencies of changes gives the median estimates of α, β, and γ of 0.500, 0.135, and 0.225. The median estimate of the difference $\alpha + \beta - \gamma$ is 0.45, 78 percent of those individual-level estimates are positive, and steady-state calculations using these parameters imply that, in the long run, unraveling to immediate defection will occur.

Learning direction theory imposes a simple structure on learning and usually predicts a majority of directional changes in other studies. However, it is hard to be thoroughly impressed by direction learning because it makes such an unsurprising prediction. The same kind of movement toward best response is built more generally into theories such as belief or EWA learning. In those theories, when the reinforcement on forgone payoffs is high enough, players will shift choice probability toward best responses just as in learning direction theory.

Furthermore, define the ex post best response

$$b_i(t) = \text{argmax}_{s_i^j} \pi_i(s_i^j, s_{-i}(t)).$$

Learning direction theory predicts only that players are likely to choose strategies between $s_i(t)$ and $b_i(t)$. But imagine a game in which some strategies in the interval $[s_i(t), b_i(t)]$ have very low payoffs. Learning direction theory does not predict anything about whether those low-payoff interior strategies will be played or not. Theories that are responsive to forgone payoffs (such as beliefs and EWA) predict precisely which strategies in the interval are more or less likely to be played. Learning direction predictions are therefore sharpened when more information is available.

6.3.4 Bayesian Learning

Cox, Shachat, and Walker (2001) did the first experimental test of Jordan's (1991) Bayesian learning model. In that model, players are uncertain what other players' payoffs are, but they have a commonly known prior and can learn over time, from actions of other players, which payoff matrix is being used. Jordan showed that the Bayesian learning process converges to a Nash equilibrium in finite games (and sometimes it refines the set of equilibria). Although Jordan's result is reassuring, it is tailored to explain only learning about what other players' *payoffs* are, rather than learning what other players *will do*. In experiments where payoffs are common knowledge, the Jordan model predicts immediate equilibration, which we rarely see. Because the model's prediction is wrong in these simpler cases, it is not the best general approach. Nonetheless, it makes interesting predictions in games with incomplete payoff information which are worth examining.

In the experiments of Cox et al., row players have payoffs given by one of four matrices with commonly known priors, and column players have payoffs given by one of two matrices. All matrices are shown in Table 6.10. Each true game is a combination of a row player payoff matrix (with priors shown in parentheses) and a column player matrix. Players know their own matrix but not the other player's matrix.

Along the Bayesian equilibrium path, players take actions but also learn about the other player's payoff matrix (and likely actions) over time. (Many theorists love this model because it characterizes "equilibrium learning"– that is, players are changing what they do, but are always perfectly anticipating what others will do given what they know.)

To illustrate, suppose the matrix combination drawn is C for row and B for column (denoted CB). Since the row player has a dominant strategy, she plays (B)ottom for sure and earns 2. Column knows there is a 3/8 chance the matrix is A, and row will play (T)op, and a 3/8 chance the matrix is C, and row will play B. In equilibrium, row also plays B when the matrix is B and T

Table 6.10. *Games used in experiments on Bayesian (Jordan) learning*

	Possible row player payoff matrices								Possible column player payoff matrices			
	A (3/8)		B (1/8)		C (3/8)		D (1/8)		B (1/2)		D (1/2)	
	L	R	L	R	L	R	L	R	L	R	L	R
T	1	2	0	3	1	0	3	0	0	2	3	1
B	0	0	2	2	2	2	1	1	3	2	0	1

Source: Cox, Shachat, and Walker (2001).

when the matrix is D (these inferences come from more delicate reasoning). If the column player anticipates these moves and their probabilities, she infers that the row moves will be T, B, B, T for row matrices A–D, so, given the priors, there is a 50–50 chance row will play either T or B. Given that guess and knowing her own payoffs are given by matrix B—in our example of the CB combination—column should play R and earn 2. Hence, the Jordan path predicts (B,R) play in period 1 when the matrix combination is CB.

Notice that if they play (B,R), column then earns 2 but also learns that the row player's matrix is either B or C. Then column infers row will keep playing B so she should switch to L and earn 3. The second-period prediction is therefore (B,L). Then there is nothing more to be learned and the players should play (B,L) (a Bayesian–Nash equilibrium) forever.

In the first period, as noted, both types of players with matrices B and D should choose B and T, or R and L, respectively. Row players make that predicted choice about 70 percent of the time and column players make it 60 percent of the time. The corresponding figures in the second period (conditional on period 1 history) are 54 percent and 69 percent. Players are therefore roughly on the Jordan path but there are many deviations.

Table 6.11 shows relative frequencies of each strategy pair and matrix pair, from the third period on (when the Jordan path is predicted to settle into equilibrium), averaging across matching protocols. Jordan predictions

Table 6.11. *Summary results in Bayesian learning experiment from period 3 on*

	Strategy pair			
Matrix pair	(T,L)	(T,R)	(B,L)	(B,R)
AB	0.03	**0.97**	0.00	0.01
AD	**0.91**	0.05	0.05	0.00
CB	0.00	0.00	**0.96**	0.04
CD	0.00	0.00	0.09	**0.91**
BB	0.13	*0.26*	**0.37**	0.23
DD	**0.70**	0.08	0.10	*0.12*
BD	0.14	0.23	0.32	0.31
DB	0.14	0.27	0.23	0.35
Mixed-strategy predictions (DB, BD)	0.11	0.22	0.22	0.44

Source: Cox, Shachat, and Walker (2001).
Note: Jordan predictions are in **bold**; Nash predictions that do not coincide with Jordan are in *italics*. Mixed-strategy predictions apply to games DB and BD, and are also Nash equilibria (but not Jordan) in DD and BB.

are in bold. When the row player has a dominant strategy, in matrix pairs (AB,AD) and (CB,CD), more than 90 percent of strategy pairs are at the Jordan and Nash prediction. In matrix pair DD the Jordan prediction of (T,L) is again rather accurate (70 percent) but in the matrix pair BB the predicted (B,L) is played only about a third of the time. In games DB and BD the Jordan and Nash predictions are mixed strategies in which (T,L) is most rare and (B,R) is most common, and the data do match the predicted rank of frequency across pairs (as in most mixed games described in Chapter 3).

The predictions of the Jordan model depend delicately on players making the right choices in the first couple of periods. Given this fragility, the results above are encouraging. At the same time, these games are only 2 × 2 and the row player sometimes has dominant strategies, so Bayesian learning is not computationally difficult. It should be easy to construct games that are only slightly more complicated in which the Jordan paths are very unlikely to emerge in the short run.

6.3.5 Measuring Beliefs Directly

Several studies in experimental economics have measured players' beliefs using incentive-compatible "scoring rules" to induce players to report thoughtfully.[18] In a pioneering study, McKelvey and Page (1990) elicited beliefs to test information aggregation. In 1988, Weigelt and I elicited beliefs to test refinement predictions about out-of-equilibrium beliefs in signaling and trust games (reported in Camerer, Ho, and Chong, 2002b). Karjalainen and I (1994) found elicited beliefs in a coordination game could be superadditive, reflecting ambiguity-aversion owing to strategic uncertainty.

Many years later, Nyarko and Schotter (2002) elicited beliefs to answer an obvious but unanswered question—do beliefs correspond to fictitious play? (The answer is no.) They used a 2 × 2 game with a unique mixed-strategy equilibrium (MSE), shown in Table 6.12. Subjects played sixty rounds in four sessions, crossing random- and fixed-matching protocols with and without belief elicitation. As in other mixed games (see Chapter 3), actual frequencies across all periods are between equal randomization and the MSE prediction.

Because beliefs are measured directly, one can fit stated beliefs to a weighted fictitious play model to see how well it explains beliefs. These fits

---

[18] For example, Nyarko and Schotter's subjects play either R(ed) or G(reen). If the player reports a belief r that the opponent will play R, they earn $0.10 - 0.10(1 - r)^2$ if R is actually played and $0.10 - 0.05(r^2 + (1 - r)^2)$ if G is played. It is easy to show that, if players are risk neutral and have a true belief b, then their expected payoff is maximized by reporting $b = r$ (e.g., Camerer, 1995).

Table 6.12. *Nyarko and Schotter's mixed-strategy game*

Row strategies	Column strategies		MSE prediction	Relative frequency
	Green	Red		
G	6,2	3,5	0.40	0.46
R	3,5	5,3	0.60	0.54
MSE prediction	0.40	0.60		
Relative frequency	0.39	0.61		

Source: Nyarko and Schotter (2002).

yield ϕ coefficients close to 1^{19} but stated beliefs and fitted beliefs are usually very far apart. A key problem is that fictitious play beliefs with ϕ close to 1 average all previous observations and settle down rapidly after about twenty periods. But stated beliefs vary wildly from period to period and do not converge. Players' actions are also more like best responses given stated beliefs, *not* like best responses given fictitious play beliefs. However, stated beliefs are slightly *worse* predictions of actual behavior by opponents than are fictitious play beliefs (i.e., subjects would have earned more money if they stated fictitious play beliefs instead of what they actually guessed).

The Nyarko and Schotter results show fictitious play is a bad model of stated beliefs in these games. Beliefs may be drawing on more information than is used in fictitious play, or may reflect time-variation of weights (see Camerer and Ho, 1999b) or sophisticated outguessing of how others are learning.

6.3.6 Population-Level Replicator Dynamics

Cheung and Friedman (1998) apply replicator dynamics to their hawk–dove and buyer–seller games and compare it with individual learning.[20] In replicator dynamics, the percentage of a population that uses a strategy increases proportionally with the relative payoff advantage of that strategy. The payoff advantage to strategy 1, which is strategy 1's expected payoff minus the population average payoff, is $(1 - S_t) \cdot R(S_t)$, where S_t is the proportion playing 1. The replicator dynamic is defined as $(S_{t+1} - S_t)/S_t = \beta \cdot (1 - S_t)R(s_t)$, where β is an adjustment speed parameter. Note that replicator dynamics predicts only how population-level averages change; it makes no predictions about how specific individuals will change what they do.

---

[19] The median $\hat{\phi}$ across subjects is 1.05 and the interquartile range is (0.98, 1.32). Inferring ϕ coefficients from choices yields a lower overall estimate of $\hat{\phi} = 0.61$ with much variability. Note that Feltovich (2000) also finds good fits from ϕ slightly greater than 1, which is odd and merits further investigation.

[20] This section benefited from discussion with Dan Friedman.

Table 6.13.   *Replicator dynamics coefficients*

	Estimate			Mean absolute deviation	
Sample	$\hat{\alpha}$	$\hat{\beta}$	$\hat{\gamma}$	Replicator	Weighted FP
Hawk–dove	−.08 (.01)	.50 (.04)	.39 (.06)	.119	.117
Buyer	.23 (.05)	.60 (.26)	.23 (.54)	.22	.16
Seller	−.07 (.51)	.49 (.03)	.48 (.14)	.19	.16

Source: Cheung and Friedman (1998).
Note: Standard errors in parentheses.

Cheung and Friedman test replicator dynamics by regressing percentage changes of the population frequency against the historical relative payoff advantage

$$\delta S_{t+1}/S_t = \alpha + \beta \cdot (1 - S_t)R(s_t) + \gamma \cdot MM \cdot (1 - S_t)R(S_t) + \epsilon_t. \text{ (6.3.4)}$$

The intercept α captures drift toward strategy 1 (which is difficult for standard replicator dynamics to explain). The variable MM is a dummy which equals 1 if the data came from the mean-matching treatment, so γ measures any variable *increase* in adjustment speed from mean-matching.

Table 6.13 shows the results and compares the accuracy of replicator dynamics with weighted fictitious play (FP). The estimates of β are within the bounds necessary to ensure stability. Positive estimates of $\hat{\gamma}$ show that adjustment speeds are larger in the mean-matching (MM) condition in which subjects have more information.

Although replicator dynamics is very popular in evolutionary game theory, there are three problems with it as a theory of population learning in the lab. First, it doesn't fit as well: The mean absolute deviations from actual population frequencies are simply higher than for the weighted fictitious play model. Second, there is no sensible reason why the intercepts $\hat{\alpha}$ should be nonzero—strictly speaking, nonzero α implies that, even when strategy 1 has no payoff advantage (e.g., at the mixed-strategy equilibrium), there is drift toward play of the first strategy (for Sellers) or away from it (in Hawk–dove and Buyer). Third, in the Buyer–Seller game the replicator dynamic is "area-preserving," which means that, if the population begins in some region of population frequencies around the equilibrium, there is no pressure for the population to move closer toward the equilibrium over time. However, actual behavior *does* move closer. These drawbacks mean it is hard to take replicator dynamics seriously, relative to individual-level models, as the best possible model of human learning in high-information conditions.

Summary: The idea that players learn in games by updating beliefs about what others will do is a natural model with a long history. Empirical papers by Crawford and Broseta, Cheung and Friedman, Cooper and Kagel, Capra et al., and Sefton concentrate on models in this class. Their work suggests that belief-based models generally improve on Nash equilibrium. Without comparing these models with others, however, it is hard to know whether they truly fit well or not; the next section shows that they usually fit worse than other models.

One study shows that Jordan's Bayesian learning model predicts well in a simple setting, but that model cannot explain learning in complete-information games and probably predicts poorly in more complex games. Nyarko and Schotter directly measure beliefs that subjects state in a 2×2 mixed-equilibrium game. Stated beliefs deviate persistently from fictitious play beliefs (even though stated beliefs are slightly less accurate guesses), which raises an important question of which models can characterize how stated beliefs change, if fictitious play cannot.

6.4 Imitation Learning

People often learn by imitating actions of others. Imitation is especially prevalent among animals and children. And imitation is often a good economizing heuristic because players need only to repeat observed strategies, rather than form beliefs and evaluate all strategies (see Schlag, 1999).

Hück, Normann, and Oechssler (1999) studied imitation in Cournot oligopoly. Four players simultaneously choose outputs $q_i(t)$ in the interval $[0, 100]$. Prices are set by an inverse demand function $P(t) = 100 - Q(t)$, where $Q(t) = \sum_{i=1}^{4} q_i(t)$ is total quantity. Marginal cost is 1 for all players, so an individual player's profit is $\pi_i(t) = q_i(t)(P(t) - 1)$. The four players choose quantities in each of forty periods. Hück et al. compare behavior in four conditions, designed to test learning theories that require use of different kinds of information. Table 6.14 shows the four main information conditions.

Table 6.14.   *Information conditions and output predictions in Hück et al.*

Condition	Information given to firm i		Predicted output $Q(t)$		Mean $Q(t)$ (std. dev.)
	Information	Outputs, profits	Cournot	Imitate-the-best	
BEST	demand, cost	$Q(t)$	79.2	n/a	82.56 (2.5)
FULL	demand, cost	$q_j(t), \pi_j(t) \forall j$	79.2	99	91.60 (6.5)
IMIT	none	$q_j(t), \pi_j(t) \forall j$	n/a	99	138.85 (31.6)
NOIN	none	$\pi_i(t)$	n/a	n/a	93.55 (14.7)

Source: Hück, Normann, and Oechssler (1999).

Simple computations (such as those many readers of this book have done as economics homework) give three benchmark predictions for total output. The Cournot–Nash equilibrium is $Q(t) = 79.2$. The Walrasian or competitive outcome (where price equals marginal cost) is $Q(t) = 99$. The collusive outcome, which maximizes total industry profit, is $Q(t) = 49.5$. The focus of Hück et al. is on the learning dynamics across information conditions. They build in inertia by allowing firms to change their output only with probability $1/3$ in each period. Inertia stabilizes Cournot best-reply dynamics.[21]

The information conditions distinguish the predictions of best-response and imitation learning. If players learn by Cournot dynamics, they can calculate best replies with BEST and FULL information, and will converge to total outputs of 79.2. Since they cannot calculate best replies in the NOIN, IMIT, and IMIT+ conditions (they know only quantities and profits, but not costs), the Cournot learning theory makes no prediction in those conditions.

Imitation dynamics predicts that in the FULL, IMIT, and IMIT+ conditions players will converge to the competitive output of 99, since they know the most successful producer's output. Since they do not know who to imitate in the BEST and NOIN conditions, imitation theories make no prediction in those cases.

In the BEST condition, outputs creep downward toward the Cournot–Nash prediction of 79. In FULL, outputs drift upward toward the Walrasian prediction of 99. Because FULL subjects know individual outputs and profits, and imitate-the-best dynamics predicts convergence to the Walrasian prediction, this is the first glimpse of evidence that imitation occurs. In IMIT and IMIT+ the fluctuations in output are very large. However, in IMIT+ there is a visible tendency to converge toward the Walrasian output of 99. In NOIN the outputs fluctuate wildly at first then drift up toward the Walrasian output of 99 as well.

Hück et al. characterize learning with an omnibus regression that relates changes in output from period to period, $q_i(t) - q_i(t-1)$, to changes predicted by the different theories. Denote subject i's best reply to period $t-1$ output by $r_i(t-1)$, the quantity of the highest-profit producer in period $t-1$ by $b(t-1)$, and the average quantity of other firms' outputs by $a_i(t-1)$. Their regression is

$$q_i(t) - q_i(t-1) = \beta_0 + \beta_1(r_i(t-1) - q_i(t-1)) + \beta_2(b(t-1) - q_i(t-1))$$
$$+ \beta_3(a_i(t-1) - q_i(t-1)) + \epsilon_{it}. \qquad (6.4.1)$$

---

[21] Vega-Redondo (1997) proved that if there is inertia (and some "mutation" or trembles), if firms imitate the quantity of the firm that is most successful, then quantities converge almost always to the Walrasian outcome. The intuition is simple—if price is above (below) marginal cost, then the largest (smallest) producer earns the most. If firms imitate the most successful producer, they are led to marginal-cost competitive pricing.

Table 6.15.   *Quantity-change regression coefficients in Hück et al.*

Variable	Coefficient	Coefficient estimates BEST	FULL	IMIT	IMIT+
Best-reply	β_1	.430	.366	—	—
		(.038)	(.044)	—	—
Imitate-the-best	β_2	—	.110	.465	.435
		—	(.038)	(.046)	(.040)
Imitate-the-average	β_3	.340	.344	.151	.273
		(.038)	(.038)	(.048)	(.047)
	R^2	.410	.507	.356	.439
	N	610	631	620	533

Source: Hück, Normann, and Oechssler (1999).
Note: Standard errors in parentheses.

The coefficients $\beta_1, \beta_2, \beta_3$ measure the extent to which quantities change in the direction predicted by best-reply, imitate-the-best, and imitate-the-average learning rules. Results pooled across subjects are summarized in Table 6.15.

All coefficients are highly significant. In the FULL condition, the best-reply effect (.366) is a lot stronger than imitating the best (.110). But imitating the best looms large in the IMIT and IMIT+ conditions where best replies can't be calculated.

Bosch-Domenech and Vriend (in press) also studied imitation in two- and three-firm (duopoly and triopoly) quantity-setting experiments. Collusive, Cournot–Nash, and competitive Walrasian outcomes are shown in Table 6.16.[22] Players chose quantities from 8 to 32 simultaneously, for twenty-two periods. Like Hück et al., they varied information conditions to see when imitation was most common. In all conditions players learned the history of output and profit for all firms. In their "easy table" condition, players also saw a profit table showing possible profits for all combinations of outputs. In the "hard table" condition they received the same information in an opaque form—"an inconveniently arranged enumeration of the market prices associated with all output levels and possible cost levels." In the IMIT+ condition (which they call "hardest") subjects were told only that prices were lower when aggregate output was higher.

Recall that imitation of the most successful firm will lead subjects, in theory, to the competitive Walrasian outcome since the most successful firm

---

[22] In their experiments the inverse demand curves were $P(Q) = 414 - 4Q$ and $P(Q) = 530 - 4Q$ and cost functions were $C(q) = 174q - 146$ and $C(q) = 174q - 266$, respectively.

Table 6.16.   *Final outputs in duopoly and triopoly experiments*

Actual output statistic	Information condition			Predictions		
	Easy table	Hard table	IMIT+	Collusive	Cournot–Nash	Walrasian
Two-firm duopoly						
Mean	18.2^a	23.4^b	22.4^b	15	20	30
Median	20	24	20			
Mode (%)	15 (39%)	20,32 (17%)	15,30 (17%)			
Three-firm triopoly						
Mean	23.7^a	24.3^{ab}	26.4^b	15	22	30
Median	23	24	27			
Mode (%)	23 (28%)	18,20,25 (11%)	24 (17%)			

Source: Bosch-Domenech and Vriend (in press).
Note: Identical letter superscripts denote outputs that are not significantly different at $p < .05$ (one-sided Wilcoxon test).

has the highest output. Bosch-Domenech and Vriend theorize that, since computing best responses (under time pressure of 1 minute per round) is more difficult in the hard-table condition, and essentially impossible in the IMIT+ condition, players will imitate the most successful player and gravitate toward higher (Walrasian) outputs more often in those conditions.

Outputs in the last two periods, shown in Table 6.16, show only weak support for that hypothesis. As it becomes harder for subjects to compute best responses—moving from the easy table to the hard table to IMIT+—outputs do rise slightly, but they are always significantly below the Walrasian output of 30.

Summary: Behavior in quantity-setting experiments shows both best-reply learning and imitation learning. These results and Stahl (2001), discussed below, suggest imitation should be taken seriously as an empirical source of learning. However, imitation may also be a heuristic shortcut to more general types of learning.

6.5 Comparative Studies

Many recent studies compare models in different types of "horse races." These comparisons are much more informative than the studies described earlier, because it is quite possible that some adaptive rule is an approximation to a similar or more general rule, and its weaknesses are revealed only by comparison.

6.5.1 Comparing Belief Models

Boylan and El-Gamal (1993) use a Bayesian procedure to draw inferences about the relative accuracy of Cournot and fictitious play. Their procedure starts with prior probabilities that each of the two theories are true. Then simulations are used to generate likelihoods for different observations. Using the priors, the simulated likelihoods, and the actual data, Bayes' rule can be used to infer the posterior probability that each theory is true. They apply this procedure to experiments on dominance-solvable games by Knott and Miller (1987) and coordination games by Cooper et al. (1990). Cournot is much worse on a dominance-solvable game and about equally good on a coordination game, so it is much worse overall.

A huge advantage of the Bayesian approach is the ability to naturally integrate results from different experiments. For example, if one theory is much better on one data set and much worse on another, by multiplying the likelihood ratios together (a procedure that assumes experiments are independent, which is sometimes unlikely) it is often possible to declare a clear overall winner rather than simply concluding that one study favored each theory.

6.5.2 Comparing Belief and Reinforcement Models

Several studies have compared belief and reinforcement learning.

Ho and Weigelt (1996) studied behavior in two-player coordination games with multiple pure-strategy equilibria (see Chapter 7). They compared four models of learning. One model is a simple form of reinforcement ("vindication") which essentially assumes very concave utility for payoffs. The other models are Cournot, reinforcement, and fictitious play, all of which are a modest improvement over a no-learning benchmark. Fictitious play fits best.

A thorough early study was done by Mookerjhee and Sopher (1997). They compared fictitious play, Cournot, and three types of reinforcement in two constant-sum games. They used games with four or six strategies, which are much better for distinguishing different theories than games with only two strategies (see Mookerjhee and Sopher, 1994; Salmon, 2001). Their games are shown in Chapter 3.

Their model is very general. Each strategy s_i^j has a score that is a weighted linear combination of the attractions $A_i^j(t-1)$ of *each* of player i's m_i strategies. Strategy s_i^j's score in period t is $S_j(t) = \sum_{k=1}^{m_i} \alpha_{jk} \cdot A_i^k(t-1)$. The probability that each strategy is chosen is a logit $P(s_i^j)(t) = e^{S_j(t)} / \sum_{k=1}^{m_i} e^{S_k(t)}$. This specification allows the attraction of one strategy k to affect the score of another strategy i, through the coefficients α_{ik}. Cross-effects occur if the attraction of one strategy affects probabilities of choosing other strategies *differently*; for example, if some strategies are regarded as more similar and treated as close strategic substitutes. Mookerjhee and Sopher use logit regression to estimate the probabilistic response model under six different hypotheses about how attractions are determined. Three hypotheses assume some kind of reinforcement learning and three correspond to types of belief learning (Cournot and ficititious play with various averaging *i*). The Cournot model fits poorly. Reinforcement fits slightly better than the belief-based model. Most individual cross-effect terms are insignificant, but the restriction that they are all 0 is often rejected at the 1 percent level. Overall, the Mookerjhee–Sopher findings are a messy win for reinforcement models.

Tang's dissertation (1996) reports experiments on three games with mixed-strategy equilibria. He specifies and estimates a dizzying variety of learning models using those data. I will not discuss the learning model estimation at length (the data are reported in Chapter 3) because it is complicated, the results are not very conclusive, and the statistic (MSD) used does not allow statistical inferences about which models are most accurate. However, variants of fictitious play do substantially worse than reinforcement models. The only models competitive with reinforcement are rule learning, in which players shift weight across different rules. None of the models is much better than just using the observed frequency of choices.

Battalio, Samuelson, and Van Huyck (2001) compared three stag hunt games with different best-response properties (see Chapter 7 for more on coordination games). The games are shown in Table 6.17. All three

Table 6.17.   *Stag hunt games of Battalio et al.*

	Player 2 choices	
Player 1 choices	X	Y
Game 2R		
X	45,45	0,35
Y	35,0	40,40
Game R		
X	45,45	0,40
Y	40,0	20,20
Game .6R		
X	45,45	0,42
Y	42,0	12,12

Source: Battalio, Samuelson, and Van Huyck (2001).

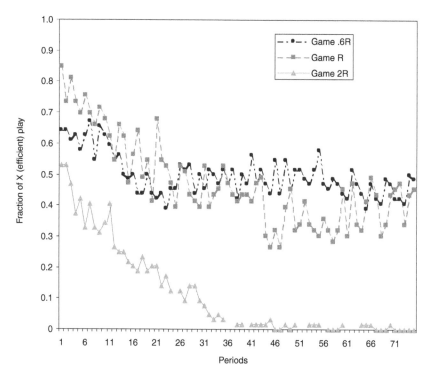

Figure 6.3. *Percentage of efficient (X) play in stag hunt games with different response gradients. Source: Based on data from Battalio, Samuelson, and Van Huyck (2001).*

games have the same Nash equilibria—an efficient equilibrium at (X,X), an inefficient equilibrium at (Y,Y), and a mixed-strategy equilibrium in which players choose X with probability .8. However, the payoff *differences* between strategies X and Y, for any belief q about an opponent's probability of choosing X, are $r(q) = 50q - 40$ in game 2R, $25q - 20$ in game R, and $15q - 12$ in game .6R. This payoff differential is twice as large in game 2R and .6 times as large in game .6R, compared with the differential in game R. Intuitively, it seems likely that convergence will be swifter when the payoff difference $r(q)$ is larger.

Figure 6.3 summarizes the results. The figures show the percentage of players choosing X across the seventy-five periods (in five-period blocks). Most of the groups began with fewer than 80 percent of the subjects playing X. Convergence is indeed more rapid when the payoff gradient is higher. In two of the .6R sessions and one R session, players hop across the "separatrix" at .80 and converge toward the efficient equilibrium despite starting out with a percentage of Y choices high enough to draw them toward (Y,Y).

Table 6.18.   *Learning model coefficients*

Model	α	Received payoff r_{it}	Expected payoff $r(y_{it})$	2R dummy	.6R dummy	Log-likelihood
Reinforcement	1.031	.173	—	−1.322	n/i	−1783
	(.07)	(.01)		(.12)		
Beliefs	1.856	—	.348	n/i	n/i	−1510
	(.09)		(.02)			
Both	2.963	.048	.422	−1.742	−1.810	−1433
	(.19)	(.01)	(.02)	(.26)	(.19)	

Source: Battalio, Samuelson, and Van Huyck (1999).
Note: Standard errors in parentheses. Player-specific intercept and response-sensitivity parameters are defined as deviations from some common term; the terms reported above are common terms. The table reports only variables that enter significantly in a stepwise procedure. Variables that are not included are denoted "n/i."

In an earlier version of their paper (1999), Battalio et al. fitted three learning models. Fictitious play is used to compute an expected earnings difference $r(y_{it})$ and then players choose strategy X with a probability

$$P_{it}(X) = e^{\alpha_i + \lambda_i r(y_{it})}/(1 + e^{\alpha_i + \lambda_i r(y_{it})}). \qquad (6.5.1)$$

The player-specific constant α_i expresses an inherent preference (or dispreference if α_i is negative) for strategy X. They also fit an average-reinforcement model in which r_{it} is the average of received payoffs. Table 6.18 summarizes fits of three models on periods 1–40, using expected payoffs $r(y_{it})$, average earnings r_{it}, and both terms together. The belief model r_{it} fits better than the average-payoff reinforcement model, and a model that combines both terms fits even better. But the combination is a lopsided mixture—like horse and rabbit stew, made with one horse and one rabbit—because the expected payoff term has an estimated coefficient almost ten times as large as the reinforcement term.

Feltovich (1999, 2000) studied two-stage games of asymmetric information. His game is interesting because a player's move in the first of the two stages both earns a payoff and (potentially) reveals information about what game is being played. Table 6.19 shows the payoffs. Nature moves first and determines a matrix, either left or right with probabilities p and $1 - p$. The row player is informed of the matrix choice but the column player is not. Players move simultaneously and play twice with the same matrix. Both players are told only their opponent's choice in the first stage, but not their payoff (to prevent the uninformed column player from learning which matrix is being used). If the row player always chooses her dominant strategies (A if left, B if right) she reveals which matrix has been chosen; if the column

Table 6.19.   *Two-stage asymmetric information game studied by*
Feltovich

	Uninformed (column) player strategies			
	Left matrix (p)		Right matrix ($1 - p$)	
Informed (row) player	A	B	A	B
A	1,0	0,1	0,1	0,1
B	0,1	0,1	0,1	1,0

Source: Feltovich (1999, 2000).

player figures this out she will choose B after observing A and A after observing B, and the row player will get 0 in the second round. So it is better to randomize in the first stage, then choose the dominant strategy in the second stage.

In equilibrium, when the prior $p = .50$, informed players should randomize equally in the first stage to hide what they know. When $p = .34$, the informed player should choose A with probability .971 when the matrix is left and randomize equally over A and B when the matrix is right.

When $p = .50$, the uninformed player should choose B in response to a first-stage choice by the informed player of A with probability β between .5 and 1, and choose A with probability $1 - \beta$. When $p = .34$ the uninformed player should randomize equally after an observed A choice and should always play A after a B choice.

Call the choice of A (or B) by player 1 after observing L (or R) the "stage-dominant action" (the choice that is a best response if the game ended right away rather than continuing to a second round). Call the choice of B (A) by player 2 after observing a player 1 choice of A (B) a "best response." In the $p = .50$ game, player 1 played her myopic choice (A if she saw L, B if she saw R) 85 percent and 77 percent of the time in the first and last twenty rounds, showing very slow convergence to the MSE prediction of 50 percent. Player 2 best-responded to the observed choice (picking A after observing B or B after A) 80–90 percent of the time. In the $p = .34$ game the corresponding fractions are 85 percent and 79 percent for player 1s (converging slowly toward the MSE of 66 percent) and 75 percent for player 2s.

Belief learning and a version of reinforcement that includes sophistication (see below) fit about equally well,[23] depending on the test statistic used. Sophisticated reinforcement fits individual choices a little better than belief learning (an 80 percent hit rate, about as accurate as predicting the most

---

[23] The reinforcement model builds in sophistication because players' first-stage strategies are reinforced by the *sum* of the payoffs from *both* stages. This means that an anticipatory strategy that anticipates how revealing information in the first stage will hurt the player's second-stage payoff gets strongly reinforced.

common choice); but belief learning generates simulated paths that are a little more accurate. These results show that when a range of models are about equally accurate—especially when equilibria are mixed, so no model can predict too accurately—the best fit is sensitive to the fit criterion.

In other studies, Nagel and Tang (1998) compared belief and reinforcement models in centipede games. They concluded that reinforcement fits best using the MSD criterion but their implementation of belief learning is odd. Ho, Wang, and Camerer (2002) showed that the EWA model fits slightly better than reinforcement on the same data, and reveals detectable individual differences. Blume et al. (2001) fitted simple reinforcement and belief models to their data on sender–receiver games (see Chapter 7). They found that reinforcement fits better.

Summary: Several studies have compared reinforcement and belief models. In games with mixed-strategy equilibria (Erev and Roth, Mookerjhee and Sopher), reinforcement models generally fit slightly better than belief models (although none of the learning models do much better than QRE equilibrium). In the coordination games studied by Ho and Weigelt and Battalio et al., belief learning does better. Three studies estimating the relative contribution of different models found that belief terms were almost ten times as important as reinforcement.[24]

Nonetheless, it is difficult to draw firm conclusions across studies because the games and details of model implementation differ. Different studies add or subtract parameters to reinforcement models and change how attractions are reinforced. Belief models are also implemented in different ways (for example, how initial beliefs or attractions are defined, and whether weighted or standard fictitious play is used). Test statistics differ. Some studies use log likelihood of fit or predicted choices, which permit statistical inferences, whereas others use squared deviations, which do not permit inference. The obvious solution is to use a wider variety of games and statistics, and to use general model specifications that include as many earlier ones as possible. This is the approach of Camerer and Ho (1999a,b) and Stahl (2000a,b), discussed next.

6.6 Experience-Weighted Attraction (EWA) Learning

Reinforcement learning assumes players ignore information about forgone payoffs. Belief learning assumes players ignore information about what they chose in the past. But players seem to use both types of information when they are available.

---

[24] See Erev and Roth (1998), Battalio, Samuelson, and Van Huyck (2001), and Munro (1999), reported in Chapter 7.

Teck Ho and I (Camerer and Ho, 1999a,b) therefore created a hybrid of reinforcement and belief models which also uses both types of information. The experience-weighted attraction (EWA) model has two variables, attractions $A_i^j(t)$ and an experience weight $N(t)$, which are updated after every period of experience.

The experience weight starts at an initial value $N(0)$ and is updated according to $N(t) = \phi(1 - \kappa) \cdot N(t - 1) + 1$, with the restriction $N(t) \leq 1/[1 - \phi(1 - \kappa)]$ so that $N(t)$ is weakly increasing.[25] Attractions start at $A_i^j(0)$ and are updated according to

$$A_i^j(t) = \frac{\phi \cdot N(t - 1) \cdot A_i^j(t - 1) + [\delta + (1 - \delta) \cdot I(s_i^j, s_i(t))] \cdot \pi_i(s_i^j, s_{-i}(t))}{N(t)}.$$

$$(6.6.1)$$

Attractions determine probabilities using the logit form $P_i^j(t + 1) = e^{\lambda \cdot A_i^j(t)}/\sum_{k=1}^{m_i} e^{\lambda \cdot A_i^k(t)}$ (but a power form fits about equally well; see Camerer and Ho, 1999b).

The weighted payoff term $[\delta + (1 - \delta) \cdot I(s_i^j, s_i(t))] \cdot \pi_i(s_i^j, s_{-i}(t))$ is crucial. The attractions of *all* strategies are updated by δ times the payoff that strategy would have yielded, even if it was not chosen. The chosen strategy $s_i(t)$ is updated by an *additional* fraction $1 - \delta$ of its payoff. Reinforcement is often justified by appeal to the "law of effect"—the regularity, discovered by behavioral psychologists, that animals tend to repeat successful strategies. Since behaviorists studied mostly animal learning, they never thought about a parallel "law of *simulated* effect"—strategies that *would* have been successful would be chosen more often. EWA allows for both effects.

Under different parameter restrictions, EWA reduces to reinforcement and weighted fictitious play. When $\delta = 0, \kappa = 1$, and $N(0) = 1$ (so $N(t) = 1$), attractions are updated by $A_i^j(t) = \phi \cdot A_i^j(t - 1) + I(s_i^j, s_i(t)) \cdot \pi_i(s_i^j, s_{-i}(t))$, which is a simple form of cumulative reinforcement model. When κ is 0 instead of 1, the attractions are weighted averages instead of cumulations, with weights $\phi/(\phi + 1)$ and $1/(\phi + 1)$.

When $\delta = 1$ and $\kappa = 0$, the updating equation is

$$A_i^j(t) = \frac{\phi \cdot N(t - 1) \cdot A_i^j(t - 1) + \pi_i(s_i^j, s_{-i}(t))}{\phi \cdot N(t - 1) + 1}.$$

$$(6.6.2)$$

[25] In our earlier work we used $\rho = \phi(1 - \kappa)$, but recently switched notation to make the model more transparent.

A little algebra shows that this updating equation is *exactly* the same as weighted fictitious play.[26] That is, a person who learns according to weighted fictitious play behaves just like an EWA learner who starts with initial attractions based on expected payoffs, reinforces each strategy equally strongly according to what it would have earned (or did earn), and takes a weighted average of previous attractions and current reinforcements.

Thus, reinforcement and belief learning are elements of a family of learning rules which are surprisingly related, like siblings raised apart or rivers that turn out to have a common source. The kinship is important because it was often suggested that the two approaches are fundamentally incompatible. For example, Selten (1991, p. 14) wrote: "In rote [reinforcement] learning success and failure directly influence the choice probabilities. . . . Belief learning is very different. Here experience strengthens or weakens beliefs. Belief learning has only an indirect influence on behavior."[27]

The parameters of EWA have psychological interpretations. The parameter δ is the weight placed on forgone payoffs (opportunity costs, in economic terms, or counterfactuals or regret in psychological terms). The weight δ is presumably affected by imagination and the reliability of information about forgone payoffs (Heller and Sarin, 2000). It may also reflect the difference between received gains and "opportunity gains" (people may underweigh lost opportunities).

The parameter ϕ reflects the decay of previous attractions owing to forgetting or to deliberate shedding of old experience when the learning environment is changing. The parameter κ controls the rate at which attractions grow. When $\kappa = 0$ attractions are weighted averages of reinforcements and decayed lagged attractions; when $\kappa = 1$ attractions cumulate. The growth rate of attractions is important because in the logit model the difference in attractions determines the spread of choice probabilities; fixing λ, players can lock in more sharply to playing one strategy frequently if κ is larger.

The initial weight $N(0)$ calibrates the strength of initial attractions in units of "experience-equivalence". When players have a Dirichlet prior, and use fictitious play, their beliefs are Bayesian and $N(0)$ is the strength of prior beliefs. Frankly, $N(t)$ was included precisely to link the model to Bayesian ideas. It usually does not contribute much to empirical fit so in recent work we usually set $N(0) = 1$.

---

[26] The trick is to first write beliefs in period t as a function of period $t - 1$ beliefs. When these beliefs are used to compute expected payoffs, and expected payoffs in period t are written as a function of period $t - 1$ expected payoffs, the belief term disappears. That is, all of the mathematical effect of belief updating is encompassed by reinforcing strategies according to forgone or received payoffs, as in equation (6.6.2).

[27] The connection was also noticed by Fudenberg and Levine (1998) and Cheung and Friedman (1997). Hopkins (in press) showed that if actual payoffs are scaled by the probability with which a strategy is chosen, so that rare strategies get a boost in cumulative attraction, then the two are roughly equivalent.

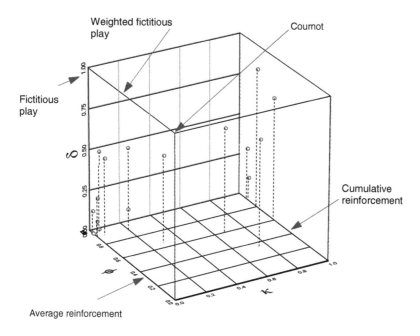

Figure 6.4. *Cube of EWA parameter configurations.*

Different learning rules can be represented as points in a cube of the three key EWA parameters (see Figure 6.4). Each point in the cube is a triple of parameter values which specifies a precise updating equation (leaving aside λ and initial conditions). The cube shows the EWA family of learning rules. Corners and vertices of the EWA cube correspond to boundary special cases. The corner of the cube with $\phi = \kappa = 0, \delta = 1$, is Cournot best-response dynamics. The corner $\kappa = 0, \phi = \delta = 1$, is standard fictitious play. The vertex connecting these corners, $\delta = 1, \kappa = 0$, is weighted fictitious play. Vertices with $\delta = 0$ and κ equal to 0 or 1 are averaging and cumulative choice reinforcement rules.

The EWA cube is a visual aid to show the relations and differences among theories. But the construction of EWA is also a bet that psychologically plausible learning rules have parameter values that might be in the interior of the cube rather than clustered on vertices and corners.

In all of our empirical estimation, the first 70 percent of each player's time series is used to estimate model parameters using maximum-likelihood estimation.[28] Initial conditions $A_i^j(0)$ are either estimated as free parameters

---

[28] In recent work we fit data from a sample of 70 percent of players, using *all* those players' choices, then forecast the entire learning path for the remaining holdout sample of 30 percent of the players.

or "burned in" by choosing attractions to fit the relative frequencies in the first period as closely as possible.

Studies with about thirty-one data sets (summarized in Camerer, Ho, and Chong, 2002a) show that EWA generally fits and predicts *out of sample* more accurately than the reinforcement and weighted fictitious play, except in games with mixed-strategy equilibrium (where no models improve much on QRE). Figure 6.4 shows twenty triples of estimates resulting when different treatments in the thirty-one data sets are collapsed together. Most points are sprinkled around the cube. Several points cluster in the average reinforcement corner where $\delta = \kappa = 0$ and ϕ is close to 1 (these are from games with mixed equilibria). Except for that cluster, there is no strong tendency for points to cluster on any special corners or vertices. This means that focusing attention on a single learning rule, because it is presumed to predict more accurately than rules with other parameter configurations, is a mistake.

Keep in mind that *all* the studies reviewed previously in this chapter compared either one point or vertex in the cube (one learning rule) with equilibrium, or two or more points in the cube with each other. These early comparisons tell us very little about which rules fit best because so few rules are being compared. Estimating best-fitting parameter values in EWA essentially compares a huge number of possible rules in one fell swoop (including all the familiar ones, and Bayesian learning).

It is tempting to conclude that any empirical improvement in EWA just shows that adding parameters always improves predictions. This claim is doubly wrong. First, forcing models to predict out of sample after parameters are estimated in-sample means that if a model is unnecessarily complex, it will fit better but *predict more poorly*. That is, adding parameters *does not* always improve predictions when predictive accuracy is judged correctly. Second, the hybrid model doesn't really add parameters because the new parameters (δ and κ) were implicit in earlier models; those parameters simply express the distinctions between models more clearly and allow new combinations.

Two games will help illustrate the strengths and weaknesses of different models.

6.6.1 Example: Continental Divide

The "continental divide game" (discussed in Chapters 1 and 7) is an order-statistic game in which each of seven players chooses integers from 1 to 14. A player's payoff depends on her number and the median number chosen by the players in her group, as shown in Table 6.20. There are two pure-strategy Nash equilibria, at 3 and 12.

Figure 6.5a shows the pooled frequencies of choices of ten groups across fifteen periods, from Van Huyck, Battalio, and Cook (1997). The data have

Table 6.20. *Payoffs in a "continental divide" experiment*

Choice	Median choice													
	1	2	3	4	5	6	7	8	9	10	11	12	13	14
1	45	49	52	55	56	55	46	−59	−88	−105	−117	−127	−135	−142
2	48	53	58	62	65	66	61	−27	−52	−67	−77	−86	−92	−98
3	48	54	60	66	70	74	72	1	−20	−32	−41	−48	−53	−58
4	43	51	58	65	71	77	80	26	8	−2	−9	−14	−19	−22
5	35	44	52	60	69	77	83	46	32	25	19	15	12	10
6	23	33	42	52	62	72	82	62	53	47	43	41	39	38
7	7	18	28	40	51	64	78	75	69	66	64	63	62	62
8	−13	−1	11	23	37	51	69	83	81	80	80	80	81	82
9	−37	−24	−11	3	18	35	57	88	89	91	92	94	96	98
10	−65	−51	−37	−21	−4	15	40	89	94	98	101	104	107	110
11	−97	−82	−66	−49	−31	−9	20	85	94	100	105	110	114	119
12	−133	−117	−100	−82	−61	−37	−5	78	91	99	106	112	118	123
13	−173	−156	−137	−118	−96	−69	−33	67	83	94	103	110	117	123
14	−217	−198	−179	−158	−134	−105	−65	52	72	85	95	104	112	120

Source: Van Huyck, Cook, and Battalio (1997).

two key features: (1) Behavior bifurcates from initial choices in the range 4–8 toward the equilibria at 3 and 12; and (2) convergence is asymmetric—it is much sharper (taller spikes in the figure) at the equilibrium of 12 than in the neighborhood of 3. In addition, the learning process "brakes" and "accelerates" quickly, in the sense that common early choices from the range 5–8 are completely extinguished by period 15, whereas choices below 4 and above 10 are rare in early periods but quickly pile up in later periods.

Table 6.21 gives parameter estimates. Restricting parameters to belief and reinforcement values gives log-likelihood (LL) values that are 180 and 249 points worse, respectively, so those simpler models fit much worse. Figure 6.5e shows predictions based on maximum-likelihood estimates (MLE) of a reinforcement model (the restriction of EWA with $\delta = \kappa = 0$, $\phi = 1$, and reinforcements divided by variability of payoffs; see Roth et al., 1999).[29] Reinforcement fits reasonably well, although it does not brake early choices or accelerate later choices as quickly as is observed in the data.

---

[29] The predicted probability for each player and period, given the parameter estimates that maximize likelihood from the first ten periods, are averaged across players to produce the figures in the plot. Note that the model does make predictions about all individuals and periods, but they are simply averaged to give an overall glimpse of model fit.

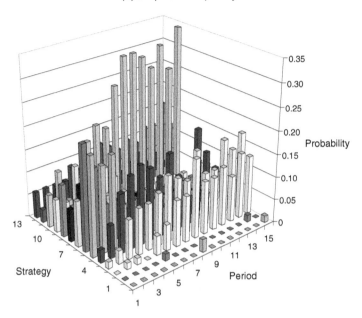

(a) Empirical frequency

(b) Adaptive EWA

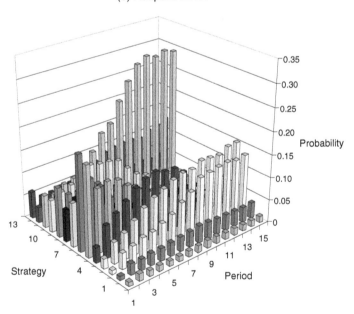

Figure 6.5. *Data and learning model fits, continental divide game. Source: Ho, Camerer, and Chong (2002).*

(c) EWA Lite

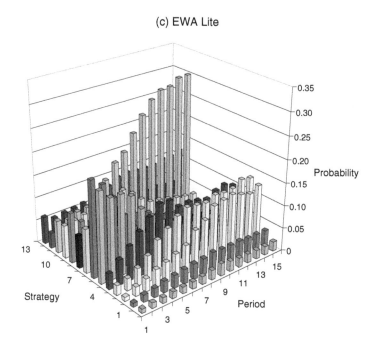

(d) Belief-based

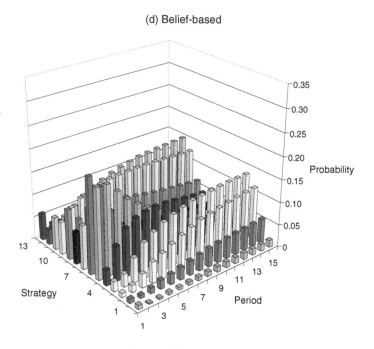

Figure 6.5 (continued)

(e) Choice reinforcement with PV

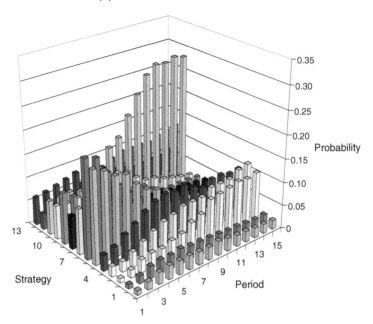

(f) Quantal response

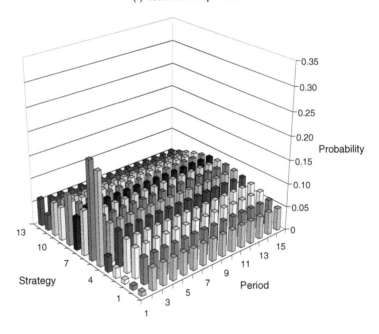

Figure 6.5 (continued)

Table 6.21. *Parameter estimates for continental divide and p-beauty contest games*

| Parameter | Continental divide game | p-Beauty contest game | | | |
| | | Inexperienced | | Experienced | |
		Sophisticated EWA	EWA	Sophisticated EWA	EWA
ϕ	0.61	0.44	0.00	0.29	0.22
δ	0.75	0.78	0.90	0.67	0.99
κ	1.00	0.00	0.00	0.04	0.00
α	—	0.24	0.00	0.77	0.00
α'	—	0.00	0.00	0.41	0.00
d	—	0.16	0.13	0.15	0.11
LL (in)		−2095.32	−2155.09	−1908.48	−2128.88
LL (out)		−968.24	−992.47	−710.28	−925.09
$\bar{p}$ (in)		0.06	0.05	0.07	0.05
$\bar{p}$ (out)		0.07	0.07	0.13	0.09

Source: Camerer, Hsia, and Ho (2002); Camerer, Ho, and Chong (2002a).
Note: QRE log likelihood in and out of sample are −2471 and −1129 (inexperienced) and −2141 and −851 (experienced).

Figure 6.5d shows predictions from the weighted fictitious play model. It captures the bifurcation toward low and high numbers, but it does not predict that convergence around 12 is sharper than around 3. It cannot explain the asymmetry because the payoff gradients around the two equilibria are *exactly* the same. In the belief model, the distribution of choices is entirely determined by the payoff gradient.[30] EWA can account for the asymmetry because sharpness of convergence is determined by the difference between received payoffs and δ-weighted forgone payoffs, and this difference is larger at the higher payoffs around the 12 equilibrium.

Figure 6.5f shows, as a static benchmark, the fit of a quantal response equilibrium model (which, by definition, makes the same prediction in each period). The model fits quite poorly because the data are roughly a mixture of high or low numbers, but the best response to such a mixture is a middle number (which are rarely chosen after the first couple of periods). The requirement that players' beliefs always be in equilibrium makes it impossible to explain these data when all the periods are pooled.

---

[30] If others are choosing 3 or 12, then choosing 1 or 2 units too high or low costs players only 2 cents or 8 cents, respectively. That is, deviations are equally costly at the two equilibria, though absolute payoffs are higher for the equilibrium at 12 (see Table 6.20).

Figures 6.5b–c show predictions of EWA. (The parametric model is the one being discussed now; the "fEWA" or "Lite" version is a one-parameter variant described below.) EWA fits only a little better than reinforcement learning, but it does predict both bifurcation and convergence asymmetry, and also brakes and accelerates quickly. Parameter estimates are summarized in Table 6.21.

The continental divide game can also be used to illustrate differences in how models are estimated and used. The maximum-likelihood estimates (MLE) method uses the actual observed history in period t to update attractions for period $t + 1$. An alternative approach is to simulate paths, essentially using artificial history generated by the model itself from period t to update attractions and predict period $t + 1$ choices. Knowing whether a model can simulate an entire path of play, without any data to work with, is important for using the model to forecast behavior in brand-new games or economic institutions.

Note, first, that if the accuracy of a model is judged by comparing the *conditional* frequencies of simulated play (i.e., frequencies after observed histories) with actual conditional frequencies, then simulating paths and forecasting period $t + 1$ from data in periods $1 - t$ produce precisely the same results.[31] Since conditional frequencies are often of interest (e.g., when does strategy switching occur?), forcing a model to predict conditional frequencies accurately is an important and tough test. Nonetheless, it is often useful to see whether models can pass an easier test of predicting unconditional frequencies.

Comparisons of fits and predictions derived from MLE, and simulated paths based on those MLE estimates, have been done by Crawford (1995), Camerer and Ho (1999b), Camerer, Hsia, and Ho (2002), and Erev and Haruvy (2001). The first three papers found no interesting differences between the two methods. The last found that models that include inertia— the frequency of a choice depends on how often it was chosen before—can be particularly bad at simulating paths because inertial models are extremely sensitive to starting points.

Teck Ho, Xin Wang, and I compared path simulation and period $t + 1$ estimation further using the continental divide game. We simulated 1,500 groups of seven subjects using five different models—EWA, a functional

---

[31] In the continental divide game, for example, suppose a particular player's choice history in the first two periods is 6 and 8, and the medians of others in her group were 7 and 9. Suppose we simulate paths and compare the simulated frequency with which the simulated players make choices 1–14 conditional on the actual history (i.e., after choosing 6 and 8, with group medians of 7 and 9) with the actual conditional frequencies of those choices. The result will be exactly the same as if attractions were updated using the actual historical data—i.e., as if we were predicting period $t + 1$ from periods 1 to t. Forecasted and (filtered) simulated results are the same because filtering out only those simulated paths with histories that match the actual history is exactly the same as using the actual history directly for updating.

Table 6.22. *Results from different model-fitting methods, continental divide game*

Model	Within-game				Cross-game		Simulated path	
	In-sample		Out-of-sample					
	LL	Rank	LL	Rank	LL	Rank	MSD($\times 100$)	Rank
EWA	−1062	1	−460	1	−1635	1	0.2416	1
fEWA	−1081	2	−470	2	−1741	2	0.2434	2
Beliefs	−1288	3	−564	3	−2147	3	0.2506	3
Reinforcement−PV	−1293	4	−573	4	−2403	4	0.5300	4
QRE	−1890	5	−808	5	−2695	5	0.5300	5

Source: Ho, Camerer, and Chong (2002); Camerer, Ho, and Wang (unpublished).

form of EWA (discussed below), belief learning, reinforcement with payoff variability, and QRE as a no-learning benchmark. Parameter values were chosen to minimize the sum of squared deviations between simulated unconditional frequencies (pooling all 10,500 simulated subjects together) and actual unconditional frequencies, summed across all strategies and periods.

Table 6.22 summarizes the statistical fits (mean squared deviations multiplied by 100) and compares them with log likelihoods (LL) derived three different ways: estimating parameters within a game; first fitting in sample then forecasting out of sample; and estimating parameters on six other games and using them to forecast fresh data from the continental divide game (see Ho, Camerer, and Chong, 2002). As it turns out, the models are ranked by the four estimation criteria in the same way. Although the ranks do not depend on whether simulated or actual data are used to update attractions, there are some interesting differences in the simulation results.

Figures 6.6a–c show the average simulated frequencies for the EWA, belief, and reinforcement models. First note that the simulated data do not match the actual frequencies as closely as when the periods $1 − t$ data are used to forecast $t + 1$. This is no surprise, of course, since in the simulations the models' errors are compounded rather than corrected by using the actual history. Belief learning also simulates better than it fits.

Reinforcement suffers because, as learning occurs, human players actually choose numbers further and further from the center because they are responsive to forgone payoffs. But in the reinforcement model, simulated players are not sensitive to forgone payoffs so they do not move quickly enough away from the middle. When the actual history is used, the sluggish tendency in the reinforcement model is corrected: The chosen strategies are not those the model predicts would be made, but they receive more

(a) EWA

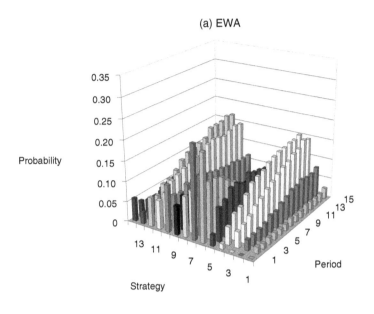

(b) Belief learning

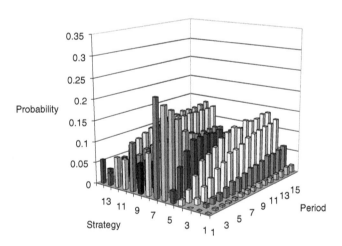

Figure 6.6.   *Average simulated paths (parameters chosen to minimize mean squared deviations), continental divide game: (a) EWA; (b) belief learning; (c) reinforcement. Source: Camerer, Ho, and Chong (unpublished).*

(c) Reinforcement

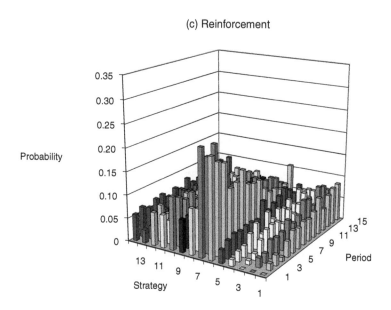

Figure 6.6 (continued)

reinforcement and constantly correct the model's mistakes. (By analogy, imagine a robot that simulates how quickly a person walks, but takes steps that are only half as long as the steps people actually take. The robot would be far behind the person it is simulating after 100 yards. But if the robot's mistake were corrected after each step—by letting the robot start afresh, where the person stood after each step—it would be only a half-step behind after 100 yards.) When the model is used to simulate paths, its sluggishness is never corrected and the resulting simulations do not create much convergence toward the high and low equilibria at 3 and 12.

Of course, *both* ways of evaluating models—predicting new history from actual history, or simulating an entire path—are useful criteria depending on one's purpose. It is even conceivable that some models perform one task well and another badly. However, I doubt that, in the domain of learning rules, some models are uniformly better than others at different types of forecasting (with the noted exception of inertial models simulating poorly). Good models will fit well both ways. And, when a promising theory does fail to predict accurately in a certain way, that failure usually contains a clue about how to improve the theory.

6.6.2 *Example: p-Beauty Contest, and Sophistication*

A second example is the *p*-beauty contest (pBC) described in Chapter 5 to study the number of steps of iterated thinking players seem to do. In the pBC games reported here, groups of seven players choose numbers from 0 to 100. The player in each group whose number is closest to *p* times the average number (for *p* = .7, .9) wins a fixed prize.

Figure 6.7a shows relative frequencies of choices by experienced subjects, pooled across several groups. Figures 6.7b–e show predicted frequencies of belief, reinforcement, EWA Lite (fEWA), and sophisticated EWA learning. (Parameter estimates are reported in Table 6.21.) Belief learning fits and predicts reasonably well, as does EWA learning. Reinforcement learning is terrible. The problem is that six of seven players earn nothing in each period, get no reinforcement, and therefore learn nothing. Something clearly has to be added to reinforcement to explain why losers are learning. EWA adds reinforcement of forgone payoffs.

The pBC also illustrates the benefits of adding "sophistication." Sophisticated players are aware that others are learning. Camerer, Ho, and Chong (2002a) include sophistication in a recursive way. In our model, a fraction α of players believe that α' of the players are sophisticated and the remaining $1 - \alpha'$ are adaptive and learn according to EWA. Sophisticated players have correct guesses about the EWA parameters but may be socially miscalibrated about how sophisticated others are. If sophisticated players are correctly calibrated, $\alpha = \alpha'$. If they overestimate how sophisticated they are relative to others (owing to overconfidence about relative skill, for example), then $\alpha > \alpha'$. If they think others are more like themselves than they really are ("false consensus"), then $\alpha < \alpha'$. The sophisticated players do not update attractions per se. Instead, they update the perceived attractions of EWA players and use them to compute choice probabilities, and calculate expected payoffs $E_i^j(t)$ according to

$$E_i^j(t) = \sum_{k=1}^{m_{-i}} [(1 - \alpha') \cdot P_{-i}^k(a, t+1) + \alpha' P_{-i}^k(s, t+1)] \cdot \pi_i(s_i^j, s_{-i}^k), \quad (6.6.3)$$

$$P_i^j(s, t+1) = \frac{e^{\lambda \cdot E_i^j(t)}}{\sum_{k=1}^{m_i} e^{\lambda \cdot E_i^k(t)}}, \quad (6.6.4)$$

where $P_{-i}^k(s, t+1)$ and $P_{-i}^k(a, t+1)$ are choice probabilities by sophisticated and adaptive (EWA) players, respectively. Note that sophistication is recursive because $P_{-i}^k(s, t+1)$ determines the expected payoff-$E_i^j(t)$, which in turn determines those probabilities through the logit response function.

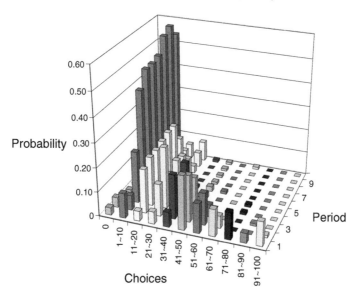

(a) Empirical frequency

(b) Belief-based

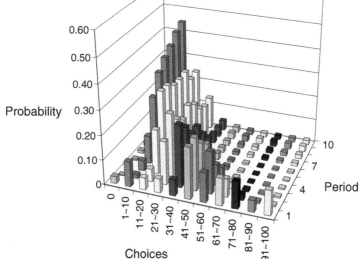

Figure 6.7. *Results of pBC beauty contest game, experienced subjects. Source: Camerer, Ho, and Chong (2002a); reproduced from* Journal of Economic Theory *with permission of Academic Press.*

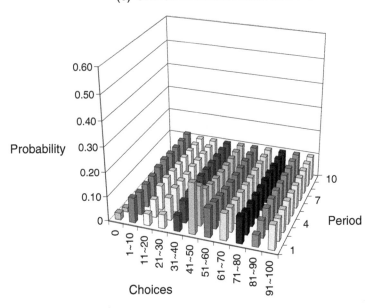

(c) Choice reinforcement with PV

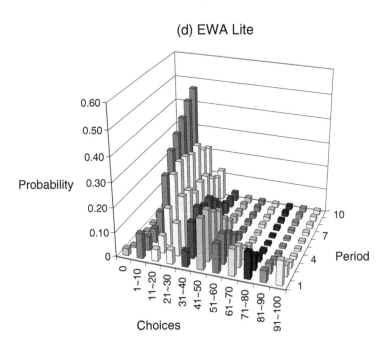

(d) EWA Lite

Figure 6.7 (continued)

(e) Sophisticated EWA

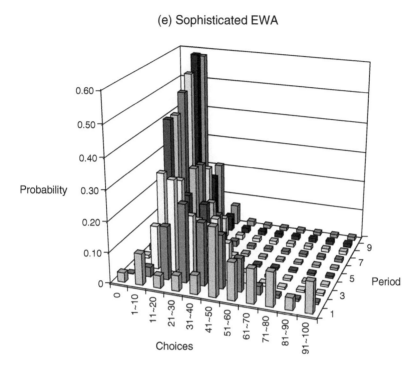

Figure 6.7 (continued)

Including sophistication in this way nests *many* special cases with only three new parameters (α, α', and a λ for sophisticates).[32] QRE is the conjunction of social calibration ($\alpha = \alpha'$) and complete sophistication ($\alpha = 1$). Adding hyperresponsiveness (large λ) is Nash equilibrium. Stahl's model of sophistication imposes $\alpha' = 0$. Fixing $\alpha = 0$ reduces to EWA and its many special cases. Estimating the full model therefore provides information on many quite different models in one fell swoop.

Table 6.21 gives parameter estimates for the sophisticated model, for both inexperienced subjects (playing a pBC for the first time) and experienced subjects (playing the second of two games). In the adaptive EWA model (with $\alpha = 0$) the estimates of δ and κ are close to 1 and 0, so the belief model restriction is reasonable but reinforcement is strongly rejected

---

[32] The three added parameters could easily be reduced to one by imposing $\alpha = \alpha'$ and using the same λ for all players, suitably rescaled.

(as the earlier figures suggested). When sophistication is included, the estimated proportion of sophisticated players, $\hat{\alpha}$, is 24 percent and 77 percent for inexperienced and experienced subjects. The increase in this percentage with experience suggests a kind of "learning about learning" or increase in sophistication over time. Furthermore, in both groups *perceived* sophistication α' is less than α, so players appear to underestimate how many others are sophisticated. The learning models also improve over QRE, although the improvement is modest when subjects are experienced.

6.6.3 Functional EWA (fEWA)

Ho, Camerer, and Chong (2002) developed a new variant, which we call fEWA, for two reasons. The first reason is that, because EWA has several parameters, many people have wondered whether it overfits, and researchers who are used to simpler models have found it hard to use in their own work.[33] So we tried to create a good theory with only one free parameter (a response sensitivity λ, which can be jettisoned in favor of a best-response rule if one's goal is simply to maximize the hit rate).

A second reason for developing fEWA is that estimated parameter values of EWA vary across games (although this is true of *all* learning models, e.g., Crawford, 1995; Cheung and Friedman, 1997; Erev and Roth, 1998). This means for cross-game prediction it is necessary to have some mapping from games to parameters.

The key ingredients in fEWA are a change-detector function $\phi_i(t)$ and an imagination weight $\delta_i(t)$ which is linked to $\phi_i(t)$. The change-detector simply compares the vector of historical frequencies of all previous choices by other players with the frequencies in the last W periods (where W is the (lowest) number of strategies that are predicted to be played in equilibrium; this feature just smoothes out fluctuations in the recent-history vector which are expected if other players are mixing).[34] The differences in these frequencies

---

[33] Of course, the too-many-parameters criticism is naive and unconstructive unless accompanied by a precise way to judge how many parameters is "too many." Fortunately, whether a theory has too many parameters is easily judged by restricting some parameters to plausible values and seeing whether the fit is much worse or not. If fit does not suffer, the theory *does* have too many parameters; otherwise, its parameters are justified statistically.

[34] The formal definition is

$$\phi_i(t) = 1 - .5 \left(\sum_{j=1}^{m_{-i}} \left[\frac{\sum_{\tau=t-W+1}^{t} I(s_{-i}^j, s_{-i}(\tau))}{W} - \frac{\sum_{\tau=1}^{t} I(s_{-i}^j, s_{-i}(\tau))}{t} \right]^2 \right).$$

The term $\sum_{\tau=t-W+1}^{t} I(s_{-i}^j, s_{-i}(\tau))/W$ is the jth element of a vector that simply counts how often strategy j was played by the others in periods $t - W + 1$ to t, and divides by W. The term $\sum_{\tau=1}^{t} I(s_{-i}^j, s_{-i}(\tau))/t$ is the relative frequency count of the jth strategy over all t periods. Note that, in games with multiple players, a frequency count of the relevant aggregate statistics can be used. For example, in median action game, frequency count

are squared and summed up across all the strategies, divided by two, then subtracted from 1. If the recent history is like all previous history, the frequency differences will be small so $\phi_i(t)$ will be close to 1. But when the recent history is quite different, the squared differences will be large, which drives $\phi_i(t)$ toward 0—i.e., the person has "detected change" and lowered the weight on old history, in effect increasing the responsiveness to the new history.

The imagination weight $\delta_i(t)$ is simply set equal to $\phi_i(t)/W$. This fits well because the parametric estimates of δ are close to 0 in games with mixed equilibria (when $W > 1$), so dividing by W pushes δ down toward 0 in those games.

The $\kappa_i(t)$ function controls the degree to which players explore different strategies (low κ) or exploit strategies that yield high payoffs (high κ). $\kappa_i(t)$ is the Gini coefficient (often used to measure income inequality) of previous choice frequencies. It is not as important empirically as the other functions and could be set to 0 or 1 without sacrificing much accuracy or insight.

These function values are then used in the EWA updating rule to update attractions after observations. Note that the functional values can differ across players and across time, so in principle they can capture individual differences and also endogenous changes in learning rules across games. For example, if ϕ starts low and grows toward 1 as behavior equilibrates, players are in effect switching from Cournot-like reinforcement rules toward fictitious play.

The model was estimated on seven games and compared with several other models. (Table 6.22 summarizes some fit results from the continental divide game.) It generally forecasts better than belief and reinforcement models which have *more* free parameters (except in mixed games where the models are equally accurate). The average values of the $\phi_i(t)$ and $\delta_i(t)$ functions also correspond rather closely, across games, to the values when their counterpart parameters are fixed and estimated in the EWA model.[35]

The dictionary definition of the phrase "ad hoc" is "for the specific purpose, case, or situation at hand, and for no other" (as in an "ad hoc committee"). Economists often misuse the term ad hoc to ridicule a new idea they didn't learn in graduate school or which does not arise from optimization. The fEWA functions are *unconventional*, but they are not ad hoc because the model is meant to apply to *all* games, not just the few it was applied to in our paper. In fact, after our paper was circulated, several readers wondered whether we might have tried so many different specifications in a search for

---

of the median strategy by all other players in each period is used. If each individual players' strategy is payoff-relevant then the vectors become matrices and an alternative form might be more parsimonious.

[35] For example, in the continental divide game the fEWA average values of ϕ, δ, and κ are 0.69, 0.69, and 0.77, compared to EWA MLE estimates of 0.61, 0.75, 1.00, and MSD-minimizing estimates from the simulations of 0.68, 0.68, 0.87.

good-fitting functions, that perhaps we overfitted the model to the sample of seven games we reported. So we invited people to submit more data sets and ended up with three more games (all dominance-solvable). fEWA fits about as well as the more complex theories on those new games too. fEWA has also been applied to learning repeated trust and entry games (see Chapter 8) with asymmetric players (where economizing on free parameters is especially desirable). It fits worse than parametric EWA, but substantially better than an equilibrium model (Camerer, Ho, and Chong, 2002b).

Summary: The EWA model is a hybrid of the key features of reinforcement and belief learning; namely, weighting received payoffs more strongly (reinforcement) and weighting forgone payoffs (belief models do this implicitly). If the simpler models were good approximations—and in mixed-equilibrium games they are—then adding parameters would not improve out-of-sample predictive accuracy, but EWA generally improves accuracy in about thirty-five games (except for mixed ones). Substituting functions of the data for the key parameters (fEWA) reduces the number of parameters that must be estimated to 1—or 0 if the criterion is to maximize hit rate—and fits as well as more complex models, or better, on a sample of ten games.

6.7 Rule Learning

Learning rules are functions from previous history and payoffs into a specific future choice. The papers discussed previously in this chapter all posit one learning rule and assume that a player sticks with the same rule throughout an experimental session (perhaps comparing models that posit different rules). Stahl (1996, 1999a,b, 2000a,b) discusses a more general approach in which players learn how various rules do, and switch among them (cf. Tang, 1996a; Erev and Barron, 2001). In rule learning, what one learns is not how well various *strategies* work, but how various *decision rules* perform (based on the performance of the strategies the rule recommends each period).

   In Stahl (1999a,b), a rule is a set of weights given to various kinds of "evidence" or scores. The scores y_0, y_1, y_2, y_3 correspond, respectively, to a weighted average of previous play by others ("imitation," y_0), expected payoffs given updated beliefs (y_1), iterated expected payoffs y_2 (given the beliefs that others are best-responding to updated beliefs), and Nash payoffs y_3. A parameter θ measures the responsiveness to recent history in belief updating ($\theta = 1$ is Cournot). Weights on the four types of evidence are $v_i, i = 0, 1, 2, 3$. Rules are reinforced by the expected payoff they would have generated in period t (taking expectations over all the possible strategies, and the actual distribution of population play) and chosen according to a logit rule.

Intuitively, think of a rule as the way a particular expert weighs different attributes or evidence (like jurors in a legal case, or critics judging films). Each expert weights evidence using their weights v_i and recommends a strategy. The total probability that the strategy is played is the probability recommended by each expert times the tendency of the player to follow each expert's recommendation. As the player learns, the experts get "reinforced" according to their performance, so the player learns to pay more and more attention to the experts whose recommendations have performed well.

Stahl runs experimental sessions in which a pair of games are each played for fifteen periods. The initial reinforcement for a rule in the second game is an average of the rule's initial reinforcement at the start of the *first* game (with weight $1 - \tau$) and the ending reinforcement at the end of the first game (weight τ). The value of τ parameterizes the strength of *transfer* of learning—about rules, not strategies—from one game to another. Transfer of learning is crucial because, taken seriously, rule learning implies that, as people go through life, they learn which rules work best across all the strategic interactions they encounter. Generally this will imply a gradual shift of weight toward more sophisticated rules. The parameter τ gives a way of resetting rule propensities or, interpreted cognitively, incorporating how well rules transfer across games that may seem different.

The econometric estimation is complicated (conquering such challenges is Stahl's great contribution to empirical analysis of experimental data from games). Initial propensities are assumed to have a common distribution in the population but evidence weights are different for each player.

An impressive feature of Stahl's experimental approach is that he sampled billions of 5×5 symmetric normal-form games to find those which were best for distinguishing among rules (see Chapter 1 appendix), and chose four "optimally informative" games (see Table 6.23). Experiments were conducted with a mean-matching protocol—players earned the average of their payoffs playing against every other player—and players learned the population history after each trial. The right-hand columns of Table 6.23 show overall choice frequencies from periods 1–8 and 9–15. Nash equilibrium play always grows over time and is modal in later periods (except for game 2).

The overall log likelihood (LL) for the model, with nine parameters for each subject, is -1896. In Stahl's parameter-rich approach, many obvious models are special cases, so the restrictions they imply can be easily tested with standard χ^2 statistics. Models in which all the players are the same, all choose Nash equilibrium with error, or all learn only from Nash evidence, all have LL worse than -3000. The hypothesis of no rule learning ($\beta_0 = 1, \beta_1 = 0$) is strongly rejected. Each parameter helps explain how players learn because restricting parameters to be zero, one at a time, always harms fit significantly.

Table 6.23. *Symmetric games used by Stahl (row payoffs only)*

Decision rule	Row player payoffs					Frequency in periods	
						1–8	9–15
Game 1							
b1	19	43	96	85	85	0.46	0.27
Nash	28	62	88	74	24	0.18	0.52
b2	67	21	38	48	38	0.17	0.14
Worldly	40	58	0	15	92	0.05	0.02
Maximax	16	15	86	99	79	0.13	0.05
Game 2							
Worldly	68	10	76	33	75	0.51	0.60
Strictly dominated	73	4	59	0	8	0.03	0.01
b2	3	92	16	15	99	0.04	0.02
Nash	86	54	25	41	6	0.06	0.14
b1	72	98	92	8	52	0.36	0.22
Game 3							
Maximax	2	31	0	99	6	0.09	0.04
b2	6	10	97	40	24	0.07	0.02
b1	98	96	38	48	19	0.23	0.07
Worldly	42	40	80	51	48	0.36	0.24
Nash	97	46	5	68	49	0.24	0.64
Game 4							
Worldly	22	79	35	56	75	0.35	0.36
b1	22	38	78	55	99	0.25	0.12
Strictly dominated	27	58	1	11	0	0.01	0.01
Nash	70	1	34	59	37	0.26	0.36
b2	56	84	60	23	2	0.13	0.14

Source: Stahl (1999a).

Table 6.24 summarizes estimated means for each of the parameters, along with the fraction of subjects whose parameter estimates are significantly different from 0 at the 5 percent level. The largest evidence weight is put on expected payoff. The weight on past history in updating beliefs, θ, and the transfer weight, τ, are around a half. A few clusters emerge.

Table 6.24.   *Mean coefficient estimates for rule-learning models*

Weighting parameter	Coefficient	Stahl (1999a)	Stahl (2001)	Stahl and Haruvy (in press)
Imitation	$\bar{v}_0$	1.12	—	—
Expected payoff	$\bar{v}_1$	1.35*	0.80	0.38
Iterated expected payoff	$\bar{v}_2$	0.19	0.07	0.00
Nash payoff	$\bar{v}_3$	0.26	0.00	0.00
Recent history	$\bar{\theta}$	0.43	0.65	0.94
Evidence weight dispersion	σ	1.15	0.77	0.80
Probability of imitation	δ_h	—	0.53	0.44
Experimentation probability	ϵ	—	0.09	0.12
Lagged propensity	β_0	1.26	1.00	1.00
Reinforcement	β_1	1.53*	0.0079	0.0047
Transfer	τ	0.47	1.00	0.31

Note: * denotes weights significant (at .05) for more than half of subjects. Significance of σ and β_0 was not tested in Stahl (1999a).

About one-third of the subjects have a particularly high value of v_1 (corresponding to belief learning). Another sixth have a flat profile with even, low evidence weights. Another sixth have a high weight on imitation (high v^0). The remaining third of the subjects show a variety of profiles that do not particularly fall into clusters.

Stahl (2000b) compares a wide variety of models using population data. Some of the models reinforce actions (strategies) and others reinforce rules, so his paper represents the largest "horse race" to date. Because the data used are relative frequencies of choices in the population, Stahl develops population-level analogues of theories previously applied to individuals (see Stahl, 2000a).

The first part of his ambitious paper compares replicator dynamics, a six-parameter aspiration-based reinforcement model from Roth and Erev (1995), and the Camerer–Ho (1999a) EWA model. He also defines a logit best-reply with inertia (LBRI) model in which choices are a mixture of inertia or habit (with weight δ_h) and logit best-reply to the population frequencies $p(t-1)$ from the last period (Cournot). Allowing best-response to θ-weighted adaptive expectations instead, $q(t) = \theta q(t-1) + (1-\theta)p(t-1)$ gives a model called LBRIAE. He also adds various sorts of trembles and mutations to these models.

Table 6.25.   *Out-of-sample performance of*
population learning models

	Measure of forecast accuracy		
Model	LL	MSD	GOP
Random	−7086		
Logit Nash	−6660		
AR(1)	−5095	0.125	−356
Replicator	−5024	0.120	−312
Reinforcement	−4868	0.099	−335
LBRI	−4834	0.091	−305
EWA	−4803	0.091	−301
LBRIAE	−4794	0.088	−300
Best possible	−4296	0.000	

Source: Stahl (2001).

Stahl tries a wide variety of criteria for evaluating goodness of fit both in and out of sample. Stahl contributes to the debate about methods for fitting models by introducing a measure GOP (goodness of prediction). GOP uses parameters estimated by MLE, simulates the entire path of fifteen-period play, and computes the log likelihood of average simulated behavior in period 15. A bad model that wanders away from the data using its own simulated history will produce a poor GOP measure (even if its conventional LL and MSD are good).

The data consist of sessions with two runs of fifteen periods on separate 5×5 and 3×3 games (see Haruvy and Stahl, 1998). Summary statistics derived from estimating parameters on part of the sample and forecasting a fresh sample of subjects and sessions are shown in Table 6.25. The random, logit Nash, and AR(1)[36] models are simply naive benchmarks to see how much the learning models are really adding.

Since these models predict population frequencies rather than individuals, it is impossible to be perfectly accurate; the model called "best possible" simply guesses the population frequency correctly but still has a substantial log likelihood (although its MSD is 0).

The replicator model is a big loser. Reinforcement does modestly worse than the LBR* and EWA models. Note also that reinforcement is particularly bad at forecasting simulated paths (the GOP measure is high), contrary to

[36] The AR(1) model simply forecasts that the population frequencies in t will be the same as in $t − 1$.

the claim of Erev and Haruvy (2001) based on simple pairwise choices. EWA is a little more accurate than LBRI but worse when adaptive expectations are added (LBRIAE).

In the second part of the paper, Stahl revises his earlier (2000a) population model in a way that encompasses the race-winning LBRIAE model. As in the earlier model, rules are combinations of evidence. Three kinds of evidence are expected payoffs, iterated expected payoffs, and Nash payoffs. Herding occurs with probability δ and is defined as following the past with probability θ and imitating the population with probability $1 - \theta$ (akin to the LBRIAE rule).[37]

Table 6.24 shows parameter estimates. There is a large herd component (δ_h is around .50). Restricting $\beta_1 = 0$ means there are rules but no learning, and degrades LL by 10 points. Eliminating level-2 and Nash evidence ($\bar{v}_2 = \bar{v}_3 = 0$) gives the LBRIAE model, which is another 42 LL points worse. However, these special cases of the rule-learning model forecast almost as well out of sample (no-learning actually forecasts better by MSD and GOP measures) so it is hard to declare a clear winner. The main feature of the data that rule learning picks up, which LBRIAE does not, is the decline of herd behavior over time and the increasing propensity to use rules that choose according to expected payoffs or iterated expected payoffs.

Stahl and Haruvy (in press) add two twists to the rule-learning model (using the Haruvy and Stahl, 1998, data): aspiration-based experimentation, and cooperation. They generate aspiration-based experimentation by reinforcing an experimentation rule by the pseudo-payoff equal to the aspiration level,[38] and generate cooperation by reinforcing a cooperative rule with the largest *total* payoff.

Results of the estimation are summarized in the right column of Table 6.24. The overall LL is -8550. Setting $\beta_1 = 0$ in the basic model chokes off rule learning (there are rules, but their propensities do not change) and reduces LL only slightly, to -8569, which means switching among rules is rare. There is little evidence for aspiration-based experimentation, but including a cooperative rule improves LL by 30 points, to -8522 (roughly as important a factor as allowing rule learning). The initial probabilistic propensity to cooperate is estimated to be 3.7 percent, within an order of magnitude of estimates of "homemade" priors by Camerer and Weigelt (1988, Chapter 8) and McKelvey and Palfrey (1992, Chapter 5).

---

[37] The key difference from his earlier paper is that herding is treated as a separate rule rather than using $\ln(q(t))$ as "evidence" which generates imitation.

[38] Then, if aspirations are high but received payoffs are low, the experimentation rule will be more strongly reinforced than other payoff-based rules, and players will experiment. Conversely, when payoffs exceed aspirations, experimentation gets less reinforcement than other rules. The tendency to experiment will be low (representing satisfaction, or "if it ain't broke don't fix it").

6.8 Econometric Studies of Estimation Properties

Most estimation of learning models described in this chapter took place *before* the econometric properties of estimators were thoroughly investigated. Thus, it is conceivable that, for a particular game and number of experimental trials, a particular econometric method may not produce accurate results, or may not be able to distinguish different models. Three recent studies have tackled this problem in the obvious way: Try to prove as much as possible about the econometric properties of different techniques, for different games and experiment lengths, then use Monte Carlo simulation when theoretical proof is not possible.

The results from the three studies range from disappointing to encouraging. The most pessimistic conclusions have come from games with mixed equilibria and small numbers of strategies, which suggests that more complex games with pure equilibria are the right ones to study (if the goal is to estimate parameters precisely). Exercises of this kind can also be used to figure out, before running experiments, which games and experimental designs are best for model identification.

Salmon (2001) compares the Mookerhjee and Sopher (1994, 1997), Cheung and Friedman (1997), and Camerer and Ho (1999a) learning rules using several data sets. Specific rules are used to create simulated data sets—reinforcement, belief learning, and population mixture models. Econometric models are then fitted to data. Good identification occurs when the right model recovers the actual rule, and does not falsely recover the wrong rule.

The two Mookerjhee–Sopher studies use 2×2, 4×4, and 6×6 games with mixed equilibria. Identification is bad. When reinforcement rules are used to generate data, the reinforcement models fit better than belief models only in the 6×6 games, and incorrect mixture models fit as well as the correct reinforcement model.

In the Cheung–Friedman games, when ϕ weights are close to 1 (fictitious play), the FP and EWA rule with fictitious play restrictions correctly show that weights are close to 1. However, when weights are 0 (Cournot) the model correctly recovers a 0 weight half the time and mysteriously misestimates a very large weight (two or more!?) half the time. When data are generated by reinforcement or mixed-population models, the estimated fictitious play weight varies a lot.

When the EWA model is fitted to data generated by either reinforcement ($\delta = 0$) or belief learning ($\delta = 1$) rules, recovery of the proper δ is excellent in the sense that the correct restriction is rejected infrequently (about 20 percent of the time) and the wrong restriction is almost always rejected. Recovery of the cumulation parameter κ is poor, however. When the EWA model is used to simulate data, the EWA model recovers correct parameters significantly about half the time. The likelihood functions for parameter *combinations* work best and almost always pick out the right model in a direct comparison.

Salmon concludes that model identification is poor on many games that have been previously studied, particularly those with mixed equilibria and a small number of strategies. Other games have better identification. Furthermore, the EWA model usually identifies the correct value of δ, the parameter that most sharply distinguishes reinforcement and belief models. Salmon concludes by noting that other types of data besides choices (such as attentional data; see Salmon 1999; Costa-Gomes, Crawford, and Broseta, 2001; Johnson et al., 2002) may help in identifying learning rules.

Cabrales and Garcia-Fontes (2000) study the EWA model of Camerer and Ho (1999). They first prove that, if ϕ is bounded below 1, estimators that either maximize log likelihood or minimize squared deviations are consistent and asymptotically normal. Of course, asymptotic normality says little about small-sample properties of these estimators; so Cabrales and Garcia-Fontes did Monte Carlo simulations. They simulated different configurations of ϕ, δ, and λ parameters, for $T = 30$ or 1,000 trials, for 2×2 coordination (stag hunt) and prisoners' dilemma games, then saw how well estimation recovers the true values. When $T = 30$, recovered estimates of ϕ are biased downward and often inaccurate; mean δ values are quite accurate but the range of values is too highly dispersed. However, when $T = 1000$ the correct values of both parameters are recovered (within .01) and the dispersion around the true mean is close to that expected by random sampling error. These results are encouraging for identifying δ, but also a reminder that good estimation is sensitive to the length of the experiment.

Blume et al. (1999) also compare belief, reinforcement, and a hybrid model on their sender–receiver data (see Chapter 7). They find poor identification in small samples, but identification improves a lot with an increased sample of subjects and span (number of periods).

Summary: Three studies show that identification of models is sometimes poor; a wrong rule can fit as well as the actual rule that generated the data. Identification is particularly poor in games with few strategies (e.g., 2 and 4) and mixed equilibria. EWA identification of the δ parameter is good in the studies by Salmon (2001) and Cabrales and Garcia-Fontes (2000) when the experiment length is long enough. The more general lesson is that exercises such as these are not difficult to do, and are worthwhile. They should also prove valuable in the future in guiding us to choose games and experimental design features (e.g., number of periods) that *do* permit more accurate model discrimination.

6.9 Conclusions

Fitting learning models to experimental data has been very informative in the past five years. The first wave of studies focused on only one class of models (typically reinforcement, belief learning, or learning direction theory). All these approaches pass an important basic test by improving on equilibrium predictions and capturing the direction of movement in data (even though the *magnitude* of predicted changes is often far off the mark). Thus, there is no doubt that simple learning rules can approximate learning better than equilibrium (which assumes none); nor is this conclusion surprising any longer.

Since many different theories all predict better than equilibrium concepts, comparative studies become crucial if the goal is to make further progress. Most comparative studies establish two results. Reinforcement models tend to predict slightly better than belief learning in games with only mixed-strategy equilibria (although no models do much better than QRE or a static observed-frequency benchmark in those games).

But belief learning generally fits better than reinforcement in coordination games and some other classes of games (e.g., market games, dominance-solvable games). The relatively good performance of choice reinforcement on some games is surprising because these models assume players learn only from the payoffs they received, but studies show that players do learn faster when they have information besides received payoffs. Therefore, it is surprising that reinforcement reproduces some features of some games, but it also means reinforcement models are incomplete in a way that can be easily remedied.

My work with Teck Ho on EWA learning is one way of using more information to avoid the empirical sluggishness of reinforcement learning. EWA is a family of learning rules that vary how strongly forgone payoffs are weighted and the degree to which payoffs are averaged or cumulated. Since EWA includes some reinforcement and belief theories as special cases (by construction), it obviously fits better within a sample of data than those special cases. It is therefore important both to penalize the more complex EWA model for its extra parameters when judging in-sample fit, and to use holdout samples to evaluate how well the model predicts fresh data (new periods, or new subjects) once the parameters are estimated. EWA predicts better in 80–95 percent of the studies in which it has been studied. It also generates reasonably accurate simulated paths (where that has been tried) and can forecast new games with parameters estimated from other games. The major exception is games with mixed equilibria, in which all the basic models predict about equally accurately (and probably only a little better than QRE).

The point of EWA is to create an approach that is more robust across many games than simpler approaches. It is easy to construct games in which simple reinforcement does poorly (the market games in Roth and Erev, 1995, are an early example). Belief learning often predicts poorly in dominance-solvable games, where convergence is predicted by belief learning and is not always observed (e.g., Nagel and Tang, 1998; Capra et al., 1999). By building in some degree of responsiveness, EWA can improve on reinforcement when that model does badly, and also improve on belief learning by not predicting sharp convergence in dominance-solvable games as belief learning does.

EWA model parameters vary across games, but parameters from *all* other models vary across games too (e.g., Cheung and Friedman, 1997; Crawford, 1995). Parametric variation presents a challenge in predicting the behavior of new games. A one-parameter theory called "functional EWA," or fEWA for short (Ho, Camerer, and Chong, 2002), makes parameters functions of players' experience rather than free parameters, and can explain why different parameter values arise in different games.

Because EWA predicts better than simpler theories (adjusting for extra parameters in several ways), there is no compelling reason, other than historical convention, to focus attention solely on reinforcement or belief models, if one's purpose is predicting behavior as accurately as possible. fEWA is easy to estimate (it has only one free parameter) and fits better than models with more free parameters.

EWA is a hybrid that "gene-splices" features of learning processes. A different kind of hybrid is rule learning. In rule learning, rules recommend strategies and are reinforced by the payoffs of the strategies they recommend. Rule learning fits population-level data a little better than a model mixing inertia and best response, which in turn fits a little better than EWA. Rule learning is an obvious way to explain "learning to learn" and certainly deserves further exploration.

An important issue is how evidence about the statistical fit of models should interact with theoretical exploration of different models. Virtually all of the theory literature focusses on models—typically evolutionary dynamics and fictitious play—that repeatedly fit experimental data much worse than other types of models. At the same time, the statistical models look too complex, and perhaps even intimidating, to theorists. (I had lunch recently with a smart young theorist who said he was embarrassed to be working on fictitious play dynamics in the light of the experimental results showing that other theories fit data better. He said he had looked at the EWA model and found it "too complicated"—this from a theorist working on deep mathematical questions involving supermodularity, stability, and so forth! What he meant, of course, was that no ready-made tools he had learned in graduate school equipped him to start working on proving theorems about the behavior of models fitted to data. But isn't rising to that challenge what innovative science is all about?) The right compromise seems to be for theorists to begin thinking about good-fitting theories, and for those of us sharpening such theories to think about which simplifications are likely to make theorizing easier.

There are two loose ends and three challenges in crafting better theories of how people actually learn. The loose ends are learning direction theory and imitation dynamics.

In learning direction theory, players know their ex post best response and move toward it (or have some intuition about the direction in which they should move). Selten suggests that direction learning is a good place to start because, in many domains, players know the direction in which to move and know little else. But learning direction theory has never been fully specified (e.g., it applies only when strategies are ordered) and its core prediction is not surprising. My hunch is that, when players know which direction to move, they typically *also* know something more about forgone payoffs from different strategies. Then a theory such as EWA could be applied.

Another loose end is imitation. Imitation dynamics are evident in the oligopoly study of Hück, Normann, and Oechssler (1999) (less so in Bosch-Domenech and Vriend, in press) and in "herd behavior" in Stahl (1999a,b, 2000a,b). A good theory could incorporate imitation indirectly. After all, imitation is most compelling when players are symmetric, and not at all sensible when players are asymmetric. (For example, children imitate the actions of adult humans, but do not instinctively imitate their pets.) This difference is an important clue: Imitation of successful players who are similar is probably a heuristic way of moving toward strategies with high forgone payoffs. Symmetric imitation could be gracefully incorporated into a theory such as EWA, where actions of similar players are proxies for forgone payoffs.

The learning models described in this chapter will have to conquer three modeling challenges before they are applicable to all situations: sophistication, imperfect payoff information, and strategy specification.

- *Sophistication* means some players understand how others are learning. Camerer, Ho, and Chong (2002a,b) and Stahl (2000a) show the advantages of modeling sophistication in a simple way, and how "teaching" in repeated games follows naturally.
- Models that require perfect information about forgone payoffs will have to adjust to environments with *imperfect information* about payoffs (Vriend, 1997). For example, EWA can be applied in low-information settings by fixing $\delta = 0$. Richer approaches use information about possible payoffs (in extensive-form games; see Ho, Wang, and Camerer,

2002) or historical payoffs (Anderson and Camerer, 2000) as proxies for forgone payoffs (Chen and Khoroshilov, in press).

- Most learning models use stage-game strategies. Broader *strategy speci-fications* are often sensible, in extensive-form games, and when there is pattern-recognition (e.g., the rule learning of Stahl, 1999a; and see Duffy and Engle-Warnick, 2000; and Engle-Warnick and Slonim, 2000). However, expanding the set of strategies from stage-game strategies typically generates combinatorial explosion. The trick is to find effi-cient methods for winnowing a large set of feasible strategies to a few psychologically plausible ones as rapidly as people seem to (e.g., ge-netic algorithms). Connecting this research to psychological research on learning, particularly connectionist neural networks (e.g., Sgroi and Zizzo, 2002), may prove useful too.

7
Coordination

GAMES WITH MULTIPLE EQUILIBRIA require coordination. Even if players have a common incentive to follow a convention or commonly understood pattern of behavior, agreeing on how to behave is not simple if there are many self-enforcing conventions, or if different players prefer different conventions. Language is a ubiquitous example: To communicate, players must choose words that are understood. Another example is economic life with "participation externalities," such as trading in markets (traders want to be where other traders are to increase liquidity) or geographic concentration (Internet whizkids move to Silicon Valley because employers expect to find the most talent there, and do). Predicting which of many equilibria will be selected is perhaps the most difficult problem in game theory. This "selection" problem is essentially unsolved by analytical theory and will probably be solved only with a healthy dose of observation.

Many approaches to the selection problem have been used. One approach is to look at features of equilibria and choose those that are desirable. For example, everyone is happier in a "payoff-dominant" equilibrium and, hence, players might know to choose it. Other equilibria are less risky and are appealing when uncertain players hedge their bets. Another approach is to ask which equilibria are more likely to be reached by adaptation or evolution. Careful treatment of this important approach is beyond the scope of this book (but see Weibull, 1995, and Fudenberg and Levine, 1998).

A third approach—the subject of this chapter—is fundamentally empirical. The empirical approach tries to infer what selection principles players are using by putting them in experiments and observing what they do.

Suppose a game is played repeatedly. An obvious selection principle is "precedent": Play the equilibrium that was played previously. Sometimes equilibria are "focal" or psychologically prominent—some strategies are culturally understood to be the ones people are likely to choose (such as equal splits in bargaining). The empirical research can be summarized as a catalog of which selection principles are used in which sorts of situations.

Coordination games illustrate why observation is useful. It is unlikely that a purely mathematical theory of rational play will ever fully identify which of many equilibria are likely to emerge because history, shared background, and the way strategies are described or made psychologically prominent surely matter. As a result, experiments and observation of the sort that naturalists do in biology can potentially do what mathematical analysis cannot—predict what will happen. As Schelling (1960, p. 164) put it, "One cannot, without empirical evidence, deduce what understandings can be perceived in a nonzero-sum game of maneuver any more than one can prove, by purely formal deduction, that a particular joke is bound to be funny."

Furthermore, precisely what people know about each other and can see are likely to affect coordination in subtle ways. Chwe (2001) is a fascinating account of how delicate details of how groups are physically organized can influence whether uprisings take place (in union organizing) or don't (in prisons).

Given the large relative payoff to experimental observation, it is surprising that coordination games have been relatively understudied compared with, say, public goods games or prisoners' dilemmas. Perhaps a bias against empirical observation arose because coordination games might be easily "solved" by communication, in principle. This prejudice is wrong in practice and in theory. In practice (at least in experiments), communication usually improves coordination but it does not *always* help, and communication rarely leads to full efficiency. In theory, communication is not really a solution because simple coordination games with few players who do not talk are really meant as micro-scale reduced-form models of large social processes in which players cannot all talk at the same time (and large public announcements may not be believed). Examples include coordinating activity in the macroeconomy, commuters responding to an unexpected closing of the Bay Bridge in San Francisco, and the use of speed limits as a coordinating device.[1]

Miscoordination can lead to inefficiencies that are hard to reverse. Language is again a good example. English has many odd features that make

---

[1] Lave (1985, p. 1159) argues that "For peculiar historical reasons, speed laws evolved as limits on driver behavior, rather than as signaling devices meant to coordinate it. . . . This paper tests these differing views of the law by examining the current effects of the 55 mph NMSL [national maximum speed limit]—should it be viewed as a coordinating mechanism or a limiting mechanism?" Lave finds that "variance kills, not speed" and concludes that speed limit laws are useful because they reduce variance (i.e., enhance coordination).

learning the language difficult. But convention rules by tyranny—if English is spoken in an odd way, and has a large "installed base" of speakers who understand its peccadillos, then new speakers must learn the peccadillos too.[2] Nowadays, English seems to be growing as the international language because of the advantage English speakers have in using the Internet. These users inherit the quirky features of English like bad genes.

Here are some examples of where coordination matters and how it arose:

- Why is the standard width (gauge) of U.S. railroad tracks 4 feet and 8.5 inches?[3] The answer is that English wagons built to carry goods and people were made about 5 feet wide, the width of two horses. Tramway builders used the same jigs and tools as the wagon makers, so they made tram lines 5 feet wide less 4 inches for track, plus a half inch for some subtle technical reason. English railroads were built by the tram builders, who used the width they knew best. English expatriates built the U.S. railroads and copied the English tracks they were familiar with. At many points along the way of this two-millennium journey, a coordinated effort to switch to a different standard could have been achieved, but wasn't. The result was that the NASA Space Shuttle is powered by two big booster rockets that are smaller than engineers would have liked them to be. Why? The rockets had to be shipped by train from a factory in Utah to the launch site. Since the train track width was determined by the construction of wagons, pulled by teams that were two horses wide, the Space Shuttle rockets were two horses wide as well. (In a sense, the shuttle was designed by a horse's ass!) An interesting twist: Russia deliberately chose a different track width—deliberately to *mis*coordinate—either to make invasions harder or to signal non-offensive intentions.
- Economic geographers are interested in why some industries are so heavily concentrated in small areas. The answer is that a small historical accident can determine a town's long-run concentration. For example, a woman in Smyrna, Georgia injured her hand and had to learn to stitch quilts in a different way. She developed a new technique which turned

---

[2] The attempt to replace different languages by the more efficient hybrid of Esperanto—which is spoken by game theorists Roger Myerson and Reinhard Selten, among others—hasn't caught on.

[3] Thanks to my sister Doreen and Giovanna Devetag for this example. A variant of this story traces the track gauge further back to Roman chariots, which supposedly carved ruts all over Europe, so the English wagon-makers were then forced to make their wagons the same width so axles wouldn't break as wheels dipped in and out of the Roman ruts. Apparently the Roman-chariot link is largely myth because the Roman chariots were not of uniform width, and there is no evidence that the English tram makers were influenced by the Romans. Furthermore, the rocket boosters were not entirely constrained by the track width (the constraint was passing through tunnels, which are typically wider than track) but the point that horse booty influenced rocket design through a long historical chain still holds. See http://www.straightdope.com/columns/000218.html for more.

out to be more efficient than the old way, and taught it to several friends. Decades later, Smyrna emerged as one of the rug-stitching capitals of the world because her technique was best taught from friend to friend (e.g., Krugman, 1992). Another famous example is Silicon Valley. Silicon Valley emerged because of the influence of local universities and some historical accidents. Being far away from the stuffy bankers in New York enabled the creation of a culture of proud scientific innovation— every "us" needs a "them"—in which cleverness, workaholic zeal, and engineering feats were valued more highly than money, fancy suits, and Ivy League pedigree. (Many early Silicon Valley pioneers were midwestern boys who had learned to cobble together inventions from scratch on the farm, out of necessity. Their do-it-yourself skills and philosophy were ideally suited to the technology of computing and new economy.) Making movies coalesced in Hollywood because the reliable, dry climate (ten days of rain a year) lowered the weather risk of shooting movies outside. Like a speck of dirt which becomes a pearl in an oyster, when there are increasing returns to scale or geographical externalities a little accident can lead to an entire industry.

- Urban gentrification often occurs in a small city (Manhattan, San Francisco), where expensive housing drives wealthy yuppies to areas where prices are cheaper because some kind of physical risk or undesirable feature drives down prices. Then a new gentry want to live where the yuppies are. Gentrification usually happens rapidly. A small critical mass can create a Schellingesque (1978) "tipping point," a point at which the percentage of people who want to do something changes rapidly from none to all. Examples include Soho in the 1970s in Manhattan, then Brooklyn; South of Market (SoMa) in San Francisco in the 1990s; Los Feliz in Los Angeles in the 1990s; Brixton in London in the late 1990s; and so on.

- A classic example of pure coordination is the emergence of conventions for driving on the left- and right-hand side of roads. (Supposedly the American convention of driving on the right, contrary to the British, emerged from having to hold a whip in the right hand to drive a wagon to market and wanting to avoid hitting a passerby if you drove on the left.) A wonderful twist on this example comes from Bolivia.[4] Ascending from the cities to mountainous areas, the roads become narrow and treacherous, with steep cliffs and frequent accidents. (When a bus driver arrives home in his village from the city, his family gathers around and celebrates the fact that he made it back alive.) In the cities drivers stay to the right (and sit in the left side of a car). But on mountain roads this convention is risky because the driver cannot see very clearly where

---

[4] Mónica Capra told me this great story.

the cliffside is. (Imagine sitting in the left side of the car, American style, and peering across the passenger side to emptiness beyond.) So the convention (which is enforced by signs) *switches* to driving on the left on mountain roads! This way both drivers can see the cliffside more clearly. Another driving example: Pittsburgh has many two-way streets with one lane in each direction. Normally drivers who are making left-hand turns must wait for oncoming traffic to pass before turning, but this rule creates long delays for those who are waiting behind the left-turner because streets have just one lane. So a convention developed—the "Pittsburgh left"—which unofficially permits drivers turning left to turn *first* (contrary to state law).

- Categorizing products is a coordination problem. Is the movie *Casino* in the "action" category at Blockbuster or in "drama"? Buyer and seller have a common interest in getting customers in and out of the store rapidly, so nobody cares how the movie is categorized as long as it's easy to find. The two sides play a coordination game in which movies must be assigned to a small number of categories, and both sides benefit if they can guess which category the other side chose.

- Usually the desire to communicate produces a preference for a common language. For example, the rise of the internet may increase widespread English speaking across the world. (Unintended consequence: Young Koreans eager to learn English are actually having their tongues loosened surgically—as funnyman Dave Barry would say, "I'm not making this up!"—hoping it will improve their pronunciation.) At other times one group of people may want to disguise what they are saying in front of others; then having an obscure, impenetrable language is better than a widely spoken one. In World War II, twenty-nine Navajo Indians were recruited as "code talkers" in the Pacific to communicate front-line commands, because their native language, Dineé, had such complex syntax and tonal subtleties that it was unusually difficult for expert Japanese code breakers to break.

In these examples, agreeing on *some choice* is often more important than what is agreed upon, but some coordinated choices are better than others. Actors and software engineers want to be where demand for their skills is (and firms will locate where they expect those skilled people to congregate); yuppies want to live in yuppie neighborhoods; and video store customers with good taste want to quickly find *Jackie Brown* (action? or blaxploitation?) and *Crouching Tiger, Hidden Dragon* (Hong Kong–style action, wu-xia flavor? or romance?); debt-heavy nations want patient investors. They all need to coordinate.

In this chapter, coordination games are divided into three categories: matching games; games with asymmetric payoffs; and games with asymmetric equilibria.

In matching games, all equilibria have the same payoffs for each player.[5] These games are useful for studying how "psychologically prominent" focal points emerge from psychophysical, semantic, and cultural considerations. In some coordination games, payoffs are asymmetric so players disagree about which equilibrium is best. The battle-of-the-sexes (BOS) game is a canonical example. In BOS, variables that distinguish one player from another—such as communication, preplay options, timing (first-mover advantages or disadvantages), or cues to bargaining power (such as past reputations)—determine which equilibrium is selected. In other games, players are symmetric but equilibria are not. A game with this feature is "stag hunt" (also called the "assurance game"). In stag hunt, two players choose risky or safe actions. If both choose the risky action they earn *more* than if they had played it safe, but if the other person doesn't choose the risky action the risk-taking player earns *less*. Selection principles that distinguish different kinds of equilibria, such as payoff-dominance and risk-dominance, are tested by these games.

Each class of games has a different source of strategic uncertainty about what others will do, which makes coordination difficult. In matching games, strategic uncertainty comes from the lack of structural ways to distinguish among equilibria. In BOS, strategic uncertainty comes from doubt about which player deserved the better outcome. In stag hunt, strategic uncertainty comes from the conflict between the shared motive for a higher payoff (expressed by payoff-dominance) and the individual motive to avoid risk (expressed by risk-dominance). Excellent overviews of work on coordination are given by Ochs (1995a) and Crawford (1997).

7.1   Matching Games

In the fall of 1988 *GAMES* magazine (1989) conducted a contest. Players could submit mock votes for each of nine celebrities, one for president and another for vice-president. From the pool of contestants who "voted" for the most popular presidential candidate, one contestant was drawn and

---

[5] Matching games as defined here are different from the kind of matching studied experimentally by Harrison and McCabe (1996a), Kagel and Roth (2000), and Haruvy, Roth, and Unver (2001), and the mathematical study of matching algorithms stretching back to the 1950s. In these matching games players seek to consummate one-to-one or many-to-one matches, but players have idiosyncratic preferences about whom to match with. (In the early game theory literature this was often called the "marriage problem" for obvious reasons, and has also been applied to matching of medical residents to hospitals, sorority "rush" matching students to sororities, College Bowl games, and so forth.) In those matching problems, the key is to find workable algorithms which guarantee some degree of Pareto-efficiency in matches. In the Schelling-type "pure matching games," *which* "match" occurs is irrelevant and so the focus is entirely on how shared focal points can guide equilibration.

Table 7.1. *Results of GAMES magazine matching contest*

President	Vice-president									Vice-president total
	Oprah	Pete	Bruce	Lee	Ann	Bill	Sly	Pee-Wee	Shirley	
Oprah Winfrey	—	35	63	218	35	247	41	110	29	778
Pete Rose	36	—	33	74	25	67	32	36	20	323
Bruce Springsteen	45	36	—	71	26	139	49	65	23	454
Lee Iaccoca	56	36	41	—	31	155	34	39	22	414
Ann Landers	48	30	37	149	—	365	29	58	28	744
Bill Cosby	122	41	83	435	41	—	53	147	21	943
Sly Stallone	36	27	66	58	27	117	—	145	20	496
Pee-Wee Herman	61	32	75	84	76	343	90	—	33	794
Shirley MacLaine	33	30	37	66	30	56	29	56	—	337
President total	437	267	435	1,155	291	1,489	357	656	196	5,283

Source: GAMES magazine (1989).

paid a dollar sum which was independent of their choice. Each contestant was trying to guess what each other contestant would guess, precisely as in Keynes's description of the stock market as a "beauty contest." The results are shown in Table 7.1. The celebrities getting the largest number of the 5,283 presidential votes were Bill Cosby (1489 votes), followed by Lee Iacocca and Pee-Wee Herman. Actress and self-proclaimed reincarnate Shirley MacLaine finished last.

The *GAMES* contest is a pure matching game because the amount earned by matching the most people was independent of what one chose. Good matching requires figuring out which of the equally profitable strategies the most people would pick (knowing others have the same goal). At the time of the game, the popular Cosby had a successful television show, which may have served as a focal principle; but so did Pee-Wee Herman and Oprah Winfrey, who finished fourth. Lee Iacocca had actually been mentioned as a possible candidate for President (of the United States), which may have directed attention toward him.

Table 7.2 shows a simple pure matching game, where strategies are labeled A and B. Choosing A or choosing B are both equilibria, and no sophisticated selection principles apply (i.e., refinements of Nash equilibrium). However, some equilibria might be "focal" or "psychologically prominent" (as Schelling pointed out in 1960) because of precedent[6] or physical or

---

[6] Pascal wrote, "Why do we follow old laws and old opinions? Because they are better? No, but they are unique, and remove sources of diversity."

Table 7.2.   A matching game

	A	B
A	1,1	0,0
B	0,0	1,1

semantic distinctions in the way strategies are labeled—e.g., middleness, upper-leftness, choose the strategy with the longest number of vowels, etc.

Despite the charm of these games, and Schelling's compelling examples, amazingly little hard evidence has been collected about how people play them. Mehta, Starmer, and Sugden (1994a,b) ran the most thorough experiments. The percentage of coordinated responses ranged from 10 percent and up in games with many strategies. For example, 29 percent picked the number 1 when asked to choose a number, 28 percent picked the time "noon" from the set of times of day, and 38 percent picked Trafalgar Square from the set of meeting places in London. Sometimes a sharp focal point sticks out—87 percent chose heads out of the set {heads,tails}, 89 percent chose Mt. Everest from the (large) set of mountains, and 89 percent chose Ford from the set of car makes.

In their 1994a paper, Mehta et al. were interested in where strategic salience, or focality, came from. They contrasted a pure picking condition, in which players simply picked (P) strategies, with a coordinating (C) condition in which subjects earned £1 for each match with another randomly chosen subject. Comparing choices by the P group and the C group enabled a test of whether some strategies are simply preferred (and hence chosen by Ps and Cs alike), or whether players know certain strategies are focal and pick them more often in the C condition.

Results from several games are shown in Table 7.3. The table shows the frequency of the most common choices, the total number of different responses given (r), and a coordination index c (the fraction of matches if responses were randomly matched). The frequency of matching is impressive. Asked to name a year, the pickers chose forty-three different years—they picked 1971 (probably the most frequent birth year among the young students) 8.0 percent of the time, and 1990 (the year of the experiment) 6.8 percent of the time. However, they managed to coordinate by picking the year 1990 61.1 percent of the time. The eighty-eight pickers chose a total of seventy-five different dates (presumably their privately known birthdays) but in the matching condition nearly half chose December 25, Christmas Day.

Slim popularity differences in the picking condition blossomed into bigger advantages in matching. Pickers chose the color blue slightly more

Table 7.3. *Results of picking (P) and coordinating (C)*

	Group P ($n = 88$)		Group C ($n = 90$)	
	Response	Proportion	Response	Proportion
Years	1971	8.0	1990	61.1
	1990	6.8	2000	11.1
	2000	6.8	1969	5.6
	1968	5.7		
	$r = 43$	$c = 0.026$	$r = 15$	$c = 0.383$
Flowers	Rose	35.2	Rose	66.7
	Daffodil	13.6	Daisy	13.3
	Daisy	10.2	Daffodil	6.7
	$r = 26$	$c = 0.184$	$r = 11$	$c = 0.447$
Dates	25 December	5.7	25 December	44.4
	10 December	1.1	10 December	18.9
	1 January	1.1	1 January	8.9
	$r = 75$	$c = 0.005$	$r = 19$	$c = 0.238$
Towns	London	15.9	London	55.6
	Norwich	12.5	Norwich	34.4
	Birmingham	8.0		
	$r = 36$	$c = 0.054$	$r = 8$	$c = 0.238$
Numbers	7	11.4	1	40.0
	2	10.2	7	14.4
	10	5.7	10	13.3
	1	4.5	2	11.1
	$r = 28$	$c = 0.052$	$r = 17$	$c = 0.206$
Colors	Blue	38.6	Red	58.9
	Red	33.0	Blue	27.8
	Green	12.5		
	$r = 12$	$c = 0.269$	$r = 6$	$c = 0.422$
Boys' names	John	9.1	John	50.0
	Fred	6.8	Peter	8.9
	David	5.7	Paul	6.7
	$r = 50$	$c = 0.002$	$r = 19$	$c = 0.264$
Coin toss	Heads	76.1	Heads	86.7
	$r = 5$	$c = 0.618$	$r = 3$	$c = 0.764$
Gender	Him	53.4	Him	84.4
	$r = 6$	$c = 0.447$	$r = 2$	$c = 0.734$

Source: Mehta et al. (1994a).

often than red but they chose red twice as often when matching (58.9 percent versus 27.8 percent). "Him" beats "her" by a small margin in picking but wins by 84.4 percent to 15.6 percent in matching.

Bardsley et al. (2001) dissected the difference between picking and matching more carefully. They used choice sets in which one of four choices was distinctive. For example, the city Bern is distinctive in the set {Bern, Barbados, Honolulu, Florida} because the last three locations are warm vacation spots and Bern is not. They compared choices in a picking condition, in a guessing condition in which subjects guessed what most people picked, and in a matching condition. (Their design adds guessing to the P and C conditions above.) If salience in matching arises from knowledge of what people like, what people believe people like, and so forth, then the modes in all three conditions will be the same; they call this condition "derivative salience." In contrast, "Schelling salience" (or nonderivative salience) is present when the mode in the matching (C) condition is different than in picking and guessing (e.g., if subjects choose Bern when matching but pick Florida and guess that others pick Florida). In fact,[7] Schelling salience predicts well. In twelve of fourteen games, the distinctive choice is the modal one, chosen about 60 percent of the time, even though distinctive choices are usually picked and guessed less often.

7.1.1 Assignment Games and Visual Selection

Some matching games are "assignment games." In an assignment game, a strategy assigns each object in a set to one category or another. Economic examples include dividing people into teams, firms choosing locations in a physical space or attribute space (e.g., Ochs, 1990), assigning objects in an estate to heirs, categorizing movies into genres in a video store, dividing assets of a bankrupt firm among creditors, and dividing community property in a divorce.

In one class of assignment games, several circles must each be assigned to a left or right square.

Some focal principles that might be used in assignment are anticipated by Hume's (1978 [1740]) analysis of justice and property. As Mehta et al. (1994b, p. 170) wrote,

Hume argues that people recognize the advantages to individual self-interest gained from interaction in society. But they also recognize that the major source of conflict in society emanates from goods with the characteristic that they can easily be transferred from person to person.

---

[7] In their experiments, focality of physical location (such as first on the list or upper left) was cleverly disabled by having stimuli "swim" around a computer screen.

He suggests convention has emerged as the means by which such conflicts may be averted: convention enables each person to recognize what
others will accept as being his or her property.

Hume suggested that property conventions arise from analogy and metaphor. Since "property of" is a relation between people and objects, natural
analogies for property relations might be found in other kinds of people–
object relations, such as spatial or temporal proximity, physical resemblance,
cultural attachment, and so forth. Spatial proximity is often used to decide
which countries or people have rights to catch fish or mine minerals. Temporal proximity is embodied in the principle of "finder's keepers" or "first
possession," which awards an object to the person who found it first. [8]

Following Hume, Mehta et al. describe three focal principles for assigning objects to "owner" A or B: *Closeness*—Assign an object to whichever of
A or B is closer; *equality*—assign half to A and half to B; and *accession*—if a
subset of objects are closely related to one another, the subset should not
be broken up.

These rules are evident in everyday bargaining and folk law assigning
assets, costs, debts, and damages to various parties. Suppose apples fall from
two trees owned by neighbors, Mr. Left and Ms. Right. The trees' branches
are spread widely and it is impossible to tell which apple fell from which tree.
Who owns which apples? The rule of closeness gives an apple to the person
whose tree it fell closest to. The rule of equality divides the apples equally.
The rule of accession insists that a cluster of apples that fell close together
not be separated. (Keeping nearby apples together is silly, but accession has
much appeal for awarding custody of siblings in a divorce or adoption, or
assigning assets that are productive complements to creditors.)

A set of questions from Mehta et al. (1994b) designed to test these
principles are shown in Figure 7.1. In each question, each of several circles
(numbered 1–5) is assigned to a square. If a subject's assignment exactly
matches the assignment of another subject (for all circles), she earns money
from a pool. Table 7.4 shows the assignments of circles predicted by each
of the three selection rules defined above, in two studies by Mehta et al.
(1994a,b). The percentages of subjects choosing consistently with each rule
are shown in parentheses. For example, in question 20 of Mehta et al.
(1994b), closeness assigns circles one and two to the left and the other three
to the right (32 percent do this), accession assigns circles four and five to
the right (43 percent do this), and equality is mute.

---

[8] Mehta et al. (1994b) quote a Humean example in which cultural "ownership" matters (cf. Kreps, 1990,
pp. 424–25): "a German, a Frenchman, and a Spaniard enter a room in which there are three bottles of
wine—Rhenish, Burgundy, and port. If they fall into a dispute about who should have which bottle, Hume
says, the obvious solution is that each should take the product of his own country" (1994b, p. 170).

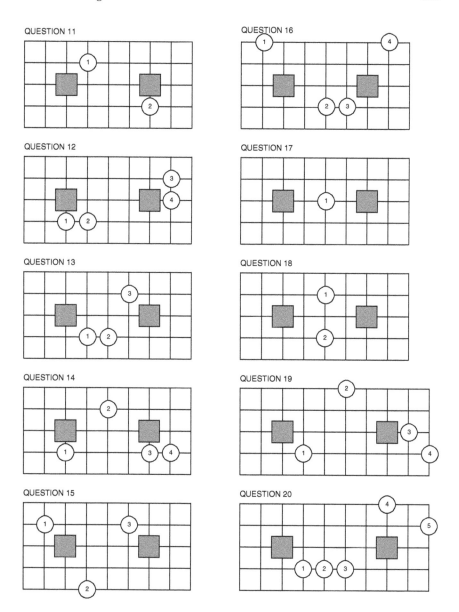

Figure 7.1. *Circle-to-square assignment games. Source: Based on Mehta, Starmer, and Sugden (1994b).*

Table 7.4.   *Choices consistent with various assignment rules*

Question	Closeness	Accession	Equality
11	LR (74)	LR (74)	LR (74)
12	LLRR (68)	LLRR (68)	LLRR (68)
13	L*R (70+)	LLR (70)	None
14	L*RR (76)	**RR (76+)	LLRR (68)
15	LLR (71)	LLR (71)	None
16	L*RR (73)	LRRR (5)	LLRR (68)
19	LRRR (29)	LRRR (29)	LLRR (45)
20	LLRRR (32)	LLLRR (43)	None

Source: Mehta et al. (1994b).
Note: Figures in parentheses show the percentage of subjects choosing consistently with each rule. * Denotes *either* L or R permitted.

When all three rules agree, about 70 percent of the subjects chose the assignment the rules imply. Some of the questions are designed to pit principles against one another. In question 19, closeness and accession predict a lopsided split, assigning the middle circle 2 to the right (because it's closer to the right square). About a third of the subjects made that assignment, but nearly half enforced equality and assigned circle 2 to the left. Question 20 is a straight choice between closeness, which assigns the middle circle 3 to its nearest square (on the right), and accession, which keeps 3 with its "siblings" and assigns it left. Accession beat closeness by a small margin, 43 percent versus 32 percent. Question 16 pits accession against equality: Does circle 2 stay with its sibling 3, and get assigned to the right, or go left to create equality? Most subjects voted for equality and only a few for accession. Looking across all the questions, it appears that equality is a primary principle that is always respected, and accession and closeness considerations are applied about equally strongly when equality is satisfied.

There are many interesting experiments on matching that could be done. Matching games could be used to measure cultural "strength": Ask subjects questions about shared values and see how well answers correlate across subjects.[9] The degree of shared understanding might also predict

[9] For example, a company's employees could be asked questions such as, "Is it appropriate to bend the rules for an angry customer even if it means costing the company a small sum?" Some cultures clearly allow this indulgence (some luxury hotel chains have rules such as "Spend up to $1,000 to solve a customer's problem"); others do not. But this measure of one employee's answer does not get at truly *shared* values, which players know that others know (and others know they know, and so on). To measure shared values,

success in relationships, such as marriages. On the *Newlywed Game* television show, two newlyweds are separated and asked questions, usually with bawdy overtones designed to draw snickers like, "In what room of your house would your wife say you two have the most fun?" If the husband's answer matches the wife's answer they win a prize. Perhaps matching tasks such as this helps predict the length of a marriage and the chance of divorce.

7.1.2   Unpacking Focality

Bacharach and Bernasconi (1997) unpack what it means for a strategy to be focal (see also theory by Gauthier, 1975; Crawford and Haller, 1990; Bacharach, 1993; Sugden, 1995). The basic elements are evident from the matching games discussed above, and from Schelling's earlier work: People make perceptual and other distinctions among strategies—labels matter—then "use" distinctions which are most likely to produce a match.

The elements in the Bacharach framework are *actions* Ω; *attributes* which partition Ω into subsets with and without the attribute; and *subtlety*, the probability that an attribute is recognized by other players. Players are assumed to randomize within a subset of options with the same available attributes, and then apply payoff-dominance. Attributes that are most distinctive are preferred as selection principles because they yield a higher chance of a match, and hence higher expected payoffs. However, since distinctive attributes are usually less recognizable, a tradeoff between the distinctiveness of an attribute and its subtlety can arise. Bacharach and Bernasconi ran experiments to test some implications of this framework. Because subjects are eager to coordinate, "nuisance" attributes which have not been controlled by the experimenter—such as the position of an action on the page—loom large. Bacharach and Bernasconi try to disable these nuisance attributes by inserting subjects' pages in their packet of experimental materials in different orientations. Then there is no natural top/bottom or left/right because each subject has privatized values of these orientations. (Computerized displays would be useful for this purpose too.)

Their results can be organized by the principles they test.

Tests of Rarity Preference

Rarity preference means subjects should choose objects that are rarer—fewer of them share the same attribute. Figure 7.2 displays a typical picture subjects saw. The display shows six flowers and eight triangles, drawn to look

---

players should be asked how *others* would answer questions. Why stop there? Players should also wonder how others think *they* will answer questions. Schelling-type matching games provide an ideal—and simple—tool for measuring shared cultural values.

Figure 7.2. *Example of a picture used to test "rarity preference" in matching games. Source: Based on Bacharach and Bernasconi (1997).*

as similar as possible. Table 7.5 reports the percentage of times that subjects chose relatively rare or frequent options in four games with varying degrees of rarity. In games such as the one pictured in Figure 7.2, strength is an increasing function of the gap between the number of rare and frequent actions. When the rare action is an "oddity," the only action with a particular attribute, the oddity is chosen 94 percent of the time.

Tests of Tradeoff

Suppose a game has an oddity—a singleton option which is the only action that has feature F—but the feature F is subtle and is recognized with probability $p(F)$. And suppose some of the other actions can be classed into a group that is relatively rare, with n elements. Then the tradeoff principle says that people decide to choose the oddity, rather than take their chances matching on one of the members of the rare set, if $p(F) > 1/n$.

Table 7.5. *Frequency of choices of rare versus frequent actions (percent)*

	Number of rare/frequent options			
	6/8	2/3	6/18	1/15
Rare	65	76	77	94
Frequent	35	24	23	6

Source: Bacharach and Bernasconi (1997).

Figure 7.3. *Example of a picture with object size differences used to test "tradeoff." Source: Based on Bacharach and Bernasconi (1997).*

Figure 7.3 shows a stimulus used to test for tradeoff. The actions are three flowers and eleven diamonds. One of the diamonds, just to the lower left of center, is slightly smaller than the rest (marked by an arrow, which subjects did not see). This size difference is a subtle feature that creates a distinctive oddity diamond if subjects notice it (and think others do too). To test tradeoff one must induce a degree of availability $p(F)$, then measure it. Bacharach and Bernasconi did so by manipulating two dimensions of the oddity objects—their size and their intensity (boldness of color)—and asking subjects whether they noticed the oddity. In the obvious conditions, 94 percent of the subjects noticed the oddity, so $p(F)$ is estimated to be .94. In the subtle conditions, 40 percent of the subjects noticed the oddity. Both sessions of each condition are pooled and reported in Table 7.6.

The table shows the number of choices of the oddity and of one of the rare options, ranked by the number of options in the rare set r (from 2–6) and by the subtlety of the oddity $p(F)$. The tradeoff principle predicts that if the percentage noticing the oddity, $p(F)$, is above $1/r$, people should pick the oddity; otherwise they should pick a rare option. Because $p(F)$ happens to be always above $1/r$, people should always choose the oddity.

The oddity is usually chosen when it is obviously unique (i.e., $p(F)$ is high; the left half of Table 7.6). However, when an oddity is only subtly unique ($p(F)$ is low; the right half of Table 7.6) it is chosen less than half the time. For example, Figure 7.3 shows a subtle size oddity (only 40 percent noticed that one diamond was smaller) and three options in the rare class (flowers). In this case, 36 percent picked the small diamond and 64 percent chose one of the flowers. As the gap between $p(F)$ and $1/r$ increases, the

Table 7.6. *Frequency of choices in tests of tradeoff, fourteen actions in total (percent)*

	Subtlety of oddity attribute								
	Number of rare options r								
	Obvious				Subtle				
	2	3	4	5	2	3	4	5	6
Rare	14	19	9	7	77	55	45	69	55
Oddity	83	79	91	88	23	31	45	19	20
Other	2	2	0	5	0	14	10	12	25
$p(F)$	0.95	0.91	0.95	0.93	0.55	0.40	0.62	0.25	0.25

Source: Bacharach and Bernasconi (1997).

oddity should be chosen more often but there is not enough variation in the size of that gap to test this prediction.

Bacharach also conjectured a property called "symmetry disqualification" but it does not appear to be widely followed.[10]

Munro (1999) reports on an unusual field study of coordination in physical matching games. He watched ten samples of bicyclists approaching from opposite directions on bike paths around a college campus in Japan. (He chose paths that did not have lines painted down the middle; on these paths, bicyclists tend to ride in the middle and have to coordinate on which direction to swerve.) When two bicyclists approached each other, did they both go left, or both go right? Or did they fail to coordinate and collide? Munro found that collisions were very rare, and bicyclists went left 80 percent of the time. People drive cars on the left in Japan (though it is a little surprising that a more uniform convention did not emerge).[11]

---

[10] Suppose there are two circles and one each of a diamond, square, and triangle. Since there is only one diamond, for example, you might think that choosing it is a good idea. But there is nothing special which distinguishes the partitions (diamond, non-diamond), (square, non-square), and (triangle, non-triangle). Symmetry disqualification says that if no feature favors any of these three partitions then even though each partition has a unique "singleton" element in it, there is only a 1/3 chance that you will coordinate on the same singleton as another player. You should "disqualify" the three singleton partitions and pick one of the two circles, where you have a 1/2 chance of matching. This principle does not predict well when it disqualifies partitions with singletons and predicts choice of one of two or more objects (e.g., only 12 percent chose one of the two circles, and more than half chose the triangle). Symmetry disqualification does predict well when it favors one of two or more singleton choices over multiple-object choices, but these patterns can be explained by other simple theories.

[11] Munro points out that virtually any learning theory predicts an increasing tendency toward one convention or the other over time, which is not evident in the data. When traffic was heavy, a strong left convention emerged spontaneously, but when the flow slowed down cyclists returned to negotiating a direction separately for each encounter. Munro also compared learning models, regressing a cyclist's

Summary: In pure matching games players choose an object from a set and win a fixed prize if they match. These games are extreme illustrations of what happens when players care *only* about coordinating, and don't care what they coordinate on. Mehta, Starmer, and Sugden found that players use shared knowledge of which choices are "focal" or "psychologically prominent" (in Schelling's terms) to match much better than chance, though matching is not perfect. They also found that coordination does not derive solely from preferences or guesses about preferences; it seems to depend on what choices are most distinctive and are noticed. Bacharach and Bernasconi also show a strong effect of labeling actions and a preference for actions with more distinctive features, and modest evidence that subjects trade off subtlety with distinctiveness.

In assignment games where different focal principles can be applied, there is a rough ranking in which equality is respected first, followed by accession and then closeness. It would also be interesting to study matching games embedded in economic contexts of special interest—division of assets or debts, division of workers into categories, or focal principles that are part of "organizational culture" (see Camerer and Vepsalainen, 1988; and Kreps, 1990). Also, it is possible that persistent failure to match one's peers may be an index of poor social acuity, perhaps linked to deficits in "theory of mind" or autism.

7.2 Asymmetric Players: Battle of the Sexes

Table 7.7 shows a "battle of the sexes," a canonical game with asymmetric player equilibria. In this modern version of BOS, two people are interested in coordinating their choice of a movie to see. Chris (playing as Column) wants to see *Waiting to Exhale* whereas Randy (Row) prefers *The Usual Suspects*. Both would like to match, but each prefers a different movie. The pure-strategy equilibria are (Exhale, Exhale), which Chris likes best, and (Suspects, Suspects), which Randy prefers. There is a third mixed-strategy equilibrium in which players mix by choosing their preferred movie with probability 3/4. In that equilibrium, the expected payoffs are 0.75, which are worse for both players than either of the pure-strategy equilibrium payoffs.

The two equilibria are symmetric, up to the identity of the players, because both yield 1 to one player and 2 to another. A dispassionate arbitrator who cared equally about the two players would be indifferent between the

---

reinforced strategy (i.e., successful left or right movement) with the fraction of observed left movements, to compare reinforcement and belief learning. Like some other studies which combine the two terms, he found that the belief term was six times larger than the reinforcement term; see Chapter 6).

Table 7.7.   *Battle of the sexes*

		Chris	
		Waiting to Exhale	*Usual Suspects*
Randy	*Exhale*	1,3	0,0
	Suspects	0,0	3,1

Table 7.8.   *Battle of the sexes (Cooper et al.)*

		Column	
		1	2
Row	1	0,0	200,600
	2	600,200	0,0

Source: Cooper et al. (1994)

two pure equilibria. Hence, only selection principles that distinguish one player from the other will help them coordinate. BOS captures an important "mixed motive" social situation—both players want to coordinate (a shared or social motive), but they disagree on which strategy to coordinate on (because of individual motives).

An elegant experimental investigation of BOS was conducted by Cooper, DeJong, Forsythe, and Ross (1990, 1994). In the 1990s the well-coordinated Cooper et al. group, based in Iowa, produced a long series of beautiful studies of coordination games. The BOS game used by Cooper et al. is shown in Table 7.8. Both players' preferred equilibrium strategy is 2. The payoffs 600 and 200 are numbers of lottery tickets.[12]

The results from several treatments are shown in Table 7.9. The table shows the numbers and percentages of pairs choosing each of the two equilibrium outcomes and either of the disequilibrium outcomes, from the last half of a twenty-two-period experiment.

Coordination failure is common. The players mismatch 59 percent of the time in BOS, very close to the 62.5 percent mismatch rate predicted by the mixed-strategy equilibrium. Even if the subjects are not deliberately

---

[12] After each round, a lottery for $1 or $2 was conducted (depending on the session conducted). In the lotteries, X tickets give the player an $X/1000$ chance of winning; the 600 payoff means a 60 percent chance of winning.

Table 7.9. *Battle of the sexes game: Last eleven periods*

Game	Outside option	(1,2)	(2,1)	(1,1) or (2,2)	Total
BOS	—	37	31	97	165
		(22%)	(19%)	(59%)	
STRAUB	—	24	13	53	90
		(26%)	(14%)	(60%)	
BOS-300	33	0	119	13	165
		(0%)	(90%)	(10%)	
BOS-100	3	5	102	55	165
		(3%)	(63%)	(34%)	
BOS-1W	—	1	158	6	165
		(1%)	(96%)	(4%)	
BOS-2W	—	49	47	69	165
		(30%)	(28%)	(42%)	
BOS-SEQ	—	6	103	56	165
		(4%)	(62%)	(34%)	

Sources: Cooper et al. (1994); Straub (1995).
Note: Numbers in parentheses refer to proportions of play of each outcome.

randomizing, the data are consistent with the idea that, as a population, they are mixing in the equilibrium proportions (as we often saw in the Chapter 2 studies of mixed games). The next row, STRAUB, reports results collected by Straub (1995) with the same payoffs, which replicate Cooper et al. very closely.

7.2.1 Outside Options

In treatment "BOS-300," the row player can take an outside option that pays 300 tickets to both players, rather than playing the BOS. Outside options are interesting because a refinement called "forward induction" predicts that the very presence of an outside option could matter for coordination, in a way that depends delicately on the size of the option. If the option is 300, then Column should reason that the Row player would reject the option only if she expected to get 600 in the BOS game. (Rejecting 300, then playing for the inferior 200 outcome, would violate the conjunction of dominance, self-interest, and dynamic consistency.) Thus, Column should confidently conclude that Row intends to play 2, and Column should best-respond by choosing 1.

Forward induction is intuitive to game theorists, but a lot can go wrong with it empirically. Row players could appreciate the argument but lack faith that Column players will think it through, and take the sure 300 rather than play BOS and risk getting 200. Columns could play 1 because they think it is unfair that Row should both have the option and, having rejected it, get the better payoff as well. Row players could violate dynamic consistency, rejecting the option then "forgetting" what they had in mind by doing so (or changing their minds about whether Columns will have reasoned it through). The third row of Table 7.9 shows that, despite these cognitive obstacles, the forward induction argument works well: Only 20 percent of the Rows chose not to play, and 90 percent of those who did got their preferred payoff (from the (2,1) equilibrium).

Of course, players in a BOS crave any tie-breaking feature that distinguishes one player from another, to break the stalemate between (2,1) and (1,2). Cooper et al. wondered whether having *any* option distinguishes the Row player, leading both players to the (2,1) equilibrium that favors Row. To test this possibility, they ran sessions in which the option pays 100 to both players. When the option value is only 100, forward induction does not apply because rejecting the option does not indicate anything about Row's beliefs about what will happen in the BOS subgame.

Row "BOS-100" in Table 7.9 shows what happened when the option is 100. Only three players picked the option. When the other 98 percent chose to play BOS, 63 percent of the pairs gravitated toward Row's preferred equilibrium, and 34 percent mismatched. These percentages are about halfway between the original BOS results and the BOS-300 results. We can conclude that roughly half of the effect of the 300 option is due to forward induction, and half to the presence of an option being used as a coordinating device that favors the Row player.

7.2.2 Communication

Communication is obviously important in coordination games. To study communication, Cooper et al. allowed either one or both players to make nonbinding preplay announcements ("cheaptalk").

The effects of communication are summarized in the rows labeled BOS-1W (one-way) and BOS-2W (two-way) in Table 7.9. One-way communication worked like a charm: 95 percent of announcements by Row were intended play of 2, and all but one actually did play 2. All but two of the Columns went along and played 1.

If a little (one-way) communication helps a lot, two-way communication must do even better, right? Wrong. Table 7.9 shows that with two-way communication the mismatch rate was 42 percent, not quite as high as the communication-free 59 percent in the baseline BOS treatment, but far short of the low 4 percent rate with one-way communication. The problem was that both players tended to announce their preferred strategies, which did not form an equilibrium and therefore left them in roughly the same position as if they'd said nothing.

7.2.3 Evolution of Meaning

Communication creates a meta-coordination problem in which players must coordinate their beliefs on what various messages mean before they can use messages to coordinate on what to do (see Farrell and Rabin, 1996). This problem is illustrated by the following story.[13] There is a dialect of Portuguese that is widely spoken in Brazil, and substantially different from the dialect spoken in Portugal. Although the Portugese were first to use their language, the Brazilian-dialect speakers outnumber the Portugese natives, so there is a conflict between "precedent" (temporal priority) and sheer numbers as principles for determining which dialect to use. So a conference was convened to agree, once and for all, on a common dialect. But what language should they speak at the conference?!

The point is that creating shared meaning from scratch is deceivingly difficult and may take a long time. Where does meaning come from? "Common sense" is not a satisfactory answer for theorizing, since we would like to know where common sense comes from and how it is sustained (i.e., why is it common?).[14]

Because pure theory seems unable to give conditions under which specific meanings arise, it is useful to put people in a situation with no meaning and see how they create it. Blume et al. (1998) did such an experiment (see also Blume et al. 2001). They were interested in whether senders in sender–receiver games could learn to create a homemade language, whose meaning would be understood by receivers.

Start with game 1 of Blume et al, shown in Table 7.10. The game shows the payoffs to senders and receivers when the sender's type is t_i and the receiver's action is a_i. (Payoffs are in units of probability of winning \$1, since they used the lottery ticket procedure.) In the experiment, senders

---

[13] Thanks to Sam Bowles for this story.

[14] There are also many examples in everyday language where speakers and listeners know that sentences mean the opposite of their literal meaning. As I write this, I am staring at an ad which says, "When we ask, 'Is that what you're wearing?' we're actually hoping it's not." The ad is part of a Virginia Slims campaign with the slogan "It's a *woman* thing" which tries to explain nonliteral female meanings to clueless men. For example, most women know that the utterance "Is that what you're wearing?"—which appears to be a question requiring a yes or no answer—is in fact a thinly veiled command: "Take those clothes off and put on something different that I would approve of." A "take it literally" assumption of meaning creation must bend to accommodate these exceptions. See Sally (2002a) for more.

Table 7.10.   *Payoffs in sender–receiver game 1 of Blume et al.*

	Receiver actions	
Sender types	a_1	a_2
t_1	0,0	0.7, 0.7
t_2	0.7, 0.7	0,0

Source: Blume et al. (1998).

observed their type and chose a preplay message from the set A,B. The receiver observed the message, but not the sender's type, and chose an action.

Game 1 is a game of common interest because both senders and receivers would prefer to have their types revealed to the receivers, so the receivers can match actions with types. Their paper describes an adaptive process which leads to an efficient separating equilibrium when there are two messages. That is, either type 1s send A and type 2s send B, or vice versa, and receivers come to know which message connotes which types, and choose action a_2 after the type 1 message and a_1 after the type 2 message. Converging to this kind of separation requires players to decide endogenously on a homemade language—either A will "mean" you are type 1 (and B means type 2) or B means you are type 1 and A means type 2.

Game 2 of Blume et al., shown in Table 7.11, complicates the situation by adding a secure action for receivers (a_3). Game 2 is still a common interest game in which players would prefer to find a meaningful language that indicates types and enables separation. Blume et al.'s adaptive process still predicts separation, as do most evolutionary theories.

In game 3 (see Table 7.12), senders would prefer to disguise their types so that receivers could not guess which type sent a message, and would choose a_3 (giving the senders .4) rather than gambling on guessing the type

Table 7.11.   *Payoffs in sender–receiver game 2 of Blume et al.*

	Receiver actions		
Sender types	a_1	a_2	a_3
t_1	0,0	0.7,0.7	0.4,0.4
t_2	0.7,0.7	0,0	0.4,0.4

Source: Blume et al. (1998).

Table 7.12. *Payoffs in sender–receiver game 3 of Blume et al.*

Sender types	Receiver actions		
	a_1	a_2	a_3
t_1	0,0	0.2,0.7	0.4,0.4
t_2	0.2,0.7	0,0	0.4,0.4

Source: Blume et al. (1998).

correctly and giving the senders only .2. The adaptive process still picks out the separating equilibrium when there are only two messages. A pooling equilibrium at a_3 cannot be sustained because it depends on both types of sender picking the same message (say, A). When one type trembles and chooses B, history-watching receivers who are active will detect that shred of revelation and respond to it (since guessing types correctly gives them a higher payoff), breaking the pooling equilibrium. Thus, when there are two messages the shrewd receivers can always use them to sort the types and separate.

Blume et al.'s experimental design required some ingenuity. Most subjects participated in a first session in which they played game 1 with messages A and B. The same subjects then participated in a second session in either game 2 with two messages or game 3 with either two or three messages. To disable any focal influence of their first-session experience, in the second session players chose messages from the set *, #, which were privately translated into A and B.

Table 7.13 shows results in periods 1, 5, 10, 15, and 20, pooled across sessions.[15] The table reports the percentages of plays consistent with separation, and the proportion of a_3 messages as an index of pooling. The results show a steady, sharp convergence toward separating in game 1 in the first session—players *are* able to create a meaningful language for expressing their types. Game 1NH is game 1 played with an own-history protocol in which players know only the history of their own matches. Without population history, convergence in 1NH to separation is sluggish; after twenty periods players separate only 72 percent of the time, about the same rate as players achieved in five periods with history. Game 2 play begins with about

---

[15] The results are standardized according to whichever message configuration emerged as the predominant one in period 20. Although this reporting convention understates the amount of temporary separation, it is the best way to show the time path of convergence to an equilibrium with a particular "meaning" that emerges later.

Table 7.13. *Percentage of plays consistent with separating in*
sender–receiver games 1 and 2 of Blume et al.

| | Period | | | | |
Game	1	5	10	15	20
First session					
Game 1	48	65	74	88	95
	(.14)	(.12)	(.17)	(.13)	(.07)
Second session					
Game 1	49	72	61	89	100
	(.28)	(.09)	(.19)	(.09)	(.00)
Game 1NH	55	55	28	55	72
	(.25)	(.09)	(.19)	(.09)	(.19)
Game 2					
Separating	44	88	88	88	94
	(.19)	(.09)	(.09)	(.09)	(.09)
Pooling	39	05	00	05	05
	(.25)	(.09)	(.00)	(.09)	(.09)

Source: Blume et al. (1998).
Note: Standard deviations are in parentheses.

equal amounts of separating and pooling, and moves toward separating,
more swiftly than in game 1.

Table 7.14 reports results from game 3 with two and three messages.
There is certainly a stronger tendency to pool (more than half) in the
divergent interest game 3 than in games 1 and 2. However, there is more
heterogeneity across sessions (masked by the averages shown in Table 7.14)
and there is greater separation in the session that followed game 1, which
suggests that the separation subjects were able to achieve in that game spilled
over to game 3.

A similar experiment on cheaptalk in sender-receiver games was done
by Kawagoe and Takizawa (1999). In their games a sender observes her type,
either 1 or 2 (equally likely), and sends one of the two messages "I am type
1" or "I am type 2." A receiver hears the message, but does not observe the
sender's type, and chooses an action A, B, or C. Payoffs for both sender
and receiver depend only on the sender's type and the receiver's action.
The messages are cheaptalk because they do not affect payoffs and are not
binding.

Table 7.14. Results in sender–receiver game 3 of Blume et al.

Number of messages	Behavior	Periods					
		1–10	11–20	21–30	31–40	41–50	51–60
Second session (after game 1)							
2	Separating	43	53	38	39		
	Pooling	33	34	41	43		
3	Separating	43	38	33	24		
	Pooling	33	37	42	60		
First session							
2	Separating	39	27	23	24	24	23
	Pooling	39	48	51	60	63	61
3	Separating	23	22	23	25	22	24
	Pooling	55	61	58	56	57	61

Source: Blume et al. (1999).

Kawagoe and Takizawa's games are designed to vary the degree of common interest and compare likely equilibria. Payoffs in three games are shown in Table 7.15. In game 1, senders and receivers have a common interest in revealing types, since senders will then choose A for type 1 and B for type 2, earning (4,4) rather than the pooling equilibrium outcome (3,3). The separating equilibrium outcomes and results are shown in bold.

Table 7.15. Sender–receiver games with cheaptalk

Sender's type	Receiver's action			Frequencies in sessions 1–3 (percent)		
	A	B	C	Separating	Babbling	Other
Game 1						
1	**4,4**	1,1	*3,3*	**86**	*11*	4
2	1,1	**4,4**	*3,3*			
Game 2						
1	**3,4**	2,1	*4,3*	**56**	*35*	9
2	2,1	**3,4**	*4,3*			
Game 3						
1	4,4	1,1	*2,3*	—	*40*	.60
2	3,1	2,4	*4,3*			

Source: Kawagoe and Takizawa (1999).

However, there is always a "babbling" equilibrium in which receivers do not think they have learned anything from the senders' messages, and choose C in response to either message; these pooling outcomes and results are marked in italics. In games where interests coincide (as in game 1), evolutionary dynamics typically lead to the separating equilibrium.

Game 2 reduces the degree of common interest, creating something akin to BOS. There is still a separating equilibrium in which types are revealed, yielding (3,4). Senders who think their message reveals their type do not want to be mislabeled (leading to a payoff of 2 rather than 3) so they should reluctantly reveal. However, the babbling equilibrium in which messages do not reveal types, and receivers choose C, gives a higher payoff to the senders (4) than the separating equilibrium does. In game 3, there is no separating equilibrium. The interesting question is whether the babbling equilibrium emerges strongly and, if not, what happens.

Message-action pairs for each subject pair were coded as separating equilibria if a type 1 (2) message led to action A (B). They were coded as babbling equilibria if receivers chose the action with the highest expected payoff given the prior type probabilities (i.e., C). The relative frequencies are shown in the right-hand columns of Table 7.15.[16] There was very sharp separation in the common interest game 1, around 80–90 percent. In game 2, there was substantial separation in the first session (66 percent) but it was reduced a lot, and babbling emerged, when the action labels were scrambled in the second session. In game 3, babbling did not emerge strongly, since only 30–55 percent of the choices were the predicted action C.

As in Blume et al. (1999), separating emerged strongly when sender and receiver interests coincided, and less strongly otherwise. Babbling did not emerge strongly when there was no separating equilibrium in game 3, but this fact can be explained by quantal response equilibrium.[17]

7.2.4 External Assignment

One interpretation of an equilibrium is a set of strategies that players would use, self-enforcingly, if an external arbiter recommended them. This definition suggests a straightforward experimental: Recommend or "assign" them in an experiment, and see what subjects do.

---

[16] No separating equilibrium statistics are reported for game 3 because there is no such equilibrium in that game.

[17] When the QRE response sensitivity λ is low, types 1 and 2 do not have an incentive to separate their messages because receivers respond so noisily that it doesn't matter which messages are chosen. When λ reaches a critical value, around 1, a noisy separating QRE emerges, in which type 1s (2s) choose A (B) about 90 percent of the time. Thus, QRE is able to suggest an explanation why Kawagoe and Takizawa *do not* find strong emergence of a babbling equilibrium. In this equilibrium, receivers play the action C only around 35–40 percent of the time, which fits the data (41 percent C) reasonably well.

Table 7.16.   *Results of assignments in games A, B, and C*

Game	Assignment	Choices (percent)		
		1	2	3
A payoffs		(5,5)	(5,5)	(5,5)
	None	30	51	19
	1	99	0	1
	2	1	99	0
	3	0	0	100
B payoffs		(9,9)	(5,5)	(1,1)
	None	97	2	1
	1	99	1	0
	2	51	48	1
	3	62	0	38
C payoffs		(7,3)	(5,5)	(3,7)
	None	10	82	8
	3 (row play)	1	63	35
	3 (column play)	0	54	46

Source: Van Huyck, Gillette, and Battalio (1992).

This is precisely what Van Huyck, Gillette, and Battalio (1992) did (see also Brandts and MacLeod, 1995). The games they used are shown in the top lines of each panel of Table 7.16. In all games, players chose strategies 1, 2, or 3 and earned nothing if they mismatched. Game A is a pure matching game where all payoffs (in multiples of $0.10) are (5,5). Game B has three (strict) equilibria which are Pareto ranked. Game C is like a BOS, with two asymmetric equilibria yielding (7,3) and (3,7), and an equilibrium with equal payoffs (5,5).

In periods with assignments, the experimenter chose one of the three strategies to assign. For strategy 1, for example, they said "Row choose row 1 and Column choose column 1. If the Row participant chooses row 1 then the best the Column participant can do is to choose column 1. If the Column participant chooses column 1 then the best the Row participant can do is to choose row 1."

Table 7.16 summarizes the results, aggregated across periods and sessions. In game A, with no assignment, subjects tended to choose the middle strategy 2 about half the time and split choices between 1 and 3 roughly equally. Hungry for a device to coordinate their choices, when one strategy is assigned they play it almost all the time (99–100 percent). Game B is different because the equilibria are Pareto ranked. When no assignment was made, subjects overwhelmingly chose the payoff-dominant strategy 1, which yielded (9,9) if both players chose it. When that strategy was assigned, they played it. When one of the Pareto-inferior strategies was assigned—2 or 3— they played the assigned strategy less than half the time.

In game C, when no assignment was made subjects tended to choose the (2,2) equilibrium yielding equal payoffs (5,5). When the strategy yielding unequal payoffs was assigned, slightly more than half continued to play the equal-payoff strategy and less than half played the assigned strategy. There was also a small self-serving asymmetry in row and column responses to the suggestion to play the strategy that yielded unequal payoffs: The column player, who benefited from the inequality, getting 7, followed the assignment 46 percent of the time, whereas the row player, who suffered by getting only 3, played it only 35 percent of the time.

Thus, assignment influences behavior strongly when it does not compete with another focal principle (in game A). But, when an assigned strategy conflicts with another focal principle—payoff-dominance (in game B) or equality of payoffs (in game C)—assignments are followed only half the time.

Suggestions by an outside authority of how to play coordination games often occur in economic and political life. For example, in 1966 Mao Tse-tung launched the Great Proletarian Cultural Revolution in Communist China. As part of the revolution (Kristof and WuDunn, 1994, p. 70), "For a time, cars were instructed to go forward at red lights and to stop at green, because red was a revolutionary color signifying action. That plan was dropped when not enough drivers got the message and pileups occurred at major intersections." As in experiments, an assignment that competes with another focal principle (in this example, historical precedent and automatic habit) does not necessarily work, even when recommended by one of the most authoritarian governments in the history of the world.

Traffic lights and communication are familiar examples of a "correlating device"—a publicly observable signal on which players can condition their strategies.[18] Correlating devices are useful in triggering collective action when tacit communication is cumbersome or even illegal. For example, in recent years there have been large-scale riots (often causing widespread injury and destruction) after both sports losses and *victories* (e.g., after the 2000 Los Angeles Lakers world championship win). One interpretion of these events is that some groups of people would like to riot, but don't want

---

[18] Conditioning strategy choices on correlating devices leads to "correlated equilibrium," an interesting generalization of a Nash equilibrium that captures the essence of many coordination problems.

to get caught. The end of a sport game—regardless of whether the outcome makes the hometown crowd happy or sad—is a good correlating device because it has sharp timing and is widely heard, like a pistol shot starting a race.

Another example: During the 2001 power crisis in California, state investigators claimed that a cartel of power companies created "artificial shortages" by taking plants off-line (allegedly for routine maintenance and so forth) when the state issued emergency alerts that more power was needed (*Los Angeles Times*, 2001). To a game theorist, it is obvious that the emergency alerts might have served as a correlating device that enabled firms to conspire by removing capacity, spiking prices sharply upward. Like sports outcomes, the emergency alerts were widely publicized and sharply timed—ideal properties in a correlating device.

7.2.5 Timing

Early in the history of game theory, von Neumann and Morgenstern made a deliberate choice to emphasize only information known at decision nodes. They reasoned that, if you did not know what another player did, you should not care whether that player had already moved, was moving just when you did, or was moving later.

More recently, several game theorists have wondered whether timing, per se, might act as a selection principle in games such as BOS, even without affecting the information players have. The first to take this idea seriously were Amershi, Sadanand, and Sadanand (1989, 1992); they introduced a generalization of Nash equilibrium that incorporated the principle that early-moving players would make choices assuming later-moving players would realize they were moving later. They also reported an informal pilot experiment showing this effect in BOS. Kreps (1990, p. 112) conjectured this effect as well and several experiments have replicated its existence and studied its cause (e.g., Rapoport, 1997; Colman and Stirk, 1998; Weber and Camerer, 2001).

Cooper et al. looked for the effect of timing in BOS. In their treatment, it was common knowledge that Row players went first, but also that Column players didn't know what Row did. The results are shown in row BOS-SEQ in Table 7.9. The mismatch rate was 34 percent, about half as large as in the timing-free BOS baseline, and 62 percent of the time the players together chose (1,2). Simply knowing that Row was moving first led pairs to move about halfway to Row's preferred equilibrium. This remarkable effect of timing overturns Von Neumann and Morgenstern's presumption.

Rapoport (1997) explored the effect of timing on perceived first-mover advantage. He studied three-player BOS games. Half the players used the

Table 7.17.   *Mean requests in sequential resource dilemmas*

	Position of player				
Previous moves	1	2	3	4	5
Known (sequential)	172	135	125	104	102
Unknown (positional)	139	122	116	103	102

Source: Rapoport (1997).

position in which people had played—though they did not observe earlier moves—to coordinate behavior on the equilibrium the first-mover preferred. Rapoport also experimented with resource dilemmas with uncertain resource totals. In these games, five players sequentially requested resources from some pool uniformly distributed between $[a, b]$. Players did not know the precise amount of resources available, but the distribution $U(a, b)$ was commonly known. If the total of their requests was larger than the amount of resource, nobody got anything; otherwise they got what they requested.[19] To test for timing, some subjects participated in a "sequential protocol" in which each player's request was known to players who made later requests. Others played under a "positional protocol" in which they moved in a specified order (their positions were known) but later movers did *not* know what earlier movers had done.

Table 7.17 summarizes the average requests in the two conditions, by players' positions in the sequence. Timing played a strong role in the sequential protocol (as predicted by subgame perfection) and a weaker, but highly significant role in the positional protocol. The gap between the first and last players' requests was roughly half as large in the positional case as in the sequential case.[20] Timing, per se, matters.

Rapoport (1997) also reports effects of pure timing in "threshold public goods games" in which a public good was provided if three out of seven players contributed. This game is like BOS because there are many equilibria—every combination of any three players contributing is an equilibrium. Rapoport tested whether players used order of moves as a correlating device to coordinate on equilibria in which the first-movers got to free ride,

---

[19] This game, which has been widely studied, is a player asymmetric coordination game like BOS, but with many more equilibria and nonzero payoffs for "mismatched" nonequilbrium strategy vectors. It is also called the "Nash demand game" (when $a = b$) and has been studied in bargaining.

[20] Rapoport also asked players to estimate how much the players playing *previously* had given, and how much players playing *subsequently* would give. Estimates of previous requests did show an effect of position, but estimates of subsequent requests did not. This asymmetry suggests that players are able to reason backward in time better than they can forecast ahead in time.

and later movers picked up the slack by contributing (even though earlier moves were not known for sure). The fractions of players contributing across the five positions were 0.15, 0.11, 0.29, 0.44, 0.32, and 0.40, so there was a strong positional effect (although it took a couple of trials to emerge).

Summary: Battle-of-the-sexes (BOS) games are the consummate mixed-motive games: Both players desire to coordinate on *some* joint outcome, but each prefers a different coordinated outcome. (Imagine choosing a movie or restaurant with your spouse.) Players tend to choose somewhere between random mixing and the mixed-strategy equilibrium (which yields many mismatches, and is less efficient than agreeing on *either* of the coordinated outcomes). Having one player announce in advance their intended choice helps a lot (the announcing player gets their preferred outcome); simultaneous announcements are not much help. Other changes in the game can improve coordination. It helps if one player has an outside option that is preferable to their inferior BOS equilibrium (then, rejecting the option and playing the BOS signals their intent to choose the preferable equilibrium, a logic known as "forward induction"). Most surprisingly, if one player moves first, *even if the second-mover does not know what the first-mover has done*, the two players tend to coordinate on the first-mover's preferred outcome, so there is a tacit—almost telepathic—first-mover advantage. Having an external "assignment" (e.g., by an experimenter, a laboratory "body double" for a government, regulatory influence, or media announcement) can also improve coordination.

Finally, some experiments have explored endogenous development of meaning. Players with different types choose announcements from a random language. When it pays for players to reveal their types they find a language that does so (i.e., one type announces one message and the other type announces a different message), but when sender and receiver players have different incentives the results are mixed.

7.3 Market Entry Games

An important class of coordination games involves entry into markets and competitions. In a typical model, there are n players and a market with capacity c. (It is easy to generalize to more than one market, and a few experiments have explored multiple markets.) Entrants earn a return which declines with the number of entrants, and is negative if more than c enter. How firms (and workers) coordinate their entry decisions in domains such as this is important for the economy. If there is too little entry, prices are too high and consumers suffer; if there is too much entry, some firms lose money and waste resources if fixed costs are unsalvageable. Public announcements of planned entry could, in principle, coordinate the right amount of entry, but announcements may not be credible because firms that *may* enter always have an incentive to announce that they surely will do so, to ward off competition. Government planning may help but is vulnerable to regulatory capture by prospective entrants seeking to limit competition.

A dramatic example in which tacit coordination failed miserably is the production of high-capacity optic cable. Too many firms laid too much cable, which is so powerful that it would take a huge expansion in use to soak up all the capacity. As the *Los Angeles Times* reported (2002):

> The cables were laid by a band of upstart companies that spent $50 billion or more in the last few years to wire the planet. . . . These upstarts bet that if they built communications networks with far more capacity, or bandwidth, than had ever been available before customers would rush to use them. . . . The problem was that too many companies had the same dream, and they built too many digital toll roads to the same destination. . . . "People have laid huge amounts of fiber in the ground," said Internet analyst Tony Marson of Probe Research Inc., "and there is a distinct possibility that quite a lot of that will never actually see any traffic."

The optic cable industry is a failure of independent firms to coordinate the right amount of entry (or perhaps a collective forecasting mistake), but other evidence suggests that errors in planning entry are common. Field studies of business entry and exit find that *most* new businesses (and plant openings by established businesses) fail, and usually fail rapidly. (For example, about 80 percent of new restaurants fail within a year.) This stylized fact suggests there is too much entry. However, since the relatively few successful entrants are often hugely successful, firm profits have a long positive "right tail" or skew. So entrants may be maximizing *expected* profits even if the failure rate is high.

Since the process by which firms coordinate entry is not well understood, and field evidence tentatively suggests too much entry, experiments are useful (see Ochs, 1999, for a review).

The first experiments on single-market games were conducted by Kahneman (1988). He was surprised that the number of players who chose to enter was very close to the number predicted by theory (i.e., around c entrants), even though the players all made their choices at the same time and could not communicate or learn from feedback. "To a psychologist," he wrote, "it looks like magic."

Rapoport (1995) created a simple single-market design and did experiments with Ph.D. students playing over several weeks. He has subsequently explored the design with various colleagues under more controlled laboratory conditions.

Denote player i's entry decision by e_i, 1 for entry and 0 for non-entry. Payoffs are v if a player stays out and $k + r(c - m)$ for entrants, where $m = \sum_{j=1}^{n} e_j$. Sundali, Rapoport, and Seale (1995) did experiments in which $v = k = 1$ and $r = 2$. Since capacity is c, the pure-strategy equilibria are for c or $c - 1$ players to enter (the marginal cth entrant is indifferent). There is also a symmetric mixed equilibrium in which players enter with probability $[r(c - 1) + k - v]/r(n - 1)$.

In their experiment, groups of twenty players made a series of simultaneous one-shot entry decisions with ten different capacity values c—the odd integers 1, 3, . . . , 19. In most experiments subjects were told how many others decided to enter after each decision. In each block they played once with each of the ten capacities, and to allow learning they played six such blocks.

Table 7.18 shows the results from the Sundali et al. experiment and from several others. In the first block, the number of entries rose erratically with capacity c, and there were too many entries at low c and too few at high c. But subjects learn fast: Pooling across blocks, the number of entries was never more than two different than the number predicted by the mixed equilibrium for all capacities c.

Rapoport, Seale, Erev, and Sundali (1998) varied the nonentry payoff v (keeping the other payoff parameters constant). When $v = 6$ many fewer players should enter than when $v = 1$ (fixing capacity c) and when $v = -6$ more should enter. Table 7.18 shows that players did respond to changes in v but, as in the earlier experiments, there was some over-entry at low c and under-entry at high c.

Seale and Rapoport (2000) used the strategy method, eliciting entry decisions for each value of c in one fell swoop. The overall entry rates were similar to those observed from asking for entry decisions for each c separately. Furthermore, the c-dependent strategies show little regularity or stability. One hypothesis about how effective coordination comes about is that players use cutoff rules, entering for some threshold capacity c^*, but variation in cutoffs generates a population profile that roughly matches the equilibrium prediction. However, the direct measurement of strategies shows that few are sharp cutoff rules.

Rapoport, Seale, and Winter (2002) experimented with an asymmetric game in which players paid different costs to enter. There were five types of players, numbered 1 through 5, and players of type (number) i paid a cost i to enter. Different costs are interesting because they imply asymmetric equilibria in which high-cost players should enter less often than low-cost players. For example, in their design low-cost players should *always* enter when $c = 9$ or above and high-cost players should *never* enter until $c = 19$. Overall entry was close to the rate predicted by equilibrium but players were remarkably insensitive to costs. Low-cost players did not enter often enough and high-cost players entered too often.

Table 7.18.   *Number of entries in market entry games*

Study	Data	Market capacity c									
		1	3	5	7	9	11	13	15	17	19
	MSE equilibrium	0	2.1	4.2	6.3	8.4	10.5	12.6	14.7	16.8	18.9
Sundali, Rapoport, and Seale (1995), $v = 1$											
Experiment 2	First block	1.3	5.7	9.7	6.7	3.7	14.0	11.3	11.3	16.0	18.0
	All blocks	1.0	3.7	5.1	7.4	8.7	11.2	12.1	14.1	16.5	18.2
Seale and Rapoport (2001), $v = 1$											
(Strategy	First block	3.7	5.7	6.2	7.0	7.7	10.2	11.0	12.2	12.7	13.9
method)	All blocks	1.9	4.1	5.1	6.8	7.6	10.9	12.5	13.5	15.1	16.0
Rapoport, Seale, and Winter (2002), $v = 1$, asymmetric entry cost											
	Pure equilibrium	0	2	4	5–6	7–8	9	11	12–13	14–15	16
	Total	0.6	2.1	4.0	6.0	8.0	9.6	11.0	13.0	14.3	16.1
	Low cost = 1 (max. 4)	0	0.3	0.8	1.2	1.5	2.0	2.6	3.3	3.4	3.4
	High cost = 5 (max. 4)	0.1	0.2	0.1	0.7	1.1	1.1	1.5	1.7	1.6	2.1
Rapoport et al. (1998), $v = -6$											
	Capacity	1	3	5	7	8	9	10	12	14	16
	MSE equilibrium	3.7	5.8	7.9	10.0	11.1	12.1	13.2	15.3	17.4	19.5
	First block	4.0	9.0	9.0	9.0	9.0	15.0	9.0	17.0	17.0	18.0
	All blocks	5.2	9.0	8.6	10.2	10.8	12.8	12.2	14.6	16.0	18.4
Rapoport et al. (1998), $v = 6$											
	Capacity	4	6	8	10	11	12	14	16	18	20
	MSE equilibrium	0.5	2.6	4.8	6.8	7.9	8.9	11.1	13.2	15.3	17.4
	First block	4.0	5.0	6.0	4.0	9.0	11.0	10.0	14.0	16.0	15.0
	All blocks	2.2	4.2	7.8	7.0	10.0	10.2	11.8	13.4	15.0	16.8

In Rapoport, Seale, and Ordóñez (2002), the nonentry payoff was a lottery (see also Rapoport, Lo, and Zwick, in press). Results were like those in earlier studies: Entry rates were close to those predicted, with over-entry at low c and under-entry at high c, and can be fit by a nonlinear transformation of probability (as is common in nonexpected utility theories; e.g., Prelec, 1998).

Rapoport and Erev (1998) ran experiments with $c = 4$ and 8 and varied information conditions, in order to compare learning models. When subjects did not know the payoff function, but got feedback about either their own payoff or the payoffs from both entering and not entering, learning was slow: Even after twenty periods with the same value of c, the number of entries was one or two away from equilibrium. Knowing the payoff function improved the speed and accuracy of convergence. The differences in speed of convergence with information show that models which assume players respond only to payoffs from chosen strategies can be improved by adding information about forgone payoffs from unchosen strategies (cf. Chapter 6).

7.3.1 *Multiple Markets*

Meyer et al. (1992) studied entry in two markets. Each of six subjects supplied a single unit to either market A or market B. Prices in each market were equal to $1.05 divided by the number of units of supply. In a pure equilibrium, players would coordinate to supply three units in each market; in the symmetric mixed equilibrium they should randomize equally over the two markets. Meyer et al. were motivated by concerns about how well decentralized allocations works. (Their example corresponds to a famous example of Marshall's in which fishermen deliver their catch to one of two islands; do quantities adjust to satisfy the law of one price?)

The total supply to market A fluctuated around three units, and did not converge in fifteen or even sixty periods. Even when subjects hit upon the even (3–3) allocation of units in one of the first few periods, they did not stick to that allocation. Why not? Subjects appeared to be roughly randomizing each period (though they repeated their previous choice more often than is predicted by random mixing). However, sharp convergence to the equal-allocation equilibrium did occur under two conditions: when subjects were experienced (i.e., they returned for a second experimental session); and when they announced their entry decisions sequentially and were allowed to change their choices.

Rapoport, Seale, and Winter (2000) ran experiments in which subjects could enter either of two markets, or sit out and earn a small return. When the two markets had the same capacity, entry decisions were close to equilibrium (except for the familiar bias of over entry at low c). When the markets had different capacities, however, initial decisions were wildly far from equilibrium at first, but converged rather closely over ten blocks.

Samuelson (1996) studied entry in market games with asymmetric information about costs. In his experiments, if there are x entrants and n players, then entrant i earns $\pi(x) - c_i = a - bx - c_i$, where c_i is entrant i's cost, drawn independently from some commonly known interval. The profit function and the number of players vary, to test whether actual entry is sensitive to these factors as predicted by equilibrium. In each case there is a symmetric cutoff equilibrium in which players with costs below a cutoff c^* enter and players with costs above the threshold stay out. For example, when the cost interval is $[1,2]$ and $\pi(x) = 2.8 - .08x$, and $n = 2$ players, the cutoff $c^* = 1.56$ (assuming risk-neutrality).[21] In the experiment, cutoff strategies were elicited explicitly. Results for several one-shot games with different numbers of players and profit functions, and hence different equilibrium values of c^*, are reported in Table 7.19.

The average cutoff values were remarkably close to those predicted by theory, although always slightly below (usually significantly so). Mean cutoff values tracked changes across treatments. An interesting case is the three middle data columns of Table 7.19, showing cutoff values from a two-period game with $n = 2$. In the two-period game the equilibrium cutoff in the first period is $c^* = 1.61$. In the second period, the equilibrium cutoff changes because subjects should learn something about other players' costs from their first-period behavior. When both subjects in a pair enter in the first period ("after both"), each should think the other's cost is low. Since the other player, if rational, will be likely to enter again in the second period, players should be hesitant to enter again unless their costs are quite low (below 1.43, a lower cutoff than the original 1.61). In fact, entry cutoffs did drop substantially in the second period after both entered (to a mean of 1.28). When neither subject enters in the first period ("after none"), subjects should be more likely to enter in the second round, raising the equilibrium cutoff to 1.74. However, the cutoff distribution after neither entered was very similar to the first-period distribution. As Samuelson notes, the failure of the other player to enter after nonentry is like the "dog that didn't bark" in a famous Sherlock Holmes story (the dog's *failure* to bark suggested an intruder knew the dog). Subjects appeared to learn less from observed nonentry than they did from observed double entry.[22]

7.3.2 Skill

The experiments described above all exclude an important feature of entry in many markets: skill. In most naturally occurring markets, entrants do not earn the same amount of money. Profits differ because of differences in costs, the ability to anticipate customer demand, and so forth. Adding skill is also important because efficient entry requires firms to anticipate their *relative* skill accurately. But many surveys and experiments indicate that av-

---

[21] At that cutoff, a player can expect no other entrant with probability .44, and earns $2.0 - c_i$ if she enters, and expects one other entrant with probability .56, and earns $1.2 - c_i$ if she enters. Since expected profits are $.56(1.2) + .44(2.0) - c_i$, or $1.56 - c_i$, she earns a tiny positive expected profit if she enters when costs are 1.56 or below.

[22] This asymmetry in learning from entry and failure-to-enter seems related to a principle in mental representations of logic problems, that people fail to explicitly represent what is false, which can lead to dramatic logical errors (see Johnson-Laird, 1994).

Table 7.19. *Cumulative frequency of entry at each cost or below in games with private costs and n players*

off cost val	$\pi(x) = 2.8 - .8x$					$\pi(x) = 2.1 - 0.2x$	$\pi(x) = 3.3 - 0.2$
		n = 2, two-period games					
				Period 2			
	n = 2	n = 4	Period 1	After both	After none	n = 11	
	0.98	0.82	0.98	0.97	0.97	0.84	0.97
	0.98	0.78	0.94	0.97	0.96	0.74	0.97
	0.90	**0.42**	0.88	0.48	0.92	**0.53**	0.94
	0.88	0.18	0.82	**0.26**	0.86	0.19	0.91
	0.74	0.12	0.74	0.20	0.78	0.11	0.86
	0.44	0.04	**0.40**	0.10	0.53	0.08	0.73
	0.00	0.04	0.00	0.04	**0.19**	0.00	**0.52**
2.0	0.00	0.00	0.00	0.00	0.04	0.03	0.31
librium	1.56	1.29	1.61	1.43	1.74	1.30	1.70
n	1.49	1.21	1.50	1.28	1.53	1.25	1.68
dard deviation	0.135	0.143	0.139	0.136	0.161	0.178	0.200
t	-3.59	-4.04	-5.74	-7.76	-8.77	-1.61	-0.63

e: Samuelson (1996).
Entries are cumulative frequencies of players choosing to enter at each cost level or below. *t*-test tests whether the me
nificantly different from the equilibrium prediction. If players are risk neutral and choose equilibrium strategies, entri
ld should be 1.0.

erage people are persistently overconfident about their relative abilities and life prospects. If firms overestimate their ability to deliver a good product, and confident firms choose to enter, there may be too much entry.

Camerer and Lovallo (1999) modified the standard paradigm to allow skill and overconfidence about skill. In their design the top c entrants shared a portion of $50 according to their *rank*.[23] Entrants below the top c lost $10. To mimic the usual design in which skill doesn't matter, in a random-rank condition ranks were determined randomly. In a skill-rank condition ranks were determined by how well subjects did in a trivia quiz. It is crucial to note that the random ranks and the trivia ranks were determined *after* subjects made all their entry decisions.

On average, about two more subjects (out of fourteen) entered when their payoff depended on relative skill than when it was random. Subjects also forecast how many others would enter (and were rewarded for accuracy), and their forecasts were quite accurate. This fact is important because it means subjects entered knowing full well that many others would enter too.

Lovallo and I also studied a phenomenon called "reference group neglect." This is illustrated by a quotation from Joe Roth, the former chairman of Disney movie studios. When asked why so many big-budget movies are released at the same time (rather than avoiding direct competition), Roth said (*Los Angeles Times*, 1996, p. F8), "Hubris. If you only think about your own business, you think, 'I've got a good story department. I've got a good marketing department, we're going to go out and do this.' And you don't think that everybody else is thinking the same thing." To study this phenomenon, when recruiting for the experiment we told subjects that their earnings would depend on how skilled they were at trivia. When the subjects arrived in the lab we reminded them of what they were told when they were recruited. We hypothesized that subjects would not adjust for the fact that other subjects self-selected to participate because they thought they were good at trivia too. In these sessions, there was far too much entry in the skill-rank condition. In 70 percent of the periods, so many subjects entered that, as a group, they *guaranteed* themselves a collective loss.[24]

This experiment shows that overconfidence about relative skill may influence entry decisions. Subjects also easily neglected the fact that their competition was self-selected based on perceptions of skill, and subjects in this condition entered far too often. A single experiment is no proof that businesses fail owing to overconfidence, but it is suggestive and, most importantly, offers an experimental paradigm in which to investigate further.

---

[23] The i-th ranked entrant earned $(c - i + 1)/(0.5c(c + 1))$ times $50.

[24] Since the top c entrants earned $50, and lower-ranked entrants lost $10, if more than $c + 5$ entered then they would lose money as a group.

Summary: In market entry games, initial entries into a single market are often remarkably close to those predicted by the symmetric mixed equilibrium, and convergence is rather sharp after learning. Players tend to slightly over-enter at low capacities and under-enter at high capacities. (These stylized facts can be explained by QRE and some models of limited thinking; see Goeree and Holt, 2000b, and Camerer, Ho, and Chong, 2001.) In multiple markets, however, entry decisions are much further from equilibrium, and in one experiment (Meyer et al., 1992) did not converge at all unless subjects were experienced. When the payoffs of entrants depend on their relative skill (at trivia), overconfidence leads players to over-enter so dramatically that, in many periods, the players as a whole are sure to lose money.

7.4 Payoff-Asymmetric Order-Statistic Games

In payoff-asymmetric coordination games, players' outcomes are the same in equilibrium, but equilibria are different. An important set of games in this class, which have been well studied, are "order-statistic games." In order-statistic games, players choose numbers and their payoff depends on their own choice and on an order statistic (such as the minimum or the median) of all the numbers.

One well-known order-statistic game is called "stag hunt" (also called "Wolf's Dilemma" by Hofstadter, 1985; see Huettel and Lockhead, 2000, for a psychological perspective). Stag hunt is named after a story in Jean-Jacques Rousseau illustrating the benefits of coordination. Two hunters can hunt for rabbit, earning 1 each, or together hunt for stag and earn 2. But since a single hunter can't catch a stag, he earns 0 unless the other hunter hunts for stag too. The Lamalera whale hunters of Indonesia actually play this sort of game all the time (Alvard, 2000). Hunting whale requires a team—a captain, a navigator, a spotter, and daring men willing to stand on the prow of a boat and throw a harpoon. A team that sails out one person short has much less chance of success. But whale hunters can always stay ashore and hunt small game or socialize. Roughly speaking, whale hunters prefer hunting whale if enough others join the expedition, but prefer to stay home and hunt on their own if the crew is short-handed.

Payoffs in a stylized stag hunt game are shown in Table 7.20. In stag hunt, (stag,stag) is a pure-strategy Nash equilibrium but (rabbit,rabbit) is also. This is an order-statistic game because, if strategies are defined as numbers, stag $\equiv 1$ and rabbit $\equiv 0$, then the payoffs depend on the minimum of the two numbers.[25] Stag hunt is also called an "assurance game" because players will

---

[25] That is, payoffs can be written as $\pi_i(s_i^j, s_{-i}^k) = 1 + 2 \cdot \min(s_i^j, s_{-i}^k) - s_i^j$.

Table 7.20.   *Stag hunt*
(assurance game)

	Stag	Rabbit
Stag	2,2	0,1
Rabbit	1,0	1,1

choose stag only if they are assured others are likely to choose stag as well. In stag hunt, strategic uncertainty arises from the conflict between the players' common motive—to somehow coordinate on (stag,stag) and earn 2 each— and the private motive to avoid the risk of getting 0 if the other person plays rabbit.

Stag hunt illustrates basic selection principles in action. The (stag,stag) equilibrium is payoff dominant, or Pareto dominant, because it is better for everyone than (rabbit,rabbit). Playing rabbit is "secure," or maximin, because it has the highest possible guaranteed (minimum) payoff. A risk-dominant equilibrium is one that minimizes players' joint risk, measured by the product of the cost of deviations by other players to any one player who does not deviate (Harsanyi and Selten, 1988). For example, if players think the equilibrium is (stag,stag) and play stag, then when another player deviates, the cost to the player who sticks to the equilibrium is $(2 - 0)$ or 2, and the product of these costs is 4. But if players think the equilibrium is (rabbit,rabbit) and play rabbit, then it costs them nothing if others deviate. Therefore, (rabbit,rabbit) is risk dominant.

Another idea which can be used as a selection principle is a QRE or noisy Nash equilibrium. In n-player stag hunt games with continuous strategies— you can choose a "degree" of hunting for stag—Anderson, Goeree, and Holt (1996) showed that there is a unique QRE. Thus, QRE is a kind of selection principle. When the cost of exerting higher effort (hunting for stag) rises, or the number of players rises, then players will be less likely to hunt for stag. As we will see below, these predictions match the experimental results, so QRE shows some promise for explaining these data and others.

Stag hunt is important because many games that are thought to be prisoners' dilemmas (PD) are actually coordination games such as stag hunt. For example, suppose players contribute to a public good but they can be excluded from consuming a public good (or fined for imposing negative externalities on others), or there are synergies from producing joint output. Suppose the cost of contributing is $c < 1$, the public good is worth P if one person contributes and $P + s$ if two contribute, and a noncontributer gets only $(1 - e)$ of the public good. Then payoffs are those shown in Table 7.21. For this game, (contribute,contribute) is a Nash equilibrium if and only if $P + s - c > P(1 - e)$, or $c < s + Pe$. This condition holds if s and e are

Table 7.21. *Public good contribution with synergy and exclusion*

	Contribute	Don't contribute
Contribute	$P + s - c, P + s - c$	$P - c, P(1 - e)$
Don't contribute	$P(1 - e), P - c$	$0, 0$

large enough. Thus, if there is enough excludability (high e) and synergy in producing the public good (high s), the public good game is actually a game of stag hunt.

Similarly, if players in a PD have homemade reciprocal social values, as in the Rabin (1993) fairness equilibrium (see Chapter 2), then cooperating is an equilibrium because somebody cooperating with me is nice, and I repay their niceness by cooperating as well. Furthermore, it is a well-known consequence of the "folk theorem" about repeated games that, if a PD is repeated with a high enough discount factor, the repeated-PD game has multiple equilibria, which can "implement" or achieve the highest possible joint payoff. Seen this way, many situations in the world that are classified as PDs are really games of coordinating on repeated-game strategies with stag hunt properties. If a PD is likely enough to be repeated, evokes emotion, or has enough synergy or excludability, it is really a stag hunt game.

Stag hunt is also the building block of economic situations with "strategic complementarities." Strategic complementarities are present when the marginal productivity of one player's strategy choice rises with the level of another's strategy choice. An example is "spatial externalities" in which firms would like to locate near one another. Locating nearby often enables a common supplier to achieve scale economies (by building a larger mine or factory, to sell to many clients). Spatial proximity also creates liquid or "thick" markets, which are useful when products are differentiated. Then many merchants come to the market because they are more likely to find a buyer for their goods, which in turn draws more buyers and fulfills the market's forecast success. (Think Ebay.) Sometimes the crucial markets are labor markets for talented workers (as in Silicon Valley or Hollywood).

Coordination games of this sort have also been studied in macroeconomics as a basis for neo-Keynesian business cycles (e.g., Bryant, 1983; Romer, 1996, Chapter 6). In full-employment equilibria, workers are employed, so they spend, which creates demand for products and keeps them employed. But if workers fear a recession, they will cut back spending, causing layoffs and fulfilling their fearful prophecy. Summers (2000) explicitly describes a stag hunt game as a model of the economic fragility of borrowers in emerging markets such as Indonesia. He writes (p. 7):

Imagine that everyone who has invested $10 with me can expect to earn $1, assuming that I stay solvent. Suppose that if I go bankrupt, investors who remain lose their whole $10 investment, but that an investor who withdraws today neither gains nor loses. . . . Suppose, first, that my foreign reserves, ability to mobilize resources, and economic strengths are so limited that if any investor withdraws, I will go bankrupt. It would be a Nash equilibrium (indeed, a Pareto-dominant one) for everyone to remain, but (I expect) not an attainable one. Someone would reason that someone else would decide to be cautious and withdraw, or at least that someone would reason that someone would reason that someone would withdraw, and so forth . . . I think that this thought experiment captures something real. On the one hand, bank runs or their international analogues do happen. On the other hand, they are not driven by sunspots: their likelihood is driven and determined by extent of fundamental weakness.

A formal way to capture the effects of the strategic uncertainty Summers describes is called "global games" (Carlsson and Van Damme, 1993; Morris and Shin, 2000). In a global game, the precise payoffs in the game are drawn from some interval, so each player isn't sure exactly what the other player's payoffs are. If the set of possible games is connected in a precise way, and one set of possible payoffs yields a dominated strategy, iterated application of dominance can lead to the risk-dominant equilibrium in stag hunt. This gives a precise way to express why a little uncertainty about what others might do (in the form of uncertainty about their payoffs, and hence behavior) can lead players to an inefficient equilibrium even when, as in Summers' example, the result is a small-scale economic catastrophe. Cabrales, Nagel, and Armenter (2001) ran experiments that support the prediction of the global games view, though the iterated process of convergence happens slowly.

7.4.1 Experimental Evidence

An elegant series of experiments on stag hunt were done by Cooper et al. (1990). Their payoffs are shown in Table 7.22. (Points were units of probability, with 1,000 points guaranteeing a win of $1.)

Data from the last eleven periods of their experiments are shown in line "CG" of Table 7.23. The inefficient equilibrium (1,1) exerts a strong pull on the subject population: 97 percent played (1,1) and *none* played the payoff-dominant equilibrium (2,2).

As with their BOS experiments, Cooper et al. experimented with two outside option treatments to test forward induction. In CG-900, the row player could opt out and award both players 900 instead of playing the stag

Table 7.22. *Stag hunt payoffs in Cooper et al.*

	1	2
1	800,800	800,0
2	0,800	1000,1000

Source: Cooper et al. (1990).

hunt game. Forward induction worked most of the time (77 percent) when players opted in; but players opted out almost half the time. CG-700 tests whether the mere presence of an outside option, even one that is dominated by a matrix strategy, has any effect (as it did in BOS). The option had two small effects: Strangely, 12 percent of row players chose the option (earning 700 instead of the 800 they could have guaranteed by opting in and playing strategy 1); and, when they rejected the option and played the matrix game, 82 percent went to the inefficient (1,1) equilibrium.

The effects of cheaptalk are explored in treatments CG-1W and CG-2W. With one-way communication by the row player, the level of efficient (2,2) play is increased from nothing to 53 percent. Communication fills the glass of efficiency half full, but also leaves it half empty. Communication

Table 7.23. *Stag hunt results: Last eleven periods*

Game	Outside option	(1,1)	(2,2)	(1,2) or (2,1)	Total
CG	—	160	0	5	165
		(97%)	(0%)	(3%)	
CG-900	65	2	77	21	165
		(2%)	(77%)	(21%)	
CG-700	20	119	0	26	165
		(82%)	(0%)	(18%)	
CG-1W	—	26	88	51	165
		(16%)	(53%)	(31%)	
CG-2W	—	0	150	15	165
		(0%)	(91%)	(9%)	

Source: Cooper et al. (1994).

Note: Numbers in parentheses refer to proportions of play in the subgame of the outside option treatments.

works only half-way because, after an announcement of intended play of 2, both players actually play 2 only about 80 percent of the time. [26] Two-way communication, however, worked like a charm. In the last eleven periods, *every* pair of players announced the intention to play (2,2), and in 91 percent of the cases both actually did.

Notice the contrast between the effects of one- and two-way communication in BOS and in stag hunt. In BOS the central problem is to resolve the asymmetry between players' preferences, which mixes their motives. One-way communication resolves this conflict (in favor of the speaker) and improves efficiency from 40 percent to almost 100 percent. Moving to two-way communication is a half-step backward because it often restores the conflict, lowering overall efficiency back down to 60 percent. In stag hunt, the problem is not resolution of the asymmetry, but providing both players with enough assurance that the other player will take the risky efficient action. One-way communication provides halfway assurance, raising efficiency to 50 percent, and two-way communication provides fuller assurance, raising efficiency further to 91 percent. Too much communication hurts in BOS, and too little hurts in stag hunt.

The stag hunt results suggest that efficiency is difficult for subjects to achieve without preplay options or explicit communication. How much does this result depend on payoffs? Straub (1995) collected data from several variants of stag hunt to answer this question. The payoffs change the number p, the probability that a player would have to attach to his partner playing the payoff-dominant action to be just indifferent to playing either action. This is an index of the "risk" inherent in playing the efficient action (and also corresponds to the mixed-strategy equilibrium proportion of playing the efficient action and the size of the "basin of attraction" from which an evolving population will be drawn to inefficiency).

When p is .8 or .75, the population converges to the inefficient outcome. But when the break-even probability p drops to .67, play converges to the *efficient* outcome. There appears to be a sharp flash point somewhere between $p = .67$ and $p = .75$, which determines which equilibrium results.

---

[26] Why do row players announce 2 then play 1? One possibility is that some row players prefer the outcome (800,0) to the outcome (1000,1000) because they like the status advantage of earning more than the player they are paired with, even though they earn less (and, hence, less than many other subjects in the same room) as a result. Such status-seeking row players might be suckering column players in, inducing the Columns to play 2 so they can achieve the (800,0) payoff they desire. Although this behavior may be part of the story (see also Weber and Camerer, 2001), the fact that we rarely see announcements of 2 and choices of 1 in the two-way communication treatment suggests that imperfections in one-way communication are due to failures of nerve or residual strategic uncertainty, rather than systematic status-seeking.

Table 7.24. *Weak-link game payoffs in Van Huyck et al.*

Your choice of X	Smallest value of X chosen (including own)						
	7	6	5	4	3	2	1
7	1.30	1.10	0.90	0.70	0.50	0.30	0.10
6	—	1.20	1.00	0.80	0.60	0.40	0.20
5	—	—	1.10	0.90	0.70	0.50	0.30
4	—	—	—	1.00	0.80	0.60	0.40
3	—	—	—	—	0.90	0.70	0.50
2	—	—	—	—	—	0.80	0.60
1	—	—	—	—	—	—	0.70

Source: Van Huyck, Battalio, and Beil (1990).

7.4.2 Weak-Link Games

The two-person stag hunt is an example of the more general "weak-link" game studied by Van Huyck, Battalio, and Beil (1990). In these games, each of n players chooses an integer x_i from a set (say, 1 to 7). Their payoff increases with the minimum of all the numbers chosen, and decreases with the deviation of their own choices from the minimum. In the payoff table used by Van Huyck et al., the payoff from choosing x_i is $\$0.60 + 0.10 \cdot \min_i(x_1, x_2, \ldots, x_7) - 0.10 \cdot [x_i - \min_i(x_1, x_2, \ldots, x_7)]$ (see Table 7.24).

The weak-link game models situations in which a group's payoff is sensitive to the "weakest link" in some productive chain. Economists will recognize this property as a feature of Cobb–Douglas production functions with large exponents (or Leontief). A common example is production of a recipe (perhaps industrial chemicals) which is sensitive to the quality of the worst ingredient. Often the "ingredients" in the recipe are *times* at which project parts are done. Imagine a group of hungry people who meet at a restaurant which won't seat them until their entire group is present. Each person wants the latest person to be there early, but nobody wants to wait around. In professional organizations such as law firms, accounting firms, and investment banks, documents are often assembled in pieces, by various people or groups, and must meet a very strict deadline. If one part of the project is late or shoddy, the whole project is sunk or jeopardized.

In the airline business, a weak-link game is played every time workers prepare an airplane for departure. The plane cannot depart on time until it has been fueled, catered, and checked for safety; passengers have been boarded; and so on. For short-haul carriers, which may use a single aircraft

Table 7.25.   *Total frequencies of choices in large-group weak-link games of Van Huyck et al.*

Choice	Period									
	1	2	3	4	5	6	7	8	9	10
7	33	13	9	4	4	4	6	3	3	8
6	10	11	7	0	1	2	0	0	0	0
5	34	24	10	12	2	2	4	1	0	1
4	17	23	24	18	15	5	3	3	2	2
3	5	18	25	25	17	9	8	3	4	2
2	5	13	17	23	31	35	39	27	26	17
1	2	5	15	25	37	50	47	70	72	77

Source: Van Huyck, Battalio, and Beil (1990).

on multiple flights in a day, each departure is also a link in the chain of multiple flights, which creates another weak-link game among different ground crews. A flight from San Jose to Las Vegas, and on to Tucson, cannot arrive in Tucson on time unless it is approximately on time in Las Vegas.

Data from seven sessions conducted by Van Huyck et al. are pooled and shown in Table 7.25. There is initial dispersion and gradual deterioration to 1 in all seven groups.

Van Huyck et al. also conducted sessions with large groups under two additional treatments. Eliminating the penalty for choosing a number above the minimum led most subjects (83 percent) to immediately choose 7; four of six groups reached a minimum of 7. Giving the subjects the entire distribution of choices people made, rather than just the minimum, *accelerated* convergence toward the inefficient minimum of 1.

Group Size

The weak-link game is unforgiving because it is sensitive to a single outlying (low) response. To see whether smaller groups might coordinate on higher (more efficient) numbers, Van Huyck, Battalio, and Beil (1990) ran one experimental session in which subjects were paired in groups of two (in a partner protocol) for seven periods. Their choices are shown in Table 7.26. The distribution of first-period choices is roughly similar to that in the large groups (shown in Table 7.25), but, after seven periods, ten of twelve pairs reached the efficient minimum of 7. A subject who chose 7 while her partner

Table 7.26.   *Choices in weak-link games for two-person groups of Van Huyck et al.*

Choice	Period						
	1	2	3	4	5	6	7
7	9	13	13	17	19	19	21
6	0	1	4	2	1	1	0
5	4	1	1	1	0	0	0
4	0	1	2	0	1	1	0
3	1	2	1	1	0	0	0
2	1	2	0	0	0	0	1
1	8	4	3	3	3	3	2

Source: Van Huyck, Battalio, and Beil (1990).

chose a lower number is more likely to wait a couple of periods for the other player to adjust upward (and usually the other player did).

Van Huyck et al. ran other sessions in which subjects were paired in two-person groups, but with random rematching. As in the large groups, initial choices were dispersed and eventually converged near 1. Thus, a small group size per se does not guarantee efficiency; the stability and mutual adjustment in fixed pairings are also required. Clark and Sefton (1999) replicated this finding in a stag hunt game.

A more complete look at group size can be had by compiling data from various studies (and some informal experiments conducted during seminar presentations; see Weber et al., 2001). The top panel of Table 7.27 shows the frequency of first-period choices in groups ranging from two to fourteen–sixteen subjects (with medians in italics). The second panel shows the frequency of various minima in the first period, and the third panel shows the frequency of minima in the fifth period. There is a strong effect of group size on first-period minima, which is exacerbated by the fifth period. In groups of six or more, the first-period minima are never above 4, and usually deteriorate to 1 by the fifth period. In groups of two or three, however, minima of 5–7 are achieved with some frequency in the first period and two-person groups usually reach efficient minima of 7 by the fifth period.

Given the strong effect of group size, the distribution of first-period choices is surprisingly invariant to the number of subjects in the group. The percentage of subjects choosing 7 ranges is about as high in fourteen–sixteen person groups as in two–three-person groups, and initial medians

Table 7.27.   *Weak-link games, various group sizes*

Group size	Number choice							Total sample size
	1	2	3	4	5	6	7	
Distribution of first-period choices (percent)								
2	28	3	3	7	*21*	0	36	28
3	8	5	8	17	7	2	41	60
6	18	7	13	*16*	7	7	39	114
9	0	11	28	*39*	5	0	17	18
12	25	4	13	*8*	16	4	29	24
14–16	2	5	5	17	*32*	9	31	104
Distribution of first-period group minima (percent)								
2	43	7	7	7	29	0	7	14
3	25	5	35	15	5	0	15	20
6	73	16	11	0	0	0	0	19
9	0	100	0	0	0	0	0	2
12	100	0	0	0	0	0	0	2
14–16	28	28	14	28	0	0	0	7
Distribution of fifth-period group minima								
2	14	0	0	0	0	0	86	14
3	30	15	20	15	0	0	20	20
6	80	10	10	0	0	0	0	10
9	100	0	0	0	0	0	0	2
14–16	100	0	0	0	0	0	0	7

(in italics) are 4–5 for all group sizes. Subjects in larger groups should realize that the minimum in a large group of choices is likely to be low, and should choose much lower numbers than in small groups.[27]

---

[27] I think subjects construe the game as a game between themselves and a single "representative" other player. There is much related work on the cognitive psychology of judgment showing that people use "representativeness" as a heuristic to make judgments of this sort. For example, they think that exemplars that are highly representative of a category—as robins are of birds, or stylish Parisian women are of Parisian women in general—are also common, and that short sequences of Bernoulli trials that match the population proportion are more likely than sequences with too many runs. They extrapolate for group size by 'cloning' or reproducing the representative player but, unless their guess about the representative player's choice has some element of variance, they will ignore the downward bias that choosing a minimum from a large group exerts.

Table 7.28.   *Weak-link payoffs for row players in Berninghaus et al.*

		Other player choices		
		Both X	One X, one Y	Both Y
Row player	X	80	60	60
	Y	10	10	90

Source: Berninghaus, Erhart, and Keser (2002).

Local Interaction

An important finding from theoretical work on social learning and evolution in games is that the nature of interaction among players can matter. This claim is verified by experiments by Berninghaus, Erhart, and Keser (2002). In their design, groups of three subjects played a weak-link or three-person stag hunt game with payoffs (shown in Table 7.28).[28] The strategy profile (X,X,X) is an (inefficient) Nash equilibrium (everyone earns 80), and (Y,Y,Y) is an efficient Nash equilibrium (everyone earns 90).

In a standard protocol, subjects are grouped into three-person groups and play for twenty periods. They learn the two choices by their partners at the end of each period (but not which partner made each choice). In a "local interaction" protocol, eight subjects are (hypothetically) arranged on a circle and play with their two nearest neighbors. Local interaction is different because a player A's two neighboring partners are influenced by the behavior of *their* distant neighbors, who do not directly affect A's payoff. Local interaction allows a kind of contagion or linkage, which permits equilibration to spread around the circle in a way that cannot happen in the standard protocol.

Equilibration in the two protocols is completely different. In the standard three-person groups, players initially play Y about three-quarters of the time, and seven out of eight groups coordinate on the Pareto-dominant all-Y equilibrium. In the local interaction groups, players start by playing Y only half the time, and play of Y falls steadily, to almost none in period 20. Players respond to their neighbors by playing X 64 percent of the time when one neighbor chose X. Like a disease that spreads through a population by close

---

[28] They report some other effects of different group sizes, and players arranged on a lattice who play the neighbors around them, which allow segregated equilibria in which "rectangles" of neighbors play the same way. Messick, Moore, and Bazerman (1999) report a very similar finding in "committee" with ultimatum bargaining.

contact—fear—the incidence of X play spreads from neighbor to neighbor, eventually infecting the entire group.

7.4.3 Mergers, Bonus Announcements, and "Leadership"

Camerer and Knez (1994) argued that weak-link games model many kinds of organizational processes. Motivated by this analogy, they studied three treatments of special interest to business researchers.

One treatment was the "merger" of two small groups into one large one. The group size effect documented above suggests that, everything else held equal, larger groups will do worse (so a merger will harm efficiency). On the other hand, players in small groups stuck in inefficient equilibria might use the merger as an opportunity to "restart" and coordinate on a better equilibrium.

In fact, mergers fail. Table 7.29 shows results. Each line shows the two minima achieved by each of two three-person groups after five periods, followed by the minima in the first and fifth periods for their merged six-person group.[29] When there was public information about previous group performance (top panel), groups usually continued to do what they had been doing after being combined, leading to low minima. When there was no information, groups picked lower numbers when they were combined. Eight of ten groups converge to the minimum of 1.

A second treatment is the public announcement of a "bonus" (by the experimenters) of $0.20 or $0.50 if everyone picks 7. Notice that, if a group has converged to a number below 7 (such as 1), there is *already* an implicit bonus, because everyone can profit if a tacit switch to 7 can be coordinated. The bonus announcement combines this added incentive with a public announcement that draws attention to 7 (much as communication did in the BOS and stag hunt experiments). Bonus announcements turn groups on a dime in one period, from 85 percent choosing 1–2 to 90 percent choosing 7. This regularity may explain why group-level bonuses in firms work surprisingly well (Knez and Simester, 2001).

A third treatment is "leadership." Much research extrapolates from case studies and other kinds of evidence to identify good and bad leaders and tries to determine their different traits. Evidence in social psychology on "attribution errors" suggests that searching for leadership qualities may be misguided. When both situational factors and personal traits contribute to

---

[29] For example, the first row shows a merger in the public information condition in which each three-person group knew the other group's period 5 minimum just before the merger. The two small groups had reached minima of 1 and 2; when combined, the six-person group had a minimum of 1 in period 1 and 1 in period 5. (The separate minima for the players in the two small groups in the first period after their combination are reported in parentheses; they were (1,3).)

Table 7.29. *Minima (MIN) after "mergers" of groups in Camerer and Knez*

Three-player groups	"Merged" six-player group	
Period 5 MINs	Period 1 MIN	Period 5 MIN
Public information about other group's minimum		
1,2	(1,3) 1	1
1,4	(1,1) 1	1
1,1	(1,2) 1	1
4,1	(4,1) 1	1
1,7	(1,7) 1	1
No information about other group's minimum		
2,4	(1,2) 1	1
7,3	(7,1) 1	1
3,2	(3,1) 1	2
7,3	(7,3) 3	3
7,3	(7,2) 2	1

Source: Camerer and Knez (1994).

a behavior, people who are trying to explain the behavior tend to attribute too much cause to personal traits and not enough cause to situational traits (e.g., Nisbett and Ross, 1991). For example, when a colleague in San Jose arrives 20 minutes late for a meeting and claims the traffic was unusually bad, people are too likely to jump to the conclusion that the colleague is chronically late, rather than blame traffic (the situation).

Weber et al. (2001) applied this idea to study misattributions of leadership ability in a weak-link game. Subjects played weak-link games with small groups of two people or large groups of eight–ten people. After each group had played two rounds, a "leader" was randomly selected to make a short speech exhorting the group to choose higher numbers so everyone could benefit. The earlier research on group size effects showed that two-person groups coordinate in weak-link games efficiently but larger groups cannot. Weber et al. guessed that subjects would mistakenly infer that their good or bad outcomes were due to the different leadership skills of the people chosen to be leaders, rather than to the difficulty of leading large groups and the ease of leading small groups.

The game had a weak-link structure in which players chose integers from 0 to 3, and earned $2.50 + 1.25 \cdot [\min_k(s^j_k) - 1] - s^j_i$ from choosing S^j_i (minus an additional 0.25 if the minimum was 0). Higher numbers lead to

Table 7.30.   *Choices and leadership ratings in weak-link game of Weber et al.*

	Large group				Small group			
	0	1	2	3	0	1	2	3
Rounds 1–2								
Frequency of choices (percent)	25	24	20	32	5	24	26	45
Leadership rating (before)		5.88				5.80		
Rounds 3–8								
Frequency of choices (percent)	47	4	0	49	6	6	6	83
Leadership rating (after)		4.53				6.17		

Source: Weber et al. (2001).

better equilibria. The results are shown in Table 7.30. In the first two rounds (top panel), the large group chose slightly lower numbers and, immediately after the leaders' short speeches, the leaders were given ratings of 5.88 (large groups) and 5.80 (small groups) on a nine-point scale where 9 is high. When they played six more times, the large groups began to choose lower numbers and the small groups chose larger numbers, consistent with the group size effect observed by Van Huyck, Battalio, and Beil (1990). Restrospective ratings of leadership ability *after* the last period differed significantly— leaders of large groups had been marked down from the post-speech rating of 5.88 to 4.53, whereas leaders of small groups got a little bit of extra credit, with ratings rising from 5.80 to 6.17.[30]

7.4.4 Median-Action Games

Van Huyck, Battalio, and Beil (1991) studied order-statistic games in which a player's payoffs depend on the *median* number picked by each member of the group. Table 7.31 shows dollar payoffs, using the payoff function $\pi_i(x_i, M) = \$0.70 + \$0.10 \cdot (M - 1) - \$0.05 \cdot (x_i - M)^2$. Every point increase in the median adds a dime to each person's earnings, and each person is penalized a nickel times the squared difference between their choice and the median. Like stag hunt, median-action games pit selection principles against one another. Payoff-dominance points to choosing 7, but "security" (or maximin) points to 3, which guarantees earnings of $0.50.

---

[30] In another study, the subjects played the eight-period game and rated the leaders. Then they were unexpectedly told they would play another eight periods and could keep the same leader or "fire" him. Subjects voted to switch leaders 32 percent of the time in the large groups and 16 percent of the time in the small group, so their ratings affected their behavior.

Table 7.31. *Payoffs in median-action game of Van Huyck et al.*

Your choice of X	Median value of X chosen						
	7	6	5	4	3	2	1
7	1.30	1.15	0.90	0.55	0.10	−0.45	−1.10
6	1.25	1.20	1.05	0.80	0.45	0.00	−0.55
5	1.10	1.15	1.10	0.95	0.70	0.35	−0.10
4	0.85	1.00	1.05	1.00	0.85	0.60	0.25
3	0.50	0.75	0.90	0.95	0.90	0.75	0.50
2	0.05	0.40	0.65	0.80	0.85	0.80	0.65
1	−0.50	−0.05	0.30	0.55	0.70	0.75	0.70

Source: Van Huyck, Battalio, and Beil (1991).

Median-action games capture economic situations in which players prefer to conform. An example is a group production process that depends on the median person's effort and people prefer to not work too hard, or too little. Subjects played in groups of nine for several periods. At the end of each period they learned only the group median. Choices from six sessions are shown in Table 7.32. Two patterns are regular. First, there was substantial dispersion in the first period, which *always* leads to first-period medians of 4 or 5. Second, there is perfect lock-in: In *every* session the tenth-period median is exactly the same as the first-period median.

Table 7.32. *Results in median-action games (six sessions pooled)*

Choice	Period									
	1	2	3	4	5	6	7	8	9	10
7	8	2	2	0	0	1	1	0	0	0
6	4	6	6	6	3	3	4	1	3	1
5	15	15	22	19	22	20	20	24[1]	23[1]	26[2]
4	19	26	22	29[1]	27[1]	30[2]	30[2]	28[2]	28[3]	27[3]
3	8	3	2	0	0	0	0	1	0	0
2	0	1	0	0	1	0	0	0	0	0
1	0	1	0	0	0	0	0	0	0	0

Source: Van Huyck, Battalio, and Beil (1991).
Note: Superscripts denote the number of groups fully equilibrated (all choosing the same number).

Table 7.33.   *First-period choices in three median-action games*

	Game					
	γ		ω		ϕ	
Number	Principle	%	Principle	%	Principle	%
7	Payoff dominance	15	Payoff dominance	52		8
6		7		4		11
5		28		33		33
4		35		11	Maximin	41
3	Maximin	15		0		8
2		0		0		0
1		0		0		0

Source: Van Huyck, Battalio, and Beil (1993).

Van Huyck et al. used two other games to study the effects of payoff dominance and maximin separately. One game (ω) is like the game shown in Table 7.31 except payoffs to actions that are not best responses are 0 (i.e., the penalty to missing the median is to earn 0). In this game, the minimum earnings for all strategies are 0, so maximin no longer selects strategy 3. Table 7.33 contrasts first-period choices in this game with those in the original game γ. Equalizing the penalty for mismatching the median shifts the distribution of choices upward. Half the subjects chose 7, compared with only 15 percent in the original game γ.

In another game ϕ, the gain from an increasing median, $\$0.10 \cdot (M - 1)$, is removed. Then all strategies pay a maximum of $\$0.70$ (i.e., the diagonal terms in Table 7.31 are all $\$0.70$), so payoff-dominance no longer favors any strategy. Results from this game are also shown in Table 7.33. The initial choices look a lot like those from the original game γ.

The three games show that a combination of selection principles guides choices. When a single selection principle points to a choice, most people pick it but there is still substantial dispersion. When selection principles point to different choices, people often pick those or—more typically—pick something in between. No single principle universally trumps the others.

7.4.5 Preplay Auctions and Entry Fees

Van Huyck, Battlio, and Beil (1992) experimented with a special form of communication—a preplay auction for the right to play a coordination game. In these experiments, eighteen subjects participated in an "English clock auction." In the clock auction, prices started at a low level, $0.05, and increased slowly. When the price rose to a price a player did not want to pay, that player dropped out of the auction and earned nothing. When nine players remained, at a price P^*, they then played a nine-person median-action game and P^* was deducted from their earnings.[31]

As players sit in the auction and watch the price rise, they should think to themselves:[32] "At the current price P, anybody who chooses to play expects to earn more than P. Then the median will be a number that enables me to earn P if I just choose that number too. So I should stay in the auction." The logical, surprising consequence of this reasoning is that prices will rise to $1.29 and all players will stay in. Nine of them will play the game, choose 7, and earn $1.30 for a tiny $0.01 net return. This is an application of "forward induction," by which players look back at forgone choices others could have made, to make educated guesses about what those players can be expected to do.

Table 7.34 shows results from the first period, in five different sessions. Each column shows the price at which only nine players were willing to play, and the distribution of numbers those players chose. Forward induction has some force: The preplay auction increased the number of high-number choices 5–7, from 50 percent in the no-auction baseline experiments reported above, to more than 80 percent with auctions.[33] On the other hand, forward induction did not drive subjects all the way to the payoff-dominant equilibrium right away. However, across trials prices rose and a median of 7 was reached in the third period, on average.

After seeing the Van Huyck et al. auction results, Gerard Cachon and I (1996) wondered whether the effect of preplay auctions was the result of forward induction reasoning, or of the fact that all players had to pay a fee to play the game. This distinction was important because psychological research shows that people do not always ignore sunk costs in making decisions. In one of the most clever studies, Arkes and Blumer (1985) randomly gave surprise discounts to people who had come to a theater box

---

[31] It is crucial that players all know that the other eight people they are playing the game with have all agreed to pay P^* as well.

[32] More formally, the application of three principles implies that subjects can use the auction to reach the payoff-dominant equilibrium where everyone plays 7 and earns $1.30. The first principle is dominance—never lose money if you can avoid it. The second principle is dynamic consistency—if nothing has changed, do what you planned to do. A player who obeys these two principles will never pay P then choose an action in the game that gives an expected payoff less than P. The third principle is iterated dominance—players believe others obey the first two principles. This implies that players can expect others always to choose numbers that give higher payoffs than P^*.

[33] Notice, however, that these results could be the result of players having dispersed beliefs about what would happen in the median-action games, and the auction mechanism screened players who had the most optimistic beliefs (and who then chose the highest numbers).

Table 7.34. *First-period prices and choices in median-action games
with preplay auctions*

	Session and prices					
Choice	10 $1.24	11 $1.00	12 $0.95	13 $1.05	14 $1.05	Overall percent
7	7	4	1	2	0	31
6	2	1	0	1	7	24
5	0d	2	6	3	1	27
4	0d	2	1	3	0	13
3	0d	0d	1	0d	1d	4
2	0d	0d	0d	0d	0d	0
1	0d	0d	0d	0d	0d	0

Source: Van Huyck, Battalio, and Beil (1991).
Note: d denotes a dominated action.

office to buy six tickets to a series of plays. If the theatergoers exhibited a
"sunk cost fallacy," those who paid the full price might feel they "had to go"
to "get their money's worth" even though the ticket cost was sunk.[34] In fact,
the full-price group went to significantly more plays.

Applied to the auction game of Van Huyck et al., having to pay a fee
might change players' behavior by making them eager to recoup the fee
by choosing higher numbers. And if players think that others exhibit such
behavior, they could use "avoid losses" (see Kahneman and Tversky, 1979)
as a selection principle, which would rule out some equilibria.[35]

Forward induction can be easily separated from loss-avoidance—just
make all the subjects pay the entry price. If players do not *choose* to pay a
price, forward induction does not apply so the mandatory fee should make
no difference.

---

[34] Economists will note that the cost is not sunk if the tickets can be resold, but there is no reason to
think the resale price varies between those who got the discount and those who paid the full price, which is
the crucial comparison.

[35] The loss-avoidance principle partitions the set of equilibria into those in which everyone loses money
(after subtracting the fee) and those in which people might profit, and selects only equilibria in the profitable
subset. Notice that payoff-dominance also partitions equilibria into "best for everyone" and "not best for
everyone" and picks "best for everyone." Seen this way, loss-avoidance uses the same intuition that underlies
payoff-dominance, but "satisfices" by allowing equilibria that are profitable but not best for everyone.

In fact, forcing subjects to pay the fee *did* lead them to choose higher numbers, almost as strongly as letting them choose whether to pay the fee. Thus, some of the efficiency-enhancing effect of preplay auctions that Van Huyck et al. observed is probably due to a sunk cost effect. Cachon and I conjectured that players use "avoid losses" as a selection principle which coordinates their beliefs on those equilibria that earn a positive profit after the fee is subtracted.[36]

7.4.6   General Order-Statistic Games

Ideally, experimental observations inspire theorizing, which in turn suggests interesting new experiments. A good example of this dialogue is the learning model of Crawford (1995), which was developed to explain the adaptive dynamics observed in the weak-link and median-action games. (See Chapter 6 for a fuller discussion of learning.) Crawford's model assumes players begin with different beliefs and strategy choices, which can be characterized statistically.[37] Van Huyck, Battalio, and Rankin (2001b) ran experiments to test the most striking fresh predictions of the Crawford model.

In their design, there are n players who choose integer numbers $x_i \in \{0, 1, 2, \dots, 100\}$. To make the results comparable to earlier work, each choice is then transformed onto a 1 to 7 scale by taking $e_i = 1 + 0.06 \cdot x_i$. The jth order statistic is denoted by $m_{j:n}$. (The weak-link experiments use the minimum or first-order statistic, $m_{1:n}$, and the nine-person median-action games used $m_{5:9}$.) The payoff to player i is $\pi_i(e_i, m_{j:n}) = \$0.30 + \$0.10 \cdot m_{j:n} - \$0.05 \cdot (m_{j:n} - e_i)^2$.

In Crawford's model, players choose a weighted mixture of their own previous choice and the previously observed order statistic, plus an idiosyncratic zero-mean term and a period-specific common drift term. Under general conditions, Crawford proves that: increasing j—that is, taking a higher number as the order statistic from which deviations are penalized—will *increase* choices; and when the order statistic is the median there is no expected change in the order statistic across periods. The median is $j = (n + 1)/2$ (for n odd). When j is below (above) that threshold, the order statistic is predicted to fall (rise) over time.

---

[36] A key part of this interpretation is that the fee is common knowledge. In some experimental sessions, subjects knew only their own prices, so they could not tell whether other people were losing money at particular equilibria. In those sessions, raising the price did *not* affect behavior significantly. This means common knowledge of losses is crucial: Loss-avoidance is a selection principle applied to infer what others will do (and what others will expect you to do, and so on), not a principle of individual choice.

[37] His model "reflects the conviction . . . that it is impossible to predict from rationality alone how people will respond to coordination problems" (Crawford, 1995, p. 105).

Table 7.35.   *Order statistics in all sessions*

| | Position of game in experimental session | | | |
| | First | | Second | |
n, j	First period	Last period	First period	Last period
5,4	78	100*	53	53
	69	80*	60	100*
	97	100*	67	100*
	95	100*	100	100*
5,2	42	43	60	100
	35	40*	48	80*
	50	100*	100*	100*
	36	36*	100	100*
7,4	80	100*	50	50
	50	50	50	90
	100	100*	96	100*
	73	73	59	59*
	50	100	—	—
	70	100	—	—
7,2	33	27	49	49*
	39	36	15	15*
	6	0	18	46
	32	33*	35	73*

Source: Van Huyck, Battalio, and Rankin (2001b).
Note: * denotes full equilibration (all subjects choosing the same number).

These predictions motivate the design of Van Huyck et al., which varies the order statistic j, either 2 or 4, and the group size n, either 5 or 7. These variations test whether choices rise with group size and fall with j, and test whether choices change over time in the predicted directions. Table 7.35 summarizes the order statistics derived from each session, in the first and last periods of the first and second game. Each line is data from one session. The games are organized from top to bottom to provide a quick visual test of the prediction that higher n and smaller j lead to lower numbers.

The order statistics differ across (n, j) conditions in ways that are consistent with the prediction of the Crawford model. Lowering j or raising n (fixing the other factor) lowers choices. Choices should also drift upward over time in the (5,4) condition, remain stable in the median-action game (7,4), and fall in the conditions (5,2) and (7,2). In fact, choices generally rise or stay constant in most sessions. Thus, Crawford's model is accurate about the *relative* tendency to drift upward, across games, but underestimates the amount of upward movement.

The contrast between the (7,4) results and the earlier results in Van Huyck, Battlio, and Rankin's (1991) nine-person median games is worth noting. In those games, the median choice (transformed to a 0–100 scale) was 58.3 whereas here the initial (7,4) mean is 69. These groups sometimes escape the irresistible path-dependence that occurred in the (9,5) games with only seven actions (causing the final median *always* to equal the first-period median). Many groups increased rising order statistics over time. Typically, once the second-period order statistic was larger than the first period, this created a common belief that the third-period statistic would be larger still, creating a precedent of (profitable!) change which often resulted in an equilibrium of 100. Van Huyck, Battlio, and Rankin speculate that the fine-grained strategy space might play a role in these dynamics. Deviating from the order statistic by even 5 units produces a tiny loss of only $\$.005 \cdot (0.3)^2 = \$0.0045$. Subjects can therefore experiment more cheaply and, in smaller groups, can nudge the order statistic upward.

Summary: In order-statistic games (Van Huyck, Battalio, et al.), players' payoffs depend on their numerical choices and how far they deviate from some order statistic of others' choices (such as the minimum or median). In minimum ("weak-link") games, large groups generally collapse to inefficient outcomes. In median games, players gravitate toward middle numbers and there is near-perfect path-dependence (medians after several periods of play are precisely the median in the initial period). Conducting a preplay auction for the right to play improves efficiency, since players know that those who have paid a high price will play efficiently (or perhaps are just more optimistic). Further experiments showed that simply *imposing* a high price on all players to play also improves efficiency, which is consistent with players using avoidance of losses as a principle to rule out some equilibria and move toward others. In a good example of the potential of two-way dialogue between data and theory, Crawford (1995) showed how these patterns could be explained by a model in which players have initial beliefs that are spread out, but respond to what they have seen. His model also predicts interesting effects in other order-statistic games, which are largely confirmed by new experiments (although players converge to more efficient outcomes than Crawford would predict).

7.5 Selecting Selection Principles

7.5.1 *Simplicity*

Early in the history of game theory, a small literature investigated the connection between games with extensive forms and games with normal forms. Dalkey (1953) showed that all extensive-form games with the same normal-form representation could be derived from one another with one or more "inessential transformations." The applied mathematicians who did this work were interested in purely formal relations among different extensive-form games which would render them equivalent (through their shared normal form). The term "inessential" conveys an implicit prediction that games which are transformations of one another will be played in the same way.

However, some games that are formally equivalent (through some inessential transformation) *are* played differently (e.g., the effects of timing described in Section 7.2.5 and Cooper and Van Huyck, 2001). The fact that representation sometimes matters raises the possibility that, in games with multiple equilibria, features of the representation of the game are used as selection principles.

Motivated by this intuition, Ho and Weigelt (1996) studied whether players use representational simplicity as a selection principle. They measure simplicity of an equilibrium in three ways: (1) the number of outcomes (terminal nodes) following from the last information set on an equilibrium's path; (2) the number of levels of iterated rationality required to make an equilibrium subgame perfect; and (3) the number of levels of knowledge of strategies required to reach an equilibrium.

Figure 7.4 illustrates their second simplicity measure, using their game G5. In game G5, there are two subgame perfect equilibria in pure strategies: outcomes (8,4) and (3,9). The equilibrium outcome (8,4) is reached if player I chooses top and II chooses top also. To make player I's top choice a best response, all she needs to think is that II will choose top (with high enough probability). Whether II is doing so rationally (forming beliefs and choosing the strategy with the highest expected utility given those beliefs) or not does not matter, so I does not need to know that II is rational. The equilibrium outcome (3,9) requires more: If both choose bottom, and play proceeds to the subgame where player I gets to move again, then player I must believe that II will move across to reach (3,9) if she gets the chance, rather than foolishly move down to (0,2). Thus, to reach (3,9) requires I to believe II is rational. Since reaching the (3,9) equilibrium requires I to think II is rational, but reaching (8,4) does not, the (8,4) equilibrium is simpler. Players will be more likely to reach the (8,4) equilibrium if they either prefer simpler equilibria, or use simplicity as a focal principle.

Ho and Weigelt's experiments used two-player games with two or three pure-strategy equilibria. In all cases the players' equilibrium payoffs add

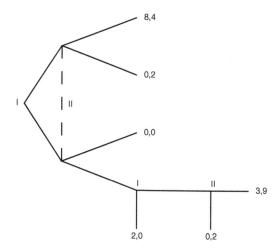

Figure 7.4.   *Game G5, illustrating simplicity as a selection principle. Source: Based on Ho and Weigelt (1996).*

to 12, but they varied the payoff disparity—payoffs were (3,9), (8,4), or (7,5)—to see whether "minimize payoff-inequality" also acted as a focal principle. Results from periods 1–5 are summarized in Table 7.36. The table shows the percentage of players choosing strategies that lead to the

Table 7.36.   *Fraction of players choosing simple equilibrium in Ho and Weigelt's games 4–6*

			Measure of simplicity			
	Equilibrium payoffs		Number of outcomes		Level of iterated rationality	
Game	Simple	Complex	Player s	Player c	Player s	Player c
G4	(3,9)	(7,5)	78	74	46	32
G5′	(3,9)	(8,4)	92	83	71	41
G6′	(8,4)	(7,5)	56	71	69	77
G5	(8,4)	(3,9)			89	84
G6	(7,5)	(8,4)			86	80
G4′	(7,5)	(3,9)	69	59	68	63

Source: Ho and Weigelt (1996).
Notes: Player s denotes player who prefers the simple equilibrium (player II in the first two games, player I in the last four games); player c denotes player who prefers the complex equilibrium. Data are fractions of choices in rounds 1–5.

simple equilibrium, reported separately for the type of player who prefers the simple equilibrium (player s) and the type of player who prefers the complex equilibrium (player c). Most fractions are above 50 percent, so there is a general tendency to choose the simpler equilibrium by either measure. Payoff-inequality is also used as a focal principle because the equilibrium with the more-equal payoffs is generally chosen more often (holding simplicity constant). There is also a slight "self-serving bias"—the players s, who get more from the simple equilibrium, choose it about 5 percent more often than players c, who get less from the simple equilibrium.

7.5.2 Empirical Comparison of Selection Principles

In the first draft of this chapter, I wrote that no single selection principle seemed to dominate others in determining what subjects chose in the first period or converged to. Consequently, studies should be designed to measure the frequency with which various principles are used. Then a paper by Haruvy and Stahl (1998) arrived in the mail, reporting exactly the kind of comparison I had in mind.

Their experiment used twenty symmetric games with three strategies in each. In each game different strategies are chosen by various selection principles. Comparing across games measures how often the various principles are used. Table 7.37 summarizes the fraction of choices consistent with each of four selection principles: payoff-dominance, risk-dominance, maximin (security), and "level-1 bounded rationality" (choose strategies with the highest expected payoff given a diffuse prior about opponent behavior). The table shows the minimum, maximum, and average frequencies of choices corresponding to each principle, across the twenty games. The level-1 principle *always* accounts for at least 62 percent of the choices, and accounts for 83 percent on average, which is twice as many as risk-dominance and maximin. Payoff-dominance predicts worst of all.

Haruvy and Stahl use these choices to fit an "evidence-based" model of first-period choices. Selection principles produce numerical evidence for different strategies. Players weight evidence and combine it to produce an overall score for a strategy, then choose strategies with probabilities given by a multinomial logit function of their scores. Estimation of the model confirms the Table 7.37 impression that level-1 is a good predictor of one-shot play. One-third of the players are estimated to use level-1 evidence exclusively, and half are "wordly" types who combine level-1 with a small sprinkling of other evidence.

Summary: A comprehensive test by Haruvy and Stahl (1998) using twenty games, comparing different selection principles, shows strong and robust support for "level-1" or Laplacean reasoning, in which players act as if

Table 7.37.   *Frequency of choices consistent with selection principles in twenty games (percent)*

| | Selection principle | | | |
Game	Payoff-dominance	Risk-dominance	Maximin	Level-1 bounded rationality
Average	28	44	53	83
Minimum	0	0	0	62
Maximum	98	98	94	98

Source: Haruvy and Stahl (1998).

others might do anything, and choose strategies that are best responses to that "diffuse prior" belief. However, there is evidence for other selection principles, such as simplicity, precedent, and assignment. It is unlikely that any theory of selection will be anything more (or less) than a statistical collage of when the different principles are used.

7.6   Applications: Path-Dependence, Market Adoption, and Corporate Culture

In this section I describe three related experiments inspired by observations made by experimenters and applied economists about the nature of coordination. The first is a creative attempt to explore the strength of path-dependence and "historical accident." The second is motivated by interest in the development of information technology for trading financial assets. The third is about development of culture, in the special form of language "codes" for rapid, memorable communication.

7.6.1   Path-Dependence: Creating a Laboratory "Continental Divide"

A clear lesson from the median-action coordination games is that the determination of medium-run equilibria can be extremely sensitive to small "historical accidents." Van Huyck, Battalio, and Cook (1997) studied this property further using a "continental divide" game. (The game was discussed in Chapter 1, and again in Chapter 6 on learning, so I'll only sketch the basic structure and results here.) Players choose integers 1–14 and their payoff depends on their choice and on the *median* choice of the seven people in their group. If the median starts at 7 or less and subjects best-respond, they will eventually work their way to a pure-strategy equilibrium at 3. If the median starts at 8 or above, however, best-responding will eventually converge to an equilibrium of 12. The payoff at 3 is about half as much as at 12. This game captures the possibility of extreme sensitivity to initial conditions (or path-dependence), which has fascinated scientists interested in chaotic dynamics and complex systems in the past fifteen years or so.

Path-dependence is often evident in physical systems. I once went mountain climbing in Alaska with a friend. We stood on the continental divide, which is the imaginary line (marked on a map) that marks the point at which the direction of water flow changes from one direction to the opposite. We poured water from a canteen right at the divide; some water trickled south and some trickled north. Eventually, the north-flowing water made it to the Arctic Ocean, and the south-flowing water to the Pacific. Molecules that began imperceptibly close together ended up a thousand miles apart.

In the experiments of Van Huyck et al., the invisible "separatrix" between choices 7 and 8 acts precisely like the continental divide. Half the groups start high and are inexorably drawn to 12–13; the other half start low and converge to 3–6. Since the low groups, in equilibrium, earn about half as much as the high groups do, tiny historical accidents that determine the initial conditions have large, persistent earnings consequences. One cannot help but wonder whether the continental divide property is related to the fact that Thailand and Vietnam prosper much more than neighboring Laos does, or the fact that in the late 1990s housing prices in Palo Alto went sky-high while across a creek, in East Palo Alto, more people murdered each other (per capita) than anywhere else in America.

7.6.2 Market Adoption

In large centralized markets for commodities, such as financial assets, most traders value the ability to make large trades cheaply (liquidity) and quickly (immediacy). To find the best price quickly, traders want to use the market that most other traders use. These "participation externalities" tend to lead to dominance of one market over another (and perhaps natural monopoly). However, changes in technology also affect liquidity and immediacy by lowering the per-trade cost. Can a new market that offers lower trading costs displace a market that has been historically active?

This question was investigated experimentally by Clemons and Weber (1996).[38] Their experiments have four buyers or four sellers. Each subject

---

[38] Indeed, their experiments are a nice example of how policy considerations lead to special features of experimental design. They were motivated by changes in information technology that make it possible for investment institutions to trade more cheaply in non-intermediated electronic off-exchange market systems such as Instinet or Posit than on the established New York Stock Exchange or London Stock Exchange

Table 7.38. *Percentage of shares traded in market Y*

Sessions	Part I periods 1–12	Part II (market Y more profitable) periods			
		1–3	4–6	7–9	10–12
1–4	48.3	62.9	67.6	71.2	73.7
5–7	45.5	52.9	56.4	60.4	57.5
T	41.2	57.1	59.6		

Source: Clemons and Weber (1996).

has ten shares to trade and can divide the ten, in any (integer) combination, into separate orders which are sent to either market X or market Y. Buyers and sellers earn a (reduced-form) profit if they trade in the market where the order imbalance benefits their side (e.g., buyers benefit if there are more sellers in the market they trade in). To simulate risks from not having orders executed in a new market, after subjects submitted orders to markets X and Y in each period a coin flip would determine whether market Y would actually open. If it did not open, orders were not executed and subjects earned no profit from these orders.

Table 7.38 shows the percentage of orders submitted to market Y—its "market share"—averaged across groups of sessions. The market share of Y in the first twelve periods of part I averaged less than half, so Clemons and Weber were able to induce subjects to trade more often in market X. After the twelfth period, incentives were changed to favor market Y. The execution risk was removed and profits were higher in market Y (with different bonuses in sessions 1–4 and 5–7).

Table 7.38 shows what happened in the next twelve periods, after this "technological advantage" was added to market Y. There is a steady movement toward market Y but the movement is not very rapid (especially in sessions 5–7, where the premium for switching is lower).[39]

Session T was an unusual session motivated by concern that student subjects behave differently than the market professionals whose behavior is ultimately of interest. Subjects in session T were eight New York Stock Exchange floor traders. They participated in only two periods in part I, and

markets, which hold a dominant share of trading volume but impose higher fees. Policy or field-motivated experimentation has been rare in game theory experiments, except for some auctions and some kinds of bargaining experiments (e.g., final-offer arbitration).

[39] An exponential model used to guess how many periods would elapse before market Y achieved an 85 percent market share forecast ten periods in sessions 1–4 and thirty-three periods in sessions 5–7.

six periods in part II. Table 7.38 shows that the traders behaved much like the students did. The estimated time for market Y to reach 85 percent share was fifteen periods, comparable to the ten periods forecast for student subjects. Their finding is one of several experiments showing that regularities established with student subjects are usually replicated when professional subjects are used (see Ball and Cech, 1996).

7.6.3 Culture

Camerer and Weber (in press) used experiments to study the development of organizational culture. In our experiments, subjects saw sixteen photographs depicting workers in offices. The pictures had similar features (office furniture, people talking) but each picture had some distinctive features. In each pair of subjects, one subject was given a list of which eight of the sixteen pictures were the targets in a particular trial. That subject had to describe the target pictures to another subject accurately enough that the listener subject could pick them out, with a penalty for being too slow. Over several trials, subjects developed a pithy homemade language to describe the pictures—a kind of jargon or slang, a feature of culture. For example, one picture showed a meeting in which a man was gesturing with his hands. In the first trial, it took about 30 seconds of description to get the listener to understand what picture was being described. After several trials, however, the talker just said "Macarena" (the name of a then-popular dance which used hand gestures similar to those in the picture).

To study cultural conflict, the talker in one group B was "fired" and the listener was combined with the group A players. The time it took to complete the task shot up because the group B listener didn't understand the language the A pair had developed. Furthermore, before the "merger" took place subjects forecast how long it would take them to complete the task. Their forecasts were too optimistic. Just as a fish swimming in water is oblivious to its liquid environment, the players were unaware of how special was the culture (language) they created, and how hard for new players to grasp. Camerer and Weber speculate that this phenomenon is a very stylized representation of the kind of surprising cultural clash that undermines many corporate mergers.

Summary: Three applications show that: small historical accidents can lead to equilibria with large payoff differentials; biasing traders toward one of two markets can lead to a handicap that is modestly, and slowly, overcome when the "bad" market suddenly becomes efficient because of technological change; and experiments can be used to create endogeneous culture and explore how merging different cultures creates surprising conflict.

7.7 Conclusion

Theory has not generally provided clear, convincing guesses about which of the multiple equilibria will occur in a coordination game with many equilibria. A high ratio of observation to theorizing is therefore necessary to understand which equilibria are selected. As a result, experimental research on coordination games represents an influential body of empirical findings. Energetic research by Cooper, De Jong, Forsythe, and Ross at Iowa; Van Huyck, Battalio, Beil, and other colleagues at Texas A&M; and many others, has provided a wealth of data on coordination games, which should keep theorists busy for some time.

Several basic conclusions have emerged from this research: Coordination failure is common—play does not usually converge reliably to a Pareto-efficient equilibrium. Risk-dominant and secure outcomes are typical in games where the risk inherent in playing the payoff-dominant equilibrium is high. In stag hunt games with a Pareto-efficient equilibrium and a risk-dominant equilibrium that is efficient, whether play converges to the efficient equilibrium seems to depend sensitively on the degree of assurance that others will play efficiently.

Adaptive dynamics generally do guide players to an equilibrium, often swiftly. The standard pattern, as Crawford (1995) noted and theorized about, is that initial choices are dispersed but players best-respond sluggishly, perhaps optimistically and noisily, to what they have observed. In large-group median-action games, for example, these dynamics imply that the group converges to a strategy choice in the middle of the strategy space; and they do. In weak-link games, where payoffs depend on the minimum number picked in a group, these dynamics imply that small groups can achieve efficiency but large groups will erode to the inefficient equilibrium; and they do.

Convergence can depend on the matching protocol and information available to players. In stag hunt games with "local interaction," in which players are located on a circle and play their two nearest neighbors, inefficiency can spread through a population like a disease.

A strong intuition is that, in coordination games with common interests in reaching some equilibrium, a little communication among players would go a long way. Although communication can enhance coordination effectively, its effects are often weaker than one might expect and depend in subtle ways on game structure. Communication works when it (1) selects a unique equilibrium and (2) provides enough assurance that players will believe the communication and act on it. The combination of these conditions means that in battle of the sexes, for example, one-way communication works well because it points to a single equilibrium (the one that the communicator prefers). But two-way communication creates almost as much conflict as no communication, so it does not help. In stag hunt games the effects of communication are opposite: One-way announcements help only partly because they do not provide full assurance; two-way announcements work beautifully because they provide enough assurance and point to a consistent outcome.

Special forms of communication have mixed effects on efficiency. Pre-play speeches by a single player in a weak-link game (a "leader") with many players do not help avoid coordination failure. (The leaders are also unfairly blamed by other subjects for the failure of their large group to coordinate, an effect predicted by research in social psychology on attribution of cause.) "Assignment" or recommendation of equilibrium by an outside authority (e.g., the experimenter) guides players to an equilibrium when the recommendation does not compete with another focal principle. When it competes with another principle, such as payoff-dominance or payoff-equality, players are usually torn between following the recommendation and following the other principle. Preplay auctions for the right to play a coordination game do enhance efficiency, but it is not clear whether the effect is the result of self-selection of players with optimistic beliefs (and, hence, optimistic actions) or of forward induction by players about the intentions of others who self-selected by paying the auction price. Efficiency is also enhanced by simply charging all players a fee to pay (with no option to quit, so forward induction does not apply). The fact that charging a fee matters suggests that "loss-avoidance" is used as a focal principle to exclude equilibria in which all players lose. (In turn, this principle implies that the way losses are "mentally accounted" for can affect equilibrium selection.)

Work on evolution of meaning shows that, even when a natural assignment of messages to behavior is not supplied to subjects, they can create a homemade language within ten–twenty experimental periods, if it is in their interest to do so.

Experiments on matching games, in which players earn a fixed prize if their choices match, so there are no payoff differences among equilibria, show the importance of understanding the cultural and cognitive bases of "common ground." In these games, thinking strategically means guessing how others will distinguish objects in a choice set, and how they think you will distinguish them, and so forth. Experiments suggest subjects are rather inventive and consistent in finding shared distinctions among objects, or principles that select focal points. Theories that pit the distinctiveness of strategy features against the jointly understood likelihood that players recognize those features (if they are subtle) promise to unpack elements of focality.

Finally, the standard approach to refinement of equilibrium concepts in coordination games is to posit selection principles that pick one equilibrium out of many. A list of selection principles includes: precedence (choose the last equilibrium played); risk-dominance (choose the equilibrium with the lowest "risk," i.e., product of deviation costs); payoff-dominance (choose the equilibrium that pays us all more than any other does); loss-avoidance (choose only equilibria that pay everyone positive profits); maximin or security (choose the equilibrium in which everyone maximizes their minimum possible payoff from that strategy); level-1 expected payoffs (choose the equilibrium that gives the highest expected payoff if others choose randomly); first-mover advantage (if there is a known first-mover, she gets her preferred equilibrium); complexity (pick "simpler" strategies).

There is evidence for each of these focal principles in various games. The paper by Haruvy and Stahl (1998) is an excellent comparison of a subset of these rules. They find that the level-1 rule does extremely well when it competes with payoff-dominance, risk-dominance, and maximin. Indeed, there is evidence from a wide range of games that people often choose strategies that are good responses to uncertain beliefs about what others will do, at least in the first period of a game (cf. Chapter 5). This can explain initial choices of preferred strategies in battle of the sexes, of 4–5 in both the median and weak-link order-statistic games, average choices distributed around 50 in the general order-statistic games, and phenomena described in other chapters—such as initial behavior in dominance-solvable *p*-beauty contests (see Chapter 4) and signaling games (see Chapter 8). The level-1 rule is appealing because it uses a lot of information about possible payoffs (indeed, every possible payoff is weighted equally). It can also be seen as a compromise between the pessimistic and optimistic intuitions of maximin and maximax, but it is more robust than those criteria because it does not depend on only one possible payoff.

Appendix: Psycholinguistics

In psycholinguistics, Herbert Clark (1996) and others take an action-oriented approach that emphasizes the idea that language is often used to coordinate joint action. The recognized precursor to Clark's action-oriented approach seems to be Mead (1934), who emphasized the fact that speakers must take the perspective of their listeners ("audience design") in choosing words.

To do so, speakers and listeners must use language that is understandable in terms of a shared "common ground." Clark argues that searching for common ground is a heuristic that halts the infinite regress of wondering whether a listener knows that the speaker know that . . . (ad infinitum), making effective speech possible. (Note the analogy to behavior in the "email game" in Chapter 5, in which players naturally coordinate on a convention that one or two steps of message-passing are enough to create "mutual-enough" knowledge for coordinated action to proceed.)

An important set of examples for investigating common ground are "indefinite references," in which a speaker refers to one object in a class without being specific about which object she is referring to. For example, Clark, Schreuder, and Buttrick (1983) showed subjects' pictures depicting four types of flowers growing next to a fence and asked them, "How would you describe the color of *this* flower?" The phrase "this flower" makes the reference indefinite because the experimenters refer to a flower, but don't say which of the four types they mean. Nonetheless, most subjects were able to induce a definite reference by using some cue about which of the four flowers was being referred to. For example, when daffodils were substantially more prominent in the picture than the other three types, half the subjects were confident that daffodils were the flowers that were being referred to. Clark and others suggest that several general heuristics are used to establish common ground.

One is "physical copresence"—two communicators assume objects that are physically observable to both people are likely to be the objects which are being referred to (see Chwe, 2001). For example, if a person at a party exclaims, "What a dress!" it probably refers to the nearest dress within looking distance of both communicators (rather than a dress that both saw earlier but has disappeared from view). "Perceptual copresence" and "linguistic copresence" are similar heuristics. "Category membership" is a way of inferring common ground, by assuming that people in the same category have a common database. This is beautifully illustrated in experiments by Kingsbury (1968). He approached people on the streets of Boston and asked for directions, speaking in either a Boston or a Missouri accent. The instructions he received were more detailed when he asked in a Missouri accent, and less detailed when he asked in a Boston accent. Bostonians inferred membership in the category "people who know their way around Boston" from the Boston accent, and were able to draw on perceived common ground to give pithier instructions.

The psycholinguistic work on common ground tends to emphasize how nimble speakers and listeners are at creating shared understanding. However, it would be useful to study two categories of lapses or mistakes. The first category is systematic mistakes in the guesses of speakers about what listeners know. For example, speakers probably take their own knowledge as prototypical and may insufficiently adjust for differences between what they know and what others know. Indeed, there tends to be a positive correlation between subjects' estimates of the percentage of people who recognize a person or object, and their forecast errors (their estimate minus the actual percentage). This correlation occurs because people who are familiar with a person, for example, don't adjust for the fact that if they are familiar then their familiarity is likely to be an upward-biased estimate of the population proportion (and oppositely if they are unfamiliar). In rational expectations terms, if forecast errors are correlated with any available information, then errors can be reduced by using the information to eliminate the correlation. In this case, their own familiarity is information they could use to give a clue about population familiarity—they should self-consciously recognize that on average, if a person is familiar to them, their recognition is to some extent a fluke and won't be commonly held. This "false consensus" bias may lead to a "curse of knowledge" in which well-informed speakers tend to confuse an audience because the speakers do not appreciate how little the listeners know. (Piaget mentioned teaching as an example of the curse of knowledge in action; and see Camerer, Loewenstein, and Weber, 1989, for more discussion.)

The language-for-coordinated-action view emphasizes coordination in which speaker and listener strive to achieve the same goal. A second kind of "mistake" in conversational matching can arise in cases, such as bargaining or confidence games, in which speakers try to exploit common ground to trick listeners into drawing the wrong inference about what they actually mean or intend to do. Some advertising works this way. In one famous case, ads for Listerine mouthwash reminded listeners that winter is a time when it is easy to get colds. Another ad explained that Carnation Instant Breakfast provides as much mineral nutrition as strips of bacon. Filling in the gap, listeners are implicitly expected to infer that Listerine prevents colds (which it doesn't) and both Carnation Instant Breakfast and bacon have healthy mineral nutrition (which they don't). Exploiting common-ground rules to establish false claims has not been explored much by the psycholinguists.

8
Signaling and Reputation

IN 1974 MICHAEL SPENCE published one of the most influential dissertations ever in economics, which eventually (in 2001) earned him a Nobel Prize (shared with George Akerlof and Joseph Stiglitz, for related work in information economics). Inspired by ideas in international relations, Spence formalized and demonstrated the usefulness of the idea of "signaling." Signals are actions players take that convey unobservable information about their "types" to other people, who can observe the signals but not the types. Spence had in mind actions that were too costly for people or countries to take unless they were serious, or *might be* serious. His central example was investing in education to signal intellectual ability (or something). In labor markets, for example, education may signal intelligence (or obedience) to prospective employers. A cheap warranty signals to consumers that a product isn't likely to break down too often. Giving flowers and small gifts (without the reminder of a splashy holiday such as Valentine's Day) means you think about her (or him). In organized crime gangs, a person's willingness to kill or maim a relative who broke the rules signals that they are more loyal to the gang than to their own kin.

Signals are credible if they satisfy two properties. First, signals must be *affordable* by certain types of people, for whom the cost of the signal is less than the benefits that result if the "receiver" decodes the signal. Education pays because it gets students jobs; warranties get firms eager customers; flowers are well worth it if she knows what they mean; and loyalty tests give killers security in their gangs. And, secondly, signals must be *too expensive* for players of the wrong type to afford. Students who really hate schoolwork cannot stand the pressure and boredom of a very academic university. People selling fake Rolexes from briefcases on the streets of New

York cannot afford to offer warranties. Regular gifts of gorgeous flowers are too high a price for a casual relationship. Some gangsters quit rather than kill their brothers.

Combining the two affordability properties, a logical observer can conclude that, if one person buys the signal and another does not, then the two people are of different types (i.e., there is a "separating" equilibrium). This gives the assurance an employer, customer, girlfriend, or gang leader might need to take action. Returning full circle to the signal buyers, the actions by observers who decode the signal fulfill the prophecy made by the signal buyers, which makes the signal worth buying in the first place. A psychologist to whom I once explained signaling equilibrium said, "But it's . . . circular!" Indeed it is. Everything fits together: the sender *should* take the action the receiver expects (that's why she expects it); the receiver's anticipated response is what makes the sender's action worthwhile. By "circular," we usually mean nothing could be ruled out. But the mutual consistency requirement actually rules out a lot of possible behaviors (as the examples below illustrate). Put differently, without the "circular" equilibrium requirement then *some* player is making a mistake—such mistakes surely *do* happen (we'll see some in the experimental data), so it makes sense to think of equilibrium as an idealized steady state reached by learning.[1]

Spence's work used tools developed by John Harsanyi (1967–68). Harsanyi proposed that a simple way to include asymmetries in information in game theory was to assume that one player observed a move by "nature," and all players knew the possible moves but only the privately informed player knew what nature had done. ("Nature" is just a metaphor for an exogenous force or player who is not an active player in the game, and is the source of the asymmetric information.) Harsanyi's idea gave theorists a powerful tool to analyze the influence of private information and is probably the most important development in noncooperative game theory after the seminal contributions of von Neumann and Morgenstern and Nash. The types-based approach also has the right degree of difficulty for challenging theorists— not too easy, not too hard.

Introducing types also provides a generic way to try to explain apparently irrational actions. Why would a gangster kill his brother? Perhaps he is trying to convey information about himself. Why would autoworkers who would genuinely prefer to work stand on a picket line, shivering, to strike

---

[1] In technical terms, signaling models are those in which the privately informed player moves first ("buying" a signal). When the uninformed player moves first, the analogous model is called a "screening" model (e.g., insurance firms offering a menu of contracts to get consumers to self-sort according to their riskiness, to limit adverse selection). I will generally ignore these distinctions in model structure and use the term "signaling" broadly.

against a firm? Perhaps the workers are trying to convey how much they feel they deserve a higher wage.

Applications of signaling models exploded in social science in the twenty-five years since Spence's book appeared (e.g., see Gibbons, 1992). Signaling is used in economics to explain activities that might seem inefficient, such as advertising (which certifies product quality, even if it does not convey information), strikes (which convey each side's seriousness or patience), education, and more. Applications in political science include a Congressional committee signaling a bill's appeal to the entire House. Signaling models have also begun to influence biology and anthropology. The theory of "costly signaling" in biology (e.g., Zahavi, 1975) explains apparently maladaptive (fitness-reducing) activities or mutations by asking what type of information they convey. Male animals often develop physical features that seem to be handicaps, such as a peacock's lush tail-feathers, or an elk's large, heavy antlers. A handicap shows females that a particular male is *so* strong or safe from predators that it can afford to bear an extra burden—the peacock's showy feathers may attract predators, the elk's heavy antlers slow it down. The equivalent for human animals is flashy Hong Kong gangsters lighting cigarettes with $100 bills in John Woo movies (showing they literally have money to burn).

Despite the ubiquity of signaling models in theoretical social science, there are relatively few direct empirical studies of them. Some studies relate predictions of models to evidence from labor strikes (e.g., Kennan and Wilson, 1990), measures of advertising, and product quality for cars (Thomas and Weigelt, 1998). There are also a small number of experimental studies. This chapter describes those experiments and what is learned from them (see Van Winden, 1998, for an earlier review).

The signaling games I shall discuss are the most theoretically difficult games described in this book. The results of these studies are therefore important for judging the descriptive accuracy of game theory when it demands the most cognition or delicate equilibration. If subjects do not behave as theory predicts in simple laboratory games, with ample feedback, one must surely question whether actual players behave that way in much more complicated naturally occurring games.

In fact, most experiments show that players do not fully reason their way toward signaling equilibria as theory conventionally assumes. However, most studies indicate *some* strategic reasoning like that assumed in the models. Players seem to realize that the signals they choose convey information, and receivers make inferences from signals. And when repeatedly playing the same game, subjects usually adapt toward equilibria.

Signaling games illustrate an important methodological point about the interplay of theory and data. As theorists began using these games to explain phenomena such as educational investment, warranties, and strikes, they quickly realized that games often had multiple equilibria. Some equilibria seemed patently implausible, although they were mathematically consistent with established equilibrium concepts (such as even sequential equilibrium). Looking back, it is easy to see that concepts such as Nash equilibrium were just too mathematically weak to pick out the likely equilibria. Refinements of the established concepts were needed to codify what "implausible" meant.

The search for refinements obsessed many game theorists during the 1980s. The papers proposing these ideas are filled with discussions of intuition and plausibility, but no data. It is strange for mathematically gifted theorists to spend years debating with each other which kinds of behavior are most plausible in different games, without occasionally putting people in those games and defining "plausible" as what most people do. The experiments reported in this chapter do just that.

Most tests have yielded pessimistic results about the ability of strong refinements to predict which equilibria players converge to. One important set of experiments (Brandts and Holt, 1993, 1994) even established that players can be systematically led to the "wrong" equilibrium (the *less* refined one). However, theories of learning provide an empirically based way to restrict out-of-equilibrium beliefs, substituting empirical arguments for the logic of mathematical refinement.

8.1 Simple Signaling Games and Adaptive Dynamics

The first thorough experimental investigations of sender–receiver games were conducted by Brandts and Holt (1992) and Banks, Camerer, and Porter (1994). Brandts and Holt (1992) were interested in the Cho–Kreps "intuitive criterion." This can be illustrated by their game 1, shown in Table 8.1.

Think of the payoffs as reflecting labor market returns to education, in the following way: A worker draws her type, either L (low intelligence) or H (high intelligence). There is a common prior probability that her type is L with probability $1/3$, and H with probability $2/3$. (That means everyone

Table 8.1. *Payoffs in Brandts and Holt's sender–receiver game 1*

	Action after message S(kip)		Action after message I(nvest)	
	C^S	D^I	C^I	D^S
Type L(ow)	140,75	60,125	100,75	20,125
Type H(igh)	120,25	20,75	140,125	60,75

Source: Brandts and Holt (1992).

knows the distribution of Ls and Hs but also knows that the worker knows her own type.) After observing her type, the worker can either skip education (S) or invest in education (I). A prospective employer does not observe the worker's type (L or H), but *does* observe whether she invested in education (S or I). Then the employer assigns the worker to either a dull (D) job that requires little skill, or a challenging (C) job that requires skill.

The employer's payoffs are simple. She wants to assign L employees to the D job and H employees to the C job. Those assignments produce a payoff for employers of 125; the opposite assignments are mismatches and produce a payoff of 75.

The worker's payoffs create a different incentive. Workers get payoffs from both wages and "psychic income." Both types earn 100 from the challenging job C and only 20 from the dull job D. In addition, L types get an added payoff of 40 if they skip college (S) and H types get an added payoff of 40 if they invest in education and go to college (I). (In addition, to match the payoffs in Brandts and Holt's game, suppose the H types who skip college get an extra payoff of 20 from the challenging job C, perhaps reflecting on-the-job learning from the challenging job which is a substitute for what they would have learned in school.) Adding up these payoffs gives those in Table 8.1.

There is a conflict of interest between senders (workers) and receivers (employers) in this game. Employers would like to know the workers' types so they can assign the Ls to job D and the Hs to job C. Since the probability is 2/3 that the worker's type is H, if the employer doesn't learn anything about the worker's type from her choice of S or I, she will assign the worker to job C.[2] Both types of workers prefer job C. Therefore, since the employer will assign a worker to job C unless she becomes fairly convinced (more than 0.5 probability) that the worker is type L, the type L workers have an incentive to "pool" with the type H workers and mimic whatever they do, so they can get the lucrative C job assignment.

There are two equilibria in which both types send the same message (called "pooling equilibria"). In one sequential equilibrium, both types choose S and employers respond with C. In addition, a Bayesian–Nash equilibrium must specify how employers respond to unexpected messages. In this sequential equilibrium, to keep H types from breaking out of the pool and choosing I, it must be that employers think that an unexpected choice of I is evidence that the worker is type L, and assigns a worker who sends message I to the dull job D. Since the payoffs to D after choosing I are lower for both types than the payoffs from C after choosing S, neither type will deviate and so the pattern of choosing S and getting job C is an

---

[2] Assigning to job C gives the employer an expected payoff of $(2/3)125 + (1/3)75$, or 108.3. Assigning to job D gives an expected payoff of $(2/3)75 + (1/3)125$, or 91.7. Essentially, since H is more likely than L, it pays for the employer to take a chance and assign everyone to the more challenging job C.

equilibrium. In Table 8.1 the equilibrium is denoted by superscripting the equilibrium employer choices after each message by S; thus, if the worker chooses S, the employer's equilibrium action is C^S, and if the worker deviates and chooses I, the employer's equilibrium action is D^S.

There is something fishy about this equilibrium pattern. Imagine a country in which nobody gets advanced education for decades. Then one person *does* choose to get educated—travelling abroad to college and then returning. Everybody knows that L types don't like education—they are bored and frustrated by school—but H types love it (they earn a higher psychic payoff, reflected by the bonus of 40 in the game). Then why would an employer think that the person who went abroad to college is an L type? The L types are earning their highest possible payoff of 140 by choosing S and getting job C, so they cannot possibly do better by deviating (going abroad to college) and choosing I. The H types, on the other hand, earn a payoff of 120 in the equilibrium but by choosing I they can conceivably earn 140. The Cho–Kreps (1987) "intuitive criterion" (also called "equilibrium dominance") says that when one type cannot possibly improve her payoff by deviating from an equilibrium, and another type might improve her payoff, then the only sensible belief about which type deviated is to assume that the deviator was the type who might benefit. (You should assume that the nonconformist who broke the rules and went to college is an H type, who might have liked it, rather than an L type who wouldn't.) In algebraic terms, the employer should have the belief $P(H \mid I) = 1$. This belief leads her to place a worker who went abroad to college, choosing I, in the job C. Anticipating this, H-type workers will deviate from the S equilibrium by choosing I, thus "breaking" the equilibrium. Because L-type workers will get placed in the low-payoff D job if they are the only ones who choose S, they too will be forced to invest in college by choosing I.

Thus, there is a second sequential equilibrium in which players pool by choosing I, employers assign everybody who chooses I to job C, and a worker who deviates by choosing S is assigned job D. This equilibrium *does* satisfy the intuitive criterion because the H types cannot possibly earn a higher payoff by deviating (by choosing I and getting job C they earn their dream payoff of 140), but the L types might earn a higher payoff. Assigning deviators who choose S to the bad job D is consistent with employers believing that anybody who deviates is an L type; and, in fact, L types are the only ones with an incentive to deviate.

Refinement concepts such as the intuitive criterion were developed to reflect intuitions about what sort of receiver beliefs were sensible after unexpected behavior. We have no idea if these intuitions are right, so the stage is set for an informative experiment.

The results from game 1 are summarized in Table 8.2 in four-period blocks, along with equilibrium predictions. In the top panel, the relative

Table 8.2.   *Results in Brandts and Holt's sender–receiver game 1*

	Message given type		Action given message		Equilibrium predictions	
Periods	$I \mid H$	$I \mid L$	$C \mid I$	$D \mid S$	Intuitive	Sequential (unintuitive)
1–4	100	25	100	74	100	0
5–8	100	58	100	100	100	0
9–12	100	75	98	60	100	0
With suggested message S, suggested actions C $\mid$ *S, D* $\mid$ *I*						
1–4	50	13	60	46	100	0
5–8	75	33	33	67	100	0

Source: Brandts and Holt (1992).

frequencies of I messages and intuitive equilibrium actions tend to support the intuitive equilibrium. The strongest evidence against it is a low frequency of I choices by L types in the early periods 1–4, but they quickly learn to pool with the Hs (who *always* choose I) by choosing I most of the time in later trials.

The bottom panel of Table 8.2 shows results from a treatment in which the experimenters read an announcement in which they "suggested" that players choose message S, and respond to S with C and to I with D. This treatment was intended to test an interpretation of game theory in which equilibria result from self-enforcing "assignments" by an outside authority (or perhaps history; see Chapter 7). The suggestion of playing the unintuitive equilibrium stress-tests the fragility of the intuitive equilibrium. Conformity with the intuitive equilibrium *is* shaken by the announcements, but I choices do rise over time. The substantial announcement effect hints that the intuitive equilibrium could be vulnerable to social forces that nudge people away from it.

In Banks, Camerer, and Porter (1994) we had an ambitious goal. Because expanding the concept of Nash equilibrium to "Bayesian–Nash equilibrium"—essentially, insisting that players have *some* belief about other players' types which justifies their moves at each information set—created many equilibria that seemed nonsensical, theorists proposed many refinements to specify precisely what kinds of beliefs were nonsensical. Banks, Porter, and I thought the refinement question begged for an empirical answer. The theorists' intuitions were mathematically clear, but based on no data, and examples used in the literature sprang ready-made into experimental designs. Banks cooked up a set of seven games, which each had two (pooling) equilibria and which tested levels of refinements—constraints on beliefs—that were mathematically nested. The games are shown in Table 8.3.

Table 8.3.   *Signaling games and equilibria in Banks et al.*

Types	Message m_1			Message m_2			Message m_3		
Game 1: unique Nash pooling (m_1)									
	a_1^N	a_2	a_3	a_1	a_2	a_3^N	a_1^N	a_2	a_3
t_1	2,1	2,0	0,2	3,1	1,0	0,0	1,2	1,1	3,0
t_2	1,2	2,0	2,1	2,1	0,0	0,6	0,2	3,1	1,1
Game 2: Nash (m_1) vs. sequential (m_3)									
	a_1	$a_2^{N,S}$	a_3	a_1	$a_2^{N,S}$	a_3	a_1^S	a_2^N	a_3
t_1	1,2	2,2	0,3	1,2	1,1	2,1	3,1	0,0	2,1
t_2	2,2	1,4	3,2	2,2	0,4	3,1	2,2	0,0	2,1
Game 3: sequential (m_2) vs. intuitive (m_1)									
	a_1^S	a_2^I	a_3	a_1^I	a_2	a_3^S	$a_1^{S,I}$	a_2	a_3
t_1	0,3	2,2	2,1	1,2	2,1	3,0	1,6	4,1	2,0
t_2	1,0	3,2	2,1	0,1	3,1	2,6	0,0	4,1	0,6
Game 4: intuitive (m_2) vs. divine (m_3)									
	a_1	a_2	$a_3^{I,D}$	a_1	a_2^D	a_3^I	a_1^D	a_2^I	a_3
t_1	4,0	0,3	0,4	2,0	0,3	3,2	2,3	1,0	1,2
t_2	3,4	3,3	1,0	0,3	0,0	2,2	4,3	0,4	3,0
Game 5: divine (m_3) vs. universally divine (m_3)									
	a_1^U	a_2^D	a_3	a_1^D	a_2	a_3^U	a_1^D	a_2^U	a_3
t_1	4,1	2,4	1,5	1,3	3,1	4,2	3,3	2,0	1,4
t_2	5,6	2,5	2,2	1,3	1,4	3,3	3,4	1,5	0,1
Game 6: universal divinity (m_3) vs. never-a-weak-best-response (NWBR) (m_2)									
	a_1^U	a_2^N	a_3	a_1^N	a_2	a_3^U	a_1	a_2^U	a_3^N
t_1	2,2	0,3	5,2	1,5	5,3	1,0	2,1	3,3	0,4
t_2	0,2	2,0	5,1	4,0	4,1	0,2	1,4	3,3	2,1
Game 7: NWBR (m_1) vs. stable (m_2)									
	a_1	$a_2^{N,S}$	a_3	a_1^N	a_2^S	a_3	a_1	$a_2^{N,S}$	a_3
t_1	1,6	2,5	2,0	0,5	3,4	1,2	4,2	1,1	0,3
t_2	2,0	2,5	0,6	1,2	3,4	0,5	1,2	0,4	3,3

Source: Banks, Camerer, and Porter (1994).

I will mention only a few basic refinements here. (The subtler ones require some serious hair-splitting.) Motivated readers can look at our paper and the original theory papers for more depth.

I have already discussed the intuitive criterion, which ties the plausibility of a receiver's beliefs about which type is likely to deviate to the possibility that the deviator's out-of-equilibrium payoff is above the equilibrium payoff. But the intuitive criterion does not go far enough. Two types may both conceivably do better after deviating, but one type's deviation seems more likely, because the set of receiver responses that make a deviation optimal is larger for that type.

This property is called "divinity"; game 4 illustrates it. In game 4 there is an intuitive (I) equilibrium in which both types send message m_2. Receivers respond with action a_3, and respond to a deviation m_1 with a_3 (because they believe the chance that any such deviation came from a type 1, denoted $\mu(t_1 \mid m_1)$, is above 0.75). This belief satisfies the intuitive criterion because both types *might* benefit from deviating to m_1.[3] Because both types could benefit from deviating, the intuitive criterion is silent about which type is more likely to deviate. But a little calculation shows that the set of responses by receivers that make a deviation profitable (including mixtures) is strictly larger for type 2 than for type 1.[4] Intuitively, imagine that types 1 and 2 are identical twins who have the same guess about what receivers will do in response to a deviation to m_1. Whenever type 1 deviates, type 2 does too. But if "their" shared belief puts less than 0.75 weight on an action a_1, but more than 0.50 on a_1 and a_2 together, then type 2 will want to deviate while type 1 will not want to deviate. In this sense, a type 2 deviation is more likely. Divinity requires that when the sets of possible action responses that support deviation are larger for one type than another, then the receiver's beliefs about which type deviated should put more weight (relative to the prior) on the type whose deviation-supporting belief set is larger. Since the intuitive equilibrium belief $\mu(t_1 \mid m_1) > 0.75$ puts too much weight on the wrong type (t_2 is more likely to deviate than t_1), it does not satisfy divinity.

Put more simply, the intuitive criterion just divides the set of types into those who would never deviate and those who might. Divinity divides those who might deviate into types who deviate "more often" than others. Divinity therefore requires more reasoning (or a learning process that leads you to that conclusion). A step farther—a step too far, in my view—is "universal divinity." Universal divinity requires that, if the set of receiver actions that make a deviation profitable is higher for one type than another, receivers

---

[3] Type 1 gets 3 in equilibrium and might get 4 after choosing m_1; type 2 gets 2 in equilibrium and might get 3 after choosing m_1.

[4] Type 1 benefits from deviating only if the receiver chooses a mixture that at least places 0.75 probability on action a_1. Type 2, in contrast, benefits from deviating for a wider set of mixtures—namely, any mixture with 0.5 probability or more on the combination of a_1 and a_2.

must believe *for sure* that a deviation came from the more likely type. (Game 5 illustrates an equilibrium that is divine but not universally divine.)

The next two refinements, "never-a-weak-best-response" (NWBR) and stability, are *extremely* subtle.[5] Divinity is as far as intuitive strategic reasoning is likely to go because going farther requires receivers to have complete faith in their ability to figure out the senders' sense of how likely it is that a deviation is profitable, which in turn affects the propensity of different types of senders to deviate. We know from experiments on dominance-solvable games (Chapter 5) that people seem instinctively to do just one or two steps of strategic thinking about others. It is therefore unlikely that senders will reason as thoughtfully about what receivers will think about—what their own signal choices imply as subtle refinements predict. Nonetheless, these refinements were taken very seriously for a while (and still are used in many applications), so seeing what happens in the lab is important. Table 8.4 summarizes the relative frequencies of more refined, less refined, and non-Nash outcomes in two five-period blocks, for all games.

Look first at the frequencies with which message-action pairs match the more and less refined equilibrium predictions in periods 1–5 and 6–10. The more refined message–action pair is played more than half the time in games 1–3, and there is substantial increase in that frequency between periods 1–5 and 6–10. The conformity with the more refined equilibrium drops sharply in game 4. At one point we thought, alliteratively, that subjects acted as if they used simple refinements but not subtler ones ("refine till divine"). That rhythmic conclusion is too simplistic. The reason is that the coarser refinements of the lower-numbered games are also satisfied by both refinements in higher-numbered games (but not vice versa). For example, the intuitive equilibrium is reached 68 percent of the time in later periods of game 3. But in games 4–7, both equilibria are intuitive, yet they are played only a total of 46–63 percent of the time; hence, there is less overall intuitive play in higher-numbered games than in game 3. With that small qualification, there is certainly not strong support for very

---

[5] The idea behind the NWBR criterion is that even when universal divinity fails to apply, because the set of receiver actions making a deviation profitable is not strictly larger for one type than another, it is sometimes the case that one type will have a receiver action response that makes a deviation just as profitable as sticking to the equilibrium message (i.e., defecting is a "weak best response") while the other type prefers the equilibrium payoff for that same action response. Note that this definition nests universal divinity because, if the two action response sets that elicit profitable deviation are strictly nested, then there will be at least one response that makes deviation by the larger-set (more likely) type a weak best response while the other type will prefer the equilibrium payoff.

The last refinement is stability. Banks, Camerer, and Porter wrote (1994, p. 11) that, "Universal divinity and NWBR were initially attempts to characterize the restrictiveness of the concept of stable equilibrium . . . The stable equilibrium concept requires that every possible 'tremble' of strategies have an equilibrium 'close to' the candidate equilibrium." The appeal of stability was that the existence of a stable equilibrium can be guaranteed, yet it is the finest-grained refinement. It is the closest theorists came to finding a Holy Grail theory that guarantees the existence of a kind of equilibrium, with as few of those equilibria as possible.

Table 8.4.   *Results in signaling games (percent)*

	More refined equilibrium				Less refined equilibrium			
	Message–action pairs in periods		Messages only	Actions only	Message–action pairs in periods		Messages only	Actions only
Game	1–5	6–10			1–5	6–10		
	Unique Nash							
1	56	76	86	84	—	—	—	—
	Sequential				*Nash*			
2	61	71	72	87	13	24	28	22
	Intuitive				*Sequential*			
3	53	68	72	91	13	4	20	9
	Divine				*Intuitive*			
4	28	38	42	47	16	8	15	18
	Universally divine				*Divine*			
5	31	27	39	44	36	36	42	75
	NWBR				*Universally divine*			
6	30	15	53	17	30	33	41	72
	Stable				*NWBR*			
7	59	56	78	64	13	7	7	23

Source: Banks, Camerer, and Porter (1994).

subtle refinements beyond the intuitive criterion. When one splits hairs by distinguishing divine from intuitive, universally divine from divine, and so forth, the tendency to play the more refined equilibrium falls, the tendency for more refined play to increase over time falls, and the fraction of non-Nash play rises. Subjects do not act as if they appreciate subtle refinements.

When the frequency of non-Nash message–action pairs is high, it is useful to ask whether it is the senders or receivers who make more non-Nash choices. Senders may choose divine messages in game 4, for example, but receivers respond to the divine message with an intuitive action (this would be scored as a non-Nash outcome). Columns 4–5 and 8–9 of Table 8.4 enable us to tell whether this is common by reporting the frequency of equilibrium messages of each type and actions of each type separately.[6] More refined

---

[6] Note that although the games are constructed so that the more and less refined messages are never the same (so their percentages can never add to more than 100), more and less refined action responses to messages sometimes overlap, so their percentages can add to more than 100.

Table 8.5.   *Brandts and Holt's games 3 and 5*

Types	Message I			Message S		
Game 3	C^I	D^S	E	C^S	D^I	E
A	45,30	15,0	30,15	30,90	0,15	45,15
B	30,30	0,45	30,15	45,0	15,30	30,15
Game 5	C^I	D^S	E	C^S	D^I	E
A	45,30	0,0	0,15	30,90	30,15	60,60
B	30,30	30,45	30,0	45,0	0,30	0,15

Source: Brandts and Holt (1993).

message and action choices are quite common in games 1–3 (70–90 percent) but these frequencies drop sharply in games 4–7.

Another important finding (which is not apparent in the table) is that senders do not really pool because type 1s and 2s tend to choose different messages in games 2–6. We tried to figure out whether subjects were using different decision rules, such as maximin or the principle of sufficient reason (level-1 reasoning in Chapter 5 jargon), but no single decision rule could account for most deviations. However, it is notable that hardly any receivers rarely violated weak dominance, and senders rarely chose messages that could be eliminated by one round of iterated dominance. Thus, there is strong conformity with a simple principle of strategic thinking—deletion of another player's dominated strategies and strong conformity to Nash equilibrium in games 1–3.

The way learning dynamics can lead to unrefined equilibria can be illustrated by two games taken from Brandts and Holt (1993), extending their earlier work. Table 8.5 shows their games 3 and 5.

In game 3, types are equally likely ($P(A) = P(B) = 0.5$) and there are two equilibria. In the sequential (S) equilibrium, both types of senders (A and B) send message S (denoted by superscripting by S). Since both types choose S, receivers infer or learn this, Bayesian-update and infer $P(A \mid S) = P(A) = 0.5$ and $P(B \mid S) = P(B) = 0.5$. Then they should choose C, which gives payoffs of 90 or 0 and hence maximizes expected utility given the Bayesian posterior beliefs. Note that, in this equilibrium, type As earn 30 and type Bs earn 45. What prevents the type As from defecting to I and earning 45 if their message is met with a response of C? The sequential equilibrium coheres only if receivers choose D in response to message I.[7] But then why would

---

[7] Note that E in response to I is strictly dominated and should never be chosen; in the experiments, it rarely is.

receivers choose D in response to I? Receivers must believe that D choices are more likely to be made by B types (more specifically, $P(I \mid B) > 2/3$ to justify a choice of D by receivers). The intuitive criterion insists that belief is wrong. Type Bs earn 45 in equilibrium (from choosing S and getting response C) and could not possibly benefit from switching to I. Type As earn 30 in equilibrium and could conceivably benefit if they choose I and meet response C, earning 45. Hence, the off-path belief $P(I \mid B) > 2/3$ is not intuitive because it shifts belief toward B types, who are least likely to benefit from having picked I.

The argument underlying the intuitive criterion is purely theoretical. It deduces from sheer payoffs the implausibility of type Bs having switched from S to I. From a learning point of view, this is sensible only if subjects have been choosing S for a long time and any history of I choices is forgotten or dismissed. But learning, by definition, allows the possibility of a pre-equilibrium convergence process that leaves an empirical trace of previous I choices. What if, during the learning process, most players who chose I happened to be type Bs? Then the intuitive criterion competes with an empirical construction of off-path beliefs, recalled from the equilibration phase (before such moves *were* out of equilibrium). It is hard to think of a compelling empirical reason why players should ignore, in the medium run, what they previously observed in favor of a purely deductive argument that flagrantly ignores history.

In game 3 there is another equilibrium in which both types choose I and are met with the response C, yielding them 45 and 30. Since type Bs could conceivably earn more (45) by choosing S instead, the equilibrium sticks only if defections to S are met with responses of D. Note that a D response to S is justified by the belief that S defections are more likely to have come from B types (i.e., D is optimal for receivers if $P(B \mid S) > 5/7$). This inference *does* satisfy the intuitive criterion because, indeed, B types might benefit by defecting from I to S whereas A types would never benefit. Hence, the equilibrium in which both types choose I does satisfy the intuitive criterion.

From an equilibrium point of view, game 5 is identical to game 3. In the game 5 sequential equilibrium, both types pick S and are met with response C, earning 30 and 45 respectively. The A types are prevented from defecting to I only if a defection is met with response D, which is justified if receivers think a defection probably came from a B type $(P(B \mid I) > 2/3)$. But in the S equilibrium, B types never do better defecting whereas A types might; so the presumption that defections were probably from Bs is unintuitive.

And, as in game 3, in game 5 there is an intuitive equilibrium in which both types choose I and are met with response C. A defection to

S makes receivers sensibly think the defectors are B's who might do better ($P(B \mid S) > 5/7$), so they choose response D, which in turn keeps both types from defecting.

Game 5 nicely illustrates how a plausible convergence path might leave "footprints" of empirical history that contradict the intuitive criterion. In the account due to Brandts and Holt (the BH dynamic), both types of players start out with (roughly) diffuse priors about the behavior of others. In game 5, suppose senders have diffuse priors about what receivers will do. Type A senders will compute expected payoffs of $(45 + 0 + 0)/3 = 15$ and $(30 + 30 + 60)/3 = 40$ for strategies I and S, and are more likely to choose S. Type B senders compute expected payoffs of $(30 + 30 + 30)/3 = 30$ and $(45 + 0 + 0)/3 = 15$, and are more likely to choose I initially. Thus, if senders have sufficiently diffuse priors they are likely to separate initially—As choose S and Bs choose I.

This first step illustrates the way in which a sensible start to the convergence process can yield empirically based off-path beliefs that are unintuitive. Recall that in the sequential equilibrium, both types pick S. This unintuitive equilibrium is held together by the odd belief that B types who would never want to revert to I, once they end up getting 45 by picking S, are more likely to have picked I. But in fact, the B types pick I in the first place. They begin doing so because the diffuse prior does not concentrate their belief on the possibility of getting 45 from S, which later becomes an equilibrium. Groping around, they begin doing something they later regret. But their early groping leaves an empirical trace that can sustain the belief that any player who picks I might be a B type.

Suppose receivers, meanwhile, have diffuse priors over the types of senders who are likely to have chosen each message. Receivers who observe I compute expected payoffs of 30, 22.5, and 7.5 for strategies C–E and, hence, choose C most often. Receivers who observe S compute expected payoffs of 45, 22.5, and 37.5 and choose C most often. Hence, in this equilibration phase A's choices of S are mostly met with C (or E) and B's choices of I are mostly met with C or D.

In the second phase, equilibration occurs as players build up empirical experience by observing what others do, and move in the direction of ex post best responses. Two things happen, probably more or less simultaneously. Receivers learn that, when they observe message S and choose C, they earn 90 because S choices come from A types. So their C choices are reinforced and become more frequent. When receivers observe message I, they earn 30 from C and 45 from D, and gradually switch to D. Meanwhile, type A senders earn 30 (or 60) from choosing S, and learn that, if they had picked I, they would have earned 45 or 0. As receivers adapt, picking D more frequently in response to I, the A types realize that a defection to I would yield 0, which

Table 8.6.   *Results in games 3 and 5: Brandts–Holt and Partow–Schotter (percent)*

Game	Periods	Message given type $I \mid A$	$I \mid B$	Action given message $C \mid I$	$D \mid S$	Equilibrium predictions Intuitive	Sequential
3 (BH)	1–4	77	26	91	60	100	0
	5–8	82	8	93	62	100	0
	6–12	89	57	91	82	100	0
3 (PS)	1–6	78	10	62	27	100	0
		$S \mid A$	$S \mid B$	$C \mid S$	$D \mid I$		
5 (BH)	1–4	87	8	74	61	0	100
	5–8	89	49	79	76	0	100
	6–12	96	59	68	74	0	100
5 (PS)	1–6	87	39	68	51	0	100

Source: Brandts and Holt (1996); Partow and Schotter (1996).

keeps them from switching. On average, then, their S choices are (relatively) reinforced and they keep choosing S. Type B senders, meanwhile, earn 30 from picking I, but realize they might have earned 45 from picking S since action C is often chosen in response. And indeed, as senders learn that S messages are chosen by A types, they learn to choose C more often in response, which intensifies reinforcement of the unchosen strategy S for B types.

Gradually, then, As stick with S and Bs switch to S as well. Eventually a pooling equilibrium results in which both types pick S and receivers, having learned that an S choice is likely to come from either type, maximize expected payoff by choosing C most of the time. The equilibrium is sustained by the fact that a sender who learned from experience would respond to an unusual I choice by presuming—based on history—that a type B picked it, and would choose D in response, which keeps both types from picking I and sustains the choice of S.

Table 8.6 shows the time path of intuitive equilibrium messages for each type $(I \mid A, I \mid B)$ and receiver actions. In game 3 senders start by initially separating by type, so that As mostly choose I and Bs rarely choose I. Anticipating this separation, or quickly learning it, receivers respond to I with C, and to S with D. That pattern of responses quickly teaches B types that choosing S yields only 15, whereas choosing I would have yielded 30, causing them to switch to I and pool with the type As. That is roughly what happens. By periods 9–12, type Bs choose I 57 percent of the time.

In game 5, the initial type-dependence is reversed, so that As strongly prefer S (which guarantees 30, and may pay 60) whereas Bs rarely choose

S because I guarantees a payoff of 30. Receivers again anticipate this separation or learn it quickly, and usually respond to S with C (which implies that type Bs would have earned 45) and to I with D (which implies that type As would have earned 0). Senders then learn these action responses. Since there is no incentive for type As to switch to I, and a stronger incentive for Bs to switch to S, there is a gradual shift toward pooling on S.

If the process fully converged, the receivers would end up responding C to S and D to the occasional I, because they would have remembered that the only types who chose I in the past were type Bs. However, once the equilibrium crystallizes, the only types with an incentive to deviate are type As. Thus, there is a sharp conflict between the force of history, which shaped beliefs about which types might deviate based on which types *did* "deviate," and the logic of the intuitive criterion, which asks which types would prefer to deviate, given the *current* equilibrium. The logic of the intuitive equilibrium is impeccable, but is no match in the short run for the force of historical observation.

Partow and Schotter (1996) noted that, in the adjustment dynamic posited by Brandts and Holt, players do not use information about other players' payoffs to sharpen their beliefs, or about what receivers will do or what types of senders might have chosen different messages. So they replicated the Brandts–Holt (BH) games 3 and 5 by telling players only their own payoffs (and fixing roles within each game). If the Brandts–Holt dynamic explains what is happening, these own-payoff games should look like the other games. Results are shown in Table 8.6. The type-dependence observed by Brandts and Holt is replicated in Partow and Schotter (PS). An important difference is that the convergence toward pooling on the intuitive equilibrium is not evident in game 3; only 10 percent of the type Bs choose I. This is driven by the fact that receivers respond to a choice of S by choosing D only 27 percent of the time, and C otherwise (which gives the type Bs their highest payoff, 45, rather than the lowest payoff of 0, so they have little incentive to switch from choosing S to choosing I).

The difference due to knowing others' payoffs suggests that the receivers are doing some strategic thinking. If they were simply keeping track of which types of senders chose I and S (which does not require them to know anything about the payoffs of the senders), they should choose D in response to S with similar frequency in BH periods 1–4 and PS periods 1–6. But even in those early periods receivers choose D much more often, which suggests that they are able to figure out, from studying the senders' payoffs, which types of senders are likely to be choosing S rather than I. They are being sophisticated rather than purely adaptive.

Anderson and I (2000) were curious whether the belief learning story of Brandts and Holt would track the equilibration path as well as other learning models described in Chapter 6, which have been applied to many other games. In experience-weighted attraction (EWA) learning, players are assumed to learn by updating a numerical measure of a strategy's attractiveness based on the payoffs they received, or the forgone payoff the strategy *would* have earned if it had been played, multiplied by an "imagination" weight δ. (Belief learning is a kind of EWA earning in which forgone payoffs are weighted as heavily as the payoffs players actually get, so it assumes "perfect imagination.") Extensive-form games present a challenge because players do not know what exactly would have happened if they had chosen a different message. However, they know the set of *possible* payoffs for an unchosen message. And if message I was chosen in the past, for example, then its historical payoff is known, so players could use this as a guess about what they would have gotten in the current round if they had chosen I. Anderson and I implemented EWA by using an agent-based model in which strategy attractions are updated separately for each type (for senders), and for each possible message (for receivers), and a proxy for forgone payoffs is used based on various models, such as the last received payoff.[8]

We replicated Brandts and Holt's experiments on games 3 and 5 for thirty-two periods, to have a longer span of data and see more learning. The thick lines in Figures 8.1a–8.1d show the results from game 5 in four-period blocks. The figures show the type-dependent relative frequencies of choosing m_1 given t_1 and choosing m_1 given t_2 (Figures 8.1a and 8.1b), and the message-dependent action frequencies (Figures 8.1c and 8.1d). Replicating Brandts and Holt's results, there is movement away from the intuitive message choices of m_1 (although the t_2 frequency time series turns sharply upward in the last four periods). Receiver action choices drift toward the unintuitive choice over time.

The figures also show the fit of three learning models which are fitted to the first twenty-four periods and used to forecast the last eight periods. The learning models are EWA, choice reinforcement (CR), and weighted fictitous-play belief learning (BB) (see Chapter 6 for details). The three models track the data about equally well, but there are small differences among them. Reinforcement does not pick up the drift over time in $m_1 | t_2$ and $a_2 | m_1$. Belief learning is too flat for $a_2 | m_1$ and overshoots on $a_1 | m_2$. EWA avoids these small mistakes and therefore fits and predicts a little better than the special case models, adjusting for its extra degrees of freedom in several ways.[9] The EWA imagination parameter δ is estimated to be 0.54 with

---

[8] We also realized that belief learning requires the strategy attraction for message choices by an "undrawn" type to be updated by the forgone payoff that type would have earned if they had chosen the same message that was chosen by the type that was actually drawn. Cross-type updating is equivalent to belief learning.

[9] The per period out-of-sample log likelihoods for EWA, reinforcement, and belief learning are -17.44, -19.20, and -20.40. (Note that the more complex model does not generally do better out of sample and, in fact, does worse if it is overfitting.) Out-of-sample hit rates are 81.6, 80.1, and 77.3. The corresponding figures for game 3 are -9.02, -9.83, and -10.28; and 91.0, 87.5, 91.0.

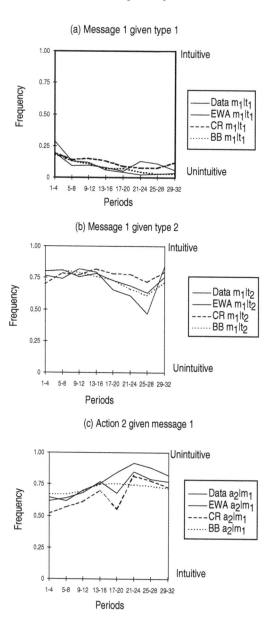

Figure 8.1. *Frequencies of messages and conditional actions (and intuitive/unintuitive equilibrium predictions) in Brandts and Holt's sender–receiver signaling game 5. Source: Anderson and Camerer (2000), p. 710, Figure 3. Reproduced with permission of Springer-Verlag.*

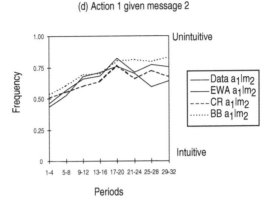

Figure 8.1 (continued)

a standard error of .05, so we can confidently reject the hypotheses that $\delta = 0$ (reinforcement) or $\delta = 1$ (belief learning).

Summary: Tests of basic signaling games yield mixed evidence about the adequacy of equilibrium refinements to predict what players will do. There is certainly much evidence of convergence toward Nash equilibria over time. However, refinements that are subtler than sequentiality do not predict reliably well in Banks, Camerer, and Porter (1994). The results very roughly match the cognitive difficulty underlying subtler refinements.[10] Brandts and Holt also showed that, if equilibration occurs through adaptive dynamics, a game can be constructed in which players are led toward the sequential equilibrium, which is not intuitive. Beliefs about likely deviations emerge from looking at history, rather than from logic applied at equilibrium to deduce which types are likely to deviate. Anderson and I showed how a precise learning model could explain this process.

---

[10] Define the difficulty of a concept by how hard it is to implement computationally. To execute the intuitive criterion, for example, a receiver must simply compare all possible payoffs from a deviation to a type's equilibrium payoff, for each type. If one type has no deviation payoffs that are larger, and another type has some, then the intuitive receiver decides the latter type must have deviated. Implementing this idea requires a receiver to classify types into "never will" or "might." Divinity is more difficult, since it requires the receiver either to construct sets of her own possible reactions that would make a deviation profitable, for each type, then test for embeddedness of the sets, or to enumerate all possible deviation responses on a checklist, and ask whether one type says "Yes, I'd deviate" every time another does and sometimes says "Yes" when the other says "No." This procedure is more complex computationally. These computational stories are metaphors for what subjects may be thinking, or rough yardsticks to calibrate difficulty—and hence likelihood of actual play. But they suggest a precise way to measure plausibility of refinements by linking them with cognitive complexity.

Table 8.7. *Payoffs in Potters and van Winden's lobbying signaling game*

	No signal		Costly signal	
Type (probability)	x_1	x_2	x_1	x_2
t_1 $(1-p)$	$0, b_1$	$a_1, 0$	$-c, b_1$	$a_1 - c, 0$
$t_2(p)$	$0, 0$	a_2, b_2	$-c, 0$	$a_2 - c, b_2$

Source: Potters and van Winden (1996).

8.2 Specialized Signaling Games

This section describes games designed to model very specific economic environments: lobbying, corporate finance, ratchet effects in multiperiod production, and limit pricing.

8.2.1 Lobbying

Potters and van Winden (1996) studied a costly signaling game inspired by theories of lobbying in politics. Senders observe their types t_1 or t_2 (which occur with probabilities $1 - p$ and p). They can then choose to send a signal which costs c. Receivers observe the signal (but not the sender's type) and choose actions x_1 and x_2. Payoffs are shown in Table 8.7 (assume $0 < c < a_1 < a_2$ and $b_1, b_2 > 0$).

The game models a lobbying group (the sender) that wants a politician (receiver) to take the action x_2. The politician wants to figure out whether the lobbying group has power or not. The politician prefers to take action x_i if the group is type i.

Define $\beta = pb_2/(1 - p)b_1$, the relative expected payoff from choosing x_2 instead of x_1 if the receiver knows only the prior probabilities of types. Assume $\beta < 1$. There are two sequential equilibria. In one, senders think the costly signal will be ignored if it is sent and, since $\beta < 1$, the receiver will choose x_1. Although the senders are not happy (getting 0), it doesn't pay to signal if their signals are ignored, so there is nothing they can do. This equilibrium is intuitive (since both types could conceivably benefit from defecting) and divine, but not universally divine.[11] In the other equilibrium, type 2s always buy the costly signal. Type 1s will attempt to pool, since

---

[11] The set of possible receiver actions that justifies a defection by type i is $p(x_2|\text{signal}) > c/a_i$, which is a lower threshold for type 2 than for type 1. Divinity therefore requires that receivers believe a defection to "signal" is more likely to have come from a type 2. This is not enough to guarantee a choice of x_2 in response to a signal, however, unless the stronger requirement of universal divinity is imposed, which requires $p(t_2|\text{signal}) = 1$.

Table 8.8.   *Results in Potters and van Winden's lobbying signaling game (percent)*

Treatment	β	c/a_1	Frequency of signals by t_1, t_2		Frequency of x_2 after no signal, signal	
			Actual	Prediction	Actual	Prediction
1	0.25	0.25	38, 76	25, 100	2, 5	0, 25
2 ($a_2 = 2c$)	0.75	0.25	46, 100	75, 100	3, 79	0, 25
2a ($a_2 = 6c$)	0.75	0.25	83, 93	75, 100	11, 54	0, 25
3	0.25	0.75	16, 85	25, 100	0, 53	0, 75
4	0.75	0.75	22, 83	25, 100	5, 80	0, 75
Averages across β		$c/a_1 = 25$			5, 46	0, 25
		$c/a_1 = .75$			2, 66	0, 75
Averages across c/a_1	$\beta = 0.25$		27, 81	25, 100		
	$\beta = 0.75$		50, 92	75, 100		

Source: Potters and van Winden (1996).

otherwise their type is revealed and they get 0. In equilibrium, receivers play x_1 after no signal and mix after receiving a signal, playing x_1 with probability $(a_1 - c)/a_1$ and x_2 with probability c/a_1. This mixture gives t_1 an expected payoff from signaling of 0, so type 1s mix by sending the signal with probability β.[12]

Potters and van Winden argue that for giving policy advice it is often sufficient to be confident that a change in a policy variable will affect behavior in the correct direction. To test the comparative static predictions, they vary parameters so that β and c/a_1 change, to see if the probability of type 1s signaling and receivers choosing x_2 after a signal respond to these changes as predicted. Table 8.8 summarizes the relative frequencies of signaling by the two types, and the choice of x_2 after no signal and a signal.

Data are pooled across all twenty periods, although there is some trend across trials (generally in the direction of equilibrium). Look at the signaling frequencies first. The universally divine equilibrium predicts that type 1s should signal β of the time, and type 2s should always signal. The type 2s *do* signal most of the time. Type 1s signal an average of 27 percent of the time when $\beta = 0.25$ and 50 percent of the time when $\beta = 0.75$, so the predictions

---

[12] Such a mixture leads to a posterior belief after observing a signal that makes receivers indifferent between x_1 and x_2. The posterior $p(t_2|signal) = 1 \cdot p/[1 \cdot p + \beta(1 - p)]$ and the expected payoffs to x_1 and x_2 are therefore equal.

do change with β as predicted, although not as sharply.[13] As predicted, receivers rarely choose x_2 if there is no signal. After a signal, they choose x_2 46 percent and 66 percent of the time, respectively, when the predicted percentages were 25 percent and 75 percent. The results again respond to $c \mid a_1$ in the correct direction, but the change is too small.

Treatments 2 and 2a vary the payoff to type 2s as a function of the signal cost. Since type 2s should always signal (for these parameter values), changing their payoff a_2 should not matter, but it does, increasing t_2 signaling from 46 percent to 83 percent. This unpredicted response is supportive of a decision-theoretic approach (à la Brandts and Holt) in which one's own payoffs matter.

Potters and van Winden note that players respond to past history. Denote the past frequency of x_2 response to signals (across both types) in periods 1 to t_1 by $r(m)_{t-1}$. Type 1 senders learning by fictitious play should then signal in period t if $r(m)_{t-1}a_1 - c > 0$. When this expected payoff was positive (negative) they did signal 46 percent (28 percent) of the time. Fictitious play learning by receivers is even stronger: they chose x_2 when its expected payoff was positive (negative) 77 percent (37 percent) of the time.

Potters and van Winden (2000) extended their study to compare the behavior of students and professionals. There have been only a few serious studies comparing the behavior of college students (the typical subject pool) and professionals (see Ball and Cech, 1996). Most studies show that students and professionals behave similarly, which is extremely important for generalizability, but it is important to know more.

The payoffs in their game are shown in Table 8.9 (payoffs were four times higher for professionals). As in their earlier study, there is an equilibrium in which neither type signals, since the receiver believes a signal came from t_1, but this equilibrium does not pass universal divinity. There is also a universally divine equilibrium in which t_1 (t_2) signal with probability 0.25 (1.00), receivers never choose x_2 when there is no signal, and choose x_2 after a signal with probabilities 0.25 and 0.75 in the low- and high-cost conditions.

The results, shown in Table 8.10, are similar to their earlier findings and show little evidence that professionals are more inclined to equilibrium play. The degree of type separation (the difference in signaling rates by t_1 and t_2) is similar in the two groups, and is about half as wide as predicted. Learning occurs because players responded to history as in their earlier study. (Students were actually twice as responsive as professionals, so they learned better.)

---

[13] Note also that the equilibrium in which senders never signal is badly rejected, which is evidence for the refinement of universal divinity relative to the weaker refinements of divinity and intuitiveness.

Table 8.9. *Payoffs in Potters and van Winden's lobbying signaling game*

Type (probability)	No signal		Costly signal	
	x_1	x_2	x_1	x_2
Low-cost signals				
t_1 (2/3)	2,3	4,1	1.5,3	3.5,1
t_2 (1/3)	1,0	7,1	0.5,0	6.5,1
High-cost signals				
t_1 (2/3)	2,3	4,1	0.5,3	2.5,1
t_2 (1/3)	1,0	7,1	−0.5,0	5.5,1

Source: Potters and van Winden (2000).

Table 8.10. *Results in Potters and van Winden's lobbying signaling game (percent)*

Subject pool	Signal cost	Frequency of signals by t_1, t_2		Frequency of x_2 after no signal, signal	
		Actual	Prediction	Actual	Prediction
Students	Low	55, 69	25, 100	6, 27	0, 25
Professionals	Low	52, 83	25, 100	8, 27	0, 25
Students	High	34, 93	25, 100	4, 50	0, 75
Professionals	High	37, 71	25, 100	25, 65	0, 75
Students	Overall	46, 70	25, 100	5, 39	0, 50
Professionals	Overall	46, 87	25, 100	13, 40	0, 50

Source: Potters and van Winden (2000).

8.2.2 Corporate Finance

Distant investors and a company's managers have very different information about the company's prospects. Theorists in corporate finance have recognized this information gap and seized on it as an explanation for why firms engage in activities to convey good news to investors (and hide bad news) even if those activities don't otherwise benefit the company. For example, guaranteeing payment of dividends from current cash flows is a way for managers to signal that cash flows are healthy (cutting the dividend is a sign of very poor financial health), even though dividend payments make little sense otherwise. (They simply transfer cash from the stockholder's share of the cash in the firm's bank account to the stockholder's own bank account, incurring a tax debt in the process.)

An influential signaling model of corporate external financing of new projects is due to Myers and Majluf (1984). They asked what happens if firms have great investment opportunities but must raise capital by issuing shares ("diluting" the firm's value to current shareholders). There are inefficient separating equilibria in which firms with good projects will fear that investors will demand too much of the firm to supply capital (or, equivalently, will pay too little for new shares) and, hence, will not offer their best projects. Then only the most mediocre projects will be offered and investors are justified in demanding a large share of the firm because the firm is not so valuable after the good project is undertaken. Note that this equilibrium is inefficient because the best projects go unfinanced.

Cadsby, Frank, and Maksimovic (1990) did the first experiments to test this theory. In their design, firms are equally likely to be high (H) or low (L) value, and need capital I to finance a new project. H and L firms are worth A_H and A_L if they pass up the project, and an additional gain (net of I) of B_H and B_L if they do the project. Investors cannot determine whether the firm is H or L and can agree to put up I in financing in exchange for a fraction S of the firm's ex post value.

Cadsby et al. used a variety of parameter values, so that unique pooling, unique separating, and both types of equilibria are possible in different sessions.[14] An example will help illustrate. In session E, L firms are worth 50 without the project and 375 with it. H firms are worth 200 and 625. The investment is 300. There is a separating equilibrium in which $S^* = 0.80$. L firms offer shares, since selling 80 percent of the firm is worthwhile (because $(1 - 0.8)375 > 50$). H firms don't offer shares because accepting only 20 percent of shares worth 625 is worth less than the no-project firm value of 200. However, if investors demand only $S^* = 0.60$ of the firm, then Ls will offer because $0.4(375) > 50$. Hs also offer since $0.4(625) > 200$, and investors get an expected value of $0.6(0.5(0.25) + 0.5(375)) = 300$, equal to their investment. Therefore, there is a pooling equilibrium in which $S^* = 0.60$

[14] First note that $S_L = I/V_L$ is the fraction of shares shareholders would want if they knew that the firm was L. $S_P = I/(0.5V - H + 0.5V_L)$, which is lower than S_L, is the fraction investors want in a pooling equilibrium. H firms will sell S shares if $S < (B_H + I)/V_H$ (H's will sell if $V_H - B_H = I$, the no-project firm value, is less than $(I - S)V_H$, giving the inequality in the text), and investors will finance even L firms at a share of S_L. If $(I/V_L) < (B_H + I)/V_H$ then there is a unique pooling equilibrium in which H and L both offer projects and the shares demanded, S^*, is S_P. If $(B_H + I)/V_H < S_P$ then there is a unique separating equilibrium in which the shares that must be offered dilute the H firm too much, so only Ls offer and the share is $S^* = I/V_L$. If both conditions are met, $I/(0.5V_L + 0.5V_H) < (B_H + I)/V_H) < I/V_L$, then there is also a semi-separating equilibrium in which a fraction $P = I/B_H - V_L(I + B_H)/B_H V_H$ of H firms offer projects, all Ls offer projects, and investors demand shares which are worth I in expected value.

and both types offer projects. There is also a semi-separating equilibrium with $S^* = 0.68$, Ls always offer, and Hs offer with probability 0.36.

Cadsby et al. first ran two baseline sessions (A and B) in which firm types *were* known to investors, as a kind of comprehension check (and to see how competitive investors were during the share auction). All firms offered and shares went to within 1 percent of predicted levels within one period. Later sessions used two distinct groups to look for effects of experience across different parametric environments. One group participated in sessions C, E, and G and a different group participated in D, F, and H. Subjects were then mixed for three more sessions, I–K. Results are summarized in Table 8.11. Each panel shows an experimental session. Since the data are extremely regular, they can be summarized as the fractions of H and L firms offering projects in periods 1–5 and 6–10, and the mean share demanded by investors (in percentage terms) in the last two periods.

The results are very supportive of equilibrium predictions, and of pooling when there are multiple equilibria. When pooling is predicted uniquely (session C), all firms offer in all periods. When separating is predicted uniquely (sessions D, G, I), type H firms offer projects in periods 1–5, but they gradually learn the shares they will get are too low, and offer few projects in periods 6–10. In the sessions with multiple equilibria (E, F, H, J), there is reliable convergence to the pooling equilibrium. The pooling happens very rapidly, generally in the very first period. The willingness of investors to bid down to the lower pooled-equilibrium share right away assures H firms that it pays to offer projects, and the equilibrium quickly crystallizes. Of course, the result may be very sensitive to the institutional structure that determines investor shares.[15]

Cadsby, Frank, and Maksimovic (1998) extended their earlier experiments to include signals. Often signals are available to the firms that are socially inefficient, but which H firms can afford while L firms cannot. (Signals include costly activities such as paying dividends, share repurchases, "road shows" in which executives tell security analysts about all their firms' wonderful prospects, and so forth.) Do H firms buy these signals? In some cases there are only pooling equilibria in which either both types of firms purchase the signal, or neither type does. In these cases, the signaling equilibrium is Pareto dominated by the no-signaling equilibrium because (by definition) the signals are wasteful, but the no-signaling equilibria do not

---

[15] The auction is *descending* in the share S, and the pooled equilibrium share S^* is always below the other equilibrium shares. An auction in which shares were determined in a way that put less downward pressure on shares, such as a sealed-bid second-price auction or bilateral bargaining, might produce less evidence for pooling. Alternatively, investors and firms may pool because doing so is efficient and increases their collective take from the experiment. Maybe they are using efficiency as an equilibrium selection principle.

Table 8.11. *Results in project financing experiments of Cadsby et al.*

Session		Percentage of firms offering new projects in periods (1–5), (6–10)		Mean share S (last two periods)
		L	H	
C	Results	100,100	100,100	28.3
	Prediction—pooling	100	100	30.0
D	Results	100,100	50,21	57.5
	Prediction—separating	100	0	75.0
G	Results	100,100	21,6	61.7
	Prediction—separating	100	0	62.5
I	Results	82,83	36,00	38.5
	Prediction—separating	100	0	40.0
E	Results	100,100	100,100	58.3
	Prediction—pooling	100	100	60.0
	separating	100	0	80.0
	semi-separating	100	36	68.0
F	Results	93,92	80,100	29.3
	Prediction—pooling	100	100	30.0
	separating	100	0	40.0
	semi-separating	100	20	36.0
H	Results	100,100	100,100	37.8
	Prediction—pooling	100	100	39.2
	separating	100	0	62.5
	semi-separating	100	9	57.1
J	Results	100,100	88,100	28.8
	Prediction—pooling	100	100	30.0
	separating	100	0	50.0
	semi-separating	100	35	37.1

Source: Cadsby, Frank, and Maksimovic (1990).

satisfy the Cho–Kreps intuitive criterion. These games pit Pareto-dominance against the intuitive criterion as a selection principle.

Cadsby et al. ran twenty-six experimental sessions using a very wide range of parameter configurations. In each round firms learned their types and chose whether to raise equity and, if so, whether to buy a costly advertisement. Then a descending-price auction was conducted in which many investors bid for the right to own a share of the firm's equity in exchange for some fixed capital.

The results from the last two periods of each session are summarized in Table 8.12. The left-hand columns show the percentage of L and H firms choosing to advertise (i.e., to signal), and the mean equity share raised in the market for firms that advertised ("if A") and did not advertise ("if no A"). The right-hand columns show the predictions about the fractions of firms of the respective types that should advertise, and the predicted equity shares (in percent). The "intuitive" column gives the intuitive equilibrium. The "other" column gives other equilibria that are not intuitive.

Take game G4 as an example. The intuitive equilibrium is a separating equilibrium in which L firms are predicted never to advertise, H firms are predicted always to advertise, and equity shares of 40 percent and 60 percent are predicted for firms that advertise and don't advertise, respectively (denoted (0, 100, 40/60)). There are two other equilibria, one in which neither firm advertises and the equity share is 48 percent, and another in which only L firms enter the equity market (H firms stay out) and the equity share is 60 percent.

There are three types of games. G1–2, BC1, GW2, and GS1 are the simplest: Firms could not advertise (replicating their earlier study). In these games, virtually all firms enter the equity market, and the mean equity share is within a few percentage points of the prediction.

In games G4–G6, GW1, and GW3, the intuitive equilibria are separating equilibria in which only H firms advertise (although there are also no-signaling pooling equilibria that are not intuitive). H firms do not advertise quite as often as predicted, but there is partial separation because the L types rarely advertise and the H types advertise about half the time.

In all other games, there are two pooling equilibria; the intuitive equilibrium requires both types to advertise. In roughly half the games there is a lot of advertisement and equity shares are fairly close to those predicted. In the other half, however, there is very little advertisement (e.g., BC2–BC4 and GW4–GW5).

To explore why players in some sessions pool on advertising and in other sessions pool on no-advertisement, Cadsby et al. computed the short-term gain for an H firm defecting from a no-advertising pooling equilibrium, assuming their advertisement is taken as a signal of high quality. This number is the dollar pressure toward convergence (by H types) *away* from the

Table 8.12. *Corporate finance games with advertising of Cadsby et al.*

	Results (last two periods)				Equilibrium predictions	
	Percent advertising (A)		Mean share (percent)		Intuitive	Other
Game	L	H	If A	If no A	(%L, %H, shares)	(%L, %H, shares)
No advertising allowed (data are entry rates)						
G1*	100	100	—	39.7	(100, 100, 40)	—
G2*	100	0	—	59.4	(1, 0, 62.5)	—
BC1*	100	100	—	28.0	(1, 1, 32)	
GW2*	100	83	—	26.3	(1, 1, 30)	
GS1*	100	100	—	59.8	(1, 1, 60)/(1, 0, 80)	
Separating equilibria are intuitive						
G4	0	44	42.5	48.0	(0, 100, 40/60)/	(0, 0, 48)/
					(0, —, 60)	(0, —, 60)
G5	0	50	30.0	56.6	(0, 1, 30/60)/	(0, 0, 40)/
					(0, —, 70)	(0, —, 75)
G6	0	75	50.0	73.8	(0, 1, 50/75)	(0, 0, 60)
GW1	14	20	31.0	32.3	(0, 1, 30/50)	(0, 0, 37.5)
GW3	0	100	51.0	74.9	(0, 1, 50/75)	(0, 0, 60)
All-advertise pooling equilibrium is intuitive						
G3	40	14	22.0	23.6	(100, 100, 24)	(0, 0, 24)
G7	75	100	23.7	58.0	(1, 1, 30)/(0, —, 80)	(0, 0, 30)
G8	33	100	50.5	76.2	(1, 1, 60)	(0, 0, 60)
BC2	0	25	17.0	24.0	(1, 1, 24)	(0, 0, 24)
BC3	0	14	48.0	51.5	(1, 1, 60)	(0, 0, 60)
BC4	0	17	60.0	60.2	(1, 1, 60)/(0, —, 75)	(0, 0, 60)
GW4	0	0	—	54.0	(1, 1, 60)	(0, 0, 60)
GW5	0	0	—	45.2	(1, 1, 48)	(0, 0, 48)
GW6	100	100	58.0	—	(1, 1, 60)	(0, 0, 60)
GW7	80	100	55.6	69.0	(1, 1, 60)	(0, 0, 60)
GW8	14	100	45.6	59.0	(1, 1, 50)	(0, 0, 50)
GS2	0	33	19.0	24.9	(1, 1, 30)	(0, 0, 30)
GS3	60	100	30.9	41.5	(1, 1, 24)	(0, 0, 24)
GS4	80	100	44.9	70.0	(1, 1, 52.2)	(0, 0, 52.2)
GS5	0	50	53.0	59.2	(1, 1, 60)	(0, 0, 60)

Source: Cadsby, Frank, and Maksimovic (1998).

no-signaling equilibrium. A regression of the fraction of H-type firms advertising against this convergence-pressure figure (where each session is a data point) yielded a coefficient significant at $p = .04$, so they have a statistical explanation for why some sessions converge to advertising whereas others don't. They also fitted an adaptive fictitious-play type model, which shows significant learning by investors in about half the sessions.

8.2.3 *Games with Ratchet Effects*

Chaudhuri (1998) studied ratchet effects in a principal–agent game with two-period output and dynamic quota-setting. His experiment is difficult to explain briefly so I'll just sketch the design and results. In each of two periods the principal sets a quota. Agents have high or low costs and produce an output in each period. A clever principal should set a low quota in the first period, since the low-cost agent will prefer to produce a lot to meet the quota and earn a big bonus, even though it means revealing their type. When their type is revealed, the principal "ratchets" up the quota in the second period and extracts more surplus from the low-cost principal.

Berliner (1957) coined the term "ratchet effects" and pointed out that in centrally-planned economies, quota schemes are often used to induce managers to produce higher output (in the absence of profit-sharing, reputational, and high-powered promotional incentives). Wise managers often create inefficiency by deliberately underproducing to avoid being ratcheted. Even in capitalist economies, quota-setting is commonly used in regulated industries. Quotas are also used inside firms in contracts between managers and individual workers whose effort is hard to observe (e.g., salespeople who work in the field). For the purposes of this book, ratcheting is interesting for another reason: It isolates two simple steps of strategic reasoning that are central in all signaling games. Agents should worry about revealing their types in early periods. In turn, principals should take actions that force agents to reveal their types and enable them to ratchet.

As in many signaling games, Chaudhuri's subjects show *some* strategic sophistication, but not as much as is generally assumed by most equilibrium concepts. The main deviation is that low-cost agents unwittingly reveal their types by producing a high output in the first period even when the quota is high (when they should be hiding their skill by underproducing). As a result, principals do not need to choose the type-revealing low quota in the first period to learn what they need to ratchet later. So ratcheting occurs, but not because the principals force revelation of information initially; it occurs because the low-cost agents just give themselves away.

Cooper, Kagel, Lo, and Gu (1999) also studied ratchet effects. Their model is a simplified form of Freixas, Guesnerie, and Tirole (1985). It models target and output decisions in a "dual-track" economy, in which firms sell all output up to a target to the state at a fixed price, and can sell additional output in an open market. Planners prefer to maximize social surplus (output up to the target minus costs), subject to a penalty for profits from output beyond the target.[16]

In their game, firms first learn their productivity type, high (H) or low (L), which are equally likely. Then firms choose an output level from 1 to 7. A planner observes the firm's output choice, but not its type, and chooses a target, easy or tough. Compared with Chaudhuri's two-period model, Cooper et al. essentially trimmed away the planner's choice of a first-period quota (it's exogeneous) and the firm's second-period output (it's assumed to be optimal) from Chaudhuri's two-period model. Their reduced form focuses attention on what inferences about the firm's type planners can draw from observed output, and whether firms anticipate these inferences and try to hide their types to avoid being ratcheted.

Payoffs are shown in Table 8.13. With these payoffs, it pays for planners to set an easy target if $P(L|\text{output})$ is above 0.325. In equilibrium, L firms will choose low outputs, either 1 or 2, and H firms should pool by choosing what L firms do most of the time. (The pooling equilibria at 1 and 2 satisfy the intuitive criterion.) Myopic K firms that ignore the inferences planners draw will choose 5, hoping for the payoff of 1328 (but receiving 1035, less than the pooling payoffs of 1108–1145, if planners set the tough target offer observing the firm's choice of 5).

Cooper et al. were interested in the effects of unusual treatments they were uniquely suited to apply. Subjects were students and factory managers in China. The factory managers were generally in their forties or fifties and worked for state-run enterprises or in joint ventures with foreign investors. Most had some higher education (typically equivalent to a trade school or community college). Because wages are low in China (relative to American research budgets!) they were able to run high-stakes treatments very cheaply. They also explored the interaction of contextual labels—compared with abstract labels, the default standard in economic experimentation—with managerial experience.

Some results are summarized in Table 8.14. Since 70–90 percent of the L firms chose the output of 2, and most H firms chose either 2 or 5, the most interesting feature of the data is the relative frequencies of H firms choosing either 2 or 5 over time. They started in periods 1–12 choosing the myopic output of 5 between 54 and 76 percent of the time, and choosing the pooling output 2 only about 10 percent of the time. Planners reacted

---

[16] The penalty from profits presumably reflects something like a social distaste for private profits in a communist society, akin to a personal distaste for inequality writ large.

Table 8.13. *Payoffs in ratchet game of Cooper et al.*

	Firm payoff			
	Low-productivity firm production target		High-productivity firm production target	
Output	Easy	Tough	Easy	Tough
1	710	542	1108	815
2	730	561	1145	852
3	697	528	1230	937
4	527	357	1308	1015
5	273	103	1328	1035
6	220	48	1298	1005
7	190	15	1250	966

	Planner payoff	
Production target	Facing low-productivity firm	Facing high-productivity firm
Easy	645	764
Tough	528	820

Source: Cooper et al. (1999).

sensibly, albeit noisily, by choosing tough targets in response to outputs of 2 and 5 about 20 percent and 80 percent of the time, respectively. Over trials 13–36 there was gradual convergence away from H choices of 5 and toward the pooling prediction of 2, but the convergence was not sharp.[17]

Students in H firms started out more strategically than older managers; they chose the pooling output of 2 more often in early periods, and they learned faster. Probit regressions of H firm choices and planner responses confirm that players learned: H firms responded to the differential rate of tough target-setting they experienced, and planners reacted to the previous distribution of H firm outputs.

Stakes had an effect because H firms learned more when stakes were higher (although planners did not). Cooper et al. suggest that the planners' reasoning problem was easier, since it required an inference only about which type of firm chose which output, whereas the firms had to anticipate

---

[17] Cooper et al. comment that learning is too fast to be explained by reinforcement models, but also too slow to be explained by fictitious play. This suggests that the hybrid EWA model will fit better than those extreme cases (see Chapter 6).

Table 8.14. Frequency of H firm outputs 2 and 5, and tough responses (percent)

| | | Periods | | | | | | Pooling prediction | |
| | | 1–12 | | 13–24 | | 25–36 | | | |
	Outputs	2	5	2	5	2	5	2	5
Older managers, generic labels									
H output of 2, 5		7	76	22	60	37	39	100	0
Frequency of tough targets		30	73	18	98	21	92	0	100
Older managers, contextual labels									
H output of 2, 5		1	70	27	46	45	38	100	0
Frequency of tough targets		19	79	25	91	18	100	0	100
Students, generic labels									
H output of 2, 5		14	54	32	40	43	37	100	0
Frequency of tough targets		·20	88	21	98	30	98	0	100
Students, context labels									
H output of 2, 5		22	62	52	31	57	30	100	0
Frequency of tough targets		11	92	18	93	20	95	0	100

Source: Cooper et al. (1999).

the thinking of the planners. Incentives therefore affected the kind of thinking that is more difficult (the firms').

Probit regressions showed that context effects were weak for students and stronger for managers. The context effects virtually disappeared when interacted with prior behavior of other subjects, however, which suggests that context was simply providing a language or vivid framework that facilitated learning from experience. The context effects on managers' choices were also stronger in their role as planners than in their role as firms. Cooper et al. speculates that this difference was because managers were less familiar with planner thinking (so context helps), but already knew from the field how to manage earnings and hide productivity. For example, many Chinese firms keep two sets of accounting books. They also maintain slush funds (*xiaojin ku*) built up from selling excess production off the books, to spend on expense categories that are carefully regulated, such as employee housing and other in-kind benefits.

8.2.4 Belief Learning in Limit Pricing Signaling Games

Cooper, Garvin, and Kagel (1997a,b) studied limit pricing in a well-known game in which monopolists have unobserved types (e.g., product costs) and choose prices or quantities to prevent entry. Table 8.15 shows the payoffs in

Table 8.15. *Payoffs in a limit pricing game of Cooper et al.*

	Player A's (monopolist) payoffs			
	High cost, M_H		Low cost, M_L	
A's choice	X (IN)	Y (OUT)	X (IN)	Y (OUT)
1	150	426	250	542
2	168	444	276	568
3	150	426	330	606
4	132	408	352	628
5	56	182	334	610
6	−188 (38)	−38 (162)	316	592
7	−292 (20)	−126 (144)	213	486

	Player B's (entrant) payoff		
B's action choice	High cost, M_H B's payoff	Low cost, M_L B's payoff	Expected value
Treatment I			
X(IN)	300	74	187
Y(OUT)	250	250	250
Treatment II			
X(IN)	500	200	350
Y(OUT)	250	250	250

Source: Cooper, Garvin, and Kagel (1997a).
Notes: Expected values were not included in experimental instructions. Payoffs in parentheses (.) are those in Cooper, Garvin, and Kagel (1997b). Payoffs are in "francs," 1 franc = $0.001.

their game (adapted from Milgrom and Roberts, 1982). A monopolist (A) learns its own type, equally likely to be either high or low (denoted M_H and M_L), and chooses a quantity from 1 to 7. After observing the quantity choice, but not the monopolist's type, an entrant B decides whether to move IN and enter, or stay OUT. In their treatment I, B (entrant) players earn 250 from staying out and either 300 from entering, if the monopolist is M_H, or 74 from entering, if the monopolist is M_L. Given these payoffs, entrants are reluctant to enter unless they are fairly certain that the monopolist is a high type. If they are risk-neutral, they must think $P(M_H) \geq 0.78$ to enter.

With the treatment I payoffs, there are a variety of equilibria. There are two pure-strategy separating equilibria in which the high type M_H chooses quantity 2, succumbing to entry, and the low type M_L chooses either 6 or

7, deterring entry. In these equilibria, the monopolist's choice reveals its type. There are also several pooling equilibria. In each of these equilibria, high and low types choose exactly the same quantity (any level from 1 to 5). Because the entrant doesn't learn anything about the monopolist's type from the observed quantity, it uses the prior probability of types, calculates an expected value of 187, and prefers to stay out and earn 250. However, these are equilibria only, if a surprise defection to a different quantity is perceived to be an indication that the monopolist is M_H; then the entrant will choose IN. Since that's worse for both types, the monopolists will stick to the pooling quantity. Refinements of sequential equilibrium allow various equilibria and exclude others.[18]

The top panel of Table 8.16 shows frequencies of choices in each of the three twelve-period cycles for inexperienced subjects. Both types of monopolists started at their "myopic maxima"—the choices that give the highest expected payoffs if the entrant is equally likely to choose in or out. Low types M_L chose 4 and high types M_H chose 2. However, Es were more likely to enter when the quantity they observed was 1–3. As a result, a choice of 2 was often met with entry and gradually M_H monopolists moved upward toward 4, trying to pool with M_L types. The learning process started up again with experienced subjects playing the same game. After three cycles, there was sharp convergence to a pooling equilibrium at the quantity 4: About two-thirds of the high types M_H chose 4, almost all the low types did, and only 6 percent of the entrants entered.

In treatment II, the payoffs are changed so that entrants should enter if the monopolist is equally likely to be either high or low. This parameter change breaks the pure pooling equilibria present in the treatment I, since any pooling equilibrium in which both types enter all the time then leads to entry. Low-type monopolists can always do better by choosing 6 or 7 and separating themselves from the high types.[19] This treatment is good for checking whether there is a natural tendency for the monopolist types to pool that is immune to experience, or whether pooling is a natural state for players to pass through while converging to a separating equilibrium.

Table 8.17 shows results from treatment II. For inexperienced subjects, the cycle 1 results look very much like those from treatment I, beginning at the monopolists' myopic maxima. This feature is important because it

---

[18] Of the separating equilibria in which M_L types choose 6 or 7, the Riley equilibrium, a single round of deletion of dominated strategies, and the Cho–Kreps intuitive criterion all exclude the possibility that M_L types choose 7. Among the pooling equilibria, the intuitive criterion allows pooling at 4–5 (as does divinity), undefeated equilibrium allows 2–4, and both perfect sequential equilibrium (Grossman and Perry, 1986) and the evolutionary model of Noldeke and Samuelson (1993), which is uniquely H-dominant, predict pooling only at 4.

[19] There are also several partial pooling equilibria in which the two monopolist types do not make exactly the same choices but the sets of choices they sometimes make overlap.

Table 8.16.   *Quantity choices and entry rates: Treatment I (percent)*

| | M_H | | | M_L | | | IN% | | |
| | Cycle | | | Cycle | | | Cycle | | |
Quantity	1	2	3	1	2	3	1	2	3
Inexperienced subjects (sessions 1–2)									
1	2	3	6	1	0	0	33	67	33
2	**69**	**50**	38	4	0	0	57	64	64
3	6	10	**10**	5	2	1	30	74	30
4	21	36	47	**76**	**86**	**91**	13	10	9
5	2	1	0	6	8	6	0	15	25
6	0	0	0	3	2	1	33	50	0
7	0	0	0	3	2	1	0	0	0
Experienced subjects (session 3)									
1	2	2	3	0	0	0	100	0	100
2	41	28	23	0	0	2	59	91	70
3	2	2	5	0	2	0	100	50	50
4	**55**	**68**	**69**	**100**	**98**	**98**	3	6	6
5	0	0	0	0	0	0	—	—	—
6	0	0	0	0	0	0	—	—	—
7	0	0	0	0	0	0	—	—	—

Notes: Numbers are estimated from Cooper, Garvin, and Kagel (1997a, Figure 1), assuming equal sample sizes in sessions 1–2. Median choices are in **boldface.**

implies that (as in treatment I) the monopolists were *not* making a sophisticated guess about how entrants would react to different quantity choices. By the third cycle, however, a small spike of data grows at 6 (15 percent), where low types M_L were beginning to separate themselves from the pack, who pooled at 4 and were entered upon about half the time. By the third cycle of experienced subjects the data have modestly converged to the separating equilibrium in which high types chose 2 and low types chose 6, with a residue of both types pooling at 4, and entrants chose IN frequently for quantities of 5 or less.[20]

[20] In further sessions, Cooper et al. put some subjects in the treatment II condition first, and observed fairly strong convergence to separating equilibria (M_H chose 2, M_L chose 5–6). Then they reverted to the treatment I payoffs, in which pooling can be an equilibrium. They observed some movement toward the pooling equilibria (a lot more M_Hs chose 4), but not much.

Table 8.17. *Quantity choices and entry rates: Treatment II (percent)*

Quantity	M_H Cycle			M_L Cycle			IN% Cycle		
	1	2	3	1	2	3	1	2	3
Inexperienced subjects (sessions 4–5)									
1	6	6	0	1	0	0	80	100	—
2	**71**	39	33	7	4	12	88	91	94
3	12	**6**	13	3	8	6	60	83	100
4	11	48	**54**	72	**67**	**67**	53	52	63
5	0	0	0	9	15	0	40	44	—
6	0	1	0	6	6	15	50	33	33
7	0	0	0	2	0	0	0	—	—
Experienced subjects (session 6)									
1	3	5	8	0	0	0	100	100	100
2	43	40	**49**	4	0	0	95	100	100
3	**13**	5	4	2	5	3	100	100	100
4	41	**40**	32	37	22	14	79	85	80
5	0	10	6	**9**	7	3	0	57	100
6	0	0	0	48	**66**	**80**	14	7	12
7	0	0	0	0	0	0	—	—	—

Notes: Numbers are estimated from Cooper, Garvin, and Kagel (1997a, Figure 1), assuming equal sample sizes in sessions 1–2. Median choices are in **boldface**.

In Cooper et al. (1997b) they extended their earlier experiments in two directions, using variants of treatment II in which pure pooling is not an equilibrium and subjects tend to separate. First, note that choices of 6 and 7 are dominated for high-type monopolists (and are rarely chosen). From a learning point of view, the speed with which low types separate by choosing high quantities (6 or 7) might depend on how frequently entrants stay out after observing such a high choice, which in turn depends on whether entrants stay out after observing such a high choice, which in turn depends on whether entrants realize that the high quantities are dominated for high types, so only low types will make those choices. Therefore, variables that affect the entrants' beliefs about which type chooses high quantities (and the low-type monopolists' beliefs about those beliefs) could affect the rate of convergence.

To test this prediction, Cooper et al. changed the high-type payoffs to the larger positive numbers shown at the bottom of Table 8.15 ("Treatment

II"). In the original treatment, the high-type payoffs to 6–7 were negative, so entrants could guess more easily that high types would never choose those quantities.[21] The positive-payoff treatment is called the "0 percent anticipation" treatment because entrants are not *told* that high-cost monopolists won't choose 6 or 7 (but they should be able to infer it). In the "100 percent anticipation" treatment, the instructions specifically forbid high-type monopolists from choosing 6 or 7, and this instruction is public knowledge. The conjecture is that since low-type monopolists know that entrants know this, they might be more willing to separate because their high-quantity choices will be taken as a signal of their low type and will deter entry.

Table 8.18 shows the results from experienced subjects only. As expected, in the 100 percent anticipation treatment subjects converged rather swiftly and sharply to the separating equilibrium in which M_H chooses 2 and M_L chooses 6 (as predicted by most refinement concepts). The swift emergence of this equilibrium, compared with the earlier results, shows that even simple steps of iterated dominance (e.g., entrants learning that high-type monopolists will obey dominance) are apparently learned only over time, because when those steps are explained to subjects overall equilibration is faster.

Summary: This section reviewed signaling games about lobbying, equity finance, ratchet effects, and limit pricing. These games are very simple models of complex processes in these economic domains which assume signaling. The results are encouraging for the combination of simple game-theoretic predictions and adaptive processes. In the lobbying games, predictions of an equilibrium that survives universal divinity are roughly accurate and behavior responds to changes in payoff parameters, although less sharply than predicted. In the equity finance games without advertising, and in games with advertising and intuitive separating equilibria, behavior in later periods is very close to predicted. In finance games with two pooling equilibria, there tends to be bifurcation to either the both-advertise equilibrium or the none-advertise equilibrium. In the ratchet effect games, players often unwittingly reveal their types, subjecting themselves to ratchet effects; and other players applying ratchets (raising production quotas for productive firms) quickly notice the separation and exploit it. Chinese managers who are used to operating in planned economies with ratchet incentives do better when contextual labels remind them the game is familiar.

In limit pricing games, players in the role of low- and high-cost firms often unwittingly separate. Learning to (partially) pool is retarded by the noisy interpretation by entrants of what they can learn from the firms'

---

[21] The implicit assumption here is that attention is drawn to negative numbers, or that entrants believe players are more motivated to avoid out-of-pocket losses than opportunity losses, compared with the case in which 6 and 7 are dominated but yield positive payoffs.

Table 8.18.   *Quantity choices and entry rates: experienced subjects (percent)*

| | M_H | | | M_L | | | IN% | | |
| | Cycle | | | Cycle | | | Cycle | | |
Quantity	1	2	3	1	2	3	1	2	3
0% anticipation of M_H not playing 6–7									
1		2	2	2	5	0	0	100	100	100
2		38	26	38	5	2	0	95	92	94
3		**11**	18	**23**	22	9	8	67	56	86
4		49	**51**	33	**68**	**33**	**52**	42	69	72
5		0	3	4	3	28	30	100	17	47
6		0	1	0	0	6	0	—	50	—
7		0	0	0	4	9	9		33	50
100% anticipation of M_H not playing 6–7									
1		0	9	2	0	0	0	—	100	0
2		**56**	**76**	**78**	0	2	0	96	100	100
3		2	4	7	0	0	3	100	100	100
4		38	12	15	26	13	12	63	92	100
5		3	0	0	0	0	0	50	—	—
6		0	0	0	**75**	**84**	**88**	8	0	5
7		0	0	0	0	0	0	—	—	—

Notes: Numbers are estimated from Cooper Garvin, and Kagel (1997b, Figure 4). Median choices are in **boldface.**

output choices. Convergence to pure separation is sharper when payoffs are changed so that dominance violation for high-cost firms is easier to infer (exploiting vividness of losses), or when dominance violations are explicitly ruled out by forbidding high-cost firms to violate dominance.

In most of the games, simple learning notions such as fictitious play, or study of subjects' incentives to break a separating equilibrium, do a good job of explaining how equilibration occurs or where it fails.

8.3   Reputation Formation

In modern game theory, a player's reputation is crisply defined as the probability that she has a certain privately observed type or will take a certain action. The precision of these reputation models comes from sequential equilibrium assumptions, which tie together a player's reputation with the actions an optimizing player is likely to take. This precision also raises the empirical question of whether such complex equilibria actually occur when people play these games. Equilibria require a delicate trapeze act linking actions of the agents cultivating reputations with Bayesian updating by players who perceive reputations of others (knowing what the agents are likely to do).

8.3.1 Trust

The first paper to explore these reputation models carefully was by Weigelt and me (Camerer and Weigelt, 1988). We used a "trust" or borrower–lender game. In each eight-period repeated game, a single borrower drew a random type, either normal (X) or "nice" (Y). The same borrower played a series of eight stage games, with a different lender player each time. The lender could either lend or not lend; if she chose to lend, the borrower then decided whether to default or repay. Payoffs are shown in Table 8.19. Not lending gives the lender 10, and lending pays 40 if the loan is repaid or -100 if the borrower defaults. A normal borrower prefers to default, since she gets 150 rather than getting 60 from repayment. A nice borrower gets 0 from defaulting and thus prefers to repay.

Sequential equilibria for the eight-period game have the following properties: Lenders and borrowers must choose strategies with the highest expected payoffs given their beliefs; lenders update their beliefs about the borrower's type (X or Y) using Bayes' rule when possible; and, loosely speaking, lenders have *some* belief about the borrower's type after out-of-equilibrium events (when Bayes' rule cannot be applied).

With these requirements in mind, the equilibrium analysis proceeds as follows. Start from period 8. Since this is the last period, lenders know the borrower will default if she is type X and gets a loan, and will repay if she is type Y. Therefore, the only question is the probability that the incumbent is a nice type, $P_8(nice)$. Simple algebra shows that, if entrants are risk-neutral, they should enter if $P_8(nice)$ is above 0.79. Define this important

Table 8.19.   *Payoffs in Camerer and Weigelt's borrower–lender (trust) game*

Lender strategy	Borrower strategy	Payoffs to lender	Payoffs to borrower Normal (X)	Nice (Y)
Lend	Default	-100	150	0
	Repay	40	60	60
Don't lend	No choice	10	10	10

Source: Camerer and Weigelt (1988).

threshold to be τ. In the second-to-last period, period 7, normal borrowers are torn between two forces: Conditional on getting a loan, they would like to default to get the highest payoff; but if they do so they reveal their type and will not get a loan in period 8. Suppose the borrower's reputation (the perceived $P_7(nice)$ in period 7) is below τ. If the normal-type borrower always repays, Bayesian updating leads lenders to have the same perception $P(nice)$ in period 8 as in period 7. But since (by assumption) this $P(nice)$ $\leq \tau$, if borrowers always repay in period 7 they will not get a loan in period 8. The trick is for borrowers to play a mixed strategy, repaying frequently enough that if they *do* repay, the updated $P(nice)$ will be equal to τ, so that lenders will be willing to lend (actually, are indifferent) in the last period. Given a particular $P(nice)$ in period 7, the normal borrower should choose a repayment probability that keeps the lender indifferent to lending and not lending in period 7, and allows Bayesian updating of his reputation to the threshold τ in period 8. Combining these two conditions gives a threshold of perceived $P_7(nice)$ that happens to be τ^2, and a mixed strategy probability of default in period 7 of 0.560.

The same argument works by induction back to period 1. In each period the lender has a threshold of perceived $P(nice)$ which makes her indifferent to lending and not lending. The path of these $P(nice)$ values is simply τ^n. Figure 8.2 shows this path (using language for entry-deterrence in

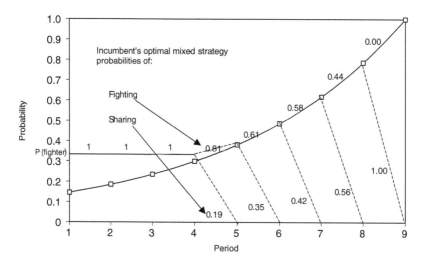

Figure 8.2. *Incumbent's optimal mixed strategy of fighting as predicted by sequential equilibrium. Source: Based on Camerer and Weigelt (1998). Note: Entrant's entering threshold =* $(.789)^{9-t}$.

which "fighter" incumbents correspond to nice borrowers and entrants correspond to lenders). The *y*-axis shows the entrant's reputation ($P(fighter)$) and the *x*-axis is the eight periods in the game (plus "period 9," which, like the 19th hole in golf, is a dummy period denoting perceptions after period 8 is over). The probabilities on the graph are the mixed-strategy probabilities of fighting by normal incumbents which keep the entrant's perceptions along this path (for an initial prior $P(fighter)$ of $1/3$).

Figure 8.2 can be used to illustrate all the key properties of this equilibrium.[22] In the first three periods, the threshold $P(nice)$ is below the prior of $1/3$, so borrowers can "afford" to always repay. Anticipating this, lenders should always lend. Beginning in period 4, normal borrowers must mix in order to boost their reputation, conditional on repaying, to stay along the equilibrium path of $P(nice)$ which increases. The probability of default rises as the last period draws near. Lenders also mix starting in period 4, lending with probability 0.643. If the borrower ever defaults, the entrant should never lend in subsequent periods.

Two patterns in the data are of primary interest. First, what is the rate of lending and default across periods (and how does it change across sequences)? And, second, do lending and repayment in each period of an eight-period sequence reflect prior history in that sequence as the equilibrium predicts?

Table 8.20 reports the conditional frequencies of lending and repayment (by normal types), from the last two-thirds of all the sequences, pooled together.[23] Actual frequencies significantly different than the prediction are marked by an asterisk.[24]

One key prediction was that lending should drop off sharply in period 5 (for experiments 3–5) or 4 (experiments 6–10). It did, but the drop was not as sharp as predicted. However, comparing the pooled periods predicted to have 100 percent lending together with those predicted to have a constant mixed rate of lending does show a sharp difference, which is close to the prediction. For example, in experiments 3–5 those pooled frequencies were

---

[22] Characteristically, there are other sequential equilibria. For example, the normal borrower might never repay, if she thinks that the entrant will perceive repayment as an indication of a normal type rather than a nice type. The intuitive criterion selects the equilibrium we discuss however, so we will casually refer to it as "the" equilibrium.

[23] The frequencies reported are conditional on within-sequence history. For lending, the frequencies are conditioned on no previous default and no failure to lend in the previous period (which, in theory, should lead lenders never to lend again in that sequence). For default, the frequencies are conditional on getting a loan, and on no previous default in the sequence.

[24] The statistical test assumes draws are independent across sequences, which is unlikely, but there is no accepted method for correcting for independence. Furthermore, dependence probably means the standard errors are too low, and hence the significance reported in the table is overstated.

Table 8.20.   *Lending and repayment rates: Camerer–Weigelt (percent)*

Experiments		Round (1 = start, 8 = end)							
		1	2	3	4	5	6	7	8
Conditional frequency of lending									
3–5	Predicted	100	100	100	100	64	64	64	64
	Actual	94	96	96	91	72	59	38*	67
6–8	Predicted	100	100	100	64	64	64	64	64
	Actual	96	99	100	95*	85*	72	58	47
9–10	Predicted	100	100	100	64	64	64	64	64
	Actual	93	92	83	70	63	72	77	33
Conditional frequency of repayment by normal (X) types									
3–5	Predicted	100	100	100	81	65	59	44	0
	Actual	95	97	98	95*	86*	72	47	14
6–8	Predicted	100	100	73	68	58	53	40	0
	Actual	97	95	97*	92*	85*	70*	48	0
9–10	Predicted	100	100	73	67	63	56	42	0
	Actual	91	89	80	77	84*	79*	48	29

Source: Camerer and Weigelt (1988).
Note: * denotes significant difference ($\text{abs}(z) > 2$) between predicted and actual frequencies.

95 and 62 percent (predicted to be 100 and 64); in experiments 6–8 the corresponding figures were 98 and 80.

Repayment rates did fall, from close to 100 percent in the first couple of periods, to nearly zero in the last period, but repayment was generally more common than predicted. We suggest an explanation for this discrepancy: Perhaps subjects act as if some proportion of players play like nice Y types instead, even when they draw normal X-type payoffs (preferring to pay back, even in the last period).[25]

The proportion of endogenous Y types necessary to explain discrepancies between the data and the predictions can be estimated from the data using a back-of-the-envelope calculation. We estimated the "homemade" $P(Y)$ to be 0.17 (that is, 17 percent of the subjects who drew the X type actually played as if they had Y-type payoffs). Based on that figure, we ran

---

[25] This is quite plausible given the evidence (see Chapter 3) that some players exhibit reciprocity, or social preferences that might make them reluctant to take an action that gives them 100 and another player −150, instead of a sacrificial action that gives them 60 and the other person 40.

experiments 9–10 in which there were *no* actual Y types at all. The predictions listed in Table 8.20 were derived from assuming that the homemade prior estimated from experiments 3–8 would then apply to experiments 9–10. This out-of-sample prediction was reasonably accurate: Predicted repayment rates were not far off (only erring significantly in periods 5–6) and predicted lending rates were quite close, averaging 90 and 67 in early and late periods when the predicted values were 100 and 64.

Weigelt and I concluded that "sequential equilibrium predicts reasonably well, given its complexity. However, formal statistical tests reject sequential equilibrium strongly for some periods of the game. Subjects failed to default as early in the game, or as often, as predicted" (Camerer and Weigelt, 1988, p. 26). The key phrase is "given its complexity." Although the equilibrium predictions are not perfectly accurate, they vary across periods in the correct direction and are not far off in magnitude. More importantly, the logic by which the predictions were derived was subtle and daring and used *no* free parameters! One can imagine many other stories about reputation-building, but they are often hard to test at all or lack the precision of the equilibrium prediction. At the time, it was hard for us to imagine a comparable theory that would deliver predictions that are just as precise and more accurate.

Neral and Ochs (1992) replicated our experiments with a critical eye on a key feature: In the later stages when players are assumed to mix, the probability $P(lend)$ should fall when the *borrower's* default payoff *falls*. (This kind of reverse payoff-dependence, in which A's mixture probabilities depend on B's payoffs, is a typical feature in games with mixed equilibria and is surely one of the more counterintuitive predictions of game theory; see Chapter 2.) Neral and Ochs tested for this perverse comparative static effect by varying the default payoff, from 150 to 100. Their design varied from ours in a few other small ways, designed to promote faster learning. They first compared the rates of four out-of-equilibrium events, which should never occur.[26] All four events are quite rare (1–13 percent), and substantially more rare than in our original study.

Table 8.21 reports the overall frequency of lending in each round of the six-round sequence and frequencies of repayment conditional on getting a loan.[27] Since Neral and Ochs's cell 1 uses the same parameters as Camerer and Weigelt (1988), the results should be the same unless the small change in design or subject pool matters. In fact, lending is a little higher in Neral and Ochs's data in middle rounds (marked by an * in CW cells), and repayment is significantly lower in one round.

---

[26] The events are not-lending in periods 1–2, loans following default, default in period 1, and final-round repayment.

[27] All frequencies are conditional on no previous defaults in the sequence and on no non-lending in the previous period.

Table 8.21. *Lending and repayment rates: Neral–Ochs (NO) and Camerer–Weigelt (CW)*

Condition	Round (1 = start, 6 = end)					
	1	2	3	4	5	6
Conditional frequency of lending						
Predicted (CW, NO-1)	100	100	64	64	64	64
Predicted (NO-2)	100	100	44	44	44	44
CW	96	89*	71*	51	32*	43
NO cell 1	100	99	88	60	70	88
NO cell 2	98	100	100	87	67	19
Cell 1–2 difference (*p*-value)	(.13)	(.81)	(.00)	(.00)	(.80)	(.00)
Conditional frequency of repayment by normal (X) types						
Predicted (all)	100	81	65	58	44	00
CW	98	92	85*	70	44	16
NO cell 1	98	97	64	51	55	00
NO cell 2	100	99	97	69	47	38
Cell 1–2 difference (*p*-value)	(.36)	(.21)	(.00)	(.09)	(.88)	(.21)

Sources: Neral and Ochs (1992); Camerer and Weigelt (1988).
Note: * denotes significant difference ($p < .02$) between CW and NO-1.

Table 8.21 also compares results from their cells 1 and 2 (with borrower default payoffs of 150 and 100, respectively). The table reminds you that lenders should lend *less* frequently in rounds 3–6 when the default payoff falls, only 44 percent of the time instead of 64 percent. The results go in the *opposite* direction of that prediction in rounds 3–5 (strongly so in two rounds, as indicated by reported *p*-values), and go significantly in the right direction in round 6. Sequential equilibrium also predicts that repayment rates should not depend on the borrower's default payoff, and this prediction is correct. Thus, the results are mixed to unfavorable for the sequential equilibrium prediction—one predicted effect fails to turn up (and often goes in the wrong direction) but the predicted non-effect on repayment is accurate.

Neral and Ochs estimated the apparent "homemade prior" of X types playing like Ys to be only 0.031, 0.019, and 0.091 in the three sessions of their cell 1, substantially lower than the 12–17 percent estimated by us. A test for pooling rejects homogeneity of these estimates at the .025 level. Thus, it appears unlikely that deviations from sequential equilibrium can be perfectly organized, across different experiments, by a single parameter.

Brandts and Figueras (1997) also studied repeated trust games. Their experiments extend our initial framework. After reviewing earlier results,

they note that "it is not clear how all these experimental results fit together."
They quote Selten's famous paper on the chain-store paradox:

> On the level of imagination a clear and detailed visualization of a se-
> quence of two, three or four periods is possible—the exact number is
> not important. A similarly clear and detailed visualization of a sequence
> of 20 periods is not possible. For a small number of periods the conclu-
> sions of the induction argument can be obtained by the visualization
> of scenarios. For a large number of periods the scenarios will either be
> restricted to several periods, e.g., at the end of the game, or the visu-
> alization will be vague in the sense that the individual periods are not
> seen in detail. (1978, p. 153)

Brandts and Figueras suggest that shorter games provide a suitable test of
sequential equilibrium because equilibria might be more visualizable or
imaginable, as Selten suggests, in games with fewer rounds. Their game uses
the basic Camerer–Weigelt structure except the lender's repayment payoff
is 55 rather than 40 and the borrower plays either three or six periods.
They vary the probability of nice type $P(Y)$ across $0, 0.25, 0.50, 0.75$. The
sequential equilibria for each of these parameter values differ dramatically.
Take the three-period games. When $P(Y)$ is 0 or 0.25 it is very likely that
the borrower is normal and won't pay back the loan, and three periods are
too few for a normal borrower to reap the rewards of paying back in the
first period, so the sequential equilibria predict lenders will never lend and
borrowers will never repay. When $P(Y)$ is 0.75, in contrast, most borrowers
are nice and it pays for the bankers to lend even in the last period. As a
result, it pays for normal borrowers to pay back in the first two periods and
for bankers always to lend. The equilibrium for $P(Y) = 0.50$ is between the
extreme cases.

Brandts and Figueras repeated the entire three six-period game seventy-
two times for each pool of subjects. Tables 8.22 and 8.23 report results averaged across the last quarter of the sessions (eighteen sequences). Asterisks
denote statistically significant deviations from the equilibrium predictions.

As they conjectured, behavior was fairly consistent with the sequential
equilibria in the extreme cases where $P(Y) = 0$ (never lend) and $P(Y) = 0.75$
(always lend), for both three- and six-period games. When $P(Y) = 0.25$ or
0.50 the picture is mixed. Bankers lent too often and borrowers repaid too
often. Brandts and Figueras estimated a homemade prior $P(Y)$ of 0.24–0.29.
However, adjusting for this effect does not generally move the (adjusted)
sequential equilibrium predictions much closer to the data.

Brandts and Figueras show that behavior *is* consistent with three basic
effects of period number, game length, and $P(Y)$. Changing variables one
at a time, there is more lending and more repayment in earlier periods,
for longer games, and as $P(Y)$ rises. Table 8.24 illustrates these properties with statistics from the last eighteen sequences of the six-period games,

Table 8.22.   *Repayment and lending rates in six-round games*

P(nice)		Round (1 = start, 6 = end)					
		1	2	3	4	5	6
Conditional frequency of lending							
0	Predicted	0	0	0	0	0	0
	Actual	61*	20	0	—	0	—
0.25	Predicted	100	100	64	64	64	64
	Actual	100	100	100*	86*	69	33
0.75	Predicted	100	100	100	100	100	100
	Actual	100	100	100	100	85	89
Conditional frequency of repayment by normal (X) types							
0	Predicted	0	0	0	0	0	0
	Actual	45*	37*	0	17	0	0
0.25	Predicted	100	98	61	55	41	0
	Actual	100	100	100*	80*	29	0
0.75	Predicted	100	100	100	100	100	0
	Actual	100	100	100	13	22	0

Source: Brandts and Figueras (1997).
Note: * denotes significant difference ($p < .02$) between predicted and actual.

smoothing the data by combining two-period pairs. Lending frequencies fell smoothly across rounds in each condition, and reneging frequencies rose. Furthermore, across the three values of $P(Y) = 0, 0.25$, and 0.75, the overall lending probabilities increased (0.37, 0.75, and 0.93) and repayment probabilities increased (0.31, 0.89, and 0.93). Brandts and Figueras concluded that behavior is consistent with basic principles of reputation formation even if it is not consistent with detailed predictions of sequential equilibrium.

8.3.2 Entry Deterrence

Jung, Kagel, and Levin (1994) ran experiments with a "chain-store" entry-deterrence game, which is a workhorse in industrial organization modeling. Chicago School economists (among others) are skeptical that monopolist firms deter entry by setting "predatory prices" or taking other unprofitable actions. The problem is that deterrence is a costly investment, and pays only if future entrants are dissuaded from deterring. But, if future entrants know that the incumbent monopolist can't lose money forever, they will enter,

Table 8.23. *Repayment and lending rates in three-round games (percent)*

		Round (1 = start, 3 = end)					
		Frequency of repayment			Frequency of lending		
P(*honesty*)		1	2	3	1	2	3
0	Predicted	0	0	0	0	0	0
	Actual	40*	0	0	17	0	0
0.25	Predicted	0	0	0	0	0	0
	Actual	91*	53*	17	85*	86*	53*
0.50	Predicted	99	41	0	100	64	64
	Actual	86	68*	0	52*	100*	64
0.75	Predicted	100	100	0	100	100	100
	Actual	100	86	0	100	100	100

Source: Brandts and Figueras (1997).
Note: * denotes significant difference ($p < .02$) between predicted and actual.

so it doesn't pay to deter in the short run. Early experiments by Isaac and Smith (1985) in a complete-information framework showed that predation was indeed rare.

  Jung, Kagel, and Levin pointed out that incomplete-information reputational models were being developed around the same time to formalize Selten's (1978) intuition that deterrence would occur until the last few periods if the game was finitely repeated. And my earlier experimental results with Weigelt suggested that reputation-formation was possible, even without an exogenous prior "type" that likes to deter. Jung, Kagel, and Levin were motivated by both the experimental results confirming some predictions of the new models and the fact that the likelihood of predatory pricing or en-

Table 8.24. *Repayment and lending rates in six-round games: Two-period pairs*

	$h = 0$			$h = 0.25$			$h = 0.75$		
Rounds	1–2	3–4	5–6	1–2	3–4	5–6	1–2	3–4	5–6
Lending frequency	46	36	29	100	93	32	100	1	78
Repayment frequency	42	27	19	100	91	25	100	93	37

Source: Brandts and Figueras (1997).

Table 8.25. *Payoffs in the chain-store game*

Entrant strategy	Incumbent strategy	Payoffs to entrant	Payoffs to incumbent	
			Normal (X)	Fighter (Y)
In	Fight	80	70	160
	Share	150	160	70
Out	No choice	95	300	300

Source: Jung, Kagel, and Levin (1994).

try deterrence is a long-standing problem in IO, which experimental data might shed light on.

Their design closely followed ours and the game-theoretic models. Table 8.25 shows payoffs. The entrants prefer to play IN if met by SHARE behavior, earning 150, but they earn the least if the incumbent fights (80) and earn an intermediate payoff of 95 from staying OUT. A "normal" incumbent earns 300 if the entrant is out, earns 160 if the entrant plays IN and she plays SHARE, and earns only 70 if she fights. Fighter-type incumbents have share and fight payoffs reversed. Payoffs were increased for entrants in two sessions.[28] With these parameters, the sequential equilibrium is very much like the one in the Camerer–Weigelt trust games: fighting for a couple of periods (and entrants staying out) followed by mixing, with an increasing tendency to share toward later periods. (The exact predictions are given in Table 8.26.)

The main treatment variables in the experiments by Jung et al. were experience (some subjects returned for a second session) and the prior $P(fighter)$, which was 1/3 in six sessions and 0 in six sessions. Results are summarized in Tables 8.26 and 8.27, reported separately for early (1–30) and late (31–end) sequences within a session.[29]

Consider $P(fighter) = 1/3$ first. Inexperienced subjects generally entered more often than predicted, because entrants shared more often than predicted. The rates of entry and sharing were also close to equal across periods within a sequence (except that entrants always shared in period 8), and showed little evidence of the early fighting predicted by the reputation-formation equilibrium. However, experienced subjects did behave as the equilibrium predicted, in later sequences (31–end): They hardly ever entered in the first four periods, and entrants never shared (i.e., always fought)

---

[28] In sessions 5–6, entrant payoffs were 150 for in–fight, 475 for in–share, and 300 for out.

[29] The entry rates are conditional on no sharing previously in the sequence, and are reported separately for subsamples in which another entrant played in or out in the previous period. Sharing rates are conditional on no previous sharing in the sequence and on entry.

Table 8.26. Entry and fighting rates: P(fighter) = 1/3 (percent)

		Round (1 = start, 8 = end)							
Experience? Sequences		1	2	3	4	5	6	7	8
Conditional frequency of entry after previous IN									
	Predicted	—	0	0	0	36	36	36	36
No	1–30 Actual	—	45*	37*	38*	41	25	16	28
No	31–end Actual	—	30*	33*	26*	40	27	38	61*
Yes	1–30 Actual	—	28*	22	20	40	33	62	60*
Yes	31–end Actual	—	0	0	0	0	33	75*	82*
Conditional frequency of entry after previous OUT									
	Predicted	—	0	0	0	100	100	100	100
No	1–30 Actual	—	77*	62*	31*	35*	45*	44*	31*
No	31–end Actual	—	62*	40*	45*	35*	28*	45*	63*
Yes	1–30 Actual	—	37*	31*	18*	21*	24*	62*	70*
Yes	31–end Actual	—	0	1	2	5*	16*	67*	100
Conditional frequency of SHARE after entry									
	Predicted	0	0	0	19	35	42	56	100
No	1–30 Actual	60*	18	17	17	10	18	20	75
No	31–end Actual	17*	18*	7	15	5	14	33	98
Yes	1–30 Actual	15	0	0	0	11	8	27	100
Yes	31–end Actual	0	0	0	0	0	18	43	93

Source: Jung, Kagel, and Levin (1994).
Note: * denotes significant difference (abs(z) > 2) between predicted and actual frequencies.

when there was entry. In periods 6–8, incumbents began to share with increasing frequency, roughly as the equilibrium predicted (though the exact sharing rates were not that close to those predicted). Entrants also began to enter more and more frequently, which was a pattern not predicted.

These data illustrate why it is always wise to run an experiment for many sequences—if you don't do so, you miss the opportunity to see what might happen if the subjects had more time to learn. In this case, the main conclusion from thirty sequences of play—that equilibrium predictions are badly rejected—was overturned by more experience.[30]

---

[30] This is *not* to say, of course, that the data from experienced subjects in later sequences are the right ones to generalize from to naturally occurring environments. Some economics is about inexperienced people making rare decisions with few learning opportunities (students choosing colleges, people getting married, deciding when to have children, buying houses, and so on). In other situations people have lots of experience

Table 8.27. *Late-sequence entry and fighting rates: P(fighter) = 0 (percent)*

Experience?	Sequences		Round (1 = start, 8 = end)							
			1	2	3	4	5	6	7	8
Conditional frequency of entry after previous IN										
		Predicted (P = 0)	—	100	100	100	100	100	100	100
		Predicted (P = 0.2)	—	0	36	36	36	36	36	36
No	31–end	Actual	—	75*	48	51	74*	58*	56	82*
Yes	31–end	Actual	—	19	21	20	47	67*	89*	100*
Conditional frequency of entry after previous OUT										
		Predicted (P = 0)	—	100	100	100	100	100	100	100
		Predicted (P = 0.2)	—	0	100	100	100	100	100	100
No	31–end	Actual	—	60*	37*	35*	37*	33*	76	78
Yes	31–end	Actual	—	27	31*	28*	35*	64*	82*	100
Conditional frequency of SHARE after entry										
		Predicted (P = 0)	100	100	100	100	100	100	100	100
		Predicted (P = 0.2)	0	19	28	31	35	42	56	100
No	31–end	Actual	59*	27*	8	21	29	27	50	79
Yes	31–end	Actual	7	30*	9	21	31	53	69	100

Source: Jung, Kagel, and Levin (1994).
Note: * denotes significant difference (abs(z) > 2) between predicted (P = 0.2) and actual frequencies.

Table 8.27 shows data from games where there were no fighter types. Following Camerer and Weigelt, Jung et al. reported predictions assuming that players think 20 percent of the subjects behave like fighter types, denoted $P = 0.2$. (The table also shows predictions from assuming no fighters, which leads to unravelling and chronic entry and sharing.) The complete unravelling idea is clearly refuted. For experienced subjects, entry rates were a little too flat across periods, and rose too much in later periods, compared with the rates predicted by the homemade prior ($P = 0.2$) theory, but they went in the right direction.

Jung, Kegel, and Levin concluded that "the data satisfy a number of qualitative implications of SE [sequential equilibrium] reputation-based arguments supporting predatory pricing"(1994, p. 90)—namely there was less entry and sharing in early periods and when the prior $P(fighter)$ was

(learning food preferences, negotiating with business partners and long-term employees). Experiments should tell us about behavior in both kinds of situations, and only long experiments do so.

higher. But they gave "the Kreps and Wilson SE model lower marks than Camerer and Weigelt did" and suggested that different parameter values might explain the difference. Most importantly for industrial organization, they noted that one can find predatory behavior by incumbent firms in suitable experimental environments.

8.3.3 Learning in Repeated Games

Weigelt and I concluded our 1988 paper by suggesting that "The data could be fit to statistical learning models, though new experiments or new models might be needed to explain learning adequately. Indeed, even equilibrium behavior could conceivably be better explained by a heuristic model in which people adapt or learn to approximate sequential equilibrium, than by sequential equilibrium itself" (Camerer and Weigelt, 1988, p. 28).

Camerer, Ho, and Chong (2002a,b) were the first to look seriously at a precise heuristic learning model that could generate the approximate adaptation that we (and others) saw in signaling games. Their theory is an extension of the experience-weighted attraction (EWA) approach described in Chapter 6. It is extended to repeated games by assuming that incumbent firms know how entrants are learning, and take into account what their current actions "teach" the entrants to expect, which creates future gains (see Fudenberg and Levine, 1989; Watson, 1993; Watson and Battigali, 1997). Strategic teaching is measured by two parameters: The fraction of incumbent players who sophisticatedly think the entrants are learning (α) (the rest of the incumbents play adaptively), and the weight placed on future payoffs (see Camerer, Ho, and Chong for details).

In the Jung et al. entry games, 27 percent of the incumbents were estimated to be teachers when subjects were inexperienced and this estimate rises to 55 percent when subjects were experienced, which means players were learning to be more sophisticated (and teach) across sessions. In the Camerer–Weigel trust games, the estimated proportion of teachers was the same as for experienced entry-game subjects, 55 percent. The out-of-sample hit rate of the teaching model was around 70 percent in most sessions, which is not bad. (Even in equilibrium, the hit rate cannot be more than about 85 percent since there is mixing.) An agent form of QRE, a benchmark static model, predicts less accurately than the teaching model in every entry game session, and in eight of ten trust game sessions.

Figures 8.3a–8.3b shows histograms of the relative frequency of lending across periods 1–8 (Figure 8.3a), averaged across ten-sequence blocks (conditional on no default earlier in the sequence), and the conditional relative frequency of default given that a loan was made in a particular period (Figure 8.3b). Loans are made in early periods (i.e., "no loan" is rare) but are increasingly rare in later periods of a sequence; and default is rare in early periods but common in later periods. There is also a slight tendency for these patterns to emerge more strongly across sequences (in particular, no-loan and default in early periods disappear across sequences). Figures 8.4c–8.4d show the predicted frequencies from the teaching model. The model gets the basic within-sequence patterns right and captures the slight trend across sequences, but predicts too few no-loans and defaults in later periods of a sequence.

Although these fits are not too visually impressive, the model persistently outpredicts agent-QRE, which by construction will always outpredict standard game-theoretic concepts. Other parameter estimates show that the EWA teaching approaches improve on other adaptive models (reinforcement and belief learning) because the parameter restrictions those models impose are confidently rejected. So, although the model leaves room for improvement, it is demonstrably more accurate than existing models.

It is conceivable that learning models in which players start with complex repeated game strategies, but learn amongst them using simple learning heuristics, could fit these data even better. The danger is that the repeated game strategies that are selected by the modeler are tailor-made to fit a particular data set. The teaching model creates such repeated-game strategies "automatically" if they are profitable for teachers and builds in sensitivity to the time horizon and other structural parameters. (For example, teachers will behave nicely in trust games, to teach lenders that lending pays, but they will also behave meanly in entry games, to teach entrants that entry does not pay.) The model also has more intuitive properties than type-based equilibrium models.[31]

Summary: Reputation-formation in repeated games is popular in applied economics, and to a lesser extent in political science, but there are amazingly few experiments compared with the large amount of theorizing. Experiments on reputation-formation in trust and entry-deterrence games are remarkably supportive of sequential equilibrium, given how complex the equilibria are. The main effects go in the right direction, but many features of the equilibria (e.g., constant entry rates within blocks of adjacent periods) are clearly wrong. Those who are skeptical of these theories as predictions of what will happen should be impressed that they work at all, in

---

[31] For example, the type-based model predicts "missed opportunity." In later periods of a sequence, if the reputation-building player does not get a chance to move—if an entrant doesn't enter, or a lender doesn't lend—then in every period after that the entrants should enter (and the incumbents share), and the lenders won't lend. Missing an opportunity to build reputation ruins one's reputation. In the teaching model, a missed opportunity means entrants learn only a little about the relative payoffs of strategies so there is not a sharp decline in the predicted incidence of not lending or not entering.

(a) Actual frequency of not lending

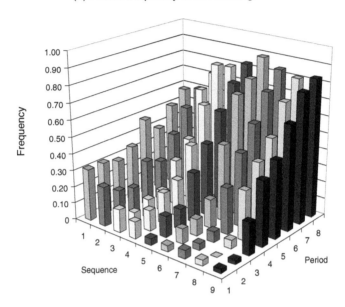

(b) Actual frequency of default (conditional on getting a loan)

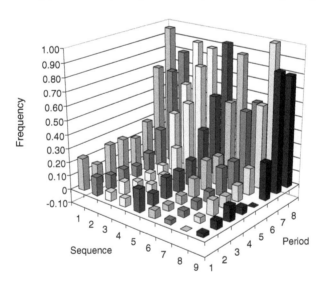

Figure 8.3. *Results and model fits in trust games. Source: Camerer, Ho, and Chong (2002a), pp. 170–71, Figure 5; reproduced with permission of Academic Press.*

(c) Predicted frequency of not lending

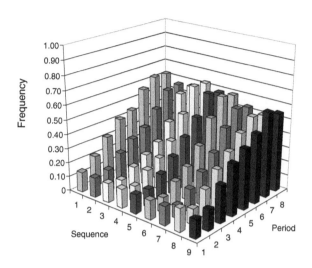

(d) Predicted frequency of default

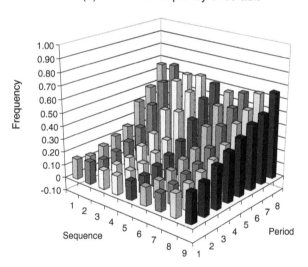

Figure 8.3 (continued)

the same way that people who thought heavier-than-air flight was impossible should be impressed that the Wright brothers' crude airplane even got off the ground.

8.4 Conclusion

In signaling games, one player observes private information and takes an action which may signal their information to a "receiver" player (who knows the distribution of the private information but not exactly what the information is). These games are common in applied social science, particularly economics. They are useful for describing the choice of price, product quality, and other features of products (e.g., warranties). They are also useful for understanding personal actions people take such as getting education and everyday gestures. Signaling games are also popular explanations for why players might appear to behave irrationally. In signaling, players use actions to generate high payoffs *and* to convey information. Sometimes the need to convey information leads to "irrational" behavior (e.g., labor strikes).

A few experiments used abstract signaling games to explore the predictive accuracy of logical "refinements." These refinements deem some equilibria to be more plausible than others, depending on whether out-of-equilibrium beliefs about which type of player deviated from an equilibrium reflect economic incentives for different types to deviate. Results from these games are supportive of very simple equilibrium refinements—particularly sequentiality (requiring receivers to have *some* belief about which types deviated). However, equilibration takes time. And games can be constructed in which players converge to unintuitive equilibria, when historical paths of which types deviated during early play conflict with logical refinement criteria.

Other experiments were modeled after specific economic phenomena—lobbying, equity financing by firms, ratchet effects in production systems with quotas, and limit pricing. In these games, equilibration is often sharp and impressive, although the ratchet and limit pricing games show limited strategic sophistication (players reveal their types unwittingly, allowing their production quotas to be ratcheted upward or entrants to enter).

In repeated games, players who have "normal" types have a strong incentive to mimic unusual types—fighting in repeated entry-deterrence games, and repaying loans in repeated trust games—when that mimicry in early periods benefits them in later periods. Behavior in these games is often remarkably consistent, with very precise, bold predictions of (intuitive) sequential equilibrium, although many subtler predictions of the reputation-formation theories are quite wrong.

The general result from these experiments is characterized thoughtfully by Cooper, Garvin, and Kagel (1997b, p. 555), who wrote:

> game theory is at its foundation a hypothesis about how people behave. In particular, it posits that individuals will attempt to anticipate the behavior of others and respond accordingly. This is the soul of game theory, and the experiments indicate that it is alive and well. What may not be so healthy are the legion of assumptions which have been added to the theory in order to get tractable results. In the rush to get theories which give sensible outcomes and are easily employed by theorists, the reality of how people actually behave may have been left behind. We do not suggest that game theory be abandoned, but rather as a descriptive model that it needs to incorporate more fully how people actually behave.

The theoretical limits that are strained by observed behavior are the limits one might expect. Players are myopic at first, rather than fully anticipating how their choices may unwittingly reveal information. Players do not make immediate (or equilibrium) inferences about what types are revealed by choices, as equilibrium theories expect. And counterintuitive properties of equilibria—such as independence of one player's mixing probabilities from their own payoffs—are generally not consistent with what players do.

In Selten's original article on the chain-store paradox (1978) he noted that, in a twenty-period entry game, backward induction leads logically to unravelling. He suggested an alternative "deterrence theory." He wrote (pp. 131–32):

> It is true that the reasoning of the induction theory is very compelling for the last periods of the game. Therefore player A [the incumbent] cannot neglect these arguments completely. He should decide on the basis of his intuition for how many of the last periods he wants to accept the induction argument. . . . Deterrence theory does not yield precise rules of behavior since some details are left to the intuition of the players, but this does not impair the practical applicability of the theory.

I think it is crucial to try to be as precise as possible about the "intuition" players are likely to have, and to make bold predictions about a variety of models. The right way to generalize the equilibrium theories and to formalize the intuition Selten wrote about is to take their basic building blocks and weaken some of the rationality assumptions.

Models such as quantal-response equilibrium or ϵ-equilibrium may explain the correspondence of actual behavior with equilibrium behavior, where it is observed, and explain observed deviations as well. These generalizations of equilibrium are certainly a step in the right direction. However, learning theories will also prove useful in explaining where equilibration occurs, and where it does not. Many of the studies in this chapter (particularly those modeled after specific economic or political games) do include a learning analysis, typically based on belief learning or EWA learning. The influence of learning is magnified when some players understand that others are learning. These "sophisticated" players have an incentive to take short-run actions that, although perhaps costly, will "teach" the players who learn what to expect in a way that benefits the teachers.

Cooper, Garvin, and Kagel also noted that, because the logics of type revelation and inference are not as empirically sharp as equilibria predict, "there may be quite a bit of room for redundant signals to help clarify messages in signaling games, a notion that is routinely dismissed in most economic models" (1997b, p. 573). If some players are boundedly rational and cannot perfectly calculate or infer what choices by others mean, then a variety of communication mechanisms can either exploit these bounds, or work around them for mutual gain.

9

Conclusion: What Do We Know, and Where Do We Go?

GAME THEORY WAS CREATED to provide a mathematical language for describing social interaction. Since then, game theory has become the standard tool in economics, is increasingly used in biology and political science, and is sporadically used in sociology, psychology, and anthropology.

This book describes a large, and rapidly growing, body of experimental data designed to address two major criticisms of game theory: first, that game theory assumes more calculation, foresight, perceived rationality of others, and (in empirical applications) self-interest than most people are naturally capable of; and, second, that in most applied domains there is too much theorizing about how rational people *would* interact strategically, relative to the modest amount of empirical evidence on how they *do* interact. (No science—*especially* the "hard" sciences economists envy most, such as physics, chemistry and biology—has flourished without a very large dose of data-constraining theorizing.)

Both criticisms can be addressed by observing how people behave in experiments in which their information and incentives are carefully controlled. These experiments test how accurately game-theoretic principles predict the behavior. When principles are not accurate, the results of the experiment usually suggest alternative principles. This dialogue between theory and observation creates an approach called "behavioral game theory," which is a formal modification of rational game theory aided by experimental evidence and psychological intuition. The modifier "behavioral" is a reminder that the theory is explicitly intended to predict behavior of people (and collectivities like firms), and draws as directly as possible on evidence from psychology to do so. The eventual goal is for game theorists to accept behavioral game theory as useful and necessary. When that time comes, the central ideas in this book will be part of every standard game theory book and the term "behavioral" can be shed.

An important preface to the summary of results that comes next is that behavioral game theory is *not* a scolding catalog of how poorly game theory describes choices. In fact, the results are uniformly mixed, in a way that encourages the view that better theory is close at hand. In "simple" games with mixed equilibria (Chapter 3) and in more complex games involving signaling of private information (Chapter 8), after a couple of hours of experimental interaction behavior is often surprisingly close to the predictions which have no business working so well. (In some of these cases, such as Rubinstein's email game, see Chapter 5, subjects start out from a bizarre equilibrium and end up close to it only two hours later.) And where game theory clearly describes badly—as in simple bargaining games (Chapter 2) and dominance-solvable games (Chapter 5)—simple parametric modifications promise to be excellent replacements for standard ideas. It appears to be easy to modify theories so self-interested people are human, and infinite steps become finite, while preserving the central principle in game theory—namely, that players think about what others are likely to do, and do so with some degree of thought.

9.1 Summary of Results

Summarizing the results in each chapter, the lessons from hundreds of experiments are the following:

9.1.1 Simple Bargaining Games

In prisoners' dilemma (PD) and public goods (PG) games, players pit their own self-interest against collective interest: Cooperating risks earning less, but yields more if others cooperate. PD and PG games have been studied in thousands of experiments, which show that people often cooperate in these games. Although these games are good models of many social situations, they cannot distinguish between players who are vindictive or negatively reciprocal and those who are simply self-interested (both types of players defect in PD and give nothing in PG). So a wider range of simple games is actually more useful than simply PD and PG for figuring out what sorts of choices people will make to express their emotional attitudes. In the dictator game—not a game at all, just a decision—one player dictates a division of a sum of money between herself and another player. Ultimatum games add a rejection option to the dictator game—a second Responder player can reject the ultimatum offer (leaving both with nothing). In trust games, the amount to be allocated by a dictator (Trustee) is determined by an investment by an

Investor. These games are the minimal building blocks of social interaction (e.g., any bargaining process with a sharp deadline, as is typical in litigation and labor–management negotiations, ends in an ultimatum game). More importantly, the games are tools that can be used to measure the structure of social preferences (i.e., how utilities for money allocations depend on one's own earnings and how much others earn, perhaps depending on the sequence of moves leading up to the allocation choice).

The basic regularities from a large body of experiments are these. Players exhibit a small degree of altruism by allocating 10–20 percent of their endowment to others in the dictator game. However, they also show negative reciprocity by rejecting ultimatum-game offers that are less than 20 percent about half the time. (Generally, players proposing ultimatum offers anticipate this rejection profile and offer 30–50 percent.) In trust games, where one player's investment determines how much a second-mover Trustee can allocate back in a dictator game, players risk about half their investment and earn essentially nothing for their investment (i.e., they get back about as much as they invested). The dictator and trust games also seem to be "weaker" social situations; hence results vary with independent variables substantially whereas ultimatum offers are relatively stable. Although Trustee repayments are often interpreted as evidence of positive reciprocity, studies that compare how much Trustees allocate to first-moving Investors (reciprocating positively) with allocations of equivalent amounts in dictator games suggest that positive reciprocity is weak. But players are more likely to reject an unfair offer in an ultimatum game, compared with their propensity to reject the same offers generated by a random device. Taken together, these data suggest that positive reciprocity is weak relative to negative reciprocity. (As in life, laboratory subjects are quicker to avenge perceived attacks than they are to write thank-you notes.)

In these experiments, there are also substantial individual differences and interesting effects of the way the game is labeled and the cultures in which subjects live. Anthropologists have investigated about a dozen simple, small-scale societies. Pure self-interest predicts that players in ultimatum games offer very little and accept whatever is offered. The fact that these primitive groups behave self-interestedly, but subjects in most developed countries do not, shows that there is a large cultural component to social preference.

Results have generated the most impressive dialogue between observation and theorizing, in the form of several models that posit a social utility function intended to explain *all* the results from different games in a parsimonious way. In "inequality-aversion" models, players care about their own earnings and their share, or the difference in earnings between themselves and others. In reciprocity-based models, players form a judgment about whether another player has treated them fairly, and respond to negative treatment with negative treatment and to positive treatment with positive treatment.

I cannot emphasize enough how important these new models are, and how rapidly they should be incorporated into mainstream economic theory. They show that concern for the payoffs (and behavior) of others *can* be modeled parsimoniously, and those models are precise enough to be falsified by new data. The models also rest on the idea that self-interest is an exception, or a heuristic outcome, rather than the rule in human behavior. Most of the models permit players to behave self-interestedly when the stakes are large, or when they do not know how much others are earning, or when their decisions cannot benefit a player they would like to help without harming somebody they would like to hurt (as in a competitive market). Thus, self-interested behavior can occur in a model in which people do care about others, when the cost of expressing that concern is too high or when the market's competitive structure makes it impossible to sacrifice one's own earnings to reduce inequality. Given the ability of these models to explain *both* self-interest and social preference, there is no good reason why these models should not immediately replace self-interest assumptions in social science as the frontier for interesting new research.

9.1.2 Mixed-Strategy Equilibria

In games with only mixed-strategy equilibria, players are assumed to randomize to prevent others from detecting some pattern in their choices, which can be exploited if the game is played repeatedly. (Or, in the modern interpretation, players may not feel as if they are consciously randomizing, but other players have uncertain beliefs about what these players will do, which are correct on average.) Although behavior in these games is often said to contradict game-theoretic predictions, my reading of the data (see Chapter 3) is quite different: In most of these games players choose strategies with proportions that lie somewhere between equal probability and the mixed-strategy prediction. Furthermore, it is hard to think of a simple theory that improves on the predictions of mixed-strategy equilibrium (though quantal response equilibrium and cognitive hierarchy models are the best bets to do so). The relative success of mixed-strategy predictions is surprising because explicit randomization seems unnatural. And people do exhibit small biases when they attempt to generate random sequences (they alternate too much, although they are closer to independent random draws when they play games against others compared with generating random sequences). The overall picture is that mixed equilibria do not provide bad guesses about how people behave, on average.

9.1.3 Bargaining

In unstructured bargaining, the precise order of moves and allowable message-passing is deliberately left uncontrolled. In structured bargaining, a specific order and message protocol is imposed. Examples of structured bargaining include alternating-offer bargaining with a "shrinking pie," or fixed bargaining costs, and models in which players have asymmetric information about their valuations. The basic finding from these studies is that offers and counteroffers are usually somewhere between an equal split of the money being bargained over and the offer predicted by subgame-perfect game theory. Many of these results are approximately equilibrium outcomes when social preferences are properly specified. But there is also clear evidence from measuring players' attention that they do not instinctively use backward induction algorithms as some game-theoretic equilibria assume, even in games much simpler than those that are routinely played in life.

9.1.4 Iterated Dominance

In many interesting games, an equilibrium choice can be predicted by sufficient iterated deletion of dominated strategies. Games in this class include simple "bets on the rationality of others," "beauty contest" guessing games, imperfect price competition, a patent race game, centipede games, "dirty faces" games adapted from logic, and Rubinstein's "email game." These games lead to a unique predicted strategy choice if dominated strategies are eliminated iteratedly (assume others will not choose dominated strategies, eliminate strategies that are dominated if that assumption holds, and so forth). In all these games, the strategies players choose are correlated with the number of steps of iterated dominance they do. The results can therefore be used to measure, indirectly, the level of iterated reasoning. Most studies indicate that players use two–three levels of iterated dominance; that is, they do not violate dominance in their own choices, but act as if they are unsure that others obey dominance or that others think *they* obey dominance. In experiments with substantial learning opportunity, however, players do converge in the direction of the dominance-solvable outcome, sometimes amazingly so.

9.1.5 Learning

An exciting area of recent research is the careful testing of precise models of how individuals learn, using experimental data. (Evolutionary models have also been tested against data rarely, but are usually strongly rejected relative to individual-level models.) My conclusions about this area of research are strongly influenced by my own work on experience-weighted attraction (EWA) learning (with Teck Ho and Kuan Chong).

There is now little doubt that any of several learning theories can account for the time path of experimental data better than equilibrium concepts can (which, of course, do not predict any change over time at all and hence represent a basic hurdle, but a low one). The central idea in our theory is that players attend to forgone payoffs from strategies they did not choose, but they also pay special attention to the strategies they did choose. The two best-known models, reinforcement and belief learning, are extremes of our hybrid approach in which players pay *no* special attention to what they actually earned (belief learning) or care *only* about what they actually earned (reinforcement learning). There is ample evidence from various sources that both of these simplifying assumptions are wrong enough that they can be easily relaxed in a slightly more general model that allows both intuitions (special attention to actual payoffs and *some* attention to forgone payoffs). As a result, the hybrid EWA model predicts new data and new games more robustly than reinforcement and belief models do, in the sense that the hybrid never forecasts much more poorly, and sometimes forecasts much more accurately.

A simpler variant of EWA theory could turn out to be very useful as a general theory of learning because it fits and predicts well, and it rests on good psychological intuitions. When sophistication is incorporated (the belief that others are learning), it nests equilibrium concepts as special no-learning benchmarks, and can also be used to understand "strategic teaching" in repeated games. However, in games where players do not know forgone payoffs—as in many naturally occurring situations—players must form some guess about forgone payoffs (perhaps using a "payoff learning" module, which may include familiar heuristics such as hill-climbing). The most interesting competitor to EWA is "rule learning," most extensively investigated in games by Dale Stahl. In rule learning, players implicitly keep track of how several different learning rules do, and gradually shift weight toward those that do better.

9.1.6 Coordination

In games with multiple equilibria, a variety of "selection principles" have been proposed to predict (or prescribe) which equilibria are most likely to arise. I distinguish three kinds of coordination games: pure matching games, in which all equilibria have the same payoffs for a player, so that only "focal" or psychologically prominent strategy labels can be used to coordinate on a particular equilibrium; stag hunt or "assurance" games, in which the payoff-dominant equilibrium is often risky; and battle-of-the-sexes (BOS) games, in which different equilibria are preferred by different players. The basic regularities are that coordination failure is common, in two senses: Players do not know how to mutually best-respond rapidly, and they converge toward payoff-dominated equilibria. However, coordination failure is typical and predictable and depends on the amount of risk in choosing a payoff-dominant equilibrium strategy and on some features of adaptive dynamics. Communication also has an interesting effect in these games: It improves coordination when strategic uncertainty can be resolved by preplay announcements (in stag hunt games), but helps resolve BOS only if one player gets to make an announcement. (In BOS, one announcement means taking charge, but two announcements create an argument.)

9.1.7 Signaling

In signaling games with asymmetric information, the sender's action may signal private information to a receiver. These games are quite prominent in many theories of economic and social phenomena—strikes, education, trust-building, entry deterrence—but have not been thoroughly tested experimentally. Evidence is particularly useful because signaling games often have several Bayesian–Nash equilibria, which can be distinguished by whether they obey certain criteria ("refinements") for the plausibility of beliefs players have about which type of sender would make a very unlikely choice. The experiments indicate that players do converge toward signaling equilibria. However, fancy refinement criteria do not help much in predicting which equilibria emerge, and it is not hard to construct games in which less refined equilibria emerge reliably.

Behavioral game theory attempts to explain this broad pattern of regularities using simple models that generalize standard tools. My basic outlook agrees wholeheartedly with the conclusion of Vince Crawford (1997, pp. 235–36)—except for one word: "the results of experiments give good reason to hope that most strategic behavior can be understood via a synthesis that combines elements from each of the leading theoretical frameworks [traditional noncooperative game theory, cooperative game theory, evolutionary game theory, and adaptive learning models] with a modicum of empirical information about behavior." My semantic quibble with Crawford's quote is the word "modicum." Its dictionary definition is "a small portion; a limited quantity" (like the amount of salt used in cooking a dish—you don't want to use too much!). I think the opposite is true—*lots* of evidence is needed, not just a small portion, to suggest which of the leading theoretical frameworks is most suitable, and to refine precisely how to generalize theory.

Some people like to cook straight from a recipe. Here is my personal recipe for using behavioral game theory. Like many cooking recipes, it is personalized (using lots of "home-grown" mathematical ingredients), but it also permits substitution of ingredients and should certainly be tinkered with. Here it is:

Are you interested in wage-setting, bargaining, tax policy, or local public good production, and looking for a parsimonious specification of social preferences? Try the Fehr–Schmidt inequality-aversion approach (the easiest to use, Chapter 2). Functional form: the utility of player i from vector X with payoff components x_k is

$$U_i(X) = x_i - \frac{\alpha}{n-1} \sum_{k \neq i} \max(x_k - x_i, 0) - \frac{\beta}{n-1} \sum_{k \neq i} \max(x_i - x_k, 0).$$

Zero-calorie parametric shortcut: try $\beta = 0, \alpha = 1/3$. Suggested substitutes: Bolton–Ockenfels ERC or Charness–Rabin Rawlsitarian, or some variant of Rabin's theory, which allows true reciprocity.

Do you want a parsimonious alternative to Nash equilibrium, to give a reasonable guess about what might happen in the first period of a game, or as initial conditions for a model of learning? Try the Camerer–Ho–Chong cognitive hierarchy approach (Chapter 5). Functional form: $f(0 \mid \tau)$ percent of players randomize across h strategies. For (integer) $k > 0$ (cap it at eight levels), the fraction $f(k \mid \tau)$ of level-k thinkers choose strategy s_i with probability $P_k(s^i) = I(s^i, s_k^*)$, where

$$s_k^* = \text{argmax}_{s^j} \sum_{m=1}^{h} \pi_i(s^j, s^m) \left[\sum_{c=0}^{k-1} f(c) P_c(s^m) \middle/ \sum_{d=0}^{k-1} f(d) \right]$$

(where $\pi_i(s^j, s^h)$ denotes i's payoff when she plays s^j and others play s^h). (That is, level-k thinkers best-respond against a normalized perceived distribution of lower-level types.) The predicted percentage of play of strategy s_i is $f(0 \mid \tau)(1/h) + \sum_{k=1}^{8} f(k \mid \tau) P_k(s_i)$. Zero-calorie parametric shortcut: try $f(k \mid \tau) = e^\tau \tau^k / k!$ (Poisson) and $\tau = 1.5$. Suggested substitute: quantal response equilibrium.

Do you want a model of learning that is flexible across games (Chapter 6)? Try the Camerer–Ho–Chong functional EWA model. Functional form of attraction updating after period t ($\kappa_{it} = 0$, $s_i(t)$ denotes actual choice of i in t):

$$A_i^j(t) = \frac{\phi_{it} \cdot N(t-1) \cdot A_i^j(t-1) + [\delta_{it} + (1 - \delta_{it}) \cdot I(s_i^j, s_i(t))] \cdot \pi_i(s_i^j, s_{-i}(t))}{N(t-1) \cdot \phi_{it} + 1}.$$

Fix $N(0) = 1$, calculate the change-detector

$$\phi_i(t) = \delta_{it} = 1 - 0.5 \left(\sum_{j=1}^{m_{-i}} \left[\frac{\sum_{\tau=t-W+1}^{t} I(s_{-i}^j, s_{-i}(\tau))}{W} - \frac{\sum_{\tau=1}^{t} I(s_{-i}^j, s_{-i}(\tau))}{t} \right]^2 \right),$$

where W is the (smallest) number of strategies in the support of Nash equilibrium. Compute choice probabilities using the logit rule $P_i^j(t+1) = e^{\lambda \cdot A_i^j(t)} / \sum_{k=1}^{m_i} e^{\lambda \cdot A_i^k(t)}$. (Initial conditions $A_i^j(0)$ can be equilibrium payoffs or expected payoffs from the cognitive hierarchy model.) Zero-calorie parametric shortcuts: try $\lambda = 1$ (for payoffs around \$1); or very large λ (best-response). Suggested substitutes: weighted fictitious play ($\phi = 0.8$) or, in a changing environment where most players get nonzero payoffs, reinforcement with payoff variability.

I'll end this book with a "top ten list" describing ten research questions that are likely to be asked, and perhaps answered, in the next ten years. Of course, forecasting is always perilous, and forecasting scientific direction is especially so. Rational forecasts *should* vary less than the variable being forecasted, so it would be surprising—and disappointing—if the most exciting new work did not veer off in directions dramatically different than those listed below. But lists are compact, useful, good, and irresistible; so here's one.

9.2 Top Ten Open Research Questions

The first five questions are more conservative, in the sense that answers are emerging rapidly. The last five are more speculative.

1. *How do people value the payoffs of others?* Theories of social preferences that answer this question are progressing nicely, in the form of precise inequality-aversion and reciprocity-based approaches (see Chapter 2). A new wave of experiments tests these approaches against each other, and will probably spawn some syntheses of these theories and a sense of which theories work well, and when.
2. *How do people learn?* Learning theories explain how people go from choices in previous periods to a choice in the current period, when they play a game repeatedly (or generalize from similar games) (see Chapter 6 for loving detail). As with social preference theories, there is a healthy variety of theories and they have been tested on many data sets in various ways. An important step would be focusing on simple versions of theories that fit robustly and well to see what their theoretical properties are. A quite different step is to explore learning

in very complex environments with limited information (where simply defining strategies is a challenge).

3. *How do social preferences vary across people and environments (e.g., cultures)?* Basic experimental protocols for measuring altruism (dictator games), negative reciprocity (ultimatums), and positive reciprocity (trust games) are now well established—we know what sorts of variables matter a lot, and which matter a little. The next move is carefully to investigate differences in these games. Amazing work of this sort is being done by anthropologists (e.g., Henrich et al., 2002) studying small-scale societies in far-flung places. (Their work will also sharpen experimental methods and provoke debate, since experimental luxuries taken for granted in university laboratories—such as subject comprehension, contagion among subjects, the influence of numerical training examples, and the ability to carry large sums of cash without being robbed—cannot be taken for granted in Africa and Papua New Guinea.)

4. *What happens when people confront "new" games?* Emerging theories of initial play rely on some combination of limited iterated thinking and quantal response. Simple rules such as choosing a strategy with a high expected payoff if others are randomizing, and iterating in some disciplined way, go a very long way to explaining first-period play (Haruvy and Stahl, 1998; Camerer, Ho, and Chong, 2001). Quantal response equilibrium is appealing because it uses only one parameter, and it avoids many of the most counterintuitive properties of standard equilibrium concepts.

5. *How exactly are people thinking in games?* An emerging literature uses detailed cognitive evidence—measuring beliefs, response times, and attention to payoffs in computer boxes—to figure out what people are thinking. These data create both an econometric challenge (identifying decision rules simultaneously with choices and cognitive measures; see Johnson et al., 2002; Costa-Gomes, Crawford, and Broseta, 2001) and an opportunity to improve model identification by using multiple measures.

6. *What game do people think they are playing?* After an experiment at Caltech on the coordination game stag hunt (Chapter 7), an uppity student wrote on a debriefing form, "I can't believe you guys are still studying the prisoners' dilemma!" Later questioning showed that, since individual rationality can lead to inefficiency in stag hunt (and *does*, if players are self-interested, in the prisoners' dilemma), the trigger-happy student had confused the two. He apparently clustered games in which rationality can (or does) lead to inefficiency into one class, a mistake no careful student of game theory would make. The student's mistake shows that the way in which games are represented or grouped is crucial to understanding what they do. (The student "defected" continually,

thinking his strategy was necessarily the best one, but of course it is not in stag hunt.) The "theory of mental representations" is an emerging body of observations, largely psychological, of how people form mental models or perceptions of elements of the game—who the players are, what the strategies are (including repeated-game strategies), what the monetary or material payoffs are, and so forth. The theory of mental representations maps raw descriptions of social situations into the kinds of familiar games theorists study and the kinds of rules people use to decide what to choose. No unified theory exists (although see Camerer, 1998; and Warglien, Devetag, and Legrenzi, 1999), but even a few crisp ideas would be helpful to explain how people and firms actually construe the interactions they face. Related to this is the important concept of the transfer of learning across games, which is presumably based on perceived similarity (the psychologist Thorndike said transfer depended on "identical elements"), which is in turn related to concepts of analogy, pattern recognition, case-based decision-making (Gilboa and Schmeidler, 2001), and so forth. Interesting recent papers along these lines include Knez and Camerer (2000), Van Huyck, Rankin, and Battalio (2000), Van Huyck and Battalio (2002), and Jehiel (2001).

7. *Can experiments sharpen the design of new institutions?* A large body of theory on how to design rules to achieve objectives ("mechanism design") has bloomed in recent years. But many of these mechanisms impose constraints on individual rationality, and presume rational response to rules, which are sometimes cognitively implausible or difficult for even designers to compute. These mechanisms won't work if people can't figure out whether to participate, or how to react to these rules. As in other domains of economic design, experiments are an efficient way to "test-bed" mechanisms and craft good theory (and hence, practice) of boundedly rational mechanism design.

8. *How do teams, groups, and firms play games?* Virtually all the experiments described in this book maintained a standard hypothesis in game theory, that whether players are genes, nonhuman animals, people, households, work groups, companies, or nation-states makes little difference to whether standard tools are applicable. So most experiments just made individual subjects responsible for their own decisions. But labs are certainly flexible enough to permit experiments in which subjects are, say, teams, to see how decision making differs (see, e.g., Bornstein and Yaniv, 1998, or Kocher and Sutter, 2000). The fact that theories of collective decision making in games are not always well-developed should not inhibit experimenters from using facts to lead theory, rather than follow it.

9. *How do people behave in very complex games?* The experiments described in this book were all constrained by the desire to use a game form that

subjects commonly know, so that equilibrium predictions that proceed from common knowledge assumptions can be compared with behavior. This approach lets theory drive design. Many other economic experiments proceed in the opposite direction (e.g., the vast body of research on complex non-Walrasian markets, which are well understood experimentally but are still not well understood theoretically). Given a wider range of new tools to predict how people are likely to behave in much more complex systems, it is useful to begin to explore them experimentally. A special example is networks, in which players can form links, then bargain or trade (e.g., Corbae and Duffy, 2002).

10. *How do socio-cognitive dimensions influence behavior in games?* Most experiments inherit the strange bias that has existed in game theory for decades—that the identity of subjects, their shared background, and what they have to say to each other before they interact either make little difference (talk is "cheap") or are so powerful that allowing such influences opens a Pandora's Box of causal influences too complex to untangle. Newer experiments allow communication, social cues, and overlapping generations (involving "parents" giving advice to "children").

There is no reason to be anything but optimistic that the synthesis Crawford described above will emerge rapidly, and that provocative findings about each of the ten questions above will emerge. The components of behavioral game theory have been carefully codified and based on evidence and psychological intuition (except, as noted, ideas about mental representation, which have yet to be actively researched). I suggest that, in the next ten years or so of experimentation, we should move past the common practice of comparing results with simple concepts such as Nash equilibrium, because the result of that comparison is now well known. Instead, researchers should compare results to a cognitive hierarchy model, to quantal response equilibrium (QRE), and to learning theories. (A version of EWA learning that includes recursively "sophisticated" players generalizes QRE and would be a reasonable, but tough, benchmark for comparison with data in the next few years.) Behavioral theories will also be useful in applications that are intended to give advice, since in strategic situations the quality of the advice depends crucially on what others are likely to do. If new behavioral tools continue to capture regularity as well as they have in recent studies, and also prove useful in theorizing, they should earn a prominent place in textbook discussions. Then the term "behavioral" will melt away. The sooner it does, the better.

Appendix: Design Details

Chapter 2

Harrison and McCabe (1996). Their experiments used groups of 16 subjects playing for 15 periods, bargaining over $20. One period was chosen randomly at the end to determine payments. Each subject played the role of both Proposer and Responder in a period, both making an offer and stating a minimum acceptable offer (MAO). This dual-role design is unusual and could account for results that are closer to self-interest.

Andreoni and Vesterlund (2001). Subjects were 70 students at Wisconsin and 72 at Iowa State, run in sessions of 34–38 subjects each. Ninety-five were male and 46 female. In each session subjects made eight dictator allocations with varying token endowment and relative token values in a double-blind protocol using claim checks that could not be linked to individual subjects. One decision was chosen at random and used to pay subjects. (Note that each subject was both a Dictator and a Recipient.)

Roth et al. (1991). To control for experimenter main effects, the three non-American experimenters conducted sessions in the United States and in their home countries. Sessions had 20 subjects playing 10 times in a fixed-role protocol with no-repetition rematching. Subjects got feedback only about their own decisions. One round was chosen at random for payment.

Buchan, Johnson, and Croson (1997). Groups of subjects played 10 times each in a fixed-role no-repetition rematching protocol, bargaining over 1,000-token amounts. Buchan et al. elicited MAOs. Subjects were students in introductory marketing courses at the universities of Tokyo and Pennsylvania.

Kagel, Kim, and Moser (1996). Subjects were University of Pittsburgh undergraduates. There were eight sessions with random rematching without repetition. One of ten trials was chosen randomly for payment.

Falk, Fehr, and Fischbacher (1999). In their experiment, 90 subjects played all four conditions, in a random order, against a different anonymous opponent each time. Since the Responder's behavior is of special interest, they used a strategy method in which each Responder stated a response to each of the two possible offers, in one condition at a time. Each point was worth 0.80 Swiss francs (about $0.56).

Snijders and Keren (1998). Subjects were 466 students at four Dutch schools (Amsterdam, Utrecht, Nijmegen, and Groningen), from many major fields of study. Subjects participated in groups of 7 or 14 in rooms where they could see each other. They played three to six games per subject in a dual-role protocol, giving decisions as both Investor and Trustee; after the trust games they did three to four other decision tasks. One game was chosen randomly for payment.

Van Huyck, Battalio, and Walters (1995, 1996). Subjects were Texas A&M undergraduates. 152 subjects participated in the commitment and discretion treatments; 48 of them participated twice to gauge the effect of experience. Sessions had ten subjects who were randomly assigned types and rematched each period. They played in three sequences of 20 periods in an ABA design (i.e., commitment–discretion–commitment, or vice versa). The reputation sessions used 90 subjects in groups of 10. They were assigned types and matched. At the end of each period the match continued with probability 5/6 (determined by a public random draw).

Cox (1999). Experiments used the double-blind mailbox procedure of Berg, Dickhaut, and McCabe (1995). In each session, they played one of the three games as individuals once, then played a trust game as a three-person group. To allow comparison of individual and group decisions, subjects had the same roles in the individual and group conditions. Subjects were 60 University of Arizona undergraduates.

Buchan, Croson, and Dawes (2000). Subjects were students in universities deemed roughly consistent in demographics and skill (128 Chinese, 140 Korean, 140 Japanese, and 140 Americans). Endowments were $10 or the equivalent in other currencies. Instructions were blindly back-translated. The American experimenter (Buchan) was present at each session, although each lead experimenter was a native of the country.

Dufwenberg et al. (2000). Subjects were 176 students at the University of Haifa, Israel (28 pairs in each complete information condition, 32 in the incomplete information condition). Subjects were endowed with 10 Israeli shekels (about $2.28).

Seinen and Schram (1999). Subjects were 168 students at the University of Amsterdam from various majors in sessions of 28. They were paired randomly across 90 rounds. After the 90th round, the experiment had a 10% chance of ending after each additional trial. Subjects were paid 20 guilders plus their earnings from 20 random trials. Payments were in Dutch cents (about 0.5 U.S. cents each).

Ho and Weigelt (2000). Subjects played in groups of 20 in the United States and China, and groups of 52–54 in Singapore. They played ten times in a no-repeat random-rematching protocol. Earnings were about US$11 and equivalent amounts in purchasing power in the other countries.

Chapter 3

Lieberman et al. (1962, 1965). Subjects in experiment 1 (Lieberman, 1962) were 20 Harvard undergraduates playing 300 times. Subjects in experiment 2 (Malcolm and Lieberman, 1965) were 18 SUNY-Stonybrook undergraduates playing in partner pairs for 200 trials. All subjects were staked $2.50 in cash and played in a fixed-match partner protocol. They played face-to-face by turning over colored cards and immediately exchanged chips depending on the game outcome after each trial.

Messick (1967). Subjects were 42 psychology undergraduates at the University of North Carolina. Subjects were staked $1.50 and payoffs were pennies.

Kaufman and Becker (1961). Subjects were students at Connecticut College. The per game maximin value was 0.95, so in each trial (a random pairing of the subject's 100 strategy allocations with the experimenter's) the expected maximin payoff was 95 points. Points were worth $0.01, but subjects' earnings were capped at $1 beyond a $1.50 guarantee. (In fact, as was common in experiments of the time, subjects were actually paid in a "tournament" style in which the difference between a player's point total and the low point-earner total, scaled by the high minus the low, determined the fraction of the $1 they got.) Subjects played each of the five games 50 times with feedback. The games were balanced for order in a Latin square and four subjects were run in each of five different orders, two each in the row and column roles.

O'Neill (1987). Subjects were 25 pairs of students at Northwestern University who played in a fixed-partner protocol 105 times, face-to-face. Subjects chose actual cards, showed them to each other, then transferred $0.05 from the loser to the winner each round. Both had an initial endowment of $2.50.

Rapoport and Boebel (1992). Subjects were 40 University of North Carolina students (20 in each win/loss condition) recruited by posted advertisements. Subjects were paired and played 10 periods for practice and 120 for money. Subjects chose physical cards corresponding to the blandly labelled strategies (C, F, L, I, and O). Cards were turned over simultaneously and wins or losses recorded. Row players became column players, and vice versa, in a second session (separated in time) with a different opponent. Sessions lasted about 100 minutes. Of the 120 money periods 3 were chosen at random for payment, so the expected win–loss differential was $0.40 per trial, eight times as large as O'Neill's payments (in nominal terms), although any player who earned less than $5 was paid $5.

Mookerjhee and Sopher (1997). Subjects were master's students at the Delhi School of Economics. Each game was played 40 times by 20 subjects, formed into 10 pairs, using a partner protocol. Game 3 (4) was the same as game 1 (2) except the stakes were doubled. Theories such as QRE, which interpret departures from equilibrium as mistakes (perhaps optimal imperfections owing to decision costs), predict that behavior will be closer to mixed-strategy equilibrium as the stakes rise. In fact, behavior in the two pairs of games was indistinguishable so they were pooled in further analysis.

Tang (1996). Subjects were 180 University of Bonn students, with five 12-subject sessions for each of the three games. Subjects were paired randomly in a fixed-role protocol. They played 150 rounds (except two sessions, which played only 100 rounds of game 1). After each round, subjects were told their opponent's choice, the average payoffs and choices of both groups (row and column) in that round, and the average payoff each of their strategies would have yielded if randomly paired with others in that round.

Binmore, Swierzbinski and Proulx (2001). Subjects were 156 students at the University of Michigan. They were recruited from various classes, which meant they probably were not familiar with game theory. Each of 13 sessions had 12 subjects interacting on a computer network. Subjects had a fixed role (row or column) for each game but their roles were randomized after each game. They played practice games 1 and 2 50 and 100 times, and all other games 150 times each (except saddlepoint game 2, which they played 75 times). Sessions took 45 minutes. This is a very fast rate of play (825 periods, plus instructions, in 45 minutes).There were 12 subjects in each session, in a random rematching protocol, and all MSE predictions are multiples of $1/6$. Thus, it is possible that MSE could be achieved by a population mixture of subjects who play pure strategies that nevertheless, averaged across the population, have the average mixture as in MSE. They played the five games in Table 3.9 plus two practice games. Payoffs were determined by a binary lottery procedure: After each game, a subject's point total determined the probability of winning a $6 prize in that game ($0.60 in the practice games). Finally, subjects were shown two graphs—a moving average of their own payoffs, and the median payoff of others in the same role, during the last six periods.

Rapoport and Budescu (1992). Subjects were 91 undergraduates at the University of Haifa (Israel), recruited from posted advertisements. All subjects participated in condition D and in one of the other two conditions, in separate sessions a week apart. Subject totals were 90, 60, and 25 in conditions D, S, and R. Condition D dyads played face-to-face in a partner protocol using red and black cards as strategy choices. (The row player earned 1 token if the card colors matched, and lost if she mismatched; the payoffs are the opposite for the column player.) Subjects were endowed with 20 New Israel shekels (NIS) and tokens were converted to one NIS each. Subjects in condition R were told that their sequence would be compared with a target sequence, and the sequence "coming as close as possible" to the target would earn 25 NIS. Note also that, in the D condition, 13 of the 45 dyads did not complete the 150 rounds because one subject lost her 20 token endowment, although these dyads completed a median of 120 periods.

Budescu and Rapoport (1994). Design details were the same as in Rapoport and Budescu (1992) except as follows: All 60 subjects participated in condition D in one session and in condition R in a subsequent session; 8 of 30 dyads in condition R did not complete all 150 periods.

Bloomfield (1994). Subjects were 72 University of Michigan undergraduates recruited from classes other than economics. Many had participated in an unrelated game a week earlier. They played 70 rounds in a random-matching protocol. Earnings from the first 20 rounds of practice play were paid at the rate of $0.015 per point. Another five of the next 50 rounds, chosen randomly, were paid at $.15 per point. Subjects had $35 subtracted from their winnings at the end, but were guaranteed a $2 payment even if their earnings were negative. Note that this convex payoff scheme could, in principle, encourage players to be more risk-seeking, which would push the MSE probabilities toward 0 and 1. Results are reported for the full-pay periods 21–70 only.

Ochs (1995b). Subjects were 48 students at the University of Pittsburgh, run in three groups of 16 subjects. Sessions took about 90 minutes. In the first session, 16 subjects played game 1 for 64 periods in a random-matching protocol, except subjects were never re-paired in consecutive periods with their opponent in the previous period. In session 2, 16 subjects played game 1 for 16 periods and game 2 for 56 periods. In session 3, 16 subjects played game 1 for 16 periods and game 3 for 64 periods. Payoffs were binary lottery payoffs, scaled by the maximum earnable points. (Note that row players using the MSE strategy in game 2, for example, could expect to earn fewer points because the maximum point was so high, so there is a small confound between the marginal point—and dollar—incentive for row players across the three games. This simply points up some added difficulty in using binary lottery and other sophisticated payoff schemes.) Players' scaled points then determined their chance of winning an additional $10 prize, beyond a base payment of $10 plus a $4 showup fee.

Shachat (2002). Subjects were University of Arizona undergraduates playing 60 periods in a fixed-partner protocol. Sessions had 6–12 participants. There were a total of 15, 16, and 15 pairs in treatments 1–3, respectively. Row players earned $0.90 from a win whereas column players earned $0.60 (which equalized expected earnings at $0.36)

McKelvey, Palfrey, and Weber (2000). Subjects were 96 Caltech undergraduates, in sessions of 12 subjects. Each session consisted of two games played 50 times each, consecutively. Each of A, B, and C were played twice, followed by each of the other two games. A and D were played together in two other sessions in counterbalanced order. Payoff units were $0.10 and subjects were also paid a $5 showup fee. Players were assigned a fixed role in a random-matching protocol, never playing the same person twice in a row.

Goeree, Holt, and Palfrey (2000). Subjects were undergraduates at the University of Virginia, Caltech, and Pasadena City College. There were 24 subjects in games 1–2 and 80 subjects in game 3. Subjects participated in groups of 10 or 12 in a fixed-role protocol, playing 10 periods. In games 1–2, and in one session in game 3, subjects were in a partner protocol; in the other sessions of game 3 the protocol was random rematching. Subjects earned $6 plus their earnings (in pennies).

Rapoport and Amaldoss (2000). Subjects were 36 students at the University of Arizona, participating in two 18-person groups. Subjects were rematched into pairs randomly, except they never played the same person twice in a row, and they played each other person approximately the same number of times. Subjects played the L and H games for 80 periods each, counterbalanced for order. Eighty payoff units were converted to $1 and subjects were also paid a $5 showup fee.

Collins and Sherstyuk (2000). Subjects were 51 University of Melbourne students, in four sessions of 9–18 subjects with random rematching in each period. Subjects knew their own location and the locations of their two competitors in each period. Earnings were A$0.01 for each 10 units sold, along with a A$3 showup fee.

Chapter 4

Roth and Malouf (1979). Subjects were second-year University of Illinois students drawn from an introductory business course. Subjects were apparently gathered in groups of two to six and bargained over four games, by sending text messages on computer terminals, in bargaining trials of 12 minutes. Subjects were re-paired with new partners after each trial, but the details of the matching protocol are not reported. Obsession with the nature of the matching protocol seems to be a post-1980 phenomenon, perhaps motivated by results in game theory around that time (e.g., Kreps et al., 1982) showing how repeated-game reputation-building could occur when players were paired with the same partner repeatedly.

Ochs and Roth (1989). Subjects were 160 Carnegie-Mellon and University of Pittsburgh undergraduates. Subjects were paid $5 for participating, along with their bargaining earnings from one of the ten rounds, chosen randomly. Each subject participated in one cell of the design (i.e., the design was "between-subjects"). The experiment was run by passing messages between player-1 and player-2 rooms.

Harrison and McCabe (1992). Subjects were 40 honors economics undergraduate students at the University of Western Ontario in Canada. Payoffs were in cents (i.e., 100 points represented $1.00) in one session and in units of probability in another session. That is, each point was one lottery ticket, in a lottery with a low prize of $1 and a high prize of $11.50. The results of the two payment schemes were similar, so I averaged them.

Carpenter (2000). Subjects were undergraduates at the University of Massachusetts. The two δ conditions were crossed with a random matching versus partner (repeated matching) condition, with 15–17 pairs in each call (a total of 130 subjects). Pies were 10 units, with an exchange rate of $0.20 per unit. They played 15 periods, starting with the ultimatum game then and alternating ultimatums and two-round games. Carpenter also pooled these data with data from 122 Arizona subjects who played only 10 periods, with the bargaining preceded by a preference revelation experiment.

Johnson et al. (2002). Subjects were 30 University of Pennsylvania undergraduates. They played eight bargaining games for periods in a role-reversal protocol with no-repeat rematching.

Zwick, Rapoport, and Howard (1992). Subjects were 54 Penn State undergraduates. They participated in groups of six. Each group had a fixed value of p. A trio of three subjects played eight times with somebody randomly chosen from the other trio (within their six-person group). Pairings were random except that no player played the same person twice in a row. Then the six groups were divided into two subgroups of three and the whole procedure was repeated twice more—a total of 24 trials. Players also alternated player-1 and player-2 roles. At the end, three trials were chosen at random and players were paid their average payoff in those three games.

Rapoport, Weg, and Felsenthal (1990). Subjects were students from the University of Haifa, Israel. Subjects participated in 18 games, rotating their role (player 1 or 2) and cost position (three games in each cost position). In their first experiment the costs in the three conditions were strong (0.10 versus 2.50), weak (2.50 versus 0.10), or equal (2.50 versus 2.50). In their second experiment the corresponding costs for strong and weak players were 0.20 and 3.0. Subjects knew that 3 of the 18 games would be chosen for actual payment, and they were paid their average earnings from those games. They actually terminated a few games (4 percent) at a random point between 9 and 13 periods.

Binmore, Shaked, and Sutton (1989). Subjects were 120 social sciences students at the London School of Economics, with students exposed to game theory or bargaining models excluded. Subjects played in pairs, only once.

Binmore et al. (1998). Subjects were University of Michigan undergraduates who participated in groups of 12. The experiment was computerized. The player with the option is denoted player 2. The players made demands simultaneously, and player 2 could choose to opt out (unbeknownst to player 1 until afterward). Players participated in blocks of ten trials with a complicated structure. In each ten-trial block, subjects were randomly re-paired. Roles were randomly determined and fixed throughout a block (except that no subject was the same type in all three blocks). In each block, two of the ten trials were chosen for payment. To encourage practice, payments were 10 percent of the nominal amounts earned in the first block, 25 percent of the nominal amounts in the second block, and full payment in the last block. Players were also "filtered" into similar-earnings groups across blocks, but the different filtered groups played similarly.

Forsythe, Kennan, and Sopher (1991a). Subjects were University of Iowa undergraduates. Groups of six–eight subjects bargained in pairs. Each pair bargained in a specific cost condition (i.e., one of the games I–IV) over three "years" (each period was a "month," so a year consisted of T "months") with different partners. The protocol fixed players in roles (strong or weak bargainer). Each month lasted 5 minutes.

Rapoport, Erev, and Zwick (1995). Subjects were 48 undergraduates at the University of North Carolina. They played six sequences of three-game triples (a total of 18 games). In each triple, each of four subjects played with each of the other three exactly once, switching roles so that each subject was a seller in half the trials and a buyer in the other half. To test the effect of δ, Rapoport et al. used three values: H (0.9), M (0.67), and L(0.33). The order of the three discount factors within each triple was balanced. Of the 48 subjects, 16 returned to participate in two additional one-hour sessions to measure the effect of experience. Buyer valuations in each trial were drawn uniformly from the integers [0,100]. Each subject was paid her earnings from three of the trials chosen at random.

Forsythe, Kennan, and Sopher (1991b). Subjects were undergraduates recruited from economics classes at the University of Iowa. Each subject played 10 or 15 periods, with fixed pie sizes and values of p, in blocks of 5 periods held on consecutive evenings. Subjects did not know the previous bargaining outcomes of their new partners in each period.

Radner and Schotter (1989). They conducted eight experimental sessions. Each session used about 20 NYU undergraduates recruited from economics courses. In each period, subjects opened an envelope, observing a specific value of either V (for buyers) or C (for sellers), then wrote down a bid v or c, which was transmitted to the other subject. Subjects learned the outcome of only their own trades. Subjects were paired with the same partner for 15 periods, to help pairs converge to an equilibrium.

Rapoport and Fuller (1995). Subjects were 60 students from the University of Arizona, who participated in groups of 10 in a fixed-role protocol. In phase I of each experiment they drew values or costs privately and submitted bids. If the seller's bid exceeded the buyer's, trade took place at the average of the two bids, and subjects were told this in each trial. After 25 trials (three of which were chosen randomly for payment), a phase II began using the strategy method in which subjects recorded bids for each of 25 values or costs

(3,7,11, . . . ,99) presented in random order. These bid functions were used to play one trial for payment.

Daniel, Seale, and Rapoport (1998). Subjects were 40 students from the University of Arizona (20 in each experiment). Each played 50 periods. To allow some between-subject comparability, each subject had the same 50 values as others in the same role. The incentive scheme is not described, although subjects earned an average of $15 each.

Valley et al. (2002). The second study used 102 undergraduates from five Boston schools. Subjects earned $10 for participating in the no-communication conditions (which took 1.5 hours) and $20 for participating in the two communication conditions (which took 3 hours). Subjects were also paid their earnings from three randomly selected periods.

Chapter 5

Beard and Beil (1994). Experiments were true one-shot games played in the extensive form: Player 2 moved only if player 1 chose L. All payoffs were in dollars. Each pair participated in only one treatment. In treatment 7, payoffs were multiplied by six but each subject earned the money from their decisions only with $1/6$ probability (to test whether playing for larger, probabilistic stakes makes a difference).

Schotter, Weigelt, and Wilson (1994). In their experiments, groups of ten subjects (NYU undergraduates) played three to five rounds in a fixed-role, random-matching protocol without replacement. Payoffs were $0.70 per point. Feedback was in terms of payoffs only, *not* opponent actions.

Rapoport and Amaldoss (1997). Two groups of 18 subjects were used, students at the University of Arizona. Subjects were divided into two groups at the beginning of each session and assigned to a fixed role (strong or weak) for 80 periods. After the first block of 80 periods, subjects switched roles and played another 80 periods. Subjects were randomly rematched each period. After each period, they learned the other player's investment (and which investment was higher, and the resulting rewards), but nothing more about the population. Payoffs were converted into dollars at a rate of $1.25 per 100 points.

McKelvey and Palfrey (1992). Each experimental session had 18 or 20 subjects who played ten times in a fixed-role, random-matching protocol without replacement. Their "zipper" design matched the ith player 1 with the ith player 2 in round 1, then slid the ith player 1 down to the $i + 1$st player 2 (and the last player 1 up to the first player 2), and so on. This simple design limits "contagion." Not only does each player play each other player only once, but no player i ever plays a player who has previously played someone who has played someone that i has already played. The game is played in the extensive form, so when one player takes the game is over.

Van Huyck, Wildenthal, and Battalio (2002). Four sessions were conducted for each of the four combinations of game and continuation conditions. Each session had ten subjects, undergraduates in business and economics at Texas A&M. In the $G(0,1)$ sessions, subjects were randomly re-paired 55 times. In the $G(5/6,2)$ sessions, random stopping points were drawn randomly in advance and were fixed across the four sessions for comparability. The result was eight sequences ranging in length from 1 period (followed, of course, by 2 periods of finite continuation) to 14 periods.

Capra et al. (2002). Their experiment used six groups of ten subjects, undergraduates in economics classes at the University of Virginia. Each subject played ten periods with fixed α in a random-rematching protocol with feedback about both prices in her pair.

Capra et al. (1999). Experimental sessions were conducted in six groups of 9–12 subjects in a random-matching protocol. Subjects were University of Virginia students recruited from economics classes. They earned $6 for participating, plus earnings from the experiment (in pennies). Subjects participated in ten rounds of a game with one value of R (denoted "part A"), followed unexpectedly by another five or ten rounds with a different value of R (part B). If R was high in part A it was low in part B, and vice versa.

Sefton and Yavaş (1996). Three sessions with different $T = 4, 8$ or 12 all used 30 subjects. Subjects were Penn State undergraduates, playing the T-period supergame 15 times (including one no-payoff practice round). Subjects were paired in a zipper design with random rematching.

Weber (2001). Weber's experiment overcame several design challenges. A basic one is how to transmit information to subjects about the types of other subjects, and to make the transmission of that information public knowledge. Weber did this by constructing a board on which players' types were concealed behind three flaps of paper that could be pulled up to show the types, and pulled down again. After the types were randomly determined by dice rolls, Weber went around the room showing each player the types of the other players. (The players whose types were being revealed could also see that the revelation was occurring.) Subjects were Caltech undergraduates who were paid the money amounts in Table 5.13 (including a $10 participation payment to ensure that they would not lose money even if they lost $5 twice). They played two consecutive sessions to see if there is much learning across sessions.

Sovik (1999). Subjects were students at the Universitat Pompeu Fabra in Barcelona. Six pairs ($n = 12$) played in a fixed-pairing session and 18 pairs ($n = 36$) in three sessions with random rematching.

Stahl and Wilson (1995). To disable learning, subjects played each game only once. Each subject played against the field, so her point total in a game was the average payoff from playing each other subject once. Payoffs were in probability points: For each game, point earnings determined a number from 0 to 100, which represented a percentage chance of winning $2. Subjects were advanced undergraduate accounting and finance majors at the University of Texas (Austin). They participated in three different sessions, with 14, 22, and 12 subjects respectively. After training, subjects were given a 10-minute screening test, then 36 minutes to make choices in all 12 games.

Costa-Gomes, Crawford, and Broseta (2001). Some games are isomorphs of one another, except that a constant was added to all payoffs; this feature enabled a test of consistency across (nearly) identical games. (Subjects did not systematically differ across isomorphs.) Subjects were students at the University of Arizona. Instructions were shown on handouts and computer screens, and were made "public knowledge" by telling subjects that everyone had the same instructions. All subjects were required to take an understanding test after the instructions, and were dismissed if they failed the test. The dismissal rates were 25 percent, 16 percent, and 53 percent in the B, OB, and TS conditions. These high rates imply a fairly large weeding out of confused and unsophisticated subjects, which may partly explain the large fraction of apparent equilibrium and sophisticated behavior mentioned in the chapter. The data reported in the chapter also excluded three trained subjects who behaved emotionally (see Costa-Gomes et al. for details). Subjects each chose one game at random and were paid for their payoff in that game (determined by random pairing with another subject). They earned $0.40 for each point. Payoffs were displayed in an unusual format, with row player payoffs on the left of the screen, and column player payoffs on the right side.

Chapter 6

Roth et al. (1999). Players were matched in a partner protocol for 500 periods. Payoffs in each stage game were probabilities of winning $0.04.

Cox, Shachat, and Walker (2001). Subjects were 120 University of Arizona undergraduates. They played in 12-person groups in a fixed-role protocol with own-history feedback. Each session had 4–5 regimes, which were random drawings of column and row matrices, followed by 15 periods of play with the same matrix. Three sessions fixed pairs within each regime and seven sessions rematched players within a regime. Payoffs were 6 payoff units = US$1 except in sessions 2–4 (10 units = US$1).

Nyarko and Schotter (2002). Subjects were 112 NYU students with no game theory training. They participated in sessions of 26–30 students with own-payoff (and opponent) history. Payoff points were worth $0.05 (about $15 from the game and $6 from predictions.)

Mookerjhee and Sopher (1997). Subjects were master's students in economics at the Delhi School of Economics. Each game was played by 20 subjects, formed into 10 pairs. Each pair played in the repeated-matching partner protocol 40 times. In addition, games 3–4 are the same as games 1–2 except the stakes are doubled.

Bosch-Domenech and Vriend (2003). Subjects were 126 undergraduates at the Universitat Pompeu Fabra in Barcelona. Each session had 18 subjects in a fixed-match protocol (either eight duopolies or six triopolies in a session, one in each information treatment). Sessions took up to two hours. Players earned 0.035 (0.025) pesetas (1,000 pesetas = US$6.40) per profit point in duopoly (triopoly) periods 1–20 and ten times as much in periods 21–22. In addition, in a seventh control treatment players with easy-table information were paid only a fixed sum if they earned the largest profit, to see whether behavior would converge strongly to competitive Walrasian. It did (all subjects chose 30 in the last two periods of this control experiment).

Selten and Stöcker (1986). Sessions had 12 subjects, divided into two subgroups of six subjects. Within each subgroup, each player was paired with each other player for the ten-period supergame, in five-pair cycles which repeated five times for a total of 25 ten-period supergames. The sessions took about four hours, unusually long for an experiment of this sort. However, it is not clear whether this unusual length had any special effect; their results look like observations in other repeated-PD experiments.

Battalio, Samuelson, and Van Huyck (2001). They ran four sessions of eight subjects (undergraduate students at Texas A&M) in each of the three games. The subjects played in a random-matching protocol for 75 periods, with own-match history.

Feltovich (2000). Subjects were 122 University of Pittsburgh undergraduates (and others). They participated in nine sessions with 8–20 subjects in each session. They earned $10 for participating, plus $10 if they won (earned one) in a single stage and game chosen at random.

Stahl (1999a). Four experimental sessions were run with 22–24 subjects in each. The sessions used a mean-matching protocol in which each player's payoff was the mean payoff from playing with each other subject, and players learned the full population history after each trial. Games 1–2 were run in counterbalanced order (1 followed by 2 in one session, and 2 followed by 1 in the other session) and games 3–4 were counterbalanced. The payoffs were in units of probability of winning a $2 prize.

Chapter 7

Mehta, Starmer, and Sugden (1994b). The subjects were 120 University of East Anglia students attending summer school. They were paired randomly (and anonymously) and played 20 matching games. The pair that matched most often shared £10.

Blume et al. (1998). Sessions consisted of 12 subjects playing for 20 periods in a random-matching, fixed-role protocol with population history information.

Kawagoe and Takizawa (1999). Their experiment used two groups of 13 subjects each, playing only with those in their group. Subjects played 13 times in a role-reversal protocol with rematching. They conducted three sessions with 26, 13, and 26 subjects in each. The three sessions varied in different ways, one of which appears to be important. In the first session subjects played all three games. Half the subjects were paid in money (about 2,000 yen) and half in probability points, in an attempt to control risk-neutrality. A second session tested the effects of scrambling action labels. In a third session subjects played only one game 13 times to look for sharper equilibration.

Van Huyck, Gillette, and Battalio (1992). They conducted nine experimental sessions with Texas A&M undergraduates, in each of which 24–30 subjects participated. Subjects played in a fixed-role protocol with pairwise matching with no repetition. In most sessions subjects played game A three times without assignments and three times with assignments in various orders. Then they played either game B or game C six times with various sequences of assignments.

Van Huyck, Battalio, and Rankin (2001b). They conducted 16 full sessions using Texas A&M undergraduates. In each session, two different groups of subjects played a game with a fixed cohort for 20 periods. Then the cohorts were scrambled (a random sample of n was taken from the $2n$ subjects present) and the new cohorts played another game for 20 periods. In each pair of groups, the group size n was fixed and j varied across the two 20-period session halves.

Samuelson (1996). Subjects were MBA students (including some executive MBAs, typically practicing managers taking night or weekend courses) at the Boston University School of Management. Students were not paid, but played in a round-robin or mean-matching protocol with each other student, and part of their course grade depended upon their point earnings in the experiment. Students played only once, but particiipated in on–four practice sessions, in which each student drew a cost and decided whether to enter, and the total number of entries was reported to all members of the group. Samuelson also reported results for cost intervals [2,3] that are quite similar to those I've selected to show.

Ho and Weigelt (1996). Subjects were University of Pennsylvania under-graduates. Players participated in groups of 11 in a random-role protocol with random-matching (with no repetition) and own-history feedback. Each game was played for ten periods and three games were played in a session (using a Latin square design to control for order effects). Games were displayed in tree form. A payoff point was worth $0.10.

Haruvy and Stahl (1998). Subjects were University of Texas undergraduates. Experiments were conducted using a mean-matching protocol, with payoffs in lottery tickets. Each of 47 subjects made a choice in each of the 20 games once, with no feedback. Subjects also had a computerized calculator which allowed them to enter "hypotheses" about the fraction of subjects who might choose various actions and compute expected payoffs to different strategies.

Van Huyck, Battalio, and Beil (1990). In the original Van Huyck et al. study, groups of 14–16 subjects played with each other ten times in seven sessions. At the end of each period, the minimum was announced and the subjects played again.

Clemons and Weber (1996). In the first 12 periods of the experiment, buyers and sellers simultaneously submitted orders—divisions of their ten shares between X and Y—and earned profits according to the scheme described in the chapter (with zero profit on Y shares if Y failed to open). Points were worth $0.0083. Subjects were University of Pennsylvania students.

Chapter 8

Brandts and Holt (1992). Subjects were undergraduates recruited for two-hour sessions from economics classes at the University of Virginia (sessions 1–5) or the Universitat Autonoma de Barcelona (sessions 6–9). Each session involved 8 or 12 participants and one monitor (a subject selected randomly to determine types by throwing a die and to oversee the experimental procedure). Subjects in the sender and receiver roles were segregated by role in separate rooms. In each phase of the experiment there were four or six matchings in a fixed-role, no-repeat-matching protocol with own-pair feedback. Types were determined randomly for each pair. After each phase, subjects switched roles. In the second phase, 15 pesetas were added to all payoffs for all players. The third-phase payoffs were the same as in the first phase. Payoffs were in pennies in Virginia and in pesetas (about 0.8 pennies at the time) in Barcelona.

Banks, Camerer, and Porter (1994). In most cases, subjects played a single game ten times, in a random-role, no-repeat-matching protocol with own-pair history only. Types were drawn independently for each pair and each period. Experiments were computerized. (In data we never published, we also tried using an incentive-compatible scoring rule to measure beliefs directly and to use those measured beliefs to test the refinements. It was a mixed success.) In 11 of 13 experimental sessions, subjects played three of the seven games in a random order (which was not counterbalanced); in two sessions they played two games, one of which lasted 20 periods rather than 10 to test for additional learning. Subjects were undergraduates at the University of Pennsylvania, Caltech, and Arizona, doctoral students at Penn, and staff scientists at the Jet Propulsion Laboratory. Data were pooled because there were no detectable differences across subject pools. Subjects earned $0.25 per point minus a $5 tax, about $20 on average for a two-hour session.

Potters and van Winden (1996). Two sessions were conducted of each of the five treatments. Payoffs were chosen so that payments equaled about 2 Dutch guilders per play (about $1.16 at the time of the experiments). Subjects were mostly (85%) undergraduate economics students at the University of Amsterdam. Seniors had 12 subjects (and one subject monitor). Seniors had two phases with ten periods in each. In each phase, subjects played in a fixed-role protocol with constrained random rematching (subjects were never matched with the same partner in consecutive periods, and never more than twice in a phase). Subjects switched roles between phases. Types were common across sender subjects in each period. They received own-pair feedback.

Potters and van Winden (2000). The design was the same as in their earlier experiment with a few minor changes. There were 12 sessions with student subjects and three with professionals, who were "public affairs and public relations directors from the private and public sector" attending conferences on public affairs in Amsterdam and The Hague. The professional sessions were run using pencil and paper, and so four of the student sessions were run that way as well (all others were run on networked computers). Students participated in two ten-round sequences with role reversal between the sequences; professionals participated in only one sequence

Cadsby, Frank, and Maksimovic (1990). Subjects were graduate economics and business students at Queen's University in Canada. In each session there were 6 firms and 8–12 investors in a fixed-rate protocol. In each of ten rounds, firms drew private random types and decided whether to offer projects; the projects were then randomly auctioned off one at a time. (Keep in mind that the investors knew H and L firms were equally likely, but did not know which firms had offered projects, or how many were being offered.) Bidding was conducted in a descending-price oral auction, in terms of the fraction of the project's value the investor would accept for an investment of 300.

Cadsby, Frank, and Maksimovic (1998). In the G* sessions, subjects were undergraduate and graduate economics students at the University of Guelph, and in the BC* sessions they were business students at the University of British Columbia. In the sessions ending in 1, subjects were inexperienced. In all later sessions in each same-lettered sequence the subjects were experienced. Each session had 6 firms and 8–16 investors in a fixed-role protocol, playing 8–14 rounds. Subjects earned C$23 for the two-hour sessions.

Cooper, Kagel, Lo, and Gu (1999). There were 21 experimental sessions, each with 12–16 subjects and 36 trials. Within six-period blocks, subjects had fixed roles in a no-repeat rematching protocol. After each block, roles were reversed. Firm types were randomly determined in each period and were common to all firms. Feedback for all pairings was provided.

Camerer and Weigelt (1988). Subjects were MBA students at NYU and a mixture of MBA and undergraduate business students at the University of Pennsylvania. Subjects played in 69–101 eight-period sequences. In each session, there were three borrowers and eight lenders in a fixed-role protocol. In each sequence, one of the borrowers was chosen from the pair of borrowers who did not play in the immediately preceding sequence (i.e., no borrower played twice in a row, and all subjects knew this). Then lenders were assigned exactly one period to play in, at random. Borrowers did not know which lender was playing in which period, and lenders did not know which borrower was playing in a particular sequence. Borrowers and lenders were in separate rooms and decisions were communicated by the experimenters, using walkie-talkies. Every decision was commonly announced to all subjects. Payoff points were worth $0.01 for lenders and $0.0015 for borrowers. The walkie-talkies turned out to be crucial in an interesting way: Because the X types often had to think for a couple of seconds about what to do in later periods, the Y type borrowers often tried to signal their type by giving very rapid (repay) responses. The experimenters therefore had to delay reporting the Y types' choices so that the speed of the response did not signal information. This is a good example of how players can "enrich" a strategy space in ways that are surprising to experimenters and not well captured by theory.

Neral and Ochs (1992). There were ten subjects in a session. There were three sessions with the borrower default payoff of 150, and four sessions with a payoff of 100. Subjects were Pittsburgh undergraduates, except for two 100-payoff sessions with Frostburg State students. In each session there were six lenders (As) and four borrowers (Bs). Since $P(honest) = 1/3$, in each sequence the four Bs were dishonest types and two honest types were played by the experimenter (who always repaid loans). As could not tell whether they were playing a dishonest-type subject or an honest-type played by the experimenter. An A and B played in a fixed pairing throughout all six rounds of a sequence. (Note that, in principle, this permits two-sided reputation-building, but it is hard to see what kind of reputation the As can build that benefits them, since punishing defaulting borrowers by withholding future loans is equilibrium behavior in any case.) Pairs played 15 sequences. The dollar payment for points was not reported.

Jung, Kagel, and Levin (1994). Subjects were MBA or senior undergraduates at the University of Houston. They were paid $4 plus their earnings from their decisions (multiplied by a points-to-dollars exchange rate), which averaged $30–50 for a $2\frac{1}{2}$ hour session. Each session had 45–90 eight-period sequences. In each session, there were seven subjects, three incumbents, and four entrants. In a given eight-period sequence, a single incumbent faced eight entry decisions, two from each of the four subjects playing in a stratified random order (each entrant played exactly once in periods 1–4 and once in periods 1–8). After nine sequences, roles were switched so that three of the four entrants became incumbents. (The fourth entrant, who was not role-switched, was made an incumbent in the *subsequent* nine-sequence block.)

Brandts and Figueras (1997). Subjects were students at the Universitat Autonoma in Barcelona. There were two–three sessions, with six or nine subjects, in each cell of the design crossing values of h, and 3 or 6 rounds (and omitting the cell with six-round games and $h = 0.5$). Three subjects were borrowers and three or six were lenders, in a fixed-role protocol. At the beginning of each sequence, a random borrower was drawn and her type determined. Lenders then played in a random order (once in each sequence). When the type was honest (Y), the borrower was forced to choose repayment if a loan was made. There were 72 sequences in each session. Points were converted to pesetas at a rate of 1.2 pesetas/point for bankers and 0.5 for borrowers.

Cooper, Garvin, and Kagel (1997a). Subjects were a broad sample of undergraduate and graduate students from Pitt and Carnegie-Mellon. Sessions had 12–16 subjects who switched roles after six periods. In each of six six-period blocks each monopolist (M) was paired with a different entrant (E). Subjects got feedback on the results of all pairs each period. Earnings averaged $17.50 for inexperienced subject sessions, which took about two hours.

Cooper, Garvin, and Kagel (1997b). Experiments were run in groups of 12–16 with University of Pittsburgh students. Most experimental sessions had a "cycle" of 12 periods, in which each subject played as a monopolist (M) for six periods, then as an entrant (E) (or vice versa). Subjects were randomly paired in each round, Ms were told their types, and after each period the Ms learned the E's decision and the Es learned the M's type. In addition, each subject's screen displayed the results of all pairs after each period.

References

Abbink, Klaus, Abdolkarim Sadrieh, and Shmuel Zamir. 1999. The covered response ultimatum game. Universität Bonn, SFB discussion paper B-416.

Abbink, Klaus, Gary E. Bolton, Abdolkarim Sadrieh, and Fang-Fang Tang. 2001. Adaptive learning versus punishment in ultimatum bargaining. *Games and Economic Behavior*, 37, 1–26.

Abreu, Dilip, and Hitoshi Matsushima. 1992a. Virtual implementation in iteratively undominated strategies I: Complete information. *Econometrica*, 60, 993–1008.

———. 1992b. A response to Glazer and Rosenthal. *Econometrica*, 60, 1439–42.

Akerlof, George. 1982. Labor contracts as partial gift exchange. *Quarterly Journal of Economics*, 97, 543–69.

Akerlof, George, and Rachel Kranton. 2000. Economics and identity. *Quarterly Journal of Economics*, 115, 715–53.

Allen, Franklin, Stephen Morris, and Hyun Song Shin. 2002. Beauty contests, bubbles and iterated expectations in asset markets. http://www.econ.yale.edu/~sm326/research.html/beauty.pdf

Alvard, Michael. 2000. Cooperative big game hunting. Texas A&M Department of Anthropology.

Alvarez, R. Michael, and Jonathan Nagler. 2002. Should I stay or should I go? Sincere and strategic crossover voting in California assembly races. In B. Cain and E. Gerber (Eds.), *California's Blanket Primary*. Berkeley: University of California Press.

Amaldoss, Wilfred, and Sanjay Jain. 2002. David versus Goliath: An analysis of asymmetric mixed strategy games and experimental evidence. *Management Science*, 49, 972–91.

Amershi, Amin, Asha Sadanand, and Venk Sadanand. 1989. Manipulated Nash equilibria, II: Applications and a preliminary experiment. University of Minnesota Department of Accounting discussion paper 1989-6.

———. 1992. Player importance and forward induction. *Economics Letters*, 38, 291–97.

Anderson, Christopher, and Colin F. Camerer. 2000. Experience-weighted attraction learning in sender–receiver signaling games. *Economic Theory*, 16, 689–718.

Anderson, John. 2000. *Cognitive Psychology and Its Implications* (5th ed.). New York: Worth.

Anderson, Simon P., Jacob K. Goeree, and Charles A. Holt. 2001. Minimum-effort coordination games: Stochastic potential and logit equilibrium. *Games and Economic Behavior*, 34, 177–99.

Andreoni, James. 1990. Impure altruism and donations to public goods: A theory of warm-glow giving. *Economic Journal*, 100, 464–77.

Andreoni, James, and John H. Miller. 1993. Rational cooperation in the finitely repeated prisoner's dilemma: Experimental evidence. *Economic Journal*, 103, 570–85.

———. 2002. Giving according to GARP: An experimental study of rationality and altruism. *Econometrica*, 70, 737–53.

Andreoni, James, and Lise Vesterlund. 2001. Which is the fair sex? Gender differences in altruism. *Quarterly Journal of Economics*, 116, 293–312.

Andreoni, James, Paul M. Brown, and Lise Vesterlund. 2002. What makes an allocation fair? Some experimental evidence. *Games and Economic Behavior*, 40, 1–24.

Arkes, Hal, and Catherine Blumer. 1985. The psychology of sunk cost. *Organizational Behavior and Human Performance*, 35, 124–40.

Arrow, Kenneth. 1974. *The Limits of Organization*. New York: W. W. Norton.

Arthur, Brian. 1991. Designing economic agents that act like human agents: A behavioral approach to bounded rationality. *American Economic Review Proceedings*, 81, 353–59.

———. 1994. On designing economic agents that behave like human agents. *Journal of Evolutionary Economics*, 3, 1–22.

Atkinson, Richard C., and Patrick Suppes. 1958. An analysis of two-person game situations in terms of statistical learning theory. *Journal of Experimental Psychology*, 55, 369–78.

Aumann, Robert J. 1990. Foreword. In A. E. Roth and M. A. Oliveira Sotomayor (Eds.), *Two-Sided Matching: A Study in Game-Theoretic Modelling and Analysis*. Cambridge, U.K.: Cambridge University Press.

Ausubel, Lawrence M., and Raymond J. Deneckere. 1992. Bargaining and the right to remain silent. *Econometrica*, 60, 597–626.

Axelrod, Robert. 1985. *The Evolution of Cooperation*. New York: Basic Books.

Ayres, Ian, and Peter Siegelman. 1995. Race and gender discrimination in bargaining for a new car. *American Economic Review*, 85, 304–21.

Ayton, Peter, Anne J. Hunt, and George Wright. 1989. Psychological conceptions of randomness. *Journal of Behavioral Decision Making*, 2, 221–38.

Babcock, Linda, and George Loewenstein. 1997. Explaining bargaining impasses: The role of self-serving biases. *Journal of Economic Perspectives*, 11, 109–26.

Babcock, Linda, George Loewenstein, and Samuel Issacharoff. 1997. Creating convergence: Debiasing biased litigants. *Law and Social Inquiry*, 22, 913–25.

Babcock, Linda, George Loewenstein, Samuel Issacharoff, and Colin Camerer. 1995. Biased judgments of fairness in bargaining. *American Economic Review*, 85, 1337–43.

Bacharach, Michael J. 1993. Variable universe games. In K. Binmore, A. Kirman, and P. Tani (Eds.), *Frontiers of Game Theory*. Cambridge, Mass.: MIT Press.

Bacharach, Michael J., and Michele Bernasconi. 1997. The variable frame theory of focal points: An experimental study. *Games and Economic Behavior*, 19, 1–45.

Ball, Sheryl, and Paula Cech. 1996. Subject pool choice and treatment effects in economic laboratory research. In R. Mark Isaac (Ed.), *Research in Experimental Economics*, Vol. 6. Greenwich, Conn.: JAI Press, 239–92.

Banks, Jeffrey, Colin F. Camerer, and David Porter. 1994. An experimental analysis of Nash refinements in signaling games. *Games and Economic Behavior*, 6, 1–31.

Bardsley, Nick, Judith Mehta, Chris Starmer, and Bob Sugden. 2001. Coordination: Derivative salience or Schelling salience? University of East Anglia working paper.

Bar-Hillel, Maya, and David V. Budescu. 1995. The elusive wishful thinking effect. *Thinking and Reasoning*, 1, 71–104.

Bar-Hillel, Maya, and Willem A. Wagenaar. 1991. Perception of randomness. *Advances in Applied Mathematics*, 12, 428–54.

Baron, James, Michael T. Hannan, and M. Diane Burton. 2001. Labor pains: Changes in organizational models and employee turnover in young, high-tech firms. *American Journal of Sociology*, 106, 960–1012.

Baron-Cohen, Simon. 1995. *Mindblindness: An Essay on Autism and Theory of Mind*. London: MIT Press.

Bates, Robert H., Avner Greif, Margaret Levin, Jean-Laurent Rosenthal, and Barry R. Weingast. 1998. *Analytic Narratives*. Princeton, N.J.: Princeton University Press.

Battalio, Raymond C., Larry Samuelson, and John Van Huyck. 1999. Optimization incentives and coordination failure in laboratory stag hunt games. Texas A&M working paper.

———. 2001. Optimization incentives and coordination failure in laboratory stag hunt games. *Econometrica*, 69, 749–64.

Bazerman, Max H., Margaret Neale, and Thomas Magliozzi. 1985. Integrative bargaining in a competitive market. *Organizational Behavior and Human Performance*, 35, 294–313.

Bazerman, Max H., Jared R. Curhan, Don A. Moore, and Kathleen L. Valley. 2000. Negotiation. *Annual Review of Psychology*, 51, 279–314.

Beard, T. Randolph, and Richard Beil. 1994. Do people rely on the self-interested maximization of others? An experimental test. *Management Science*, 40, 252–62.

Beard, Randolph, Richard Beil, and Yoshiharu Mataga. 1998. Reliant behavior in the United States and Japan. *Economic Inquiry*, 39, 270–79.

Becker, Gary. 1974. A theory of social interaction. *Journal of Political Economy*, 82, 1063–93.

Berg, Joyce E., John Dickhaut, and Kevin McCabe. 1995. Trust, reciprocity, and social history. *Games and Economic Behavior*, 10, 122–42.

Berg, Joyce E., Lane Daley, John Dickhaut, and John O'Brien. 1986. Controlling preferences for gambles on units of experimental exchange. *Quarterly Journal of Economics*, 101, 281–306.

Berliner, J. S. 1957. *Factory and Manager in the Soviet Union*. Cambridge, Mass.: Harvard University Press.

Berninghaus, Siegfried K., Karl-Martin Erhart, and Claudia Keser. 2002. Conventions and local interaction structures: Experimental evidence. *Games and Economic Behavior*, 39, 177–205.

Bewley, Truman. 1998. Why not cut pay? *European Economic Review*, 42, 459–90.

Binmore, Kenneth, and Larry Samuelson. 1997. Muddling through: Noisy equilibrium selection. *Journal of Economic Theory*, 74, 235–65.

———. 2001. Coordinated action in the electronic mail game. *Games and Economic Behavior*, 34, 200–26.

Binmore, Kenneth, Ariel Rubinstein, and Asher Wolinsky. 1986. The Nash bargaining solution in economic modelling. *RAND Journal of Economics*, 117, 176–88.

Binmore, Kenneth, Avner Shaked, and John Sutton. 1985. Testing noncooperative bargaining theory: A preliminary study. *American Economic Review*, 75, 1178–80.

———. 1989. An outside option experiment. *Quarterly Journal of Economics*, 104, 753–70.

Binmore, Kenneth, Joe Swierzbinski, and Chris Proulx. 2001. Does maximin work? An experimental study. *Economic Journal*, 111, 445–64.

Binmore, Kenneth, Peter Morgan, Avner Shaked, and John Sutton. 1991. Do people exploit their bargaining power? An experimental study. *Games and Economic Behavior*, 3, 295–322.

Binmore, Kenneth, Christopher Proulx, Larry Samuelson, and Joe Swierzbinski. 1998. Hard bargains and lost opportunities. *Economic Journal*, 108, 1279–98.

Binmore, Kenneth, John McCarthy, Giovanni Ponti, Larry Samuelson, and Avner Shaked. 2002. A backward induction experiment. *Journal of Economic Theory*, 104, 48–88.

Bloomfield, Robert. 1994. Learning a mixed strategy equilibrium in the laboratory. *Journal of Economic Behavior and Organization*, 25, 411–36.

Blount, Sally. 1995. When social outcomes aren't fair: The effect of causal attributions on preference. *Organizational Behavior and Human Decision Processes*, 63, 131–44.

Blume, Andreas, Douglas DeJong, Yong-Gwan Kim, and Geoffrey B. Sprinkle. 1998. Evolution of the meaning of messages in sender–receiver games. *American Economic Review*, 88, 1323–40.

———. 2001. Evolution of communication with partial interest. *Games and Economic Behavior*, 27, 79–120.

Blume, Andreas, Doug DeJong, George Neumann, and N. Savin. 1999. Learning in sender–receiver games. University of Iowa working paper.

Bohnet, Iris, and Bruno S. Frey. 1999a. The sound of silence in prisoner's dilemma and dictator games. *Journal of Economic Behavior and Organization*, 38, 43–57.

———. 1999b. Social distance and other-regarding behavior in dictator games: Comment. *American Economic Review*, 89, 335–39.

Bolle, Friedel. 1995. Does trust pay? Discussion paper, Frankfurt (Oder). http://www.econ-euv-frankfurt-0.de/bolle/does_trust_pay.pdf

Bolton, Gary E. 1991. A comparative model of bargaining: Theory and evidence. *American Economic Review*, 81, 1096–1136.

———. 1998. Bargaining and dilemma games: From experimental data towards theoretical synthesis. *Experimental Economics*, 1, 257–81.

Bolton, Gary E., and Axel Ockenfels. 2000. ERC: A theory of equity, reciprocity, and competition. *American Economic Review*, 90, 166–93.

Bolton, Gary E., and Rami Zwick. 1995. Anonymity versus punishment in ultimatum bargaining. *Games and Economic Behavior*, 10, 95–121.

Bolton, Gary E., Jordi Brandts, and Axel Ockenfels. 1998. Measuring motivations for the reciprocal responses observed in a simple dilemma game. *Experimental Economics*, 1, 207–19.

Bolton, Gary E., Elena Katok, and Rami Zwick. 1998. Dictator game giving: Rules of fairness versus acts of kindness. *International Journal of Game Theory*, 27, 269–99.

Börgers, Tilman, and Rajiv Sarin. 1997. Learning through reinforcement and replicator dynamics. *Journal of Economic Theory*, 77, 1–14.

———. 2000. Naive reinforcement learning with endogenous aspirations, *International Economic Review*, 41, 921–50.

Bornstein, Gary, and Ilan Yaniv. 1998. Individual and group behavior in the ultimatum game: Are groups more "rational" players? *Experimental Economics*, 1, 101–8.

Bosch-Domenech, Antoni, and Nicolaas J. Vriend. In press. Imitation of successful behavior in Cournot markets. *Economic Journal*.

Botelho, Anabela, Glenn W. Harrison, Marc A. Hirsch, and Elisabet E. Rutström. 2002. Bargaining behavior, demographics, and nationality: What can the experimental evidence show? Univeristy of South Carolina working paper. http://dmsweb.badm.sc.edu/lisa/research/bargain.htm

Boyd, Robert, and Peter Richerson. 1985. *Culture and the Evolutionary Process*. Chicago: Chicago University Press.

Boylan, Richard T., and Mahmoud A. El-Gamal. 1993. Fictitious play: A statistical study of multiple economic experiments. *Games and Economic Behavior*, 5, 205–22.

Brandenburger, Adam. 1992. Knowledge and equilibrium in games. *Journal of Economic Perspectives*, 6, 83–101.

Brandenburger, Adam, and Barry Nalebuff. 1996. *Co-opetition*. New York: Currency/Doubleday.

Brandts, Jordi, and Neus Figueras. 1997. An exploration of reputation formation in experimental games. Institut d'Analisi Economica (CSIC).

Brandts, Jordi, and Charles Holt. 1992. An experimental test of equilibrium dominance in signaling games. *American Economic Review*, 82, 1350–65.

———. 1993. Adjustment patterns and equilibrium selection in experimental signaling games. *International Journal of Game Theory*, 22, 279–302.

———. 1994. Naïve Bayesian learning and adjustment to equilibrium in signaling games. University of Virginia Department of Economics.

———. 1995. Limitations of dominance and forward induction: Experimental evidence. *Economics Letters*, 49, 391–95.

Brandts, Jordi, and W. Bentley MacLeod. 1995. Equilibrium selection in experimental games with recommended play. *Games and Economic Behavior*, 11, 36–63.

Brandts, Jordi, and Carla Sola. 2001. Reference points and negative reciprocity in simple sequential games. *Games and Economic Behavior*, 36, 138–57.

Brayer, A. Richard. 1964. An experimental analysis of some variables of maximin theory. *Behavioral Science*, 9, 33–44.

Broseta, Bruno. 2000. Adaptive learning and equilibrium selection in experimental coordination games: An ARCH(1) approach. *Games and Economic Behavior*, 32, 25–50.

Brown, George. 1951. Iterative solution of games by fictitious play. In T. C. Koopmans (Ed.), *Activity Analysis of Production and Allocation*. New York: Wiley.

Brown, James N., and Robert W. Rosenthal. 1990. Testing the minimax hypothesis: A re-examination of O'Neill's game experiment. *Econometrica*, 38, 1065–81.

Brown, Martin, Armin Falk, and Ernst Fehr. 2002. Contractual incompleteness and the nature of market interactions. University of Zurich working paper.

Brown-Kruse, Jamie, M. B. Cronshaw, and David J. Schenk. 1993. Theory and experiments on spatial competition. *Economic Inquiry*, 31, 139–65.

Bryant, John. 1983. A simple rational expectations Keynes-type model. *Quarterly Journal of Economics*, 98, 525–28.

Buchan, Nancy R., Rachel T. A. Croson, and Robyn M. Dawes. 2000. Who's with me? Direct and indirect trust and reciprocity in China, Japan, Korea, and the United States. University of Wisconsin working paper.

Buchan, Nancy R., Eric Johnson, and Rachel T. A. Croson. 1997. Culture, power, and legitimacy: Contrasting influences on fairness beliefs and negotiation behavior in Japan and the United States. University of Wisconsin Department of Marketing working paper.

Budescu, David V., and Amnon Rapoport. 1994. Subjective randomization in one- and two-person games. *Journal of Behavioral Decision Making*, 7, 261–78.

Budescu, David V., Irit Freiman, and Amnon Rapoport. 1993. The "interference" explanation of subjective randomization behavior. University of Illinois, Champaign Department of Psychology working paper.

Burnham, Terence. 1999. Testosterone and negotiation: An investigation into the role of biology in economic behavior. Harvard University, JFK School of Government.

Bush, Robert, and Frederick Mosteller. 1955. *Stochastic Models for Learning*. New York: Wiley.

Cabrales, Antonio, and Walter Garcia-Fontes. 2000. Estimating learning models from experimental data. University of Pompeu Fabra working paper.

Cabrales, Antonio, Rosemarie Nagel, and Roc Armenter. 2001. Equilibrium selection through incomplete information in coordination games: An experimental study. University of Pompeu Fabra working paper.

Cabrera, Susana, C. Mónica Capra, and Rosarie Gómez. 2002. The effects of common advice on one-shot traveler's dilemma games: Explaining behavior through an introspective model with errors. Washingtion & Lee University working paper.

Cachon, Gerard, and Colin Camerer. 1996. Loss-avoidance and forward induction in experimental coordination games. *Quarterly Journal of Economics*, 111, 165–94.

Cadsby, Charles B., Murray Frank, and Vojislaw Maksimovic. 1990. Pooling, separating, and semiseparating equilibria in financial markets: Some experimental evidence. *Review of Financial Studies*, 3(3), 315–42.

———. 1998. Equilibrium dominance in experimental financial markets. *Review of Financial Studies*, 11, 189–232.

Camerer, Colin F. 1987. Do biases in probability judgment matter in markets? Experimental evidence. *American Economic Review*, 77, 981–97.

———. 1989. Does the basketball market believe in the "hot hand"? *American Economic Review*, 79, 1257–61.

———. 1995. Individual decision making. In J. H. Kagel, and A. E. Roth (Eds.), *Handbook of Experimental Economics*. Princeton, N.J.: Princeton University Press.

———. 1997. Progress in behavioral game theory. *Journal of Economic Perspectives*, 11, 167–88.

———. 1998. Mental representations of games. Unpublished working paper.

———. 1999. Behavioral economics: Reunifying psychology and economics. *Proceedings of the National Academy of Sciences*, 96, 10575–77.

Camerer, Colin F., and Teck Ho. 1994. Isolation effects and violations of compound lottery reduction. Unpublished working paper.

———. 1998. EWA learning in games: Heterogeneity, time-variation, and probability form. *Journal of Mathematical Psychology*, 42, 305–26.

———. 1999a. Experience-weighted attraction learning in games: Estimates from weak-link games. In D. Budescu, I. Erev, and R. Zwick (Eds.), *Games and Human Behavior: Essays in Honor of Amnon Rapoport*. Mahwah, N.J.: Lawrence Erlbaum.

———. 1999b. Experience-weighted attraction learning in normal-form games. *Econometrica*, 67, 827–74.

Camerer, Colin F., and Robin M. Hogarth. 1999. The effects of financial incentives in economics experiments: A review and capital–labor-production framework. *Journal of Risk and Uncertainty*, 18, 7–42.

Camerer, Colin F., and Risto Karjalainen. 1994. Ambiguity-aversion and non-additive beliefs in non-cooperative games: Experimental evidence. In B. Munier and M. Machina (Eds.), *Models and Experiments on Risk and Rationality*. Dordrecht: Kluwer, 325–58.

Camerer, Colin F., and Marc Knez. 1994. Creating "expectational assets" in the laboratory: "Weakest-link" coordination games. *Strategic Management Journal*, 15, 101–19.

Camerer, Colin F., and George Loewenstein. 1993. Information, fairness, and efficiency in bargaining. In B. Mellers and J. Baron (Eds.), *Psychological Perspectives on Justice: Theory and Applications*. Cambridge, U.K.: Cambridge University Press, 155–79.

———. 2003. Behavioral economics: Past, present, future. In C. F. Camerer, G. Loewenstein, and M. Rabin (Eds.), *Advances in Behavioral Economics*. New York/Princeton, N.J.: Russell Sage Foundation/Princeton University Press.

Camerer, Colin F., and Daniel Lovallo. 1999. Overconfidence and excess entry: An experimental approach. *American Economic Review*, 89, 306–18.

Camerer, Colin F., and Ari Vepsalainen. 1988. The efficiency of cultural contracting. *Strategic Management Journal*, 9, 77–94.

Camerer, Colin F., and Roberto Weber. In press. Organizational culture: An experimental approach. *Management Science*.

Camerer, Colin F., and Keith Weigelt. 1988. Experimental tests of a sequential equilibrium reputation model. *Econometrica*, 56, 1–36.

———. 1991. Information mirages in experimental asset markets. *Journal of Business*, 64, 463–93.

———. 1993. Convergence in experimental double auctions for stochastically lived assets. In D. Friedman and J. Rust (Eds.), *The Double Auction Market: Theories, Institutions and Experimental Evaluations*. Redwood City, Calif.: Addison-Wesley, 355–96.

Camerer, Colin F., Teck Ho, and Kuan Chong. 2001. Behavioral game theory: Thinking, learning and teaching. Caltech working paper. http://www.hss.caltech.edu/~camerer/camerer.html

———. 2002a. Sophisticated experience-weighted attraction learning and strategic teaching in repeated games. *Journal of Economic Theory*, 104, 137–88.

————. 2002b. Strategic teaching and equilibrium models of repeated trust and entry game experiments. Unpublished. http://www.hss.caltech.edu/~camerer/camerer.html

Camerer, Colin F., David Hsia, and Teck Ho. 2002. EWA learning in bilateral call markets. In R. Zwick and A. Rapoport (Eds.), *Experimental Business Research*. Dordrecht: Kluwer, 255–84.

Camerer, Colin F., George Loewenstein, and Martin Weber. 1989. The curse of knowledge in economic settings: An experimental analysis. *Journal of Political Economy*, 97, 1232–54.

Camerer, Colin F., Eric J. Johnson, Talia Rymon, and Sankar Sen. 1994. Cognition and framing in sequential bargaining for gains and losses. In K. Binmore, A. Kirman, and P. Tani (Eds.), *Frontiers of Game Theory*. Cambridge, Mass.: MIT Press, 27–47.

Cameron, Lisa A. 1999. Raising the stakes in the ultimatum game: Experimental evidence from Indonesia. *Economic Inquiry*, 27, 47–59.

Capra, C. Mónica. 1999. Noisy expectation formation in one-shot games. Ph.D. thesis.

Capra, C. Mónica, Jacob K. Goeree, Rosario Gomez, and Charles Holt. 1999. Anomalous behavior in a travelers' dilemma? *American Economic Review*, 89, 678–90.

————. 2002. Learning and noisy equilibrium behavior in an experimental study of imperfect price competition. *International Economic Review*, 43, 613–36.

Carlsson, Hans, and Eric Van Damme. 1993. Equilibrium selection in stag hunt games. In K. Binmore, A. Kirman, and P. Tani (Eds.), *Frontiers of Game Theory*. Cambridge, Mass.: MIT Press, 237–54.

Carpenter, Jeffrey P. 2000. Bargaining outcomes as the results of coordination expectations: An experimental study of sequential bargaining. Middlebury College Department of Economics working paper.

Carter, John R., and Michael D. Irons. 1991. Are economists different and if so, why? *Journal of Economic Perspectives*, 5, 171–77.

Carter, John R., and Shannon A. McAloon. 1996. A test for comparative income effects in an ultimatum bargaining experiment. *Journal of Economic Behavior and Organization*, 31, 369–80.

Cason, Timothy, and Daniel Friedman. 1999. Learning in a laboratory market with random supply and demand. *Experimental Economics*, 2, 77–98.

Cason, Timothy N., and Vai-Lam Mui. 1998. Social influence and the strategy method in the sequential dictator game. *Journal of Mathematical Psychology*, 42, 248–65.

Cason, Timothy N., and Arlington W. Williams. 1990. Competitive equilibrium convergence in a posted-offer market with extreme earnings inequities. *Journal of Economic Behavior and Organization*, 14, 331–52.

Chamberlin, Edward H. 1948. An experimental imperfect market. *Journal of Political Economy*, 56, 95–108.

Charness, Gary, and Ernan Haruvy. 2002. Altruism, equity and reciprocity in a gift-exchange experiment: An encompassing approach. *Games and Economic Behavior*, 40, 203–31.

Charness, Gary, and Mathew Rabin. 2002. Understanding social preferences with simple tests. *Quarterly Journal of Economics*, 117, 817–69.

Charness, Gary, Guillaume R. Frechette, and John H. Kagel. 2001. How robust is laboratory gift exchange? Ohio State University working paper.

Chatterjee, Kalyan, and William Samuelson. 1983. Bargaining under incomplete information. *Operations Research*, 31, 835–51.

Chaudhuri, Ananish. 1998. The ratchet principle in a principal agent game with unknown costs: An experimental analysis. *Journal of Economic Behavior and Organization*, 37, 291–304.

Chen, Hsiao-Chi, James W. Friedman, and Jacques-Francois Thisse. 1996. Boundedly rational Nash equilibrium: A probabilistic choice approach. *Games and Economic Behavior*, 18, 1832–54.

Chen, Kay-Yut, and Charles Plott. 1998. Nonlinear behavior in sealed bid first price auctions. *Games and Economic Behavior*, 25, 34–78.

Chen, Yan, and Yuri Khoroshilov. In press. Asynchronicity and learning in cost sharing mechanisms. *Games and Economic Behavior*.

Cheung, Yin-Wong, and Daniel Friedman. 1997. Individual learning in normal form games: Some laboratory results. *Games and Economic Behavior*, 19, 46–76.

———. 1998. A comparison of learning and replicator dynamics using experimental data. *Journal of Economic Behavior and Organization*, 35, 263–80.

Chiappori, Pierre, Steve Levitt, and Tim Groseclose. 2001. Testing mixed strategy equilibria when players are heterogeneous: The case of penalty kicks. University of Chicago working paper.

Cho, In-Koo, and David Kreps. 1987. Signaling games and stable equilibria. *Quarterly Journal of Economics*, 102, 179–221.

Chwe, Michael Suk-Young. 2001. *Rational Ritual: Culture, Coordination, and Common Knowledge*. Princeton, N.J.: Princeton University Press.

Clark, Herbert H. 1996. *Using Language*. Cambridge, U.K.: Cambridge University Press.

Clark, Herbert, and Catherine R. Marshall. 1981. Definite reference and mutual knowledge. In A. K. Joshi, B. L. Webber, and I. A. Sag (Eds.), *Elements of Discourse Understanding*. Cambridge, U.K.: Cambridge University Press, 10–63.

Clark, Herbert H., Robert Schreuder, and Samuel Buttrick. 1983. Common ground and the understanding of demonstrative reference. *Journal of Verbal Learning and Verbal Behavior*, 22, 1–39.

Clark, Jeremy. 1997. Fairness preference and optimization skills: Are they substitutes? University of British Columbia working paper.

Clark, Kenneth, and Martin Sefton. 1999. Matching protocols in experimental games. University of Manchester working paper.

Clemons, Eric K., and Bruce W. Weber. 1996. Alternative securities trading systems: Tests and regulatory implications of the adoption of technology. *Information Systems Research*, 7, 163–88.

Clotfelter, Charles, and Phillip Cook. 1993. The "gambler's fallacy" in lottery play. *Management Science*, 39, 1521–25.

Collins, Richard, and Katerina Sherstyuk. 2000. Spatial competition with three firms: An experimental study. *Economic Inquiry*, 38, 73–94.

Colman, Andrew M. 1995. *Game Theory and Its Applications in the Social and Biological Sciences*. Oxford, U.K.: Butterworth–Heinemann.

———. In press. Cooperation, psychological game theory, and limitations of rationality in social interaction. *Behavioral and Brain Sciences*.

Colman, Andrew M., and J. A. Stirk. 1998. Stackelberg reasoning in mixed-motive games: An experimental investigation. *Journal of Economic Psychology*, 19, 279–93.

Cooper, David J., and Carol Stockman. 1999. Fairness, learning and constructive preferences: An experimental examination. Case Western Reserve University working paper.

Cooper, David, and John Van Huyck. 2001. Evidence on the equivalence of the strategic and extensive form representation of games. Weatherhead School of Management, Case Western Reserve University working paper.

Cooper, David, Susan Garvin, and John Kagel. 1997a. Signalling and adaptive learning in an entry limit pricing game. *RAND Journal of Economics*, 28, 662–83.

———. 1997b. Adaptive learning vs. equilibrium refinements in an entry limit pricing game. *Economic Journal*, 107, 553–75.

Cooper, David J., John H. Kagel, Wei Lo, and Qing Liang Gu. 1999. Gaming against managers in incentive systems: Experimental results with Chinese students and Chinese managers. *American Economic Review*, 89, 781–804.

Cooper, Russell, Douglas DeJong, Bob Forsythe, and Thomas Ross. 1990. Selection criteria in coordination games: Some experimental results. *American Economic Review*, 80, 218–33.

———. 1994. Alternative institutions for resolving coordination problems: Experimental evidence on forward induction and preplay communication. In J. Friedman (Ed.), *Problems of Coordination in Economic Activity*. Dordrecht: Kluwer.

Corbae, Dean, and John Duffy. 2002. Experiments with network economies. University of Pittsburgh working paper. http://www.pitt.edu/~jduffy/papers .html

Costa-Gomes, Miguel, and Klaus Zauner. 2001. Ultimatum bargaining behavior in Israel, Japan, Slovenia, and the United States: A social utility analysis. *Games and Economic Behavior*, 34, 238–69.

———. In press. Learning, non-equilibrium beliefs, and non-pecuniary payoffs in an experimental game. *Journal of Economic Theory*.

Costa-Gomes, Miguel, Vince Crawford, and Bruno Broseta. 2001. Cognition and behavior in normal-form games? *Econometrica*, 69(5), 1193–1235.

Cournot, Augustin. 1838. *Recherches sur les principes mathématiques de la théorie des richesses.* Translated into English by N. Bacon as *Researches in the Mathematical Principles of the Theory of Wealth.* London: Haffner, 1960.

Cox, James C. 1999. Trust, reciprocity and other-regarding preferences of individuals and groups. University of Arizona Department of Economics.

Cox, James C., Jason Shachat, and Mark Walker. 2001. An experiment to evaluate Bayesian learning of Nash equilibrium play. *Games and Economic Behavior*, 34, 11–33.

Crawford, Vincent P. 1985. Learning behavior and mixed-strategy Nash equilibria. *Journal of Economic Behavior and Organization*, 6, 69–78.

———. 1990. Equilibrium without independence. *Journal of Economic Theory*, 50, 127–54.

———. 1995. Adaptive dynamics in coordination games, *Econometrica*, 63, 103–44.

———. 1997. Theory and experiment in the analysis of strategic interactions. In D. Kreps and K. Wallis (Eds.), *Advances in Economics and Econometrics: Theory and Applications*, Seventh World Congress, Vol. I. Cambridge, U.K.: Cambridge University Press.

Crawford Vincent P., and Bruno Broseta. 1998. What price coordination? The efficiency-enhancing effect of auctioning the right to play. *American Economic Review*, 88, 198–225.

Crawford, Vincent P., and Hans Haller. 1990. Learning how to cooperate: Optimal play in repeated coordination games. *Econometrica*, 58, 571–95.

Crick, Francis. 1988. *What a Mad Pursuit: A Personal View of Scientific Discovery.* New York: Basic Books.

Croson, Rachel T. A. 1996. Information in ultimatum games: An experimental study. *Journal of Economic Behavior and Organization*, 30, 197–212.

———. 1999. Theories of altruism and reciprocity: Evidence from linear public goods games. University of Pennsylvania working paper.

Cross, John G. 1973. A stochastic learning model of economic behavior. *Quarterly Journal of Economics*, 87, 239–66.

———. 1983. *A Theory of Adaptive Economic Behavior.* New York/London: Cambridge University Press.

Dalkey, Norman. 1953. Equivalence of information patterns and essentially determinate games. Contributions to the Theory of Games II. *Annals of Mathematical Studies*, 28, Princeton, N.J.: Princeton University Press.

Damon, William. 1980. Patterns of change in children's social reasoning: A two-year longitudinal study. *Child Development*, 51, 1010–17.

Daniel, Terry E., Darryl A. Seale, and Amnon Rapoport. 1998. Strategic play and adaptive learning in the sealed-bid bargaining mechanism. *Journal of Mathematical Psychology*, 42, 133–66.

Davis, Douglas D., and Charles Holt. 1993. *Experimental Economics.* Princeton, N.J.: Princeton University Press.

Davis, Douglas D., and Bart J. Wilson. In press. Mixed strategy Nash equilibrium predictions as a means of organizing behavior in posted-offer market experiments. In C. Plott and V. L. Smith (Eds.), *Handbook of Experimental Economics Results.* New York: Elsevier.

Dawes, Robyn, and Richard Thaler. 1988. Cooperation. *Journal of Economic Perspectives,* 2, 187–97.

Dixit, Avinash, and Susan Skeath. 1999. *Games of Strategy.* New York: W. W. Norton.

Duffy, John, and Jim Engle-Warnick. 2000. Using symbolic regression to infer strategies from experimental data. In S. H. Chen (Ed.), *Evolutionary Computation in Economics and Finance.* New York: Springer-Verlag.

Dufwenberg, Martin, and Uri Gneezy. 2000. Measuring beliefs in an experimental lost wallet game. *Games and Economic Behavior,* 30, 163–82.

Dufwenberg, Martin, and Georg Kirchsteiger. 1998. A theory of sequential reciprocity. Tilburg Center for Economic Research discussion paper 9837.

Dufwenberg, Martin, Uri Gneezy, Werner Güth, and Eric Van Damme. 2000. An experimental test of direct and indirect reciprocity in case of complete and incomplete information. Humboldt-Universität zu Berlin economics discussion paper 158.

Eckel, Catherine C., and Philip Grossman. 1996a. Altruism in anonymous dictator games. *Games and Economic Behavior,* 6, 181–91.

———. 1996b. The relative price of fairness: Gender differences in a punishment game. *Journal of Economic Behavior and Organization,* 30, 143–58.

———. 2001. Chivalry and solidarity in ultimatum games. *Economic Inquiry,* 39, 171–88.

———. In press. Differences in the economic decisions of men and women: Experimental evidence. In C. Plott and V. Smith (Eds.), *Handbook of Experimental Results.* New York: Elsevier.

Eckel, Catherine C., and Charles Holt. 1989. Strategic voting in agenda-controlled experiments. *American Economic Review,* 79, 763–73.

Edgeworth, Francis Y. 1881. *Mathematical Psychics: An Essay on the Application of Mathematics to the Moral Sciences.* London: Kegan Paul.

El-Gamal, Mahmoud, and David Grether. 1995. Are people Bayesian? Uncovering behavioral strategies. *Journal of the American Statistical Association,* 90, 1137–45.

El-Gamal, Mahmoud A., Richard D. McKelvey, and Thomas R. Palfrey. 1993. A Bayesian sequential experimental study of learning in games. *Journal of the American Statistical Association,* 88(442), 428–35.

Engle-Warnick, Jim, and Robert Slonim. 2000. Inferring repeated game strategies from actions: Evidence from trust game experiments. Nuffield College economics paper W13.

Ensminger, Jean. 2000. Experimental economics in the bush: Why institutions matter. In Claude Menard (Ed.), *Institutions and Organizations*. London: Edward Elgar.

Erev, Ido, and Greg Barron. 2001. On adaptation, maximization and reinforcement learning among cognitive strategies. Technion working paper. http://listserv.ac.il/~barron/RELACS.htm

Erev, Ido, and Ernan Haruvy. 2001. On the application and interpretation of learning models. In Rami Zwick and Amnon Rapoport (Eds.), *Advances in Experimental Business Research*. Boston: Kluwer.

Erev, Ido, and Alvin E. Roth. 1998. Predicting how people play games: Reinforcement learning in experimental games with unique, mixed-strategy equilibria. *American Economic Review*, 88, 848–81.

Erev, Ido, Yoella Bereby-Meyer, and Alvin E. Roth. 1999. The effect of adding a constant to all payoffs: Experimental investigation, and implications for reinforcement learning models. *Journal of Economic Behavior and Organization*, 39(1), 111–28.

Estes, William. 1957. Of models and men. *American Psychologist*, 12, 609–17.

Falk, Armin, and Urs Fischbacher. 1998. A theory of reciprocity. University of Zurich, IEER working paper.

Falk, Armin, Ernst Fehr, and Urs Fischbacher. In press. On the nature of fair behavior. *Economic Inquiry*.

Farnsworth, Ward. 1999. Do parties to nuisance cases bargain after judgment? A glimpse inside the cathedral. *University of Chicago Law Review*, 66, 373–436.

Farrand, Michael (Ed.). 1996. *Records of the Federal Convention*, Vols. I–III. New Haven, Conn.: Yale University Press.

Farrell, Joseph, and Matthew Rabin. 1996. Cheaptalk. *Journal of Economic Perspectives*, 10, 103–18.

Fehr, Ernst, and Armin Falk. 1999. Wage rigidity in a competitive incomplete contract market. *Journal of Political Economy*, 107, 106–34.

Fehr, Ernst, and Simon Gächter. 2000a. Do incentive contracts crowd-out voluntary cooperation? University of Zurich working paper.

———. 2000b. Fairness and retaliation: The economics of reciprocity. *Journal of Economic Perspectives*, 14, 159–81.

———. 2000c. Cooperation and punishment in public goods experiments. *American Economic Review*, 90(4), 980–94.

Fehr, Ernst, and Klaus M. Schmidt. 1999. A theory of fairness, competition and cooperation. *Quarterly Journal of Economics*, 114, 817–68.

Fehr, Ernst, and Elena Tougareva. 1995. Do high stakes remove reciprocal fairness—Evidence from Russia. University of Zurich working paper.

Fehr, Ernst, Simon Gächter, and Georg Kirchsteiger. 1997. Reciprocity as a contract enforcement device. *Econometrica*, 65, 833–60.

Fehr, Ernst, Georg Kirchsteiger, and Arno Reidl. 1993. Does fairness prevent market clearing? An experimental investigation. *Quarterly Journal of Economics*, 108, 437–60.

Feltovich, Nick. 1999. Equilibrium and reinforcement learning in private-information games: An experimental study. *Journal of Economic Dynamics and Control*, 23, 1605–32.

———. 2000. Reinforcement-based vs. beliefs-based learning models in experimental asymmetric-information games. *Econometrica*, 68, 605–41.

Fershtmann, Chaim, and Uri Gneezy. 2001. Discrimination in a segmented society: An experimental approach. *Quarterly Journal of Economics*, 116, 351–77.

Fey, Mark, Richard D. McKelvey, and Thomas R. Palfrey. 1996. An experimental study of constant-sum centipede games. *International Journal of Game Theory*, 25, 269–87.

Fischbacher, Urs, Simon Gächter, and Ernst Fehr. 2001. Are people conditionally cooperative? Evidence from a public goods experiment. *Economics Letters*, 71, 397–404.

Forsythe, Robert, John Kennan, and Barry Sopher. 1991a. Dividing a shrinking pie: An experimental study of strikes in bargaining games with complete information. In R. Mark Isaac (Ed.), *Research in Experimental Economics*, Vol. 4. Greenwich, Conn.: JAI Press, 223–67.

———. 1991b. An experimental analysis of strikes in bargaining games with one-sided private information. *American Economic Review*, 81, 253–78.

Forsythe, Robert, Thomas Palfrey, and Charles Plott. 1982. Asset valuation in an experimental market. *Econometrica*, 50, 37–68.

Forsythe, Robert, Thomas A. Rietz, and Thomas W. Ross. 1999. Wishes, expectations, and actions: A survey on price formation in election stock markets. *Journal of Economic Behavior and Organization*, 39, 83–110.

Forsythe, Robert, Joel L. Horowitz, N. E. Savin, and Martin Sefton. 1994. Fairness in simple bargaining experiments. *Games and Economic Behavior*, 6, 347–69.

Fouraker, Lawrence E., and Sidney Siegel. 1963. *Bargaining Behavior*. New York: McGraw-Hill.

Frank, Robert. 1988. *Passions within Reason: The Strategic Role of Emotions*. New York: W. W. Norton.

Freixas, Xavier, Roger Guesnerie, and Jean Tirole. 1985. Planning under incomplete information and the ratchet effect. *Review of Economic Studies*, 52, 173–91.

Frey, Bruno, and Iris Bohnet. 1995. Institutions affect fairness: Experimental investigations. *Journal of Institutional and Theoretical Economics*, 151(2), 286–303.

———. 1997. Identification in democratic society. *Journal of Socio-Economics*, 26, 25–38.

Friedman, Daniel, and Shyam Sunder. 1993. *Experimental Methods: A Primer for Economists*. Cambridge, U.K.: Cambridge University Press.

Frohlich, Norman, and Joe Oppenheimer. 2001. Some doubts about measuring self-interest using dictator experiments: The costs of anonymity. *Journal of Economic Behavior and Organization*, 46, 271–90.

Fudenberg, Drew, and David Kreps. 1995. Learning in extensive-form games. I. Self-confirming equilibria. *Games and Economic Behavior*, 8, 20–55.

Fudenberg, Drew, and David Levine. 1989. Reputation and equilibrium selection in games with a patient player. *Econometrica*, 57, 759–78.

———. 1997. Measuring players' losses in experimental games. *Quarterly Journal of Economics*, 112, 507–36.

———. 1998. *The Theory of Learning in Games*. Cambridge, Mass.: MIT Press.

Fudenberg, Drew, and Jean Tirole. 1991. *Game Theory*. Cambridge, Mass.: MIT Press.

Fussell, Susan R., and Robert M. Krauss. 1989. Understanding friends and strangers: The effects of audience design on message comprehension. *European Journal of Social Psychology*, 19, 509–26.

Gächter, Simon, and Arno Reidl. 2000. Moral property rights in bargaining. University of St. Gallen, Switzerland, working paper.

Gale, John, Kenneth Binmore, and Larry Samuelson. 1995. Learning to be imperfect: The ultimatum game. *Games and Economic Behavior*, 8, 56–90.

Gallistel, Randy. 1990. *The Organization of Learning*. Cambridge, Mass.: MIT Press.

Gauthier, David. 1975. Coordination. *Dialogue*, 14, 195–221.

GAMES. (1989). From November: Look who's running. January/March, p. 54.

Geanakoplos, John, David Pearce, and Ennio Stacchetti. 1989. Psychological games and sequential rationality. *Games and Economic Behavior*, 1, 60–79.

Gibbons, Robert. 1992. *Applied Game Theory for Economists*. Princeton, N.J.: Princeton University Press.

Gilboa, Itzhak, and David Schmeidler. 2001. *A Theory of Case-Based Decisions*. Cambridge, U.K.: Cambridge University Press.

Gilligan, Carol. 1982. *In a Different Voice*. Cambridge, Mass.: Harvard University Press.

Gilovich, Thomas, Robert Vallone, and Amos Tversky. 1985. The hot hand in basketball: A judgment of representativeness. *Cognitive Psychology*, 3, 430–54.

Gintis, Herbert. 1999. *Game Theory Evolving*. Princeton, N.J.: Princeton University Press.

Glaeser, Edward, David Laibson, Jose Scheinkman, and Christine Soutter. 2000. What is social capital? The determinants of trust and trustworthiness. *Quarterly Journal of Economics*, 115, 811–46.

Glazer, Jacob, and Motty Perry. 1996. Virtual implementation in backwards induction. *Games and Economic Behavior*, 15, 27–32.

Glazer, Jacob, and Robert W. Rosenthal. 1992. A note on Abreu–Matsushima mechanisms. *Econometrica*, 60, 1435–38.

Glazer, Jacob, and Ariel Rubinstein. 1996. An extensive game as a guide for solving a normal game. *Journal of Economic Theory*, 70, 3–42.

Gneezy, Uri. 2002. On the relation between guessing games and bidding in auctions. University of Chicago working paper. http://gsbwww.uchicago.edu/fac /uri.gneezy/vita/

Goeree, Jacob K., and Charles A. Holt. 1999. Stochastic game theory: For playing games, not just for doing theory. *Proceedings of the National Academy of Sciences*, 96, 10564–67.

———. 2000a. An explanation of anomalous behavior in binary-choice games: Entry, voting, public goods, and the volunteers' dilemma. University of Virginia Department of Economics working paper.

———. 2000b. Altruism and noisy behavior in one-shot public goods experiments. University of Virginia working paper.

———. 2000c. Asymmetric inequality aversion and noisy behavior in alternating-offer bargaining games. *European Economic Review*, 44, 1079–89.

———. 2001. Ten little treasures of game theory and ten intuitive contradictions. *American Economic Review*, 91, 1402–22.

Goeree, Jacob K., Charles A. Holt, and Thomas R. Palfrey. 2000. Risk aversion in games with mixed strategies. University of Virginia Department of Economics.

Gould, Stephen Jay. 1985. *The Flamingo's Smile*. New York: W. W. Norton.

Grether, David M. 1981. Financial incentive effects and individual decision making. California Institute of Technology working paper no. 401.

Grossman, Sanford J., and Motty Perry. 1986. Sequential bargaining under asymmetric information. *Journal of Economic Theory*, 39, 120–54.

Güth, Werner, and Steffen Hück. 1997. From ultimatum bargaining to dictatorship—An experimental study of four games varying in veto power. *Metroeconomica*, 48, 262–79.

Güth, Werner, and Eric Van Damme. 1998. Information, strategic behavior and fairness in ultimatum bargaining: An experimental study. *Journal of Mathematical Psychology*, 42, 227–47.

Güth, Werner, Steffen Hück, and Peter Ockenfels. 1996. Two-level ultimatum bargaining with incomplete information. *Economic Journal*, 106, 593–604.

Güth, Werner, Nadege Marchand, and Jean-Louis Rulliere. 1998. Equilibration et dependance du contexte: Une evaluation experimentale du jeu de negociation sous ultimatum [Equilibration and context dependency: An experimental investigation of the ultimatum bargaining game. With English summary]. *Revue Economique*, 49, 785–94.

Güth, Werner, Rolf Schmittberger, and Bernd Schwarze. 1982. An experimental analysis of ultimatum bargaining. *Journal of Economic Behavior and Organization*, 3, 367–88.

Halpern, Joseph. 1986. Reasoning over knowledge: An overview. In J. Halpern (Ed.), *Theoretical Aspects of Reasoning about Knowledge*. San Francisco, Calif.: Morgan Kaufmann, 1–18.

Hamermesh, Daniel S., and Jeff E. Biddle. 1994. Beauty and the labor market. *American Economic Review*, 84, 1174–94.

Hannan, Lynn, John Kagel, and Donald Moser. In press. Partial gift exchange in experimental labor markets: Impact of subject population differences, productivity differences, and effort requests on behavior. *Journal of Labor Economics*.

Harbaugh, William T., Kate Krause, and Steve Liday. 2000. Children's bargaining behavior: Differences by age, gender, and height. University of Oregon working paper. http://harbaugh.uoregon.edu/papers/%20bargaining.pdf

Harless, David W., and Colin F. Camerer. 1994. The predictive utility of generalized expected utility theories. *Econometrica*, 62, 1251–89.

———. 1995. An error rate analysis of experimental data testing Nash refinements. *European Economic Review*, 39, 649–60.

Harley, Calvin B. 1981. Learning the evolutionarily stable strategy. *Journal of Theoretical Biology*, 89, 611–33.

Harrison, Glenn. 1989. Theory and misbehavior of first-price auctions. *American Economic Review*, 79, 749–62.

Harrison, Glenn, and Kevin McCabe. 1992. Testing noncooperative bargaining theory in experiments. In R. Mark Isaac (Ed.), *Research in Experimental Economics*, Vol. 5. Greenwich, Conn.: JAI Press.

———. 1996a. Stability and preference distortion in resource matching: An experimental study of the marriage problem. In R. M. Isaac (Ed.), *Research in Experimental Economics*, Vol. 6, Greenwich, Conn.: JAI Press, 53–129.

———. 1996b. Expectations and fairness in a simple bargaining experiment. *International Journal of Game Theory*, 25, 303–27.

Harsanyi, John. 1967–68. Games with incomplete information played by Bayesian players, I–III. *Management Science*, 14, 159–82, 320–34, 486–502.

Harsanyi, John C., and Reinhard Selten. 1988. *A General Theory of Equilibrium Selection in Games*. Cambridge, Mass.: MIT Press.

Haruvy, Ernan, and Dale O. Stahl. 1998. An empirical model of equilibrium selection in symmetric normal-form games. University of Texas Department of Economics working paper.

Haruvy, Ernan, Alvin E. Roth, and M. Utku Unver. 2001. The dynamics of law clerk matching: An experimental and computational investigation of proposals for reform of the market. Harvard University working paper. http://papers.ssrn.com/sol3/papers.cfm?abstract_id=286282

Heller, Dana. 1998. An evolutionary analysis of the returns to learning. Unpublished Ph.D. thesis, Stanford University.

Heller, Dana, and Rajiv Sarin. 2000. Parametric adaptive learning. University of Chicago working paper.

Henrich, Joseph. 2000. Does culture matter in economic behavior? Ultimatum game bargaining among the Machiguenga of the Peruvian Amazon. *American Economic Review*, 90, 973–79.

Henrich, Joseph, Robert Boyd, Samuel Bowles, Colin Camerer, Ernst Fehr, Herbert Gintis, and Richard McElreath. 2001. In search of homo economicus: Behavioral experiments in 15 small-scale societies. *American Economic Review*, 91(2), 73–78.

Henrich, Joseph, Robert Boyd, Samuel Bowles, Colin Camerer, Ernst Fehr, Herbert Gintis, Richard McElreath, Michael Alvard, Abigail Barr, Jean Ensminger, Kim Hill, Francisco Gil-White, Michael Gurven, Frank Marlowe, John Q. Patton, Natalie Smith, and David Tracer. 2002. "Economic man" in cross-cultural perspective: Behavioral experiments in 15 small-scale societies. Working paper. http://webuser.bus.umich.edu/henrich/gameproject .htm

Hertwig, Ralph, and Andreas Ortmann. 2001. Experimental practices in economics: A methodological challenge for psychologists? *The Behavioral and Brain Sciences*, 24, 383–403.

Hicks, John R. 1932. *The Theory of Wages*. London: Macmillan.

Hirshleifer, Jack. 1987. The emotions as guarantors of threats and promises. In J. Dupré (Ed.), *The Latest on the Best*. Cambridge, Mass.: MIT Press.

Ho, Teck, and Kuan Chong. In press. A parsimonious model of SKU choice. *Journal of Marketing Research*.

Ho, Teck, and Keith Weigelt. 1996. Task complexity, equilibrium selection, and learning: An experimental study. *Management Science*, 42, 659–79.

———. 2000. Population level trust building among strangers. University of Pennsylvania working paper.

Ho, Teck, Colin Camerer, and Kuan Chong. 2002. Functional EWA: A one-parameter theory of learning in games. Caltech working paper.

Ho, Teck, Colin Camerer, and Keith Weigelt. 1998. Iterated dominance and iterated best-response in experimental "p-beauty contests." *American Economic Review*, 88, 947–69.

Ho, Teck, Xin Wang, and Colin F. Camerer. 2002. Individual differences in EWA learning with partial payoff information. Caltech working paper. http://www.hss.caltech.edu/~camerer/camerer.html

Hoffman, Elizabeth, and Matthew Spitzer. 1982. The Coase theorem: Some experimental tests. *Journal of Law and Economics*, 25, 73–98.

———. 1985. Entitlement, rights and fairness: An experimental examination of subjects' concepts of distributive justice. *Journal of Legal Studies*, 14, 259–97.

Hoffman, Elizabeth, Kevin McCabe, and Vernon L. Smith. 1996a. On expectations and monetary stakes in ultimatum games. *International Journal of Game Theory*, 25, 289–301.

———. 1996b. Social distance and other-regarding behavior. *American Economic Review*, 86, 653–60.

———. 1998. Behavioral foundations of reciprocity: Experimental economics and evolutionary psychology. *Economic Inquiry*, 36, 335–52.

————. 2000. The impact of exchange context on the activation of equity in ultimatum games. *Experimental Economics*, 3, 5–9.

Hoffman, Elizabeth, Kevin McCabe, Keith Shachat, and Vernon L. Smith. 1994. Preferences, property rights and anonymity in bargaining games. *Games and Economic Behavior*, 7, 346–80.

Hofstadter, Douglas. 1985. *Metamagical Themas: Questing for the Essence of Mind and Pattern*. New York: Basic Books.

Holt, Charles A. 1995. Industrial organization. In J. H. Kagel and A. Roth (Eds.), *Handbook of Experimental Economics*. Princeton, N.J.: Princeton University Press.

Holt, Charles A., and Fernando Solis-Soberon. 1992. The calculation of equilibrium mixed strategies in posted-offer auctions. In R. Mark Isaac (Ed.), *Research in Experimental Economics*, Vol. 5. Greenwich, Conn.: JAI Press, 189–229.

Holt, Debra. 1999. An empirical model of strategic choice with an application to coordination games. *Games and Economic Behavior*, 27, 86–105.

Hopkins, Ed. In press. Two competing models of how people learn in games. *Econometrica*.

Hsia, David. 1999. Learning in single call markets. Unpublished Ph.D. dissertation, University of Southern California.

Hück, Steffen. 1999. Responder behavior in ultimatum offer games with incomplete information. *Journal of Economic Psychology*, 20, 183–206.

Hück, Steffen, Weiland Müller, and Nicolaas J. Vriend. 2002. The East end, the West end, and King's Cross: On clustering in the four-player Hotelling game. *Economic Inquiry*, 40, 231–40.

Hück, Steffen, Hans-Theo Normann, and Jörg Oechssler. 1999. Learning in Cournot oligopoly—An experiment. *Economic Journal*, 109, C80–95.

Huettel, Scott, and Gregory Lockhead. 2000. Psychologically rational choice: Selection between alternatives in a multiple-equilibrium game. *Cognitive Systems Research*, 1, 143–60.

Hume, David. 1978. *A Treatise of Human Nature, 1740*. Oxford: Oxford University Press.

Isaac, R. Mark, and Vernon L. Smith. 1985. In search of predatory pricing. *Journal of Political Economy*, 93, 320–45.

Jacobson, Eva, and Abdolkarim Sadrieh. 1996. Experimental proof for the motivational importance of reciprocity. University of Bonn.

Jehiel, Phillipe. 2001. Analogy-based expectation equilibrium. CERAS, Paris, working paper. http://www.enpc.fr/ceras/jehiel/working_papers.htm

Jenni, Karen, and George Loewenstein. 1997. Explaining the identifiable victim effect. *Journal of Risk and Uncertainty*, 14, 235–57.

Johannesson, Magnus, and Bjorn Persson. 2000. Non-reciprocal altruism in dictator games. *Economics Letters*, 69, 137–42.

Johnson, Eric J., and John W. Payne. 1985. Effort and accuracy in choice. *Management Science*, 35, 395–414.

Johnson, Eric J., Colin F. Camerer, Sankar Sen, and Talia Rymon. 2002. Detecting failures of backward induction: Monitoring information search in sequential bargaining experiments. *Journal of Economic Theory*, 104, 16–47.

Johnson-Laird, Philip. 1994. Mental models and probabilistic thinking. *Cognition*, 50, 189–209; also http://cognet.mit.edu/MITECS/Entry/johnson-laird

Jordan, James S. 1991. Bayesian learning in normal form games. *Games and Economic Behavior*, 3, 60–81.

Josephson, Jens. 2001. A numerical analysis of the evolutionary stability of learning rules. Stockholm School of Economics SSE/EFI paper no. 474. http://swopec.hhs.se/hastef/abs/hastef0474.htm

Jung, Yun Joo, John H. Kagel, and Dan Levin. 1994. On the existence of predatory pricing: An experimental study of reputation and entry deterrence in the chain-store game. *RAND Journal of Economics*, 25, 72–93.

Kagel, John. 1995. Auctions: A survey of experimental research. In J. Kagel and A. Roth (Eds.), *Handbook of Experimental Economics*. Princeton, N.J.: Princeton University Press, 501–86.

Kagel, John, and Dan Levin. In press. *Common Value Auctions and the Winner's Curse.* Princeton, N.J.: Princeton University Press.

Kagel, John, and Alvin E. Roth (Eds.). 1995. *Handbook of Experimental Economics.* Princeton, N.J.: Princeton University Press.

———. 2000. The dynamics of reorganization in matching markets: A laboratory experiment motivated by a natural experiment. *Quarterly Journal of Economics*, 115, 201–35.

Kagel, John, and Katherine Wolfe. 2001. Tests of fairness models based on equity considerations in a three-person ultimatum game. *Experimental Economics*, 4, 203–19.

Kagel, John, Chung Kim, and Donald Moser. 1996. Fairness in ultimatum games with asymmetric information and asymmetric payoffs. *Games and Economic Behavior*, 13, 100–110.

Kahneman, Daniel. 1988. Experimental economics: A psychological perspective. In R. Tietz, W. Albers, and R. Selten (Eds.), *Bounded Rational Behavior in Experimental Games and Markets*. New York: Springer–Verlag, 11–18.

Kahneman, Daniel, and Shane Frederick. 2002. Representativeness revisited: attribute substitution in intuitive judgment. In T. Gilovich, D. Griffin, and D. Kahneman (Eds.), *Heuristics and Biases: The Psychology of Intuitive Judgment*. Cambridge, Mass.: Cambridge University Press.

Kahneman, Daniel, and Amos Tversky. 1979. Prospect theory: An analysis of decision under risk. *Econometrica*, 47, 263–91.

Kahneman, Daniel, Jack L. Knetsch, and Richard Thaler. 1986. Fairness as a constraint on profit seeking: Entitlements in the market. *American Economic Review*, 76, 728–41.

———. 1990. Experimental tests of the endowment effect and the Coase Theorem. *Journal of Political Economy*, 98, 1325–48.

Kalai, Ehud, and Meir Smorodinsky. 1975. Other solutions to Nash's bargaining problem. *Econometrica*, 43, 513–18.

Kalisch, Gerhard, John W. Milnor, John Nash, and Evar D. Nering. 1954. Some experimental *n*-person games. In R. M. Thrall, C. H. Coombs, and R. L. Davis (Eds.), *Decision Processes*. New York: Wiley.

Katok, Elena, Martin Sefton, and Abdullah Yavaş. 2002. Implementation by iterative dominance and backward induction: An experimental comparison. *Journal of Economic Theory*, 104, 89–103.

Kaufman, Herbert, and Gordon M. Becker. 1961. The empirical determination of game-theoretical strategies. *Journal of Experimental Psychology*, 61, 462–68.

Kawagoe, Toshiji, and Hirokazu Takizawa. 1999. Instability of babbling equilibrium in cheap talk games: An experiment. Saitama University Department of Economics.

Kennan, John. 1980. Pareto optimality and the economics of strike duration. *Journal of Labor Research*, 1, 77–94.

Kennan, John, and Robert Wilson. 1990. Theories of bargaining delays. *Science*, 249, 1124–28.

Keynes, John Maynard. 1936. *The General Theory of Employment, Interest, and Money*. London: Macmillan.

Kingsbury, David. 1968. Manipulating the amount of information obtained from a person giving directions. Unpublished honors thesis, Harvard University.

Knack, Steven, and Philip Keefer. 1997. Does social capital have an economy payoff? A cross-country investigation. *Quarterly Journal of Economics*, 112, 1251–88.

Knez, Marc J., and Colin F. Camerer. 1995. Social comparison and outside options in 3-person utimatum games. *Games and Economic Behavior*, 10, 165–94.

———. 2000. Increasing cooperation in prisoner's dilemmas by establishing a precedent of efficiency in coordination games. *Organizational Behavior and Human Decision Processes*, 8, 194–216.

Knez, Marc J., and Duncan Simester. 2001. Mutual monitoring. *Journal of Labor Economics*, 19, 743–72.

Knez, Marc J., and Vernon. L. Smith. 1987. Hypothetical valuations and preference reversals in the context of asset trading. In A. E. Roth (Ed.), *Laboratory Experimentation in Economics: Six Points of View*. Cambridge, U.K.: Cambridge University Press.

Knott, Jack, and Gary Miller. 1987. The dynamics of convergence and cooperation: Rational choice and adaptive incrementalism. Michigan State University working paper.

Kocher, Martin, and Mathias Sutter. 2000. When the "decision maker" matters: Individual versus team behavior in experimental "beauty-contest" games. University of Innsbruck working paper.

Koford, Kenneth. 1998. Trust and reciprocity in Bulgaria: A replication of Berg, Dickhaut and McCabe (1995). University of Delaware Department of Economics working paper.

Konow, James. 2000. Fair shares: Accountability and cognitive dissonance in allocation decisions. *American Economic Review*, 90, 1072–91.

———. 2001. Fair and square: The four sides of distributive justice. *Journal of Economic Behavior and Organization*, 46, 137–64.

Kreps, David. 1990. *Game Theory and Economic Modelling*. Oxford, U.K.: Oxford University Press.

Kreps, David, and Robert Wilson. 1982a. Sequential equilibrium. *Econometrica*, 50, 863–94.

———. 1982b. Reputation and imperfect information. *Journal of Economic Theory*, 27, 253–79.

Kreps, David, Paul Milgrom, John Roberts, and Robert Wilson. 1982. Rational cooperation in the finitely repeated prisoners' dilemma. *Journal of Economic Theory*, 27, 245–52.

Kristof, Nicholas D., and Sheryl WuDunn. 1994. *China Wakes: The Struggle for the Soul of a Rising Power*. New York: Vintage Books.

Krueger, Alan, and Lawrence P. Summers. 1987. Reflections on the inter-industry wage structure. In K. Lang and J. Leonard (Eds.), *Unemployment and the Structure of Labor Markets*. New York: Basil Blackwell.

Krugman, Paul. 1992. *Geography and Trade*. Cambridge, Mass.: MIT Press.

Larrick, Richard P., and Sally Blount. 1997. The claiming effect: Why players are more generous in social dilemmas than in ultimatum games. *Journal of Personality and Social Psychology*, 72, 810–25.

Lave, Charles A. 1985. Speeding, coordination, and the 55 mph limit. *American Economic Review*, 75, 1159–64.

Lea, Stephen, R. M. Tarpy, and Paul Webley. 1987. *The Individual in the Economy: A Textbook of Economic Psychology*. Cambridge, U.K.: Cambridge University Press.

Ledyard, John. 1995. Public goods experiments. In J. Kagel and A. Roth (Eds.), *Handbook of Experimental Economics*. Princeton, N.J.: Princeton University Press.

Leininger, Wolfgang, Peter Linhart, and Roy Radner. 1989. Equilibria of the sealed-bid mechanism for bargaining with incomplete information. *Journal of Economic Theory*, 48, 63–106.

Levine, David K. 1998. Modeling altruism and spitefulness in experiments. *Review of Economic Dynamics*, 1(3), 593–622.

Lieberman, Bernhardt. 1962. Experimental studies of conflict in some two-person and three-person games. In J. H. Criswell, H. Solomon, and P. Suppes (Eds.), *Mathematical Models in Small Group Processes*. Stanford, Calif.: Stanford University Press, 203–20.

Lin, Haijin, and Shyam Sunder. 2002. Using experimental data to model bargaining behavior in ultimatum games. In Rami Zwick and Amnon Rapoport (Eds.), *Experimental Business Research*. Dordrecht: Kluwer, 373–97.

List, John A., and Todd L. Cherry. 2000. Learning to accept in ultimatum games: Evidence from an experimental design that generates low offers. *Experimental Economics*, 3, 11–31.

Littlewood, John E. 1953. *A Mathematician's Miscellany*. London: Methuen.

Loewenstein, George, and Jennifer Lerner. 2002. The role of emotion in decision making. In R. J. Davidson, H. H. Goldsmith, and K. R. Scherer (Eds.), *The Handbook of Affective Science*. Oxford, U.K.: Oxford University Press.

Loewenstein, George, and David Schkade. 1999. Wouldn't it be nice? Predicting future feelings. In D. Kahneman, E. Diener, and N. Schwartz (Eds.), *Well-being: The Foundations of Hedonic Psychology*. New York: Russell Sage Foundation.

Loewenstein, George, Samuel Issacharoff, Colin Camerer, and Linda Babcock. 1993. Self-serving assessments of fairness and pretrial bargaining. *Journal of Legal Studies*, 22, 135–59.

Los Angeles Times. 1996. Going after the big one. December 31, pp. F1, F8.

———. 1999a. Tight labor market shakes up workplace drug testing. December 15, pp. A1, A45.

———. 1999b. Many happy returns for lost and found. November 29, pp. A1, A6.

———. 2001. PUC chief alleges plot to raise prices. May 18, pp. A1, A20.

———. 2002. Telecom's fiber pipe dream. April 1, pp. A1, A13.

Luce, R. Duncan, and Howard Raiffa. 1957. *Games and Decisions*. New York: Wiley.

Lucking-Reilly, David. 2000. Vickrey auctions in practice: From nineteenth-century philately to twenty-first-century e-commerce. *Journal of Economic Perspectives*, 14, 183–92.

McAllister, Patrick H. 1991. Adaptive approaches to stochastic programming. *Annals of Operations Research*, 30, 45–62.

McCabe, Kevin A., Stephen J. Rassenti, and Vernon L. Smith. 1998. Reciprocity, trust and payoff privacy in extensive form bargaining. *Games and Economic Behavior*, 24, 10–24.

McClintock, Charles G. 1972. Social motivation—A set of propositions. *Behavioral Science*, 17, 438–54.

McKelvey, Richard D., and R. Talbot Page. 1990. Public and private information: An experimental study of information pooling. *Econometrica*, 58, 1321–39.

McKelvey, Richard D., and Thomas R. Palfrey. 1992. An experimental study of the centipede game. *Econometrica*, 60, 803–36.

———. 1995. Quantal response equilibria for normal form games. *Games and Economic Behavior*, 7, 6–38.

———. 1998. Quantal response equilibria for extensive form games. *Experimental Economics*, 1, 9–41.

McKelvey, Richard D., Thomas R. Palfrey, and Roberto Weber. 2000. The effects of payoff magnitude and heterogeneity on behavior in 2×2 games with unique mixed strategy equilibria. *Journal of Economic Behavior and Organization*, 42, 523–48.

Malcolm, David, and Bernhardt Lieberman. 1965. The behavior of responsive individuals playing a two-person zero-sum game requiring the use of mixed strategies. *Psychonomic Science*, 2, 373–74.

Marwell, Gerald, and David R. Schmitt. 1968. Are "trivial" games the most interesting psychologically? *Behavioral Science*, 13, 125–28.

Mead, George Herbert. 1934. *Mind, Self, and Society: From the Standpoint of a Social Behaviorist*. C. W. Morris (Ed.). Chicago: University of Chicago Press.

Mehta, Judith, Chris Starmer, and Robert Sugden. 1992. An experimental investigation of focal points in coordination and bargaining: Some preliminary results. In J. Geweke (Ed.), *Decision Making under Risk and Uncertainty: New Models and Findings*. Norwell, Mass.: Kluwer, 211–20.

―――. 1994a. The nature of salience: An experimental investigation of pure coordination games. *American Economic Review*, 84, 658–73.

―――. 1994b. Focal points in pure coordination games: An experimental investigation. *Theory and Decision*, 36, 163–85.

Messick, David M. 1967. Interdependent decision strategies in zero-sum games. A computer-controlled study. *Behavioral Science*, 12, 33–48.

Messick, David M., Don Moore, and Max H. Bazerman. 1997. Ultimatum bargaining with a committee: Underestimating the importance of decision rule. *Organizational Behavior and Human Decision Processes*, 69, 87–101.

Meyer, Donald M., John Van Hyuck, Raymond C. Battalio, and Thomas R. Saving. 1992. History's role in coordinating decentralized allocation decisions. *Journal of Political Economy*, 100, 292–316.

Milgrom, Paul, and John Roberts. 1982. Limit pricing and entry under incomplete information: An equilibrium analysis. *Econometrica*, 50, 443–59.

―――. 1991. Adaptive and sophisticated learning in normal form games. *Games and Economic Behavior*, 3, 82–101.

―――. 1992. *Economics, Organization and Management*. Englewood Cliffs, N.J.: Prentice-Hall.

Milgrom, Paul, and Nancy Stokey. 1982. Information, trade and common knowledge. *Journal of Economic Theory*, 26, 17–27.

Miller, George A. 1956. The magical number seven, plus or minus two: Some limits on our capacity for processing information. *Psychological Review*, 63, 81–97.

Mitzkewitz, Michael, and Rosemarie Nagel. 1993. Experimental results on ultimatum games with incomplete information. *International Journal of Game Theory*, 22, 171–98.

Monderer, Dov, and Dov Samet. 1989. Approximating common knowledge with common beliefs. *Games and Economic Behavior*, 1, 170–90.

Mookerjee, Dilip, and Barry Sopher. 1994. Learning behavior in an experimental matching pennies game. *Games and Economic Behavior*, 7, 62–91.

―――. 1997. Learning and decision costs in experimental constant-sum games. *Games and Economic Behavior*, 19, 97–132.

Morgan, John, and Martin Sefton. 2002. An empirical investigation of unprofitable games. *Games and Economic Behavior*, 40, 123–46.

Morris, Stephen, and Hyun Song Shin. 2000. Global games: Theory and applications. Yale University Department of Economics working paper. http://www.econ.yale.edu/~sm326/research.html/seattle.pdf

Moulin, Herve. 1986. *Game Theory for Social Sciences*. New York: New York University Press.

Munro, Alistair. 1999. Cycling with rules of thumb. University of East Anglia, Department of Economics.

Murnighan, J. Keith, and Michael Scott Saxon. 1998. Ultimatum bargaining by children and adults. *Journal of Economic Psychology*, 19, 415–45.

Murnighan, J. Keith, Alvin E. Roth, and Francoise Schoumaker. 1988. Risk aversion in bargaining: An experimental study. *Journal of Risk and Uncertainty*, 1, 101–24.

Myers, Stewart, and Natalia Majluf. 1984. Corporate financing and investment decisions when firms have information that investors do not have. *Journal of Financial Economics*, 13, 187–221.

Myerson, Roger. 1978. Refinement of the Nash equilibrium concept. *International Journal of Game Theory*, 7, 73–80.

———. 1979. Incentive compatibility and the bargaining problem. *Econometrica*, 47, 61–73.

Myerson, Roger, and Mark Satterthwaite. 1983. Efficient mechanisms for bilateral trading. *Journal of Economic Theory*, 29, 265–81.

Nagel, Rosemarie. 1995. Unravelling in guessing games: An experimental study. *American Economic Review*, 85, 1313–26.

———. 1999. A survey of research on experimental beauty-contest games. In D. Budescu, I. Erev, and R. Zwick (Eds.), *Games and Human Behavior: Essays in Honor of Amnon Rapoport*. Mahwah, N.J.: Lawrence Erlbaum.

Nagel, Rosemarie, and Fang-Fang Tang. 1998. An experimental study on the centipede game in normal form—An investigation on learning. *Journal of Mathematical Psychology*, 42, 356–84.

Nagel, Rosemarie, Antonio Bosch-Domenech, Albert Satorra, and José García-Montalvo. 1999. One, two, (three), infinity: Newspaper and lab beauty-contest experiments. University of Pompeu Fabra working paper 438. http://www.econ.upf.es/leex/working.htm

Nasar, Sylvia. 1998. *A Beautiful Mind: A Biography of John Forbes Nash Jr*. New York: Simon & Schuster.

Nash, John F. 1950. The bargaining problem. *Econometrica*, 18, 155–62.

———. 1951. Non-cooperative games. *Annals of Mathematics*, 54, 286–95.

Neelin, Janet, Hugo Sonnenschein, and Matthew Spiegel. 1988. A further test of noncooperative bargaining theory: Comment. *American Economic Review*, 78, 824–36.

Neral, John, and Jack Ochs. 1992. The sequential equilibrium theory of reputation building: A further test. *Econometrica*, 60, 1151–69.

Neumann, John von, and Oskar Morgenstern. 1944. *The Theory of Games and Economic Behavior*. Princeton, N.J.: Princeton University Press.

Neuringer, Alan. 1986. Can people behave "randomly"? The role of feedback. *Journal of Experimental Psychology: General*, 115, 62–75.

Nisbett, Richard E., and Lee Ross. 1991. *The Person and the Situation*. New York: McGraw-Hill.

Noldeke, Georg, and Larry Samuelson. 1993. An evolutionary analysis of backward and forward induction. *Games and Economic Behavior*, 5, 425–54.

Nowak, Martin A., and Karl Sigmund. 2000. Shrewd investments. *Science*, 288, 819–20.

Nyarko, Yaw, and Andrew Schotter. 2002. An experimental study of belief learning using elicited beliefs. *Econometrica*, 70, 971–1005.

Nydegger, Rudy V., and Guillermo Owen. 1975. Two person bargaining: An experimental test of the Nash axioms. *International Journal of Game Theory*, 3, 239–349.

Ochs, Jack. 1990. The coordination problem in decentralized markets: An experiment. *Quarterly Journal of Economics*, 105, 545–59.

———. 1995a. Coordination problems. In J. H. Kagel and A. E. Roth (Eds.), *Handbook of Experimental Economics*. Princeton, N.J.: Princeton University Press.

———. 1995b. Games with unique, mixed strategy equilibria: An experimental study. *Games and Economic Behavior*, 10, 202–17.

———. 1999. Entry in experimental market games. In D. Budescu, I. Erev, and R. Zwick (Eds.), *Games and Human Behavior: Essays in Honor of Amnon Rapoport*. Mahwah, N.J.: Lawrence Erlbaum.

Ochs, Jack, and Alvin E. Roth. 1989. An experimental study of sequential bargaining. *American Economic Review*, 79, 355–84.

O'Neill, Barry. 1987. Nonmetric test of the minimax theory of two-person zerosum games. *Proceedings of the National Academy of Sciences*, 84, 2106–9.

Ortmann, Andreas, John Fitzgerald, and Carl Boeing. 2000. Trust, reciprocity, and social history: A re-examination. *Experimental Economics*, 3, 81–100.

Osborne, Martin, and Ariel Rubinstein. 1995. *A Course in Game Theory*. Cambridge, Mass.: MIT Press.

Ostrom, Elinor. 2000. Collective action and the evolution of social norms. *Journal of Economic Perspectives*, 14, 137–58.

Palacios-Huerta, Ignacio. 2001. Professionals play minimax. Brown University working paper.

Palfrey, Thomas R., and Howard Rosenthal. 1988. Private incentives in social dilemmas: The effects of incomplete information and altruism. *Journal of Public Economics*, 35, 309–32.

Partow, Zeinab, and Andrew Schotter. 1996. Does game theory predict well for the wrong reasons? An experimental investigation. New York University, C.V. Starr Center for Applied Economics, working paper 93-46.

Persico, Nicola, Andrew Postlewaite, and Dan Silverman. 2001. The effect of adolescent experience on labor market outcomes: The case of height. University of Pennsylvania working paper.

Pilutla, Madan M., and Xiao-Ping Chen. 1999. Social norms and cooperation in PDs: The effect of context and feedback. *Organizational Behavior and Human Decision Processes*, 78, 81–103.

Porter, David, and Vernon L. Smith. 1994. Stock market bubbles in the laboratory. *Applied Mathematical Finance*, 1, 111–27.

———. 1995. Futures contracting and dividend uncertainty in experimental asset markets. *Journal of Business*, 68, 509–41.

Potters, Jan, and Frans Van Winden. 1996. Comparative statics of a signaling game: An experimental study. *International Journal of Game Theory*, 25, 329–53.

———. 2000. Professionals and students in a lobbying experiment. *Journal of Economic Behavior and Organization*, 43, 499–522.

Prasnikar, Vesna. 1999. Binary lottery payoffs: Do they control risk-aversion? Unpublished.

Prelec, Drazen. 1998. The decision weighting function. *Econometrica*, 66, 497–527.

Prendergast, Canice. 1999a. The provision of incentives in firms. *Journal of Economic Literature*, 37, 7–63.

———. 1999b. Restricting the means of exchange within organizations. *European Economic Review*, 43, 1007–19.

Putnam, Robert. 1995. The case of the missing social capital. Unpublished manuscript.

Rabin, Matthew. 1993. Incorporating fairness into game theory and economics. *American Economic Review*, 83, 1281–1302.

———. 2000. Risk-aversion for small stakes: A calibration theorem. *Econometrica*, 68, 1281–92.

———. 2002. Inference by believers in the law of small numbers. *Quarterly Journal of Economics*, 117, 775–816.

Rabin, Matthew, and Joel Schrag. 1999. First impressions matter: A model of confirmatory bias. *Quarterly Journal of Economics*, 114, 37–82.

Radner, Roy, and Andrew Schotter. 1989. The sealed-bid mechanism: An experimental study. *Journal of Economic Theory*, 48, 179–220.

Raiffa, Howard. 1953. Arbitration schemes for generalized two-person games. In H. W. Kuhn and A. W. Tucker (Eds.), *Contributions to the Theory of Games, II*. Princeton, N.J.: Princeton University Press, 361–87.

———. 1982. *The Art and Science of Negotiation*. Cambridge, Mass.: Belknap Press.

Rapoport, Amnon. 1995. Individual strategies in a market entry game. *Group Decision and Negotiation*, 4, 117–33.

————. 1997. Order of play in strategically equivalent games in extensive form. *International Journal of Game Theory*, 26, 113–36.

Rapoport, Amnon, and Wilfred Amaldoss. 1997. Competition for the development of a new product: Theoretical and experimental investigation. Hong Kong University of Science and Technology, Department of Marketing.

————. 2000. Mixed strategies and iterative elimination of strongly dominated strategies: An experimental investigation of states of knowledge. *Journal of Economic Behavior and Organization*, 42, 483–521.

Rapoport, Amnon, and Richard B. Boebel. 1992. Mixed strategies in strictly competitive games: A further test of the minimax hypothesis. *Games and Economic Behavior*, 4, 261–83.

Rapoport, Amnon, and David V. Budescu. 1992. Generation of random series in two-person strictly competitive games. *Journal of Experimental Psychology: General*, 121, 352–63.

————. 1997. Randomization in individual choice behavior. *Psychological Review*, 104, 603–17.

Rapoport, Amnon, and Ido Erev. 1998. Coordination, "magic" and reinforcement learning in a market entry game. *Games and Economic Behavior*, 23, 146–75.

Rapoport, Amnon, and Mark A. Fuller. 1995. Bidding strategies in a bilateral monopoly with two-sided incomplete information. *Journal of Mathematical Psychology*, 39, 179–96.

Rapoport, Amnon, Terry E. Daniel, and Darryl A. Seale. 1998. Reinforcement-based adaptive learning in asymmetric two-person bargaining with incomplete information. *Experimental Economics*, 1, 221–56.

Rapoport, Amnon, Ido Erev, and Rami Zwick. 1995. An experimental study of buyer–seller negotiation with one-sided incomplete information and time discounting. *Management Science*, 41, 377–94.

Rapoport, Amnon, Alison King Chung Lo, and Rami Zwick. 2002. Choice of prizes allocated by multiple lotteries with endogenously determined probabilities. *Organizational Behavior and Human Decision Processes*, 87, 180–206.

Rapoport, Amnon, Darryl A. Seale, and Lisa Ordóñez. 2002. Tacit coordination in choice between certain outcomes and endogenously determined lotteries. *Journal of Risk and Uncertainty*, 25, 21–46.

Rapoport, Amnon, Darryl A. Seale, and Eyal Winter. 2000. An experimental study of coordination and learning in iterated two-market entry games. *Economic Theory*, 16, 661–87.

————. 2002. Coordination and learning behavior in large groups with asymmetric players. *Games and Economic Behavior*, 39, 111–36.

Rapoport, Amnon, James A. Sundali, and Richard E. Potter. 1996. Ultimatums in two-person bargaining with one-sided uncertainty: Offer games. *International Journal of Game Theory*, 25, 475–94.

Rapoport, Amnon, James A. Sundali, and Darryl A. Seale. 1996. Ultimatums in two-person bargaining with one-sided uncertainty: Demand games. *Journal of Economic Behavior and Organization*, 30, 173–96.

Rapoport, Amnon, Eythan Weg, and Dan S. Felsenthal. 1990. Effects of fixed costs in two-person sequential bargaining. *Theory and Decision*, 28, 47–71.

Rapoport, Amnon, Darryl A. Seale, Ido Erev, and James A. Sundali. 1998. Equilibrium play in large group market entry games. *Management Science*, 44, 129–41.

Rapoport, Amnon, William E. Stein, James E. Parco, and Thomas E. Nicholas. In press. Equilibrium play and adaptive learning in a three-person centipede game. *Games and Economic Behavior*.

Rapoport, Anatol, O. Frenkel, and J. Perner. 1977. Experiments with cooperative 2 × 2 games. *Theory and Decision*, 8, 67–92.

Rasmusen, Eric. 1994. *Games and Information* (2nd ed.). Cambridge, Mass.: Oxford University Press.

Robinson, Julia. 1951. An iterative method of solving a game. *Annals of Mathematics*, 54, 296–301.

Romer, David. 1996. *Advanced Macroeconomics*. New York: McGraw-Hill.

Rosenthal, Robert W. 1981. Games of perfect information, predatory pricing, and the chain store paradox. *Journal of Economic Theory*, 25, 92–100.

———. 1989. A bounded rationality approach to the study of noncooperative games. *International Journal of Game Theory*, 18(3), 273–92.

Ross, Bruce M., and Nissim Levy. 1958. Patterned predictions of chance events by children and adults. *Psychological Reports*, 4, 87–124.

Roth, Alvin E. 1985. Toward a focal-point theory of bargaining. In A. E. Roth (Ed.), *Game-Theoretic Models of Bargaining*. Cambridge, U.K.: Cambridge University Press.

———. 1995a. Introduction. In J. H. Kagel and A. E. Roth (Eds.), *Handbook of Experimental Economics*. Princeton, N.J.: Princeton University Press.

———. 1995b. Bargaining experiments. In J. H. Kagel and A. E. Roth (Eds.), *Handbook of Experimental Economics*. Princeton, N.J.: Princeton University Press.

Roth, Alvin E., and Ido Erev. 1995. Learning in extensive-form games: Experimental data and simple dynamic models in the intermediate term. *Games and Economic Behavior*, 8, 164–212.

Roth, Alvin E., and Michael Malouf. 1979. Game-theoretic models and the role of information in bargaining. *Psychological Review*, 86, 574–94.

Roth, Alvin E., and J. Keith Murnighan. 1982. The role of information in bargaining: An experimental study. *Econometrica*, 50, 1123–42.

Roth, Alvin E., and Francoise Schoumaker. 1983. Expectations and reputations in bargaining: An experimental study. *American Economic Review*, 73, 362–72.

Roth, Alvin E., and Marilda Sotomayor. 1990. *Two-Sided Matching: A Study in Game-Theoretic Modelling and Analysis*. Cambridge, U.K.: Cambridge University Press.

Roth, Alvin E., and Xiaolin Xing. 1994. Jumping the gun: Imperfections and institutions related to the timing of market transactions. *American Economic Review*, 84, 992–1044.

Roth, Alvin E., Ido Erev, Robert L. Slonim, and Gregg Barron. 1999. Equilibrium and learning in economic environments: The predictive value of approximations. Harvard University Department of Economics.

Roth, Alvin E., Vesna Prasnikar, Masahiro Okuno-Fujiwara, and Shmuel Zamir. 1991. Bargaining and market behavior in Jerusalem, Ljubljana, Pittsburgh and Tokyo: An experimental study. *American Economic Review*, 81, 1068–95.

Rubinstein, Ariel. 1982. Perfect equilibrium in a bargaining model. *Econometrica*, 50, 97–109.

———. 1985. A bargaining model with incomplete information about time preferences. *Econometrica*, 53, 1151–72.

———. 1989. The electronic mail game: Strategic behavior under "almost common knowledge." *American Economic Review*, 79, 385–91.

———. 1991. Comments on the interpretation of game theory. *Econometrica*, 59, 909–24.

———. 1998. *Modelling Bounded Rationality*. Cambridge, Mass.: MIT Press.

———. 1999. Experience from a course in game theory: Pre- and postclass problem sets as a didactic device. *Games and Economic Behavior*, 28, 155–70.

Ruffle, Bradley J. 1999. Gift giving with emotions. *Journal of Economic Behavior and Organization*, 39, 399–420.

———. 2000. Some factors affecting demand withholding in posted-offer markets. *Economic Theory*, 16, 529–44.

Rutström, Lisa, Tanga McDaniel, and Melonie Williams. 1994. Incorporating fairness into game theory and economics: An experimental test with incentive compatible belief elicitation. University of South Carolina, Department of Economics, unpublished manuscript.

Sally, David. 1995. Conversation and cooperation in social dilemmas: A meta-analysis of experiments from 1958 to 1992. *Rationality and Society*, 7, 58–92.

———. 2002a. "What an ugly baby!": Risk dominance, sympathy, and the coordination of meaning. *Rationality and Society*, 14, 79–109.

———. 2002b. Two economic applications of sympathy. *Journal of Law, Economics, and Organization*, 18, 455–87.

Salmon, Tim. 1999. Evidence for "learning to learn" behavior in normal form games. Caltech working paper.

———. 2001. An evaluation of econometric models of adaptive learning. *Econometrica*, 69, 1597–1628.

Samuelson, Larry. 2001. Adaptations, analogies and anomalies. *Journal of Economic Theory*, 97, 320–66.

Samuelson, William F. 1996. Market entry under incomplete information. In R. J. Zeckhauser, R. L. Keeney, and J. K. Sebenius (Eds.), *Wise Choices: Decisions, Games, and Negotiations*. Cambridge, Mass.: Harvard Business School Press, 272–301.

Sarin, Rajiv, and Farshid Vahid. 2000. Strategy similarity and coordination. Texas A&M University, manuscript.

———. 2001. Predicting how people play games: A simple dynamic model of choice. *Games and Economic Behavior*, 34, 104–22.

Schelling, Thomas. 1960. The strategy of conflict. Cambridge, Mass.: Harvard University Press.

———. 1978. *Micromotives and Macrobehavior*. New York: W. W. Norton.

Schlag, Karl. 1999. Which one should I imitate? *Journal of Mathematical Economics*, 31, 493–522.

Schotter, Andrew, and Yale M. Braunstein. 1981. Economic search: An experimental study. *Economic Inquiry*, 19, 1–25.

Schotter, Andrew, and Barry Sopher. 2000. Creating culture in the lab: Evidence from intergenerational ultimatum games. New York University working paper.

Schotter, Andrew, Blaine Snyder, and Wei Zheng. 2000. Bargaining through agents: An experimental study. *Games and Economic Behavior*, 30, 248–92.

Schotter, Andrew, Keith Weigelt, and Charles Wilson. 1994. A laboratory investigation of multiperson rationality and presentation effects. *Games and Economic Behavior*, 6, 445–68.

Schotter, Andrew, Avi Weiss, and Inigo Zapater. 1996. Fairness and survival in ultimatum and dictatorship games. *Journal of Economic Behavior and Organization*, 31, 37–56.

Schweitzer, Maurice, and Sara Solnick. 1999. The influence of physical attractiveness and gender on ultimatum game decisions. *Organizational Behavior and Human Decision Processes*, 79, 199–215.

Seale, Darryl A., and Amnon Rapoport. 2000. Elicitation of strategy profiles in large group coordination games. *Experimental Economics*, 3, 153–79.

Sefton, Martin. 1999. A model of behavior in coordination game experiments. *Experimental Economics*, 2, 151–64.

Sefton, Martin, and Abdullah Yavaş. 1996. Abreu–Matsushima mechanisms: Experimental evidence. *Games and Economic Behavior*, 16, 280–302.

Seinen, Ingrid, and Arthur Schram. 1999. Social status and group norms: Indirect reciprocity in a mutual aid experiment. Unpublished working paper, CREED, University of Amsterdam.

Selten, Reinhard. 1965. Spieltheoretische Behandlung eines Oligoplmodells mit Nachfrageträgheit. *Zeitschrift für die Gesamte Staatswissenschaft*, 12, 301–24.

———. 1975. Re-examination of the perfectness concept for equilibrium points in extensive games. *International Journal of Game Theory*, 4, 25–55.

———. 1978. The chain store paradox. *Theory and Decision*, 9, 127–59.

———. 1986. Anticipatory learning in 2-person games. University of Bonn, discussion paper Series B.

———. 1991. Evolution, learning, and economic behavior. *Games and Economic Behavior*, 3, 3–24.

Selten, Reinhard, and Joachim Buchta. 1999. Experimental sealed bid first price auctions with directly observed bid functions. In D. V. Budescu, I. Erev, and R. Zwick (Eds.), *Games and Human Behavior: Essays in Honor of Amnon Rapoport*. Mahwah, N.J.: Lawrence Erlbaum.

Selten, Reinhard, and Rolf Stöcker. 1986. End behavior in sequences of finite prisoner's dilemma supergames: A learning theory approach. *Journal of Economic Behavior and Organization*, 7, 47–70.

Selten, Reinhard, Abdolkarim Sadrieh, and Klaus Abbink. 1999. Money does not induce risk neutral behavior, but binary lotteries do even worse. *Theory and Decision*, 46, 211–49.

Sen, Jayanta. 2002. The equity volume puzzle. Ohio State working paper.

Sgroi, Daniel, and Daniel J. Zizzo. 2002. Strategy learning in 3 × 3 games by neural networks. Cambridge University, Department of Applied Economics working paper No. 0207.

Shachat, Jason M. 2002. Mixed strategy play and the minimax hypothesis. *Journal of Economic Theory*, 104, 189–226.

Shaked, Avner. 1982. Existence and computation of mixed strategy Nash equilibrium for 3-firms location problem. *Journal of Industrial Economics*, 31, 93–97.

Shapley, Lloyd S. 1964. Some topics in two-person games. In M. Dresher, L. S. Shapley, and A. W. Tucker (Eds.), *Advances in Game Theory*. Princeton, N.J.: Princeton University Press, 1–28.

Slembeck, Tilman. 1998. As if playing fair—Experimental evidence on the role of information in ultimatum bargaining. ELSE, University College of London working paper.

Slonim, Robert L. 2001. Competing against experienced and inexperienced players. Case Western Reserve Department of Economics working paper.

Slonim, Robert L., and Alvin E. Roth. 1998. Learning in high stakes ultimatum games: An experiment in the Slovak Republic. *Econometrica*, 66, 569–96.

Smith, Cedric, 1961. Consistency in statistical inference and decision. *Journal of the Royal Statistical Society*, series B, 23, 1–37.

Smith, Kip, John Dickhaut, Kevin McCabe, and Jose Pardo. 2002. Neuronal substrates for choice under ambiguity, risk, certainty, gains and losses. *Management Science*, 48, 711–18.

Smith, Vernon L. 1962. An experimental study of competitive market behavior. *Journal of Political Economy*, 70, 111–37.

———. 1976. Experimental economics: Induced value theory. *American Economic Review*, 66, 274–79.

Smith, Vernon L., and James M. Walker. 1993. Rewards, experience and decision costs in first price auctions. *Economic Inquiry*, 31, 237–44.

Smith, Vernon L., and Arlington W. Williams. 1990. Boundaries of competitive price theory: Convergence expectations and transaction costs? In L. Green and J. H. Kagel (Eds.), *Advances in Behavioral Economics*, Vol. 2. Norwood, N.J.: Ablex.

Snijders, Chris, and Gideon Keren. 1998. Determinants of trust. In D. V. Budescu, Ido Erev, and Rami Zwick (Eds.), *Games and Human Behavior: Essays in Honor of Amnon Rapoport*. Mahwah, N.J.: Lawrence Erlbaum, 355–85.

Sobel, Joel. 2001. Interdependent preferences and reciprocity. University of California–San Diego working paper. http://weber.ucsd.edu/~jsobel/Papers /IPR.pdf

Solnick, Sara J. 2001. Gender differences in the ultimatum game. *Economic Inquiry*, 39, 189–200.

Sonsino, Dorin, Ido Erev, Sharon Gilat, and Galia Shabtai. 1998. On the likelihood of repeated zero-sum betting by adaptive (human) agents. Technion, Israel Institute of Technology.

Sopher, Barry. 1990. Bargaining and the joint-cost theory of strikes: An experimental study. *Journal of Labor Economics*, 8, 48–74.

Sovik, Yiva. 1999. Impossible bets: An experimental study. University of Oslo, Department of Economics.

Spence, Michael. 1974. *Market Signaling*. Cambridge, Mass.: Harvard University Press.

Stahl, Dale O. 1993. Evolution of $smart_n$ players. *Games and Economic Behavior*, 5, 604–17.

———. 1996. Boundedly rational rule learning in a guessing game. *Games and Economic Behavior*, 16, 303–30.

———. 1999a. Sophisticated learning and learning sophistication. University of Texas at Austin working paper.

———. 1999b. Evidence based rules and learning in symmetric normal form games. *International Journal of Game Theory*, 28, 111–30.

———. 2000a. Rule learning in symmetric normal-form games: Theory and evidence. *Games and Economic Behavior*, 32, 105–38.

———. 2000b. Action-reinforcement learning versus rule learning. University of Texas at Austin working paper.

———. 2001. Population rule learning in symmetric normal-form games: Theory and evidence. *Journal of Economic Behavior and Organization*, 45, 19–35.

Stahl, Dale O., and Ernan Haruvy. In press. Aspiration-based and reciprocity-based rules in learning dynamics for symmetric normal-form games. *Journal of Mathematical Psychology*.

Stahl, Dale O., and Paul Wilson. 1995. On players' models of other players: Theory and experimental evidence. *Games and Economic Behavior*, 10, 218–54.

Stähl, Ingolf. 1972. *Bargaining Theory*. Stockholm: Economic Research Institute.

Stigler, George. 1981. Economics or ethics? In S. McMurrin (Ed.), *Tanner Lectures on Human Values*. Cambridge, U.K.: Cambridge University Press.

Straub, Paul. 1995. Risk dominance and coordination failures in static games. *Quarterly Review of Economics and Finance*, 35, 339–65.

Straub, Paul, and Keith Murnighan. 1995. An experimental investigation of ultimatum games: Information, fairness, expectations, and lowest acceptable offers. *Journal of Economic Behavior and Organization*, 27, 345–64.

Sugden, Robert. 1982. On the economics of philanthropy. *Economic Journal*, 92, 341–50.

———. 1995. A theory of focal points. *Economic Journal*, 105, 533–50.

Summers, Lawrence. 2000. International financial crises: Causes, prevention and cures. *American Economic Review Papers and Proceedings*, 90, 1–16.

Sundali, James A., Amnon Rapoport, and Darryl A. Seale. 1995. Coordination in market entry games with symmetric players. *Organizational Behavior and Human Decision Processes*, 64, 203–18.

Suppes, Patrick, and Richard Atkinson. 1960. *Markov Learning Models for Multiperson Interactions*. Stanford, Calif.: Stanford University Press.

Tang, Fang-Fang. 1996a–c. Anticipatory learning in two-person games: An experimental study, I, II, III. University of Bonn working papers.

———. 2001. Anticipatory learning in two-person games: Some experimental results. *Journal of Economic Behavior and Organization*, 44, 221–32.

Thomas, Louis, and Keith Weigelt. 1998. An empirical examination of advertising as a signal of product quality. *Journal of Economic Behavior and Organization*, 37, 415–30.

Thompson, Leigh, and George Loewenstein. 1992. Egocentric interpretations of fairness in interpersonal conflict. *Organizational Behavior and Human Decision Processes*, 51, 176–97.

Tversky, Amos, and Daniel Kahneman. 1982. Judgements of and by representativeness. In D. Kahneman, P. Slovic, and A. Tversky (Eds.), *Judgment under Uncertainty: Heuristics and Biases*. Cambridge, U.K.: Cambridge University Press, 84–98.

Valley, Kathleen, Leigh Thompson, Robert Gibbons, and Max H. Bazerman. 2002. How communication improves efficiency in bargaining games. *Games and Economic Behavior*, 38, 127–55.

Van Damme, Eric. 1999. Game theory: The next stage. In L. A. Gerard-Varet, Alan P. Kirman, and M. Ruggiero (Eds.), *Economics beyond the Millennium*. Oxford, U.K.: Oxford University Press, 184–214.

Van Huyck, John B., and Raymond C. Battalio. 1999. What does it take to eliminate the use of a strategy strictly dominated by a mixture? *Experimental Economics*, 2, 129–50.

———. 2002. Prudence, justice, benevolence, and sex: Evidence from similar bargaining games. *Journal of Economic Theory*, 104, 227–46.

Van Huyck, John B., Raymond C. Battalio, and Richard Beil. 1990. Tacit cooperation games, strategic uncertainty, and coordination failure. *American Economic Review*, 80, 234–48.

———. 1991. Strategic uncertainty, equilibrium selection, and coordination failure in average opinion games. *Quarterly Journal of Economics*, 106, 885–909.

———. 1993. Asset markets as an equilibrium selection mechanism: Coordination failure, game form auctions, and forward induction. *Games and Economic Behavior*, 5, 485–504.

Van Huyck, John B., Raymond C. Battalio, and Joseph Cook. 1997. Adaptive behavior and coordination failure. *Journal of Economic Behavior and Organization*, 32, 483–503.

Van Huyck, John B., Raymond C. Battalio, and Frederick W. Rankin. 2001a. Selection dynamics and adaptive behavior without much information. Texas A&M University manuscript. http://econlab10.tamu.edu/JVH_gtee/OS6.htm

———. 2001b. Evidence on learning in coordination games. Texas A&M University manuscript. http://econlab10.tamu.edu/JVH_gtee/OS5.htm

Van Huyck, John B., Raymond C. Battalio, and Mary F. Walters. 1995. Commitment versus discretion in the peasant–dictator game. *Games and Economic Behavior*, 10, 143–70.

———. 2001. Is reputation a substitute for commitment in the peasant–dictator game? Unpublished manuscript.

Van Huyck, John B., Ann B. Gillette, and Raymond C. Battalio. 1992. Credible assignments in coordination games. *Games and Economic Behavior*, 4, 606–26.

Van Huyck, John B., Frederick Rankin, and Raymond C. Battalio. 2000. Strategic similarity and emergent conventions: Evidence from payoff perturbed stag hunt games. *Games and Economic Behavior*, 32, 315–37.

Van Huyck, John B., John Wildenthal, and Raymond C. Battalio. 2002. Tacit cooperation, strategic uncertainty, and coordination failure: Evidence from repeated dominance solvable games. *Games and Economic Behavior*, 38, 156–75.

Van Winden, Frans. 1998. Experimental studies of signaling games. In L. Luini (Ed.), *Uncertain Decisions, Bridging Theory and Experiments*. Boston: Kluwer, 147–73.

Vega-Redondo, Fernando. 1997. The evolution of Walrasian behavior. *Econometrica*, 65(2), 375–84.

Von Winterfeldt, Detlof, and Ward Edwards. 1973. Flat maxima in linear optimization models. University of Michigan, Engineering Psychology Laboratory technical report 0113131-4-T.

Vriend, Nick. 1997. Will reasoning improve learning? *Economics Letters*, 55, 9–18.

Wagenaar, Willem. 1984. *Paradoxes of Gambling Behavior*. Mahwah, N.J.: Lawrence Erlbaum.

Walker, Mark, and John Wooders. 2001. Minimax play at Wimbledon. *American Economic Review*, 91, 1521–38.

Warglien, Massimo, Giovanna Devetag, and Paolo Legrenzi. 1999. Mental models and naive play in normal form games. University of Trento, Computable and Experimental Economics Laboratory working paper.

Watson, Joel. 1993. A "reputation" refinement without equilibrium. *Econometrica*, 61, 199–205.

Watson, Joel, and Pierpaolo Battigali. 1997. On "reputation" refinements with heterogeneous beliefs. *Econometrica*, 65, 363–74.

Weber, Roberto. 2001. Behavior and learning in the "dirty faces" game. *Experimental Economics*, 4, 229–42.

Weber, Roberto, and Colin F. Camerer. 2001. First-mover advantage and virtual observability in ultimatum bargaining and "weak-link" coordination games. Unpublished.

Weber, Roberto, Colin F. Camerer, Yuval Rottenstreich, and Marc J. Knez. 2001. The illusion of leadership: Misattribution of cause in coordination games. *Organizational Science*, 12, 582–98.

Wedekind, Claus, and Manfred Milinski. 2000. Cooperation through image scoring in humans. *Science*, 288, 850–52.

Weg, Eythan, Amnon Rapoport, and Dan S. Felsenthal. 1990. Two-person bargaining behavior in fixed discounting factors games with infinite horizon. *Games and Economic Behavior*, 2, 76–95.

Weibull, Jörgen. 1995. *Evolutionary Game Theory*. Cambridge, Mass.: MIT Press.

———. 2000. Testing game theory. Stockholm School of Economics working paper No. 382.

Weisbuch, Gerard, Alan Kirman, and Dorothea Herreiner. 2000. Market organization and trading relationships. *Economic Journal*, 110, 411–36.

Weizsacker, Georg. 2000. Ignoring the rationality of others: Evidence from experimental normal-form games. Harvard Business School working paper.

Wellman, Henry M. 1990. *The Child's Theory of Mind*. Cambridge, Mass.: MIT Press.

Willinger, Marc, Christopher Lohmann, and Jean-Claude Usunier. 1999. A comparison of trust and reciprocity between France and Germany: Experimental investigation based on the investment game. University Louis Pasteur, Strasbourg, France, BETA working paper.

Yamagishi, Toshio. 1986. The provision of a sanctioning system as a public good. *Journal of Personality and Social Psychology*, 51, 110–16.

Young, H. Peyton. 1993. The evolution of conventions. *Econometrica*, 61, 57–84.

Young, H. Peyton, and Mary A. Burke. 2001. Competition and custom in economic contracts: A case study of Illinois agriculture. *American Economic Review*, 91, 559–73.

Zahavi, Amotz. 1975. Mate selection—A selection for a handicap. *Journal of Theoretical Biology*, 53, 205–14.

Zauner, Klaus. 1999. A payoff uncertainty explanation of results in experimental centipede games. *Games and Economic Behavior*, 26, 157–85.

Zeuthen, Frederik. 1930. *Problems of Monopoly and Economics*. London: Routledge.

Zizzo, Daniel J. 2002. Racing with uncertainty: A patent race experiment. *International Journal of Industrial Organization*, 20, 877–902.

Zwick, Rami, Amnon Rapoport, and John C. Howard. 1992. Two-person sequential bargaining behavior with exogenous breakdown. *Theory and Decision*, 32, 241–68.

Index

Page numbers for entries occurring in figures are followed by an *f;* those for entries occurring in notes are followed by an *n;* those for entries occurring in tables are followed by a *t.*

www.ingramcontent.com/pod-product-compliance
Ingram Content Group UK Ltd.
Pitfield, Milton Keynes, MK11 3LW, UK
UKHW020322040125
452908UK00003B/191